PACEMAKER®

United States History

Fourth Edition

TEACHER'S ANSWER EDITION

GLOBE FEARON
Pearson Learning Group

Contents

Pacemaker® United States History Fourth Edition

Reviewers

We thank the following educators, who provided valuable comments and suggestions during the development of this book:

Lawrence Broughton, North Chicago Community High School, North Chicago, Illinois
Dr. Dorothy Fields, Miami Dade Public Schools, Miami, Florida
Nadine Liebow, Indio High School, Indio, California
Paula Young, Orange County Public Schools, Orlando, Florida

Subject Area Consultant: Peter Myers, Department of History, Palo Alto College, San Antonio, Texas
Pacemaker® Curriculum Adviser: Stephen C. Larsen, formerly of The University of Texas at Austin

ISBN 0-13-024421-X

Printed in the United States of America

5 6 7 8 9 10 11 11 10 09 08

Globe Fearon
Pearson Learning Group

1-800-321-3106
www.pearsonlearning.com

PACEMAKER®

United States History

Fourth Edition

This comprehensive U.S. history program helps students of all abilities meet academic content standards and improve their performance on standarized tests.

Pacemaker® United States History offers a complete course in the fundamentals of the history of our country and its people. With content that fully correlates to the NCSS standards, *Pacemaker® United States History* is built on an effective approach to learning centered on the premise that students learn best at a pace that is right for them.

Pacemaker® United States History
helps make required content accessible to all students:

★ Helps students progress at a pace that works for them through a manageable and consistent format and design

★ Offers extensive skills practice to reinforce students' understanding

★ Makes content accessible to all students with text written at a controlled reading level

★ Features strong vocabulary instruction to prepare students for understanding content

★ Organizes chapter content with clear learning objectives to guide students through the chapter

★ Reinforces comprehension with frequent opportunities to assess students' understanding

★ Fosters primary and secondary source understanding by having students work with quotes, maps, charts, graphs, and timelines, and answer document-based questions

★ Brings history to life for students with engaging features that tie content to students' interest and life experiences

Globe Fearon Social Studies Programs

Globe Fearon offers a wide array of social studies programs covering American history, world history, government, economics, geography, and much more. Our effective, student-friendly instruction in key social studies content helps students of all ability levels develop important skills such as comprehension, critical thinking, reading, and writing.

SUPPORTS No Child Left Behind

AMERICAN HISTORY

Pacemaker® United States History

Globe Fearon American History

Using Primary Sources with Document-Based Questions, Level B

WORLD HISTORY AND GEOGRAPHY

Pacemaker® World History

Globe Fearon World History

Pacemaker® World Geography and Cultures

GOVERNMENT AND ECONOMICS

Pacemaker® American Government

Unlocking the Constitution and the Declaration of Independence

Pacemaker® Economics

The Pacemaker® Social Studies Curriculum

Pacemaker® is a standards-based parallel curriculum offering core-content instruction for students of diverse learning styles and abilities to help them meet content standards and improve their performance on state tests.

See the chart below for available Pacemaker® social studies titles and their program components.

	PACEMAKER® TITLES					
COMPONENTS	U.S. History, 4th Edition	American Government	World History	World Geography and Cultures	U.S. Geography	Economics
Full-color Student Edition	◆	◆	◆	◆		◆
2-color Student Edition					◆	
Full-color Teacher's Answer Edition	◆	◆	◆	◆		◆
Classroom Resource Binder	◆	◆	◆	◆	◆	◆
Interactive Classroom Resources	◆					
Teacher's Planning Guide	◆					
Workbook	◆	◆	◆	◆	◆	◆
Spanish Supplement	◆		◆	◆		
ESL/ELL Teacher's Guide	◆	◆	◆	◆		◆
ESL/ELL Teacher Package	◆	◆	◆	◆		◆
Audio CD Program	◆		◆	◆		
Answer Key	◆	◆	◆	◆	◆	◆

Globe Fearon offers additional materials to help customize instruction to meet the diverse needs of your students. For more information regarding Globe Fearon's materials, please call 1-800-321-3106 or visit www.pearsonlearning.com.

What is "considerate text"?

SUPPORTS No Child Left Behind

Anderson and Armbruster developed the concept of "considerate text." A considerate text provides the reader with a clear, well-organized, coherent, and compelling body of information.[1, 2]

Pacemaker® curriculum offers

- A text that students can read and navigate successfully
- Required content made accessible through a controlled reading level, strong vocabulary instruction, extensive practice and review, and frequent opportunities for assessment
- Depth of coverage, instructional design, and pedagogy specifically designed and improved over time to enable students of all ability levels to meet the academic content standards
- Flexible teacher support to meet the needs of individual students

How does the Pacemaker® curriculum improve my students' understanding?

According to Tyree, Fiore, and Cook, textbooks that contain the following features increase student comprehension.[3]

- A preview of goals and objectives
- Explicit statements of steps and procedures
- Embedded questions
- Written conclusions and summaries

Pacemaker® curriculum offers

- Learning objectives and goals that are clearly presented and pre-taught at the beginning of every chapter
- Concise, single-concept lessons that engage students with a clear, straight-forward approach
- A variety of integrated comprehension questions that provide numerous opportunities to measure students' content understanding
- Chapter summaries in a graphic format that help students organize the main chapter ideas

Pacemaker® Providing solutions for success!

Research extracted from the Pacemaker® Research Paper written by Dr. Marty Beech, Center for Performance Technology, Florida State University.

[1] Anderson, T. H., and B. B. Armbruster. 1986. "Readable Textbooks, or Selecting a Textbook Is Not Like Buying a Pair of Shoes." In *Reading Comprehension: From Research to Practice*. J. Orasanu, ed. Hillsdale, NJ: Lawrence Erlbaum Associates, Inc. 151–162.

[2] Armbruster, B. B. and T. H. Anderson, 1988. "On Selecting 'Considerate' Content Area Textbooks." Remedial and Special Education, 9(1): 47–52.

[3] Tyree, R. B., T. A. Fiore, and R. A. Cook. 1994. "Instructional Materials for Diverse Learners." Features and Considerations for Textbook Design. Remedial and Special Education, 15(6): 363–377.

Each unit has an engaging opener and practical review.

Unit Opener lists chapters for planning.

High-interest visual is shown with a critical thinking question.

Unit 1 Settling the Americas

Chapter 1 **Early America** Prehistory–1492
Chapter 2 **Colonies Are Settled** 1519–1733
Chapter 3 **Growth of Colonial Society** 1630–1760
Chapter 4 **The Struggle for Freedom** 1754–1783

This painting shows what one artist believed North America looked like before Europeans arrived. What feeling about the land does the artist want to give you?

"There are valleys and plains streaming with sweet springs . . . hills and mountains . . . of hidden treasure, never yet searched . . . there is a world of means to set many thousands to work."

—from a pamphlet published by The London Company in 1609

Unit 1 Review

Critical Thinking
Give one reason why each of the following events happened.

1. In the 1400s, European explorers began to travel far from home.
2. The colony of Georgia was settled.
3. England bought raw materials from the colonies in America.
4. The Second Continental Congress chose George Washington as a military leader.

Building Your Skills
Draw a timeline with the following information. Then give the timeline a title.

1488 Bartolomeu Dias navigates western coast of Africa
1492 Christopher Columbus sails to the Americas
1419 Prince Henry of Portugal establishes school for navigators
1501 Amerigo Vespucci sails to South America
1498 Vasco da Gama sails to India

Answer one of the following essay topics.

1. Discuss the effects of the Ice Age on the first people in the Americas.
2. Explain why Great Britain felt it was right to regulate trade in its colonies in the Americas.

Linking Past and Present
Discuss why people from other countries migrate to the United States today. Compare the reasons why people come to the United States today with the reasons why people came in the past.

80 Unit 1 • Settling the Americas

Primary source quotation sets the stage for unit content.

Unit Review provides a variety of assessment opportunities.

Linking Past and Present provides connections to today.

Sample pages from Unit 1 of the Student Edition

Motivating openers draw students into chapter content.

Captivating visual sparks students' interest.

Detailed caption supports understanding, prompts critical thinking, and provides a springboard for discussion.

The painting above shows early settlers arriving in North America. The cradle to the right belonged to a baby born on the ship Mayflower. *What difficulties do you think early settlers faced in making such a long sea voyage?*

Historical artifact gives a personal perspective to history.

Settlement of the Americas

Timeline places chapter content in a graphical context.

1510 – **1550** – **1590** – **1630** – **1670**

- **1519** Cortés conquers Aztecs
- **1540** Spanish explore the Southwest
- **1607** English settle Jamestown
- **1608** French settle Quebec
- **1620** Pilgrims settle Massachusetts
- **1638** Swedish settle Delaware
- **1664** English take over New Amsterdam from Dutch

Sample pages from Chapter 2 of the Student Edition

Chapter opener previews chapter concepts.

Chapter 2

Colonies Are Settled
1519–1733

Words to Know introduces students to key vocabulary in the chapter.

Words to Know

conquer

mission

convert

joint-stock company

charter

cash crop

indentured servant

treaty

debtor

Learning Objectives

- Explain the defeat of the Aztec Empire by Spanish conquerors.
- Identify reasons for Spanish and French settlements in the Americas.
- Describe the English colonies at Jamestown, Plymouth, and Massachusetts Bay.
- Identify the colonies in the New England, Middle, and Southern regions.
- Explore how colonial medicine affected the colonists' lives.

Clear Learning Objectives that aid goal-setting and assessment are provided.

1681 William Penn settles Pennsylvania

1710

1750

1733 Georgia, last English colony, settled

Portfolio Project

Different ways of life developed in the regions of the New England, Middle, and Southern colonies. You are a merchant traveling through the colonies to find new goods. You keep a travel journal. Choose one region. Describe the people, the way of life, and the geography of the region. Your journal should have one entry for each colony in a region.

High-interest Portfolio Project motivates students to learn chapter concepts.

Chapter 2 • Colonies Are Settled • **1519–1733** 21

Manageable sections make content accessible.

Vocabulary is pretaught at the start of every section for student retention.

Margin notes provide timely reminders.

Section 3 The Growth of the Thirteen Colonies

Words to Know

treaty	a written agreement between two or more nations
debtor	a person who owes money to others

There were 13 English colonies established along the Atlantic coast between 1607 and 1733. The 13 English colonies were divided into three regions: the New England, Middle, and Southern colonies.

The New England Colonies

Remember
The Puritans settled the Massachusetts Bay Colony in 1630.

Massachusetts

In the last section you read that the Massachusetts Bay Colony became the first of the New England colonies. At that time, the colony included all the land in present-day Massachusetts and part of present-day Maine. The other New England colonies grew out of the Massachusetts colony.

Rhode Island

After Massachusetts was settled, many people who were unhappy with Puritan life moved to other areas. Others were forced to leave. In 1635, a minister, Roger Williams, was ordered to leave Massachusetts. This is what Williams believed.

1. The established churches had too much power.
2. The state, or government, should be separate from the church, or religion.
3. All people should be free to practice their own beliefs.

32 Unit 1 • Settling the Americas

Sample pages from Chapter 2 of the Student Edition

Williams and his followers built a settlement called Providence. The colony of Rhode Island grew out of that settlement. Here all people were free to follow their religious beliefs.

Anne Hutchinson was also forced to leave Massachusetts. She did not agree with the religious ideas of the Puritan leaders.

Connecticut

In 1636, another minister, Thomas Hooker, led a group of people out of Massachusetts. Hooker and his followers felt that Puritan leaders had become too powerful. This group settled a new colony that had a Native American name meaning "long river place." That colony was Connecticut.

Content in narrative form engages students with a clear, straightforward approach.

Great Names in History

ANNE HUTCHINSON

Anne Hutchinson lived in the Massachusetts Bay Colony. She was a Puritan. However, she did not agree with all the beliefs of the Puritan ministers.

Hutchinson began to hold meetings in her home. She discussed why she did not agree with the church sermons. Those who followed her were also unhappy with the beliefs of the Puritan ministers.

The Puritan leaders felt that anyone who went against them was wrong. They were also unhappy that a woman was spreading these different ideas.

Eventually, Hutchinson was put on trial. She was found guilty. As a result, she and her family had to leave the colony in 1638. With a group of followers, she helped to settle a new colony in Rhode Island.

Anne Hutchinson

Critical Thinking Do you think the Puritan leaders were right to be unhappy with Anne Hutchinson? Explain.

Boxed features such as Great Names in History, History and You, Citizenship Link, and A Closer Look make social studies come alive.

Content is enhanced by map and chart skills.

Comprehension questions assess students' content understanding.

Headings divide and preview section content.

In 1639, settlers in Connecticut wrote a document called the Fundamental Orders of Connecticut. This document allowed men in the colony to elect their leaders. The people of Connecticut agreed to live by the rules in this document. The Fundamental Orders became the first written system of government in North America.

New Hampshire

In 1623, King James I of England sent two fish merchants and others to explore the coast of present-day New Hampshire. Soon communities were established there. Some people came to these fishing communities from Massachusetts. They did not want to follow the rules of the Puritan Church. New Hampshire became a colony in 1741.

Why did people leave Massachusetts?

The Middle Colonies

New York

During the 1600s, much of the land between Virginia and New Hampshire was claimed by people from the Netherlands. They were called the Dutch.

In 1609, Henry Hudson, an English explorer who was paid by the Dutch, sailed up a river that was later named for him. He claimed the land on both sides of the river. In 1626, the land was named New Netherlands.

The largest town in that colony was settled on an island where the Manhattan group of Native Americans lived. The new town was called New Amsterdam.

New Jersey

The land claimed by the Netherlands did not stay under Dutch control for long. In 1664, English forces took control of New Amsterdam and the rest of the colony. They broke the land into two colonies—New York and New Jersey. The large town at the mouth of the Hudson River was renamed New York City.

Sample pages from Chapter 2 of the Student Edition

New Jersey, like New York, attracted people from different places. Many colonists from the New England colonies moved to New Jersey. They were looking for better farmland. People from many European nations also came to New Jersey.

Pennsylvania

In England, a religious group called the Quakers was led by a wealthy man named William Penn. Penn wanted to travel to America to follow his beliefs. He asked the English king to give him land in America. In 1681, the king allowed Penn to settle a colony called Pennsylvania.

The Thirteen Colonies, 1733

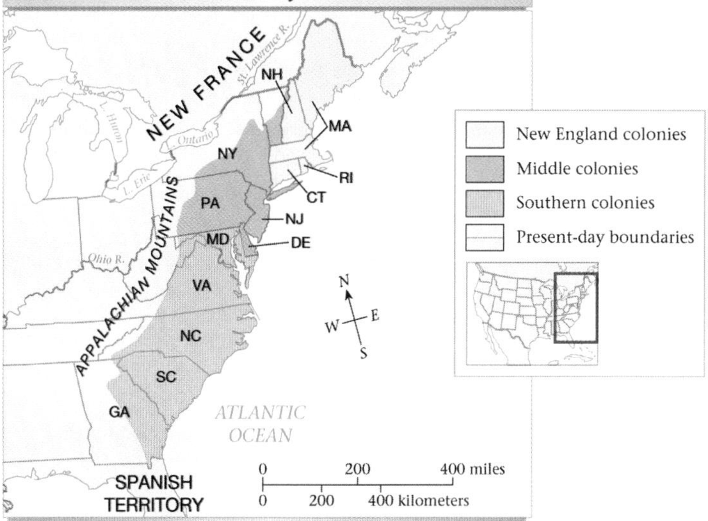

Map Study

1. Name the New England, Middle, and Southern colonies.
2. What geographical feature is west of the colonies?

Accessible full-color maps, which include locator prompts, give students geographical context.

Map Study questions focus on map comprehension and critical-thinking skills.

Ample opportunities for review are in every lesson.

Engaging visuals tied directly to content makes history relevant.

Vocabulary words are boldfaced and defined the first time they appear in the text.

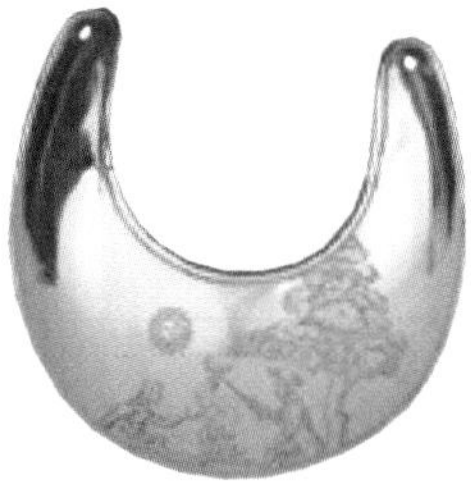

This metal collar was a gift from the Quakers of Pennsylvania to the Native Americans.

The Quakers believed all people should be treated fairly. They were against slavery. The Quakers also believed that Native Americans should be treated with respect. When the Quakers landed in the new colony, they signed a peace **treaty,** or written agreement between two or more nations, with Native Americans. Pennsylvania became a colony known for its freedom.

Delaware

Settlers from Sweden came to present-day Delaware in 1638. They built a settlement, which they named Fort Christina. The Swedes built other settlements.

For a short time, the Dutch took over the Swedish settlements. Next, the English took over. In 1682, the Duke of York gave the Swedish settlements to William Penn. Some settlers in areas south of Pennsylvania asked for the right to set up their own colony. Penn and other Quaker leaders agreed. Delaware became a colony in 1704.

What groups of people settled the Middle colonies?

The Southern Colonies

Virginia

The first English colony of Virginia began with the Jamestown settlement in 1607, which you read about in Section 2. Jamestown began to attract settlers from the New England and Middle colonies. More settlers also came from England.

Maryland

In England, Catholics were also punished for their religious beliefs. In 1632, Lord Baltimore, a rich English Catholic, was given a charter. He settled the colony of Maryland.

In 1649, Lord Baltimore saw to it that the Toleration Act was passed in Maryland. This act guaranteed freedom of religion to all Christians, both Catholic and Protestant, in the colony of Maryland.

Sample pages from Chapter 2 of the Student Edition

The Carolinas

In 1663, King Charles of England gave eight rich English lords the right to settle land south of Virginia. The land was beautiful and the soil was good. It was named Carolina after the English king.

Settlers in Carolina were allowed religious freedom. Many people came to Carolina for that freedom. They also came to farm the rich soil in the area. So many people arrived that, in 1712, Carolina was broken into two colonies—North Carolina and South Carolina.

Georgia

The last of the 13 colonies, Georgia, was settled to give a home to **debtors.** These are people who had been jailed for not paying money owed to others.

An English general named James Oglethorpe felt it was unfair to put debtors in jail. He asked the king to allow people to settle in America and get a new start. In 1733, Georgia, named after King George II, became the thirteenth English colony.

How was Georgia different from the other English colonies?

Economics Fact

In colonial Georgia, 16-year-old boys became taxpayers and served in the army. Sixteen-year-old girls were usually married.

Margin notes, such as Economics Facts, Geography Facts, and History Facts give students new perspectives on content.

Section 3 Review

1. Into what three regions were the 13 colonies divided?
2. Name two leaders who left Massachusetts. Where did each go?
3. **Critical Thinking** How were the Middle colonies different from the New England colonies?
4. **Write About History** Write a pamphlet to attract people to live in one of the 13 colonies.

A variety of review questions measure students' mastery of section content.

Features provide relevant connections to today's world.

Feature lessons connect history to a variety of discipline areas, such as economics, language, technology, government, and geography.

Content helps students grasp the relationship of history to other curriculum areas.

Questions assess students' understanding of feature content.

Sample page from Chapter 2 of the Student Edition

CONNECTING HISTORY AND SCIENCE
Colonial Medicine

Getting sick in colonial times was risky. Women often grew special plants, called herbs, which they used as medicine. They believed that elderberry helped a fever, North American ginseng relieved pain, and black snakeroot healed a snake bite.

Many of the cures used by the colonists were learned from local Native Americans. They taught the colonists new uses for the roots, bark, and leaves of plants.

Sometimes patients turned to doctors. Unlike the doctors of today, colonial doctors did not understand the human body. For example, they used walnuts to treat headaches because the walnut looked like a brain.

In case a doctor was hard to find, there was the local barber. The barber could pull rotten teeth and could bleed pati
bleeding patients with lee
person. Usually, it made a

Colonists believed ther
person feel better. If elder
you could try eating sever
sad, gathering ants by the
improve your mood.

Answer the questions

1. What cures did colo
2. How did colonial do

CHALLENGE Are any
colonial times still u

Sample page from Chapter 3 of the Student Edition

VOICES FROM THE PAST
Anna Green Winslow

Anna Green Winslow was a young girl in 1772. She lived in Boston. Like other colonial girls in New England, she spent her days going to school or church and learning how to sew, knit, and read. She read books such as *The Pilgrim's Progress*, a story about the importance of leading a good life. Anna's diary describes a young girl's view of life in colonial Boston.

"**January 11, 1772** I have attended my school every day this week except Wednesday afternoon. I made a visit to Aunt Sulky, and was dressed just as I was to go to the ball. I heard Mr. Thatcher preach our lecture last evening.

February 9, 1772 My right hand is in bandages, but my left is free. My aunt says it will be a nice opportunity when it improves to learn to spin flax [a fiber spun into thread]. I am pleased with the proposal.

I have read my Bible to my aunt this morning (as is the daily custom) and sometimes I read other books to her.

February 22, 1772 I have spun 30 knots of linen and mended a pair of stockings for Lucinda, read a part of *The Pilgrim's Progress*, copied part of my text journal. Played some, laughed enough. . . ."

A colonial woman works at a spinning wheel.

Answer the questions below.

1. What did Anna's diary describe?
2. How do you know that education and religion were important in Anna's life?

CHALLENGE What kind of person was Anna? Explain.

Quotes help students experience firsthand diaries, speeches, letters, and other primary source documents.

Challenge question prompts higher-order thinking skills.

Every unit includes instruction on key social studies skills.

Sample page from Chapter 9 of the Student Edition

BUILDING YOUR SKILLS
Reading a Map: The Compromise of 1850

Full-page feature provides essential practice of valuable social studies skills.

A map gives information about places. Some maps show the physical features of an area. Some maps give information about the economy or population. The following information will help you read a map.

1. The *key* tells what the colors on the map stand for.
2. The *compass rose* shows direction—north, south, east, and west.
3. The *scale* shows how distances on the map represent real distances.

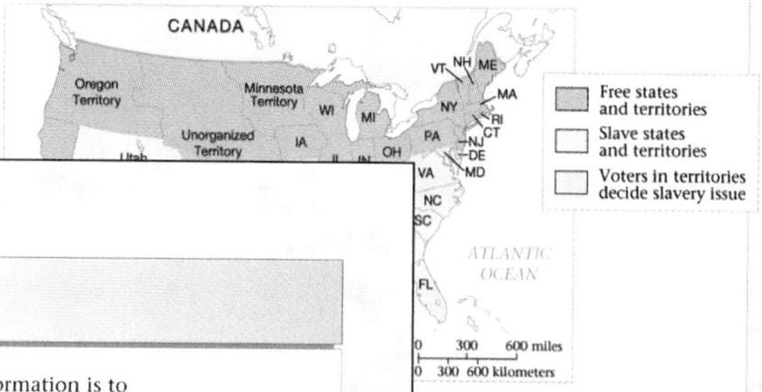

Apply the Skill
Write two questions that can be answered by the map on this page. Trade questions with a partner.

Engaging activity provides an opportunity to extend the lesson.

BUILDING YOUR SKILLS
Reading a Chart

One of the best ways to understand information is to organize facts on a chart. Charts can show how important ideas connect to one another.

Here is how to make a main idea and details chart.

- Choose a topic. Use it for the title.
- List the main idea at the top of the chart. List the details that support the idea below the main idea.
- Use the information on the chart to help answer any questions you have about the material you have read.

Government Under the Articles of Confederation

Main Idea	The Articles of Confederation was a plan of government.
Supporting Details	1. The government is run by Congress. 2. Approval of all 13 states is needed to make changes to the Articles of Confederation.

Answer the questions below, using the information on the chart.

Questions assess students' mastery of the skills.

1. What is the main idea of the chart?
2. What are the supporting details?

CHALLENGE Copy the chart on a sheet of paper. Find two more details about government under the Articles of Confederation to add to the chart.

Apply the Skill
Create a main idea and details chart, using what you have read about the Northwest Ordinance on page 86.

Sample page from Chapter 5 of the Student Edition

Chapter Review assesses understanding.

Chapter Review assesses concept retention, builds study skills, and provides test preparation.

Chapter Summary provides a graphic presentation of main chapter ideas to use as a study aid.

Essential Vocabulary Review reinforces word retention.

Chapter 2 Review

Summary: Settlers came to America looking for wealth, religious freedom, and land. Different ways of life developed in each region.

Section 1: Spanish explorers destroyed the Aztec Empire in search of wealth and power. Spaniards settled New Spain. The French settled New France.

Section 2: The English settled their first colony in North America at Jamestown, Virginia. The Pilgrims and the Puritans settled in New England to follow their religious beliefs.

Section 3: Other colonies were settled in New England, and in the Middle and Southern regions. A different way of life developed in each region.

- cash crop
- mission
- charter
- indentured servant
- debtor

Vocabulary Review

Complete each sentence with a term from the list.

1. King James of England gave a group of settlers a ____ allowing them the right to set up a colony.
2. One of the main crops in Virginia was tobacco, which became an important ____ for land owners.
3. In England a ____ could be jailed for not paying money owed to others.
4. Someone who worked for others to pay for passage to America was called an ____.
5. A Spanish priest could set up a church-run settlement, or a ____, in North America.

Sample pages from Chapter 2 of the Student Edition

Chapter Quiz questions assess chapter objectives.

Chapter Quiz

Write your answers in complete sentences.

1. What did Spain do to run farms in the colonies in the Americas?
2. What did John Smith do for people in the Jamestown colony?
3. Where were the 13 colonies located?
4. **Critical Thinking** If you were a Native American living around 1600, would you have wanted to live in lands colonized by people from Spain, France, or England? Explain.
5. **Critical Thinking** Why were all 13 colonies developed along the coast and not farther inland?

Test Tip
Before you begin a test or quiz, look it over. Decide how much time you can spend on each question.

Useful test-taking tips help students succeed on tests.

Writing Tip
You can support the main points with facts and examples.

Writing Tips help students plan and revise their writing.

Using the Timeline

Use the timeline on pages 20–21 to answer the questions.

1. How many years after the English settled Jamestown did the English take over New Amsterdam?
2. What European countries were exploring and settling in the Americas?

Timeline questions help students manage sequence of chapter events.

Group Activity

Your group is part of a new colony. Meet to discuss the name of the colony and how it will be governed. With your group, write a compact that lists and describes each of the laws of the colony.

High-interest Group Activity fosters collaborative learning.

Student Edition includes a comprehensive reference section.

U. S. and world maps provide geographical reference points for students.

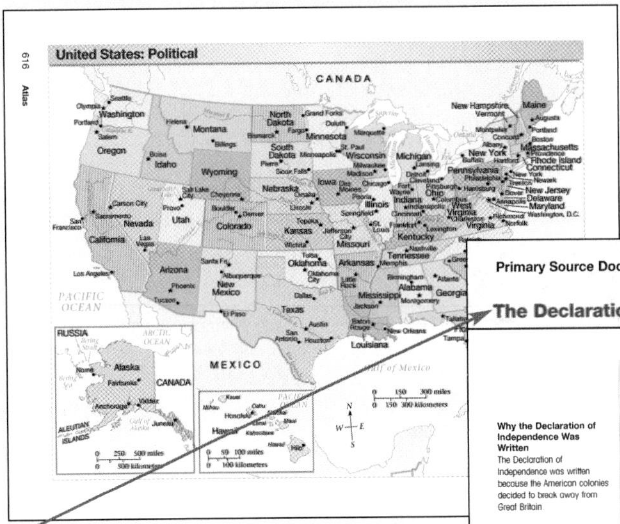

Primary source documents encourage students to become active historians.

Primary Source Document

The Declaration of Independence

Why the Declaration of Independence Was Written
The Declaration of Independence was written because the American colonies decided to break away from Great Britain.

Purposes of Government
The colonists wanted a government that protected the rights of the people. These rights included the rights of life, liberty, and the chance to seek happiness.

In Congress July 4, 1776

The Unanimous Declaration of the Thirteen United States of America

When in the course of human events, it becomes necessary for one people to dissolve the political bands which have connected them with another, and to assume among the powers of the earth, the separate and equal station to which the laws of nature and of nature's God entitle them, a decent respect to the opinions of mankind requires that they should declare the causes which impel them to the separation.

Political Theory of the Declaration

We hold these truths to be self-evident, that all men are created equal, that they are endowed by their Creator with certain unalienable rights, that among these are life, liberty, and the pursuit of happiness. That to secure these rights, governments are instituted among men, deriving their just powers from the consent of the governed. That whenever any form of government becomes destructive of these ends, it is the right of the people to alter or to abolish it, and to institute new government, laying its foundation on such principles and organizing its powers in such form, as to them shall seem most likely to effect their safety ... Prudence, indeed, will dictate that ... ng established should not be changed ... ansient causes; and accordingly all ... shown, that mankind are more ... er, while evils are sufferable, than to ... s by abolishing the forms to which they ... But when a long train of abuses

Margin notes help students unlock the language of historical documents.

Primary Source Document

The Constitution of the United States of America

Preamble
This Constitution was written to see that all citizens are treated fairly, to keep the country safe, and to keep people free for all times.

Preamble

We the people of the United States, in order to form a more perfect Union, establish justice, insure domestic tranquility, provide for the common defense, promote the general welfare, and secure the blessings of liberty to ourselves and our posterity, do ordain and establish this Constitution for the United States of America.

Article I

The Legislative Branch

SECTION 1. All legislative powers herein granted shall be vested in a Congress of the United States, which shall consist of a Senate and House of Representatives.

House of Representatives

SECTION 2. (1) The House of Representatives shall be composed of members chosen every second year by the people of the several states, and the electors in each state shall have the qualifications requisite for electors of the most numerous branch of the state legislature.

Section 2. (2)
To be a member of the House of Representatives, a person must:
- Be at least 25 years old.
- Be a U.S. citizen for at least seven years.
- Live in the state he or she represents.

(2) No person shall be a representative who shall not have attained to the age of twenty-five years, and been seven years a citizen of the United States, and who shall not, when elected, be an inhabitant of that state in which he shall be chosen.

(3) Representatives *~~[and direct taxes]~~ shall be apportioned among the several states which may be included within this Union, according to their respective numbers, ~~[which shall be determined by adding to the whole number of free persons, including those bound to service for a term of years, and excluding Indians not~~

* The blue lines indicate portions of the Constitution changed by amendments to the document.

624 Reference Center

Sample pages from Reference Center of the Student Edition

The Presidents of the United States

	Years in Office	Vice President
1. George Washington Born: 1732 Died: 1799	1789–1797	John Adams
2. John Adams Born: 1735 Died: 1826	1797–1801	Thomas Jefferson
3. Thomas Jefferson Born: 1743 Died: 1826	1801–1809	Aaron Burr, George Clinton
4. James Madison Born: 1751 Died: 1836	1809–1817	George Clinton, Elbridge Gerry
5. James Monroe Born: 1758 Died: 1831	1817–1825	Daniel D. Tompkins
6. John Quincy Adams Born: 1767 Died: 1848	1825–1829	John C. Calhoun
7. Andrew Jackson Born: 1767 Died: 1845	1829–1837	John C. Calhoun, Martin Van Buren
8. Martin Van Buren	1837–1841	Richard M. Johnson
	1841	John Tyler
	1841–1845	None
	1845–1849	George M. Dallas
	1849–1850	Millard Fillmore
	1850–1853	None
	1853–1857	William R. King

hile in office *** resigned while in office

Information about our country's Presidents provides a political overview through time.

The Fifty States

State (U.S. government abbreviation)	Date of Entry into Union (Order of entry)	Total Area in Square Miles (Rank)	Population (in thousands)	Capital City	State Nickname
Alabama (AL)	1819 (22)	52,423 (30)	4,447	Montgomery	Heart of Dixie
Alaska (AK)	1959 (49)	656,424 (1)	627	Juneau	The Last Frontier
Arizona (AZ)	1912 (48)	114,006 (6)	5,131	Phoenix	Grand Canyon State
Arkansas (AR)	1836 (25)	53,182 (29)	2,673	Little Rock	Natural State
California (CA)	1850 (31)	163,707 (3)	33,872	Sacramento	Golden State
Colorado (CO)	1876 (38)	104,100 (8)	4,301	Denver	Centennial State
Connecticut (CT)	1788 (5)	5,544 (48)	3,406	Hartford	Constitution State
Delaware (DE)	1787 (1)	2,489 (49)	784	Dover	First State
Florida (FL)	1845 (27)	65,756 (22)	15,982	Tallahassee	Sunshine State
Georgia (GA)	1788 (4)	59,441 (24)	8,186	Atlanta	Empire State of the South
Hawaii (HI)	1959 (50)	10,932 (43)	1,212	Honolulu	Aloha State
Idaho (ID)	1890 (43)	83,574 (14)	1,294	Boise	Gem State
Illinois (IL)	1818 (21)	57,918 (25)	12,419	Springfield	Prairie State
Indiana (IN)	1816 (19)	36,420 (38)	6,080	Indianapolis	Hoosier State
Iowa (IA)	1846 (29)	56,276 (26)	2,926	Des Moines	Hawkeye State
Kansas (KS)	1861 (34)	82,282 (15)	2,688	Topeka	Sunflower State
Kentucky (KY)	1792 (15)	40,411 (37)	4,042	Frankfort	Bluegrass State
Louisiana (LA)	1812 (18)	51,843 (31)	4,469	Baton Rouge	Pelican State
Maine (ME)	1820 (23)	35,387 (39)	1,275	Augusta	Pine Tree State
Maryland (MD)	1788 (7)	12,407 (42)	5,296	Annapolis	Old Line State
Massachusetts (MA)	1788 (6)	10,555 (44)	6,349	Boston	Bay State
Michigan (MI)	1837 (26)	96,705 (11)	9,938	Lansing	Wolverine State
Minnesota (MN)	1858 (32)	86,943 (12)	4,919	St. Paul	Gopher State
Mississippi (MS)	1817 (20)	48,434 (32)	2,845	Jackson	Magnolia State
Missouri (MO)	1821 (24)	69,709 (21)	5,595	Jefferson City	Show Me State
Montana (MT)	1889 (41)	147,046 (4)	902	Helena	Treasure State
Nebraska (NE)	1867 (37)	77,358 (16)	1,711	Lincoln	Cornhusker State
Nevada (NV)	1864 (36)	110,567 (7)	1,998	Carson City	Silver State
New Hampshire (NH)	1788 (9)	9,351 (46)	1,236	Concord	Granite State
New Jersey (NJ)	1787 (3)	8,722 (47)	8,414	Trenton	Garden State

Information about each of the 50 states gives students a reference tool in chart form.

Sample pages from Reference Center of the Student Edition

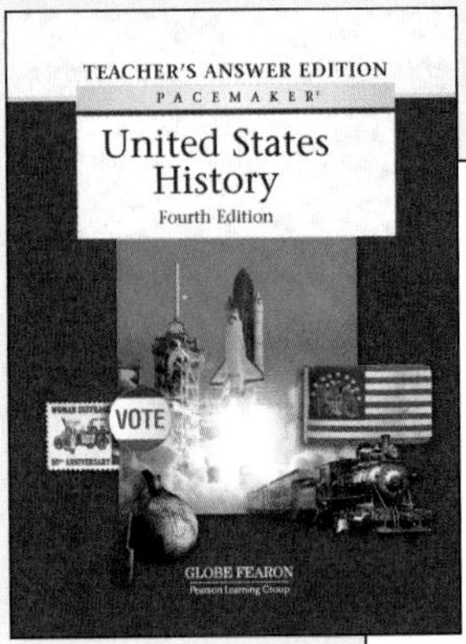

Getting Started note introduces each section.

Section 3 The Growth of the Thirteen Colonies

Words to Know

treaty	a written agreement between two or more nations
debtor	a person who owes money to others

Getting Started Have students look at the world map on pages 614–615 of the book. Ask students to think about where they would look for land in the Americas if they lived in England. Discuss why the English colonies were established on the Atlantic coast.

Remember
The Puritans settled the Massachusetts Bay Colony in 1630.

There were 13 English colonies established along the Atlantic coast between 1607 and 1733. The 13 English colonies were divided into three regions: the New England, Middle, and Southern colonies.

The New England Colonies

Massachusetts

In the last section you read that the Massachusetts Bay Colony became the first of the New England colonies. At that time, the colony included all the land in present-day Massachusetts and part of present-day Maine. The other New England colonies grew out of the Massachusetts colony.

Rhode Island

After Massachusetts was settled, many people who were unhappy with Puritan life moved to other areas. Others were forced to leave. In 1635, a minister, Roger Williams, was ordered to leave Massachusetts. This is what Williams believed.

1. The established churches had too much power.
2. The state, or government, should be separate from the church, or religion.
3. All people should be free to practice their own beliefs.

Sample pages from Chapter 2 of the Teacher's Answer Edition

The Carolinas

In 1663, King Charles of England gave eight rich English lords the right to settle land south of Virginia. The land was beautiful and the soil was good. It was named Carolina after the English king.

Settlers in Carolina were allowed religious freedom. Many people came to Carolina for that freedom. They also came to farm the rich soil in the area. So many people arrived that, in 1712, Carolina was broken into two colonies—North Carolina and South Carolina.

Economics Fact Before 1640, most European males in the colonies had a fifty-fifty chance of dying during their first year of residence. Half of all marriages were ended by the death of one partner before the seventh anniversary.

Annotations provide more in-depth teacher information for content instruction.

Georgia

The last of the 13 colonies, Georgia, was settled to give a home to **debtors.** These are people who had been jailed for not paying money owed to others.

An English general named James Oglethorpe felt it was unfair to put debtors in jail. He asked the king to allow people to settle in America and get a new start. In 1733, Georgia, named after King George II, became the thirteenth English colony.

Economics Fact

In colonial Georgia, 16-year-old boys became taxpayers and served in the army. Sixteen-year-old girls were usually married.

How was Georgia different from the other English colonies? English people who were debtors were allowed to settle there.

Hardcover Teacher's Answer Edition has answers at point of use.

Section 3 Review

1. Into what three regions were the 13 colonies divided?
2. Name two leaders who left Massachusetts. Where did each go?
3. **Critical Thinking** How were the Middle colonies different from the New England colonies?
4. **Write About History** Write a pamphlet to attract people to live in one of the 13 colonies.

1. New England, Middle, Southern
2. Roger Williams went to Rhode Island. Thomas Hooker went to Connecticut.
3. Middle: Religious freedom; people from different European countries; farming
   New England: Puritan rule, fishing, small farms
4. Student responses should show an understanding of religious and political life in the colonies.

More Review is provided in Exercise 8 of the Workbook.

Additional annotations refer to other support throughout the program.

Workbook provides practice for every lesson.

Concise review of the key concepts of each section is boxed.

Name ____________________ Date ____________

Section 3: The Growth of the Thirteen Colonies

Exercise 8

Beginning in 1635, other English colonies were settled. The colonies were divided into the New England, Middle, and Southern colonies.

Complete the chart below. Some facts are already included.

Colony	Founders/First Settlers	Year Founded
Rhode Island		1635
Connecticut		
New Hampshire	Members of a fishing community	
New York		
New Jersey		1664
Pennsylvania		
Delaware	Settlers from areas south of Pennsylvania	
Maryland		
The Carolinas	Eight rich English lords	
Georgia		

CRITICAL THINKING

Do you think the Puritan leaders were right to force people who disagreed with them to leave the Massachusetts colony? Explain. Write your answer on a separate sheet of paper.

8 Chapter 2 • Colonies Are Settled • **1519–1733**

A variety of comprehensive exercises encourages students to apply their knowledge.

Name ____________________ Date ____________

Using a Map: The Thirteen Colonies, 1733

Exercis

A. Fill in these place names on the lines on the map.

Pennsylvania (PA) Georgia (GA) Virginia (VA) Atlantic Ocean

The Thirteen Colonies, 1733

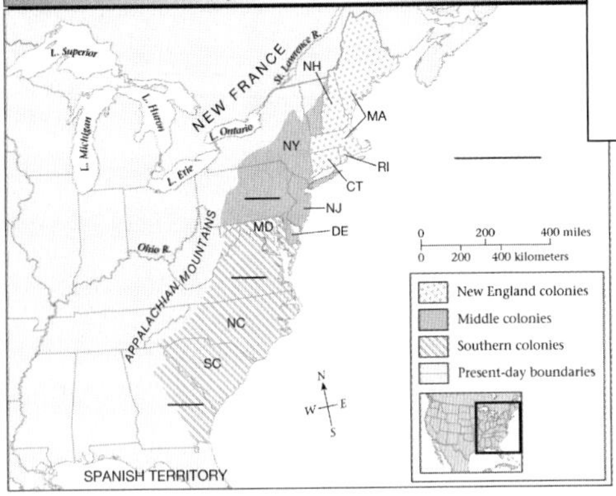

B. Use the map to answer the questions below.

1. Which colony was closer to the Appalachian Mountains, Connecticut or Pennsylvania? ____________
2. Which colony was the farthest north? ____________
3. Which group of colonies was North Carolina a part of? ____________
4. Which group of colonies was New Jersey a part of? ____________
5. Which three colonies shared a boundary with Connecticut? ____________

Chapter 2 • Colonies Are Settled • **1519–1733** 9

Critical Thinking exercises extend skills.

Comprehension questions reinforce content understanding.

Sample pages from Chapter 2 of the Workbook

Classroom Resource Binder extends and supports lessons.

Words to Know exercises assess vocabulary mastery for each chapter.

Name ______________________ Date ______________

CHAPTER 2

Words to Know

8

A. Match each term with its meaning. Write the correct letter on the line.

____ **1.** treaty — **a.** a settlement, built by a church, from which people teach their religion to others

____ **2.** conquer — **b.** to take over and control

____ **3.** mission — **c.** to change from one religion or belief to another

____ **4.** debtor — **d.** a written agreement giving certain rights

____ **5.** convert — **e.** a person who owes money to others

____ **6.** charter — **f.** a written agreement between two or more nations

B. Complete each sentence with a term from the box.

joint-stock company	charter	cash crop	indentured servant

7. Tobacco became a ______________ for the Virginia colony.

8. People give money to share costs in a ______________.

9. The ______________ from the king allowed the settlers to form a colony.

10. An ______________ helped the farmer grow tobacco.

Name ______________________ Date ______________

The Declaration of Independence

1

Part I

Study the Declaration of Independence on pages 618–623 of your textbook. Answer the questions below. Circle the letter of the correct answer.

1. What is the most important idea in the Declaration of Independence?

(a) The King of Great Britain treated the colonies badly for too long a time.

(b) All men are created equal.

(c) Human rights is a privilege, not a right.

...ns cannot vote new leaders ...overnment until the old ...s die.

...g to the Declaration, when ...e allowed to change their ...ent?

...they no longer admire that ...ment's rulers

...they disagree with a law

...a new ruler tells them to

...that government treats ...ople badly for too long

...most colonists blame for ...ir situation?

...itish public

...ns and Native Americans

...George III and the British ...ment

...s Jefferson

4. Which statement is an important reason colonists wanted independence?

(a) King George III would only pass certain laws if the colonists gave up representation in Parliament.

(b) Colonists were being forced to join Parliament.

(c) Colonial lawmakers did not think King George III was a good leader.

(d) King George III enforced all laws the same way.

5. Which of the following was a law the colonists felt they could not obey?

(a) the extra tax on people they traded with

(b) not being taxed on the money they made

(c) raising taxes without asking for their agreement or vote

(d) paying a tax for British troops living in their homes

Document-Based Questions • **DBQ 1**

Document-Based Questions offer reinforcement of primary source understanding.

Sample page from Document-Based Questions of the Classroom Resource Binder

Name ______________________ Date ______________

CHAPTER 2

Comprehension Check

9

A. Read each sentence. If it is about Spain, write *Spain*. If it is about France, write *France*. If it is about England, write *England*.

________ **1.** This country used cannons and guns to conquer the Aztec Empire.

________ **2.** The settlers from this country wrote the Mayflower Compact.

________ **3.** This country's colony, Quebec, was a small fort.

________ **4.** An explorer from this country named a land of flowers and wildlife Florida.

________ **5.** One of this country's explorers claimed the St. Lawrence River.

________ **6.** This country's king gave land to a Quaker to start a colony.

B. Complete each sentence by writing the correct letter on the line.

____ **7.** Plymouth and Massachusetts Bay colonies were settled by
- (a) people who wanted religious freedom.
- (b) tobacco farmers.
- (c) people from Sweden.

____ **8.** The colony named after a king and later split into two was
- (a) Georgia.
- (b) New York.
- (c) Carolina.

____ **9.** Massachusetts, Connecticut, New Hampshire, and Rhode Island were called the
- (a) Southern colonies.
- (b) New England colonies.
- (c) Middle colonies.

____ **10.** The New York colony was originally settled by the
- (a) Dutch.
- (b) Spaniards.
- (c) French.

Chapter 2 • Colonies Are Settled • 1519–1733 41

Comprehension Check worksheets review chapter content.

Sample pages from Chapter 2 of the Classroom Resource Binder

Interactive Classroom Resources builds classroom success!

The Pacemaker® Interactive Classroom Resources provides electronic support for *Pacemaker® United States History*.

PACEMAKER® INTERACTIVE Classroom Resources

The Interactive Classroom Resources offers all the worksheets from the Classroom Resource Binder and Workbook in a printable format for easy reproduction.

Worksheets, quizzes, and tests can be modified using the ExamView® test generator software to support individual students' ability levels.

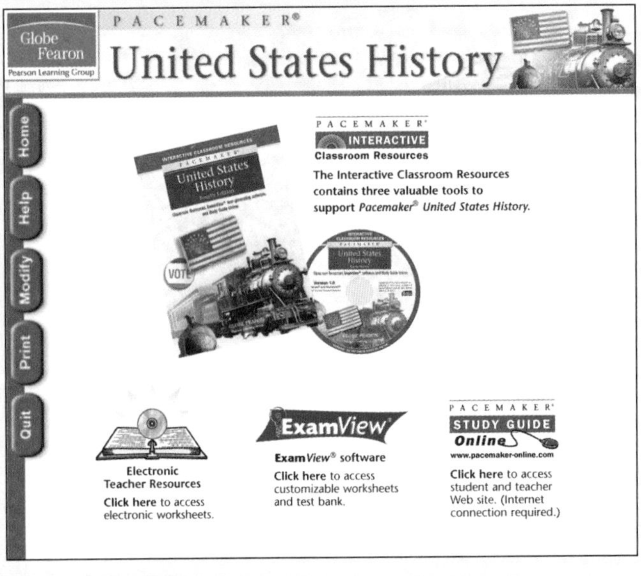

The Pacemaker® Interactive Classroom Resources also offers a Web link to the Pacemaker® Online Study Guide. The Pacemaker® Online Study Guide provides extensive practice, review, and feedback for students to use at their own pace.

PACEMAKER® STUDY GUIDE Online
www.pacemaker-online.com

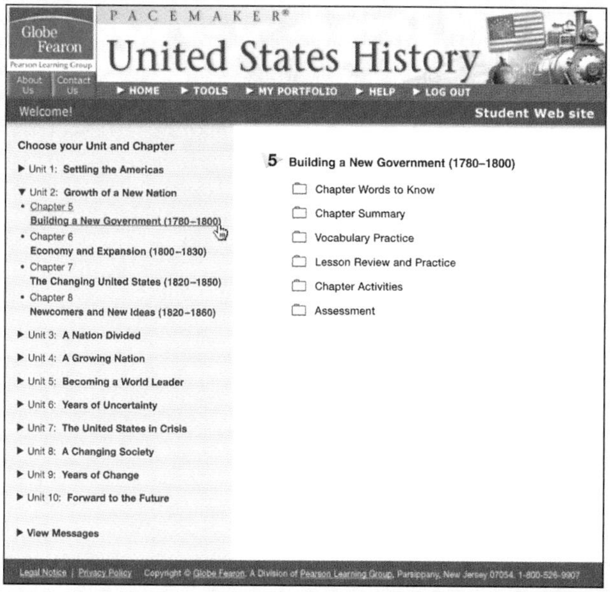

The Pacemaker® Online Study Guide also includes

- Vocabulary practice and review to improve comprehension
- Practice and review for every chapter to foster student success
- Chapter activities to reinforce key concepts
- An online student portfolio to help students track their own performance and to help teachers monitor their progress

The Pacemaker® Interactive Classroom Resources helps all students succeed by allowing them to access required content in the format that works best for them. At the same time, it helps teachers save time on day-to-day preparation and classroom management.

ESL/ELL Teacher's Guide enhances instruction for ELL students.

Students' prior knowledge is related to new concepts.

Vocabulary section teaches and reinforces high-frequency academic words, idioms, and expressions.

Visual aids and graphic organizers enhance students' comprehension.

ESL/ELL

Chapter 2 Colonies Are Settled (1519–1733)

pages 20–39

Introducing the Chapter

Tapping Prior Knowledge
Ask students to preview the chapter by reading the headings and subheadings and by looking at the art and photos (on pages 20, 22, 23, 26, 28, 29, 31, 33, and 36 of the Student Edition), the timeline (on pages 20–21 of the Student Edition), the numbered lists (on pages 22, 29, and 32 of the Student Edition), the chart (on page 24 of the Student Edition), and the map (on page 35 of the Student Edition). Then, direct students to the paintings on pages 20 and 28 of the Student Edition. Ask students, *What problems or dangers do immigrants have when they come to a new country?*

Preteaching Vocabulary
Personalizing Vocabulary Begin by asking students to preview the chapter for five unfamiliar words or phrases and to record them in their Word Logs. Once students have identified these words and phrases, ask them to use their dictionaries to define them.

Identifying Essential Vocabulary Go over the pronunciation and meaning of each word and phrase in the box below. Then, ask each student to write a sentence for each word. Have students rewrite their sentences, leaving a blank space in place of the vocabulary term. Then, ask students to exchange sentences with a partner and fill in the blanks in the sentences their partner wrote.

Word or Phrase	Meaning
claimed	declared (p.22)
in search of	looking for (p.23)
wildlife	animals and plants that live in nature (p.23)
settler	a person who makes a place his or her home (p.24)
forced	made to do something (p.24)
water route	a path made of water (p.25)
religious beliefs	the way people feel about faith (p.27)
agreement	understanding (p.28)

Applying Content Knowledge

From the Chapter: Connecting History and Science (page 31)
Ask students to read Connecting History and Science: Colonial Medicine on page 31 of the Student Edition. Then, have students work in groups to list the medical cures that today we know were useless or even foolish. Next, have students predict five cures we use today that will probably appear to be foolish 200 years from now. These include radiation, surgery, vaccinations, antibiotics, and chemotherapy. Ask students, *Why do you believe that the cures you listed will be useless or seem foolish 200 years from now?*

Organizing Information
Explain to students that a chart can give essential information in a short form. Ask students to make a five-column chart of the three early English settlements in North America. Ask students to label the columns **Name of the Colony, Date of Settlement, Reason for Settlement, Leader,** and **Problems**. You may wish to distribute the four-column chart on page 70 of this guide and have students draw an additional column.

Personalizing the Lesson
Ask students to work in small groups to make a list of reasons that explain why people came to North America to live during the 1700s. Tell them to also list the dangers or problems involved in such a move. After their lists are complete, ask students to decide which reasons or problems/dangers still apply today and

4 **Unit 1** • U.S. History

Chapter content activities that parallel the Student Edition help to ensure understanding of appropriate grade-level content.

ESL/ELL

Assessing Content Knowledge

Ask students to respond to the following questions. You may wish to encourage students with higher language proficiency to help beginning level students understand the questions.

Beginning Level Questions
Encourage students at this level to think about the answers to these questions and offer short verbal responses.

1. Look at the chart on page 24. Who are four Spanish explorers? (Juan Ponce de León, Hernán Cortés, Francisco Pizarro, and Francisco de Coronado)
2. Look at the picture on page 26. Who is the person? (John Smith, leader of Jamestown)
3. Look at page 27. Who settled in Plymouth? (the Pilgrims)
4. Look at pages 32–37. How many colonies were there? (13)
5. Look at the map on page 35. What three regions are shown? (New England, Middle, Southern)

Intermediate Level Questions
Encourage students at this level to offer verbal responses or short written responses to the following questions.

1. Look at Section 1. Why did Spain want to conquer, or take over, the Aztecs? (for their gold and silver)
2. Look at Section 1. Why were a small number of Spanish soldiers able to conquer the Aztecs? (The Spanish soldiers used cannons, guns, and swords that were more powerful than the bows, arrows, and spears used by the Aztecs; the Aztecs were frightened by the Spanish soldiers' horses; and many Aztecs died from measles and smallpox.)
3. Look at Section 2. What are three things that the Native Americans showed the Pilgrims? (how to grow corn; where to hunt turkey and deer; and ways to fish for food)
4. Look at Section 2. What group of settlers came to New England in 1628? (the Puritans)
5. Look at Section 3. What are the names of the 13 colonies? (Massachusetts, Rhode Island, Connecticut, New Hampshire, New York, New Jersey, Pennsylvania, Delaware, Virginia, Maryland, North Carolina, South Carolina, and Georgia)

Advanced Level Questions
Encourage students at this level to provide written responses in complete sentences to the following questions.

1. What are three European countries that made settlements in the Americas? (Three European countries that made settlements in the Americas are Great Britain, Spain, and France.)
2. What was the Mayflower Compact? (The Mayflower Compact was an agreement written by the leaders of the Pilgrims that stated that all laws of the new colony would be fair and equal.)
3. How did Native Americans help the colonists? (The Native Americans showed the colonists how to grow corn; where to hunt turkey and deer; and ways to fish for food.)
4. What are four religious groups that were established in the colonies? (The four religious groups that were established in the colonies were the Pilgrims, the Catholics, the Puritans, and the Quakers.)
5. How was the colony of Georgia unusual? (It was settled by debtors.)

Closing the Chapter

Ask students to use the chart they created in the Organizing Information activity on page 4 of this guide to write a paragraph about what they learned in the chapter.

Chapter 2 • U.S. History 5

Three levels of questions help to assess the comprehension of students with varying levels of fluency.

Sample pages from Chapter 2 of the ESL/ELL Teacher's Guide

Chapter closing activities promote critical thinking.

PACEMAKER®
ESL/ELL Online
www.ESL-ELL.com

Spanish Supplement fosters content understanding.

The Spanish Supplement provides Spanish translations of the Words to Know, Learning Objectives, Vocabulary Review, Chapter Summary, Chapter Quiz, Unit Review, and more for each chapter in *Pacemaker® United States History*.

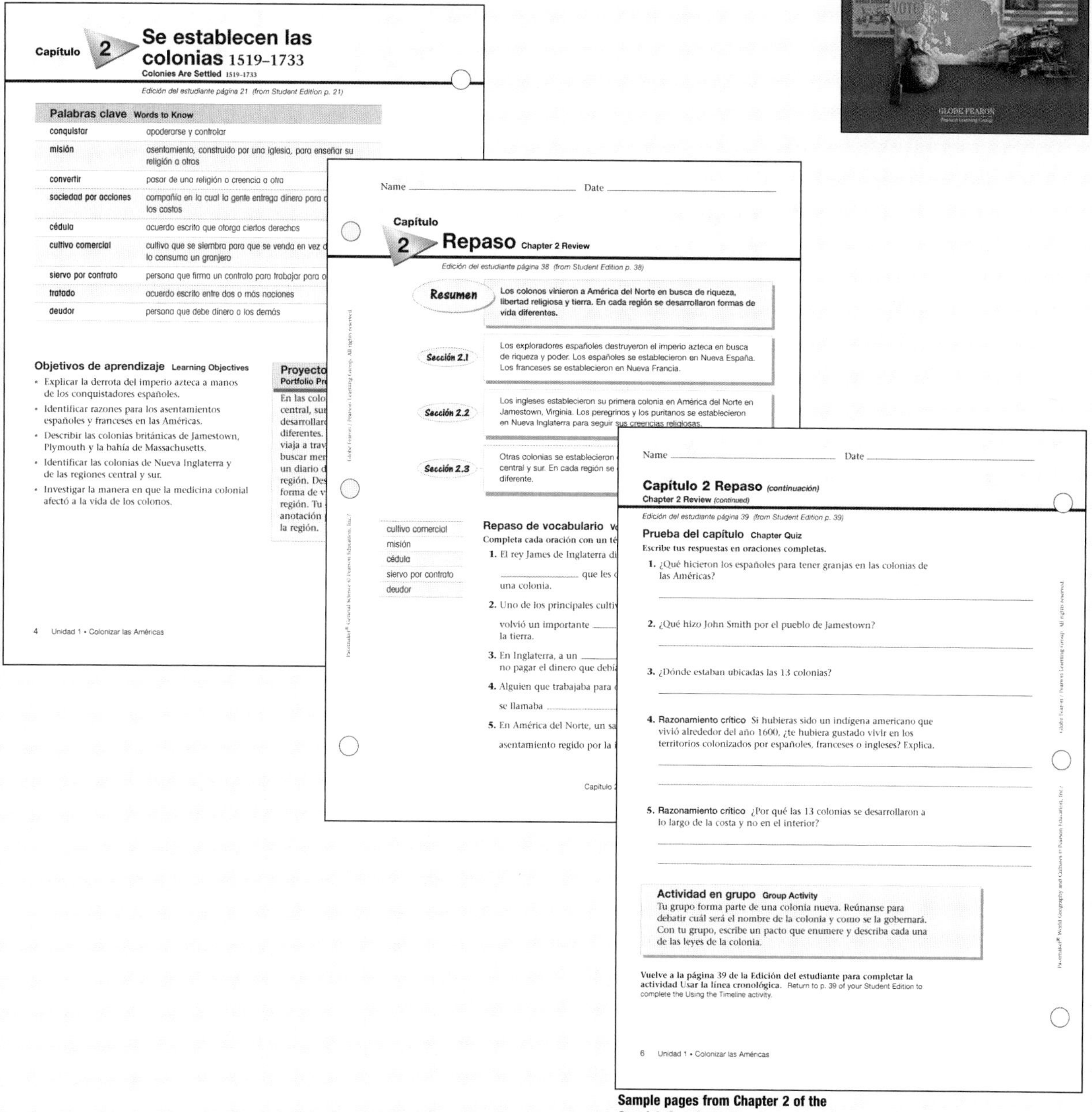

Capítulo 2 **Se establecen las colonias** 1519–1733
Colonies Are Settled 1519–1733

Edición del estudiante página 21 (from Student Edition p. 21)

Palabras clave Words to Know

conquistar	apoderarse y controlar
misión	asentamiento, construido por una iglesia, para enseñar su religión a otros
convertir	pasar de una religión o creencia a otra
sociedad por acciones	compañía en la cual la gente entrega dinero para c… los costos
cédula	acuerdo escrito que otorga ciertos derechos
cultivo comercial	cultivo que se siembra para que se venda en vez d… lo consuma un granjero
siervo por contrato	persona que firma un contrato para trabajar para o…
tratado	acuerdo escrito entre dos o más naciones
deudor	persona que debe dinero a los demás

Objetivos de aprendizaje Learning Objectives
- Explicar la derrota del imperio azteca a manos de los conquistadores españoles.
- Identificar razones para los asentamientos españoles y franceses en las Américas.
- Describir las colonias británicas de Jamestown, Plymouth y la bahía de Massachusetts.
- Identificar las colonias de Nueva Inglaterra y de las regiones central y sur.
- Investigar la manera en que la medicina colonial afectó a la vida de los colonos.

Proyecto… Portfolio Pr…
En las colo… central, su… desarrollar… diferentes. viaja a trav… buscar men… un diario d… región. Des… forma de v… región. Tu anotación … la región.

4 Unidad 1 • Colonizar las Américas

Name ________________ Date ________________

Capítulo 2 **Repaso** Chapter 2 Review

Edición del estudiante página 38 (from Student Edition p. 38)

Resumen Los colonos vinieron a América del Norte en busca de riqueza, libertad religiosa y tierra. En cada región se desarrollaron formas de vida diferentes.

Sección 2.1 Los exploradores españoles destruyeron el imperio azteca en busca de riqueza y poder. Los españoles se establecieron en Nueva España. Los franceses se establecieron en Nueva Francia.

Sección 2.2 Los ingleses establecieron su primera colonia en América del Norte en Jamestown, Virginia. Los peregrinos y los puritanos se establecieron en Nueva Inglaterra para seguir sus creencias religiosas.

Sección 2.3 Otras colonias se establecieron … central y sur. En cada región se … diferente.

cultivo comercial
misión
cédula
siervo por contrato
deudor

Repaso de vocabulario V…
Completa cada oración con un té…
1. El rey James de Inglaterra di… ________ que les … una colonia.
2. Uno de los principales culti… volvió un importante ____ la tierra.
3. En Inglaterra, a un ________ no pagar el dinero que debí…
4. Alguien que trabajaba para … se llamaba
5. En América del Norte, un sa… asentamiento regido por la i…

Capítulo 2

Pacemaker® General Science © Pearson Education, Inc. / Globe Fearon / Pearson Learning Group. All rights reserved.

Name ________________ Date ________________

Capítulo 2 Repaso *(continuación)*
Chapter 2 Review *(continued)*

Edición del estudiante página 39 (from Student Edition p. 39)

Prueba del capítulo Chapter Quiz
Escribe tus respuestas en oraciones completas.

1. ¿Qué hicieron los españoles para tener granjas en las colonias de las Américas?
2. ¿Qué hizo John Smith por el pueblo de Jamestown?
3. ¿Dónde estaban ubicadas las 13 colonias?
4. **Razonamiento crítico** Si hubieras sido un indígena americano que vivió alrededor del año 1600, ¿te hubiera gustado vivir en los territorios colonizados por españoles, franceses o ingleses? Explica.
5. **Razonamiento crítico** ¿Por qué las 13 colonias se desarrollaron a lo largo de la costa y no en el interior?

Actividad en grupo Group Activity
Tu grupo forma parte de una colonia nueva. Reúnanse para debatir cuál será el nombre de la colonia y como se la gobernará. Con tu grupo, escribe un pacto que enumere y describa cada una de las leyes de la colonia.

Vuelve a la página 39 de la Edición del estudiante para completar la actividad Usar la línea cronológica. Return to p. 39 of your Student Edition to complete the Using the Timeline activity.

Pacemaker® World Geography and Cultures © Pearson Education, Inc. / Globe Fearon / Pearson Learning Group. All rights reserved.

6 Unidad 1 • Colonizar las Américas

Sample pages from Chapter 2 of the Spanish Supplement

Teacher's Planning Guide saves you preparation time . . .

Planning the Chapter

Chapter 2 · Colonies Are Settled 1519–1733

Chapter at a Glance

Unit 1

An overview of the sections and features in the chapter is provided.

Learning Objectives

- Explain the defeat of the Aztec Empire by Spanish conquerors.
- Identify reasons for Spanish and French settlements in the Americas.
- Describe the English colonies at Jamestown, Plymouth, and Massachusetts Bay.
- Identify the colonies in the N... England, Middle, and Southe... regions.

Social Studies Skills

- Compare and contrast medic... practices in colonial times wi... present technology.
- Read a timeline that illustrat... settling of the Americas .
- Describe the people, econom... geography of the New Englan... Middle, and Southern coloni...

Writing Skills

- Write a list of reasons for coming to the Americas.
- Write a class compact and explain how these rules will benefit each class member.
- Write a pamphlet describing what...

Concise Learning Objectives help target instruction for individual needs.

Resource Planner

Chapter 2 Colonies Are Settled

Use the Correlating Program Resources for reinforcement, reteaching, or enrichment. Additional activities for customizing the lessons can be found in this guide.

Key: Reteaching = ; Reinforcement = ; Enrichment =

Sections	Program Resources: Workbook Exercises	Teacher's Planning Guide	Classroom Resource Binder
Spain and France Begin Colonies	6	p. 11	Outline Map 5 *North America*
The First English Colonies	7	p. 12	Transparency 13 *U.S. Political Outline*
Connecting History and Science Colonial Medicine		p. 13	Connecting History and Science *Making Soap*
The Growth of the Thirteen Colonies	8, 9	p. 14	Transparency 2 *The Thirteen Colonies*
Chapter Review		p. 15	Vocabulary 8 Chapter Test A, B 12, 13

Correlations to other program resources make planning easy.

Customizing the Chapter

Opening the Chapter

Student Edition pages 20-21

Photo Activity

Invite students to guess why a cradle was selected to accompany a painting of Pilgrims from the *Mayflower*. Explain that the cradle was supposedly brought on the *Mayflower* by Susanna and William White who were anticipating the birth of their child. Mention that their son was born on the *Mayflower* in 1620 after the ship landed in Provincetown Harbor. Because of this momentous journey, the White's named their son Peregrine, which means "traveler" or "pilgrim." Since space and weight were concerns, the Pilgrims could bring very few prized possessions. Ask students what they would have brought with them if they had been traveling on the Mayflower. Make a class list of all the possessions, ranking the items according to the ones students think are most important. Then have students categorize the items according to their purpose.

Words to Know

Review the Words to Know on page 21 of the Student Edition. To help students remember the words, invite pairs to find the words in the Glossary on page 00. Have them take turns giving clues that tell about a vocabulary term, without using any part of the term itself. Ask each pair of students to keep track of the number of clues it takes to guess each key term. The following words and definitions are covered in this chapter.

10 · Unit 1

Sample pages from Chapter 2 of the Teacher's Planning Guide

. . . and adapts lessons for diverse learning styles.

Activities for each lesson address diverse learning styles.

Hands-on activities bring social studies to life.

Traditional and alternative assessment tools check students' understanding of chapter content.

Activities and assessments close the chapter.

Reteaching Activity

Have students list the colonies that were settled by the English. Next to each colony ask students to list the problems that colonists faced and how these problems were solved.

Alternative Assessment

Students write journal entries from the perspective of settlers in one of the colonies. They discuss what an average day is like, describing the work, the hardships faced, family life, and favorite activities.

CONNECTING HISTORY AND SCIENCE: COLONIAL MEDICINE

Student Edition, page 31

Objectives

- Social Studies Skill: Outline health conditions aboard a ship in colonial times by writing a report.
- Social Studies Skill: Depict colonial and contemporary medical practices by drawing two scenes.
- Social Studies: Compare and contrast medical [...]ctices in colonial times with present-day [...]hnology and practices.

[...]tivities

[...]n and Now

[...]rials: reference materials (Bibliography, page [...]nternet sites)

[...]dure: Have students work in pairs to do [...]rch about colonial medicine. Each pair lists [...]ical practices in colonial and contemporary [...]s. Students in each pair then assume the role [...]ther a colonial or contemporary doctor and [...]-plays with their partner, discussing the [...]rences in medical practices-then and now.

[...]here a Doctor in the House?

[...]dure: Invite students to think of a medical [...]dition, such as a sore throat, and how it might [...]eated in both colonial and contemporary times. [...]e them draw two scenes, depicting how a doctor [...]ld treat a patient-then and now. Ask students to [...]l each scene with the treatment or remedy.

Let's Inspect It

Procedure: Ask students to assume the role of a colonial health inspector assigned to passenger ships traveling from Europe to the colonies.

Students can write a brief report that includes their observations aboard ship, an evaluation of conditions on the ship and of the passengers, and recommendations for improvements.

Practice

Have students complete Connecting History and Science from the Classroom Resource Binder.

Unit 1

SECTION 3: The Growth of the Thirteen Colonies

Student Edition pages 32-37

Section Objectives Activity objective(s) starred.

- Describe the people, economy, and geography of the New England, Middle, and Southern colonies.
- Explain why people left Massachusetts to establish other New England colonies.
- Identify reasons why the Middle colonies were settled.
- Explain how farming differed in the three colonial regions.
- Identify the 13 colonies of the New England, Middle, and Southern regions.

Words to Know

treaty, debtors

Cooperative Group Activity

Who's Who

Materials: reference materials (Bibliography list, pate 00; Internet sites)

Procedure: Explain to the class that *Who's Who* is a listing of important people. Divide the class into three groups and assign each group a region: New England, Middle colonies, and Southern colonies.

- Groups assume the role of editors at *Who's Who*. They need to decide which people from their region should be listed in *Who's Who*.
- Students research their choices and write short, two-paragraph biographies on five people.
- One student from the group presents the *Who's Who* for their region to the class.

Chapter 2 • 13

Customizing the Activity for Individual Needs

ESL To help ESLstudents learn about the *Who's Who* choices, have them write the names of their group's *Who's Who* choices on index cards. Then, have ESL students summarize their group's biographies on the other side of the index cards.

Learning Styles Students can:

- look at pictures of their *Who's Who* choices. What can they tell about each person by their picture?
- design a memorial for one of the *Who's Who* choices. The memorial should incorporate the reason the person made the *Who's Who* list.
- role-play the *Who's Who* choices for one region. Each group member role-plays one *Who's Who* choice. Each group member tells the rest of the group who he/she is and why he/she made the *Who's Who* list.

Reinforcement Activity

Divide students into three groups. Have each group think of "Who Am I" trivia questions about colonists in each of the colonies found in their region. Have them write questions about life in the colonies on one side of an index card, with the answers on the back. Then have each group take turns playing a trivia game with the other two groups, awarding points for every correct answer.

Example: We are a group of people in Pennsylvania who are against slavery. Who are we?

Answer: the Quakers

Alternative Assessment

Students can state the names of the 13 American colonies and tell one fact about each colony.

Example: Virginia

Answer: First colony settled by the English.

Closing the Chaper

Student Edition pages 38-39

Chapter Vocabulary

Review with students the Words to Know on page 21 of the Student Edition. Then have students quiz each other in pairs.

Have students complete the Vocabulary Review questions on page 38 of the Student Edition by completing each sentence with a term from the list.

For more vocabulary practice, have them complete the vocabulary exercise on page 00 in the Classroom Resource Binder.

Test Tip

In pairs, have students practice the test tip when completing the Chapter Quiz. Tell students they have 30 minutes to complete the Chapter Quiz. Have students approximate how much time they can spend on each question.

Learning Objectives

Have the students review their Chapter Goals Worksheet found on page 00 in the Classroom Resource Binder. They can check off the goal they have reached. Note that each section of the quiz corresponds to a Learning Objective.

Group Activity

Summary: Students create a new colony, name it, and decide how it will be governed by creating a compact describing its laws.

Materials: Butcher paper, markers

Procedure: Divide the class into groups and ask them to brainstorm a name for a new colony and decide how they will be governed. On butcher paper students write a list of the most important laws they think are needed to govern the colony. Students then write their colony's compact on paper. Each member signs and dates the document. Students choose one group member to read the compact to the rest of the class.

Assessment: Use the Group Activity Rubric found on page xii of this guide. Fill in the rubric with the following additional information. For this activity, students should have:

- divided the writing tasks so that each student wrote and contributed information about the new colony.
- worked together to combine the i[...] into a coherent compact, listing la[...] newly formed colony.

RELATED MATERIALS See the Un[...] page for related Globe Fearon books[...] used to enrich and extend the mate[...] chapter.

14 • Unit 1

Assessing the Chapter

Traditional Assessment

Chapter Quiz

The Chapter Quiz on page 39 of the Student Edition can be used as an open-book test, a closed-book test, or a homework assignment. Use the quiz to identify concepts in the chapter that students need to review. Chapter Tests can be found in the Classroom Resource Binder on pages 00-00. Workbook pages 00-00 can be used for additional practice.

Chapter Tests

Use Chapter 2 Tests A and B in the Classroom Resource Binder to further assess mastery of chapter concepts.

Additional Resources

Use the Resource Planner on page 11 in this guide to assign additional exercises from the Classroom Resource Binder and Workbook.

Alternative Assessment

Interview the Student

Give each student a slip of paper on which the name of one of the 13 colonies is written. Ask:

- When was this colony settled?
- Who settled the colony?
- What problems did the colonists face?

Create a Timeline

- Students scan the chapter and list pertinent dates and events that happened between 1519 and 1733.
- Students list reasons why the colonies were established.
- Students draw timelines that outline the people, places, and events that occurred in the colonies.

Unit 1

Chapter 2 • 15

Sample pages from Chapter 2 of the Teacher's Planning Guide

▶ Audio CD Program helps all students access the content.

Help all your students succeed with this new, flexible approach to access *Pacemaker® United States History* content! Simply place the audio CD into any computer or CD player and go directly to a specific chapter or lesson.

The *Pacemaker® United States History Audio CD Program*

- Includes complete unabridged content from the *Pacemaker® United States History* Student Edition
- Allows fast access to specific chapters and lessons
- Enhances comprehension for struggling readers and students with diverse learning styles
- Provides targeted instruction for ESL/ELL students
- Supports learning for visually impaired students
- Helps you meet requirements of the No Child Left Behind Act by helping all your students make adequate yearly progress

With the *Pacemaker® United States History Audio CD Program*, the Pacemaker® curriculum becomes an ideal example of universal design, providing flexible content in a variety of formats.

PACEMAKER®

United States History

Fourth Edition

GLOBE FEARON
Pearson Learning Group

Pacemaker® United States History Fourth Edition

Reviewers
We thank the following educators, who provided valuable comments and suggestions during the development of this book:

Lawrence Broughton, North Chicago Community High School, North Chicago, Illinois
Dr. Dorothy Fields, Miami Dade Public Schools, Miami, Florida
Nadine Liebow, Indio High School, Indio, California
Paula Young, Orange County Public Schools, Orlando, Florida

Subject Area Consultant: Peter Myers, Department of History, Palo Alto College, San Antonio, Texas
Pacemaker® Curriculum Adviser: Stephen C. Larsen, formerly of The University of Texas at Austin

The following people have contributed to the development of this product:
Art & Design: Patricia Battipede, Evelyn Bauer, Susan Brorein, Jenifer Hixson, Angel Weyant
Editorial: Elaine Fay, Jane Petlinski, Jennie Rakos
Manufacturing: Mark Cirillo
Marketing: Katie Erezuma
Production: Irene Belinsky, Karen Edmonds, Suellen Leavy, Jennifer Murphy
Publishing Operations: Travis Bailey, Thomas Daning, Kate Matracia

About the Cover: *United States History* is the story of how our country became what it is today. The images on the cover represent the first people who lived in the Americas, the earliest days of a democratic nation, advances in transportation, the granting of voting rights to women, exploration into new frontiers, and finally, the active participation of all citizens. What other images can you think of that could represent important events in United States History?

ISBN 0-13-024410-4

Printed in the United States of America
6 7 8 9 10 11 11 10 09 08

Globe Fearon
Pearson Learning Group

1-800-3321-3106
www.pearsonlearning.com

Contents

Resource Center 613

Maps

Charts

Timelines

A Note to the Student

The purpose of this book is to help you understand the history of the United States. You will learn how our country began, how men and women contributed to its growth and development, and how the United States became a powerful world leader. You will see links between the past and the present. These links will help you understand how history continues to affect our lives today and into the future.

In every chapter of this book, there are special features that show you how history relates to your life. For example, you may have wondered how history connects to other subjects. **The Connecting History and . . .** feature shows how history relates to other areas of study, such as science, environment, economics, language, and technology. Maybe you want to know what people from the past thought about the times they lived in. In **Voices From the Past,** you will read the ideas and opinions of people throughout history.

You probably hear a lot about social studies skills in school. Do you wonder what this has to do with you? Whether you are taking a test or reading a map, you need skills to guide you. *United States History* has many activities that allow you to practice these social studies skills. These activities can be found in the **Building Your Skills** pages of your book.

Throughout the book you will find notes in the margins of the pages. Some of these handy **margins notes** are there to remind you of something you already learned in this book. Other margin notes teach you unusual facts about the time period of each chapter.

You will also find several study aids in the book. At the beginning of every chapter, you will find **Learning Objectives.** They will help you focus on the important points in the chapter. You will also find **Words to Know,** a look ahead at the vocabulary you may find challenging. The colorful photos, maps, and charts in the book make history come to life. **Test Tips** and **Writing Tips** in the Chapter Reviews will help you prepare for—and succeed on—tests.

Everyone who put this book together worked hard to make it useful, interesting, and enjoyable. The rest is up to you. We wish you well in your studies. Our success is in your accomplishment.

Unit Opener Use the primary source to set the tone for the time period.

Unit 1 Settling the Americas

Chapter 1 **Early America** Prehistory–1492

Chapter 2 **Colonies Are Settled** 1519–1733

Chapter 3 **Growth of Colonial Society** 1630–1760

Chapter 4 **The Struggle for Freedom** 1754–1783

This painting shows what one artist believed North America looked like before Europeans arrived. What feeling about the land does the artist want to give you? The land is beautiful, peaceful, vast.

> *"There are valleys and plains streaming with sweet springs . . . hills and mountains . . . of hidden treasure, never yet searched . . . there is a world of means to set many thousands to work."*
>
> —from a pamphlet published by The London Company in 1609

Primary Source The London Company was a charter company that wanted English settlers to come to Virginia. Words such as these appealed to people seeking land and wealth.

Native Americans lived in villages in the Americas for thousands of years before Europeans arrived. Native American people made this pottery from clay. What do the photographs show about the way these Native Americans lived? They built homes from materials they found in their environment. They made objects from the clay nearby.

Early America

◀ B.C. | A.D. ▶

15,000 B.C.
Nomads cross land bridge from Asia

1200 B.C.
Olmec civilization develops

250
Maya civilization develops

15,000 B.C. — 500

◀ B.C. | A.D. ▶

Additional activities and strategies to customize lessons can be found in the Teacher's Planning Guide.

Chapter 1 Early America Prehistory–1492

ESL Note To help students understand the concept of migration, have pairs or small groups discuss why a group of people might leave their homes and migrate to explore, or settle in, a new land. Encourage students to discuss their own family's migration to the United States.

Words to Know

nomad

glacier

civilization

empire

colony

navigator

compass

geography

astronomy

Words to Know These words are defined in the section in which they appear, as well as in the Glossary. Point out to students that the words *navigator, compass, geography,* and *astronomy* are related to exploring.

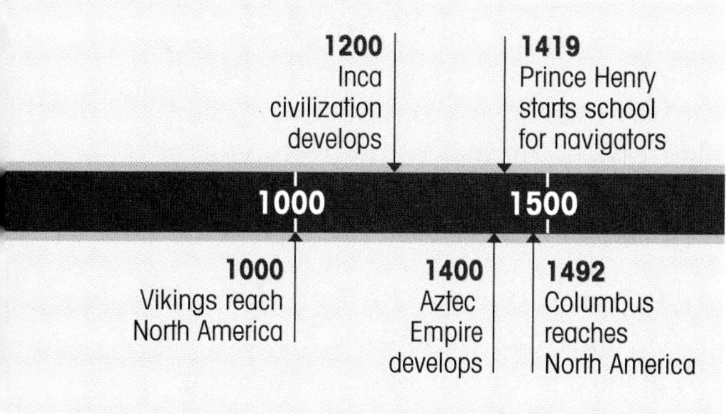

Learning Objectives

- Explain how the first people may have reached the Americas.
- Discuss how the first people may have lived in the Americas.
- Identify the different types of Native American civilizations.
- Describe the reasons Europeans came to the Americas.
- Read a timeline.

Project Students can begin work on the project after completing Section 3. To help them get started, encourage them to study the illustrations in the chapter.

Portfolio Project

You are setting out on a voyage to an unknown land. Write a series of letters to your family explaining what you expect to see. As you learn more about the land you are in, write additional letters that describe how your first ideas have changed.

Timeline The A.D. side of the timeline is divided into intervals of 500 years. The events take place over a period of 16,500 years. Point out that B.C. stands for "before Christ" and that A.D. stands for *Anno Domini*, or "in the year of the Lord."

Section 1 The First Americans

Words to Know

nomad	a person who travels all the time in search of food
glacier	a huge sheet of moving ice
civilization	the way of life of a people in one place and time
empire	the territories and people under the control of one ruler

Getting Started Have students make guesses as to why early people traveled as nomads, or in bands that searched constantly for food. Discuss why people today can settle in one place and stay there over a period of time.

The history of the nation we call the United States begins long before there was such a country. It begins long before European explorers landed on the shores of North and South America.

The first people in the Americas arrived many thousands of years ago. After they arrived, they spread out slowly through the Americas. This took thousands of years. During this time they developed different ways of life.

Crossing a Land Bridge From Asia

Not everyone agrees about how and when people first came to the Americas. Some Native Americans believe that their people have always lived in North and South America. However, many scientists believe that the first people in the Americas came from Asia. They were **nomads.** A nomad is a person who travels all the time in search of food.

The first nomads arrived thousands of centuries ago during the Ice Age. At that time, there were many **glaciers** on Earth. A glacier is a huge sheet of moving ice. Some of Earth's water was trapped in the glaciers.

Many scientists believe that as the amount of water in the oceans dropped, a land bridge between Asia and North America appeared. The nomads walked across the land bridge to North America. They were following herds of animals that they hunted for food.

About 10,000 years ago, the glaciers began to melt. By that time, thousands of people lived in the Americas. Today these people are called Native Americans. They were the first people to live in the Americas.

Why did nomads travel to North America? They were following herds of animals to hunt for food.

Land Bridge to the Americas

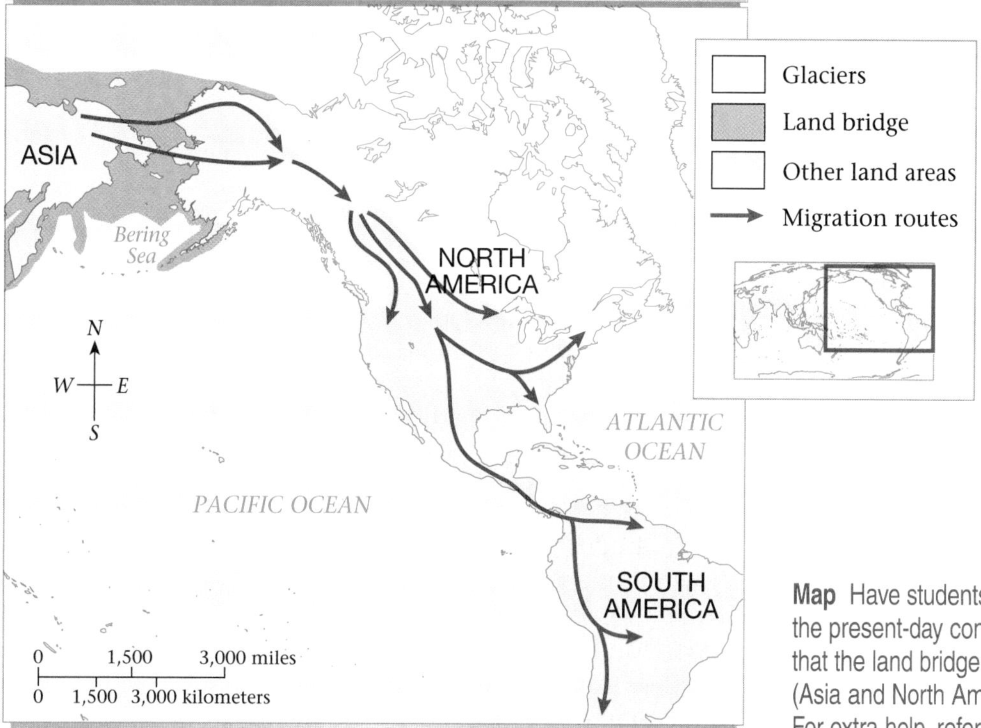

Map Study

1. In which direction did the nomads travel to reach the Americas?
2. What body of water did the nomads cross?

Map Have students name the present-day continents that the land bridge connects. (Asia and North America) For extra help, refer to the world map in the Classroom Resource Binder or the atlas at the back of this book.

1. South and east
2. The Bering Sea

Native American Groups

After the Ice Age, many Native Americans changed their ways of life. As nomads, they had followed herds of animals. When the climate became warmer, some of the animals died out. Native Americans began hunting smaller animals. They fished and gathered food in a smaller area. As time passed, some Native Americans began to farm, or plant and harvest crops.

Planting and harvesting food meant that people could remain in one area. Groups built shelters, and families gathered into villages. In villages, people were able to do jobs besides hunting or gathering food. Some could make pots and baskets or weave cloth. Others could make tools.

How did the lives of nomads change after they arrived in North and South America? Hunted smaller animals, began farming, lived in villages, could do more jobs

A Closer Look

PEOPLE WHO STUDY THE PAST

Not all people who study the past agree that the first Americans were from the eastern part of Asia. Possibly, people from Europe and other regions of Asia arrived first. Some people made the long, hard journey by walking. Some people made the difficult sea voyage across the Atlantic Ocean.

Archaeologists are people who study the past. They continue to find tools and bones showing that many different types of people may have lived in the Americas. Southern Asians, East Asians, and perhaps Europeans found new homes in the Americas. If this is true, then the Americas may have been the first lands where people of different backgrounds lived and worked.

Ancient stone tools

Critical Thinking Why do you think it is important for people to study the past? Student responses should include discovering new information about history and our culture.

Groups Live in Different Ways

Native Americans lived in areas with different kinds of lands and climates. They developed ways of life that were suited to each area.

Some groups of Native Americans lived along the Pacific coast of northwestern North America. They ate fish, wild berries, and nuts. Food was easy to find, and they raised few crops. Wood from nearby forests was used to make shelters to keep out the rain.

Native Americans who lived in northeastern North America hunted for food in thick forests filled with deer, elk, and other animals. They grew crops of corn, squash, and beans in the good soil. Shelters were made of animal skin, bark, or wood to keep out the snow and cold of winter.

In the Southwest, Native Americans hunted rabbits, deer, and other animals for food. They grew crops such as corn and beans. The climate was hot and there was little rain, so they dug ditches to bring water to the fields. There were only a few forests for wood, so shelters were built from stone and sun-dried clay bricks.

Why did early Native Americans begin to live in different ways? They needed to live in ways that were suited to different kinds of lands and climates.

History Fact

Five Native American groups joined to form the League of the Iroquois. Their plan was to keep peace among themselves.

History Fact The League operated as a representative group. There was a council of 50 members, chosen by women, who made decisions for the League.

Early Native American Civilizations

Mexico, Central America, and South America became the home of many Native Americans. Over hundreds of years, these people developed important **civilizations.** A civilization is the way of life of a people in one place and time.

The Olmecs

The first large civilization in Mexico was the Olmec civilization. They accomplished many things by about 1200 B.C.

1. They built stone temples.
2. They carved huge statues.
3. They developed a number system.
4. They developed a calendar system.
5. They developed a writing system.

The Maya, Aztecs, and Incas

Map Explain that the Maya civilization existed in the area known today as Guatemala. There are still many Mayan ruins throughout Guatemala that people can visit.

The Maya

Many centuries after the Olmecs, about A.D. 250, the Maya civilization developed. The Maya lived in the rain forests of Central America. They accomplished many things.

1. They planted crops such as corn, tomatoes, cocoa, squash, and cotton.
2. They dug ditches to carry water to their fields.
3. They formed cities and began trading goods.
4. They built large temples and stone courtyards.
5. They used a calendar with 365 days in a year.

Hundreds of years after the Maya civilization, two important **empires** developed from civilizations in the Americas. Empires are territories and people under the control of one ruler. The people of these empires were known as the Incas and the Aztecs.

The Incas

In South America, about A.D. 1200, the Inca civilization developed. Here are the things the Incas did.

1. They planted crops on mountainsides. They used step-like levels for farming.

2. They mined gold and silver.

3. They built roads thousands of miles long.

4. They built palaces that had beautiful gardens and bathing rooms with running water.

The Aztecs

By about A.D. 1400, the Aztecs developed an empire near the lands that once belonged to the Olmecs and the Maya. The Aztecs lived in the area that today we call Mexico. Here is what the Aztecs accomplished.

1. They built a capital city called Tenochtitlán. It is where Mexico City is today. Tenochtitlán was built in the marshes of a huge lake with floating gardens, markets, and drawbridges.

2. They developed a written language.

3. They knew mathematics.

Religion was the center of Aztec life. The Aztecs fought wars to make their gods happy and to enlarge their empire. The Aztecs controlled millions of people.

What Native American civilizations developed in Mexico and in Central and South America? The Olmec, Maya, Inca, and Aztec civilizations

Section 1 Review

1. Why did nomads travel all the time?

2. What is one difference between the Aztecs and the Incas?

3. **Critical Thinking** Why do you think Native American families gathered into larger groups when they settled in certain areas?

4. **Write About History** Write a paragraph about a day in the life of a Mayan worker.

1. To hunt animals and gather food, by following herds
2. Student responses might mention location, time period, and which group planted crops.
3. Student responses should show an understanding of the need for protection, companionship, sharing of work, and so on.
4. Paragraphs might mention planting crops, digging ditches, building, trading, going to temple, using a calendar.

More Review is provided in Exercise 1 of the Workbook.

BUILDING YOUR SKILLS
Reading a Timeline

A timeline appears at the beginning of each chapter of this book. A timeline lists important events in the order in which they happened.

Use this information to read a timeline.

1. Notice how much time the timeline covers. To read the timeline, look at the earliest date. It is shown on the left. Then continue to read the events and dates from left to right.

2. Like a ruler, the timeline is divided into equal units. These equal units are called intervals. Intervals may be one year, five years, or any other block of time.

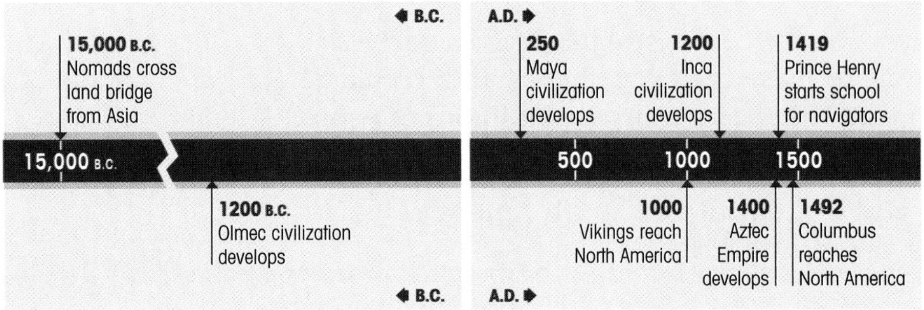

Answer the questions below.

1. Which civilization developed first, the Maya or the Olmec?

2. How many years were there between the time the Vikings reached North America and the time Columbus reached North America?

CHALLENGE Which two Native American civilizations developed about 200 years apart?

Apply the Skill
Create a timeline of the months of the school year. Put at least 5 school events that are important to you on the timeline.

1. The Olmec **2.** 492 years **CHALLENGE** Inca and Aztec

Section 2 Europeans Explore New Routes

Words to Know

colony	a settlement ruled by people from another land
navigator	a person who plans the direction of a ship

Getting Started Have students think about how they would feel if they were among the first explorers. Point out that they would be traveling in ships across waters that no one, to their knowledge, had ever crossed before.

At the time early Native American empires were growing, life was different for people in other places. In Europe, most people lived in small villages. There was hardly any trade between countries in Europe. Only a small number of Europeans traveled far from the area in which they lived. Gradually, Europeans began to explore the world.

Vikings Reach North America

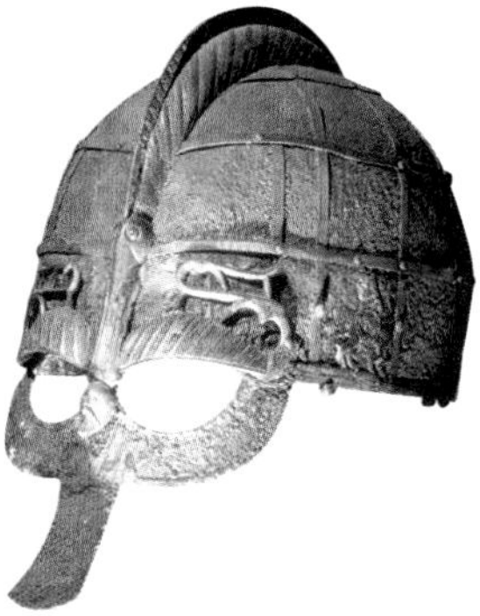

Viking leaders wore helmets made of metal.

Visual Most Viking warriors wore helmets made from animal hides. Only Viking leaders wore helmets and coats of mail, or metal armor.

The Vikings were a seagoing people of Scandinavia, in northern Europe. When farmland became scarce at home, some Vikings began to look for other areas in Europe for settlement and trade. Then in the 900s, the Vikings sailed to Greenland and Iceland. They built **colonies** there. A colony is a settlement ruled by people from another land.

About A.D. 1000, Leif Ericson, a Viking leader, sailed from Greenland to the Atlantic coast of North America. Some historians think that Viking **navigators** discovered ways to sail along the coast. A navigator is a person who plans the direction of a ship.

Ericson and his men spent a winter on the coast, on the land he called Vinland. The colony of Vinland may have been in the place we know today as Newfoundland, in Canada. It may have been as far south as Cape Cod, in Massachusetts.

This old map shows Marco Polo crossing Asia by camel.

Visual On one of Marco Polo's adventures, he, his father, Niccolo Polo, and his uncle, Maffeo Polo, escorted the wife of a khan, or ruler, of Persia in 1292.

Although the Vikings tried several times to settle Vinland, they never could. Changing weather patterns made the climate much colder, and the Vikings and the Native Americans did not get along. For these reasons, the Vikings left Vinland and ended their trips to the coast of North America.

Why did the Vikings explore other areas?
For settlement and trade

Marco Polo Explores Asia

In the late 1200s, an Italian explorer named Marco Polo traveled to Asia. He spent 20 years there. He wrote a book about his travels that told of visits to China and to islands called the Indies. Marco Polo described food spices that were not known to Europeans. He wrote about a beautiful cloth called silk. He described jewels, carpets, and other treasures.

Marco Polo's adventures may have made many European traders wish to find a shorter way or route to Asia. Some people believed that the shortest route was by sea.

Merchants, or people who buy and sell goods, crossed the Mediterranean Sea to Asia. They gained control of trade with Asia. These merchants charged high prices. Other European countries wanted to find another route to Asia.

However, few ships sailed far from the shores of Europe. Some Europeans believed the earth was flat, like a table. They were afraid that if they sailed too far from land, they would fall off the edge.

What information did Marco Polo take back from Asia to Europe? Information about visits to Asia and spices, silk, jewels, carpets, and other goods he found there

Section 2 Review

1. How did the Vikings arrive in America?
2. Why were some European traders interested in Marco Polo's adventures?
3. **Critical Thinking** If you lived during Marco Polo's time, would you believe his stories about China? Why or why not?
4. **Write About Geography** You are a Viking navigator. Write an entry in your journal describing why you are risking sailing across the Atlantic Ocean.

More Review is provided in Exercise 3 of the Workbook.

1. By ship from Greenland or Iceland
2. Wanted to find a short route to Asia so they could trade in the goods he described
3. Student responses should show an understanding of the limited experience and information most Europeans had about the rest of the world.
4. Student responses might mention a desire for farmland, new settlements, and trade as well as a spirit of adventure; a love of the sea.

Section 3 Europeans Search for Wealth

Words to Know

compass	an instrument that shows direction
geography	the study of climates and land forms
astronomy	the study of stars and planets

Getting Started Discuss with students what they already know about Christopher Columbus. Have them explain why we celebrate Columbus Day.

West African Kingdoms 1000–1600

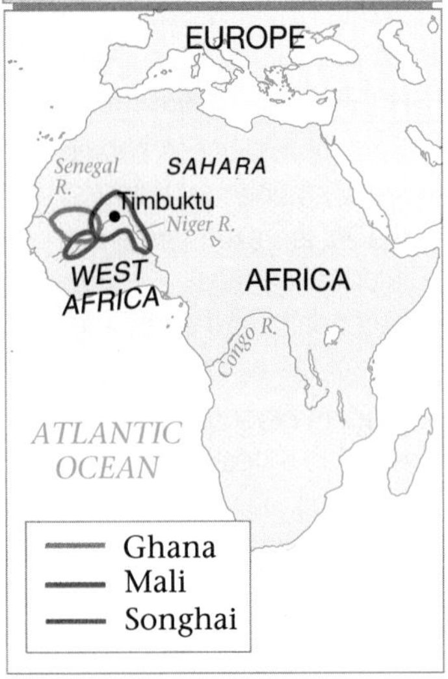

Map Each of these early kingdoms of West Africa reached the height of its power in different time periods.

In the early 1400s, Europeans began to explore new places. Explorers traveled far from Europe in search of a shorter route to Asia. Portugal was one of the first European countries to send explorers to sea.

Portugal Explores Africa

Prince Henry of Portugal set up a school for navigators in 1419. The students learned to use a **compass**, an instrument that shows direction. They learned about **geography** and studied **astronomy.** Geography is the study of climates and land forms. Astronomy is the study of stars and planets.

During the 1400s, the Portuguese were the first to search for a water route to Asia. They believed they could reach Asia by sailing around Africa. Bartolomeu Dias was influenced by these ideas. He was the first explorer to sail around the southern tip of Africa. Later, the explorer Vasco da Gama sailed around the southern tip of Africa to India, in Asia.

The first part of Africa the Portuguese explored was the western coast. During the years from about 1000 to 1600, three empires, or kingdoms, controlled West Africa. These West African kingdoms were Ghana, Mali, and Songhai.

All three kingdoms were powerful. They had gold, which they used for trade. Each kingdom traded its gold for salt. Salt was valuable because it was used to keep meat from spoiling. People almost everywhere needed salt to protect their food supplies from rotting.

Portuguese explorers started colonies along the western coast of Africa during the 1400s. The area became known as the Gold Coast because it had gold. It also had salt and slaves. Slaves had already been used in Africa for many years. Usually, slaves were prisoners of war or criminals. Sometimes people sold themselves into slavery to pay off their debts, or money they owed someone. As the 1400s came to an end, Europeans were using enslaved Africans to farm the islands off the coast of Africa.

Why were the Portuguese interested in exploring the continent of Africa? To get to Asia; for its valuable goods

Early Explorers

Explorer	Year	Sending Country	Place Reached
John Cabot	1497	England	North America
Amerigo Vespucci	1502	Portugal	South America
Vasco Núñez de Balboa	1513	Spain	Pacific Ocean
Ferdinand Magellan	1519–1522	Spain	Philippines His expedition was the first to sail around the world.

Chart Study

1. What country sent Vespucci on a voyage to South America?
2. Whose expedition was the first to sail around the world?

Chart Ask students to refer to the atlas at the back of the book to locate the place each explorer reached. Use the blackline master in the Classroom Resource Binder to trace the explorer's route from his sponsoring country to the place he reached.

1. Portugal
2. Magellan's expedition

Columbus Sails to America

Christopher Columbus lived in Italy. He dreamed of becoming a wealthy explorer. He believed he could find a shorter route to Asia by sailing west across the Atlantic Ocean.

Remember
Some European explorers were interested in Asia after learning about Marco Polo's voyage there.

At first no one listened to Columbus's ideas. He tried to get money from the rulers of England and Portugal to pay for a voyage across the Atlantic. He was turned away. Finally, King Ferdinand and Queen Isabella of Spain agreed to help Columbus. In return, Columbus promised to claim for Spain any lands he discovered.

In early October 1492, Columbus and his ships—the *Niña*, the *Pinta*, and the *Santa María*—landed on an island in North America. Columbus believed that he had landed somewhere close to Japan, in Asia. He claimed the island for Spain and named it San Salvador.

History and You

THE COLUMBIAN EXCHANGE

Today, you eat foods from many parts of the world. Before Columbus arrived in the Americas in 1492, most people ate only the foods that were grown close to home.

When Columbus arrived in the Americas, an exchange of foods and seeds for growing food crops began. As a result, the nutrition of people all over the world improved. The exchange of seeds, goods, and ideas among Africa, Asia, Europe, and the Americas is known as the Columbian Exchange.

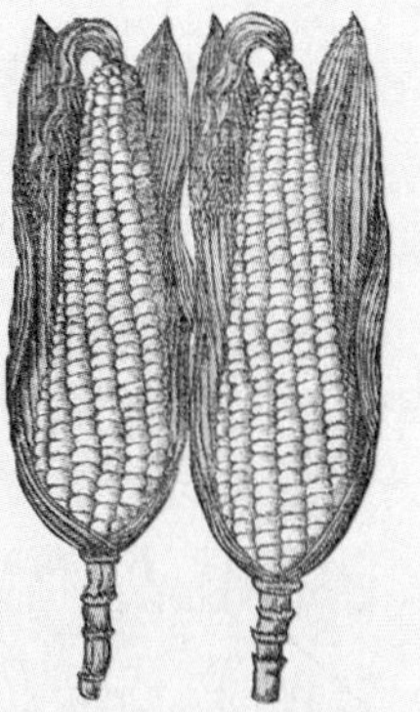

Native American corn

Some food crops that came from the Americas are corn, tomatoes, beans, peppers, potatoes, and pumpkins. Food crops that came from Europe, Africa, and Asia include wheat, onions, carrots, lettuce, yams, okra, rice, and oranges.

Critical Thinking Why do you think the Columbian Exchange was important? Student responses should show an understanding of increased nutrition and variety from the exchange.

Columbus believed he had landed in the East Indies. When he met the people on the island, he called them Indians. Their real name was Arawak. The Arawaks lived on the chain of islands that stretches from Florida to South America.

The Arawaks welcomed Columbus. However, Columbus did not return their kindness. Like most Europeans of his time, Columbus thought he should defeat other groups of people and control them. Columbus and his men treated the Arawaks badly.

In the following years, Columbus returned to North America three more times. Yet Columbus never found great wealth. By the early 1500s, almost all the Arawaks died out. Many other Native Americans had also died. Thousands of Native Americans were killed by battles with Spanish soldiers, European diseases, and enslavement. Columbus died in 1506. He still believed that he had found a short route to Asia.

What happened when Christopher Columbus landed in North America? He met people he called Indians because he thought he was in the East Indies.

Section 3 Review

1. What did students learn in Prince Henry's school?
2. What did Columbus hope to find on his voyage?
3. **Critical Thinking** Why do you think early explorers studied astronomy and geography?
4. **Write About History** You are a sailor on one of Columbus's ships. Write a journal entry about the day you first saw land.

1. How to use a compass, geography, astronomy
2. The shortest route to Asia
3. Student responses should show an understanding that geography and astronomy would help explorers navigate.
4. Journal entries might include reactions to finally sighting land after a long voyage and reactions to the new land and its people.

More Review is provided in Exercise 4 of the Workbook.

Chapter

1 Review

Summary Have students use this graphic organizer to outline the main ideas and details of the chapter.

Summary: In the late 1400s, Europeans explored lands that were not known to them. They came upon Native Americans who had developed their own cultures.

Section 1: Native American civilizations developed in the Americas. Different ways of life developed according to the climate and geography of an area.

Section 2: Around A.D. 1000, the Viking explorer Leif Ericson reached the Atlantic coast of North America. He settled a colony called Vinland.

Section 3: In the early 1400s, Europeans began a time of exploration and discovery. The Portuguese explored the western coast of Africa. In 1492, Christopher Columbus reached the Americas.

- geography
- glacier
- nomad
- empire
- colony

More Vocabulary Review is provided in Exercise 1 of the Classroom Resource Binder.

Vocabulary Review

Complete each sentence with a term from the list.

1. A ____ is a person who crossed a land bridge to the Americas in search of food. nomad
2. A ____ is a huge sheet of moving ice. glacier
3. Vinland was a Viking ____. colony
4. The study of climate and different land forms is called ____. geography
5. The Aztec ____ controlled much of the land known today as Mexico. Empire

1. By walking across a land bridge pp. 4–5 **2.** No longer nomads, raised crops, hunted, developed different cultures pp. 6–7 **3.** For religious reasons, to enlarge their empire p. 9 **4.** Possible answer: Increased knowledge of geography and astronomy; available training in navigation; and European desire for easier access to foreign goods pp. 14–15 **5.** Student responses should show understanding of resistance to new ideas. p. 16

Chapter Quiz

Write your answers in complete sentences.

1. How do scientists think people reached North America?
2. How did life change when Native Americans began living in villages?
3. Why did the Aztecs go to war?
4. **Critical Thinking** In the early 1400s, what led European countries to explore new places?
5. **Critical Thinking** Why do you think Christopher Columbus had a difficult time getting money and supplies for his voyage?

Test Tip
As you study for a test, use a dictionary to find words you do not understand.

Writing Tip
List the most important points you want to cover before you begin a paragraph.

Using the Timeline

Use the timeline on pages 2–3 to answer the questions.

1. How many years passed between the time Prince Henry started a school for navigators and Columbus reached North America? 73 years
2. Which Native American civilizations developed before the Vikings arrived in North America? Olmec and Maya

Group Activity See the Teacher's Planning Guide for a scoring rubric for this activity.

Group Activity

Form groups to act out a scene in which Columbus and his crew ask for money for their voyages. One group will be the rulers of England, Portugal, and Spain. The other group will be Christopher Columbus and his crew.

The painting above shows early settlers arriving in North America. The cradle to the right belonged to a baby born on the ship Mayflower. *What difficulties do you think early settlers faced in making such a long sea voyage?* Some difficulties were storms at sea, unsanitary conditions, crowding, spoiled foods, and medical problems.

Settlement of the Americas

1510 · 1550 · 1590 · 1630 · 1670

- **1519** Cortés conquers Aztecs
- **1540** Spanish explore the Southwest
- **1607** English settle Jamestown
- **1608** French settle Quebec
- **1620** Pilgrims settle Massachusetts
- **1638** Swedish settle Delaware
- **1664** English take over New Amsterdam from Dutch

Additional activities and strategies to customize lessons can be found in the Teacher's Planning Guide.

Chapter 2 Colonies Are Settled 1519–1733

ESL Note Discuss with students the various challenges that occur when people of different cultures live together in one country, such as the United States. (Differences in language, food, religion, politics, skills.) Have students discuss a situation made difficult because of two cultures.

Words to Know

conquer

mission

convert

joint-stock company

charter

cash crop

indentured servant

treaty

debtor

Words to Know These words are defined in the section in which they appear, as well as the Glossary. Point out to students that the terms *joint-stock company, charter, cash crop,* and *indentured servant* have to do with the economy of the new colonies.

Timeline This timeline is divided into 40-year intervals. The events take place over a period of 214 years. Point out that Spain and France settled large areas in the Americas.

1681 William Penn settles Pennsylvania

1710

1750

1733 Georgia, last English colony, settled

Learning Objectives

- Explain the defeat of the Aztec Empire by Spanish conquerors.
- Identify reasons for Spanish and French settlements in the Americas.
- Describe the English colonies at Jamestown, Plymouth, and Massachusetts Bay.
- Identify the colonies in the New England, Middle, and Southern regions.
- Explore how colonial medicine affected the colonists' lives.

Project Students will be able to begin work on the project after completing Section 3. Encourage students to take notes about the areas described.

Portfolio Project

Different ways of life developed in the regions of the New England, Middle, and Southern colonies. You are a merchant traveling through the colonies to find new goods. You keep a travel journal. Choose one region. Describe the people, the way of life, and the geography of the region. Your journal should have one entry for each colony in a region.

Section 1 Spain and France Begin Colonies

Words to Know

conquer	to take over and control
mission	a settlement, built by a church, from which people teach their religion to others
convert	to change from one religion or belief to another

Getting Started Discuss how students would feel if a group of people came to this country to take away their land and wealth.

During the 1500s, explorers from Spain and France set out to find riches in the Americas. They claimed large parts of the Americas for their countries. Each country had different ways to reach its goal.

The Fall of the Aztecs

It was the year 1519 when the Spanish explorer Hernán Cortés led his army into Mexico. This band of men planned to **conquer**, or take over and control, the Aztec Empire. Once the Spaniards had control, they would claim the Aztec gold and silver.

How did such a small group of men win a battle against thousands of Aztecs?

1. The Spaniards used cannons, guns, and swords. These weapons were more powerful than the bows, arrows, and spears that the Aztecs used.
2. The Aztecs had never seen horses. They were frightened by the Spaniards on horses.
3. The Aztecs had no resistance to European diseases. Many died from measles and smallpox.

Visual The Aztec word for "spear-thrower" is *Atlatl* (pronounced like "atlantic"). The Aztecs had every member of their army carry an atlatl in its holder.

This is an Aztec spear-thrower.

By 1521, Cortés had destroyed the Aztec Empire and captured the Aztec king, Montezuma. Montezuma died two years after he was taken prisoner. Cortés and his soldiers then took most of the empire's riches for Spain. In its place was a colony called New Spain. Mexico City became the capital of Spain's new empire.

How were the Aztecs defeated by the Spaniards?
Overpowered by Spanish weapons, European diseases, fear of horses

Spain's Power Grows

Throughout the 1500s, Spain sent more and more conquerors to the Americas in search of gold. In South America, Francisco Pizarro destroyed the powerful Inca Empire. This defeat brought great wealth to the Spanish king and Spain grew into one of the most powerful countries in the world.

Stories spread about cities of gold in other parts of the Americas. In 1513, Juan Ponce de León sailed in search of gold and also for a Fountain of Youth. He had heard that water from this fountain would make old people young again. Ponce de León never found gold nor the Fountain of Youth. He did find a beautiful land of flowers and wildlife. He called the land Florida. *Florida* means "full of flowers" in Spanish.

Spanish explorers also explored areas farther west. In 1540, Francisco de Coronado claimed a large area of what is now the United States for Spain.

Not all those who traveled with the explorers were conquerors. Some were Catholic priests who set up **missions.** A mission is a settlement, built by a church, from which people teach their religion to others. By building missions, Spain hoped to **convert,** or change the beliefs of, Native Americans to Christianity.

Why did Spain send explorers to the Americas? To look for gold and silver, and to convert Native Americans

History Fact

Aztec warriors believed a chocolate drink would make them strong in battle.

History Fact The Aztecs drank their chocolate hot or cold. Often they would add other ingredients to make different flavors and improve the taste.

The Spanish explorer Juan Ponce de León, searched for the Fountain of Youth.

Visual Tell students that the modern city of Ponce, Puerto Rico, is named for Ponce de León, who sailed from there to Florida.

Chart Ask students to refer to the atlas at the back of the book to find each place mentioned on the chart. You may wish to use the map transparency of the world in the Classroom Resource Binder.

1. 1513–1540
2. Juan Ponce de León, Hernán Cortés, Francisco Pizarro, Francisco de Coronado

Spanish Explorers

Explorer	Year	Place Reached
Juan Ponce de León	1513	Florida
Hernán Cortés	1519	Mexico
Francisco Pizarro	1535	South America
Francisco de Coronado	1540	Southwestern U.S.

Chart Study

1. What period of time does this chart cover?
2. Which Spanish explorers conquered land in the Americas?

Spanish Rule

As Spain's power grew in the Americas, more settlers came. Spaniards who settled in New Spain wanted to live the way they had lived in Europe. That meant that they would run large farms cared for by workers.

The Spaniards forced Native Americans to work for them. The workers were often treated poorly and paid only enough to stay alive. Many Native Americans died from diseases brought by the settlers.

Native Americans were also forced to work in silver mines. In 1546, a Spanish miner discovered silver in Mexico. Soon thousands of silver mines across Mexico were sending this valuable metal back to Spain. Many Native American miners died from work accidents, poor treatment, and disease.

Since the need for workers in New Spain was so great, Spaniards brought Africans to their colonies. Africans worked as slaves on the farms and in the mines. The practice of slavery spread throughout the Spanish lands and other places in European colonies.

? How did the Spaniards treat Native Americans?
Poorly—they worked under terrible conditions

Other Explorers in North America

Spain was not the only country to claim lands in the Americas. France sent explorers to North America to find a water route that would lead to Asia. In 1534, French explorer Jacques Cartier explored the St. Lawrence River. He hoped it would lead to the Pacific Ocean. Cartier claimed the St. Lawrence and the land we now call Canada for France.

In 1608, another French explorer, Samuel de Champlain, sailed up the St. Lawrence River. There he built a small fort, which he named Quebec. Fishing and fur trading with Native Americans soon developed. This helped Quebec grow into a large settlement. Champlain named the land he explored New France.

French settlers came slowly to New France. Some settlers hoped to become rich from the fur trade. Others came to set up Catholic missions. The French got along well with Native Americans. They did not make Native Americans slaves, as the Spanish had done. The fur trade helped to make France a rich country.

Why did the French come to North America?

For furs and converts

Geography Fact

The St. Lawrence River is about 800 miles long and is located in two countries, Canada and the United States.

Geography Fact Have students use the map of the United States in the back of this book to locate the St. Lawrence River. Ask them to trace its route.

Section 1 Review

1. What were the differences in the way Spanish and French explorers treated Native Americans?
2. What were the different reasons the Spanish and French came to the Americas?
3. **Critical Thinking** What brings people to a new place to live?
4. **Write About History** List the reasons why an explorer might have come to the Americas.

1. The Spanish explorers were cruel and made the Native Americans slaves. The French were fair.
2. The Spanish wanted gold and wealth. The French wanted furs and converts.
3. Student responses should mention jobs, opportunity, and religious belief.
4. Student answers should include a desire for wealth, adventure, furs, and land.

More Review is provided in Exercise 6 of the Workbook.

Section 2 The First English Colonies

Words to Know

joint-stock company	a company in which people give money to share costs
charter	a written agreement giving certain rights
cash crop	a crop grown for sale rather than for use by a farmer
indentured servant	a person who signs a contract to work for others

Getting Started Ask students what they know about the stock market. Point out that today's stock market operates in about the same way that joint-stock companies did.

The English began to settle colonies in North America nearly 100 years after Spain did. To pay for the cost of starting a colony, **joint-stock companies** were formed. In this way, many people gave money to share the costs. As part owners in the colony, the people also shared the profits and risks.

John Smith was the leader of Jamestown.

Visual By the time John Smith came to Virginia at age 27, he had already fought in several wars.

The Growth of Jamestown

The London Company was a joint-stock company. The owners had a **charter** from the king of England. A charter is a written agreement giving certain rights. It gave the settlers the right to form a colony. In 1607, three English ships landed in what is today called Virginia. The settlers named the colony Jamestown to honor King James of England.

The Jamestown settlers faced problems right away. The land was filled with swamps and was too poor for growing food crops. There was hardly any fresh water. Many settlers died from hunger and disease that first year.

Jamestown was saved by John Smith, the leader of the colony. Smith made friends with the Native Americans. He met with Powhatan, the powerful chief of the Algonquins, and traded with him for corn. He got enough food to help the colonists live through the winter. When spring arrived, Smith warned the colonists that anyone who did not work to plant crops would not get food to eat.

In 1612, some settlers decided to grow a crop that they had seen Native Americans grow. The crop was tobacco. It grew well in the swampy soil. By 1619, tobacco was Jamestown's biggest **cash crop.** A cash crop is grown for sale rather than for use by a farmer.

Tobacco was an important crop for Jamestown. As the colony grew, more workers were needed to plant and care for the tobacco fields. Tobacco growers offered to pay for workers to come from England to Jamestown. The workers would work for up to seven years to pay off the cost of traveling from England. Then they were free to settle and farm on their own. These people were known as **indentured servants.**

In 1619, the first Africans arrived in Jamestown. They had been captured from their homeland and forced into slavery. Soon African slaves were doing much of the work in the tobacco fields and farms of the growing colony. Most farmers found it better to have slaves than indentured servants.

How did the tobacco crop help Jamestown survive? It provided a cash crop for colonists to purchase the things they needed to survive.

Pilgrims Settle in Plymouth

In the 1500s and early 1600s, people in England could be punished for their religious beliefs. Many people did not agree with the beliefs of the Church of England. One group that separated from the Church of England was the Pilgrims. In September 1620, the Pilgrims were among the 101 passengers on the ship *Mayflower.* The Pilgrims were going to America because they wanted to be free to follow their own religious beliefs.

History Fact The Pilgrims decided against settling in the English colony of Virginia. They thought they would face religious persecution there.

History Fact

The Pilgrims first thought of settling in South America. They decided against it because of the hot climate.

The Mayflower *landed at Plymouth Harbor after a long, difficult sea voyage.*

Visual The *Mayflower* had the latest sailing ship design. It carried 101 passengers and a crew of 34. Thirty-one of the passengers were children. The storage area held clothing, cooking utensils, guns, tools, seed, 20,000 pounds of dried biscuits, and 30 bushels of oatmeal.

About two months later, the *Mayflower* sailed into the area we know today as Massachusetts. Before leaving the ship, the leaders of the Pilgrims wrote an agreement saying that the laws of the new colony would be fair and equal. All the men on board voted to follow the laws. This agreement was called the Mayflower Compact. It established the idea in America that people are allowed to govern themselves.

The Pilgrim colony was named Plymouth. It faced serious problems. The settlers had come to America with only a few supplies. Since they had landed in November, it was too late to plant crops. The weather was cold, there was not enough food, and many settlers became ill. However, they were lucky. The Native Americans living in that area helped the Pilgrims through the first winter. Still, by spring, more than half of the Pilgrims had died. As the weather became warmer, Native Americans helped the colonists survive.

Native Americans showed the Pilgrims

1. how to grow corn.

2. where to hunt turkey and deer.

3. ways to fish for food.

By the fall of 1621, the Pilgrims had made it through one full year in Plymouth. They were happy about having lived through this difficult time. To celebrate, the Pilgrims held a three-day harvest festival. This is what many people today think of as the first Thanksgiving.

Why did the Pilgrims settle in Plymouth? They wanted to be free to follow their own religious beliefs.

Citizenship Link

SELF-GOVERNMENT IN AMERICA

Self-government in America began with the Mayflower Compact. A vote was taken to decide if the laws of the Mayflower Compact should be followed.

As the New England colonies grew, citizens took part in town meetings. They discussed issues that affected their towns. They voted on laws that would be part of their government.

Town meetings are still held today. Whenever necessary, people in communities gather to discuss, debate, and vote on local issues.

This old drawing shows the first meetinghouse in New England.

Critical Thinking What important questions do you think might have been debated in the early town meetings? Student responses should include choosing leaders, choosing ways of protecting the settlement, forming new laws, voting.

Puritans Settle Massachusetts Bay Colony

In 1628, another group of settlers came to New England. Like the Pilgrims, members of this group wanted to be free to follow their religious beliefs. They called themselves the Puritans because they wanted to make the Church of England more "pure." By 1630, the Puritans had settled a large colony they called the Massachusetts Bay Colony.

By 1630, the Puritans began to build settlements near their most important town, Boston. At the center of each town was a Puritan meetinghouse.

Even though Puritans came to America for religious freedom, their leaders did not want to give other people a choice. Other groups living in the colony had to follow Puritan ways. Only Puritans were allowed to vote. Anyone who did not follow church laws was punished. Because of the strict laws of Puritan leaders, many settlers began to move to other areas of New England.

Why did the Puritans come to America? To be free to follow their religious beliefs.

Section 2 Review

1. What difficulties did the colonists face in establishing the Jamestown colony?
2. How did the Puritans treat others in their colony?
3. **Critical Thinking** Why did the Pilgrims think it was important to write the Mayflower Compact?
4. **Write About Citizenship** The Pilgrims wrote laws for the good of the colony. With your class, write a classroom compact. Explain how its rules will be good for members of your class.

1. Farming was difficult; diseases spread.
2. Puritans punished anyone in the colony who did not follow their church laws.
3. Student responses should mention that the Pilgrims needed laws to govern themselves once they settled their colony.
4. Student responses should show an understanding of how groups come to a decision on issues and of the process involved in self-government.

More Review is provided in Exercise 7 of the Workbook.

CONNECTING HISTORY AND SCIENCE
Colonial Medicine

Getting sick in colonial times was risky. Women often grew special plants, called herbs, which they used as medicine. They believed that elderberry helped a fever, North American ginseng relieved pain, and black snakeroot healed a snake bite.

Many of the cures used by the colonists were learned from local Native Americans. They taught the colonists new uses for the roots, bark, and leaves of plants.

Sometimes patients turned to doctors. Unlike the doctors of today, colonial doctors did not understand the human body. For example, they used walnuts to treat headaches because the walnut looked like a brain.

This woman used leeches for bloodletting.

In case a doctor was hard to find, there was the local barber. The barber could pull rotten teeth and could bleed patients. People thought bleeding patients with leeches would cure a sick person. Usually, it made a person feel worse.

Colonists believed there were other ways to make a person feel better. If elderberry did not cure your fever, you could try eating seven insects. If you were feeling sad, gathering ants by the light of the moon might improve your mood.

Answer the questions below.

1. What cures did colonists learn from Native Americans?

2. How did colonial doctors try to cure patients?

CHALLENGE Are any practices from the medicine of colonial times still used today? Explain.

1. Plants and herbs **2.** They used walnuts to cure patients' headaches. **CHALLENGE** Some people still use herbal medicines.

Section 3 The Growth of the Thirteen Colonies

Words to Know

treaty	a written agreement between two or more nations
debtor	a person who owes money to others

Getting Started Have students look at the world map on pages 614–615 of the book. Ask students to think about where they would look for land in the Americas if they lived in England. Discuss why the English colonies were established on the Atlantic coast.

Remember
The Puritans settled the Massachusetts Bay Colony in 1630.

There were 13 English colonies established along the Atlantic coast between 1607 and 1733. The 13 English colonies were divided into three regions: the New England, Middle, and Southern colonies.

The New England Colonies

Massachusetts

In the last section you read that the Massachusetts Bay Colony became the first of the New England colonies. At that time, the colony included all the land in present-day Massachusetts and part of present-day Maine. The other New England colonies grew out of the Massachusetts colony.

Rhode Island

After Massachusetts was settled, many people who were unhappy with Puritan life moved to other areas. Others were forced to leave. In 1635, a minister, Roger Williams, was ordered to leave Massachusetts. This is what Williams believed.

1. The established churches had too much power.
2. The state, or government, should be separate from the church, or religion.
3. All people should be free to practice their own beliefs.

Williams and his followers built a settlement called Providence. The colony of Rhode Island grew out of that settlement. Here all people were free to follow their religious beliefs.

Anne Hutchinson was also forced to leave Massachusetts. She did not agree with the religious ideas of the Puritan leaders.

Connecticut

In 1636, another minister, Thomas Hooker, led a group of people out of Massachusetts. Hooker and his followers felt that Puritan leaders had become too powerful. This group settled a new colony that had a Native American name meaning "long river place." That colony was Connecticut.

Great Names in History

ANNE HUTCHINSON

Anne Hutchinson lived in the Massachusetts Bay Colony. She was a Puritan. However, she did not agree with all the beliefs of the Puritan ministers.

Anne Hutchinson

Hutchinson began to hold meetings in her home. She discussed why she did not agree with the church sermons. Those who followed her were also unhappy with the beliefs of the Puritan ministers.

The Puritan leaders felt that anyone who went against them was wrong. They were also unhappy that a woman was spreading these different ideas.

Eventually, Hutchinson was put on trial. She was found guilty. As a result, she and her family had to leave the colony in 1638. With a group of followers, she helped to settle a new colony in Rhode Island.

Critical Thinking Do you think the Puritan leaders were right to be unhappy with Anne Hutchinson? Explain. Student responses should mention Puritan leaders' intolerance of different ideas.

In 1639, settlers in Connecticut wrote a document called the Fundamental Orders of Connecticut. This document allowed men in the colony to elect their leaders. The people of Connecticut agreed to live by the rules in this document. The Fundamental Orders became the first written system of government in North America.

New Hampshire

In 1623, King James I of England sent two fish merchants and others to explore the coast of present-day New Hampshire. Soon communities were established there. Some people came to these fishing communities from Massachusetts. They did not want to follow the rules of the Puritan Church. New Hampshire became a colony in 1741.

Why did people leave Massachusetts? Because they were unhappy with Puritan life

The Middle Colonies

New York

During the 1600s, much of the land between Virginia and New Hampshire was claimed by people from the Netherlands. They were called the Dutch.

In 1609, Henry Hudson, an English explorer who was paid by the Dutch, sailed up a river that was later named for him. He claimed the land on both sides of the river. In 1626, the land was named New Netherlands.

The largest town in that colony was settled on an island where the Manhattan group of Native Americans lived. The new town was called New Amsterdam.

New Jersey

The land claimed by the Netherlands did not stay under Dutch control for long. In 1664, English forces took control of New Amsterdam and the rest of the colony. They broke the land into two colonies—New York and New Jersey. The large town at the mouth of the Hudson River was renamed New York City.

New Jersey, like New York, attracted people from different places. Many colonists from the New England colonies moved to New Jersey. They were looking for better farmland. People from many European nations also came to New Jersey.

Pennsylvania

In England, a religious group called the Quakers was led by a wealthy man named William Penn. Penn wanted to travel to America to follow his beliefs. He asked the English king to give him land in America. In 1681, the king allowed Penn to settle a colony called Pennsylvania.

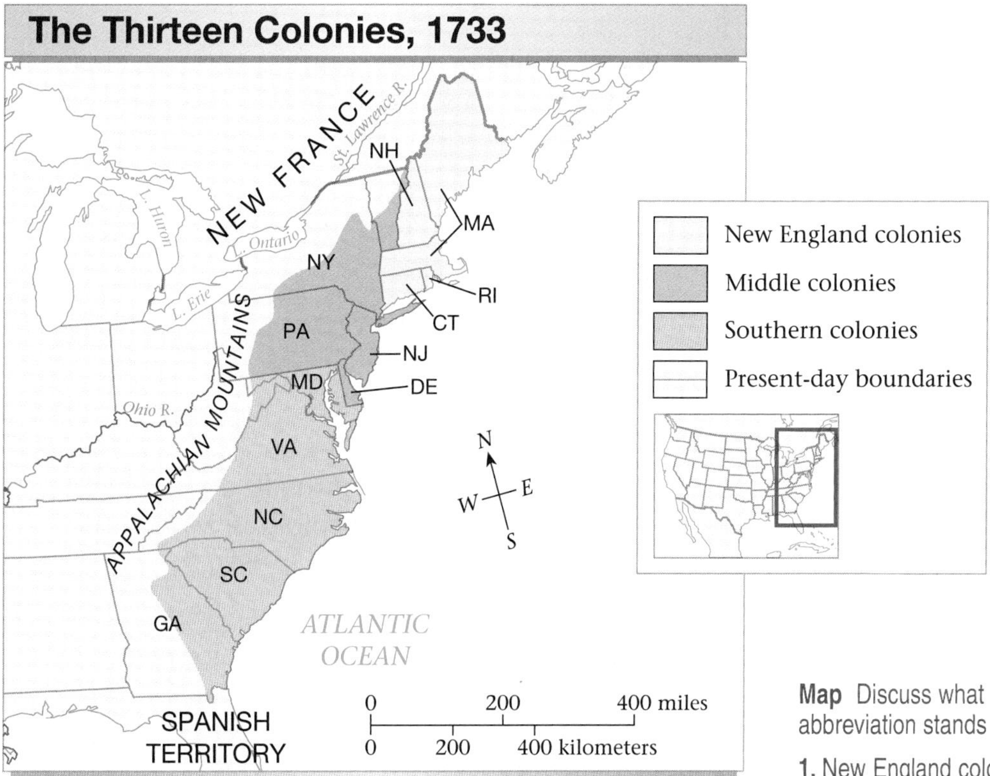

Map Study

1. Name the New England, Middle, and Southern colonies.
2. What geographical feature is west of the colonies?

Map Discuss what each state abbreviation stands for.

1. New England colonies: CT, RI, MA, NH; Middle colonies: NY, NJ, PA, DE; Southern colonies: MD, VA, NC, SC, GA
2. Appalachian Mountains

This metal collar was a gift from the Quakers of Pennsylvania to the Native Americans.

Visual Point out that the collar was used by the Quakers as a token of peace to help avoid conflicts with Native Americans.

The Quakers believed all people should be treated fairly. They were against slavery. The Quakers also believed that Native Americans should be treated with respect. When the Quakers landed in the new colony, they signed a peace **treaty**, or written agreement between two or more nations, with Native Americans. Pennsylvania became a colony known for its freedom.

Delaware

Settlers from Sweden came to present-day Delaware in 1638. They built a settlement, which they named Fort Christina. The Swedes built other settlements.

For a short time, the Dutch took over the Swedish settlements. Next, the English took over. In 1682, the Duke of York gave the Swedish settlements to William Penn. Some settlers in areas south of Pennsylvania asked for the right to set up their own colony. Penn and other Quaker leaders agreed. Delaware became a colony in 1704.

What groups of people settled the Middle colonies?
The Dutch, the Quakers, and the Swedes

The Southern Colonies

Virginia

The first English colony of Virginia began with the Jamestown settlement in 1607, which you read about in Section 2. Jamestown began to attract settlers from the New England and Middle colonies. More settlers also came from England.

Maryland

In England, Catholics were punished for their religious beliefs. In 1632, Lord Baltimore, a rich English Catholic, was given a charter. He settled the colony of Maryland.

In 1649, Lord Baltimore saw to it that the Toleration Act was passed in Maryland. This act guaranteed freedom of religion to all Christians, both Catholic and Protestant, in the colony of Maryland.

The Carolinas

In 1663, King Charles of England gave eight rich English lords the right to settle land south of Virginia. The land was beautiful and the soil was good. It was named Carolina after the English king.

Settlers in Carolina were allowed religious freedom. Many people came to Carolina for that freedom. They also came to farm the rich soil in the area. So many people arrived that, in 1712, Carolina was broken into two colonies—North Carolina and South Carolina.

Economics Fact Before 1640, most European males in the colonies had a fifty-fifty chance of dying during their first year of residence. Half of all marriages were ended by the death of one partner before the seventh anniversary.

Georgia

The last of the 13 colonies, Georgia, was settled to give a home to **debtors.** These are people who had been jailed for not paying money owed to others.

An English general named James Oglethorpe felt it was unfair to put debtors in jail. He asked the king to allow people to settle in America and get a new start. In 1733, Georgia, named after King George II, became the thirteenth English colony.

Economics Fact

In colonial Georgia, 16-year-old boys became taxpayers and served in the army. Sixteen-year-old girls were usually married.

How was Georgia different from the other English colonies? English people who were debtors were allowed to settle there.

Section 3 Review

1. Into what three regions were the 13 colonies divided?
2. Name two leaders who left Massachusetts. Where did each go?
3. **Critical Thinking** How were the Middle colonies different from the New England colonies?
4. **Write About History** Write a pamphlet to attract people to live in one of the 13 colonies.

1. New England, Middle, Southern
2. Roger Williams went to Rhode Island. Thomas Hooker went to Connecticut.
3. Middle: Religious freedom; people from different European countries; farming
   New England: Puritan rule, fishing, small farms
4. Student responses should show an understanding of religious and political life in the colonies.

More Review is provided in Exercise 8 of the Workbook.

Chapter 2 Review

Summary Have students use this graphic organizer to outline the main ideas and details of the chapter.

Summary	Settlers came to America looking for wealth, religious freedom, and land. Different ways of life developed in each region.
Section 1	Spanish explorers destroyed the Aztec Empire in search of wealth and power. Spaniards settled New Spain. The French settled New France.
Section 2	The English settled their first colony in North America at Jamestown, Virginia. The Pilgrims and the Puritans settled in New England to follow their religious beliefs.
Section 3	Other colonies were settled in New England, and in the Middle and Southern regions. A different way of life developed in each region.

- cash crop
- mission
- charter
- indentured servant
- debtor

More Vocabulary Review is provided in Exercise 8 of the Classroom Resource Binder.

Vocabulary Review

Complete each sentence with a term from the list.

1. King James of England gave a group of settlers a ____ allowing them the right to set up a colony. charter

2. One of the main crops in Virginia was tobacco, which became an important ____ for land owners. cash crop

3. In England, a ____ could be jailed for not paying money owed to others. debtor

4. Someone who worked for others to pay for passage to America was called an ____. indentured servant

5. A Spanish priest could set up a church-run settlement, or a ____, in North America. mission

1. They forced Native Americans to work for them. p. 24 **2.** He made friends with the Native Americans and got enough food to live through the winter. pp. 26–27 **3.** They were located along the Atlantic coast of North America. p. 32 **4.** Answers will vary. pp.24, 25, 29 **5.** They were developed along the coast because they were closer to water and had easier access to trade. pp. 32–37

Chapter Quiz

Write your answers in complete sentences.

1. What did Spain do to run farms in the colonies in the Americas?
2. What did John Smith do for people in the Jamestown colony?
3. Where were the 13 colonies located?
4. **Critical Thinking** If you were a Native American living around 1600, would you have wanted to live in lands colonized by people from Spain, France, or England? Explain.
5. **Critical Thinking** Why were all 13 colonies developed along the coast and not farther inland?

Test Tip
Before you begin a test or quiz, look it over. Decide how much time you can spend on each question.

Writing Tip
You can support the main points with facts and examples.

Using the Timeline

Use the timeline on pages 20–21 to answer the questions.

1. How many years after the English settled Jamestown did the English take over New Amsterdam? 57 years
2. What European countries were exploring and settling in the Americas? Spain, France, Sweden, Holland, England

Group Activity See the Teacher's Planning Guide for a scoring rubric for this activity.

Group Activity

Your group is part of a new colony. Meet to discuss the name of the colony and how it will be governed. With your group, write a compact that lists and describes each of the laws of the colony.

The painting above shows a street in the city of Philadelphia in the 1700s. Rich people ate from silver bowls like the one to the right. How is city life today different from city life then?
Today most people ride in cars instead of wagons and on horseback, streets are paved, there are many stores and tall buildings, clothing styles are different, there is more traffic.

The Colonies Grow and Change

1636
Harvard College established in Massachusetts

1693
College of William and Mary established in Virginia

1620 — 1640 — 1660 — 1680 — 1700

1651
England passes first Navigation Acts

Additional activities and strategies to customize lessons can be found in the Teacher's Planning Guide.

Chapter 3 Growth of Colonial Society 1630–1760

ESL Note To help students understand the economy of a society, have them make a list of household products. Discuss how these products are made. Explain that a society's economy is based on its ability to make goods and provide services.

Words to Know

economy

export

frontier

barter

import

common

political rights

jury

mercantilism

regulate

tax

Words to Know These words are defined in the section in which they appear, as well as in the Glossary. Point out to students that the words *export, barter, import,* and *mercantilism* have to do with trading goods in the new colonies.

Learning Objectives

- Identify the economy of each colonial region.
- Explain triangular trade.
- Describe a colonial town.
- Discuss how cities grew from towns.
- Explain how new ideas about political and economic rights changed the colonists.
- Explore a young girl's view of life in colonial Boston.

Project Students can use information they have learned so far as well as information from this chapter to complete their projects. To help them organize their thoughts, suggest that they review section titles.

Portfolio Project

As you read, think about the different kinds of changes taking place in the colonies. Choose one way in which the colonies are changing. Then, from the point of a colonist, write a diary entry. Describe how you feel about the change.

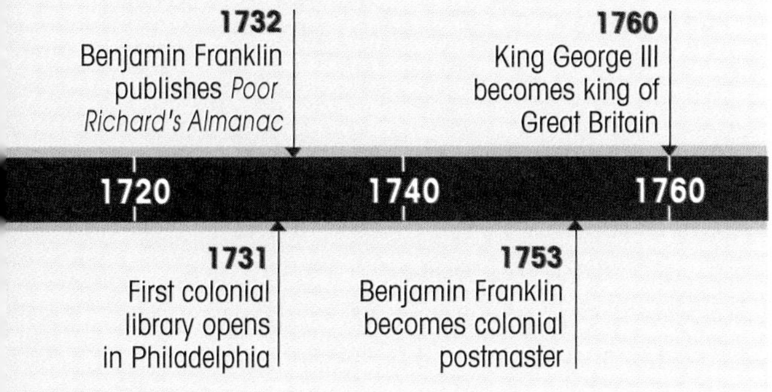

Timeline The timeline is divided into intervals of 20 years. The events take place over a period of 124 years. Four out of seven entries pertain to education and learning. Point out that education and learning were an important part of colonial life.

Section 1 Economies of the Colonies

Words to Know

economy	the way goods, wealth, and services are created and used
export	to send goods to another region or country
frontier	a newly settled or lightly settled area just outside an area of older settlements

Getting Started Discuss examples of major industries upon which state or regional economies rely today, such as the automobile industry in Michigan, the film industry in California, and agriculture in Iowa. Discuss reasons for the development of different regional economies in the colonies as students read the section.

The first explorers to reach North America came in search of gold and other riches. However, by the time the 13 colonies were formed, colonists knew that there was little gold to be found along the East coast. Fortunately, as the colonies grew, colonists learned that there was much of value in their new home.

Each region had different climates, land, and natural resources. These differences in geography affected the **economy** of each region. The economy of a place is the way goods, wealth, and services are created and used.

Economy of the New England Colonies

Remember
The colonies were divided into three regions. They were the New England, the Middle, and the Southern colonies.

Settlers in New England grew or made most of the things they needed. Most of the settlers had enough food and clothing. They were able to keep their houses warm.

In New England, the soil was rocky and the growing season was short. Settlers learned to farm the land, but the farming was so difficult that most of the farms were small. Although the land was poor for farming, New England did have important resources, or things people use, to make what they needed. The great forests and the nearby Atlantic Ocean helped the economy. That is why the lumber, fishing, and shipbuilding industries developed there.

Shipping became important too. Boston, the largest city in Massachusetts, became a major colonial port. Each year, many ships loaded with animal hides, whale oil, and lumber sailed from Boston to England. The ships returned to Boston with cloth, clothing, furniture, dishes, and other supplies.

The wooded areas of New England provided the lumber used by shipbuilders.

Visual Early ships were roughly made. Wooden planks were hewn by hand, then shaped and fitted with a broad axe and a plane.

What was New England's economy like? Small farms, lumbering, fishing, shipbuilding, and shipping were important.

Economy of the Middle Colonies

The Middle colonies had some of the richest farmland of all the regions. The climate was warmer than the climate of New England. Farmers in the Middle colonies had a longer season for growing crops.

Farms in the Middle colonies were usually larger than New England farms. Landowners in the Middle colonies sometimes needed to hire workers to help with planting and harvesting crops. Some enslaved Africans worked on farms in the Middle colonies, but most farm workers were hired by the landowners.

Grains such as wheat and rye were important crops. These grains were ground into flour, and the flour was used to make bread. The Middle colonies were sometimes known as the Bread Colonies or the Breadbasket Colonies. That is because they **exported** so much flour to other colonies and to other countries. To export means to send goods to another region or country. Goods from the Middle colonies were shipped from the cities of Philadelphia and New York.

Who worked on the farms of the Middle colonies? Mostly hired workers, some enslaved Africans

Two Economies of the Southern Colonies

The Southern colonies had the warmest weather and the longest growing season of all the regions. Farming was the most important part of the economy. Two different economies developed in the Southern colonies.

1. There were large plantations in the east. They used enslaved workers.

2. There were small farms in the west. They did not use enslaved workers.

Large Plantations

Along the coast, white landowners used enslaved Africans to work large plantations. There, the enslaved Africans raised tobacco, rice, cotton, indigo, and other crops for use on the plantation and for sale. Indigo is a plant used to make blue dye. Plantation owners sold crops to other colonies and to England. Charleston, South Carolina, was an important southern port for shipping goods.

Economics Fact

The Southern colonies exported more goods to England than the other regions did.

Economics Fact One product shipped to England was indigo. Indigo was first grown in the colonies by Eliza Lucas. While she was in her teens, Lucas managed three large plantations, owned by her father, in South Carolina.

At first, plantation owners hired workers to farm the fields along with enslaved Africans. But as the plantations grew larger, the owners wanted more slaves. By the 1700s, enslaved Africans were doing most of the work on the large plantations of the South.

The enslaved Africans had no rights. They were considered nothing more than property to be bought and sold. Many owners treated their enslaved workers like animals.

Small Farms

On the **frontier** farther west, farmers worked small pieces of land to raise food crops for their families and perhaps for sale. A frontier is a newly settled or lightly settled area just outside an area of older settlements. Frontier farmers did not use enslaved workers to plant and harvest their crops.

Europeans who arrived in the Southern colonies in the late 1600s discovered that most of the good farmland on the coast was taken. They moved inland toward the Appalachian Mountains and started small farms there.

What were the two kinds of economies that developed in the Southern colonies? Plantations with enslaved workers; smaller farms with no enslaved workers

Triangular Trade

The economy of the colonies depended on trade with other colonies, with England, and with other countries. Some trade came to be known as triangular trade because three separate voyages were involved.

A Closer Look

SLAVE SHIPS

Africans were brought to America on large ships. They were treated cruelly from the moment they boarded the ships. Africans were crammed in the below deck, as shown in the diagram below. They were so close together they could hardly breathe. Diseases spread. Many Africans died on board ship.

If the Africans tried to rebel, they would be beaten and sometimes thrown overboard. Sometimes, through great effort, the Africans won out. There were more than 100 successful revolts at sea.

Critical Thinking What does the diagram of the inside of a slave ship show about the treatment of enslaved Africans? They were treated as cargo. They were so cramped that they had no room to move and scarcely any air to breathe.

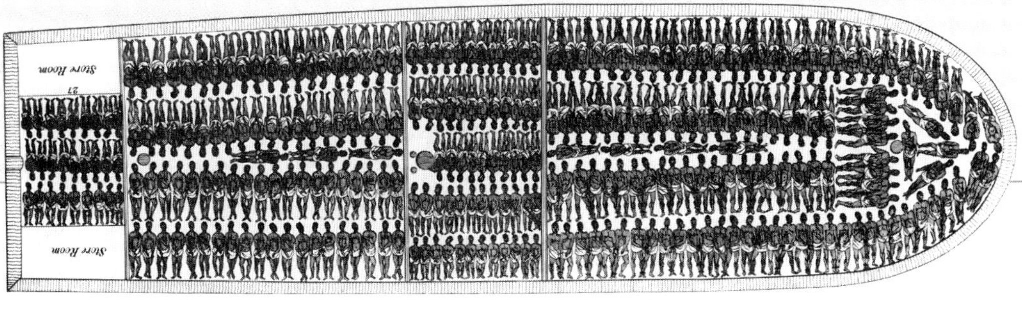

A Triangular Trade Route, 1700s

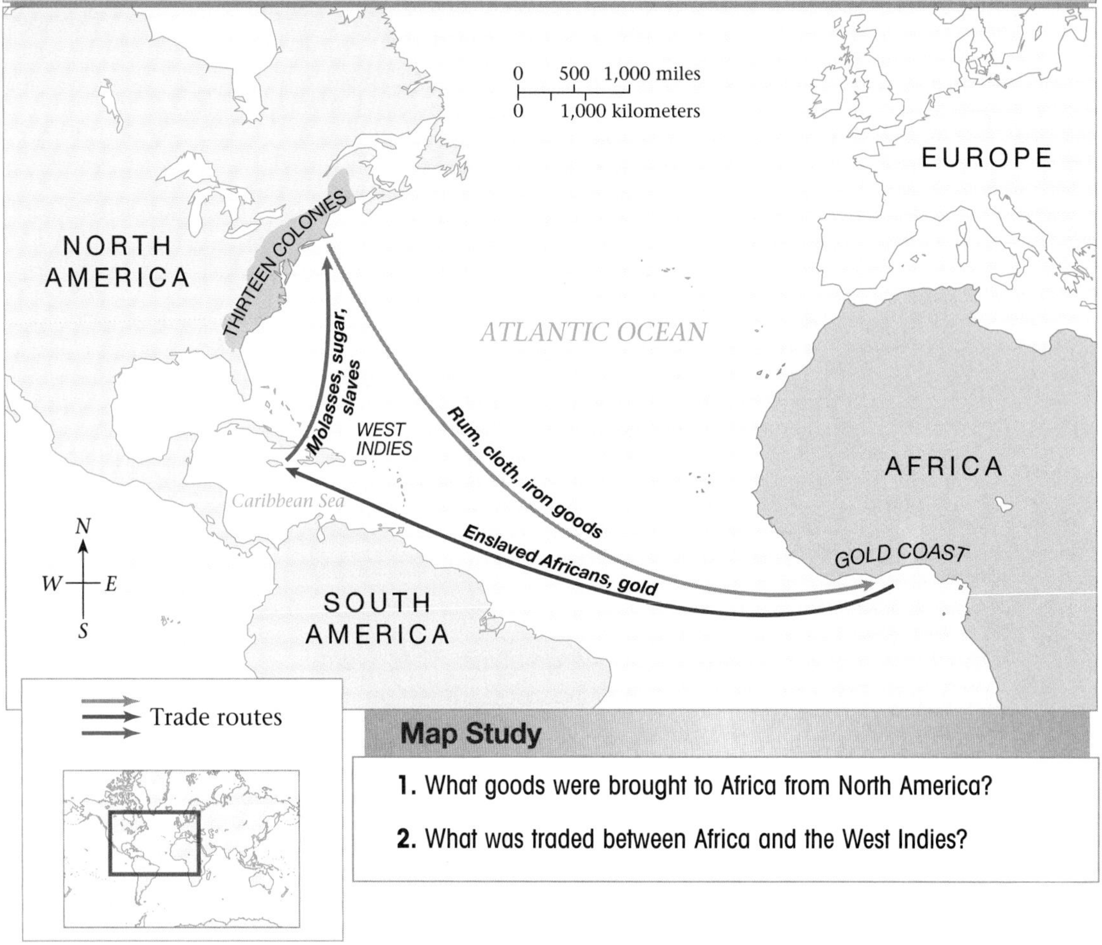

Map Study

1. What goods were brought to Africa from North America?
2. What was traded between Africa and the West Indies?

1. Rum, cloth, iron goods
2. Enslaved Africans, gold

Map The map shows a major trade route that moved goods and people between North America, Africa, and the West Indies.

These voyages formed three points of a great triangle on the Atlantic Ocean. One triangular route connected the colonies to West Africa and to the West Indies.

On the first part of the route, ships carried goods from the colonies to West Africa. There, the goods were traded for enslaved Africans. On the second part of the route, ships leaving West Africa carried enslaved Africans to sell in the West Indies. This part of the trip was called the Middle Passage.

On the third part of the route, the enslaved Africans who had not been sold in the West Indies were transported to the colonies in North America. They were then sold in the colonies.

What was triangular trade? A trade route where goods and slaves were bought and sold at three destinations

Women and the Colonial Economy

Women were important workers in the economy of the 13 colonies. Women did all the household jobs, such as sewing, cooking, and cleaning. Some unmarried women worked as shopkeepers, printers, and even shipbuilders. In many families, women worked beside their husbands, planting and harvesting crops. On the frontier, women also had to know how to hunt.

Colonial women had few rights. Women could not vote. When a woman married, she had to give all of her property to her husband.

What kinds of work did women do in the colonies? They worked as shopkeepers, printers, shipbuilders; they farmed and did all household jobs.

Section 1 Review

1. Why were most farms in New England small?
2. How was farming in the Middle colonies different from plantation farming?
3. **Critical Thinking** Why do you think trade with England was important to the economy of the colonies?
4. **Write About Economics** Write a paragraph about a settler coming to a Southern colony during the late 1600s.

More Review is provided in Exercise 10 of the Workbook.

1. Farming was difficult due to rocky soil and a short growing season.
2. Farms in the Middle colonies used fewer enslaved workers and more hired workers. The products were different.
3. Student responses should mention that colonists shipped goods to England; brought back needed supplies and goods.
4. Student responses should mention shortage of good farmland, started small farms, raised crops for food and sale.

Section 2 The Growth of Towns and Cities

Words to Know

barter	to trade a product or service for another product or service
import	an item brought into a country or region from another country or region
common	an open area shared by all the villagers

Getting Started Point out to students that an economic system based on trade works only when each trading partner has goods the other partner wants. Discuss with students items they may have traded such as baseball cards, video games, or CDs, and what motivated them to trade.

Gradually, some of the settlements in the 13 colonies became towns and cities. These towns and cities developed in different ways. As people arrived in the colonies from different countries, they brought their own ways of doing things. From town to town, people talked differently, dressed differently, and acted differently. In many larger towns and in cities, people of different backgrounds borrowed from one another.

From Settlement to Town

There were many kinds of towns in colonial America. In New England, each town was a community of people who knew each other well. In the Middle colonies, some towns grew to be large trade towns, where people came to trade goods from miles away. In all the regions, there were port towns. Goods were shipped to and from port towns.

In all the 13 colonies, farmers brought items to town to trade. Some of these items were fruits, vegetables, meat, eggs, quilts, baskets, and other things they had grown or made. People wanted to **barter**, or trade a product or service for another product or service.

There was not much money in the colonies. England did not allow the colonies to make their own money. England also did not allow the colonists to bring English money to America.

As towns grew, people set up shops, sometimes on the ground floor of their homes. Some of these people were barrel makers and shoemakers. A general store sold a variety of items, including some **imports.** An import is an item brought into a country or region from another country or region.

Many towns had a gristmill, a place where grain was ground into flour and meal. Some towns also had a sawmill, where logs were cut into lumber.

Most towns had at least one church. In the Middle colonies, towns often had people of many backgrounds. In those towns, there might be several churches of different faiths.

What goods and services were in colonial towns? Goods: food, handmade products, barrels; Services: grinding grain

A colonial barrel

Visual In colonial times, barrel makers were called *coopers.* Coopers built containers for flour, tobacco, cider, butter, and other products.

New England Towns

People in New England built their towns in a special way. The church, the meetinghouse, and the school were built around a **common.** A common is an open area shared by all the villagers. A volunteer army trained at least once a year in the common. Houses were built around the common too. Fields lay just outside the town. There, people raised crops.

Town meetings were held at the meetinghouse. During town meetings, colonists elected town leaders and voted on laws for the town. New Englanders felt they had the right to make their own decisions about government.

How was the town common used? A church, meetinghouse, school, and houses were built around it; volunteer army trained there

The Growth of Cities

History Fact

Benjamin Franklin published *Poor Richard's Almanac,* which included common sense sayings and farming advice.

History Fact Some of Franklin's sayings, or proverbs, were: "A penny saved is a penny earned" and "Early to bed and early to rise, makes a man healthy, wealthy, and wise."

As more colonists arrived in the 13 colonies, some port towns became cities. These cities grew quickly. Colonial economy depended on the shipping and trade that took place in cities such as Boston and New York. Philadelphia also grew from a colonial town to a well-organized city. One of the most famous colonists, Benjamin Franklin, had many ideas for making Philadelphia a better city in which to live. Some of his plans included adding street lights, a fire company, and a library.

Colonial cities became centers of learning. The first universities in North America began there. In 1636, Harvard College was established in the city of Cambridge in Massachusetts. In 1693, the College of William and Mary was established in Williamsburg, Virginia, not far from the Jamestown colony. Only young men were allowed to attend college.

What were two of the important colonial cities?
Boston, New York, and Philadelphia

Section 2 Review

1. What kind of towns were in colonial America?
2. What is a New England town meeting?
3. **Critical Thinking** If you were an educated person living in a colonial city, what new ideas might you be talking about?
4. **Write About History** You are a farmer in colonial America. Write a list of things you can do when you go to town.

1. Trade towns, port towns, communities where people knew one another
2. A meeting of townspeople to vote on leaders and laws
3. Possible answers might include how to organize cities; relations with England.
4. Student answers might include selling and buying goods, bartering, using the services of a shoemaker or barrel maker.

More Review is provided in Exercise 12 of the Workbook.

VOICES FROM THE PAST
Anna Green Winslow

Anna Green Winslow was a young girl in 1772. She lived in Boston. Like other colonial girls in New England, she spent her days going to school or church and learning how to sew, knit, and read. She read books such as *The Pilgrim's Progress*, a story about the importance of leading a good life. Anna's diary describes a young girl's view of life in colonial Boston.

"**January 11, 1772** I have attended my school every day this week except Wednesday afternoon. I made a visit to Aunt Sulky, and was dressed just as I was to go to the ball. I heard Mr. Thatcher preach our lecture last evening.

February 9, 1772 My right hand is in bandages, but my left is free. My aunt says it will be a nice opportunity when it improves to learn to spin flax [a fiber spun into thread]. I am pleased with the proposal.

I have read my Bible to my aunt this morning (as is the daily custom) and sometimes I read other books to her.

February 22, 1772 I have spun 30 knots of linen and mended a pair of stockings for Lucinda, read a part of *The Pilgrim's Progress*, copied part of my text journal. Played some, laughed enough. . . ."

A colonial woman works at a spinning wheel.

Answer the questions below.

1. What did Anna's diary describe?

2. How do you know that education and religion were important in Anna's life?

CHALLENGE What kind of person was Anna? Explain.

1. A young girl's view of life in colonial Boston **2.** Anna goes to school everyday, listens to the minister, and reads her Bible. **CHALLENGE** Answers will vary but can include that Anna cared about her family, education, and religion; she liked to have fun and learn new things.

Section 3 New Ideas in the Colonies

Words to Know

political rights	rights given to people by the government
jury	a group of people who decide whether a person on trial is guilty or innocent
mercantilism	the idea that a nation becomes stronger by building up its gold supply and increasing its trade
regulate	to control
tax	money that must be paid to a government

Getting Started Conduct a discussion about the freedoms that many of us take for granted, such as freedom of religion, freedom of speech, freedom of the press, and freedom from unreasonable search and seizure. Discuss what these freedoms allow us to do.

As the colonies grew, colonists began to move away from English ways of life. America was far away, separated by an ocean from England. The population in the colonies was made up of people from many different countries, as well as Native Americans. By the middle of the 1700s, people in the colonies began to think of themselves as different from other English people. Some colonists began to be attracted to new ideas, especially ideas about freedom and equality.

The Great Awakening and the Enlightenment

The first settlers came to the colonies for religious freedom. However, by the early 1700s, religion was not so important to many colonists. Fewer people were members of a church. Religious faith was no longer so important in daily life.

In the 1730s, some ministers, especially in New England, tried to get colonists to believe again in the importance of religion. These ministers spoke in an exciting way. They said that a person's belief was more important than following a certain religion.

The ministers tried to awaken a feeling of religion in colonists. This time period became known as the Great Awakening. Many new religious groups formed during this period.

Colonists were also interested in other new ideas. The Enlightenment was a new way of thinking that came from people in Europe. These people believed that knowledge was power. They said that if people used reason, the government and society would improve. They encouraged people to question others and to believe that government should protect "lives and liberty and property."

What was the Great Awakening? A time when ministers tried to awaken a feeling of religion in colonists, a time when many new religious groups formed

Visual Whitefield was best known for attracting huge outdoor audiences. According to some historical accounts, as many as 19,000 people attended his sermons at any one time.

George Whitefield was a popular preacher during the Great Awakening.

Political Rights

Many colonists began to feel they had the right to govern themselves. They believed they had the same **political rights** as any English person. Political rights are rights given to people by the government.

In England, voters elected people to represent them in making laws. In the colonies, voters also had that right. However, eight of the 13 colonies were ruled by governors who were chosen by the king of England. These men could throw out lawmakers who did not follow English laws. Many colonists believed this was unfair.

People in England had a right to trial by **jury.** A jury is a group of people who decide whether a person on trial is guilty or innocent. Colonists felt that they should also have that right.

What political rights did men in England have that colonial men did not? Rights to representation, trial by jury

Economic Rights

The colonists wanted to be allowed to sell their products wherever they wished and for the most money. They wanted to make finished goods that they could sell. But English rulers believed in **mercantilism**, or the idea that a nation becomes stronger by building up its gold supply and increasing its trade.

England had established the colonies in North America to make England rich. English rulers passed laws to **regulate**, or control, trade in the colonies. The English told the colonists what goods they could export and import. In most cases, the colonies exported raw materials, such as fur, lumber, and cotton, to England. The English used the raw materials to make finished products which they sold for high prices.

Why did England establish colonies? To increase the wealth of Great Britain

The Navigation Acts

The British also passed laws called the Navigation Acts to regulate trade. These laws said that only English ships or ships made in the colonies could carry goods to and from the colonies. Ships from other countries had to stop in England before going to the colonies. Those ships had to pay **taxes** to England on their cargo. A tax is money that must be paid to a government. The tax meant that colonists had to pay more money for goods that came from other countries.

In 1760, King George III became king of Great Britain. England was part of Great Britain. Many colonists had been thinking about new ideas of freedom and equality. Some of the colonists began to think about what true independence from Great Britain might mean.

How did the Navigation Acts control trade? The colonies had to pay more money for goods from other countries; only English ships could carry goods to and from colonies.

Section 3 Review

1. How did the Great Awakening affect the colonies?
2. Why did England tell the colonies what goods they could import and export?
3. **Critical Thinking** Explain why the right to a trial by jury was important to colonists.
4. **Write About Economics** You are a colonist. Write a letter to King George III, persuading him to let the colonies make their own rules about trade.

More Review is provided in Exercise 13 of the Workbook.

History Fact

In 1707, Scotland joined England and Wales to become Great Britain, or Britain.

History Fact Students might note that, in this textbook, the terms Great Britain and British replace the terms England and English to describe the country and its people.

1. New religious groups formed.
2. So England could become rich by buying cheap raw materials from the colonies and using them to make finished products, which England sold for high prices
3. Student responses should show an understanding of the importance of being judged by people in one's own community, and the feeling of entitlement to the same rights as the English.
4. Student responses should show an understanding that colonists might feel that the Navigation Acts were unfair.

Chapter 3 Review

Summary Have students use this graphic organizer to outline the main ideas and details of the chapter.

Summary	Colonial settlements grew into cities and towns. The colonists developed new ways of doing things. They began to think of themselves as separate from England.
Section 1	The 13 colonies were divided into three regions. These were the New England, Middle, and Southern colonies. Each region had its own climate, economy, and way of life.
Section 2	There were many changes in the colonies from 1630 to 1760. Some settlements became towns. Some towns along the Atlantic coast became cities.
Section 3	By the middle of the 1700s, many colonists no longer felt like a part of Great Britain. There were new ideas about religion, politics, and economics.

More Vocabulary Review is provided in Exercise 14 of the Classroom Resource Binder.

Vocabulary Review

Write *true* or *false*. If the statement is false, change the underlined term to make it true.

1. The colonies <u>exported</u> raw materials to England. True
2. At the town markets, farmers would <u>regulate</u> or trade one product for another. False: barter
3. Colonists wanted the right to a trial by <u>jury</u>. True
4. The <u>common</u> was a lightly settled area outside an area of older settlements. False: frontier

1. People farmed in all three regions. pp. 42–44 2. General store, a church, a grist mill, a meeting house p. 49 3. They said religion was important, but personal belief was more important than belonging to a certain religion. pp. 52–53 4. Possible answer: It was profitable; colonists sold goods; goods were brought back to colonies; slavery increased. pp. 45–46 5. Student responses should show an understanding that the colonists were more willing to question authority and to fight for liberty. pp. 52–54

Chapter Quiz

Write your answers in complete sentences.

1. How were the economies of the New England, Middle, and Southern colonies alike?
2. What kinds of buildings might be in a colonial town?
3. What did the ministers of the Great Awakening preach about religion?
4. **Critical Thinking** How did triangular trade affect the colonists?
5. **Critical Thinking** How do you think the Enlightenment changed the colonists' ideas?

Test Tip
A good way to study for a test is to turn the titles of sections into questions. Look for the answers as you read.

Writing Tip
When writing a paragraph, state your main idea at the beginning.

Using the Timeline

Use the timeline on pages 40–41 to answer the questions.

1. How many years after Harvard College was established did King George III become king of Great Britain? 124 years
2. What three events on the timeline show how important education was in the colonies? Harvard College was established, College of William and Mary was established, first colonial library opened in Philadelphia.

Group Activity See the Teacher's Planning Guide for a scoring rubric for this activity.

Group Activity

Your group lives in a colonial town. You meet in the general store, where you talk about political rights in the colonies. What will your group say? Write a skit and perform it for the rest of the class.

During the Boston Tea Party, colonists threw tea into Boston Harbor to protest a British tax. The slogan on the teapot on the right protests the Stamp Act. Why do you think the colonists felt angry about British laws and acts? Colonists had to pay taxes to the British but had no say in the government.

The Road to Freedom

- **1750**
- **1754** French and Indian War begins
- **1760**
- **1763** French and Indian War ends
- **1770**
- **1770** The Boston Massacre
- **1773** Boston Tea Party
- **1774** Intolerable Acts passed
- **1775** War for Independence begins
- **1776** Congress approves the Declaration of Independence

Additional activities and strategies to customize lessons can be found in the Teacher's Planning Guide.

Chapter 4 The Struggle for Freedom 1754–1783

ESL Note To help students understand the concept of change, have them work in pairs to describe the emotions associated with change—fear, excitement, confusion. Tell students to keep these feelings in mind as they learn why the American colonists broke away from Britain.

Words to Know

ally
cede
proclamation
representative
repeal
declaration
revolution
militia
blockade
Loyalist
Patriot
neutral

Words to Know These words are defined in the section in which they appear, as well as in the Glossary. Point out the root word *loyal* within *Loyalist.*

Learning Objectives

- Identify the causes of the French and Indian War.
- Explain how Great Britain gained control of most French lands in North America.
- Identify British laws that angered the colonists.
- Identify the events leading to the War for Independence.
- Explore how Thomas Jefferson wrote the Declaration of Independence.

Project Help students select an important event for their articles such as the French and Indian War or the Proclamation of 1763. To help students get started, have them look at the timeline for key events.

Portfolio Project

Find an exciting event in the chapter. Consider that you are there, watching the event. Write a news article about what you see and hear. Write an exciting headline for your article. Answer the questions *who, what, when, where, why,* and *how* in your article. Read the article to your classmates.

Timeline The timeline is divided into intervals of 10 years. The events take place over a period of 29 years. Point out to students that two wars took place on U.S. soil within this time period.

Section 1 The French and Indian War

Words to Know

ally	a nation that joins with other nations for the same cause
cede	to surrender something

Getting Started Ask students to think how they might settle an argument between two people who wanted to build a house on the same plot of land. Discuss why nations would be willing to go to war over land.

French fur trader

Visual French fur traders at this time were known as *coureurs de bois* or "travelers of the forest." The voyagers were usually unmarried and in their twenties.

As more British settlers came to North America, they traveled farther west. By the middle of the 1700s, they had pushed over the Appalachian Mountains into the Ohio River valley. However, France had already explored that region. Now two enemies from Europe—Great Britain and France—fought in those less settled areas of North America.

Trouble in the Ohio Valley

French explorers were some of the first Europeans to land in North America. However, the French explorers were not looking for gold. They were looking for furs. After building a settlement at Quebec, in Canada, French fur traders traveled in canoes across the Great Lakes and down the Ohio River to the Mississippi River.

Each year, fur traders paddled back to Quebec with canoes full of animal furs. The fur trade became important to France's economy. French rulers hoped to control the Ohio River valley to continue their fur trade. This meant that British settlements would have to be limited to land along the Atlantic coast.

The fur traders got along well with many Native Americans. They traded fairly for furs and treated the Native Americans as equals. French traders set up many forts and trading posts along the Ohio River valley.

The French made a great deal of money from the fur trade. However, the fur trade did not bring large numbers of French settlers to North America. By 1754, about 65,000 settlers from France lived in the Ohio River valley. On the other side of the Appalachian Mountains, there were more than one million people in the 13 British colonies.

Why did French rulers want to control the Ohio River valley? To continue the fur trade that was important to the French economy

War Breaks Out

During the 1750s, fur traders from Great Britain began to cross the Appalachian Mountains. Soon Great Britain claimed the land that the French had named New France. Both France and Britain wanted to control the valley. That led to war.

The conflict, or fight, between Great Britain and France began in 1754. The first fighting was in the Ohio River valley. The two nations also fought in Europe as well as in the British colonies. In America, some Native American groups were **allies** of the French. An ally is a nation that joins with other nations for the same cause. The Native Americans felt that it was better to trade with the French than to lose their lands to British settlers. For this reason, the war became known as the French and Indian War.

The two sides fought battles in different ways. British soldiers marched into battle in large groups to the beat of drums. They dressed in uniforms with bright red coats. The French and Native Americans fought differently. They used surprise attacks, shooting from hiding places. Their battle clothes were not easily seen. The French had learned the fighting style of the Native Americans.

Why did the French and Indian War begin? Both France and Britain wanted to control the Ohio River valley.

French soldiers and Native Americans attacked this British fort during the French and Indian War.

Visual During the French and Indian War, the Acadians, French-speaking settlers in the British Canadian colony of Nova Scotia, refused to swear loyalty to the British government. The British forced them to resettle in the 13 colonies. Cajuns in Louisiana are descendants of Acadians. The word *Cajuns* comes from the word *Acadians.*

Great Britain Wins the War

At first, France seemed to be winning the war. In one battle, the French forces beat the colonial troops led by a young officer named George Washington. In another battle, French and Native American forces attacked and killed about 900 British soldiers.

Soon Great Britain began to send more troops and supplies to the colonies. Then, in 1760, British troops and colonists attacked the large French post in Quebec. The French lost control of Quebec.

By 1763, the fighting had ended. France's power in North America was over. The British claimed the Ohio River valley. France had to **cede**, or surrender, other land east of the Mississippi River. Great Britain also took control of Canada.

What lands did Great Britain control after winning the French and Indian War? The 13 colonies, the Ohio River valley, other lands east of the Mississippi River, and Canada

1. British wanted to settle beyond Appalachian Mountains
2. Ohio River Valley, Quebec, English colonies, Europe
3. Great Britain might have won the war very quickly.
4. Student charts should include: Native Americans keep British from taking their land and continue trade with the French. French and British both wanted control of the Ohio River valley. Colonists wanted right to settle in Ohio River valley.

Section 1 Review

1. Why did the British want the French out of the Ohio River Valley?
2. Where was the French and Indian War fought?
3. **Critical Thinking** What might have happened if Native Americans had not helped the French fight the British?
4. **Write About History** Prepare a chart with four columns. List the headings as Native Americans, French, British, Colonists. List what each group expected to gain when the French and Indian War began.

More Review is provided in Exercise 14 of the Workbook.

Section 2 The Colonists Unite

Words to Know

proclamation	an official government announcement
representative	a person selected to act for others
repeal	to end
declaration	a public statement
revolution	a sudden, complete change of government

Getting Started Discuss with students whether they feel taxes are necessary, and how much they think people should pay for various programs such as social security and Medicaid. Have them compare their opinions about taxes to the colonists' response to the taxes imposed by the British.

After the French and Indian War, King George III passed a law saying that colonists could not settle in the Ohio River valley. The king's law was called the Proclamation of 1763. A **proclamation** is an official government announcement. The colonists were angry. Other British laws would make them even angrier.

New Acts Seem Unfair

The Proclamation of 1763 was passed for two reasons. Great Britain did not want colonists moving too far west. British leaders thought colonists who moved west would not follow British laws or buy as many British goods. Great Britain would lose money. The colonists did not obey the proclamation. They settled and traded in the Ohio River valley anyway.

The Proclamation of 1763 was only the beginning of new laws. Over the next several years, British rulers passed four more acts or laws. These included the Sugar Act, the Stamp Act, the Quartering Acts, and the Townshend Acts.

Why was the Proclamation of 1763 passed? To prevent colonists from moving too far west

Chart After students read the next section, have them add an additional column titled "Reaction of the colonists" on a separate sheet of paper. They can add the following answers in the new column: Proclamation of 1763, "Ignore proclamation"; Sugar Act, "Protest taxation without representation"; Stamp Act, "Boycott British goods"; the Quartering Acts, "Protest in assemblies"; and Townshend Acts, "Boycotts, Boston Massacre."

1. Townshend Acts
2. Stamp Act and Quartering Acts

British Acts Against the Colonies

Name of Act	Year	What It Said
Proclamation of 1763	1763	Colonists are not allowed to settle in the Ohio Valley.
Sugar Act	1764	Colonists are taxed on sugar and molasses.
Stamp Act	1765	Colonists must buy stamps for all printed material.
Quartering Act	1765	Colonists must give quarters, or food and shelter, to British soldiers.
Townshend Acts	1767	Colonists are taxed on paint, glass, paper, and tea.

Chart Study

1. Which act taxed colonists on tea?
2. Which acts were passed in 1765?

Colonists Protest British Acts

Most of the money collected in taxes went back to Great Britain. The colonists wanted to use the money to improve life in the colonies.

The colonists protested, or spoke and acted against, the British acts. Some colonists refused to buy British goods. Others refused to pay the taxes. Protest groups called the Sons of Liberty were formed.

Colonial leaders, such as Patrick Henry and Samuel Adams, spoke out against the taxes. "No taxation without representation" became a famous saying. The colonists did not have **representatives** in the British government. A representative is a person selected to act for others. The colonists had no way to vote against the tax laws.

Why did British taxes make the colonists angry?
Taxes went to Britain; colonists had no way to vote against them.

The Boston Massacre

Bad feelings soon became strong between colonists and British soldiers. On March 5, 1770, a crowd of colonists in Boston began to yell insults at a group of British soldiers. Someone began to throw snowballs.

Suddenly a British soldier was hit with a rock. Shots rang out. Five colonial men died in what became known as the Boston Massacre. A massacre is the killing of people who cannot defend themselves. The first to fall was Crispus Attucks, a runaway slave.

After the Boston Massacre, the British understood how angry the colonists were. The British decided to **repeal**, or end, most of the Townshend Acts. However, King George III said the tax on tea had to remain. It would remind the colonists that they were still under British control.

What happened in the Boston Massacre? Angry colonists attacked British soldiers and five people were killed.

Visual There were approximately 50 members of the Boston Committee of Correspondence—led by Samuel Adams—at the Boston Tea Party. This small band—in a very orderly and quiet fashion—emptied three ships worth and 342 chests of British tea into Boston Harbor.

The Colonies Are United

The colonists continued to grow angry with the British. The British passed a new law that said only a British company could supply the colonists with tea. This meant that colonial tea merchants would be put out of business. Colonists wondered how long it would be before other colonial businesses were closed. Many colonists refused to buy British tea.

Finally, colonists took matters into their own hands. One night in December 1773, colonists dressed as Native Americans boarded British ships in Boston Harbor. The ships were loaded with tea. The colonists threw all the tea overboard. This action, led by Samuel Adams of Boston, became known as the Boston Tea Party.

Colonists emptied tea from bottles such as this one.

British leaders punished Boston by passing even stricter laws. Colonists were no longer allowed to hold public meetings. Boston Harbor was closed and more

British soldiers were sent to the city. The colonists called the British laws that were passed after the Boston Tea Party the Intolerable Acts.

How did colonists show anger with British tea laws?
Refused to buy tea, threw tea overboard in Boston Harbor

The First Continental Congress

In 1774, colonial leaders met in Philadelphia, Pennsylvania. George Washington, Samuel Adams, and Patrick Henry were among the leaders.

This meeting was the First Continental Congress. Representatives from every colony except Georgia came to the meeting. Those who met sent a Declaration of American Rights to Great Britain. The **declaration,** or public statement, listed all the unfair treatment that the colonists faced. The declaration did not change the actions of the British government. At that point, colonists began to think of the idea of **revolution,** or a sudden, complete change of government.

Why did the First Continental Congress meet?
To discuss ways the colonists could be given the same rights as British citizens

Section 2 Review

1. How did the colonists feel about the Proclamation of 1763?
2. How did the colonists protest British acts against the colonies?
3. **Critical Thinking** If you were a colonist, how would you protest British control?
4. **Write About Citizenship** You are at the First Continental Congress. Write a short speech to get people to support your cause.

More Review is provided in Exercise 15 of the Workbook.

1. They did not like it and did not obey it.
2. Refused to buy British goods, refused to pay taxes, formed Sons of Liberty, spoke out, attacked British soldiers, dumped tea into Boston Harbor
3. Student responses might mention organizing a march or writing newspaper editorials or taking up arms against the British.
4. Student speeches should show an understanding of the need for unity against unfair British control.

Section 3 The War for Independence

Words to Know

militia	an army of citizens used in emergencies
blockade	an action to keep supplies from getting into or out of an area
Loyalist	a colonist who remained loyal to Great Britain
Patriot	a colonist who wanted independence from Great Britain
neutral	not favoring either side in a quarrel or war

Getting Started Ask students how they would feel about being ruled by a government that was thousands of miles away. They might feel that a remote government could not understand what life was like across the ocean in the colonies.

The problems between Great Britain and the colonies did not get better. Angry feelings grew throughout the colonies. In one speech, Patrick Henry demanded freedom from Great Britain. He ended his speech by crying out, "Give me liberty or give me death!" Those words rang throughout the colonies.

Colonists Prepare to Fight

Patrick Henry was not the only colonist ready to die for freedom. In Massachusetts, groups called Minutemen were formed in most towns. These colonists, between the ages of 16 and 60, could be ready to fight at a minute's notice. The Minutemen began to store guns and bullets in Concord, a town about 20 miles outside of Boston.

British General Thomas Gage heard about the guns being stored in Concord. He ordered his troops to march from Boston in a surprise raid to destroy the guns.

On the night of April 18, 1775, about 700 British soldiers marched out of Boston. They did not know that they were being watched. Colonists had come up with a plan to warn the Minutemen of a British attack. Lanterns in the tower of a Boston church would be lit as a warning signal. One lantern meant the British were heading north by land. Two lanterns in the tower meant they were heading north by sea.

Remember
The British were called redcoats because of their red-colored uniforms.

One lantern lit the tower. The Minutemen had to be warned! A colonist by the name of Paul Revere jumped onto his horse and galloped into the darkness. He rode 16 miles, crying out the warning "The Redcoats are coming!" When he reached Lexington, Revere was joined by William Dawes. The two men rode toward Concord shouting the alarm.

Revere and Dawes were captured. However, Samuel Prescott continued the ride. He warned the other towns.

Who were the Minutemen? Groups of colonial men between the ages of 16 and 60 who could fight at a minute's notice

Battles at Lexington and Concord

On the morning of April 19, 1775, the British arrived at Lexington Green. Seventy men were waiting to stop the large British force. American Captain John Parker gave orders. "Stand your ground. Don't fire unless fired upon. But if they want war, let it begin here!"

No one knows who fired the first shot. But within a few minutes, eight colonists lay dead. One British soldier had been hurt. The Minutemen scattered in defeat. General Gage's troops marched on to Concord.

However, the colonists were not beaten. As the British reached North Bridge in Concord, they were met by a large force of Minutemen. More than 450 farmers, shopkeepers, and others had rifles ready. They charged across North Bridge, forcing the British to turn back to Boston.

Along the road, more Minutemen joined the fight, shooting at the British from behind trees and stone walls. By the time Gage's men reached Boston, 300 British soldiers were dead or wounded. The colonists had 90 men killed or wounded.

What happened at Lexington and Concord? Lexington: First battle between colonists and British; Concord: colonists won

The Second Continental Congress

About a month after the battles of Lexington and Concord, colonial leaders met again in Philadelphia. This meeting was called the Second Continental Congress. War had not yet been declared between Great Britain and the colonies. Many leaders at the meeting did not want war.

However, the colonial leaders also knew that since fighting had begun, war could easily follow. They decided to ask Great Britain to help find a peaceful solution to their problems. The solution the colonists offered the British was called the Olive Branch Petition. At the same time, the colonial leaders decided to prepare for war. They chose George Washington, a Virginia planter, as their military leader. Washington had fought bravely as a military leader during the French and Indian War.

What happened at the Second Continental Congress? Colonial leaders wrote the Olive Branch Petition. They also prepared for war.

Battle of Bunker Hill

While the Second Continental Congress was meeting in Philadelphia, more fighting was breaking out in Boston. Since the first battles in April, British forces had remained in the city. In June, British leaders ordered the troops to break out of the city. To do that, they would have to defeat the colonial **militia**, which was an army of citizens used in emergencies. The colonial militia was camped on Bunker Hill and Breed's Hill in the city.

Visual In 1782, General George Washington devised the Purple Heart or the Badge of Military Merit. The badge specifically honored the lower ranks, signifying that the road to glory in a Patriot army was open to all.

Colonial soldiers who fought bravely received this special badge of honor.

The colonists faced the British at Bunker Hill. The British won the battle.

Visual The Battle of Bunker Hill actually took place on nearby Breed's Hill. Some historians believe the colonial general chose the wrong hill, because they had to fortify it at night. Another theory is that the map was incorrect. Most likely, Breed's Hill was simply closer to where the British ships were. This gave the colonists a better attacking position.

After a bloody battle, British forces took Bunker Hill on June 17, 1775. The British lost twice as many soldiers as the colonists. The colonists felt that even though they had lost the battle, they might win a war against Great Britain.

The British losses shocked King George III. He ordered the British navy to keep all supply ships from reaching the colonies. He also hired German soldiers called Hessians to help control the colonists.

When colonial leaders learned of King George's actions, they knew that war would probably occur. Great Britain had set up a shipping **blockade,** or an action to keep supplies from getting into or out of an area.

The British sent 30,000 more troops to the colonies. The colonists felt it was time to declare their independence from British rule.

Why was the Battle of Bunker Hill important to the colonists? The colonists thought they had a chance to win a war because the British lost so many soldiers.

Colonists Declare Independence

In January 1776, Thomas Paine published a pamphlet called *Common Sense*. In it he said that colonists should rule themselves by setting up their own government. He said kings only brought misery to their people and should be overthrown. Congress read Paine's pamphlet, and many of the members agreed with his ideas.

In June 1776, the Second Continental Congress gave a young colonist from Virginia an important job. His name was Thomas Jefferson. He was asked to write a declaration explaining why the colonies should be free from British rule.

In the declaration, Jefferson tried to speak for all colonists. He said that colonists believed in equality. He said that colonists believed they had the right to life, liberty, and the pursuit of happiness.

At that time, equality and liberty were thought by some to be the rights of white men only. The Declaration of Independence did not mention African Americans, Native Americans, or women.

Finally, on July 4, 1776, all the members of the Second Continental Congress signed the Declaration of Independence. The colonists who signed it told Great Britain, and the world, "that these united colonies are, and of right ought to be free and independent states." The 13 colonies had declared independence.

What did Thomas Jefferson do for the Second Continental Congress? Wrote the Declaration of Independence

Loyalists and Patriots

Some colonists wanted to remain part of Great Britain. A colonist who remained loyal to Great Britain was called a **Loyalist.** Some Loyalists fought on the side of the British. Others were forced to go to Canada by colonists who wanted freedom.

The colonists who wanted independence from Great Britain called themselves **Patriots.** Some Patriots joined the colonial army. Others served in their local, or town, militia.

There were also colonists who did not care which side won the war. At the beginning of the war, about one of every three colonists was **neutral.** That meant these colonists did not favor either side in the war.

Soldiers carried gunpowder in powderhorns made from the horn of an ox or cow.

Visual Gunpowder was developed in 9th-century China. Europeans began to use gunpowder in the 14th century.

What did the Loyalists and Patriots want? Loyalists wanted to remain with Great Britain; Patriots wanted independence.

Early Battles of the War for Independence

The colonists were fighting against one of the toughest and best-trained armies in the world. George Washington knew that his best chance of defeating the stronger British forces was with surprise attacks.

The War for Independence, which is also called the Revolutionary War, was a hard-fought war. It ended in victory for the Americans. These are the major battles of the War for Independence.

Summer 1776: Battle of New York

A powerful British fleet, or group of ships, sailed into New York Harbor and sent thousands of troops ashore. General Washington was badly outnumbered. He ordered a retreat. If not for the retreat, colonial forces could have been destroyed and the war would have quickly been lost.

December 25, 1776: Battle of Trenton

On Christmas Eve, Washington ordered a surprise attack on Hessian soldiers in Trenton, New Jersey. American troops crossed the Delaware River in the dark of night. They marched to Trenton and captured more than 900 Hessians. Only four Americans were wounded. Trenton was the first American victory since independence had been declared. It raised the hopes of Patriots everywhere.

October 17, 1777: Battle of Saratoga

A force of American volunteers met a large British force in Saratoga, New York. The battle was fought off and on for several weeks. Finally, British forces surrendered to the Americans.

This battle was called the turning point of the war because it sent an important message to other countries. France, one of Great Britain's enemies, started to believe that Americans could win the war. The French began to send supplies to the Americans.

At Saratoga, General Benedict Arnold led the American troops. But Arnold soon became a traitor to the Americans. A traitor is a person who secretly helps the enemy. Arnold joined the British forces and gave away American military secrets.

Why was the Battle of Saratoga the turning point of the war? France and other countries began to believe the Americans could win. They wanted to help the Americans.

Visual The first mention of a military musical organization used in connection with battle in the U.S. Army occurred after the capture of Fort Ticonderoga in 1775. A fife and drum corps was used.

Drummer boys used drums and a small flute to call soldiers to battle.

From Valley Forge to Yorktown

Winter 1778: Valley Forge

A few months after the victory at Saratoga, American forces hit their lowest point, in Valley Forge, Pennsylvania. While the British troops were safe and warm in nearby Philadelphia, thousands of Americans froze to death in the cold. Americans had no shoes, no blankets, and very little food or shelter.

Major Battles of the Revolutionary War

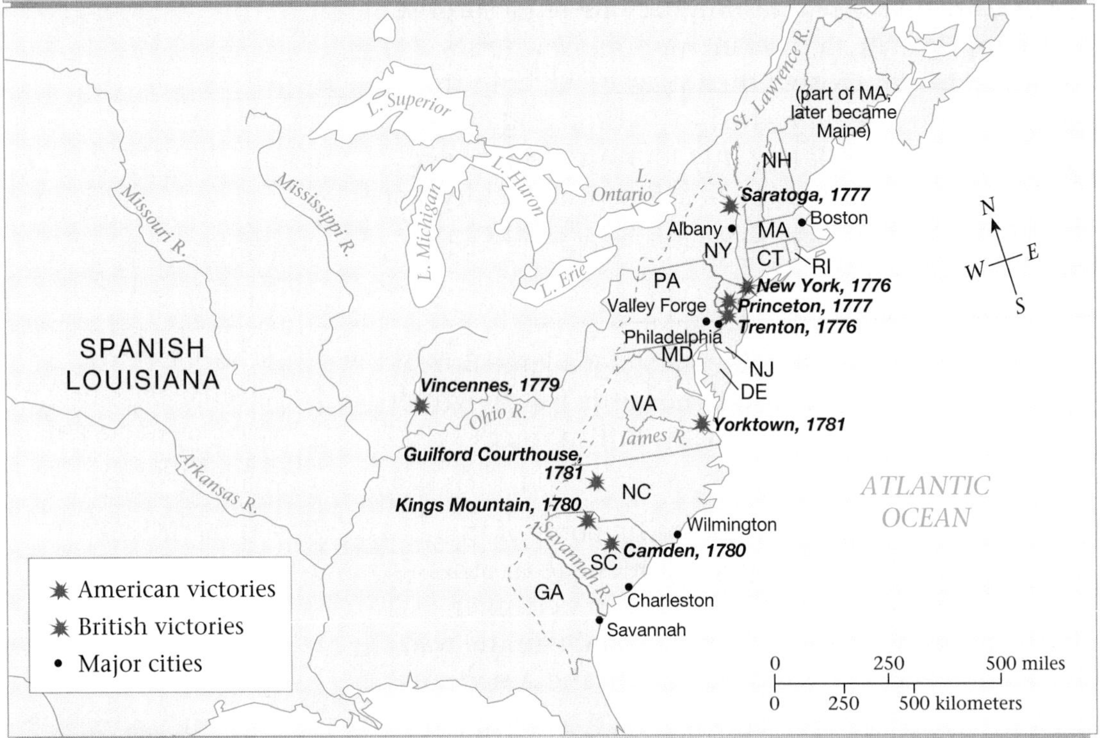

Map Study

1. Who won the Battle of Camden? The British

2. In what year was the battle of Princeton fought? 1777

Map The map shows the major battles of the Revolutionary War. Students should identify the locations as well as the names of the battles.

Washington spent the winter at Valley Forge too. "You can tell where the American army has been," he said, "by the footprints of blood in the snow."

February 1778: France enters the war

After the American victory at Saratoga, Benjamin Franklin went to France to get help for the United States. He worked with French leaders to put together a treaty between the United States and France. The French were then ready to join the American fight for independence.

A French nobleman, Marquis de Lafayette had come to Virginia to join the Americans a year earlier. When French troops arrived, he led them against British forces in the South.

1778: Other nations follow France

Once France decided to help the American side, it opened the way for other countries to join the war. Spain and Holland lent money to help the Americans. The German military leader Baron von Steuben served as a leader for American troops. So did military leaders from Poland, including Count Pulaski and Thaddeus Kosciusko.

Fall 1781: Battle of Yorktown

British General Lord Cornwallis marched through the South. Finally he was trapped on a piece of land near Yorktown, Virginia, that was surrounded on three

History and You

NAMES FROM THE REVOLUTION

Have you ever considered how your county got its name? The people of the United States often name counties after military heroes and civilian heroes.

George Washington's name is the most popular name for counties in the United States. There are 31 states with counties named Washington. Naming a county after Washington honors his service during the War for Independence.

Foreign heroes from the War for Independence have also had U.S. counties named in their honor. For example, 17 counties are named for Marquis de Lafayette. He was a French officer who fought with the colonists.

This is a bronze statue of George Washington.

Critical Thinking Why is it an honor to have a county named after you? Student responses should show an understanding that the county is recognizing your accomplishments.

sides by water. The French navy blocked British ships from rescuing Cornwallis's troops. The British were trapped. On October 19, 1781, Cornwallis surrendered.

Who were some military leaders in the war?
Washington, Lafayette, von Steuben, Pulaski, Kosciusko; Cornwallis

The Treaty of Paris

King George III could have gone on fighting, but he saw that the British people had become tired of the war. A group of Americans met British leaders in Paris to prepare a treaty to end the war. Finally, in 1783, the Americans and the British signed the Treaty of Paris. Under the treaty, Great Britain agreed to recognize the colonies as an independent nation.

The United States of America was now a free country. Americans had fought and defeated the most powerful country in the world. The cause of freedom had been won after a long and hard fight.

What was the Treaty of Paris of 1783? A peace agreement between Great Britain and the United States

Section 3 Review

1. What did Thomas Paine's pamphlet *Common Sense* say the colonists should do?
2. What happened at the Battle of Yorktown?
3. **Critical Thinking** Why do you think the Second Continental Congress tried to keep peace with Great Britain?
4. **Write About History** Think about the Loyalists, Patriots, and those who remained neutral. Make a chart comparing and contrasting them.

More Review is provided in Exercise 17 of the Workbook.

1. Colonists should set up their own government.
2. The British general Lord Cornwallis had to surrender after being trapped.
3. Student responses might mention that many colonists were still not sure about independence; would be fighting a stronger, better-trained navy.
4. Student charts should include the following: Loyalists—wanted to remain with Britain, fought on British side, some forced to go to Canada. Patriots—wanted independence from Britain, joined local militia, fought on American side. Neutral colonists—didn't care which side won.

VOICES FROM THE PAST
Thomas Jefferson

In 1776, delegates at the Second Continental Congress asked Thomas Jefferson to write the Declaration of Independence. The Declaration was the colonists' announcement that the colonies were becoming a separate nation—the United States of America.

Jefferson wrote the Declaration in several parts. In the introduction, Jefferson stated that the colonists had no choice but to break away from Great Britain. He then stated the colonists' reasons for such an important step.

Thomas Jefferson

Next, the Declaration described the colonists' main ideas about government. Jefferson wrote:

"We hold these truths to be self-evident, that all men are created equal, that they are endowed [given] by their Creator with certain unalienable [not able to be taken away] Rights, that among these are Life, Liberty, and the pursuit of Happiness."

Then the declaration lists the "long train of abuses," or the unfair things that the British King George III had done. It also describes the colonists' efforts to get justice. Jefferson finished by declaring that for all these reasons the 13 colonies were no longer a part of Great Britain. You can read the whole Declaration of Independence on pages 618–623 at the back of this book.

1. What was the purpose of the Declaration of Independence?

2. How did Thomas Jefferson support the colonists?

CHALLENGE What did Thomas Jefferson mean when he said "all men are created equal"?

1. To announce that the colonies were becoming a separate nation **2.** By listing the abuses of King George III and the efforts colonists had made to get justice **CHALLENGE** White men are equal under the law.

Chapter

4 Review

Summary Have students use this graphic organizer to outline the main ideas and details of the chapter.

Summary	The colonists began to struggle for freedom after the French and Indian War. The colonists finally won their freedom in a war against Great Britain.
Section 1	From 1754 to 1763, Great Britain and France fought the French and Indian War. The colonists fought along with the British. Great Britain won the war.
Section 2	After the French and Indian War, Great Britain passed a series of laws and taxes. The new acts made the colonists angry. There were protests, such as the Boston Massacre and the Boston Tea Party, that soon followed.
Section 3	In 1775, the War for Independence began. Colonists fought hard for freedom. The British surrendered at Yorktown in 1781.

More Vocabulary Review is provided in Exercise 20 of the Classroom Resource Binder.

Vocabulary Review

Write *true* or *false*. If the statement is false, change the underlined term to make it true.

1. Patrick Henry, Thomas Jefferson, and Paul Revere were <u>Patriots</u>. True
2. A <u>declaration</u> is a sudden change of government. False: revolution
3. Angry colonists wanted Great Britain to <u>repeal</u> unfair laws and taxes. True
4. A colonial <u>blockade</u> was a citizen army used in emergencies. False: militia

1. The French were there first and had built a fur trade and small settlements. pp. 60–61 2. Colonists became angry, refused to pay the taxes or buy English goods, joined protest groups p. 64 3. France and Great Britain were enemies. At the Battle of Saratoga, the colonists had shown that they might be able to win. pp. 73–75 4. Possible answer: The Declaration spoke for white men in the colonies. p. 71 5. Possible answer: Saratoga was a turning point; Yorktown was the final battle. pp. 72–76

Chapter Quiz

Write your answers in complete sentences.

1. Why did the French think they had a right to control the Ohio River valley?
2. What did the colonists do when the British passed new acts after the French and Indian War?
3. Why did France and other European nations decide to help the Americans fight the British?
4. **Critical Thinking** Jefferson tried to speak for all colonists in the Declaration of Independence. Do you think he succeeded in doing this? Explain.
5. **Critical Thinking** What do you think was the most important battle of the War for Independence? Why?

Test Tip
As you study for a test, write questions you have. When you finish each chapter, answer the question or ask questions in class to get answers.

Writing Tip
Think of your audience as you write. An essay for school should be formal. Do not use slang. Answer in complete sentences.

Using the Timeline

Use the timeline on pages 58–59 to answer the questions.

1. When were the Intolerable Acts passed? 1774
2. Which took place first, the Boston Massacre or the Boston Tea Party? The Boston Massacre

Group Activity See the Teacher's Planning Guide for a scoring rubric for this activity.

Group Activity

Form groups to be members of the Second Continental Congress. Turn to the Declaration of Independence, on pages 618–623. Choose a part of the Declaration. Discuss it with the other members of Congress and vote to accept it or reject it. Write a group discussion.

Critical Thinking **1.** To find a short route to Asia **2.** To give a home to debtors **3.** To make finished goods to sell all over the world **4.** He had already shown he was a good leader in the French and Indian War.

Unit 1 Review

Critical Thinking

Give one reason why each of the following events happened.

1. In the 1400s, European explorers began to travel far from home.

2. The colony of Georgia was settled.

3. England bought raw materials from the colonies in America.

4. The Second Continental Congress chose George Washington as a military leader.

Building Your Skills

Draw a timeline with the following information. Then give the timeline a title.

1488 Bartolomeu Dias navigates western coast of Africa

1492 Christopher Columbus sails to the Americas

1419 Prince Henry of Portugal establishes school for navigators

1501 Amerigo Vespucci sails to South America

1498 Vasco da Gama sails to India

Timelines should show events in order. Suitable titles include European Exploration, 1419–1501.

Who Did It?

Write the name of the person who took each action below.

1. He was the first European explorer to reach North America. Leif Ericson

2. She angered Puritan leaders and was forced to leave the Massachusetts Bay Colony. Anne Hutchinson

3. He was the first person to die in the Boston Massacre. Crispus Attucks

Writing an Essay

Answer one of the following essay topics.

See the Answer Key for a detailed answer.

1. Discuss the effects of the Ice Age on the first people in the Americas.

2. Explain why Great Britain felt it was right to regulate trade in its colonies in the Americas.

Linking Past and Present

Discuss why people from other countries migrate to the United States today. Compare the reasons why people come to the United States today with the reasons why people came in the past. Students may discuss political, social, economic, and religious reasons.

Unit Opener Use the titles, visual, and caption to engage students in a discussion of the time period.

Unit 2 Growth of a New Nation

Chapter 5 **Building a New Government** 1780–1800

Chapter 6 **Economy and Expansion** 1800–1830

Chapter 7 **The Changing United States** 1820–1850

Chapter 8 **Newcomers and New Ideas** 1820–1860

This painting shows William Clark, Meriwether Lewis, and their Native American guide Sacajawea exploring lands west of the Mississippi River. How do you think Sacajawea helped Lewis and Clark? She seems to be greeting the Native Americans. She knew the customs and the best way to communicate with them.

> *"No people in the world have made such rapid progress as the Americans."*
>
> —from *Democracy in America*, a book by the French historian Alexis de Tocqueville about his travels in the United States during 1831 and 1832

Primary Source *Democracy in America* tells how free societies work. It discusses the good and bad aspects of social equality. In it, Tocqueville warns that democracy has a tendency to smother individuality and personal freedom.

The Constitution of the United States was signed in 1787. At that time, quill pens and inkstands were used to write. What does the painting tell you about the signing of the document? It was a very formal event and people were focused on the signing of the Constitution.

Forming a Government

- **1780**
- **1781** Articles of Confederation ratified
- **1785**
- **1786** Shays's Rebellion starts
- **1787** Constitution written
- **1787** Northwest Ordinance passed
- **1789** George Washington elected first President
- **1790**
- **1791** Bill of Rights added to the Constitution

Additional activities and strategies to customize lessons can be found in the Teacher's Planning Guide.

Chapter 5 Building a New Government 1780–1800

ESL Note To help students understand the concept of compromise, ask pairs of students to discuss examples of compromises they have made at home or school. Explain that the United States relied on compromise to form a new government.

Words to Know

constitution

territory

convention

compromise

legislative branch

executive branch

judicial branch

ratify

amendment

Cabinet

alliance

Words to Know These words are defined in the section in which they appear, as well as in the Glossary. Point out that the word *Cabinet* is capitalized because it is a proper noun.

Learning Objectives

- Discuss the purpose of the Articles of Confederation.
- Analyze the weaknesses of the Articles of Confederation.
- Explain how the Constitution was created.
- Discuss the Bill of Rights.
- Identify the problems facing the first leaders of the nation.
- Read a main idea and details chart.

Project To read the Constitution and Bill of Rights in full, students may wish to refer to pages 624–654 in the back of their book.

Portfolio Project

When the American colonists declared their independence from Great Britain in 1776, they had to plan a government of their own. First they wrote the Articles of Confederation. Then they wrote the U.S. Constitution. Finally, the Bill of Rights was added to the Constitution. In your journal, tell how each document affected U.S. government.

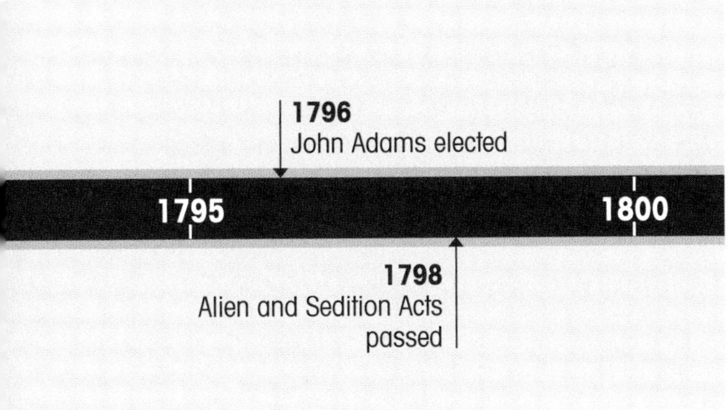

Timeline The timeline is divided into intervals of 5 years. The events take place over a period of 17 years. Discuss what the timeline is about by reading the title and entries with students.

Section 1 The Articles of Confederation

Words to Know

constitution	the laws and plan of a nation's government
territory	land that belongs to a national government but is not a state

Getting Started Ask students to think about forming a club centered on a favorite sport or hobby. Discuss how the club might be organized and what rules members might need. Point out that a government also has a set of rules.

Visual Maryland refused to sign the Articles of Confederation in 1777 unless states such as New York and Virginia turned over their western land claims to the federal government.

The Articles of Confederation were signed in 1777.

When the War for Independence ended, the 13 colonies won their freedom from Great Britain. However, there was still a great deal of work to do. The colonies had to create a new government.

The Articles of Confederation

The Second Continental Congress continued to meet throughout the War for Independence. In 1777, colonial leaders finished writing a plan of government called the Articles of Confederation. This was America's first national **constitution.** A constitution is made up of the laws and plan of a nation's government.

Under the Articles, the states thought of themselves as separate countries. They did not want a strong national government controlling them. After all, they had just fought a war to get rid of a king.

Under this plan, the government was run by a congress. The Congress was controlled by representatives from individual states. Each of the 13 states had one vote in Congress. Before Congress could pass any law, nine of the 13 states had to approve it.

What were the Articles of Confederation? America's first constitution

Problems After the War

The United States faced many problems after the war. Here are some of them.

1. Great Britain closed its ports to America. The United States had to find new trading partners.
2. Debts could not be paid because Congress could not collect taxes.
3. Each state printed its own money. However, the money was worthless in other states.
4. There were no courts to settle arguments between states.

The Articles of Confederation could not handle these problems. It soon became clear that a stronger national government was needed.

What were some problems the United States faced at the end of the War for Independence? Get new trading partners, pay its debts, organize a monetary system, establish courts

Shays's Rebellion

One of the most violent revolts against the new government occurred in Massachusetts in 1786. That state had borrowed money during the war. State leaders decided to raise taxes to pay off those debts.

If people could not pay the taxes, they would lose their land. Many farmers in western Massachusetts were unable to pay the higher taxes. They decided to protest the taxes. A farmer named Daniel Shays led the revolt, or uprising. He and his followers made plans to attack an arsenal, which is a place where weapons are stored.

The U.S. government learned about the plans. Finally a militia group hired by Massachusetts businessmen stopped the rebellion.

Why did the farmers in Massachusetts revolt? Farmers could not pay the higher taxes levied by state leaders of Massachusetts.

Visual Before they were stopped by government troops, Daniel Shays and others protested at courthouses. The courts were making judgments against debtors.

Daniel Shays led angry farmers in a violent uprising in 1786.

The Northwest Ordinance

Another problem that the new government had to solve was what to do about land north of the Ohio River and east of the Mississippi River. This area was called the Northwest Territory. A **territory** is land that belongs to a national government but is not a state. The British had controlled this area before the war. Now American settlers were claiming the land.

The Northwest Ordinance was passed in 1787. An ordinance is a set of laws. It was a plan to create a government for this land. The Northwest Ordinance described the steps which new states would have to take to be formed. It stated that the territory would be divided into smaller territories. After 5,000 freemen of voting age settled an area, they could elect a legislature. Territories could ask for statehood after reaching a population of 60,000. The Northwest Ordinance allowed settlers to buy one square mile of land for $640. No slavery was allowed anywhere in the territory.

What was the purpose of the Northwest Ordinance?
Described how the Northwest Territory would become a state

Section 1 Review

1. What was the first plan for governing the 13 states after the Revolutionary War?
2. Why did Congress have trouble paying its debts after the war?
3. **Critical Thinking** If you were a settler in the Northwest Territory, would you have welcomed the Northwest Ordinance? Explain.
4. **Write About Citizenship** Write a paragraph explaining whether you think Daniel Shays was right or wrong to break the law.

1. Articles of Confederation
2. Congress could not collect taxes.
3. Student answers should show an understanding of the Northwest Ordinance.
4. Possible answers supporting Shays may state that taxes should be equally placed. Answers against Shays may say it is the responsibility of citizens to support government.

More Review is provided in Exercise 18 of the Workbook.

BUILDING YOUR SKILLS
Reading a Chart

One of the best ways to understand information is to organize facts on a chart. Charts can show how important ideas connect to one another.

Here is how to make a main idea and details chart.

- Choose a topic. Use it for the title.
- List the main idea at the top of the chart. List the details that support the idea below the main idea.
- Use the information on the chart to help answer any questions you have about the material you have read.

Government Under the Articles of Confederation	
Main Idea	The Articles of Confederation was a plan of government.
Supporting Details	**1.** The government is run by Congress. **2.** Approval of all 13 states is needed to make changes to the Articles of Confederation.

Answer the questions below, using the information on the chart.

1. What is the main idea of the chart?

2. What are the supporting details?

CHALLENGE Copy the chart on a sheet of paper. Find two more details about government under the Articles of Confederation to add to the chart.

Apply the Skill
Create a main idea and details chart, using what you have read about the Northwest Ordinance on page 86.

1. The Articles of Confederation was a plan of government. **2.** Government run by Congress, approval of all states needed for changes. **CHALLENGE** Approval of nine states to pass a law; each state has one vote in Congress

Section 2 The Constitution and the Bill of Rights

Words to Know

convention	a large gathering of people for a particular reason
compromise	a settling of differences where both sides give up something
legislative branch	the part of government that makes laws
executive branch	the part of government that carries out laws
judicial branch	the part of government that settles differences about the meanings of laws
ratify	to approve
amendment	a change or addition to a document

Getting Started Discuss with students ways to overcome challenges. Have them read on, looking at the strategies America's founders used in response to the challenges of creating the Constitution.

In May 1787, 55 representatives, or delegates, from 12 states gathered in Philadelphia for a convention. A **convention** is a large gathering of people for a particular reason. The purpose of the convention was to come up with a better plan for the government of the United States.

The Constitutional Convention

Remember
Benjamin Franklin helped turn Philadelphia into a well-organized city.

George Washington was chosen to run the Constitutional Convention. James Madison of Virginia was there. He became known as the Father of the Constitution. Years later he would be elected the fourth President of the United States. Benjamin Franklin attended also. He was still serving the nation at age 81.

On the first day of the meeting, the delegates agreed on two ideas. First, they would keep the doors to the meeting hall locked and the windows nailed shut. Even though the summer heat would be terrible, the men did not want anyone to hear their discussions. Second, they all agreed that the talks would remain secret until the new Constitution was completed. After that day, though, the delegates hardly ever agreed again.

Who were some of the famous delegates at the Constitutional Convention? George Washington, James Madison, Benjamin Franklin

Big States Against Small States

The first and most important question at the meeting was how the new Congress would be set up. Most delegates agreed that Congress should have two houses, or parts. However, the delegates could not agree on how representatives should be chosen.

Delegates from Virginia came up with a plan that gave more power to the large states. This plan was called the Virginia Plan. These delegates felt that states with more people should have more votes in Congress.

Small states came up with a different plan. Each state would have one vote in Congress. The number of people in a state should not matter. This plan was called the New Jersey Plan.

The argument went on for six weeks. Luckily, Roger Sherman, a delegate from Connecticut, came up with a plan called the Great Compromise. A **compromise** is a settling of differences where both sides give up something. Sherman's compromise called for two houses of Congress. In the Senate, each state had the same number of votes. In the House of Representatives, votes were determined by the number of people in the state. The delegates accepted Sherman's compromise.

What problem did the Great Compromise solve? How representatives in Congress should be chosen

History Fact

In 1776, Sherman served with Thomas Jefferson on a committee to write the Declaration of Independence.

History Fact John Adams, Benjamin Franklin, and Robert Livingston were the other members of the committee.

The Three-fifths Compromise

Another problem soon arose. In coming up with the population of a state, how were enslaved people to be counted? Northerners said Southerners treated enslaved Africans as property, so they should not be counted. Southerners wanted to count enslaved Africans as part of the population. That way the South would have more votes in Congress.

The delegates agreed on another compromise. When counting the population of a state, five enslaved persons would count as three people. This became known as the Three-fifths Compromise.

What was the Three-fifths Compromise? Five enslaved people would equal three free people in population counts.

Checks and Balances

As the summer passed, the delegates agreed that the government should have three branches, or parts. The **legislative branch**, or Congress, would make laws. The **executive branch**, led by the President, would carry out laws. The **judicial branch**, which is made up of the courts, would settle differences about the meanings of laws.

The delegates agreed that dividing the government into three branches would balance the powers of all three branches. In this government, no one branch would have more power than another. This idea came to be known as the system of checks and balances.

Finally, the plan for the new United States government was written down. The delegates took the new Constitution back to the leaders of their states. Under the rules, nine of the 13 colonies had to **ratify**, or approve, the Constitution for it to go into effect.

What is the purpose of the system of checks and balances? To help legislative, executive, and judicial branches work together as equal partners

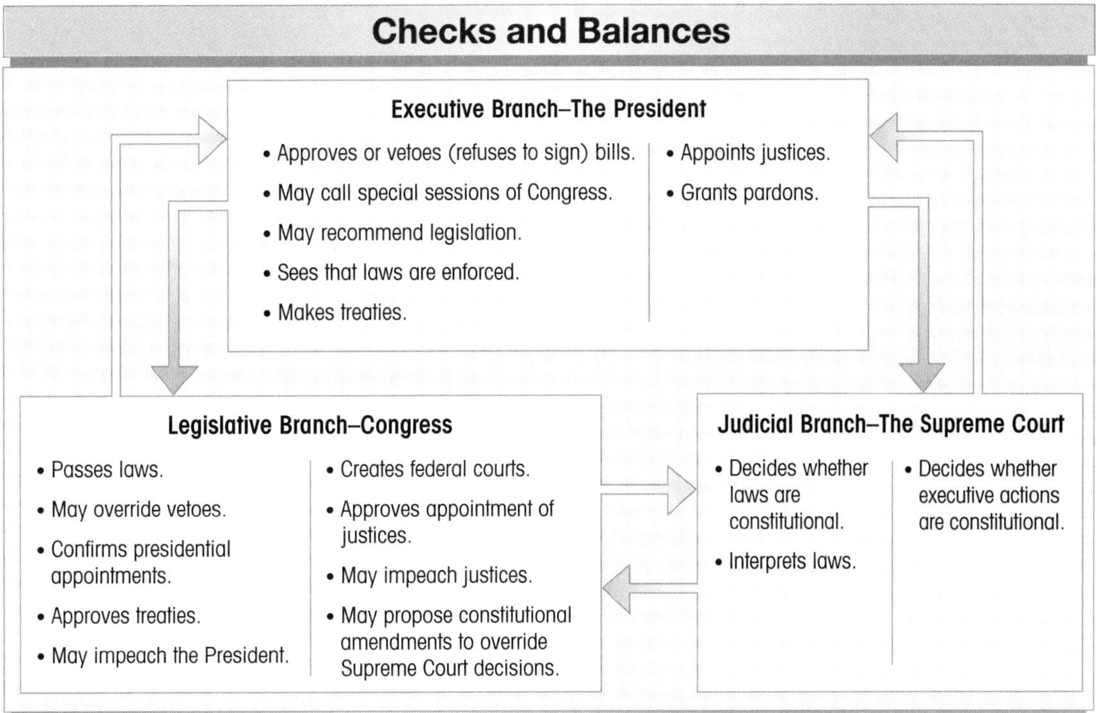

Chart Study

1. Which branch of government can decide whether laws are constitutional? Judicial branch
2. Which branch approves treaties? Legislative branch

Federalists and Anti-Federalists

Over the next few months, the Constitution was discussed in all 13 states. Those in favor of the Constitution and a strong national government were called Federalists. The Federalists were wealthy landowners, merchants, and lawyers who supported the Constitution. They wanted a strong central government that would keep the country united.

Those who were against a strong national government were called Anti-Federalists. The Anti-Federalists were mostly farmers who did not support the Constitution. They wanted more power for states.

Chart Point out the arrows and discuss what they link. Discuss reasons why this system was called "Checks and Balances." Ask individual students to read the job of each branch of government.

The vote to ratify the Constitution was very close. However, by 1790 all the states finally agreed to become a united country.

Who were the Federalists and the Anti-Federalists? Federalists wanted a strong national government; Anti-Federalists were against it.

The Bill of Rights

You can read the U.S. Constitution and Bill of Rights on pages 624–654.

Even though the Constitution was ratified, some Americans wanted to add a bill of rights to the Constitution. The Bill of Rights lists actions that the government is not allowed to take. It guarantees freedom of speech and religion and the right to a fair trial to every American.

The Bill of Rights are the first ten **amendments** of the Constitution. An amendment is a change or addition to a document. The amendments were added to the Constitution in 1791. Many amendments have been added since then.

What is the Bill of Rights? The first ten amendments to the Constitution

Section 2 Review

1. What were two of the compromises during the Constitutional Convention?
2. Why is the Bill of Rights important?
3. **Critical Thinking** Why did the constitutional delegates include a system of checks and balances?
4. **Write About History** Suppose you are either a Federalist or an Anti-Federalist. Write a letter to a newspaper, describing your views about ratification of the Constitution.

More Review is provided in Exercise 19 of the Workbook.

1. The Great Compromise and the Three-fifths Compromise
2. The Bill of Rights guarantees freedom of speech and religion and the right to a fair trial.
3. The system of checks and balances guaranteed no one branch of government would have more power than another.
4. Federalist letters should support a strong national government. Anti-Federalist letters should support powerful state governments.

Section 3 The New Government Begins

Words to Know

Cabinet	a group of people chosen by the President to give advice
alliance	a partnership

Getting Started Have students discuss whether they have ever gone into the voting booth with family members who were voting. Discuss why family members voted for a particular candidate. Have students brainstorm a list of qualities they think are important for the leader of a country to have.

The new government of the United States had much to do to repair the damage done by the Articles of Confederation. Building a powerful, united country was most important. A large part of that job meant creating a strong political system and a strong economy.

The First President

On April 6, 1789, George Washington was elected the first President of the United States. John Adams, who finished second in votes, became Vice President.

Washington took on a difficult job. He had no examples to follow. Washington had to find money to pay war debts. He had to work out trade agreements with foreign countries. He had to make decisions that were best for all the states. Washington knew he could not do his job alone. He chose a **Cabinet.** A Cabinet is a group of people chosen by the President to give advice.

Washington chose his advisers wisely. His Cabinet was made up of Thomas Jefferson, Alexander Hamilton, Henry Knox, and Edmund Randolph. Washington also chose John Jay as Chief Justice, or head, of the Supreme Court. Every President since Washington depends on a Cabinet.

Why did George Washington choose a Cabinet?
To receive the advice of experts

George Washington traveled to New York to be sworn in as the first President.

Visual When George Washington was sworn in, debates arose over how to address him in his new position. The Senate had three suggestions: "His Highness," "His Excellence," and "His Elective Majesty." The title "Mr. President" was finally chosen.

The New Government

Each Cabinet member had a different job. Thomas Jefferson became Secretary of State. He advised Washington on how to deal with foreign countries. Alexander Hamilton became Secretary of the Treasury. He advised Washington on the economy. Henry Knox became Secretary of War. He advised Washington about keeping a strong army and navy. Edmund Randolph became Attorney General. He advised Washington on the laws that were passed.

Washington served for two four-year terms as President. During that time the country became stronger. George Washington accomplished the following during his terms in office.

1. He kept the United States out of war.
2. He raised enough money to pay off the country's war debt.
3. He established a national bank.
4. He set up a money system.

After two terms, Washington decided not to run again for President. This decision set an example for other Presidents. For more than 140 years, Presidents left office after two terms. Later, the Constitution would be changed so that no President could serve more than two terms in office.

What did George Washington accomplish as President? Kept the country out of war; paid off the war debt; established a national bank; set up a money system

Citizenship Link

A NEW CAPITAL

New York City was the first capital of the United States. Then, between 1790 and 1800, Philadelphia served as the nation's capital.

In 1800, the capital was moved to the banks of the Potomac River, where Virginia and Maryland had each given land for a new city to be built. Washington, D.C., or District of Columbia, was not part of any state. It was its own district, so no state could claim it. At first, the capital was to be called Federal City, but it was changed to Washington, D.C., in 1800 to honor the first President.

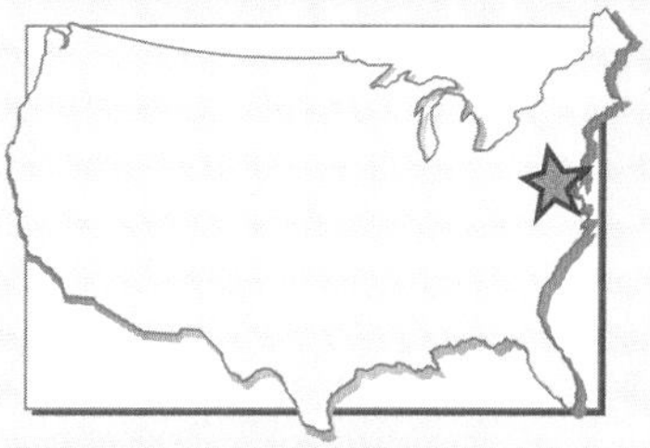

Washington, D.C. became the nation's capital in 1800.

Critical Thinking Why was Washington, D.C., a good place for the nation's capital? It was its own district; not part of any state.

Political Parties

Two of Washington's most important advisers were Thomas Jefferson, the Secretary of State, and Alexander Hamilton, the Secretary of the Treasury. Even though they advised the President, they did not agree with each other. They had different ideas about how the nation should be governed.

Hamilton believed in a strong national government. He also felt that only well-educated landowners knew enough to take part in governing. He did not think the average person was smart enough to serve in the government.

Jefferson wanted everyone to have a voice in government, not just the rich. He worried that the national government would become too powerful. He did not want the government to spend more money than it could raise in taxes.

The people who supported Hamilton and his views formed the Federalist party. Those who supported Jefferson's ideas formed the Democratic-Republican party. These different beliefs were the beginning of political parties in the United States. Every President since Washington has belonged to a political party.

What were the differences between the Federalists and the Democratic-Republicans? The Federalists were for a strong national government; Democratic-Republicans were against it.

John Adams Becomes President

In 1796, George Washington decided to step down as President of the United States. Before leaving office, he prepared a written report called his Farewell Address. In his Farewell Address, Washington advised the leaders of the United States to stay away from permanent **alliances**, or partnerships, with foreign countries.

John Adams was elected the second President in 1796. Adams belonged to the Federalist party. During his presidency, the Alien and Sedition Acts were passed. The Alien Act was passed in 1798. The act said that a person arriving in the United States had to wait 14 years to become a citizen. The old waiting period had been 5 years. Newcomers to the United States felt unwanted because of this law.

The Sedition Act made it a crime for anyone to write or print articles criticizing the government. Angry citizens said that this violated the right of free speech in the Constitution.

The Alien and Sedition Acts made Adams unpopular. In 1800, he lost the election when he tried to win a second term. As a new century began, Thomas Jefferson took office as the third President of the United States.

Why were the Alien and Sedition Acts unpopular?
The Alien Act made the waiting period to become a citizen longer. Many Americans felt the Sedition Act violated their right to free speech.

Section 3 Review

1. What problems did George Washington face as President?
2. What were the first two political parties?
3. **Critical Thinking** If you were a wealthy landowner during Washington's presidency, would you have supported Hamilton or Jefferson? Explain.
4. **Write About History** Write a news article about the Alien and Sedition Acts during John Adams' presidency.

1. War debts, trade agreements, decisions that were best for all states
2. Federalists and Democratic-Republicans
3. Possible answers: Supporting Hamilton would make for a strong national government; supporting Jefferson would give all Americans a voice in government.
4. Student answers should show an understanding of the Alien and Sedition Acts.

More Review is provided in Exercise 21 of the Workbook.

Chapter

5 Review

Summary Have students use this graphic organizer to outline the main ideas and details of the chapter.

Summary
Americans designed a new kind of government. A Constitution was written that still protects the rights of Americans today.

Section 1
The Articles of Confederation provided the first government for the United States. However, these Articles created a government that was too weak to collect taxes, set up a money system, or settle disputes.

Section 2
In 1787, state delegates met to create a new government. There were disagreements and compromises among these people. Eventually, the Constitution was completed and all 13 states ratified it.

Section 3
George Washington became the nation's first President. His leadership made the nation strong.

Cabinet
compromise
ratify
amendment

More Vocabulary Review is provided in Exercise 28 of the Classroom Resource Binder.

Vocabulary Review

Complete each sentence with a term from the list.

1. The members of Washington's _____ were not always in agreement. Cabinet
2. It took time and much debate before all the states decided to _____ the Constitution. ratify
3. The large states and the small states reached a _____ that created separate houses in Congress. compromise
4. The Constitution has remained law for more than 200 years because a change, or an _____, can be added. amendment

1. They believed in a strong national government. p. 91 **2.** He advised the country on avoiding foreign alliances. p. 96 **3.** John Adams p. 97 **4.** They had been ruled harshly by a monarchy in which the power rested with only one person. p. 84 **5.** Not all the leaders agreed on whether power should be vested in a central government or in the states, whether people's individual rights should be identified. pp. 89–92

Chapter Quiz

Write your answers in complete sentences.

1. What were the views of the Federalists?
2. What suggestion did George Washington make in his Farewell Address?
3. Who became President after George Washington?
4. **Critical Thinking** Why do you think many people in the United States were worried about a strong central government having too much power?
5. **Critical Thinking** Why do you think the first leaders of our country faced difficult problems?

Test Tip
Make your own timeline of the period you are studying. Add the most important dates and events.

Writing Tip
Think about your answers before you begin writing.

Using the Timeline

Use the timeline on pages 82–83 to answer the questions.

1. How many years after the Constitution was written was the Bill of Rights added? 4 years
2. Which was passed first, the Northwest Ordinance or the Alien and Sedition Acts? Northwest Ordinance

Group Activity See the Teacher's Planning Guide for a scoring rubric for this activity.

Group Activity

Form five groups that will represent five states at the Constitutional Convention. Decide what your state wants to gain at the convention. Make a list of your ideas. Select a spokesperson to present your ideas. Conduct a meeting in which all the spokespersons argue for their states' interests.

These machines prepared cotton for spinning in early factories. Workers packed lunches in pails. Who were the workers in this factory? Women and young girls

A New Nation Grows

- **1800** Thomas Jefferson elected
- **1803** United States buys Louisiana Territory from France
- **1804** Lewis and Clark expedition begins
- **1808** James Madison elected
- **1812** War of 1812 begins
- **1814** Treaty of Ghent ends War of 1812
- **1816** James Monroe elected
- **1819** Spain gives Florida to United States

1800 | 1805 | 1810 | 1815 | 1820

Additional activities and strategies to customize lessons can be found in the Teacher's Planning Guide.

Chapter 6 Economy and Expansion 1800–1830

ESL Note To help students understand the concept of goal setting, invite them to describe a time when they or someone they know worked hard to accomplish a goal. The settling of the West and advances in transportation and communication occurred because of hard work.

Words to Know

- elector
- impressment
- embargo
- nationalism
- doctrine
- industry
- textile
- interchangeable part
- mass production
- cotton gin
- overseer

Words to Know These words are defined in the section in which they appear, as well as in the Glossary. Point out that the words *industry, interchangeable part,* and *mass production* show the shift from worker power to machine power in the United States.

Learning Objectives

- Explain how the United States grew in the early nineteenth century.
- Describe the events that led to the War of 1812.
- Discuss how the Industrial Revolution affected the economies in the North and South.
- Explore how the cotton gin changed the economy of the South.

Project Students will be able to begin work on the project after completing Section 3. To help them get started, discuss where and how people lived, and what they did to make a living.

Portfolio Project

You are living in the United States in the early 1800s. You have heard about the Louisiana Purchase, the Lewis and Clark expedition, the War of 1812, and mass production of goods. Write a diary entry expressing how you feel about two of these events and why.

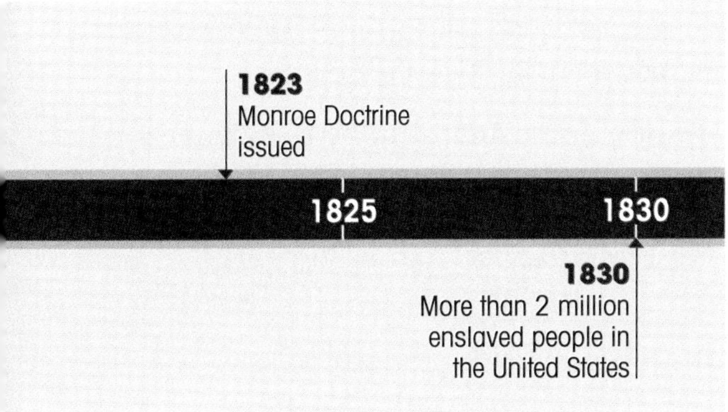

Timeline The timeline is divided into intervals of 5 years. The events take place over a period of 30 years. Discuss the main idea of this timeline. Point out that the United States gained more land with its acquisition of the Louisiana Territory and Florida.

Section 1 Growth and Conflict

Words to Know

elector	a person selected to vote for the President and Vice President
impressment	the act of forcing a person into public service, especially into a navy
embargo	a government order that stops trade with other countries
nationalism	pride in one's country
doctrine	a set of beliefs

Getting Started Have students discuss the ways their neighborhood or community has changed in the past few years. Point out that big changes, whether in a country, region, or neighborhood, often create both conflicts and new expectations.

Remember
The Federalist party believed in a strong national government. The Democratic-Republican party was against this.

Between 1800 and 1830, the United States was growing quickly and in many ways. Many changes took place. Some changes caused problems among Americans. Others caused problems between the United States and foreign nations. The United States tried to solve these problems.

The Election of 1800

In 1800, there were two political parties in the United States. They were the Federalist party and the Democratic-Republican party. The election of 1800 was the first real contest between the two parties.

The Federalists wanted John Adams to be President for a second term, with Charles C. Pinckney as Vice President. The Democratic-Republicans supported Thomas Jefferson for President and Aaron Burr for Vice President.

The U.S. Constitution provided for a way to select the President and Vice President. It called for an electoral college. The electoral college is a group of people called **electors.** An elector is a person selected to vote for the President and Vice President. When the electors voted, the person who received the most electoral votes became President. The runner-up became Vice President.

In 1800, when the votes were counted, Jefferson and Burr had the same number of votes. The decision was left to the House of Representatives. The House voted 35 times. Each time there were the same number of votes for Jefferson and Burr. Finally, Jefferson received more votes than Burr. Thomas Jefferson was chosen President. Aaron Burr became Vice President.

Why did the House of Representatives decide the election of 1800? Jefferson and Burr had the same number of electoral votes.

Citizenship Link

THE ELECTORAL COLLEGE

Each state in the United States sends representatives to the electoral college. The number of electors for each state is equal to the number of that state's senators and representatives in Congress. For example, a state having 12 representatives and two senators would have 14 electors.

This button tells people to vote.

Electors are expected to vote for the candidate who wins the popular election, or the election in which ordinary citizens vote, in their state.

If a candidate does not win in a popular election in a state, he or she will receive no electoral votes from that state. If the candidate wins more than half the state's popular votes, he or she gets all its electoral votes.

Critical Thinking Why might some voters want to get rid of the electoral college? So that citizens could vote directly for the candidates of their choice

The Louisiana Purchase

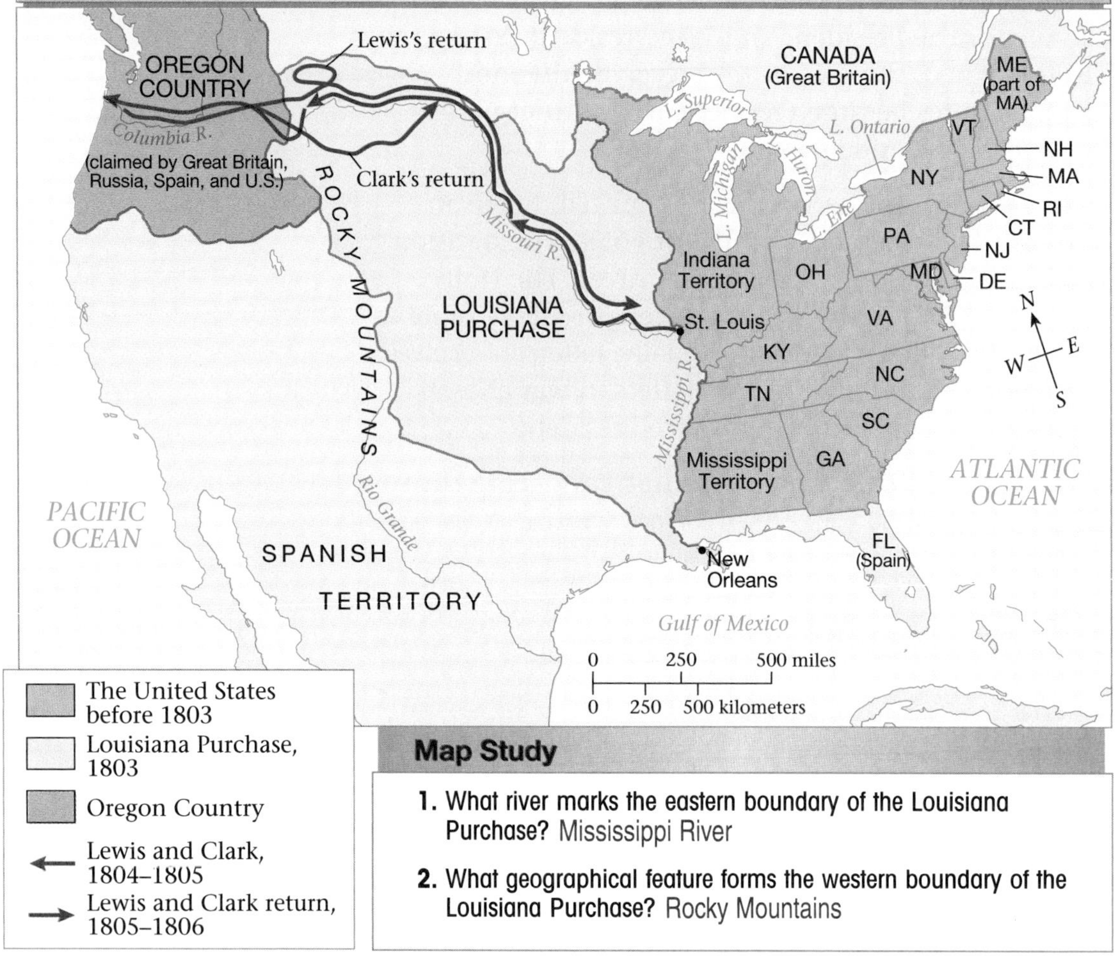

Map Study

1. What river marks the eastern boundary of the Louisiana Purchase? Mississippi River
2. What geographical feature forms the western boundary of the Louisiana Purchase? Rocky Mountains

Map Give students a copy of the outline map of the physical United States found in the Classroom Resource Binder. Have them draw the routes of Lewis and Clark, based on information from this map.

The Louisiana Purchase

When Thomas Jefferson became President, the western boundary of the United States was the Mississippi River. The region west of the Mississippi was under the control of Spain.

In 1801, Spain turned a large part of the area over to France. Jefferson did not want a strong military power, like France, bordering the United States. So he sent people to France to offer to buy the land. Napoleon, the French emperor, offered to sell all the land known as

Louisiana for $15 million. His armies were fighting in Europe, and he needed the money to continue fighting.

Congress quickly approved the sale and the Louisiana Purchase became part of the United States on December 20, 1803. It doubled the size of the United States. The new land had to be explored. In 1804, President Jefferson sent Captain Meriwether Lewis and Lieutenant William Clark on an expedition, or long journey.

Lewis and Clark had some help along the way. A Native American woman named Sacajawea became their guide. She traveled with them from what is now North Dakota through Oregon.

In November 1805, Lewis and Clark reached the Pacific Ocean. By September 1806, they were back in St. Louis. Later, they met with President Jefferson. They had made maps and gathered plant and animal samples. For years, settlers studied that information when they traveled to the Pacific coast.

Why did President Jefferson send Lewis and Clark on an expedition? To explore the land in the Louisiana Purchase

Great Names in History

SACAJAWEA

We do not know much about Sacajawea. We do know that, in North Dakota, Lewis and Clark hired a fur trapper as a guide. They let the trapper's young Native American wife, Sacajawea, and her baby boy come on the expedition.

Sacajawea was a member of the Shoshone nation. Since she knew the Shoshone language, she helped Lewis and Clark buy the food and horses they needed. She also showed Lewis and Clark the best route for crossing the Rocky Mountains.

A page from Lewis and Clark's journal

Critical Thinking How did Sacajawea's knowledge of the Shoshone nation help Lewis and Clark? She knew the Shoshone language and helped Lewis and Clark buy food and horses.

Problems with Great Britain

As President, Thomas Jefferson faced a problem with Great Britain. Great Britain and France had been at war for several years. Great Britain needed more sailors to fight its war against France.

To get more sailors, British ships took American sailors and forced them to serve on British warships. This practice was called **impressment.**

Jefferson ordered an **embargo** on all goods that were traded with other countries, especially Great Britain and France. An embargo is a government order that stops trade with other countries.

When James Madison became President in 1808, the conflict between the United States and Great Britain was an even bigger problem. The embargo hurt the United States because American businesses lost money. In 1809, President Madison lifted the embargo.

In addition, British leaders in Canada were causing trouble for Americans. They were giving weapons and other supplies to Native Americans in the West. Many Americans believed that the British were helping Native Americans attack settlements there.

Why did British ships stop American ships at sea? To force American sailors to serve on British warships

The War of 1812

On June 18, 1812, after months of debate, Congress declared war on Great Britain. The vote was close, but there were enough votes to start the war.

Before the United States declared war, Great Britain had agreed to stop impressing Americans. The agreement arrived too late. The War of 1812 between Great Britain and the United States had begun.

Both the United States and Great Britain had problems while fighting the War of 1812. The war lasted only two and a half years. There was no winner and no loser. In 1814, the Treaty of Ghent was signed, ending the War of 1812.

Two important results came from the War of 1812. The war weakened the powers of Great Britain. The United States also won new respect around the world. That respect created a feeling of **nationalism** in the United States. Nationalism is pride in one's country. Americans were proud that the United States was their country.

What were the results of the War of 1812? Weakened Great Britain; increased feelings of nationalism in U.S.

The Monroe Doctrine

In 1816, James Monroe was elected President. In 1819, the United States signed a treaty with Spain. By that treaty, Spain ceded, or gave Florida to the United States. The United States paid Florida settlers the money that Spain owed them. The total amount was $5 million.

During this time, many colonies in the Americas were controlled by European nations. By 1823, almost all colonies belonging to Spain had won their freedom.

The War of 1812

American Problems	British Problems
The army was small and poorly trained.	There were not enough troops. Some were already fighting against France.
There was not enough money to spend on weapons and supplies.	There were not enough warships. Some were used to fight the French.

Chart Study

1. What did the Americans need money for?
2. Who was Great Britain fighting at the same time?

Chart Point out to students that neither side had the advantage in the War of 1812. Have students read aloud each side's problems and predict the outcome of the War of 1812.

1. Weapons and supplies
2. France

The United States wanted European countries out of the Americas. In 1823, President Monroe gave a speech. In that speech he

1. promised to protect the freedom of countries on the American continents.
2. warned Europe not to start new colonies, try to get back old ones, or enlarge any still there.
3. promised, in return, that the United States would stay out of European problems.

This speech is known as the Monroe Doctrine. A **doctrine** is a set of beliefs. It guided U.S. foreign decisions for many years.

What was the main purpose of the Monroe Doctrine?
To keep the American continents for Americans

Section 1 Review

1. How was the election of 1800 decided?
2. What new territories became part of the United States in the early 1800s?
3. **Critical Thinking** Do you think the United States should have declared war on Great Britain in 1812? Explain.
4. **Write About History** Write a paragraph about the importance of the Monroe Doctrine.

More Review is provided in Exercise 22 of the Workbook.

1. By the House of Representatives
2. Louisiana and Florida
3. Yes: U.S. felt confident, British army already in war with France, tired of British impressing U.S. sailors
   No: U.S. army weak, not enough money for weapons and supplies
4. Student responses should show an understanding that the Monroe Doctrine was an important statement of American foreign policy and an expression of self-reliance and national spirit.

Section 2 Northern Manufacturing

Words to Know

industry	the making or producing of goods by businesses and factories
textile	woven cloth
interchangeable part	a part that can be used in place of another part in manufactured products
mass production	a method of making large numbers of goods quickly and cheaply

Getting Started Have students look around the classroom and identify any object that was made by a machine. Explain that people take machine-made products for granted but that the widespread use of machinery is only about 200 years old.

In 1800, the United States was a nation of farmers. However, during the next 30 years, people began to move to cities. By 1830, one out of every five Americans lived in cities. What brought about changes in the way people lived and worked?

The Industrial Revolution

Before 1800, most goods were made by hand at home or in small shops. After 1800, **industry** changed the way people worked. Industry is the making or producing of goods by businesses and factories.

The Industrial Revolution began when inventors made machines that could do the jobs that people had always done. At first, water power ran these machines. Then more powerful energy sources, such as steam, oil, and gas, were found.

These machines were too big to be used at home or in small shops. Business owners began to build factories where large numbers of workers made goods.

Steamboats, such as the Savannah, *were powered by steam engines.*

Visual Robert Fulton built the first commercially successful steamboat, the *Claremont.* He launched it on the Hudson River in August 1807. It traveled 300 miles in 62 hours.

One machine invented during this time was the steam engine. This engine used coal to heat water. The steam from the heated water could drive machines. Factories no longer had to be built only on rivers. They could be built anywhere. Soon steam engines were also powering ships and railroads.

When did the Industrial Revolution begin? It began in the 1800s when products were made in factories with machines.

Factories Grow in the North

The War of 1812 helped American industry to grow. Great Britain blocked American ports and kept goods from reaching the United States. American factories had to keep up with the demand for goods.

The first industry to develop was the **textile**, or woven cloth, industry. Francis Lowell, a Boston merchant, believed that all the jobs needed to make one product could be done in one factory. He built a huge textile factory in Massachusetts.

Most workers in the Lowell factory were young, single women or teenage girls. They were usually the daughters of local farmers. They could earn more money in the mills than they could earn on farms. However, working conditions at the factory were often hard. This created many problems for the workers, who worked 12 hours a day. Many workers developed breathing problems because of the dusty air.

Factories began to produce goods in a different way. Eli Whitney had an idea to save time. He owned a gun-making factory in Connecticut where gun parts were made alike so that they could be used in any gun the factory made. The parts were called **interchangeable parts.** This idea led to **mass production**, or making large numbers of goods quickly and cheaply.

What event helped factories grow in the North? The blockade of American ports by Great Britain during the War of 1812.

Section 2 Review

1. How did the invention of the steam engine affect factories?

2. How did mass production work?

3. Critical Thinking How might a worker, used to making a product by hand, feel about working in a factory?

4. Write About History Write two paragraphs that compare and contrast life on a farm and life in a factory during the 1800s.

More Review is provided in Exercise 24 of the Workbook.

Economics Fact

The first textile factory in the United States that was a success was built in Pawtucket, Rhode Island. It opened in 1793. It produced cloth from cotton.

Economics Fact Britain manufactured textile machines before the United States did and forbade foreigners from learning their technological secrets. A young textile worker, Samuel Slater, outwitted the British. He came to the United States and created textile machines from memory.

1. Factories could be built anywhere because steam could drive machines.
2. Through the use of interchangeable parts, factories could turn out vast quantities of identical goods.
3. Student responses should reflect the understanding that factory work could bring workers closer together. However, making the same item everyday could stifle creativity.
4. Students should mention length of workday, working conditions, earnings working in textile mill.

Section 3 Southern Agriculture

Words to Know

cotton gin	a machine that separates cotton from its seeds
overseer	a person who watches over and directs the work of others

Getting Started Have students think of a situation in which they protested something they believed was wrong. Next have them talk about a time when they went along with something they felt was unfair. Point out that some Americans went along with slavery even though they felt it was wrong.

This is a cotton plant.

Visual The word *cotton* is a name for a shrubby plant, for the fibers surrounding the seeds, and for the cloth woven from the spun fibers.

By 1800, the economy of the South was in trouble. Crops such as tobacco, rice, and indigo were no longer selling well. Two other crops, wheat and corn, did not bring in enough money for planters. The South needed a new cash crop.

Southern Economy Changes

The answer to the South's need was cotton. The Industrial Revolution increased the demand for cotton. Textile mills used cotton to make cloth and other goods. The climate and rich soil of the South were perfect for growing cotton. However, removing the cotton seeds from the fiber had to be done by hand. Fiber is the soft part of the cotton used to make thread and yarn. It was difficult and expensive to remove the seeds.

A new machine invented by Eli Whitney made cotton the main cash crop of the South. It was called the **cotton gin.** A cotton gin is a machine that separates cotton from its seeds. The cotton gin made it faster to remove seeds from cotton. Plantation owners built huge cotton gins. They used enslaved workers to help with the demand for more cotton.

How did the cotton gin change the economy of the South during the 1800s? It gave the South the means to meet a great demand for cotton; made the South wealthy

Conditions of Slavery

As the number of cotton plantations grew in the South, so did the number of enslaved workers. In 1800, there were about 894,000 African Americans held in slavery in the United States. Thirty years later there were a little more than two million enslaved people in the United States. About one out of every six persons living in the United States was an enslaved African.

Most families in the South did not have enslaved workers. However, large plantation owners needed enslaved people to work in the fields. Enslaved people played an important part in raising and harvesting crops. They were the most important workers in the economy of the South.

Some enslaved African Americans worked as servants in plantation houses. Women became cooks, maids, and child-care workers. Men became blacksmiths, carpenters, and painters. Some slaveholders hired out their enslaved workers to work in factories or mills. The owners kept the money the enslaved workers earned.

Most enslaved people, however, worked long, hard days in the fields. An **overseer**, or a person who watches over and directs the work of others, kept close watch over them. Anyone who did not work hard was punished.

Enslaved workers who spoke out or disobeyed orders could be whipped. They might even be sold as punishment. There was always the danger that children could be taken from their parents, or husbands separated from their wives.

Where did most enslaved African Americans work?
In the fields of large southern plantations

Slave Protests

Enslaved workers found different ways to protest. Some struck back in small ways, by breaking tools or equipment. Others ran away, although that was dangerous. Runaways who were captured were often beaten, whipped, and sometimes killed.

Several groups of enslaved people tried to fight against the system of slavery. In 1800, a man named Gabriel Prosser, along with about 1,000 other enslaved African Americans, tried to take over Richmond, Virginia. The attack failed. Prosser and some of his followers were put to death. In 1822, Denmark Vesey, a free African American, also planned a rebellion. It also failed.

In 1831, Nat Turner led a large slave revolt. Turner and five followers attacked and killed several families of Virginia planters. More enslaved African Americans joined Turner, and the attacks went on for several days. About 60 slaveholders were killed before Turner was captured. He was hanged for leading the revolt.

Who led some of the slave revolts? Gabriel Prosser, Denmark Vesey, and Nat Turner

Section 3 Review

1. How did the Industrial Revolution affect the South?
2. How did enslaved people live?
3. **Critical Thinking** Why do you think enslaved Africans rebelled, even though they were unlikely to succeed?
4. **Write About Economics** Create an ad that Eli Whitney might have used to sell his invention, the cotton gin. Describe what it could do.

1. The Industrial Revolution led to a greater demand for cotton, which was grown in the South, and a new dependence on slavery.
2. Life was hard. Enslaved people were expected to work long hours every day for no pay. They were treated harshly and often punished.
3. Student responses should recognize that the desire for freedom and justice is a need of all human beings.
4. Student responses should include in the ad the speed, convenience, and profitability offered by the cotton gin.

More Review is provided in Exercise 25 of the Workbook.

CONNECTING HISTORY AND ECONOMICS
The Cotton Gin

In the late 1700s, the number of textile factories in the North grew. These mills needed more raw cotton fiber from the South.

The kind of cotton that grew best in the South was filled with sticky seeds. A worker took a whole day to clean one pound of raw cotton fiber by hand. That made cotton growing expensive.

The cotton gin

The cotton gin, which was invented in 1793 by Eli Whitney, changed that. It cleaned 50 pounds of cotton in a day.

After being cleaned, the raw cotton fiber was woven into cloth. The cloth was sent to clothing manufacturers in the North. Then, cloth was made into clothing for markets around the world. The great demand for cotton made both southern planters and northern textile-mill owners rich.

More plantation owners began to grow cotton. On many farms, enslaved people did the tasks that the cotton gin could not do. They tended, picked, and cleaned the cotton. As the profits from the cotton economy grew, slavery became more important than ever before.

Answer the questions below.

1. Before the cotton gin, why was growing cotton expensive?

2. Why did the practice of slavery increase after the invention of the cotton gin?

CHALLENGE Do you think machines have made life today easier or harder? Explain.

1. It took a worker a whole day to clean one pound of raw cotton fiber by hand. **2.** More workers were needed to plant, tend, and pick cotton. **CHALLENGE** Easier: Machines make it possible to produce at a faster rate. Harder: Machines have caused many workers to lose jobs.

Chapter

6 Review

Summary Have students use this graphic organizer to outline the main ideas and details of the chapter.

Summary New land and new inventions changed the way Americans lived in the 1800s.

Section 1 The Louisiana Purchase gave the United States control of the land west of the Mississippi River. The War of 1812 increased feelings of nationalism.

Section 2 Inventions changed the way goods were made. Factories brought more and more people to cities and towns.

Section 3 The southern economy became more dependent on cotton and enslaved workers to harvest it. The invention of the cotton gin shortened the time needed to pick cotton. It allowed landowners to grow more cotton.

- textile
- embargo
- industry
- overseer
- nationalism

More Vocabulary Review is provided in Exercise 35 of the Classroom Resource Binder.

Vocabulary Review

Complete each sentence with a term from the list.

1. One result of the British _____ was that U.S. industry grew stronger. embargo
2. James Monroe was President during a period of strong _____ after the War of 1812. nationalism
3. Many young women and teenage girls once worked in _____ factories. textile
4. The _____ watched over the enslaved workers on a plantation. overseer
5. After 1800, _____ changed the way people worked. industry

1. It jump-started the Industrial Revolution, which made the factory rather than individual workers the main feature of the American economy. p.110 **2.** North: many people began to work in factories; South: many people continued to farm pp.110–113 **3.** The demand for cotton in the textile industry made it the cash crop in the South. p.112 **4.** The U.S. saw westward expansion as an opportunity to develop the country. pp.104–108 **5.** The U.S. had new feelings of nationalism, industry developed, and the U.S. gained respect from other countries. pp.107–110

Chapter Quiz

Write your answers in complete sentences.

1. How did the War of 1812 change the economy in the United States?

2. How did life in the North and the South become different during the Industrial Revolution?

3. How did cotton change the economy of the South?

4. **Critical Thinking** Why do you think the United States was so interested in moving westward in the early 1800s?

5. **Critical Thinking** Why do you think the United States was a stronger nation after the War of 1812?

Test Tip
Read the directions carefully. Underline or circle the important words in the questions.

Writing Tip
Be sure you understand the assignment. Do you need to write a paragraph or a short answer? Plan to give the right answer.

Using the Timeline

Use the timeline on pages 100–101 to answer the questions.

1. For how many years was Thomas Jefferson President? 8

2. What documents affected U.S. foreign policy?
Monroe Doctrine and Treaty of Ghent

Group Activity See the Teacher's Planning Guide for a scoring rubric for this activity.

Group Activity

In your group, make a chart of some improvements that resulted from America's growth during the early 1800s. Then have another group name a problem that was caused by each improvement.

During the 1840s, families traveled west in covered wagons. Lanterns were used to give light. How were their wagons pulled? Oxen and horses

The United States Expands Westward

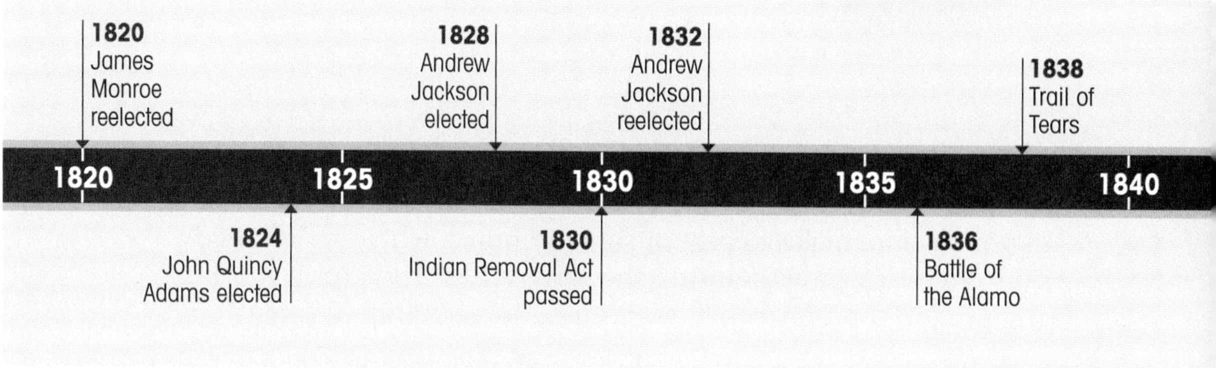

Additional activities and strategies to customize lessons can be found in the Teacher's Planning Guide.

Chapter 7 The Changing United States 1820–1850

ESL Note Discuss with students the difficulty of arriving in another land and struggling to learn the spoken language. Until they learn it, they feel isolated. Remind students that much of the land in the South and West of the United States was once possessed by Spain. People who lived on these lands mostly spoke Spanish.

Words to Know

tariff

spoils system

canal

mountain man

forty-niner

ranch

Words to Know These words are defined in the section in which they appear, as well as in the Glossary. Point out that three of these terms (*mountain man*, *spoils system*, and *forty-niner*) are made up of smaller familiar words. Have students use what they know about the smaller words to help define these terms.

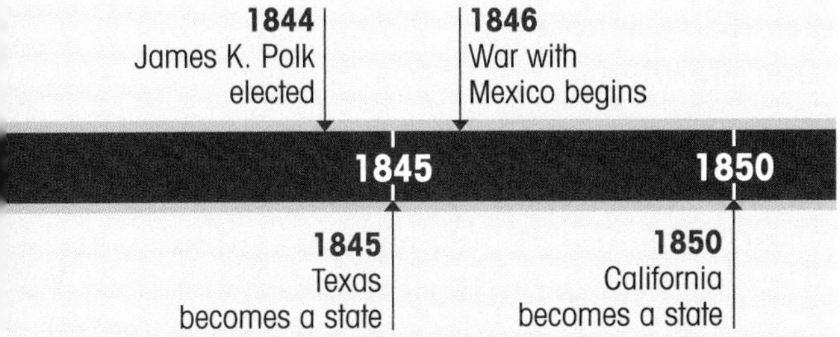

Learning Objectives

- Explain how Andrew Jackson was different from other Presidents.
- Identify ways people traveled west.
- Explain why people moved west.
- Discuss the reasons for and the results of the war with Mexico.
- Discuss how the discovery of gold led to California becoming a state.
- Explore the point of view of a Choctaw district chief.

Project Students can begin work on the project after completing Section 1 and the Voices From the Past feature. To help them get started, review with students that a poem or song is divided into stanzas and sometimes follows a rhyming pattern.

Portfolio Project

As more settlers moved west, they changed the lives of people already living there. Write a song or a poem about the settlers or Native Americans. Describe how they might have felt about their land in the 1800s. Use the information in this chapter for your ideas.

Timeline The timeline is divided into intervals of 5 years. The events take place over a period of 30 years. Point out to students that most of the events deal with the consequences of settlers moving West.

Section 1 The Policies of Adams and Jackson

Words to Know

tariff	a tax on goods brought into a country
spoils system	the system of giving government jobs to people who had helped to get the winner elected

Getting Started This section discusses the ways Native Americans responded to expanding settlements. Explain to students that growth and expansion may have some negative results. Have students discuss why some people may resist this type of change.

In 1824, John Quincy Adams was elected the sixth President. Four years later, in 1828, Andrew Jackson, a hero of the War of 1812, was elected President. His way of governing, or running the country, was different from past Presidents. Jackson believed in helping the common man.

John Quincy Adams

Around the time of the 1824 election, the nation was becoming more and more divided. Each section had its own favorite candidate, or person running for public office. The candidates were John Quincy Adams, who was the son of John Adams, William Crawford, Henry Clay, John C. Calhoun, and Andrew Jackson.

Remember
Electors were selected from each state to vote for the President and the Vice President.

When all the votes were counted, no one had more than one half of the electoral votes. Henry Clay, who was Speaker of the House of Representatives, convinced members of Congress to vote for Adams. With Clay's votes, Adams became President.

Adams was not a popular President. He was a quiet, wealthy man who was not interested in pleasing the crowd. As Adams was completing his first term, Congress passed the Tariff of 1828. It put a **tariff**, or a tax, on some goods coming into the United States from other countries. The tariff raised the price of these products.

The Tariff of 1828 was unpopular. It made goods imported from Europe cost more. This affected manufacturing in the North and farming in the South and West.

How did Adams win the election of 1824? Henry Clay convinced members of Congress to vote for Adams.

Andrew Jackson

The year 1828 was an election year. The Tariff of 1828 made John Quincy Adams even less popular. In the election, Andrew Jackson received twice as many electoral votes as Adams and became President.

This political cartoon shows that some people felt President Jackson acted like a king.

Visual Discuss with students how a political cartoon makes a point about an issue. Point out that President Jackson is dressed in a king's robe. The suggestion is that he feels he is above the Constitution.

Jackson was unlike any other President. He was the first person from the West to be elected President. Jackson understood the common or ordinary man. He believed a person did not have to come from the upper class in order to lead the country. This belief was part of what became known as Jacksonian democracy.

Jackson was a war hero from the War of 1812. He was known as a tough, brave man who was used to getting his way. Many of his enemies called him King Andrew when he took office.

How was Jackson different from past Presidents? From the West; believed in the common man

The Spoils System

One of Jackson's goals was to give many ordinary people jobs in government. He believed that the winners of elections should be able to give government jobs to people who had helped to get them elected. That practice came to be known as the **spoils system.**

Jackson did not like most of his official Cabinet members. So, he did not have regular Cabinet meetings. He preferred to talk about government matters with a small group of trusted friends. The group told Jackson what the people were thinking.

People who disliked Jackson called his group of friends the "Kitchen Cabinet." That was a way of criticizing them. Kitchen Cabinet meant that the group did not enter the White House through the front door. They entered through the back door and met secretly.

Who were Jackson's advisers? Jackson's advisers were a group of trusted friends, called the "Kitchen Cabinet."

Jackson's Native American Policies

Visual The Cherokees were well established in Georgia before they were forced to leave. They had built roads, schools, and churches. They had a system of representational government. They were farmers and cattle ranchers. They had a written Cherokee alphabet which was perfected by Sequoyah, a member of the Cherokee nation.

When Andrew Jackson took office in 1828, about 125,000 Native Americans lived east of the Mississippi River. About 60,000 lived in the South. These Native Americans lived in an area of about 33 million acres of land. Jackson wanted to take land away from Native Americans and give it to settlers.

Under pressure from Jackson, Congress passed the Indian Removal Act in 1830. The act said that all

The Cherokees were forced to move to Oklahoma on what came to be known as the Trail of Tears.

Native Americans east of the Mississippi River had to give up their land. It also said that all Native Americans would be given new land west of the Mississippi River.

Some Native Americans went to the Supreme Court to speak out against the Indian Removal Act. The Supreme Court agreed with the Native Americans. Jackson ignored the Supreme Court decision and ordered the removal.

In 1838, more than 15,000 Cherokees were forced to leave their homes in parts of North Carolina, Georgia, Tennessee, and Alabama. They walked all the way to what is now Oklahoma. About 4,000 Cherokees died along the way. The Cherokees' terrible journey became known as the Trail of Tears. By 1840, more than 60,000 Native Americans had been removed.

What was the Indian Removal Act? The act that forced thousands of Cherokees to leave their homeland and resettle.

Section 1 Review

1. Why was John Quincy Adams an unpopular President?
2. Why did Andrew Jackson support the spoils system?
3. **Critical Thinking** Why did Andrew Jackson's enemies call him "King Andrew"?
4. **Write About Citizenship** Write a paragraph in which you interview a person who voted for Jackson. Why does the person think Jackson will be a good President?

More Review is provided in Exercise 26 of the Workbook.

1. He did not set out to please the crowds.
2. He believed his supporters should be rewarded.
3. Jackson ignored the Supreme Court concerning the Indian Removal Act. He did not listen to his Cabinet members and relied on friends for advice.
4. Possible answer: Jackson's popularity as a war hero, champion of the common man; his potential for bringing change to the country.

VOICES FROM THE PAST
George M. Harkins

In 1830, the government presented the Choctaws with the Treaty of Dancing Rabbit Creek. The treaty promised the Choctaws land in the West. The U.S. government said it would not protect the Choctaws if they stayed in their homeland. It warned that their nation most likely would be destroyed.

The Choctaws felt they had to sign the treaty. George M. Harkins was district chief of the Choctaw nation. He understood the Choctaws' feelings. The following is a part of his speech in which he expresses the sadness of his people:

"Friends, my attachment to my native land is strong—that cord is now broken; and we must go as wanderers in a strange land! I must go—let me entreat [beg] you to regard us with feelings of kindness, and when the hand of oppression [the cruel or unjust use of authority] stretched against us, let me hope that every part of the United States, . . . will echo and stop."

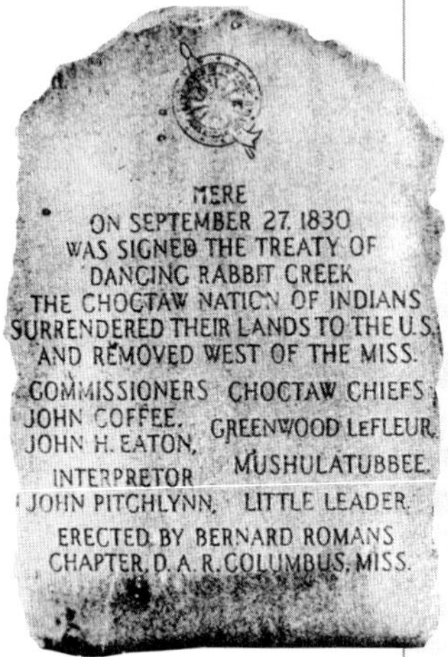

This memorial stands where the treaty of Dancing Rabbit Creek was signed.

Answer the questions below.

1. What did the Treaty of Dancing Rabbit Creek promise the Choctaws?

2. What did George M. Harkins hope would happen once others learned of what had taken place?

CHALLENGE Why do you think the Choctaws felt as if they had no choice but to move West?

1. Land in the West **2.** That they would be sympathetic toward the Choctaws and put an end to their exile **CHALLENGE** Student responses should reflect the powerlessness that the Choctaws felt against President Jackson, especially after he ignored the Supreme Court decision.

Section 2 Moving West

Words to Know

canal	a human-made waterway
mountain man	a fur trapper and trader who lived in the mountains and knew the wilderness

Getting Started Have students discuss how their lives would be different without cars, buses, telephones, e-mail, and other forms of transportation and communication. Point out to students that great improvements in transportation and communication occurred during the early 1800s.

It took eight years to build the Erie Canal.

Visual After the Erie Canal was built, the freight charge for goods dropped from $100 a ton to $10 a ton.

The mid-1800s was an exciting time in the United States. More and more Americans headed west. They wanted to know what the land was like. Was it good for farming? Could families settle there?

Different Ways of Traveling

To move west, Americans needed to develop better ways of traveling. In 1811, the federal government began building the National Road. By the 1830s, the road ran west from Maryland to the Mississippi River. Families traveled the road west in covered wagons.

For the first part of the 1800s, Americans had to travel long distances by water. Many people moved west along rivers. Americans also traveled along **canals**, or human-made waterways.

Travel by canal was slow. Boats only traveled about five miles per hour. In the winter, when the canals were blocked by ice, travel was impossible.

In 1817, work began on the Erie Canal. It was finished in 1825. The Erie Canal was more than 350 miles long. It joined the Great Lakes with the Hudson River. It was the best way to move products between the Midwest and eastern cities.

Why did Americans need better ways to travel?
To move westward

Railroads

In April 1830, Peter Cooper tested his invention. It was a steam-powered train that traveled on iron rails. The train raced a wagon pulled by a horse. The train lost. However, the idea of a steam-powered train traveling over mountains caught on.

Soon "railroad fever" spread everywhere east of the Mississippi. Trains could run in almost any weather. They were faster than wagons or canal boats. Trains could go wherever tracks had been laid down. By the 1850s, the cities of Cleveland, Detroit, Chicago, and St. Louis were all joined to the East coast by railroads.

How did railroads improve transportation? They made it faster to travel.

Trails West

After travelers crossed the Mississippi River, they faced problems. Roads became narrow trails. The rivers were either too shallow or too rough. There were no railroads.

In the early 1800s, most people who traveled west were fur trappers and traders. Fur-trading companies usually hired these **mountain men** to travel through the Rocky Mountains. Mountain men lived in the mountains and knew the wilderness. They hunted, explored, and traded from the Great Plains to the Pacific coast. The Great Plains was a huge grassland that stretched from Canada into Texas and from the Missouri River to the Rocky Mountains. Mountain men helped to find trails that settlers would follow.

Who were the mountain men? Men hired by fur-trading companies to trap beaver and other animals in the Rocky Mountains

Settling the Far West

In the late 1830s, people began to travel from the East to the far West. They sent back news of green farmland and thick forests in the Oregon Territory.

To get to the Oregon Territory, people traveled about 2,000 miles over a trail called the Oregon Trail. The trip took about six months. It was often filled with hardship and danger. Travelers had to cross a desert and rough rivers. They often faced rainstorms.

The Santa Fe Trail carried travelers to the Southwest. Wagons traveled from Independence, Missouri, to Santa Fe, New Mexico. There the trail joined the Old Spanish Trail. That trail crossed a desert to the present-day city of Los Angeles on the Pacific coast. It was a difficult journey. Still, by 1850, thousands of Americans had made their way to the far West.

What were the two main trails to the far West?
Oregon Trail and Santa Fe Trail

Map Have students use the political map of the United States in the back of their book to identify which present-day states were included in each territory.

Expansion of the United States

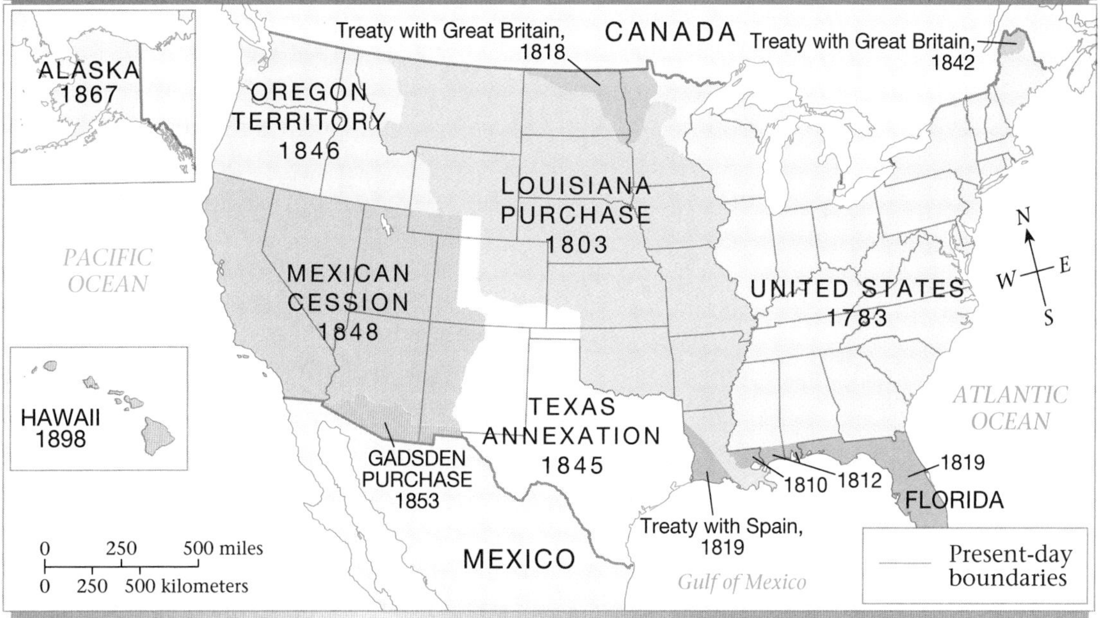

Map Study

1. Which territory did the United States gain first? Louisiana Purchase
2. Which territories border the Pacific Ocean? Oregon Territory and Mexican Cession

Manifest Destiny

There were several reasons why many Americans moved west in the 1830s and 1840s.

At the end of Jackson's presidency, the economy became worse. Many banks failed. Farmers and business people lost millions of dollars. For many people, moving west was a way to start over.

In the 1840s, many Americans were proud of their country. They wanted it to grow from coast to coast. In fact, they believed that Americans had the right to live on any land between the Atlantic and the Pacific oceans. This belief was called Manifest Destiny.

What was Manifest Destiny? Americans' belief that they could live on any land between the Atlantic and Pacific oceans

Americans in Texas

In the early 1800s, the land that we now call the state of Texas belonged to Mexico. In 1820, a businessman named Moses Austin traveled to the settlement of San Antonio. He talked with its governor about starting a U.S. colony there. The plan was approved, but Austin died the following year.

After Austin's death, his son, Stephen F. Austin, carried out his father's plan. Young Austin went to San Antonio. There he arranged with the governor to take over some land. Austin was told that U.S. settlers would have to follow the laws of Mexico.

Austin returned to the United States. He advertised in several newspapers for settlers for his colony. Many Americans moved to his colony. By 1836, there were more settlers from the United States than from Mexico.

Americans who settled in Texas wanted to break away from Mexico. They wanted independence. They formed an army led by Sam Houston.

How did Americans settle Texas? Stephen Austin advertised for people to come to a colony he was forming in Mexico.

The Alamo

Antonio López de Santa Anna was a Mexican general. He wanted to show the Americans in Texas how powerful his army was. He planned to crush the U.S. settlers.

In 1836, a force of about 200 Texans were in their fort, the Alamo. With more than 4,000 men, Santa Anna attacked the fort. The Texans fought hard and held out for 13 days. However, the Mexican army was too strong. On March 16, 1836, the Mexicans defeated the Texans who were all killed.

Santa Anna thought his victory would stop the rebels in Texas. He was wrong. "Remember the Alamo!" became the battle cry of Sam Houston's men. A few months after the Alamo, the Texans defeated the Mexican army at the battle of San Jacinto.

The Texans took Santa Anna prisoner. Texas declared itself an independent nation in 1836. In 1845, Texas became the twenty-eighth state in the Union.

What happened at the battle of the Alamo?
The Mexicans defeated the Texans.

Sam Houston

Visual As a teenager, Sam Houston served as a negotiator between the Cherokees and the U.S. government regarding land claims and agreements.

War With Mexico

The United States and Mexico did not agree on the boundary between their countries. Disagreements finally led to war between the United States and Mexico in 1846. President James Polk sent U.S. troops under General Zachary Taylor to take over the lands near Mexico.

The fighting in Texas spread into other lands that Mexico owned in the Southwest. The Mexicans were defeated in several battles. However, they refused to give up. Finally, in 1847, U.S. troops marched into Mexico City, Mexico's capital. Mexico surrendered in 1848.

Geography Fact

The Rio Grande is the longest river in Texas and the second longest river in the United States.

Geography Fact Have students use the physical map of the United States in the back of their book. Help them use the scale to compute the length of the Rio Grande.

The Treaty of Guadalupe Hidalgo ended the war. The treaty listed the following main points.

1. The Mexican government must give up all claims to Texas and to all land between Texas and California.
2. The Rio Grande will become the southern boundary of Texas.
3. The United States must pay Mexico $15 million for the new land.

In 1853, the United States bought more land from Mexico for $10 million. The land makes up the southern parts of present-day New Mexico and Arizona. This was known as the Gadsden Purchase.

In ten years, the United States had stretched its borders from the Atlantic Ocean to the Pacific Ocean. Americans began to move west in growing numbers.

What started the war with Mexico? The United States and Mexico did not agree on the boundary between their countries.

Section 2 Review

1. How did people travel west in the first half of the 1800s?
2. Who fought at the battle of the Alamo?
3. **Critical Thinking** As a settler living under Mexican rule in the Southwest, why might you have wanted your own independent state?
4. **Write About Geography** Write a paragraph in which you describe how the natural features of the land between the Mississippi River and the Pacific coast might have helped you or made your journey difficult.

1. Railroads and canals
2. The Mexicans and the Texans
3. Student responses might include that U.S. residents felt no loyalty to Mexico, didn't know Spanish language or customs, probably didn't like following Mexican laws.
4. Student responses will probably describe large rivers, hot deserts, huge mountains, and bad weather, which made it difficult to travel. Travel was not as difficult over the Great Plains, where land was usually flat.

More Review is provided in Exercise 27 of the Workbook.

Section 3 Gold and California

Words to Know

forty-niner	a person who went to California in 1849 to find gold
ranch	a large farm with grazing land for raising horses, cattle, or sheep

Getting Started Discuss the meaning of get-rich-quick schemes with students. Give examples. Remind them that the odds against winning are very high. Explain that in 1848 people caught "gold fever" and believed they could get rich quickly. Have students predict what happened to most of these people.

As the 1840s came to an end, more and more wagon trains continued to head west. Some settlers moved to the wide-open spaces of Texas. Some traveled north to Oregon. Others traveled to the Southwest on the Santa Fe Trail. Then, in 1848, a discovery turned almost all travel toward California.

A Discovery at Sutter's Mill

In 1848, the huge territory of California had fewer than 20,000 people. However, things soon began to change. John Sutter owned many acres of land on the American River, near Sacramento. In January of that year, he ordered workers to build a sawmill on his property.

James Marshall was the leader of the work crew. One morning Marshall made an exciting discovery. Beneath the cold waters of the American River, he found two gold nuggets, each the size of a pea. Marshall showed the two nuggets to Sutter. He begged Sutter to keep the discovery a secret.

The discovery did not remain a secret for long. Other workers had seen what Marshall had found. News of that discovery traveled quickly from one person to the next. Then the news traveled through newspapers and letters. Soon almost everyone in California knew about the discovery.

At first, people from San Francisco rushed to the river near Sutter's Mill. Later, people came from other parts of California and other parts of the world. For example, nearly 20,000 Chinese immigrants arrived in California. Most planned to return to China with the money they earned.

What happened at Sutter's Mill? James Marshall found two tiny nuggets of gold while supervising the construction of a sawmill.

History and You

DENIM PANTS

In 1847, Levi Strauss came to New York City from his home in Germany. Less than a year after he had arrived in the United States, gold was discovered in California.

Strauss and his family decided to travel to California. Soon they began a small business in San Francisco. They sold pants, shirts, blankets, and household items.

In 1873, Strauss received a letter from Jacob Davis, a tailor in Nevada. Davis made sturdy clothing for miners. He used rivets, or pieces of metal, to fasten the pockets on the pants. Davis asked Strauss to be his business partner. Strauss and Davis made pants from denim.

Levi Strauss' denim pants were worn by miners.

The sturdy fabric and rivets made the pants perfect for miners. Miners were not the only ones wearing pants made by Strauss. Traders carried the news of the pants to the Southwest and Texas. Cowboys liked their comfortable fit. Little by little, other workingmen, and later women, wore clothing made by Levi Strauss. People still wear denim pants today.

Critical Thinking Why would miners need strong pants? Miners needed strong pants that would not rip during the hard, physical labor they did daily. Also, strong pockets held the tools miners needed.

The Gold Rush

By 1849, news of the discovery of gold spread quickly. People hurried to California. They wanted some of the riches. The California gold rush had begun. More than 70,000 people traveled to California. These people became known as the **forty-niners** because they went to California in 1849 to find gold.

Some forty-niners were lucky enough to strike it rich. Most found that searching for gold was hard, dirty, and dangerous work. Many forty-niners gave up gold digging and turned to farming. Others found work on **ranches.** A ranch is a large farm with grazing land for horses, cattle, or sheep.

After the 1849 gold rush, the population of California grew quickly. Within two years, the population rose to 200,000. Soon California had enough people to ask to become a state. On September 9, 1850, California became the thirty-first state.

Why were people who went to California to seek gold called forty-niners? Because the first group went to California in 1849

Miners searched for gold in mountain streams.

Visual In 1850, fewer than two percent of gold prospectors were women. Most of the women who did travel to California accompanied their husbands.

Section 3 Review

1. Where was John Sutter's sawmill located?
2. Why did the population of California increase so much after the discovery of gold?
3. **Critical Thinking** If you had been living in 1849, might you have traveled to California to seek gold? Explain.
4. **Write About Citizenship** Write a letter home, telling how you feel when you first find gold in California.

1. On the American River, near Sacramento, CA
2. People arrived in hopes of finding gold.
3. Student responses should show an awareness of a sense of adventure that the discovery inspired.
4. Student responses should include the excitement of the discovery and the plans that such a discovery might lead to.

More Review is provided in Exercise 29 of the Workbook.

Chapter

7 Review

Summary Have students use this graphic organizer to outline the main ideas and details of the chapter.

Summary

Settlers moved westward because of improvements in transportation, land in Texas, and the discovery of gold in California. The United States expanded from the Atlantic to the Pacific coast.

Section 1

John Quincy Adams became President in 1824. He lost the election of 1828 to Andrew Jackson. Jackson ordered the removal of Native Americans from their land.

Section 2

The mid-1800s was a period of great expansion into the West. The area now known as Texas won its independence from Mexico.

Section 3

Gold was discovered in California in 1848. Thousands of people rushed to California, hoping to get rich. In 1850, California became the thirty-first state.

More Vocabulary Review is provided in Exercise 41 of the Classroom Resource Binder.

Vocabulary Review

Write *true* or *false*. If the statement is false, change the underlined term to make it true.

1. A person who traveled to California hoping to find gold was a <u>forty-niner</u>. True
2. A large farm for raising cattle is a <u>canal</u>. False: ranch
3. A <u>mountain man</u> was a fur trapper or trader who knew the wilderness. True
4. A tax on goods brought into a country is called a <u>spoils system</u>. False: tariff

1. The Tariff raised the prices on goods from other countries. pp.120–121 2. Settlers wanted to settle the land and start farms. pp.122–123 3. The Oregon and Santa Fe trails p.127 4. People went to Texas to establish homes and start a new life. People went to California with the idea of getting rich quickly and returning to their homes. pp.128, 131–133 5. The spirit of nationalism was strong; people felt it was their right to continue moving west. p.128

Chapter Quiz

Write your answers in complete sentences.

1. Why was the Tariff of 1828 unpopular?
2. Why did President Jackson force Native Americans off their land?
3. What trails did people use to travel west of the Mississippi River?
4. **Critical Thinking** How was the settlement of Texas different from the settlement of California?
5. **Critical Thinking** Why do you think Americans believed in Manifest Destiny?

Test Tip
As you review what you have read, try to write the main idea of a paragraph in your own words.

Writing Tip
Use a capital letter for the first word of every new sentence. End each sentence with a period, question mark, or exclamation point.

Using the Timeline

Use the timeline on pages 118–119 to answer the questions.

1. When did the Battle of the Alamo take place? 1836
2. How many years after the passing of the Indian Removal Act did the Trail of Tears take place? 8 years

Group Activity See the Teacher's Planning Guide for a scoring rubric for this activity.

Group Activity

Work with two or three classmates. Together make travel plans that settlers might have made to start a new life in the West. When you have finished, present your plans to the entire class and ask for comments.

European immigrants came to the United States with all their possessions. This is a soup bowl one family brought from their homeland. How would they have felt coming to a new land? Excited, scared

Improving American Society

1821 Troy Female Seminary opens

1831 Cyrus McCormick invents reaper

1837 John Deere invents steel plow

1841 Dorothea Dix starts her reforms

1820 · 1825 · 1830 · 1835 · 1840 · 1845

Additional activities and strategies to customize lessons can be found in the Teacher's Planning Guide.

Chapter 8 Newcomers and New Ideas 1820–1860

ESL Note To help students understand the ways people hope to achieve their dreams, have them discuss in pairs what dreams they have and what obstacles might prevent them from becoming a reality. Tell students that immigrants who traveled to the United States in the 19th century had hopes and dreams for a better life.

Words to Know

- rural
- urban
- immigrant
- famine
- equal rights
- suffrage
- reformer
- temperance

Words to Know These words are defined in the section in which they appear, as well as in the Glossary. Point out to students that the words *suffrage*, *equal rights*, and *temperance* are associated with movements for social reform.

Learning Objectives

- Discuss reasons that cities grew between 1820 and 1860.
- Identify the main immigrant groups who came to the United States in the mid-1800s.
- Describe the struggle of women for equal rights.
- Discuss the movement to reform U.S. society.
- Explore Elizabeth Cady Stanton's views on raising young girls.

Project After students make their list, remind them that a time capsule can hold objects as well as written documents.

Portfolio Project

Create a time capsule to help future generations understand U.S. history between 1820 and 1860. First, make a list of the events that you think others would be most interested in. Be sure to include something from each section in the chapter.

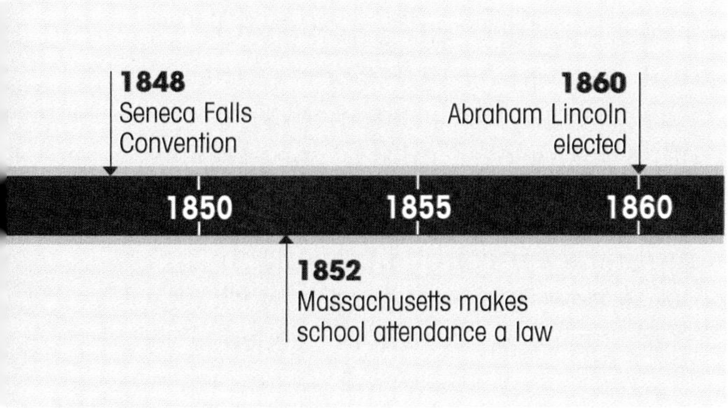

Timeline The timeline is divided into 5-year intervals. The events take place over a period of 39 years. Point out to students that events related to social and economic reform are highlighted on the timeline.

Section 1 New Ways and New People

Words to Know

rural	having to do with the country
urban	having to do with the city
immigrant	a person who comes to a country for the purpose of living there
famine	a time when people in a place starve because there is not enough food

Getting Started Discuss with students why people might move from one location to another. Explain that immigrants came to the United States for many different reasons in the 19th century.

By the mid-1800s, many Americans had moved into the growing cities of the United States. Farming was no longer the main way of life. People found new opportunities in the city. Many immigrants chose to live in the cities as well.

Cities Grow and Farms Change

In 1820, only eight cities in the United States had more than 10,000 people. New York was first in population with about 120,000 people. Thirty years later, in 1850, the population of New York was more than 500,000.

Many Americans who moved to cities in the mid-1800s came from **rural**, or country, areas. Some of these people moved to cities to enjoy the excitement that **urban**, or city, life offered. However, most of the people left their homes in rural areas to find work in cities.

Not all workers in rural areas could find work on farms. That was because new inventions made work on farms easier. As a result, fewer workers were needed.

In 1831, Cyrus McCormick invented a reaper, or grain-cutting machine. The machine could harvest, or gather, more wheat in one day than a person could harvest in two weeks. There no longer was the need for hiring large numbers of workers at harvest time.

In 1837, John Deere made the first steel plow. The blade on the plow was made of highly polished steel. This prevented the soil from sticking to the blade. It made plowing time shorter. Farmers no longer had to stop to scrape the soil from the plow.

The new inventions were in great demand. They had to be produced, or made, in factories, which were in cities. Thousands of people who worked on farms went to cities to work in factories.

Why did many people move to cities? To find work

This is an advertisement for Cyrus McCormick's reaper.

Visual Part of the reaper's success was due to McCormick's door-to-door sales and a written guarantee for his machines.

Immigrants From Europe

In the mid-1800s, many people in the United States moved from rural to urban areas. People also moved from other countries to the United States. The hope of a better life brought many **immigrants** to the United States. An immigrant is a person who comes to a country for the purpose of making a home.

People had many different reasons for coming to the United States. Most immigrants, however, were poor. They had decided that they could make a better life for themselves in the United States. Another reason that immigrants left their homes and came to the United States was for greater freedom.

Between 1830 and 1860, nearly five million immigrants came to the United States. Most of the immigrants came from the northern and western parts of Europe. Many came from Germany and Ireland.

History Fact

From 1820 to 1930, the United States received about 60 percent of the world's immigrants.

History Fact By the 1840s, the arrival of so many immigrants started a wave of resentment among many Americans. They were concerned that competition for jobs would drive wages down.

German Immigrants

In the early 1840s, many German immigrants came to the United States. They came mainly to escape both political and economic problems in their country. In 1830, a revolution broke out in Germany. For several years before the revolution, there were floods in summer and bad weather in the winter which had been destroying their crops.

Many German immigrants were farmers. They were interested in starting farms on the frontier. There they could buy land cheap. They could also enjoy living under a democratic government. Present-day cities, such as St. Louis, Chicago, and Milwaukee, became the homes of many German immigrants.

Irish Immigrants

In 1845, a plant disease began to wipe out the potato crop in Ireland. Potatoes had been the main food of poor Irish people. The loss of the potato plant caused a **famine**, or a time when people in a place starve because there is not enough food. About one million people in Ireland died during the famine. Over one million people left Ireland for the United States.

Most Irish immigrants were farmers in Ireland. However, when they came to the United States, few of them had the money to buy farmland. Instead, they settled where they landed, chiefly in eastern cities, such as New York and Boston. Most Irish immigrants took low-paying jobs. Many men became laborers. They built railroads and unloaded ships. Many Irish women worked as servants, or maids, in the homes of wealthy people.

Why did German and Irish immigrants come to the United States between 1830 and 1850? For political or economic reasons

Immigrants From Asia

The Chinese people were among the millions who hurried to look for gold in California in 1849. Most of the Chinese immigrants were young men. They expected to make their fortune in the United States and then return to China. Some did make a lot of money and did return. However, many stayed in California.

Remember
The discovery of gold in California led to the Gold Rush of 1849.

Not all Chinese immigrants who came to California dug for gold. Many were merchants. They sold supplies to the miners. Some Chinese immigrants were carpenters. They helped to build villages that grew near the gold mines.

Still other Chinese immigrants were farmers. Chinese farmers helped turn swampland in California into farms. Some Chinese newcomers opened businesses. Others made a living as traveling salespeople.

Why did young Chinese men come to California in the mid-1800s? To mine gold and to become rich

Section 1 Review

1. Why did many people in rural areas go to cities to find work?
2. What three groups of immigrants came to the United States in the 1840s?
3. **Critical Thinking** What was a major difference between the lives of German immigrants and Irish immigrants in the United States?
4. **Write About History** You are an immigrant from China in the 1840s. Write a paragraph describing your life in the United States. Include reasons for leaving your homeland.

More Review is provided in Exercise 30 of the Workbook.

1. New labor-saving inventions eliminated many jobs on farms and the need for many farm workers.
2. German, Irish, and Chinese immigrants
3. German immigrants were able to buy farmland and continue to farm in the United States as they had in Germany. Irish immigrants were too poor to buy farmland. They had to work as laborers or servants in the homes of wealthy residents.
4. Possible answer: Left homeland to seek fortune in the United States. Opportunities here include becoming a merchant, farmer, carpenter, salesman. It is lonely without one's family.

Section 2 Women and Political Rights

Words to Know

equal rights	rights that all people in a society should have
suffrage	the right to vote

Getting Started Declare to students that for the duration of class all students wearing blue do not have the right to earn wages, own property, have a career, vote, or have an equal say about current issues. Encourage students wearing blue to describe to the rest of the class what it feels like not to be treated as an equal. Tell students this was probably how women felt in the 19th century.

At the start of the 1800s, white women and all African Americans had few of the rights given to white men. As the 1800s moved on, women began to speak out about unfair treatment.

Women Fight for Equal Rights

In the early 1800s, girls were expected first to be good daughters and good sisters. Later, as adult women, they were to be good wives and good mothers. They had few of the rights that women today take for granted.

Women wanted to improve their lives and the lives of others. Many women felt slavery was wrong. This gave them a reason to come together. In the 1820s and 1830s, many women raised their voices against slavery and for **equal rights.** Equal rights are rights all people in a society should have.

Women worked hard to gain equal rights for all U.S. citizens. However, they were still without one important right. That was the right to vote. The right to vote is called **suffrage.**

What was one reason that women came together to gain equal rights? They felt slavery was wrong.

Women Who Worked For Equal Rights

Susan B. Anthony	She was a leader in the women's rights movement.
Angelina Grimké	In 1838, she became the first woman to speak to a lawmaking group about equal rights.
Sarah Grimké	She wrote for newspapers on the equality of all men and women.
Lucretia Mott	She was president of the Philadelphia Female Anti-Slavery Society. She helped organize the Seneca Falls Convention.
Elizabeth Cady Stanton	In 1854, she became the first woman to speak before the state legislature of New York. She organized the Seneca Falls Convention.
Lucy Stone	She helped to strengthen the anti-slavery movement and the women's rights movement.
Sojourner Truth	She was once an enslaved person. She later traveled to the North and spoke out against slavery. She was also a supporter of women's rights.

Chart Study

1. Who spoke before the state legislature in 1854?
2. Why was Lucy Stone a leader for equal rights?

Chart Go over the names and accomplishments of the women on the chart. Point out the ways that they got their message out: organizing, writing for newspapers, and public speaking.

1. Elizabeth Cady Stanton
2. She wanted to end slavery and gain rights for women.

The Seneca Falls Convention

In 1848, Elizabeth Cady Stanton and Lucretia Mott organized the first American women's rights convention. They held the meeting near Stanton's home in Seneca Falls, New York.

Two hundred women and 40 men came to the meeting. The group spent two days discussing women's rights. Toward the end of the convention, Stanton read a statement called the Declaration of Sentiments. The statement was based on the United States Declaration of Independence. However, there was an important difference.

Elizabeth Cady Stanton spoke before the first women's rights convention in the United States.

Visual Stanton and Mott met in 1840 at the World Anti-Slavery Convention in London. At the convention, women were denied admittance. Stanton and Mott decided to organize a convention to give women a forum. In 1848, they held the Seneca Falls Convention.

The Declaration of Independence reads, "We hold these truths to be self-evident, that all men are created equal." Stanton rewrote that part to read, "We hold these truths to be self-evident, that all *men and women* are created equal." The Declaration of Sentiments also said that it was not fair for women to obey laws "in which they had no voice."

After the Seneca Falls Convention, many other women were interested in joining the women's movement and the anti-slavery movement. The woman who became the leader in the struggle for women's rights and suffrage was Susan B. Anthony.

In 1851, Elizabeth Cady Stanton and Susan B. Anthony met. Soon they began working together for women's rights. In New York, Anthony and Stanton helped get a law passed that protected the right of women to own property. It would be a long time, however, before women would win the right to vote.

Besides meeting to talk about issues, women worked hard to get new laws passed that would give them more rights. In 1860, a law was passed in New York State protecting women's property rights. This is what the law provided.

1. Married women could own property.
2. Women could collect their own wages.
3. Women could sue in court.
4. Women could enter into contracts.

Women in several other states were able to get similar laws passed.

Why did the Seneca Falls Convention meet? To discuss women's rights issues

Section 2 Review

1. Why did many women come together in the 1820s and 1830s?
2. What was one result of the Seneca Falls Convention?
3. **Critical Thinking** Why do you think Elizabeth Cady Stanton used the Declaration of Independence as a guide for writing the Declaration of Sentiments?
4. **Write About Citizenship** Create a poster encouraging women to attend the Seneca Falls Convention. Include the date, place, and reason for the convention.

1. To oppose slavery and to work for women's rights
2. Many other women were drawn to the struggle for women's rights.
3. Student responses might include that the Declaration of Independence was a highly respected document that reflected the strongly held belief that all people had inalienable rights.
4. Poster information should include that the convention was held in 1848, in Seneca Falls, New York.

More Review is provided in Exercise 31 of the Workbook.

VOICES FROM THE PAST
Elizabeth Cady Stanton

Elizabeth Cady Stanton was a leader in the struggle for women's rights. She believed that one of the reasons women were not treated equally was because of the way they were raised as children. In the speech below she gives ideas on raising girls.

"The childhood of women must be free and unrestrained [not held down]. The girl must be allowed to romp and play, skate, climb, and swim. Her clothes must be more like those of a boy—strong, loose-fitting garments, thick boots—so that she may be out at all times to enter freely into sports. Teach her to go alone, by night or day, on the lonely highway or through the busy streets of the crowded city.

Elizabeth Cady Stanton

Better to suffer [permit] occasional insults or die outright than live the life of a coward or never move without a protector. The best protector any woman can have is courage. This she must get by her own experience.

Do you think women educated [like this] would remain weak? By no means. Depend upon it, they would not be long in finding their true level in political and social life."

Answer the questions below.

1. What were some things Stanton recommended young girls should be allowed to do?

2. What does Stanton's speech say about the way girls were raised in the 1840s?

CHALLENGE What does Stanton mean when she says "the best protector any woman can have is courage"?

1. To romp, play, skate, climb, and swim; to wear loose clothes; to go out alone **2.** Girls were protected and restricted. **CHALLENGE** Student responses should include that women are most successfully protected by their own inner resources, which include courage.

Section 3 Working for Reform

Words to Know

reformer	a person who works for a cause that improves the way something is done in a society
temperance	a reform movement that is against drinking alcohol

Getting Started Have students describe activities in which they have given time or money to improve the lives of others. Tell students that many Americans in the 1800s worked to improve the lives of others.

The first half of the 1800s brought many changes to the United States. There were changes in U.S. boundaries, industry, and population. Changes also came because some people wanted to improve the way things were done in U.S. society.

PICTORIAL PRIMER

9 and 9 make 18

10 and 10 make 20

STEAMBOAT.

Here is a Steamboat full of passengers, how swift it glides along, and makes the water foam. Steamboats were invented by Robert Fulton, and the first one was built in New-York.

This is a page from an early school book.

Visual The most popular school books in the 1800s were McGuffey's readers which taught reading, writing, and arithmetic. The readers also contained moral lessons.

Working for Change

The fast growth of the United States in the first half of the 1800s made many citizens proud of their country. They saw how the United States was expanding from coast to coast. They saw that farmlands were producing foods to feed the nation.

Still, there were people who wanted changes in the country. These people were **reformers.** A reformer is a person who works for a cause that improves the way something is done in a society. In the mid-1800s, reformers believed that education made good citizens. They believed alcohol was harmful and that mentally ill people were treated unfairly.

Most reformers believed that people did bad things only because they lived in bad conditions. Reformers believed that if conditions were improved, people would act better. They began speaking out for changes.

What did reformers believe about people? That people did bad things only because they lived in bad conditions

Public Education Reform

During the early 1800s, not all children went to public schools. Most children from wealthy families went to private schools. Many poor children received no education outside of home.

In the 1830s, many people began to see the need for free public schools. People said that without an education people could not be good citizens. Most reformers believed that education was the best way to prevent crime and other social problems. In 1852, Massachusetts became the first state where children between the ages of eight and fourteen were required to attend school.

Many women wanted to give girls more opportunities. In order to meet this goal, Emma Willard opened the Troy Female Seminary in Troy, New York, in 1821. It was a school just for girls.

How did some people feel about education? They believed people could not be good citizens without an education.

Great Names in History

HORACE MANN

Horace Mann of Massachusetts was a leader in the struggle to set up public schools for all children. Mann called education "the great equalizer." He said that democracy would not work without educated citizens. In 1848, Mann wrote,

"If we do not prepare children to become good citizens—if we do not develop their [skills], if we do not enrich their minds with knowledge, [fill] their hearts with the love of truth and duty . . . then our [country] must go down to destruction. . . ."

Horace Mann

Critical Thinking What did Mann mean when he called education "the great equalizer"? It gave all people opportunities to advance economically, socially, and personally.

Other Reform Movements

In the 1820s, many reformers believed that the use of alcohol caused poor health, crime, and other social problems. Some reformers wanted to limit the sale of alcohol. Others wanted states to outlaw the sale completely. Their beliefs led to the **temperance** movement, which is a reform movement that is against drinking alcohol.

A shocking experience made Dorothea Dix a different kind of reformer. In 1841, she went to a prison in Massachusetts to give lessons to female prisoners. She discovered that some prisoners were there only because they were suffering from mental illness. Dix worked to improve conditions for mentally ill people. She visited some prisons in Massachusetts. Two years later she reported to the state legislature the horrible scenes she had seen. As a result of her investigation, some mentally ill people in Massachusetts were taken out of prisons. They were placed in hospitals called asylums. There they could be treated as sick people and receive good care.

What conditions did Dorothea Dix help to reform?
Conditions among imprisoned people suffering from mental illness

Section 3 Review

1. What conditions did reformers in the 1800s hope to improve?
2. How did Dorothea Dix improve conditions for people who were mentally ill?
3. **Critical Thinking** Why do you think some people might not have liked the reformers?
4. **Write About Citizenship** Write a letter to the editor of a local newspaper telling why you support public education.

More Review is provided in Exercise 33 of the Workbook.

1. Lack of education, alcohol abuse, mistreatment of mentally ill people
2. By observing mentally ill people and by presenting a report to the Massachusetts state legislature
3. Student responses should mention that people who like to tell other people how to live are not always popular and not always respected.
4. Student responses should mention that people would learn how to read, become aware of different issues, vote, become productive workers.

Chapter

8 Review

Summary Have students use this graphic organizer to outline the main ideas and details of the chapter.

Summary

Between 1820 and 1860, important social changes took place. Many people moved from rural to urban areas. Many immigrants came to the United States. There were reform movements aimed at giving people more rights.

Section 1

Beginning in the 1830s, many Americans moved from rural areas to cities. Immigrants came to the United States from Germany, Ireland, and China.

Section 2

Women worked for equal rights for all Americans. In 1848, a convention was held at Seneca Falls, New York, to discuss women's rights.

Section 3

Reformers spoke out for free public education, temperance, and better conditions for mentally ill people.

More Vocabulary Review is provided in Exercise 47 of the Classroom Resource Binder.

Vocabulary Review

Write *true* or *false*. If the statement is false, change the underlined term to make it true.

1. Most people who live in <u>urban</u> areas are farmers. False: rural
2. The <u>famine</u> in Ireland caused people to leave. True
3. Susan B. Anthony wanted American women to be granted <u>temperance</u>, or the right to vote. False: suffrage
4. Making education free to American children was a goal of some <u>immigrants</u>. False: reformers
5. Angelina Grimké wanted <u>equal rights</u> for women. True

1. Land for farming, jobs, and political freedom pp. 139–140 2. It offered women the opportunity to meet and to discuss how they might gain equal rights with men. pp. 143–145 3. People who were not educated could not be good citizens. p. 148 4. Women still did not have the right to vote in public elections; therefore, they could not directly influence public policies. pp. 142–145 5. The anti-slavery movement made women aware that they didn't have full political and social rights. p. 142

Chapter Quiz

Write your answers in complete sentences.

1. What did the United States offer European immigrants of the mid-1800s?
2. What was the importance of the Seneca Falls Convention?
3. Why did people begin to see the need for public education?
4. **Critical Thinking** Women accomplished many things between 1820 and 1860. Why do you think they felt that they still had a long way to go before they gained equality?
5. **Critical Thinking** How did the anti-slavery movement affect the women's rights movement?

Test Tip
Before you begin a test, look it over. Try to set aside enough time to complete all the questions.

Writing Tip
Support a main idea with facts and examples.

Using the Timeline

Use the timeline on pages 136–137 to answer the questions.

1. Which state was the first to pass a school attendance law? Massachusetts
2. How many years were there between the invention of the reaper and the invention of the steel plow? 6

Group Activity See the Teacher's Planning Guide for a scoring rubric for this activity.

Group Activity

Form small groups. Create storyboards of four or five frames. Show several women and several men at the Seneca Falls Convention. Describe how they think people may respond to the news of the meeting.

Critical Thinking 1. He was protesting the higher taxes that farmers in Massachusetts were required to pay. 2. Great Britain was seizing U.S. ships and impressing U.S. seamen. 3. The United States wanted to keep the Western Hemisphere for Americans. 4. Women wanted to discuss women's rights and to draw up a list of demands.

Unit 2 Review

Critical Thinking

Give one reason why each of the following events happened.

1. Daniel Shays led a rebellion in Massachusetts.
2. The War of 1812 began.
3. The Monroe Doctrine was a warning to European nations.
4. The Seneca Falls Convention was held in 1848.

Building Your Skills

Make a chart that tells how each of the following people helped to improve the lives of other Americans. Give the chart a title.

1. John Deere Made farming easier by inventing the steel plow
2. Elizabeth Cady Stanton Struggled to gain equal rights for women
3. Horace Mann Worked to bring about reforms in education
4. Dorothea Dix Worked to improve the lives of people who were mentally ill

Who Did It?

Write the name of the person who took each action below.

1. He suggested that Congress be divided into two houses. Roger Sherman
2. She helped Lewis and Clark. Sacajawea
3. He led Mexican troops in the Battle of the Alamo. General Santa Anna
4. She led the fight for women's suffrage. Susan B. Anthony

Writing an Essay

Answer one of the following essay topics.
See the Answer Key for a detailed answer.

1. Describe how the writers of the Constitution made sure that no state or no branch of the government would become too powerful.
2. Discuss the reasons why many Americans moved west in the years leading up to 1850.
3. Describe the work of many people between 1820 and 1860 to improve the lives of Americans.

Linking Past and Present

Today, U.S. citizens enjoy rights that people in the 1840s did not have. Discuss some of the rights that you especially value in your life. Students may discuss: right to a free public school education, voting at age 18, right to a minimum wage, right to a driver's license.

Unit Opener Use the chapter titles and dates to set up a unit timeline.

Unit 3 A Nation Divided

Chapter 9 **North and South Disagree** 1820–1861

Chapter 10 **The Civil War** 1861–1865

Chapter 11 **Rebuilding a Divided Nation** 1865–1877

The North and the South could not agree on the issue of slavery. A bitter war began in 1861. What does this painting show you about the way battles were fought during the Civil War? Large groups fought hand to hand, using swords and rifles.

> *"A house divided against itself cannot stand. I believe this government cannot endure . . . half slave and half free."*
>
> —Abraham Lincoln, 1858

Primary Source This quote comes from a speech Abraham Lincoln gave in his campaign in Illinois for the U.S. Senate. Lincoln lost the election to Stephen Douglas.

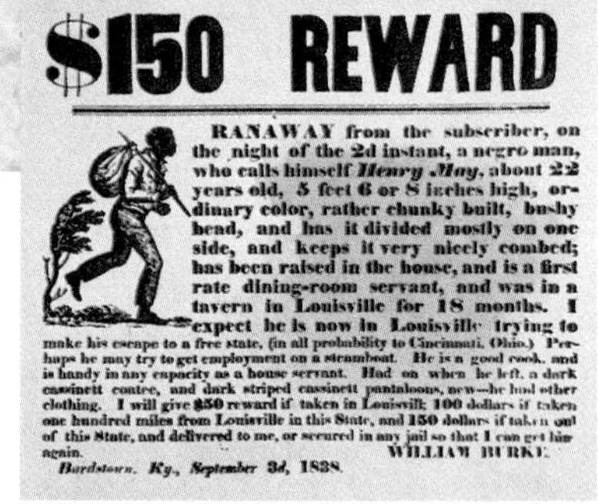

$150 REWARD

RANAWAY from the subscriber, on the night of the 2d instant, a negro man, who calls himself *Henry May*, about 22 years old, 5 feet 6 or 8 inches high, ordinary color, rather chunky built, bushy head, and has it divided mostly on one side, and keeps it very nicely combed; has been raised in the house, and is a first rate dining-room servant, and was in a tavern in Louisville for 18 months. I expect he is now in Louisville trying to make his escape to a free state, (in all probability to Cincinnati, Ohio.) Perhaps he may try to get employment on a steamboat. He is a good cook, and is handy in any capacity as a house servant. Had on when he left, a dark cassinett coatee, and dark striped cassinett pantaloons, new—he had other clothing. I will give $50 reward if taken in Louisville; 100 dollars if taken one hundred miles from Louisville in this State, and 150 dollars if taken out of this State, and delivered to me, or secured in any jail so that I can get him again.

WILLIAM BURKE.

Bardstown, Ky., September 3d, 1838.

The painting shows enslaved African Americans escaping from the South. The poster offers a reward for the return of an escaped slave. What dangers might enslaved African Americans have faced during their escape?
Capture, illness, fatigue, hunger

The North and the South Grow Apart

Additional activities and strategies to customize lessons can be found in the Teacher's Planning Guide.

Chapter 9 North and South Disagree 1820–1861

ESL Note To help students understand what it means to be strongly committed to an issue, have them discuss some local issues in their own community or at home. Encourage them to take a stand and describe how they would resolve the issue. Explain that the nation was divided over the issue of slavery.

Words to Know

free state

slave state

sectionalism

fugitive

abolitionist

Underground Railroad

popular sovereignty

extremist

secede

civil war

Words to Know These words are defined in the section in which they appear, as well as in the Glossary. Explain that the *-ist* ending refers to a person. Point out to students words with the *-ist* ending.

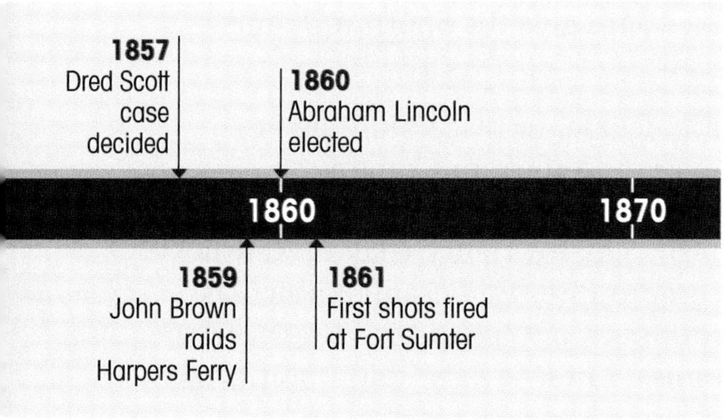

Learning Objectives

- Describe how lawmakers tried to settle slavery issues.
- Identify reasons why slavery divided the country.
- Explain how abolitionists worked to end slavery.
- Discuss how Abraham Lincoln's election in 1860 affected the Union.
- Read a map.

Project Some of the important people in this chapter include Abraham Lincoln, Henry Clay, and Harriet Tubman. Have students research the person they choose.

Portfolio Project

As you read the chapter, list the important people mentioned. Choose the person who interests you most. Suppose you could talk with that person. What questions would you ask? What answers would the person give? Write a dialogue between you and the person you have chosen.

Timeline The timeline is divided into intervals of 10 years. The events take place over a period of 42 years. Point out to students that efforts to resolve the issue of slavery had been going on since colonial times.

Section 1 Expansion and Compromise

Words to Know

free state	a state in which slavery was not allowed
slave state	a state in which slavery was allowed
sectionalism	loyalty to one region of a country instead of to the whole country
fugitive	a person who runs away or escapes

Getting Started Invite students to identify either a personal or political conflict that became worse. Discuss what happened. Point out to students that the conflict in the United States over slavery gradually became worse.

By 1819, there were 22 states in the United States of America. There were 11 **free states,** in which slavery was not allowed. There were 11 **slave states,** in which slavery was allowed. As the United States grew larger, more territories wanted to become states. Lawmakers could not agree if new states should allow slavery.

The Missouri Compromise of 1820

Remember
The Louisiana Territory was the area from the Mississippi River west to the Rocky Mountains and from New Orleans to Canada.

In 1819, Missouri asked to become a state. In 1820, Maine asked to become a state. Missouri wanted to join the Union, or the United States, as a slave state. Missouri was part of the Louisiana Territory. Northern lawmakers did not want Missouri to become a state. They said that 12 slave states would give the South too much power in making laws.

There was a long debate, or discussion of the reasons for and against an idea, in Congress. Lawmakers from the North and the South could not agree. Then, in 1820, Senator Henry Clay of Kentucky came up with a compromise. He became known as the Great Compromiser. Clay called his idea the Missouri Compromise. These are the main points of the Missouri Compromise.

1. Missouri would enter the Union as a slave state.

2. Maine would enter the Union as a free state.

3. The rest of the Louisiana Territory would be divided by a line. No slavery would be allowed in the states north of that line.

The Missouri Compromise kept the balance between slave and free states in the Senate.

What were the main points of the Missouri Compromise? Missouri would enter Union as slave state, Maine would enter as free state, a line would divide Louisiana Territory, no slavery would be allowed north of that line

Map Remind students that the Missouri Compromise applied only to the territories included in the Louisiana Purchase. Students may need to refer to the map of the Louisiana Purchase on page 104 of this book.

Missouri Compromise, 1820

Map Study

1. In what year was Missouri admitted as a slave state? 1821

2. What territory is south of the Missouri Compromise line? Arkansas Territory

The Debate Continues

In 1838, Texas asked to join the Union as a slave state. The Missouri Compromise only applied to the land north of the dividing line in the Louisiana Territory. It did not apply to Texas. Another debate started. It lasted until 1845, when Texas entered the Union as a slave state.

Arguments grew stronger between the North and the South. When Northerners called for an end to slavery, southern leaders accused them of trying to destroy the southern way of life. Feelings of **sectionalism** grew deeper. Sectionalism is loyalty to one region of a country instead of to the whole country.

Not all of the arguments were about slavery. The North and the South were growing apart. The two sections had different economies and needs. In the North, industry was growing. In the South, farming continued to be the main way of life.

The North and the South had different ideas about how to run the government. The North wanted a strong federal government. The South wanted each state to have more power.

As more states in the West began to join the Union, a new type of sectionalism developed. Westerners had their own needs. Their needs were different from the needs of people in the North and the South.

Many people in the West owned small farms. They did not depend on slave labor to help run their farms. Many Westerners felt the people in the territories should decide if they wanted slavery.

Which three regions of the Union continued to debate sectional issues? Northern, southern, and western regions

What Each Region Wanted

Issue	The North	The South	The West
Taxes on goods from other countries	Wanted higher taxes. **Reason:** Northern products could sell for less than foreign products.	Wanted lower taxes. **Reason:** Southerners could buy cheap foreign goods.	Wanted higher taxes. **Reason:** The extra tax money could be used to build railroads.
Immigration to the United States	Wanted more immigrants. **Reason:** There would be more workers for northern factories.	Wanted fewer immigrants. **Reason:** If more immigrants came, the North would gain population and power.	Wanted more immigrants. **Reason:** Immigrants could settle lands in the West.
Slavery in territories and new states	Wanted no more slave states and territories. **Reason:** Disliked slavery; wanted to get more power to make laws.	Wanted more slave states and territories. **Reason:** Favored slavery; wanted to get more power to make laws.	Wanted to make own decisions about slavery. **Reason:** Westerners wanted to control their own area.

Chart Study

1. How did each region feel about taxes on goods from other countries?
2. How did the North and the South each think they could get more power to make laws?

The Compromise of 1850

In 1849, there were 15 free states and 15 slave states. California wanted to join the Union as a free state. California was part of a large area that the United States had won from Mexico.

Lawmakers from the North wanted California to be a free state. That would give them enough power to pass a law that would stop the sale of slaves in Washington, D.C., which was the nation's capital.

Lawmakers from the South disagreed. They felt that slavery should be allowed in the nation's capital. They also wanted to pass a law that would make Northerners return escaped slaves to slaveholders. This law was called the Fugitive Slave Law. A **fugitive** is a person who runs away or escapes.

1. North and West wanted higher taxes, South wanted lower taxes
2. North: By keeping out new slave states so all new states would be free South: By having more slave states

Chart Discuss the needs of each region. Point out the similarities between what the North and West wanted. (They both wanted higher taxes, more immigrants, and the option to disallow slavery.) Remind students that their reasons for wanting these things were different.

The Senate debated the issue of slavery. Senator John Calhoun, from South Carolina, did not think the North should stop slavery. Daniel Webster, a senator from Massachusetts, thought there should be a compromise. He said that if the North and the South did not work out their problems, there would be a terrible war.

Senator Henry Clay and others came up with another compromise. The Compromise of 1850 said:

1. California would join the Union as a free state.
2. In the rest of the territory from Mexico, people would decide whether or not to allow slavery.
3. The slave trade would be banned in Washington, D.C.
4. Congress would pass the Fugitive Slave Law.

What did the Compromise of 1850 state? California: free state; Washington, D.C: slave trade banned; Other territory from Mexico: decide on slavery itself; Congress to pass Fugitive Slave Law

Section 1 Review

1. Why was Senator Henry Clay called the Great Compromiser?
2. What was the Fugitive Slave Law?
3. **Critical Thinking** Do you think there is sectionalism in the United States today? Give a reason or example to support your answer.
4. **Write About Economics** You own a factory in the North. Make a sign to let your workers know how you feel about taxes on goods from other countries.

More Review is provided in Exercise 34 of the Workbook.

1. He sponsored laws that were compromises between the North and South. He tried to give each region something it wanted.
2. Law stating that Northerners must return escaped slaves to slaveholders
3. Student responses may be yes or no. Reasons and examples might relate to different regions and include environmental, cultural, or other issues in those regions.
4. Student signs might make the following points: With higher taxes on foreign goods, our goods will sell better, jobs will be secure, pay increases may result.

BUILDING YOUR SKILLS
Reading a Map: The Compromise of 1850

A map gives information about places. Some maps show the physical features of an area. Some maps give information about the economy or population. The following information will help you read a map.

1. The *key* tells what the colors on the map stand for.
2. The *compass rose* shows direction—north, south, east, and west.
3. The *scale* shows how distances on the map represent real distances.

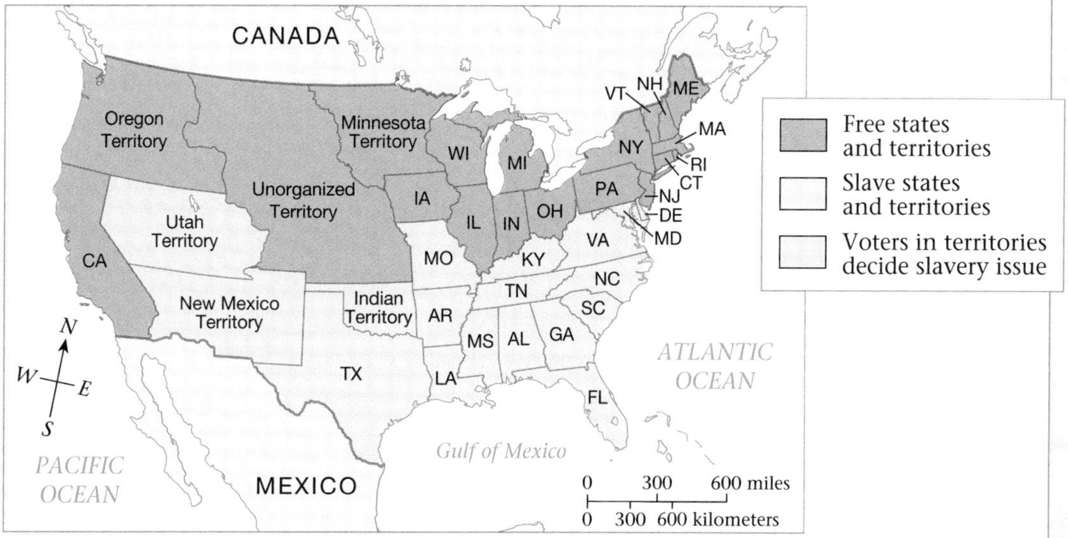

Answer the questions below.

1. What is the largest free territory?
2. Which slave states border free states?

CHALLENGE Write a title for the map. Why is this a good title?

Apply the Skill

Write two questions that can be answered by the map on this page. Trade questions with a partner.

1. Unorganized Territory **2.** MO, KY, VA, MD, DE **CHALLENGE** Titles may include States and Territories, 1850; Free and Slave, 1850. Students should mention that a title should tell what the map is about.

Section 2 Northerners Change Their Thinking

Words to Know

abolitionist	a person who wanted to end slavery
Underground Railroad	a network of secret escape routes enslaved African Americans followed to reach freedom in the North

Getting Started Point out to students that many Americans risked their lives to hide slaves escaping to freedom. Have students brainstorm challenges faced by either an escaping slave or by someone helping a slave to escape.

As the 1850s came to an end, the nation was deeply divided over the question of slavery. The Union was in danger of breaking apart.

Action Against Slavery

Some people in the North wanted to abolish, or end, slavery. These people were called **abolitionists.**

William Lloyd Garrison was a famous abolitionist. He started an anti-slavery newspaper called the *Liberator*. In 1833, he helped start the American Anti-Slavery Society. Many Northerners became involved in the abolition movement because of Garrison.

Not all abolitionists were from the North. Sarah and Angelina Grimké were the daughters of a South Carolina slaveholder. The Grimké sisters spoke out against slavery.

Abolitionists wanted to help African Americans escape from slavery. Abolitionists worked together to set up a network of secret routes for enslaved African Americans to escape to freedom in the North or in Canada. This was called the **Underground Railroad.**

? **Who were the abolitionists?** People who wanted to end slavery

Books Change Thinking in the North

The abolitionist movement in the North grew stronger. Many Northerners began to read books that changed their minds about slavery. One writer who helped to turn people against slavery was Frederick Douglass.

Douglass was an abolitionist leader who had escaped from slavery. When he was a boy, he was taught how to read by a slaveholder's wife. When his master found out, Douglass was not allowed to read anymore. Douglass was determined to escape to freedom.

When he was 21 years old, Douglass made his escape. He became a leader in the Massachusetts Abolitionist Society. He spoke about why slavery was wrong. Douglass wrote the *Narrative of the Life of Frederick Douglass,* a book about his experiences as a slave.

Frederick Douglass was a well-known speaker and abolitionist.

Visual Frederick Douglass was such a powerful speaker that some people questioned whether he really had been a slave. To counter those people, he wrote his autobiography.

A Closer Look

THE UNDERGROUND RAILROAD

Like a real railroad, the Underground Railroad had "tracks," "stations," and "conductors." The tracks were the secret routes slaves took to escape from the South. These routes started in the South and went through a number of northern states. The stations were secret hiding places in houses, churches, and caves.

About 100,000 slaves used the Underground Railroad to escape to freedom.

Harriet Tubman was one famous conductor. Tubman was an escaped slave. Even though she was free, Tubman returned to the South 19 times to help more than 300 enslaved African Americans to escape.

Harriet Tubman

Critical Thinking Why do you think Harriet Tubman, who escaped from slavery, returned South to help others?

Possible answer: The desire to help others, to rescue family members and friends

Solomon Northup, a freed African American who lived in the North, wrote *Twelve Years a Slave*. While he was visiting Washington, D.C., slave traders kidnapped him and took him to New Orleans. There, a planter bought him. For the next twelve years, Northup worked as a slave. He regained his freedom with the help of a family friend.

Uncle Tom's Cabin by Harriet Beecher Stowe was another famous anti-slavery book. The book was published in 1852. Stowe's book told a story about Uncle Tom and other enslaved African Americans. The book showed the cruelty of slavery in a way that Northerners had not seen before. Many people questioned how it was possible for one human to own another human.

What writers wrote books that turned many Americans against slavery? Frederick Douglass, Solomon Northup, Harriet Beecher Stowe

Section 2 Review

1. How did the Underground Railroad help enslaved African Americans escape to the North?
2. What did Frederick Douglass do to convince Northerners that slavery was wrong?
3. **Critical Thinking** How could a book show the cruelty of slavery to people who lived in areas with no slavery?
4. **Write About Citizenship** Write a short editorial for an abolitionist newspaper. Remember that an editorial gives your opinions, or ideas, for or against something. Be sure to give reasons for your opinion.

More Review is provided in Exercise 36 of the Workbook.

1. Slaves escaped along routes. There were conductors to lead them and stations, or hiding places, along the way.
2. He was a leader in the Massachusetts Abolitionist Society, spoke against slavery, wrote book about his life as a slave.
3. Student responses should show an understanding that a book could tell a story about the lives of slaves or relate the true experiences of a slave.
4. Student editorials might be anti-slavery and explain why slaves should be free.

Section 3 Troubles Build

Words to Know

popular sovereignty	a system that allowed people in a territory to make their own decisions
extremist	a person whose opinions are very different from those of most people
secede	to break away from, as a state leaving the Union
civil war	a war between regions or groups of people in the same country

Getting Started Discuss what happens when two people argue and do not listen to each other's points of view. Point out that when compromise and communication break down, a more serious conflict can ensue. By the late 1850s, the North and the South could find no way to compromise on slavery. The result was the Civil War.

In 1856, Senator Charles Sumner of Massachusetts made a strong speech against slavery. He criticized many southern lawmakers. One of the people he criticized was Senator Andrew Butler of South Carolina. Butler's nephew, Congressman Preston Brooks, did not like Sumner's speech. He went into the Senate and started beating Sumner with his cane. Sumner was badly hurt by the attack. The debate over slavery was becoming violent.

The Kansas-Nebraska Act

In 1854, Senator Stephen Douglas of Illinois wanted to organize Nebraska into a territory. Douglas wanted to see a railroad built from Illinois through the Nebraska Territory to the Pacific. He felt the railroad would increase settlement in the West.

Douglas suggested dividing the territory into the Nebraska Territory and the Kansas Territory. To gain the support of Southern lawmakers, Douglas decided slavery in the territory could be decided by **popular sovereignty.** Popular sovereignty was a system that allowed the people in a territory to make their own decisions.

Nebraska was too far north to have plantations. The people of Nebraska wanted a territory that was without slavery. Kansas was farther south. Plantations could be built there. As soon as the Kansas-Nebraska Act was passed, thousands of people rushed to claim land in Kansas. Some wanted slavery in the territory. Others were against slavery. Since a vote of the people would decide if Kansas would be pro-slavery or anti-slavery, each side wanted to get the most votes.

What was the Kansas-Nebraska Act? New territories to use popular sovereignty

Bleeding Kansas

By 1855, there were 9,000 people in the Kansas Territory. The population was large enough to vote for a government. Before the election, groups of armed men rode into Kansas. These men were **extremists**, or people whose opinions were very different from those of most people.

When the voting was held, the extremists went to the voting places. They warned people not to vote against slavery. They voted themselves, even though they did not live in Kansas.

The pro-slavery voters were people who wanted to allow slavery in the territory. The pro-slavery voters won, but the vote was unfair. Only about 1,500 men were supposed to vote in Kansas, but a little over 6,000 votes were counted. In spite of the unfair vote, a pro-slavery government was set up. The people against slavery also set up a government.

Now, Kansas had two governments—one for slavery and one against it. Each claimed to be the legal government. Violence broke out. In May 1856, about 700 pro-slavery extremists attacked Lawrence, Kansas, which was the capital of the anti-slavery government. The attackers robbed people and destroyed property.

Several days later, an anti-slavery group murdered five pro-slavery men and boys. Bloody battles and killings began. The territory became known as "Bleeding Kansas." More than 200 people were killed.

What happened after the unfair vote for slavery in Kansas? Two governments were set up: one for slavery, one against it

The Dred Scott Case

Dred Scott was a slave in Missouri who went to court to ask for his freedom. Scott said he was free because the slaveholder had taken him to live in a free state for four years. He said that since he had lived in a free state, he was no longer enslaved. He said it did not matter that the slaveholder later took him back to a slave state.

Dred Scott went to court asking for his freedom.

Visual The Dred Scott ruling by the U.S. Supreme Court was only the second time in American history that the Supreme Court had ruled an act of Congress unconstitutional.

Two state courts made different decisions about Scott. One court said he was free. Another said that he was still a slave. Scott went to the U.S. Supreme Court in 1857. Chief Justice Roger Taney of the Supreme Court made a decision.

1. Scott could not bring a case to court because he, as an enslaved African, was not a U.S. citizen.
2. The law considered slaves property. The owner could move anywhere and still own his property.
3. The Missouri Compromise was against the law. Congress did not have the power to decide where slavery could be allowed.

The Dred Scott decision meant that all territories were opened up to slavery once again. Northern lawmakers would not be able to keep slavery out of the territories.

Why did the Dred Scott case have to go to the Supreme Court? Two state courts made two different decisions about it

The Lincoln-Douglas Debates

In 1858, two men ran for the U.S. Senate in the state of Illinois. One was a Democrat named Stephen Douglas. As a senator, Douglas helped pass the Kansas-Nebraska Act. He was for popular sovereignty in the territories. The Republican running against him was a lawyer named Abraham Lincoln. Lincoln taught himself the law by reading law books.

Lincoln and Douglas traveled around Illinois, debating the question of slavery. Douglas believed that new territories should make their own decisions about slavery. Lincoln believed that slavery should not be allowed in the new territories. "If slavery is not wrong, nothing is wrong," he said.

Lincoln lost the election. However, many Republicans began to think Lincoln would make a good candidate for President.

? **What did Lincoln and Douglas each believe about slavery?** Lincoln: no slavery in new territories; Douglas: new territories should decide about slavery for themselves

John Brown's Raid

John Brown was strongly against slavery. He believed that it was his duty to end slavery. He led armed men in Kansas who murdered five pro-slavery men.

In October 1859, Brown and 21 followers attacked a building that held army weapons in Harpers Ferry, Virginia. Brown planned to take the weapons and give them to enslaved African Americans. He wanted to lead a rebellion against slaveholders.

Brown's attack failed. Soldiers, led by an officer named Robert E. Lee, trapped Brown in the army weapons building. Several of Brown's men were killed. Brown was hanged a short time later.

Even though Brown failed, many Southerners were worried. Southerners believed that the abolitionists would do anything in their power to destroy slavery.

Why did John Brown attack a building at Harpers Ferry, Virginia? To capture army weapons, which he would give to slaves and then lead them in a rebellion against slaveholders

The Election of 1860

The election of the President in 1860 tested people's feelings about slavery. Northern Democrats picked Stephen Douglas to run. He supported popular sovereignty. Southern Democrats chose John Breckinridge. He supported slavery. The Republicans picked Abraham Lincoln to run. He was against allowing slavery in new territories. However, he would not end it in the South.

Lincoln won the election, but he did not win any southern states. Now, Southerners felt that they were becoming powerless. They had lost the power they once had in the election of Presidents. The population of the North was much larger than that of the South. Southerners felt that this gave Northerners a greater chance to force changes in the South.

Soon after the election, many southern leaders decided the South should **secede**, or break away from, the Union. In December 1860, South Carolina became the first state to secede. By February 1861, Georgia, Florida, Mississippi, Louisiana, Alabama, and Texas had also left the Union.

In February, delegates from the seceding states met. They named their group of states the Confederate States of America, or the Confederacy. They wrote a constitution similar to the U.S. Constitution and chose Jefferson Davis as the president of the Confederacy.

Why did many southern states secede in 1860? They felt powerless after Lincoln became President.

History Fact

While campaigning in the 1860 election, Lincoln received a letter from a little girl. The letter said that Lincoln should grow a beard because his face was so thin.

History Fact In 1860, Lincoln met the little girl, Grace Bedell. He kissed her and thanked her for her advice.

The Confederate attack on Fort Sumter in 1861 pushed the nation into war.

Visual Fort Sumter was a victory for the Confederates in 1861. However, in 1865, the fort was retaken by Union forces.

The Civil War Begins

Lincoln became President in March 1861. By that time, the Confederacy had already taken over U.S. forts, post offices, and other government buildings in the South. Lincoln believed that the southern states had broken the law by seceding. However, he knew if he sent soldiers to the South, war could break out. Lincoln wanted to avoid a **civil war,** or a war between regions or groups of people in the same country. However, President Lincoln said that he would hold on to all U.S. government property.

Fort Sumter was U.S. government property. The fort was on an island, guarding the harbor of Charleston, South Carolina. Confederate forces gathered across the water. The Confederates knew the fort was running low on supplies. They planned to attack the supply ships when they arrived. The Union commander of the fort, Major Robert Anderson, told President Lincoln that he would have to give up the fort if the President did not send supplies.

Lincoln decided to send food, but not to send weapons or soldiers. In fact, he sent the food in unarmed ships, hoping the Confederates would let the ships through. Lincoln even let the governor of South Carolina know about his plan. He did not want a battle to start. However, before the Union supply ships even got to Fort Sumter, the Confederates demanded that Anderson surrender the fort to them. He refused.

On April 12, 1861, the Confederates opened fire on Fort Sumter. The Union soldiers surrendered the next day. The Civil War had begun.

How did the Civil War begin? The Union commander refused to surrender Fort Sumter. The Confederates fired on the fort. The Union forces surrendered.

Section 3 Review

1. Why was Kansas called "Bleeding Kansas"?
2. Why did the Dred Scott decision anger northern lawmakers and abolitionists?
3. **Critical Thinking** Why did Southerners want a Democrat for President in 1860?
4. **Write About History** You are a young Union soldier at Fort Sumter. It is April 12, 1861. Write a journal entry describing the first shots of the war. Tell how you felt when you heard them.

More Review is provided in Exercise 37 of the Workbook.

1. In 1856, pro-slavery and anti-slavery groups attacked each other. More than 200 people were killed.
2. The decision opened up territories to slavery. It took away the power of the Congress to limit slavery.
3. Democrats supported popular sovereignty, or the right of new states to decide the issue of slavery for themselves.
4. Student responses should show an understanding of the events at Fort Sumter and of the feelings that a young soldier might have at the start of a war, such as fear and excitement.

Chapter 9 Review

Summary Have students use this graphic organizer to outline the main ideas and details of the chapter.

Summary

Between 1820 and 1860, slavery became a bitter issue between the North and the South. In 1861, the first shots of the Civil War were fired.

Section 1

More territories wanted to enter the Union as states. Lawmakers worked out compromises to keep a balance between slave states and free states.

Section 2

The differences between the North and the South grew as the abolitionist movement gained strength. Abolitionist writings helped to turn many Northerners against slavery.

Section 3

The North and the South continued to disagree about slavery. Abraham Lincoln's election caused many southern states to secede. This action led to the Civil War.

- sectionalism
- fugitive
- abolitionist
- secede
- extremist

More Vocabulary Review is provided in Exercise 55 of the Classroom Resource Binder.

Vocabulary Review

Complete each sentence with a term from the list.

1. Southern leaders felt that the only way to keep slavery was to ____ from the Union. secede

2. An enslaved person who had escaped from a slaveholder was a ____ from the law. fugitive

3. An ____ believed that slavery was wrong. abolitionist

4. A person who turned to violence was an ____. extremist

5. The North and the South grew apart as feelings of ____ grew stronger. sectionalism

1. Join the Union as a state pp. 156–157 2. He helped found the American Anti-Slavery Society, started the *Liberator* p. 162 3. Extremists warned Kansas residents not to vote. Then the extremists voted themselves, even though they did not live in Kansas. pp. 166–167 4. Responses should show an understanding of the Compromise of 1850. pp. 159–160 5. Abolitionists felt slavery was unacceptable under any circumstances, so would not agree that people could vote to choose slavery. p. 166

Chapter Quiz

Write your answers in complete sentences.

1. What did Missouri want to do in 1819?
2. What did William Lloyd Garrison do for the abolitionist movement?
3. In 1855, why was the vote on slavery in Kansas unfair?
4. **Critical Thinking** Did the North or the South gain more from the Compromise of 1850?
5. **Critical Thinking** Why do you think the abolitionists would not accept the idea of popular sovereignty?

Test Tip
Look over the test before you begin to write. Read the direction lines to be sure you know what to do.

Writing Tip
To answer a question that asks you to tell why, you can restate the question. Then use the word *because*.

Using the Timeline

Use the timeline on pages 154–155 to answer the questions.

1. What event happened between the Compromise of 1850 and the Dred Scott decision?
   Kansas-Nebraska Act passed
2. How many years were there between Nat Turner's rebellion and John Brown's attack on Harpers Ferry? 28 years

Group Activity See the Teacher's Planning Guide for a scoring rubric for this activity.

Group Activity

Form groups of five. In each group, three people are judges. A fourth person is a lawyer arguing for the freedom of Dred Scott. A fifth person is a lawyer arguing for the slaveholder. After the case is presented, each judge gives his or her opinion.

These soldiers are resting in a Union camp before going to battle against Confederate soldiers. These are the hats worn by the Union (top) and Confederate (bottom) soldiers. What do you think these soldiers thought about as they rested before battle? Their families and loved ones, their homes, whether or not they would survive the battle

War Divides the Nation

1861 — 1862 — 1863 — 1864

- **April 12, 1861** Civil War begins at Fort Sumter
- **July 21, 1861** Battle of Bull Run
- **Sept. 17, 1862** Battle of Antietam
- **Jan. 1, 1863** Lincoln issues Emancipation Proclamation
- **July 1-3, 1863** Battle of Gettysburg
- **July 4, 1863** Vicksburg falls to northern troops
- **Nov. 19, 1863** Lincoln gives Gettysburg Address

Additional activities and strategies to customize lessons can be found in the Teacher's Planning Guide.

Chapter 10 The Civil War 1861–1865

ESL Note To help students understand reasons for the Civil War, ask them if the country from which they, their relatives, or friends came had civil war. In small groups, encourage them to comment on similarities and differences between events in these countries and the United States.

Words to Know

border state

martial law

casualty

civilian

conscription

discrimination

total war

assassinate

veteran

Words to Know These words are defined in the section in which they appear, as well as in the Glossary. Point out that the words *casualty*, *total war*, *conscription*, *martial law*, *civilian*, and *veteran* all have to do with war.

Learning Objectives

- Identify the strengths of the North and the South.
- Identify the important battles of the early war years.
- Describe life at home during the war.
- Discuss how the war ended.
- Explore how new technology made the Civil War the first modern war.

Project Suggest to students that they use the learning objectives and headings to identify which events to include. Students should select the most important events. If students prefer, their timeline can focus on the events of a single year.

Portfolio Project

The Civil War lasted for four years. The timeline on this page lists some of the main events. As you read the chapter, make notes about other important events that took place. When you finish the chapter, make your own Civil War timeline. Include at least five new entries.

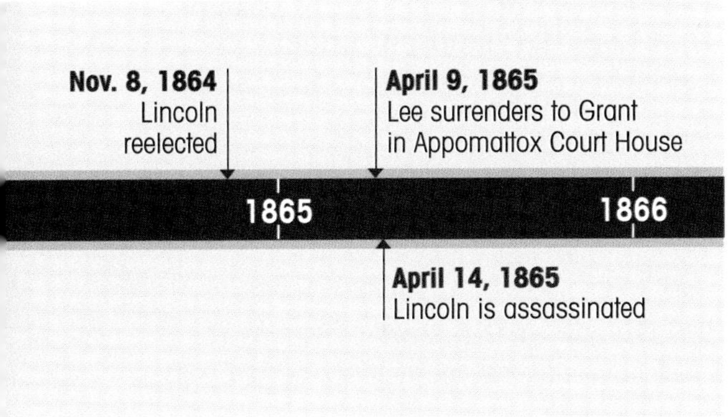

Timeline The timeline is divided into 1-year intervals. The events cover a period of 5 years. Point out that 1863 was the war's turning point.

Section 1 Preparing for War

Words to Know

border state	a slave state between the North and the South that remained in the Union during the Civil War
martial law	rule by an army instead of by elected officials

Getting Started Ask students why people join the armed forces today. Tell students that Civil War soldiers joined in the fight because of feelings of patriotism and a sense of adventure.

After the Confederate cannons fired on Fort Sumter in 1861, there would be no more compromises between the North and the South. The Civil War had begun.

The Nation Continues to Divide

Three days after the Confederates attacked Fort Sumter, President Lincoln asked for 75,000 volunteers to fight the South. Lincoln's call for volunteers led the southern states of Virginia, North Carolina, Tennessee, and Arkansas to secede from the Union. Four slave states did not secede. They were Missouri, Kentucky, Delaware, and Maryland. They became known as **border states,** because they were located on the border between the North and South.

Maryland bordered Washington, D.C., the Union's capital. It was very important for Maryland to remain in the Union. Lincoln had Maryland put under **martial law.** Martial law is rule by an army instead of by elected officials.

As the war began, the North and the South each had some strengths. These strengths influenced the way the war was fought.

How did the nation divide at the start of the war?
VA, NC, TN, AK joined southern states that seceded. MO, KY, DE, MD stayed in the Union.

Strengths of the North and South

North	South
1. Strong central government; President Lincoln would show his strength as time passed.	1. Strong military leaders, such as Robert E. Lee.
2. Large population; more soldiers to fight the war.	2. Experience with horses and weapons. Most southern men were farmers and hunters.
3. Money to pay for war.	3. Strong beliefs about fighting to protect the land.
4. Factories and workers to build weapons.	4. To win, Southerners only needed to hold onto their land. Northerners needed to invade the South and then defeat it.
5. Railroads to carry supplies to soldiers.	

Chart Study

1. What were two strengths of the North? Students should choose two points from Column 1 of the chart.
2. What were two strengths of the South? Students should choose two points from Column 2 of the chart.

Chart Remind students that Union troops had to travel to the South to win. Use the U.S. physical map at the back of this book to point out the distance Northerners had to travel.

Battle of Bull Run

President Lincoln felt that if Union forces could capture the Confederate capital of Richmond, Virginia, the war would end.

The first big battle of the war took place in July 1861, near a creek named Bull Run, in Virginia. Bull Run was only 20 miles away from Washington, D.C. Members of Congress and other Union supporters went to the battlefield to watch. Soldiers on both sides fought hard. However, the Union soldiers were poorly trained. When new Confederate troops, or soldiers, arrived, the Union soldiers retreated, or turned back. Union supporters began to understand that the war would not be won quickly. After Bull Run, many Southerners thought they could win the war.

What did the Union supporters learn from the Battle of Bull Run? The Union would not win the war quickly.

The North's Plan and the South's Plan

Remember
The South's economy depended on exporting goods to England.

President Lincoln and other Union leaders developed the Anaconda Plan. An anaconda is a large snake that wraps itself around its food and squeezes it. The plan was to squeeze the Confederacy. The Anaconda Plan had three main goals.

1. Blockade the southern ports. A blockade of the southern Atlantic coast would cut off southern supplies from getting in and out by sea.
2. Attack the South along the Mississippi River to split the Confederacy into two parts.
3. Continue to attack the Confederates in the East, with the plan to capture the capital at Richmond.

At the beginning of the war, the South had a simpler plan. It was to hold onto southern land. The South hoped the North would quickly get sick of fighting the war and quit.

What was each side's plan? North: To blockade southern ports, attack along Mississippi River, and capture Richmond; South: To hold onto southern land

Section 1 Review

1. Why was it important for Maryland to remain in the Union?
2. What was the first big battle of the Civil War?
3. **Critical Thinking** Why would President Lincoln need to pay attention to the four border states?
4. **Write About Geography** Turn to the map of the United States on page 617 of this book. In a paragraph, describe how the Anaconda Plan used geography to try to defeat the South.

More Review is provided in Exercise 38 of the Workbook.

1. Maryland bordered Washington, D.C., the capital of the Union.
2. Battle of Bull Run
3. Student responses should show an understanding that the war was not only about slavery. Lincoln needed to be careful in what he said and did regarding slavery or he would lose the border states.
4. Student answers should show an understanding of how a blockade and an attack along the Mississippi River would hurt the South.

Section 2 The Early Years of War

Words to Know

casualty	a person killed, injured, or captured in war
civilian	a person who is not a soldier

Getting Started Discuss with students what life is like for families whose breadwinners are away. Point out that many people in the North and South thought that the war would be a short one. However, for years, the war seemed to continue with no end in sight, and the men who were in the military could not earn much money or take care of the family.

In the first years of the Civil War, the North and the South fought in the southeast, at sea, and in the Mississippi River valley. The South won some battles. The North won others. Neither side could totally defeat the other.

Battles in the Southeast

After the Battle of Bull Run, President Lincoln picked General George B. McClellan to lead the Union army in the East.

Robert E. Lee, the southern general, felt that the South's best chance to win the war was to do it quickly. If the war went on too long, the North would have a greater chance of winning. With its large population and many factories, the North could replace soldiers and supplies for a longer time than the South. So Lee began to attack McClellan's forces as often and as hard as he could.

Two important battles were the Seven Days' Battle and the Battle of Antietam. In the Seven Days' Battle in late June 1862, Lee's troops attacked Union forces east of Richmond. The Union forces retreated. The South declared a victory. However, both sides had many **casualties**, or people killed, injured, or captured in war. Now both sides knew that the war would be costly.

Early Battles of the Civil War

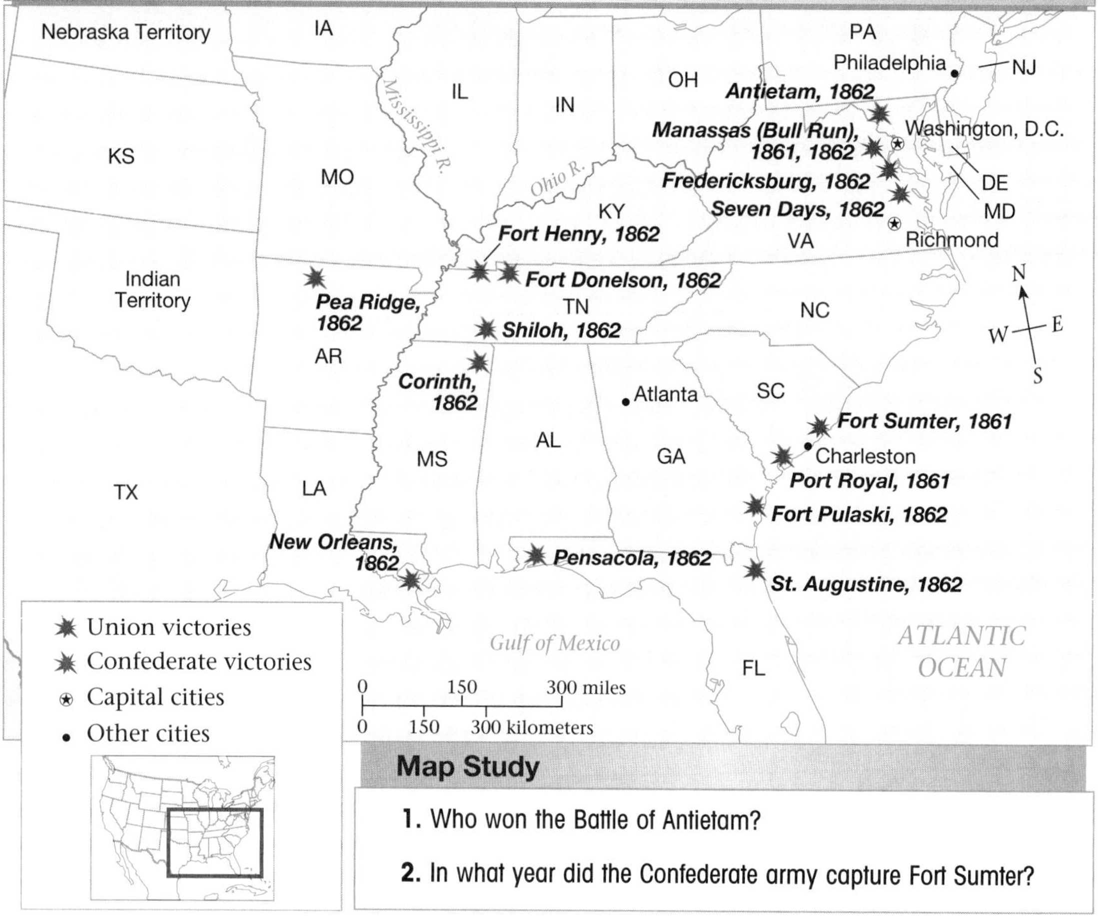

Map Study

1. Who won the Battle of Antietam?
2. In what year did the Confederate army capture Fort Sumter?

Map Ask students how they know that the Union had won almost three times as many battles as the Confederacy at this stage in the Civil War.

1. Union army

2. 1861

In September 1862, Confederate and Union forces faced each other at Antietam Creek in Maryland. Union General George McClellan received a copy of Lee's battle plan. Union forces ran through a cornfield to attack the Confederate troops. The Confederates fought back. There were more than 23,000 causalities.

In the end, Lee's troops retreated. The North declared a victory in the Battle of Antietam.

What was General Lee's plan for winning the war?
Quickly, by attacking northern forces as often as possible

Sea Battle of the Ironclads

The Union blockade of southern ports caused problems for the South. Many foreign ships could not get to southern ports. Southern soldiers and **civilians** had to go without supplies and food that they needed. A civilian is a person who is not a soldier. Southern ships carrying cotton could not get through the blockade. The South had hoped to earn money by sending cotton to Great Britain and France.

To break the blockade, Southerners built ironclad warships, or ships covered with iron plates. Most other ships at the time were covered with wood.

The first ironclad warship in the nation was named the *Virginia*. It had been a Union ship named the *Merrimac*, which had sunk. The Confederates recovered the ship, covered it with iron, and renamed it the *Virginia*. In 1862, the *Virginia* attacked Union ships. Cannonballs from the Union guns bounced off the sides of the *Virginia*. The *Virginia's* guns sank two Union warships.

The next day, the Union ironclad ship named the *Monitor* appeared. The *Virginia* and the *Monitor* shot at each other for several hours. Neither could sink the other. The Confederates' hope of ending the blockade was over.

What happened in the battle between the *Virginia* and the *Monitor?* The two ships shot at each other. Neither could sink the other.

Fighting Along the Mississippi

Union forces were fighting in the Mississippi River valley. During 1861 and 1862, they captured two Confederate forts. Under General Ulysses S. Grant, Union forces won an important battle at Shiloh, Tennessee. These victories gave the Union control of the northern Mississippi River valley.

Meanwhile, Admiral David Farragut led Union warships at the Battle of New Orleans. New Orleans, Louisiana was an important supply point for Confederate troops. The North captured New Orleans and took control of the southern Mississippi River valley.

The Mississippi River could no longer be a supply route for the South. However, the North could not use the river safely either. The Union needed to capture Vicksburg, Mississippi, to be in control of the entire river. After six weeks, Union forces under General Grant won at Vicksburg.

Visual The night before the Confederate army surrendered at Vicksburg, General Grant offered General Pemberton and his soldiers parole instead of an unconditional surrender. Pemberton chose to surrender.

Why was New Orleans important to the South?
It was an important supply point.

After the Battle of Vicksburg in 1863, the Union army controlled the Mississippi River.

The Turning Point

By July 1863, General Lee decided to invade the North, attack Union troops, and force the Union to make peace.

On July 1, 1863, the bloodiest battle of the Civil War began. At the small town of Gettysburg, Pennsylvania, Lee's forces met Union forces, led by George Meade. The battle lasted for three days. Confederate troops were badly beaten. Lee's army would never again be strong enough for a big attack on the North. The Battle of Gettysburg was the turning point of the Civil War.

On November 19, 1863, President Lincoln attended a ceremony at Gettysburg honoring Union soldiers who died in the battle. Lincoln gave a speech known today as the Gettysburg Address. The speech lasted a little over two minutes. Lincoln said the Civil War had to be fought to make sure that "government of the people, by the people, for the people, shall not perish [die] from the earth."

Why was the Battle of Gettysburg important? The South would never be strong enough to attack the North again.

Section 2 Review

1. Why was the capture of Vicksburg important for the North?
2. What did the fight between the *Virginia* and the *Monitor* show?
3. **Critical Thinking** Why did General Lee go to Gettysburg?
4. **Write About History** Write a news article about a battle in the southeast. Decide whether you are writing for a northern or a southern newspaper. Read your article to the class.

1. To gain full control of Mississippi River
2. That the South couldn't break the blockade
3. He thought he needed to attack in the North to end the war quickly.
4. Student responses should feature one battle and answer the questions *who, what, where, when, why,* and *how.*

More Review is provided in Exercise 39 of the Workbook.

Section 3 Life at Home

Words to Know

conscription	drafting of people for military service
discrimination	unjust treatment of a person based on false ideas about a particular group

Getting Started Discuss with students how the people behind the scenes in a production, whether it be a TV show or a play, are an important part of the production. Point out to students that this is also true for the Civil War. Women at home played an important role in the war.

In this cartoon, the Copperheads, shown as large snakes, rise up against the North, shown as the woman with a shield.

Visual Copperhead membership was strongest in Kentucky, Illinois, Indiana, Ohio, and Missouri.

Throughout the North and the South, almost everyone knew of a son, a brother, or a father who had died in the war. In some small towns, all the young men had been killed in a single battle. Many lives were lost on the battlefield. At home, life was difficult as well. Both the North and the South had problems.

Opposing the War

In the North, people who were against the war were called Copperheads. A copperhead is a poisonous snake. Copperheads wanted to end the war at any price. Some Copperheads believed in slavery. Others thought states had a right to leave the Union. Still other Copperheads felt the war was not worth all the soldiers who were being killed and wounded. The Copperheads did different things to show they were against the war. Some gave speeches. Others smuggled, or sneaked, guns into the South.

In the South, most wealthy landowners supported the Confederacy. However, there were many southern people, including African Americans and poor whites, who favored the Union.

Why were some Northerners against the war? Some believed in slavery, others believed South had the right to secede

Women During the War

During the war, northern and southern women worked hard to care for themselves and their families. Many stayed home taking care of the family farm. In the South, many women saw their farms burned and their fields destroyed by Union troops. Some women took jobs making uniforms and weapons. Other women worked in government offices, doing work that had always been done by men in the past.

Some women worked as battlefield nurses. In the North, Dorothea Dix became the leader of all the Union nurses. Dr. Elizabeth Blackwell trained nurses for Union hospitals. One volunteer nurse, Clara Barton, began the American Red Cross. In the South, Sally Tompkins started a small hospital. She was made a captain in the Confederate army.

Some women were spies during the war. Belle Boyd went behind Union lines to get information for the Confederacy. Pauline Cushman spied for the North by pretending to be an actress traveling in the South. Harriet Tubman, an Underground Railroad conductor, also served as a spy for the Union.

What did some northern and southern women do in hospitals and on battlefields? Worked as nurses, founded Red Cross, started hospitals and clinics, were spies

Raising Troops to Fight

At the beginning of the war, volunteers did most of the fighting on both sides. As more men were killed or injured, it became difficult to get volunteer troops. The South had to pass **conscription** laws. The North followed. Conscription is the drafting of people for military service. On both sides, some people complained that the laws were unfair.

In the South, plantation owners with more than 20 slaves could get out of serving in the military. Many

Economics Fact

More children worked in mills and factories during the Civil War than ever before.

Economics Fact There were early efforts to organize labor during the mid–nineteenth century. In 1866, the National Labor Union was formed. However, it was not until much later that any labor issue, including child labor laws, became a national issue.

poor southern farmers felt that the rich were not doing their fair share of the fighting.

In the North, a man could pay the government to get out of military service. A man could also hire someone else to go in his place. Only wealthy men could afford to do either of those things.

Northern feelings against the draft sometimes led to violence. White workers heard that African Americans would take their jobs when they were drafted. In 1863, a riot broke out in New York City to protest the draft. The riot lasted several days. More than 100 people were killed in the riot.

How were some men in the North and in the South able to stay out of the armed forces? North: Men could pay government, find a substitute; South: Large plantation owners

Economics Fact

On both sides, soldiers were paid less than $15 a month. Southern soldiers were always hungry and short of shoes and clothing.

Economics Fact Soldiers in the Union army were supposed to be paid every two months in the field. In reality, they often were paid in four-month intervals—sometimes six and eight months could go by without pay. Payment in the Confederate army was less regular and even slower.

The Emancipation Proclamation

By the summer of 1862, President Lincoln had decided to take steps to end slavery in southern states that were still held by the Confederacy. Lincoln thought that if southern slaves were freed, they would refuse to work in the fields. Then plantations would not be able to grow food for southern troops. Lincoln also thought that freeing the slaves would help many Northerners understand why the war was important.

As a result, President Lincoln issued the Emancipation Proclamation. This was a public statement that freed enslaved African Americans in the rebelling states, or the Confederacy. It said that on January 1, 1863, all slaves in the Confederate states would be "forever free." The Proclamation did not actually set any slaves free because the Union had no way to enforce the proclamation. The proclamation did not apply to slaves in the border states because Lincoln needed the support of these states.

What did the Emancipation Proclamation state? All slaves in the Confederate states would be "forever free."

African Americans in the Union Army

At about the same time that President Lincoln issued the Emancipation Proclamation, he decided to allow African American soldiers to serve in the Union army. Nearly 180,000 African Americans enlisted, or volunteered. Many of them were escaped slaves.

African American soldiers faced **discrimination** in the army. Discrimination is unjust treatment of a person based on false ideas about a particular group. At first, African American soldiers were not allowed to be officers. They served in all-African American units, or groups, under white officers. One of these units was

Great Names in History

THE 54TH MASSACHUSETTS VOLUNTEERS

The best-known African American soldiers were the 54th Massachusetts Volunteers. These soldiers were free African Americans. Frederick Douglass's two sons fought in the unit. Colonel Robert Shaw was the officer of the unit.

Despite the danger for African Americans fighting in the South, members of the 54th led several attacks in South Carolina. In July 1863, they attacked Fort Wagner in South Carolina. They climbed the walls of the fort and fought against the Confederate soldiers inside. When no other Union troops came to help them, the 54th Massachusetts Volunteers had to retreat.

These African Americans served as infantry soldiers during the Civil War.

Nearly half the soldiers in the 54th were killed during that battle, including Shaw. Even though the unit did not win the battle, the bravery of the 54th Massachusetts Volunteers earned its members respect and fame.

Critical Thinking How did members of the 54th Massachusetts Volunteers show their bravery? Attacked Fort Wagner, climbed walls of fort, fought against Confederate soldiers inside the 54th Massachusetts Volunteers. The weapons and horses that African American soldiers received were not as good as those given to white soldiers. Also, African American soldiers did not receive the same pay as white soldiers.

There were added dangers for African American soldiers and their white officers. The Confederacy warned that white officers would be punished or killed for serving with African Americans. The Confederacy also said that captured African American soldiers would be killed or sold into slavery.

In June 1864, Congress said that African American soldiers had to be paid as much as white soldiers. By the end of the war, African Americans could become officers.

What added danger did African American soldiers face? They might be killed or sold into slavery.

Section 3 Review

1. Who were the Copperheads?
2. What work did women do at home in the North and the South?
3. **Critical Thinking** What does the discrimination faced by African Americans in the Union army tell you about the North?
4. **Write About History** Create a poster urging volunteers to join the Union or Confederate army. Include reasons to encourage men to join.

More Review is provided in Exercise 41 of the Workbook.

1. Northerners who were against the war
2. Many stayed home taking care of the family farm. Some women took jobs making uniforms and weapons. Other women worked in government offices.
3. Student responses should show an understanding that the North was not free from prejudice against African Americans.
4. Student responses should show an understanding that the North was fighting to preserve the Union, the South to keep a way of life.

CONNECTING HISTORY AND TECHNOLOGY
The Technology of War

The Civil War is often called the first modern war. It was fought after the Industrial Revolution, which you learned about in Chapter 6.

During the Civil War, many inventions were used for the first time in war. For example, railroads delivered supplies, carried troops, and served as hospitals. Telegraphs sent messages to the generals in the field. Lighter-than-air balloons were used to spy on the enemy. Some things were actually invented during the war. For example, the Gatling gun, a mechanical machine gun, was invented.

A light-air balloon

By the time the Civil War ended, more than 618,000 soldiers had been killed. One reason for the high number of deaths was not enough medical care. The huge number of men who fought in battles was another reason. Still another reason was that weapons were more deadly than ever before. Armies used long-range rifles, steam-powered gunboats, and new bullets called minié balls. Minié balls could travel more than half a mile. These inventions made it possible to add distance between fighting soldiers. Soldiers could now kill their enemies without actually seeing them.

Answer the questions below.

1. How were railroads used during the Civil War?

2. Why did so many soldiers die in the Civil War?

CHALLENGE How do you think the technology of the Civil War changed the way later wars were fought?

1. Delivered supplies, carried troops, served as hospitals **2.** Huge armies, limited medical care, deadlier weapons **CHALLENGE** Possible answer: The world wars of the twentieth century were more impersonal, many soldiers were killed, new weapons were used.

Section 4 The End of the War

Words to Know

total war	the destruction of food, equipment, and anything else of use to soldiers and civilians
assassinate	to murder a political leader like a President
veteran	a person who has served in the armed forces

Getting Started Point out that when people are at war, those who do not bear arms are also affected by the conflict. Discuss with students what life might be like after so many people have died and so much land had been destroyed.

After the Union victories at Vicksburg and Gettysburg, the war was still far from over. Lincoln looked for a general to command all the Union armies. In March 1864, Lincoln met with General Ulysses S. Grant. Grant had two main plans for winning the war. He and George Meade would move toward Richmond and attack Lee's forces. General William Tecumseh Sherman would march from Atlanta to the Atlantic Ocean.

History Fact

Most people got their news of the war from newspapers. Although photography had been invented, newspapers did not yet know how to show photographs.

History Fact Matthew Brady, in 1861, became the first person to create a photographic record of a war.

Grant Attacks Lee

General Grant believed that to win, the North would need to use **total war.** Total war means the destruction of food, equipment, and anything else of use to soldiers and civilians. The people of the South would suffer as much as the Confederate soldiers in a total war. However, the Union would be saved, and the war would come to an end.

Grant's troops pushed Lee's army into Petersburg, Virginia, a town about 20 miles south of Richmond. Both sides had already lost many men. Lee's army could not make any advances. All it could do was hold off Grant's troops.

Why was Grant willing to use total war against the South? To end the war and save the Union

Sherman's March Through Georgia

While Grant fought Lee, Union General William Sherman pushed across the South toward Atlanta, Georgia. Atlanta was an important center for railroads and factories. Sherman's troops destroyed Atlanta in November 1864. Much of the city was burned. The people were forced to leave. Sherman then began his march to the Atlantic Ocean.

As Sherman marched across Georgia, Union forces used total war. They tore up railroad tracks, blew up bridges, burned barns, destroyed crops, and killed

Chart Remind students that most of the major battles of the Civil War (6 out of the 8 presented here) were fought on southern soil.

Major Battles of the Civil War

Battle	Date	Place	Description
Fort Sumter	April 12–14, 1861	South Carolina	Opening shots; Civil War declared
Bull Run	July 21, 1861	Virginia	First major Civil War battle; Confederates show strength
Hampton Roads	March 8–9, 1862	Virginia	First major naval battle, *Virginia* vs. *Monitor*
Battle of Shiloh	April 6–7, 1862	Tennessee	23,000 casualties; Union victory
Antietam	Sept. 17, 1862	Maryland	23,000 casualties in bloodiest one-day battle; Lincoln claims victory
Vicksburg	May 18–July 4, 1863	Mississippi	Union victory; the South is cut in two
Gettysburg	July 1–3, 1863	Pennsylvania	Union victory; more soldiers killed than at any other battle
Chattanooga	Nov. 23–25, 1863	Tennessee	Union sends more troops; wins control of key railway center in the South

Chart Study

1. What was the bloodiest one-day battle? Antietam
2. On what date was the first major Civil War battle fought? July 21, 1861

animals. After marching through Georgia, Sherman's troops turned north and began marching through South Carolina and North Carolina. Then they headed toward Richmond.

What happened when Sherman went to Atlanta? The city was destroyed and the people were forced to leave.

Surrender at Appomattox

By the spring of 1865, the Confederacy was beaten. Its armies were running out of troops and supplies. On April 3, Union troops entered Richmond, the Confederate capital. Lee and his men retreated until they were cornered at the village of Appomattox Court House, in central Virginia.

On April 9, 1865, Lee and Grant met at a house in Appomattox Court House. They agreed to end the war. Grant did not believe in punishing the South. Grant and Lee agreed to these terms of surrender.

1. Southern soldiers must give up their weapons.
2. Southern soldiers could keep the horses or mules if they owned them.
3. Southern officers could keep their pistols, swords, and horses.
4. All southern soldiers would be fed.

When Union troops began firing their guns to celebrate, Grant stopped them. "The long war is over," he said. "The rebels are our countrymen again."

What terms of surrender ended the war? Southern troops would give up weapons, keep their horses, be fed

Loss and Change

Five days after the Civil War ended, President Lincoln went to a play at Ford's Theater in Washington, D.C. At the play, he was **assassinated,** or murdered, by John Wilkes Booth who was a Confederate supporter.

Lincoln died the next day, April 15, 1865, of a gunshot wound to the head. In the North, there was great shock and some anger toward the South.

More than 618,000 men were killed during the Civil War. More than 375,000 men were wounded. The Union spent almost $8 billion on the war. The Confederacy spent more than $2 billion. The United States would be paying for the war for many years. In addition, the United States would need to give **veterans**, or people who have been soldiers in war, what the government had promised them.

The Civil War left a lot of the South ruined. Throughout the South, people wandered in search of shelter and food. A lot of land and property had been destroyed. Major cities like Charleston, Richmond, and Atlanta were in ruins. The reunited country would need to begin the work of rebuilding the South.

What were some of the results of the war in the North and the South? President Lincoln dead; million men killed or wounded; lots of money spent; much of the South in ruins

Section 4 Review

1. What were Grant's two main plans to end the war?
2. What did Sherman's troops do on their march to the sea?
3. **Critical Thinking** Why did Grant allow southern soldiers to keep their animals?
4. **Write About Economics** The United States government needed to spend a lot of money to pay for the Civil War. List three or more things the government needed to do. Put a star next to the one that is most important. Explain why.

More Review is provided in Exercise 42 of the Workbook.

1. He and Meade would capture Richmond. Sherman would take Atlanta and march to the Atlantic Ocean, destroying everything along the way.
2. Destroyed Atlanta, tore up railroad tracks, blew up bridges, burned barns, destroyed crops, killed animals
3. Student responses should show an understanding that for soldiers to travel home and resume their lives as farmers they would need their animals.
4. Student responses may include caring for veterans, paying the debt, rebuilding the South. Any starred item is acceptable if students can give a reason for their choice.

Chapter

10 Review

Summary Have students use this graphic organizer to outline the main ideas and details of the chapter.

Summary	The Civil War began in 1861 and ended in 1865. President Lincoln wanted to save the Union. The war cost a lot in lives, property, and money.
Section 1	When the war began, the North and the South each had different strengths. The North developed the Anaconda Plan to defeat the Confederacy.
Section 2	Southern General Robert E. Lee wanted to win the war before men and supplies ran out. The turning point of the war came at Gettysburg. Union forces won. Lee's forces were badly weakened.
Section 3	Both sides were forced to draft men. Lincoln issued the Emancipation Proclamation. African Americans and women played important roles in the war.
Section 4	Union General William Sherman marched through the South, destroying cities, crops, animals, bridges, and rail lines. Lee surrendered to Grant at Appomattox Court House, on April 9, 1865. President Lincoln was assassinated.

assassinated

conscription

veteran

discrimination

More Vocabulary Review is provided in Exercise 62 of the Classroom Resource Binder.

Vocabulary Review

Complete each sentence with a term from the list.

1. A soldier who served in the armed forces is a ____. veteran

2. President Lincoln was ____. assassinated

3. African Americans soldiers faced ____. discrimination

4. The drafting of people for military service is ____. conscription

1. North: Anaconda plan, blockades, split Confederacy in two, and capture the capital; South: hold onto land, hope the North would get tired p.178 2. The North could control the Mississippi River and stop the South from getting supplies. pp.181–182 3. It was difficult to get volunteer troops. p. 185 4. Possible answer: To end the war, hoped freed slaves would leave southern plantations, hoped it would help Union cause p.186 5. For the Union to survive, the North and the South would need to work together. p.192

Chapter Quiz

Write your answers in complete sentences.

1. How did the North and the South each plan to win the war?
2. Why was the Battle at Vicksburg an important victory for the Union forces?
3. Why were conscription laws passed?
4. **Critical Thinking** Why did Lincoln want to free the slaves in the Confederacy?
5. **Critical Thinking** Do you think it was a good idea for Grant to give the South generous terms of surrender? Explain your answer.

Test Tip
A good way to study for a test is to turn section titles into questions. Then look for the answers as you read.

Writing Tip
When writing a paragraph, state your main idea at the beginning. The main idea often answers the questions *who? what? when? where?* or *why?*

Using the Timeline

Use the timeline on pages 174–175 to answer the questions.

1. How many years did the Civil War last? 4 years
2. On the timeline, which two events happened in 1865? Lee surrenders. Lincoln is assassinated.

Group Activity See the Teacher's Planning Guide for a scoring rubric for this activity.

Group Activity

Organize into groups. In each group, some people will represent the South and some will represent the North. Debate if total war is fair. Give reasons for your point of view.

At the end of the Civil War, Richmond, Virginia and other southern cities were destroyed. Confederate states printed paper money, like the five dollar bill shown here. How would this destruction make it difficult for the South to recover? With most cities destroyed, everything had to be rebuilt; it would be costly and take a very long time.

Reconstruction

- **1865** Thirteenth Amendment passed
- **1866** Congress passes Civil Rights Act
- **1868** Fourteenth Amendment passed
- **1868** Ulysses S. Grant elected
- **1869** Fifteenth Amendment passed

1865 — 1870 — 1875

Additional activities and strategies to customize lessons can be found in the Teacher's Planning Guide.

Chapter 11 Rebuilding a Divided Nation 1865–1877

ESL Note To help students understand the concept of reconstruction, remind them that the prefix *re-* means "again," as in the words "rebuilding" and "reconstruction." Point out that after the Civil War the country had to build, or construct, itself again.

Words to Know

Reconstruction

black codes

civil rights

impeach

segregation

carpetbagger

scalawag

freedman

sharecropping

poll tax

Words to Know These words are defined in the section in which they appear, as well as in the Glossary. Point out that the words *carpetbagger, black codes, civil rights, poll tax, freedman,* and *sharecropping* are compound nouns.

Learning Objectives

- Compare the plans of President Lincoln, President Johnson, and Congress for rebuilding the South.
- Identify the Thirteenth, Fourteenth, and Fifteenth Amendments.
- Discuss the impeachment trial of Andrew Johnson.
- Identify how the lives of African Americans changed after the Civil War.
- Explore the feelings of a freed slave after the Civil War.

Project Help students narrow their focus before they begin writing. Some suggestions include the Freedmen's Bureau, black codes, Civil Rights Act, or sharecropping.

Portfolio Project

You are a historian. You write down the stories people tell you about their lives. This week, you visited an African American family in the South after the Civil War. Write one story the family shared. Draw pictures to go with the story, if you wish.

Timeline The timeline is divided into 5-year intervals. The events take place over a period of 13 years. Point out that three amendments to the Constitution were added at this time.

Section 1 Reconstruction Begins

Words to Know

Reconstruction	the time period after the Civil War when the United States began to rebuild the South
black codes	a series of southern laws to limit the freedom of African Americans
civil rights	rights belonging to all citizens

Getting Started Ask students to think of ways to help unite two angry groups who must work together. How would they get them to cooperate and to get over their anger?

After the Civil War, the United States had many problems. President Lincoln was dead. The South was in ruins. In 1865, Congress passed the Thirteenth Amendment to the Constitution, outlawing slavery. President Lincoln had approved it. However, now that the war was over, many people wondered if freed African Americans would gain all their rights.

Lincoln's Plan

Before Lincoln died, he had a plan for **Reconstruction.** Reconstruction is the time period after the Civil War when the United States began to rebuild the South. Lincoln wanted to make it easy for southern states to rejoin the Union. Here is his plan.

1. Southerners had to promise to end slavery.
2. Southerners had to take a loyalty oath before they could be forgiven.
3. Southern states could set up a new government after 10 percent of the voters took the loyalty oath.
4. Property (but not slaves) would be returned to former Confederates who took the loyalty oath.

Under his plan, Lincoln had also suggested that the southern states would give freed African Americans the right to vote.

Under Lincoln's plan, when could southern states set up a new government? Southern states could not set up governments until 10 percent of the voters had taken a loyalty oath to the Union.

Johnson's Plan

After Abraham Lincoln's death, Vice President Andrew Johnson became the new President. Rebuilding the South became his job.

Johnson was a Democrat from the state of Tennessee. He had remained loyal to the Union during the Civil War. However, he had also owned slaves at one time. Johnson's plan for the South was much like Lincoln's, but it did not make southern states give African Americans the right to vote. The states were allowed to decide that for themselves. Johnson's plan also required each southern state to ratify the Thirteenth Amendment, which ended slavery.

President Andrew Johnson

Visual Johnson's family could not afford to pay for his formal education. As an adult, his wife helped him to improve his reading, writing, and arithmetic skills.

What did Johnson's plan require of southern states? Southern states had to ratify the Thirteenth Amendment.

Radical Republicans Disagree

A large group of U.S. congressmen did not like Johnson's plan. This group was called the Radical Republicans. The Radical Republicans wanted stronger action to punish former Confederate leaders in the South. The Radical Republicans also wanted more rights for African Americans. They wanted to make the South give African Americans the right to vote.

While Congress was away from Washington, D.C., Johnson's plan went into effect. Soon, former Confederate leaders formed new state governments in the South.

What did the Radical Republicans want? To punish former Confederate leaders, gain rights for African Americans in the South

The South Under Johnson's Plan

While Johnson's plan was in effect, white southern lawmakers wrote laws called **black codes.** These laws took away many rights of freed African Americans. They could not vote or serve on juries. The black codes made it difficult for African Americans to go to school. They were a lot like the old slave laws.

In some states, black codes kept freed slaves out of good jobs. In South Carolina, the black codes said African Americans had to pay between $10 and $100 for a license to hold any job other than servant or farmer. Most African Americans could not afford to pay for the licenses.

Members of the Ku Klux Klan openly threatened and harmed African Americans.

Visual In this political cartoon, the words "Worse Than Slavery" are drawn on a shield. The cartoonist, Thomas Nast, indicates that KKK lynchings and other acts of violence made life for African Americans worse than it had been during slavery.

African Americans did not feel safe in the South. Some white Southerners formed secret groups to frighten African Americans. One group was called the Ku Klux Klan, or KKK. Members of this group wore hoods to hide their faces. They beat or hanged African Americans and burned their homes and churches.

What happened to African Americans under Johnson's plan to rebuild the South? Lost many freedoms; attacked by secret groups

The Civil Rights Act

The Radical Republicans blamed President Johnson for the passage of black codes and other strict laws. In March 1866, Congress passed the Civil Rights Act. **Civil rights** are rights that all citizens should have. The Civil Rights Act said that African Americans should have the same legal rights as white Americans.

President Andrew Johnson refused to sign the act into law. Instead he chose to veto it. However, Congress was able to pass the Civil Rights Act over the President's veto.

What rights did the Civil Rights Act of 1866 give African Americans? The same legal rights as white Americans

The Fourteenth Amendment

Next, Congress wrote the Fourteenth Amendment to the Constitution. This is what the Fourteenth Amendment said.

1. All people born in the United States are citizens.
2. State governments cannot take away the rights of any citizens.
3. States that prevent any male citizens, including African Americans, from voting will lose representatives in Congress.
4. Former Confederate leaders cannot hold office.

President Johnson was against the Fourteenth Amendment. However, it was signed by most states.

How did the Fourteenth Amendment protect the rights of citizens? States could not take away the rights of any citizens

Section 1 Review

1. How did President Lincoln feel about allowing the South to rejoin the Union after the war?
2. What did the Fourteenth Amendment say about state representatives in the U.S. Congress?
3. **Critical Thinking** Why do you think President Andrew Johnson refused to sign the Civil Rights Act into law?
4. **Write About Citizenship** Write a letter to the editor of a northern newspaper about conditions in the South under the Johnson plan. Explain what you think should be done about it.

More Review is provided in Exercise 43 of the Workbook.

1. He wanted to make it as easy as possible for the South to rejoin the Union.
2. It said that if African Americans weren't allowed to vote, the states would lose representatives in Congress.
3. Student responses may show an understanding that if African Americans had the same legal rights as white people, southern whites might lose political power. Johnson did not seem to want white Southerners to lose power.
4. Student letters should describe the black codes and the formation of secret organizations to frighten and even kill African Americans.

Section 2 Congress Takes Charge

Words to Know

impeach	to accuse a high public official (like the President of the United States) of a crime
segregation	the separation of people by race
carpetbagger	a name for a Northerner who went to the South after the Civil War
scalawag	a name for a white Southerner who supported Reconstruction government

Getting Started Discuss with students why Southerners may have felt like conquered territories, removed from the country after the Civil War. Suggest that students test their predictions as they read.

For almost two years after Abraham Lincoln's death, the southern states were able to remain free of Union control. Under Andrew Johnson's plan, the southern states formed governments like the ones they had before the war. In spite of the Civil Rights Act and the Thirteenth and Fourteenth Amendments, southern laws controlled African Americans. Finally, Congress took charge.

Congress Passes Reconstruction Acts

The Radical Republicans did not feel that Johnson's plan was working. In 1867, Congress passed the first of many Reconstruction Acts. All those states that did not accept the Fourteenth Amendment were under military rule. This meant that the South was divided into five military districts, or regions. United States troops occupied, or controlled, the South.

The act also said that all adult African American males and all qualified adult white males could vote. Whites and African Americans would run the state governments in the South. However, whites who had held Confederate office would not be able to vote or hold office. Whites who supported the Confederacy could not vote. Southern states had to approve the Fourteenth Amendment before they could be allowed back into the Union. By 1870, all former Confederate states had been readmitted to the Union.

According to the Reconstruction Act, who would not be able to vote or hold office in the South?
Whites who had held Confederate office

Congress Impeaches President Johnson

President Johnson did not like the Reconstruction Acts. He said they gave the U.S. government more powers than it should have. Johnson did not want to punish former Confederate officers. He even tried to help them get back their land.

Johnson's actions made the Radical Republicans angrier. Other Republicans in Congress were upset too. They fought back by trying to remove Johnson from office. To do this, they would have to **impeach** the President, or accuse him publicly of a crime.

Johnson was saved from being removed from office by one vote. He finished his term as President, but being impeached hurt his reputation.

Why did the House vote to impeach Johnson?
Johnson's actions made the Radical Republicans angry.

Republican State Governments

Under the Reconstruction Acts, new state governments were formed in the South. Republicans controlled most of them. The Republicans in the South were made up of African Americans, Northerners who moved to the South, and white Southerners who sided with the Republicans.

African Americans voted in large numbers. Many ran for office and won. Mississippi sent two African Americans to Congress in Washington, D.C. They were Hiram R. Revels and Blanche K. Bruce.

Visual Revels was seated in the Senate in 1870. During his term, he supported improvement of education and amnesty for Confederates who swore loyalty to the United States.

Hiram R. Revels was the first African American senator to represent Mississippi.

The Republican state governments passed laws against **segregation.** Segregation is the separation of people by race. However, not everyone followed these segregation laws. The new government also set up public school systems and tried to bring businesses and jobs to the South. The new governments did not have enough money or experience to take care of all the problems of the region.

Who made up the Republican party in the South?
Northerners, African Americans, and white Southerners with Republican ideas

Carpetbaggers and Scalawags

Some Northerners went to the South to start schools, build railroads, or work to protect the rights of African Americans. Some started businesses that provided jobs for Southerners. However, many white Southerners,

A Closer Look

THE IMPEACHMENT PROCESS

The Constitution tells how a President is removed from office. There are two parts. It begins in the House of Representatives, where the President is accused of a crime. The President is impeached if most of the representatives feel he has broken laws. Then the Senate puts the President on trial. If two thirds of the senators feel that the President broke the law, he is removed from office.

Andrew Johnson was the first President in U.S. history to be impeached. In 1998, President Bill Clinton became the second President to be impeached. Both Johnson and Clinton were acquitted, or found not guilty, in the Senate.

This is a ticket from President Johnson's impeachment trial.

Critical Thinking Why do you think the Constitution made it difficult to remove a President from office? To maintain a stable government, keep a balance of power, to keep political enemies from getting rid of a President without good reasons especially former Confederates, disliked the northern newcomers. The Southerners called the Northerners who came to the South **carpetbaggers.** The name came from the Northerners' small cloth-covered suitcases made of carpeting. Many white Southerners felt carpetbaggers were in the South just to make money.

Another group that many white Southerners disliked was the **scalawags.** The word *scalawag* means "liar" or "troublemaker." Scalawags were white Southerners who supported Reconstruction governments. Many of them were business people or small farmers. Former Confederates blamed the scalawags for allowing Northerners and African Americans to hold political office.

Why did many white Southerners dislike people they called carpetbaggers and scalawags? They thought carpetbaggers were in the South just to make money. They thought scalawags were putting Northerners and African Americans in office.

Section 2 Review

1. According to the Reconstruction Acts, who would control state governments in the South?
2. Why did Johnson not like the Reconstruction Acts?
3. **Critical Thinking** How did the impeachment of President Johnson affect his popularity?
4. **Write About Citizenship** Explain in writing why most African Americans supported the Republican party during Reconstruction.

More Review is provided in Exercise 45 of the Workbook.

1. Whites and African Americans, but not whites who had held office in the Confederacy.
2. He said they gave too much power to the federal government.
3. Student responses should show an understanding of lost reputation.
4. Student responses should show an understanding of Republicans' attempt to give African Americans full civil rights. Republicans passed laws giving African Americans the right to vote, take part in the government, and passed laws against segregation.

Section 3 African Americans Work to Build New Lives

Words to Know

freedman	a person freed from slavery
sharecropping	farming someone else's land while paying a share of the crops raised for rent
poll tax	a tax paid before someone can vote

Getting Started Discuss with students the kinds of challenges recently freed African Americans might face. Students should compare their ideas with information they read in the section.

History Fact

In Texas, some African Americans did not find out they were free until June 19, 1865. Once they knew, they celebrated. Today, African Americans in Texas and many other states still celebrate the Juneteenth holiday.

History Fact Juneteenth has been an official Texas state celebration since 1979.

With the end of the Civil War, four million African Americans were free. Some of these **freedmen** had skills they could use to make a living. A freedman was a person freed from slavery. However, most freedmen had no education or jobs. African Americans worked hard to begin new lives. During Reconstruction, Congress tried to help. At the same time, many powerful white Southerners tried to limit the freedom of African Americans.

The Freedmen's Bureau

Lawmakers in Washington, D.C. knew that freed slaves would face problems after the war. A short time before President Abraham Lincoln's death, Congress took action to begin rebuilding the South. In March 1865, Congress set up the Freedmen's Bureau. This bureau was the first federal, or national, office set up to help people in need. It gave food, clothing, and medicine to freed slaves and poor whites. The bureau also helped people find jobs.

The Freedmen's Bureau played an important role in starting schools for African Americans who had been enslaved. Most of the schools were elementary schools. It had been against the law to educate enslaved African Americans. As a result, most African Americans in the South could not read or write. Now they were happy to have a chance to make their lives better through education. One Freedmen's Bureau teacher said of her students, "I never saw children so eager to learn.... It is wonderful how they have so great a desire for knowledge."

By 1869, more than 300,000 African Americans attended Freedmen's Bureau schools. African Americans and poor whites voted and held public office. It looked as though the South really was being reconstructed.

How did the Freedmen's Bureau help African Americans after the war? Gave food, clothing, and medicine to freed slaves; helped them find jobs; started schools

Visual Some of the freedmen who attended schools founded by the Freedmen's Bureau became civic or religious leaders. Others taught at public schools or new universities serving African American students.

Students of all ages attended classes in Freedmen's Bureau schools like this one.

African Americans Look for Jobs

When slavery ended, many African Americans left the plantations to look for family members who had been sold. Couples were married legally, which had not been allowed during slavery. Children went to school, and sometimes their parents and grandparents went too.

Some freedmen found jobs in cities. Often they had to take the hardest and most dangerous work, such as digging wells and laying sewers. Many African Americans wanted to be their own boss. They did not want to work for former slaveholders. Some African Americans did buy their own land, but most could not afford it.

What kinds of jobs were open to African Americans in southern cities after the war? The lowest-paid, most dangerous jobs

History Fact

Part of the Radical Republicans' plan was to give all freedmen "forty acres and a mule." President Johnson did not approve the plan.

History Fact The Radical Republicans had given some freedmen abandoned property from southern landowners. President Johnson ordered that the tens of thousands of freedmen be evicted from the land.

Sharecropping

Many African Americans had to return to the plantations where they had been enslaved. White landowners still needed workers on their farms. Many landowners were too poor after the war to pay their workers. A system of farming called **sharecropping** developed. In this system, a person farmed the landowner's land and paid a share of the harvest for rent. The person doing the work was called a sharecropper. Usually the sharecropper had to buy seed, tools, food, clothing, and many other things from the landowner.

Sharecroppers led hard lives. Often, at harvest time their share of the crop was just enough to pay for rent and food. Without money to pay for anything else, they had to buy what they needed on credit. Credit is buying things with the promise to pay later. In many ways, sharecropping was not much better than slavery.

How did the system of sharecropping work? A person or family farmed someone else's land and paid a share of the harvest for rent

The Fifteenth Amendment

Many white Southerners refused to accept that slavery had ended. They hated the power that the federal government had over the South. Because of those angry feelings, some white Southerners kept fighting the changes that were brought on by the end of the war.

Leaders in Congress worried that African Americans were losing their legal rights. In 1869, Congress passed the Fifteenth Amendment, which said that the right of a person to vote could not be denied "on account of race, color, or previous conditions of servitude." Congress also passed a law against the Ku Klux Klan.

What did the Fifteenth Amendment say? People could not be denied the right to vote because of race, color, or having been enslaved.

Reconstruction Ends

Military leader Ulysses S. Grant was elected President in 1868. As a Republican, Grant had supported Reconstruction. By 1868, many Northerners lost interest in Reconstruction. People worried more about the economy. By the early 1870s, all southern states had rejoined the Union. Radical Republicans had lost power. When Grant was reelected in 1872, he no longer wanted to keep federal troops in the South.

Remember
Ulysses S. Grant was the commanding general of the Union forces during the Civil War.

In 1876, Republican Rutherford Hayes ran against Democrat Samuel Tilden in the presidential election. The election was very close. Congress formed a special committee to decide the winner. The committee said that Hayes won the election. Hayes promised that when he became President, he would withdraw federal troops from the South. Hayes kept that promise. Federal troops were removed from the South. When this happened, Reconstruction came to an end.

Why did Reconstruction end? Radical Republicans lost power. Hayes withdrew federal troops from the South.

Taking Away African American Rights

White southern Democrats took control of the state governments. By the early 1880s, state lawmakers began to take away African American rights. They passed **poll taxes.** A poll tax is a tax paid before someone can vote. This meant that African Americans had to pay money to vote. Southern lawmakers also passed segregation or Jim Crow laws to keep white and African American people separate. Whites and African Americans were separated in schools, restaurants, hospitals, hotels, and on trains.

African Americans lived in fear. Innocent people were lynched, or hanged, for crimes they had not committed.

Segregation was dividing the South into two worlds, one white and one African American. In the North discrimination and segregation were present too. It would be a very long time before African Americans gained their full civil rights.

How did southern white lawmakers take away the rights of African Americans? Took away voting rights, passed segregation laws

Section 3 Review

1. What did most African Americans do after they were freed?
2. How did the end of Reconstruction affect whites and African Americans in the South?
3. **Critical Thinking** Do you think sharecropping was a good system for landowners? Why or why not?
4. **Write About History** Create a newspaper story that talks about the Freedmen's Bureau.

More Review is provided in Exercise 46 of the Workbook.

1. Leave plantations, go to school, look for lost family members, get legally married, find jobs
2. Whites gained power. African Americans lost rights they gained during Reconstruction.
3. Student responses should mention that landowners benefited financially at the expense of African Americans.
4. Students' answers should include provided food, clothing, medicine, and help with finding jobs; opened schools.

VOICES FROM THE PAST
Tempie Cummins

After the Civil War, some enslaved people did not know that they had been freed. Once they were told they were free, many former slaves did not know what to do. Some had no food, jobs, homes, or protection.

Tempie Cummins was a young slave from Texas. The slaveholder tried to keep news of freedom from his slaves. He needed the slaves to stay on to harvest his crops. However, Cummins's mother discovered the slaveholder's secret plans. She risked her life by telling everyone the news of freedom. This is what Cummins said in an interview:

Tempie Cummins, shown here in Jasper, Texas, about 70 years after she was freed.

"Mother was workin' in the house, and she cooked too. She say she used to hide in the chimney corner and listen to what the white folks say. When freedom was [de] 'clared, marster wouldn' tell' em, but mother she hear him. . . . she slip out of the chimney corner and crack her heels together four times and shouts, 'I's free, I's free.' Then she runs to the field, gainst marster's will and tol' all the other slaves and they quit work. Then she run away and in the night she slip into a big ravine [ditch] near the house and have them bring me to her. Marster, he come out with his gun and shot at mother but she run down the ravine and gits away with me."

Answer the questions below.

1. Why did Cummins's slaveholder want to keep his enslaved workers?

2. Why do you think the slaveholder shot at Cummins and her mother?

CHALLENGE What were some difficulties Cummins and her mother might have faced after they escaped?

1. He wanted the enslaved workers to harvest his crops. **2.** To stop them from leaving or to punish them for trying to leave **CHALLENGE** Cummins's mother would need to find a job. She would have to find a home, food, and clothing.

Chapter 11 Review

Summary Have students use this graphic organizer to outline the main ideas and details of the chapter.

Summary: During Reconstruction, the work began to reunite the nation.

Section 1: President Andrew Johnson and the Radical Republicans in Congress disagreed about how to rebuild the South.

Section 2: Congress impeached President Johnson, but he was acquitted and served out his term. Under Reconstruction, African Americans gained rights. White Southerners grew angry.

Section 3: African Americans worked to build new lives. The Freedmen's Bureau helped them get an education. However, many African Americans were forced to become sharecroppers. After Rutherford Hayes's election, Reconstruction ended.

- carpetbagger
- impeach
- poll tax
- segregation

More Vocabulary Review is provided in Exercise 68 of the Classroom Resource Binder.

Vocabulary Review

Complete each sentence with a term from the list.

1. To keep African Americans and white people apart, southern states wrote _____ laws. segregation
2. Southern lawmakers made African Americans pay a _____ to vote. poll tax
3. The House of Representatives can _____ a President accused of a crime. impeach
4. Southerners called a Northerner who came to the South a _____ . carpetbagger

1. Both wanted to make it easy for the South to rejoin the Union. pp.198–199 2. To give African Americans civil rights p.201 3. Possible answer: No money, education, land, or job; groups like the Ku Klux Klan; white southern lawmakers took away their rights pp.200, 206–208 4. Student responses should show an understanding of the disagreements between the President and the Radical Republicans. pp. 199–200, 202–203 5. Student responses should show an understanding of the reasons Northerners went to the South. pp.204–205

Chapter Quiz

Write your answers in complete sentences.

1. How were Lincoln's and Johnson's plans to rebuild the South alike?
2. Why did Radical Republicans pass the Civil Rights Act and the Fourteenth Amendment?
3. What made it hard for people who had been enslaved to rebuild their lives?
4. **Critical Thinking** Do you think President Johnson should have been impeached? Explain your answer.
5. **Critical Thinking** If you lived in the North, would you have gone to the South during Reconstruction? Explain your answer.

Test Tip
When you are looking for details in the text, look through the material quickly. Look for names, dates, and facts that will help you answer questions.

Writing Tip
Sometimes you may have to use sequencing when writing a paragraph. This means writing about events in the order in which they happened.

Using the Timeline

Use the timeline on pages 196–197 to answer the questions.

1. When was the Thirteenth Amendment passed? 1865
2. What amendments were added to the Constitution during Reconstruction? Thirteenth, Fourteenth, and Fifteenth Amendments

Group Activity See the Teacher's Planning Guide for a scoring rubric for this activity.

Group Activity

Form two groups. Each group takes one of the following positions: a supporter of Andrew Johnson, or a supporter of the Radical Republicans. Write a short statement describing their position on Reconstruction. Then have each group share their position with the class.

Critical Thinking 1. Northern, southern lawmakers could not agree about slavery in Missouri 2. Decision fit views of white Southerners regarding slavery 3. He thought slaves wouldn't work in southern fields; might increase northern support 4. To prevent states denying male African Americans the right to vote

Unit 3 Review

Critical Thinking

Give one reason why each of the following events happened.

1. Senator Henry Clay suggested the Missouri Compromise.
2. The South favored the Dred Scott decision.
3. President Lincoln issued the Emancipation Proclamation.
4. The Fifteenth Amendment was passed.

Building Your Skills

Use the map on page 161. Write the answers to the questions below on a separate sheet of paper.

1. What is the map about?
   The Compromise of 1850
2. What do the colors in the map key stand for? Colors: Free states, slave states, voters decide slavery issue
3. What does the map scale show?
   How distances on the map represent real distance
4. Name three places shown on the map. Accept areas shown on map

Who Did It?

Write the name of the person who took each action below.

1. He led a raid on the weapons storehouse at Harpers Ferry.
   John Brown
2. She wrote a book that told about the terrible conditions of slavery.
   Harriet Beecher Stowe
3. He led a march across Georgia destroying everything in his path.
   General William Sherman
4. He was the first African American senator in U.S. history. Hiram Revels

Writing an Essay

Answer one of the following essay topics.

See the Answer Key for a detailed answer.

1. Describe the effects of the Fugitive Slave Law on Northerners and Southerners.
2. Compare the effects of the Civil War on the North and the South.
3. Discuss the ways African American lives changed after the Civil War.

Linking Past and Present

Think about the impeachment of President Andrew Johnson in 1868. How was it similar to the impeachment of President Bill Clinton in 1998? How was it different? Students responses may include that the difference was the subject of the impeachment.

Unit Opener Use the primary source to set the tone for the time period.

Unit 4 A Growing Nation

This painting shows a train traveling across the Great Plains. How do you think railroads helped the United States to grow? Railroads made it easier for travel. Population grew in western settlements; economy thrived.

> *"While the old nations of earth creep on at a snail's pace [speed], the United States thunders past with the rush of an express [train]."*
>
> —Andrew Carnegie, one of the richest, most powerful business leaders in the world during the late 1800s

Primary Source Carnegie emigrated from Scotland with his family at the age of 13. His first job paid $1.20 a week. He understood the potential for wealth in the fast-growing country.

Frontier families lived in sod houses which were made of chunks of grass and covered dirt. Frontier families used iron stoves such as the one shown on the right. How would you describe the land? Hills, no trees, flat areas

Westward Movement

1860 | 1865 | 1870 | 1875 | 1880

- **1862** Homestead Act passed
- **1865** Andrew Johnson becomes President
- **1867** The Grange organized
- **1869** First transcontinental railroad finished
- **1876** Battle of Little Bighorn
- **1876** Rutherford B. Hayes elected
- **1877** Chief Joseph surrenders

Additional activities and strategies to customize lessons can be found in the Teacher's Planning Guide.

Chapter 12 Americans Move West 1860–1890

ESL Note To help students understand the concept of the relocation of Native Americans, ask them to relate experiences in which they or someone they know was forced to relocate and start over. In pairs, have students discuss problems and feelings at that time.

Words to Know

transcontinental

prairie

homesteader

reservation

tradition

prospector

boom town

Words to Know These words are defined in the section in which they appear, as well as in the Glossary. Point out to students the word parts of *transcontinental*, *homesteader*, *reservation*, and *prospector*. These parts will help students define the larger word.

Learning Objectives

- Discuss reasons for the first transcontinental railroad.
- Describe how railroads affected the West.
- Identify events that forced Native Americans onto reservations.
- Describe what life was like in mining towns.
- Identify the ways that groups of farmers helped one another.
- Distinguish fact from opinion.

Project Students will be able to begin work on the project after completing Section 3. Students should take notes throughout the chapter to help them prepare their displays.

Portfolio Project

You are one of the first travelers on a journey by train from Omaha, Nebraska, to Sacramento, California. You want to make a museum display describing your trip. Prepare notes that you can use to describe the sights that you see from the train window.

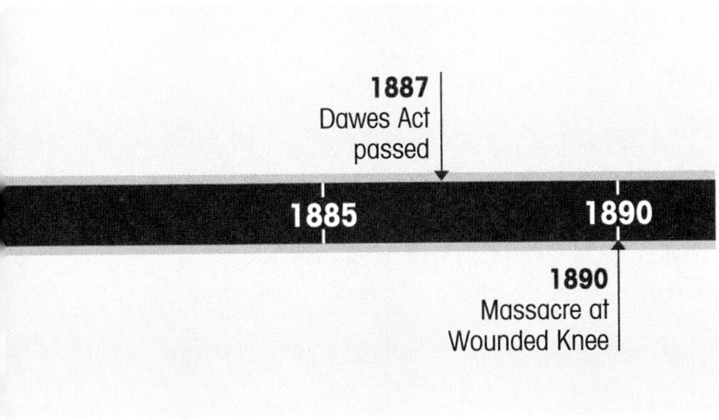

Timeline The timeline is divided into 5-year intervals. The events take place over a period of 28 years. Point out that with the exception of Johnson's and Hayes's election, all the events after 1876 show the struggles between U.S. soldiers and Native Americans.

Section 1 Joining the Nation Together

Words to Know

transcontinental	across a continent
prairie	a large area of level or slightly rolling land
homesteader	a person who received land under the Homestead Act of 1862

Getting Started Have students list different kinds of transportation they use. Next to each one, tell how far they could go on each one. Explain how the railroad made it easier to move westward.

In the mid-1800s, most Americans would say that the frontier began west of the Mississippi River. They thought of the land as flat and treeless. Settlers traveling to the West soon discovered that not all areas were flat. When workers began to build a railroad joining the East and the West, they had to cut through mountains.

Building a Railroad

At the start of the Civil War, there were about 35,000 miles of railroad track in the United States. Most of the track was east of the Mississippi River.

For years, Americans had dreamed of a **transcontinental** railway. Transcontinental means across a continent. The railroad would run across the entire continent, joining the east coast and the west coast of the country.

The hard work of joining the two coasts by rail began. One company, the Central Pacific Railroad Company, started building east from Sacramento, California, in 1863. Two years later, the Union Pacific Railroad Company started building west from Omaha, Nebraska.

Each company hired thousands of workers. Most of the workers on the Union Pacific were Irish immigrants.

The Central Pacific workers were mostly Chinese immigrants. Mexican Americans, African Americans, and Native Americans also worked on the huge project.

Building the railroad tracks was hard and dangerous work. Workers on the Central Pacific had to dig around the mountains and sometimes go right through them with only pick axes and shovels.

Finally, on May 10, 1869, the two railroad lines met at Promontory Point, in Utah. There, at 12:47 P.M., workers drove an iron spike into the last railroad tie that joined the two railroad lines. Soon other transcontinental railroads were built. By 1895, many railways crossed the country. Now it was easier for Americans to travel to the West.

Visual California Governor Leland Stanford tried to hammer in the golden spike at Promontory Point. He missed the first time, but hit it directly the second time. Afterward a telegraph message was sent across the country. It read, "Dot. Dot. Dot. . . . Done."

Who were the workers hired to build the transcontinental railroad? Irish and Chinese immigrants, Mexican Americans, African Americans, Native Americans

The transcontinental railroad was completed at Promontory Point in 1869.

Visual Buffalo "chips" were used for fuel because wood was scarce in most prairie locations. Hay twists were also used for fuel. The hay was twisted so it would burn longer when put into the fire.

Pioneer women collected buffalo chips. They used them for soil or fuel.

Settling the Great Plains

The area between the Mississippi River and the Rocky Mountains was a huge **prairie** known as the Great Plains. A prairie is a large area of level or slightly rolling land. The Great Plains looked like an ocean of grass. However, the soil was good for farming and raising cattle and other animals.

During and after the Civil War, the United States government encouraged farmers to move west. In 1862, Congress passed the Homestead Act. It gave men who were at least 21 years old 160 acres of land. The men had to pay $10, settle on the land for five years, build a home within six months, and grow crops. Hundreds of thousands of families began moving onto the Great Plains after the Homestead Act was passed. These people were called **homesteaders.** A homesteader is a person who received land under the Homestead Act of 1862.

What was the purpose of the Homestead Act?
To encourage farm settlement on the Great Plains

Section 1 Review

1. How did railroads help the United States grow?
2. Why did settlers move to the Great Plains after 1862?
3. **Critical Thinking** Why did Congress want people to settle on the Great Plains?
4. **Write About Geography** Draw a poster that encourages settlers to move to the Great Plains.

More Review is provided in Exercise 47 of the Workbook.

1. Railroads joined the eastern and western parts of the United States. They enabled many more people to travel west and settle the Great Plains.
2. To take advantage of the Homestead Act of 1862
3. Student responses should mention that more people meant more taxes and more power in Congress through votes.
4. Student answers should mention the chance to own land, start a farm, raise cattle, good soil.

BUILDING YOUR SKILLS
Distinguishing Fact From Opinion

It is important to tell the difference between a fact and an opinion. A fact is information that can be proved. An opinion is what someone thinks about a subject.

Follow these steps to decide if a statement is a fact or an opinion.

- When you read a statement, decide if the statement can be proved. If it can be proved, the statement is a fact. *Abraham Lincoln was President during the Civil War* is a statement that can be proved.
- A statement that is an opinion may have words such as *believe* or *think, like* or *dislike.* The statement cannot be proved. *Abraham Lincoln was the greatest President in U.S. history* is an opinion because it cannot be proved.

Read statements A and B below and answer the questions that follow.

A. The land now held by the railroads is more than they need. The land should be held for settlers only.

B. By 1872, Congress had given railroads more than 170 million acres of land.

1. Which statement is a fact? How do you know?

2. Which statement is an opinion? How do you know?

CHALLENGE Who might have been the speaker in statement A, a settler or a railroad president? How do you know?

Apply the Skill

Choose two statements from Chapter 12 that are facts. Rewrite each statement so that it becomes an opinion.

1. B; because it can be proved **2.** A; because it tells how someone feels about the railroad land
CHALLENGE A settler; settlers wanted land for themselves

Section 2 Problems on the Great Plains

Words to Know

reservation	public land set aside by the government for the use of a particular group of people
tradition	the handing down of information, beliefs, and customs from one generation to another

Getting Started Discuss with students how they would feel if they were forced to move out of their homes to a smaller area. How would they react if they were prevented from following the customs and ways of life they have always known?

Remember
The Indian Removal Act in 1830 forced Native Americans to move west.

Settlers and railroads changed the land as they moved west. They also changed the lives of the Native Americans who had lived there for centuries. Native Americans were forced onto land that was far from the land they knew.

Broken Promises

Before the Civil War, the U.S. government set aside land on the Great Plains for Native Americans. In the late 1860s, the government decided to allow settlers to live on that land. Lawmakers then set aside small areas of land called **reservations** for Native Americans. A reservation is public land set aside by the government for the use of a particular group of people.

However, many settlers moved onto the land that had been promised to Native Americans. Native Americans did not want to leave the place where they had lived. Their **traditions** were important to them. A tradition is the handing down of information, beliefs, and customs from one generation to another.

During the 1860s, many Native Americans began to fight to protect their land and traditions. In 1864, gold miners moved onto Native American land near Sand

Creek, Colorado. Several hundred Cheyenne and Arapahos were settled there. Soon fighting broke out.

U.S. troops attacked a Native American village at Sand Creek. The Native American chief saw that his village was in great danger. He raised a white flag as a signal that he did not want to fight. However, the soldiers did not stop their attack. Hundreds of Native American men, women, and children were killed.

Many Americans spoke out against the killings at Sand Creek. U.S. lawmakers agreed that the attack was wrong. However, they also said Native Americans in that area of the southern Great Plains had to leave. Native Americans were forced to move to reservations.

What promises made to Native Americans were broken in the 1860s? The right to live on land that had been promised to them

A Closer Look

THE END OF THE BUFFALO

For Native Americans living on the Great Plains, nothing was more important than the buffalo. The huge animals were used for food, clothing, and blankets. However, buffalo were trouble for railroads. Large buffalo herds tore up tracks. They kept trains from moving along the rails.

Hunters were hired to kill the buffalo. "Buffalo Bill" Cody once killed thousands of buffalo in a year. In the 1860s, there were about 160 million buffalo on the Great Plains. By 1890, fewer than one thousand buffalo were left.

Native Americans depended on the buffalo for many things.

Today, buffalo live in national parks. Laws have been passed to protect them.

Critical Thinking Why did Native Americans fight to keep railroads off their land? The buffalo was the source of food and shelter for the Native Americans. Settlers wanted to kill buffalo because they were trouble for the railroads.

Chief Sitting Bull

Visual Chief Sitting Bull distinguished himself as a leader at an early age. He killed his first buffalo at ten years of age. He once said, "In my early days, I was eager to do things, and therefore I learned quickly."

Victory and Defeat

A great battle was fought after the Lakota, a Native American group, moved to a reservation in the Black Hills of South Dakota. In 1874, miners discovered gold on the reservation. Thousands of miners rushed in to take the land.

In June 1876, Colonel George Custer, a U.S. officer, led a group of about 225 soldiers against the Lakota. The Lakota, led by Chiefs Sitting Bull and Crazy Horse, fought Custer and his men at the Little Bighorn River, in Montana. They killed Custer and all of his men. The Battle of Little Bighorn was one of the most famous battles between Native Americans and white soldiers in U.S. history.

It was becoming harder for Native Americans to fight against whites who were claiming their land. By the 1870s, more and more Native Americans were giving up. In 1877, the Nez Percé were ordered to pack up and leave their land. Chief Joseph, their leader, refused. Several battles were fought between the Nez Percé and U.S. soldiers. The months of fighting were hard on the Nez Percé. Finally on October 5, 1877, Chief Joseph surrendered. At his surrender he said, "I am tired of fighting. . . . My heart is sick and sad. From where the sun now stands, I will fight no more forever."

Why is the Battle of Little Bighorn remembered? Native Americans successfully defended their land against Custer and his troops.

Changing Native American Ways

By 1880, most Native Americans in the United States lived on reservations. Because of this, a movement grew to stop the use of reservations. Reformers, such as Sarah Winnemucca, wanted Native Americans to have more rights. In 1887, the Dawes Act was passed. Here is what the Dawes Act said.

1. Native Americans are to be educated.

2. Native Americans are to become farmers.

3. Native Americans can become U.S. citizens.

4. Native Americans cannot sell their land for 25 years.

The Dawes Act, which reformers wanted, did not work. It did not work because Native Americans wanted to keep their own traditions. Also, Native Americans, who had been hunters, did not want to become farmers.

Why did reformers want to change the way Native Americans were treated? They thought Native Americans were being treated unfairly.

Great Names in History

SARAH WINNEMUCCA

Sarah Winnemucca spoke out for the rights of her people, the Paiutes of northern Nevada. She was born in western Nevada around 1844. When she was a child, her family moved to California. There, Winnemucca observed the ways of people who were not Native Americans. She learned their languages, which were English and Spanish.

In 1859, silver was discovered in Paiute territory. Soon war broke out between the Native Americans and the miners. The U.S. Army asked Winnemucca to interpret the Paiute language for them. Winnemucca went to Washington, D.C. There she spoke with President Rutherford B. Hayes. She asked for better treatment for her people.

In 1885, Winnemucca opened a school for Paiute children near today's Lovelock, Nevada. She wanted to teach them their own traditions and the traditions of white people.

Sarah Winnemucca

Critical Thinking Why did Winnemucca want to teach Paiute children their own traditions and the ways of white Americans? She wanted the Paiutes to remain loyal to their culture and to be able to live among white people.

History Fact

Wovoka was a Paiute religious leader. He taught that if the Paiute lived good lives, the white settlers would not disturb them. He preached holding on to Native American traditions.

History Fact Wovoka's Ghost Dance movement inspired the Ghost Dance shirt, which Native American warriors wore in battle. It was believed that the shirts would protect warriors from bullets.

1. As more settlers moved west, they wanted the Native American land for their farms.
2. Chief Joseph felt that his people had already suffered too much to continue the fighting.
3. Student responses should include the fact that the unprovoked murder of hundreds of men, women, and children convinced many Native Americans that they could not win against white Americans.
4. Student responses could include an account of the leaders, casualties, and outcome.

The Ghost Dance

As time passed, Native Americans lost more of their land. In the late 1880s, a Native American leader named Wovoka taught his followers a special dance. The dance was to help the Plains people live peacefully and joyously. The dance was called the Ghost Dance.

In 1890, U.S. lawmakers heard about the Ghost Dance. They believed it was a secret war dance. They ordered all Native Americans in the Plains area near the Wounded Knee Creek to turn over their weapons. As the soldiers began taking the weapons, a shot rang out. The U.S. soldiers opened fire, killing hundreds of men, women, and children.

The deaths at Wounded Knee were the end of hope for Native Americans. Their land and their traditions had almost disappeared. One Native American leader spoke for many Native Americans after Wounded Knee when he said, "I can see something else died there in the mud. . . . A people's dream died there."

What happened at Wounded Knee? More than 300 Native Americans were killed.

Section 2 Review

1. Why were Native Americans forced onto smaller and smaller areas of land?
2. Why did Chief Joseph surrender?
3. **Critical Thinking** What did the words "a people's dream died there," spoken at Wounded Knee, mean?
4. **Write About History** You are a reporter who has just heard about the Battle of Little Bighorn. Write a news story about what happened at the Battle of Little Bighorn.

More Review is provided in Exercise 48 of the Workbook.

Section 3 Life on the Great Plains

Words to Know

prospector	a person who searches for gold, silver, or other valuable minerals
boom town	a camp that grows into a town almost overnight

Getting Started Discuss with students some jobs they might think are exciting. Discuss drawbacks to those jobs.

The wide-open lands of the Great Plains and the West drew many people. Some were farmers who found the rich soil perfect for growing crops. Others were drawn by the chance for great wealth. One chance was raising cattle. The other chance was mining for gold and silver.

Beef Business Grows

Cattle first arrived in North America with Spanish settlers. Later, large ranches were started in the southern part of the United States, especially in Texas. The flat, grassy land was a perfect feeding area for raising cattle. By the mid-1800s, ranchers had turned much of the plains of Texas into a region for raising cattle.

At first, the cattle were raised for their skins. Cattle leather was used in clothing, shoes, and other goods. However, as the country's population grew, more people began to eat beef. After the Civil War, the demand for beef increased.

Cattle became very valuable. A steer that cost $4 in Texas could be sold for $40 in large cities, such as Chicago or New York. Cattle raising became an important industry in Texas.

Why did the beef business grow during the mid-1800s? It was easier to raise cattle; there was a greater demand for beef as the population grew.

Nat Love was an African American cowhand. He won several roping contests in South Dakota.

Visual In addition to taking care of cattle, cowhands were required to feed chickens and milk cows. Many felt these chores were beneath them.

A Cowhand's Life

As the beef business grew, so did the need for workers. Cattle workers were called cowhands. Most cowhands were young men, usually in their early twenties. They worked through dust storms, blazing heat, and icy blizzards. Most of the year, cowhands kept the cattle from getting lost or being stolen. Once a year, cowhands went on a cattle drive. They rounded up the cattle into herds and guided them to towns where there were rail lines. A cattle drive often lasted two or three months. Cattle drives were difficult. Cattle were lost, stolen, or died from disease.

In the mid-1880s, water holes dried up and grasslands turned to desert. Blizzards in 1886 and 1887 killed thousands of cattle. By the end of the 1880s, the cowhand's way of life had disappeared.

Why did the cattle business end? Weather conditions killed thousands of cattle.

A Cowhand's Life on a Cattle Drive

Hours of work	At least 18 hours each day
Food	Fried bacon, boiled beans, biscuits, black coffee
Special clothing	A *sombrero,* or wide-brimmed hat; *chaparajos,* or leather trousers without a seat, worn over ordinary trousers; a *bandanna,* or large colored handkerchief worn at the throat
Sleeping quarters	The ground
Wages	About 25 dollars a month plus all the food a cowhand could eat

Chart Study

1. About how many hours a day did a cowhand work on a cattle drive?
2. About how much money did a cowhand earn?

Chart Point out to students that *sombrero* and *chaparajos* are Spanish words. They show the influence of the Spanish settlers on the cattle industry.

1. At least 18

2. About $25 a month

Mining Towns

In 1858, gold was discovered at Cherry Creek, Colorado, near Denver. As news of the discovery spread, thousands of miners rushed to Colorado. Few people "struck it rich," but Colorado became a mining area.

Map This map identifies cattle trails and mining areas. Point out to students that all the cattle trails originated in Texas and then spread north.

Cattle Trails and Mining Areas, 1870s

Map Study

1. Which cattle trail starts in Texas and ends in Nebraska? Western Trail
2. How many mining areas are in Washington Territory? One

Economics Fact

Not everyone who came to boom towns worked at mining. Some people set up businesses. They sold food, clothing, and tools to miners.

Economics Fact A former enslaved woman named Clara Brown washed clothes and cooked for the prospectors. She invested the tips she received and made enough money to move her entire family to Colorado.

Mining was often difficult and deadly work. Miners worked underground in darkness. Poison gases, cave-ins, and accidents were part of daily life. In the 1870s, one miner out of every 30 died.

Thousands of **prospectors** crossed the Great Plains to the Rocky Mountains to mine gold and, later, silver. A prospector is a person who searches for gold, silver, or other valuable minerals. Prospectors set up camps in what are now the states of Colorado, Idaho, Utah, and Nevada. The camps grew into towns almost overnight. These new towns were called **boom towns.**

How did mining create boom towns? Thousands of prospectors set up camps near mining centers.

Life in a Boom Town

Since boom towns grew quickly, there were no law officers at first. Thieves, outlaws, and dishonest gamblers often broke the law. In many towns, citizens formed vigilante committees. These committees were groups of people who joined together to keep order and punish criminals. However, they did so without any authority. Members of vigilante committees hunted down lawbreakers. Often the vigilantes had lawbreakers hanged or shot without a trial.

The mining boom was over by the end of the 1800s. Much of the wealth from mining in Colorado went to large mining companies. Large companies were able to hire the men needed to dig for gold.

Many men who traveled west to get rich ended up working in mines. Only a few became wealthy. By the end of the 1800s, boom towns and most mines did not exist.

Why did some people in boom towns take the law into their own hands? Boom towns were set up so quickly that there were no law officers at first. Vigilantes took it upon themselves to punish lawbreakers.

The Grange

Farming was more difficult than most settlers thought it would be. The weather was one of the biggest problems. Summer heat, tornadoes, and floods destroyed crops. Another problem was insects.

Families who found life too difficult moved farther west or returned to the East. Those homesteaders who stayed joined together to help one another through hard times. In 1867, they formed a group called the Grange. The Grange held meetings for families to get to know one another. It helped to solve problems that all the farmers faced. Members worked to keep railroad companies from charging too much money to ship farm crops. Smaller markets were set up where farmers could sell their goods to one another.

By the late 1880s, several groups of farmers had formed organizations. These groups used their power to help elect lawmakers who understood farming.

How did the Grange help farming families? It united farmers, brought them together to help each other though hard times.

Section 3 Review

1. Where did cattle raising become a major industry?
2. Why was the life of miners difficult?
3. **Critical Thinking** Why were low shipping prices on railroads important to farmers?
4. **Write About Geography** You are a cowhand in Montana. Write a letter to your family in which you discuss land features, the weather, and ways of earning a living in Montana.

More Review is provided in Exercise 49 of the Workbook.

1. Texas
2. Miners worked underground in dark, hot mines where poison gases, cave-ins, and accidents were common.
3. Student answers should mention that farmers had to pay the cost for shipping their goods to cities.
4. Student responses should mention that Montana is located in both the Great Plains and Rocky Mountains. The summers can become very hot and the winters are very cold. The leading economic activities of Montana are cattle ranching and mining.

Chapter 12 Review

Summary Have students use this graphic organizer to outline the main ideas and details of the chapter.

Summary	Railroads helped the West grow after the Civil War. Settlers turned to farming, ranching, and mining. Native American traditions were destroyed.
Section 1	Work began on the transcontinental railroad. Many workers, including immigrants, helped to build it. The Homestead Act gave land to settlers on the Great Plains.
Section 2	Settlers pushed Native Americans onto smaller areas of land. Some Native Americans fought back. By 1890, the Native American way of life was over.
Section 3	Cattle ranching, mining, and farming were the chief ways of earning a living in the West. Boom towns grew. Farmers joined together for more power.

More Vocabulary Review is provided in Exercise 76 of the Classroom Resource Binder.

Vocabulary Review

Write *true* or *false*. If the statement is false, change the underlined term to make it true.

1. <u>Transcontinental</u> means "across a continent." True
2. A <u>prospector</u> was a person who received 160 acres of land in the West to grow crops. False: homesteader
3. A <u>prairie</u> is public land set aside by the government for the use of a particular group of people. False: reservation
4. <u>Boom towns</u> were built in the West almost overnight. True

1. The railroad would join the east and west coasts of the country. p. 218 **2.** Railroads helped to lure settlers west, which lead to the growth of towns and cities. p. 220 **3.** Gold miners moved onto Native American land. U.S. government gave settlers land that belonged to Native Americans. p. 222 **4.** Possible answer: It would be exciting; there was danger and disorder. pp. 229–230 **5.** Possible answers: Life on the Great Plains was not easy; groups formed to learn from one another and support one another p. 231

Chapter Quiz

Write your answers in complete sentences.

1. Why were Americans so interested in building a transcontinental railroad?
2. How did railroads help the Great Plains and the West grow quickly?
3. Why were Native Americans forced to move to reservations?
4. **Critical Thinking** Do you think you would have liked to live in a mining town in the 1870s? Why or why not?
5. **Critical Thinking** Why do you think farmers on the Great Plains formed organizations?

Test Tip
Before you begin a test, look it over. Try to set aside enough time to complete all the questions.

Writing Tip
You can support the main points in a paragraph with facts and examples.

Using the Timeline

Use the timeline on page 216–217 to answer the questions.

1. In which year did Native Americans win a major battle? 1876
2. How many years after land was given to homesteaders was an act passed that required Native Americans to become farmers? 25 years

Group Activity See the Teacher's Planning Guide for a scoring rubric for this activity.

Group Activity

With your group, write help-wanted ads for these jobs: railroad worker, soldier, cowhand, miner, and farmer. Make the jobs sound exciting, not difficult or dangerous.

In the 1850s, a new way to make steel changed the way buildings and bridges were built. This gear, which is part of a machine, is made from steel. Why do you think making steel is important today?
Steel is a strong material used for buildings, railroads, bridges, and other items such as nails and wire.

Inventions and Industries

1865 — 1870 — 1875 — 1880 — 1885

- **1865** Pullman invents railroad sleeping car
- **1869** Knights of Labor started
- **1872** Westinghouse invents air brake
- **1876** Bell invents telephone
- **1877** Edison invents phonograph
- **1879** Edison invents electric light bulb
- **1884** Grover Cleveland elected President

Additional activities and strategies to customize lessons can be found in the Teacher's Planning Guide.

Chapter 13 The Growth of Industry 1860–1900

ESL Note To help students understand the concept of an indust today's economy in different countries of the world. Review the m difference from an economy that is rural or farming.

Words to Know

patent

pollution

corporation

monopoly

company town

labor union

strike

Words to Know These words are defined in the section in which they appear, as well as in the Glossary. Point out to students that all of these words relate to the rise of big business in the United States.

Lear

- Expl char
- Expl indu
- Identify ways that powerful business leaders controlled the lives of workers.
- Describe how the rise of industries affected workers.
- Explore the ideas of Andrew Carnegie.

Project Direct students to take notes on both sides of the issue as they read through the chapter.

Portfolio Project

Take notes for a speech on social conditions in the 1880s. Choose the point of view of a wealthy business owner or a factory worker. Include reasons why you think social conditions are bad or good.

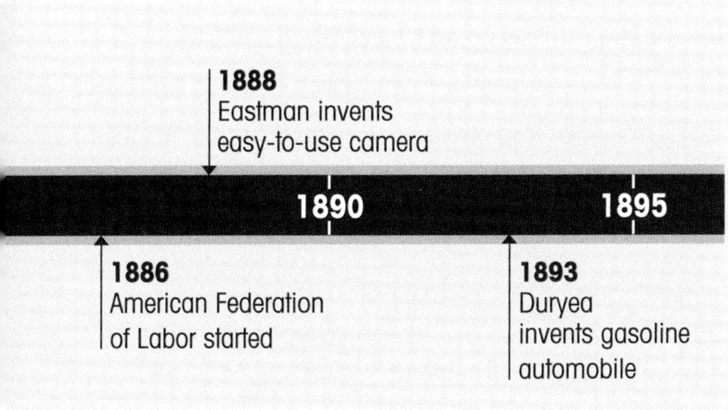

Timeline The timeline is divided into 5-year intervals. The events take place over a period of 28 years. Point out the many important inventions that developed at this time.

Section 1 The Machine Age

Words to Know

patent a government grant that allows only the inventor to make, use, and sell an invention for a certain time

pollution damage to the land, air, and water from harmful materials

Getting Started Have students brainstorm a list of inventions we use everyday. Discuss what might have prompted inventors to create new machines or products.

Thomas Edison invented the light bulb.

Visual Some other famous inventions from Edison's lab include: the stock ticker and a motion picture camera.

Between 1860 and 1900, the United States changed from an economy based on farming to an economy based on industry. Inventions and industry changed the way Americans lived, worked, and traveled.

Inventions and Change

Many changes took place in the United States in the years after the Civil War. Settlers moved to the West. Railroads joining the Atlantic coast and the Pacific coast crossed the Great Plains. Mining, farming, and ranching changed the American way of life.

Other changes took place too. Inventors improved earlier inventions and created new ones. The U.S. government began to give out thousands of **patents** for inventions. A patent is a government grant that allows the inventor to make, use, and sell an invention for a certain time.

How was an inventor's work protected? The government granted the inventor a patent.

A Remarkable Inventor

Thomas Alva Edison probably invented more things than any other person in history. In his lifetime, Edison received 1,093 patents in the United States. This is more than any other person has ever received.

Edison's invention of the electric light bulb in 1879 changed life in U.S. cities. Electric lights on city streets made people feel safe. Large buildings could be lighted with less danger of fire. Rooms and halls without windows were made brighter at night.

Thomas Edison built what he called his "invention factory" in Menlo Park, New Jersey. There, he worked on many inventions. He soon became known as the Wizard of Menlo Park.

Why is Thomas Alva Edison such an important name in history? His many inventions made life better.

Some American Inventions, 1865–1893

Invention	Year	Inventor
Railroad sleeping car	1865	George Pullman
Typewriter (patented)	1868	Christopher Sholes, Carlos Glidden, Samuel Soulé
Air brake	1868	George Westinghouse
Device that oils engines	1872	Elijah McCoy
Telephone	1876	Alexander Graham Bell
Phonograph	1877	Thomas Alva Edison
Electric light bulb	1879	Thomas Alva Edison
Cash register	1879	James J. Ritty
Easy-to-use camera	1888	George Eastman
Ballpoint pen	1888	John Loud
Gasoline-powered automobile	1893	James Duryea

Chart Study

1. Which was invented first, the telephone or the easy-to-use camera?
2. Which inventor made the most inventions between 1865 and 1893?

Chart Discuss which of these inventions are still in use today. Ask what our lives might be like without them.

1. Telephone
2. Thomas Alva Edison

The Brooklyn Bridge, finished in 1883, was made with steel bars and cables.

Visual The Brooklyn Bridge was the first steel-wire suspension bridge in the world. It took 14 years to build and was completed in 1883. It goes over the East River in New York City.

Remember
Gold was discovered in California in 1848. People from all over the world rushed there. They wanted to get rich quick.

The Oil Industry

The oil industry began in 1840. A man observed a thick, dark liquid bubbling up from under the ground near Titusville, Pennsylvania. People in the area called the oil "black gold." At first, no one knew what to do with it.

In 1859, Edwin Drake drilled the first oil well in Titusville, Pennsylvania. People came from all over to drill for oil. It was like the gold rush all over again. Soon people in the area had more oil than they knew what to do with. As the country grew over the next ten years, so did the uses for oil. Oil helped machines run smoothly. It also was used for lighting lamps and heating homes.

What were two early uses of oil? To help machines to run smoothly; for light and heat

The Steel Industry

For centuries, iron had been used for building. However, it rusted easily and was difficult to bend into shapes. Many builders would have used steel, but it was expensive to make. In the late 1850s, an inventor found a way of making iron into steel cheaply and easily. The method was called the Bessemer process. Large factories began turning out millions of tons of steel a year. Steel became the building material used in most tall buildings, bridges, and railroad tracks.

The growth of the oil and steel industries in the late 1800s brought some problems. The owners of the oil and steel companies became wealthy men. Yet, they paid their workers poorly. Workers were often forced to do dangerous jobs.

In addition, the oil and steel industries also caused **pollution.** Pollution is damage to the land, air, and water from harmful materials. Oil that leaked into water and soil poisoned some areas. Smoke from steel plants made the air unhealthy in many places.

Why was the Bessemer process important? The Bessemer process made it possible to make iron into steel easily and cheaply.

Section 1 Review

1. How did patents help inventors?
2. How did the oil and steel industries cause pollution?
3. **Critical Thinking** What were two ways that inventions changed the lives of Americans?
4. **Write About Economics** You are a young worker in a steel plant. Write a newspaper editorial describing your experiences at your job.

More Review is provided in Exercise 52 of the Workbook.

1. It protected their right to their work.
2. Oil leaked into water and soil; smoke from steel plants made air unhealthy
3. Student responses might mention any invention listed in the chart on page 237.
4. Student editorials should mention pollution, low wages, and the feeling of exploitation.

Section 2 The Rise of Big Business

Words to Know

corporation	a large company formed by a group of investors
monopoly	the complete control of an industry by one company or person

Getting Started Ask students to think of a business they might like to start someday. Discuss what they would do to be successful.

This is an advertisement for a Singer sewing machine.

Visual The first sewing machine was invented by Thomas Saint in 1790. He was an English cabinetmaker. In 1851, Isaac M. Singer invented a type of sewing machine that made sewing faster and easier.

The changes brought about by inventions and industry allowed some businesses to grow very large. As businesses grew, they often bought smaller companies in the same industry. As a result, owners of these businesses grew very rich.

Power and Wealth

Until the late 1800s, most businesses were small. Usually there was one owner and a few employees. However, in the last half of the 1800s, business leaders changed the way businesses worked.

One business that grew was the Singer Sewing Machine Company. It had several factories and thousands of workers who made more than one million sewing machines a year. Companies in the railroad, steel, and oil industries were even bigger. The new companies became **corporations.** A corporation is a large company formed by a group of investors.

Business leaders who ran the largest corporations were men of great power. Many people disliked the rich business owners. They felt that the owners had become rich because of the work of low-paid workers. They called the owners "robber barons."

How did many small businesses change in the late 1800s? They grew very large; their leaders became very rich.

Leaders of Big Business

Two of the richest and most powerful business leaders in the 1800s controlled the two most important businesses in the United States. Andrew Carnegie controlled most of the steel industry. John D. Rockefeller controlled the oil industry. Both men came up with new ways of making money.

Many people admired Carnegie and Rockefeller for their success. However, many people who believed that the men's success had come unfairly disliked them.

Andrew Carnegie

When the steel industry was just getting started, Andrew Carnegie built a big steel mill outside of Pittsburgh, Pennsylvania. He had complete control over the cost of making steel. He did not have to pay mining companies, railroads, or shippers to bring supplies to his mills. That was because he owned all the companies that took part in making steel. By the 1890s, Carnegie had many steel mills.

A Closer Look

CAPITAL AND STOCKS

As corporations become larger, they need larger amounts of capital. Capital is money used to run a business. To get the money, many companies sell stock. A stock is a share, or part, of the ownership of a company. People who buy stocks are called stockholders. They have a right to share in the money a corporation makes. They also have the right to vote for a group of leaders to run the corporation.

Stockholders own stock certificates, like this one.

Critical Thinking How might stockholders feel about a wealthy, powerful person running the corporation in which they hold stock? Students should consider the reason stockholders own stock in a corporations.

Oil taken from oil wells was used to make fuel for stoves and lamps.

Visual Some people called oil "black gold." Just as people had tried to get rich quick during the California gold rush, people now searched for oil to get rich quick. Black is the color of oil.

John D. Rockefeller

By the late 1800s, John D. Rockefeller controlled almost the entire oil industry in the United States. Rockefeller named his business the Standard Oil Company.

Rockefeller ran his company by paying close attention to every part of his business. He bought the rights to oil from oil wells drilled by others. He also bought forests for timber to build oil barrels. He even bought ships to carry oil around the world. When he retired, Rockefeller was worth more than $1 billion.

What industries did Andrew Carnegie and John D. Rockefeller control? Carnegie controlled most of the steel industry; Rockefeller controlled the oil industry.

Big Business Grows

For most of the nation's history, Americans wanted government to leave businesses alone. They believed that companies, farms, and factories should be free to make as much money as possible.

Many business leaders in the late 1800s believed that the success of industry meant more jobs for more people. Because many business leaders were wealthy and powerful, lawmakers left industry alone. When businesses continued to grow larger and larger, some Americans became worried. They thought that the government should control big business.

Farmers asked for government action. They complained that they had to pay high costs to ship their goods to markets. However, a wealthy business person like Rockefeller paid less to ship oil on rail lines. Rockefeller could force railroad owners to lower their prices. Farmers could not.

Why did farmers want the government to control big businesses? It was unfair that they had to pay high costs to ship goods, while wealthy business people could force lower prices.

Controlling Big Business

Some people were unhappy when a big business became a **monopoly.** A monopoly is the complete control of an industry by one company or person. For example, Rockefeller had a monopoly on the oil industry. A powerful monopoly could control prices.

In the late 1880s, U.S. lawmakers took some steps to control big business. Here are some of the laws that Congress passed.

1. Railroads that traveled through several states had to set prices that were fair to everyone.
2. Railroads had to make the prices they charged public so that everyone would know how much they charged.
3. Large companies could not interfere with the business of smaller companies.

Many people agreed with the ideas behind the new laws. However, making the laws work against wealthy and powerful business leaders was difficult.

How did the government try to control big business?
Set fair railroad prices, publicized prices, protected smaller companies from larger companies

Section 2 Review

1. Why did some people call rich, powerful businessmen "robber barons"?
2. How did John D. Rockefeller run his business?
3. **Critical Thinking** Do you think big business helps or hurts industries? Explain.
4. **Write About Economics** You are a farmer about to speak to lawmakers. Write a short speech giving your opinion of monopolies.

More Review is provided in Exercise 54 of the Workbook.

1. They thought big business owners became rich as a result of the work of low-paid workers.
2. Rockefeller paid close attention to every detail of his business.
3. Student answers might mention big businesses can produce goods more cheaply and thereby sell goods to customers for less than small businesses.
4. Student speeches might mention that big businesses control the prices of shipping goods to market, keep the small farmers poor.

VOICES FROM THE PAST
Andrew Carnegie

Andrew Carnegie

Andrew Carnegie was born in Scotland in 1835. When he was 12, his family moved to the United States. They settled near Pittsburgh, Pennsylvania. By the time he was 30, Carnegie was a millionaire. In "How I Served My Apprenticeship," Carnegie describes his first job.

"My father entered a cotton factory. I soon followed, and served as a 'bobbin-boy' . . .

For a lad of twelve to rise and [eat] breakfast every morning, except the blessed Sunday morning, and go into the streets and find his way to the factory and begin work while it was still dark outside, and not be released until after darkness came again in the evening, [with a] forty minutes' [break] only being allowed at noon, was a terrible task.

But I was young and had my dreams, and something within [me] always told me that this would not, could not, should not last—I should some day get into a better position. Besides this, I felt myself no longer a mere boy, but quite a little man, and this made me happy."

1. What was Carnegie's first job?

2. How did Carnegie describe his walk to work?

CHALLENGE What advice do you think Carnegie might have given to a young worker at his steel company?

1. He was a "bobbin-boy" in a cotton factory. **2.** It was in the very early morning hours while it was still dark. **CHALLENGE** Student responses might mention not giving up your dreams and working to make yourself a better person.

Section 3 The Work Force

Words to Know

company town	a community set up and run by a company for its workers
labor union	a group of workers that tries to help its members
strike	to refuse to work until certain demands, such as higher wages or better working conditions, are met

Getting Started Discuss the ways workers in the United States today are protected from poor working conditions such as poor ventilation or working in buildings that are fire hazards. Explain that workers' conditions in the late 1800s led to unrest and the formation of labor unions.

One reason that industries grew quickly was that there was a big supply of workers. By 1880, nearly five million men, women, and children worked in factories and at other jobs. Most workers faced terrible conditions on the job every day.

Poor Working Conditions

By the late 1800s, many workers worked 12-hour shifts. As they left at the end of their shift, another group came to work.

Working conditions in most factories were unsafe. Factories had poor lighting and little fresh air. Poor lighting and unsafe machinery were often the cause of accidents. Air pollution could mean illness or even death to workers.

Workers had few rights. If they became ill at work or were injured, they lost their jobs. The owners of factories or mills simply hired new workers. However, for most workers, a dangerous job was better than no job at all.

What made working conditions dangerous in factories? Poor lighting, unsafe machinery, and air pollution

Company Towns

In some places, especially in coal-mining areas, workers were forced to live in company-owned houses. The houses were part of communities known as **company towns.** A company town was a community set up and run by a company for its workers.

In company towns, workers had to give some of their wages as rent for the company houses they lived in. They could only shop at the company stores. Part of their pay was in scrip. Scrip was paper that could be used only to pay for goods in company stores.

Workers in company towns often ended up owing money to the company. If they complained about their jobs or working conditions, they could be fired. Company towns gave companies great control over workers.

What were conditions like in company towns?
Workers had to use part of their wages as rent; shop in company store

New Workers on the Job

Growing industries meant a growing need for workers. At that time, most workers did not need to be skilled to do the jobs in factories. Company owners could pay very low wages to people who badly needed jobs.

Some of the lowest wages did not go to men. They went to women and children. Both of these groups could be paid far less in wages than men.

Inventions of the time did provide new jobs for some women. One invention, the typewriter, created thousands of jobs for women as secretaries in offices. Another invention, the telephone switchboard, created new jobs for women as operators. Most women took jobs in textile mills, food-packing plants, and factories. Women faced the same long hours and dangerous conditions as men but earned much less.

Economics Fact

In 1900, 8.6 million women worked in the United States. By 1910, almost two million children were working.

Economics Fact Although some states had child labor laws, the laws did not apply to companies that did business in more than one state.

New machines did not take a great deal of strength to run. Owners often had very young children run machines. For many jobs, the pay for children was as low as ten cents for an eight-hour day.

There were some laws to protect children in the workplace. However, few officials bothered to make companies follow the laws.

Why did company owners hire women and children?
Company owners could pay women and children less than men.

Workers Join Unions

Some workers decided that the best way to improve poor working conditions was to form **labor unions.** A labor union is a group of workers that tries to help its members. Labor unions try to help their members by seeking higher pay and better working conditions.

A Closer Look

THE BREAKER BOYS

The coal industry often employed young boys called breaker boys. Usually they were under the age of 13. The boys did not work in the mine itself. They sat on hard wooden benches and picked out rocks and other objects from coal as it flowed beneath their feet from long chutes of coal trains.

Often the moving coal would cut their fingers. At the end of the work day, the boys could hardly stand up straight after leaning over the coal all day long.

Today child labor laws would not permit mines to employ breaker boys. A lot has been done to show Americans how serious a problem child labor is.

Breaker boys at a coal mine in Pennsylvania

Critical Thinking Why do you think young boys were used as breaker boys? Student responses should mention that young boys were small and were cheap to employ.

In 1869, a group of skilled and unskilled workers formed a union that they called the Knights of Labor. The Knights fought for the rights of all workers.

At first, many labor unions were small. They did not have much power. Most of the members were workers who did not have skills. In 1886, Samuel Gompers founded the American Federation of Labor (AFL). The members of the AFL were skilled workers, such as carpenters and cigar makers.

Why did workers join labor unions? Workers thought that together they could work better to improve their working conditions.

Violence Breaks Out

If company owners did not improve conditions in the factories, the union members might agree to **strike**, or stop work, until their demands were met. Workers did not earn any pay during a strike. However, if enough workers went on strike, the company owners would not make money either. Sometimes violence broke out between owners and unions.

Haymarket Square Riot

Visual Someone threw a bomb in the incident. Eight men were indicted and convicted for the crime. Four of the accused were hanged. One committed suicide in jail. Three were sentenced to life in prison.

The Haymarket Square Riot

In 1886, union workers in Chicago met in a large group to protest against a company that made farm machines. Union members went on strike to support an eight-hour workday. At the end of the day, strikers attacked workers leaving the factory. Two people were killed. The next day, workers met to protest the police action. Violence broke out and more than 60 people were hurt. Seven police officers died.

The Homestead Strike

In 1892, a manager at Andrew Carnegie's steel mill in Pennsylvania demanded that union members accept lower wages. Union workers went on strike. The company brought in private guards to fight the strikers. Strikers fired on the guards. People on both sides were killed.

The Pullman Strike

In 1894, George Pullman, the owner of a company that made railroad cars, decided to cut workers' pay. However, he did not lower the rents and high prices in the company town he set up for his workers. The workers were angry. They went on strike.

The railroad workers' union joined the strike a month later. All across the United States, railroad workers went on strike. Trains stopped running.

The railroads asked the U.S. government for help. President Grover Cleveland sent troops to take action against the strikers. In the violence that followed, people were hurt and killed. Hundreds of railroad cars were burned.

The violence that broke out did not help the unions. Many workers felt that it was dangerous to be a union member. By 1900, unions had lost much of their power.

How did strikes affect company owners? Company owners would lose workers and money.

Section 3 Review

1. Why did many workers continue to work under the poor working conditions in mills and factories?
2. What inventions made it possible for women to get better jobs?
3. **Critical Thinking** If you were a company owner, why would you be against your employees joining a union?
4. **Write About Citizenship** Explain in writing the effect of violence and riots on strikes.

More Review is provided in Exercise 55 of the Workbook.

1. Workers felt that a job under those conditions was better than no job at all.
2. Inventions of the time, such as the typewriter and the telephone switchboard, enabled thousands of women to work as secretaries or as telephone operators.
3. Unions were run by people who would disrupt your company. Workers could make demands, strike, and cause you to lose money.
4. Student responses might mention that violence and riots not only cause damage to property and people but also breed hatred.

Chapter 13 Review

Summary Have students use this graphic organizer to outline the main ideas and details of the chapter.

Summary: Many inventions between 1865 and 1893 led to the growth of industries and big businesses. Workers formed labor unions to protect themselves and to increase pay.

Section 1: Inventions changed the way that most Americans lived and worked. The rise of the steel and oil industries changed workplaces.

Section 2: Some businesses grew very large. Andrew Carnegie and John D. Rockefeller became two of the richest and most powerful business leaders in the world.

Section 3: Working conditions in factories were poor. Many workers who were forced to work under poor conditions joined labor unions.

patent
pollution
monopoly
company town
labor union

More Vocabulary Review is provided in Exercise 83 of the Classroom Resource Binder.

Vocabulary Review

Write a term from the list that matches each definition below.

1. The complete control of an entire industry monopoly
2. An organization of workers that protects the rights of its members labor union
3. A government grant that allows only the inventor to make, use, and sell an invention for a certain number of years patent
4. Damage to land, air, and water from harmful materials pollution
5. A community owned by an industry company town

1. The streets were safer because there were street lamps; people could light their homes p. 237 2. They created companies that controlled these industries. pp. 241–242 3. Powerful companies enforced strict working rules; intimidated workers; companies owned company towns. pp. 239, 246 4. Possible answer: Managers brought in the police to break up the protests; there was violence; workers lost money pp. 248–249 5. Possible answer: Company towns exploited workers; the owners would profit. p. 246

Chapter Quiz

Write your answers in complete sentences.

1. How did Thomas Alva Edison's invention of the electric light bulb change the lives of Americans?
2. How did Carnegie and Rockefeller gain control of the steel and oil industries?
3. How did powerful companies control the lives of workers?
4. **Critical Thinking** Why do you think workers gained so little from the strikes in the late 1800s?
5. **Critical Thinking** If you had been a factory worker, would you want to live in a company town? Explain.

Test Tip
As you study, make an outline. An outline helps you remember important information.

Writing Tip
When you finish a paragraph, close by stating your main idea in the last sentence.

Using the Timeline

Use the timeline on pages 234–235 to answer the questions.

1. When did Thomas Alva Edison invent the phonograph? 1877
2. How many years after the Knights of Labor did the American Federation of Labor start? 17

Group Activity See the Teacher's Planning Guide for a scoring rubric for this activity.

Group Activity

With your classmates, form two groups. One group is union workers at a steel mill. The second group is the steel mill managers. Have a meeting to debate the mill's decision to lower workers' wages. Make a list of your ideas for the debate.

The Statue of Liberty was one of the first sights many newcomers to the United States saw. Many immigrants brought their belongings in trunks like the one shown. What do you think the sight of the statue meant to them?
Hope; chance for a new beginning

The Age of Immigration

1882 Chinese Exclusion Act passed

1883 Brooklyn Bridge completed

1886 Statue of Liberty erected

1892 Ellis Island opens

1905 African Americans meet in Niagara Falls, Canada

1880 — 1885 — 1890 — 1895 — 1900 — 1905

Timeline The timeline is divided into 5-year intervals. The events take place over a period of 38 years. Point out the events that are associated with immigration.

Additional activities and strategies to customize lessons can be found in the Teacher's Planning Guide.

Chapter 14 Cities and Immigration 1880–1920

ESL Note To help students understand the concept of immigration, encourage partners to share with each other how their family's life or that of someone they know may have changed after coming to a new country. Compare their experiences with the facts presented in the chapter.

Words to Know

ghetto

tenement

skyscraper

nativism

exclusion

migration

racism

Words to Know These words are defined in the section in which they appear, as well as in the Glossary. Point out that the suffix *-ion* means the act or result of (*exclusion*, *migration*) and the suffix *-ism* means the doctrine or theory of (*racism*, *nativism*).

Learning Objectives

- Explain reasons for immigration to the United States in the late 1800s.
- Identify problems and advantages of city life.
- Explain reasons for Asian and Latin American immigration.
- Describe why some native-born Americans disliked the new immigrants.
- Discuss why many African Americans moved to the North.
- Explore ways that technology changed U.S. cities.

1909 National Association for the Advancement of Colored People (NAACP) begins

1910 1915 1920

1911 Triangle Shirtwaist Company Fire

1919 Violence in Chicago between African American and white people

Portfolio Project

Immigrants who arrived in the United States during the late 1880s saw many sights for the first time. Write five journal entries about experiences in the United States.

Project Students can begin work on their project after reading Section 3. To help students get started, have them take notes about things they would experience as new arrivals in America as they read each section.

Section 1 Immigrants From Southern and Eastern Europe

Words to Know

ghetto	a neighborhood where people of the same race, religion, or country live
tenement	an apartment house with poor safety, sanitation, and comfort conditions
skyscraper	a very tall building with many floors, elevators, and a steel frame

Getting Started Discuss with students the positive and negative aspects of life in a city. Explain that, for many new immigrants to the United States during the 1800s, the promise of a new life in the city proved to be disappointing and difficult.

Most early immigrants came to the United States from northern and western Europe. Beginning in the 1880s, immigrants arrived from southern and eastern Europe. These newcomers were different in some ways from the earlier immigrants.

New Immigrants

Fewer than one million immigrants came to the United States between 1790 and 1840. Then between 1840 and the 1870s, most immigrants came from Great Britain, Ireland, and Germany. These immigrants started many of the early customs that became part of the American way of life.

The people who arrived from the 1880s on were often called "new" immigrants. The word *new* was used to show that the immigrants were different in some ways from the old, or earlier, immigrants. The new immigrants came from such countries as Russia, Poland, Italy, and Greece. Most of the new immigrants settled in New York City, New York, or Newark, New Jersey. Other new immigrants went to Cleveland, Detroit, or Chicago.

These newcomers were alike in several ways.

1. Their religions were mostly Catholic, Jewish, and Greek Orthodox.

2. Most of the new immigrants did not speak English.

3. Most new immigrants were used to living and working conditions that were different from those of people living in the United States.

The new immigrants left their homelands for many reasons, just as the old immigrants had. Wars, violence, and religious freedom caused many people to leave their homes. They saw the United States as a place to begin a new life.

In what ways were the new immigrants alike?
Most were from southern and eastern Europe; they were Catholic, Jewish, or Greek Orthodox; few spoke English

Where Immigrants Came From

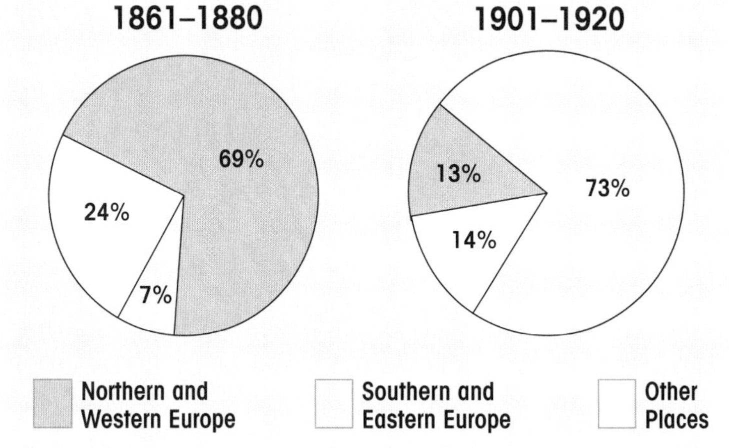

Source: *Historical Statistics of the United States*

Chart Study

1. Between 1861 and 1880, did most immigrants come from northern and western Europe or southern and eastern Europe?
2. Between 1901 and 1920, what percentage of immigrants came from southern and eastern Europe?

Chart Point out to students that the pie charts show immigration shifting from a primarily northern and western European origin to a southern and eastern European origin.

1. Most immigrants came from northern and western Europe.
2. 73 percent

Coming to America

Most of the immigrants entered the United States through New York. Those who arrived after 1892 landed on a small island near the Statue of Liberty. This place was called Ellis Island. There the immigrants were checked for disease. Records of their arrival were kept. Ellis Island became a gateway to America for millions of immigrants for the next 60 years.

Visual So many immigrants passed through Ellis Island between 1892 and 1954 that many Americans today have family members who passed through Ellis Island.

Only a few of the new immigrants ever saw their dreams come true. Most did not speak English. Most were not skilled workers. Many immigrants did not

After arriving in the United States, these immigrants are waiting in a room on Ellis Island.

have enough money to buy land to farm. Most immigrants ended up living in cities and working at low-paying factory jobs.

What happened to most immigrants who came to the United States? They lived in cities and worked at low-paying jobs.

Changing Cities

With the coming of new immigrants, the population of many U.S. cities increased almost overnight. Most immigrants settled in cities, near people from their homeland. They wanted to share their language, religion, and customs with people they knew. Between 1870 and 1920, the number of people living in U.S. cities grew from almost 10 million to more than 50 million.

Often immigrants settled in the parts of a city that were set apart from other areas of the city. The areas in which the immigrants lived became known as **ghettos**. A ghetto is a neighborhood where people of the same race, religion, or country live.

Even though many ghettos were poor places, they were places where immigrants could get used to life in their new country. Getting used to the new life was not easy. Sometimes dishonest Americans cheated the newcomers by charging them higher prices for goods. Often immigrants were targets of hate from people who disliked newcomers.

Why were ghettos important to immigrants in the late 1800s? Ghettos were places where immigrants could share with people from their homeland their language, religion, and customs.

Living in Cities

Cities grew quickly between 1860 and 1900. The rapid growth of cities led to problems. Often there were not enough places for people to live. **Tenements** were built quickly to provide homes for the many people moving

History Fact

In 1890, four out of five children in New York had been born in another country or had a parent who had been born in another country.

History Fact Today one of every five children under the age of 18 living in the United States is an immigrant or has immigrant parents.

to the cities. A tenement is an apartment house with poor safety, sanitation, and comfort conditions.

Usually, tenements were poorly built. Many families were crammed into the buildings. The rooms in tenements were small with little light or air. Tenements were in neighborhoods that were dirty and crowded. There was lots of noise, rotting garbage, and bugs and rats. The unclean conditions led to disease as well.

Unsafe Workplaces

Most of the new immigrants took jobs in factories. They worked long hours for little pay. Workers often found themselves working in poorly lit buildings with little fresh air.

Fire

Fire was always a danger in overcrowded cities. In 1911, a fire broke out in the Triangle Shirtwaist Company in New York City. Workers in the clothing factory could not leave the building quickly because

A Closer Look

THE TRIANGLE SHIRTWAIST COMPANY FIRE

It was a Saturday just before the end of the work day. Fire suddenly broke out on the eighth floor of a building in New York City. Smoke filled the air as flames spread quickly. Frightened women could not get out because the doors were locked.

Firefighters could do nothing. Their tallest ladders only reached the sixth floor. Many women jumped in an attempt to escape. "I thought I saw a bundle of burning cloth falling," said one person. "Then I saw it was a young girl." In the ashes of the fire, firefighters found several engagement rings.

The burning Triangle Shirtwaist Company

Critical Thinking What new laws might have been passed as a result of this fire? Laws that would make buildings safer for workers most of the doors were locked. More than 140 workers, mostly young women, were killed in the fire.

Crime

Crime was a big problem for people living in poor, crowded neighborhoods. Thieves stole wallets and purses. Street gangs often attacked and robbed people. Many cities added more officers to their police departments to fight crime. However, crime rose too fast for the police to control.

While cities had problems, they also had many good points. In the growing cities, people found excitement and new opportunities. Cities had public schools and colleges, museums, libraries, theaters, shops, and sports fields.

The growth of the steel industry and the development of electric power helped to bring taller buildings to cities. **Skyscrapers** rose high above city streets. A skyscraper is a very tall building with many floors, elevators, and a steel frame.

What was city life like? Problems: poor housing conditions, crime, unsafe workplaces, and the possibility of fires; Opportunities: schools, libraries, theaters, shops, sports fields

Section 1 Review

1. What did the new immigrants hope to find in America?
2. Why did most new immigrants settle in cities?
3. **Critical Thinking** What challenges did people in cities have to face?
4. **Write About History** You are a reporter who is at the Triangle Shirtwaist Company fire. Write a news article about the event.

More Review is provided in Exercise 56 of the Workbook.

1. The new immigrants hoped to find a better life, free of war and violence.
2. There were more jobs in cities; chance to be near people from their homeland who settled there
3. Student responses might mention poor housing, crime, fires, unsafe workplaces.
4. Student responses might include a description of flames bursting from the building; the heat; panic-filled faces of workers and spectators; the sight of young women falling to their deaths.

CONNECTING HISTORY AND TECHNOLOGY
Skyscrapers, Streetcars, and Bridges

Before the Civil War, no building in the United States stood more than five stories tall. The first skyscraper was built in Chicago, Illinois. It was ten stories tall. Three things made it possible to build tall buildings.

- Steel frames could hold up the weight of the building.
- New materials could make the building walls fireproof.
- Electric elevators could carry people up and down.

The Home Insurance Building was the first skyscraper.

Skyscrapers made it possible for cities to build *up*. Other inventions helped people to move around cities. For example, before the electric streetcar, people did not travel very far outside the area where they lived. Streetcars powered by electric lines carried people from place to place. People were able to commute, or travel to and from work, over longer distances. Steel was also used to build bridges that carried people into and out of cities.

Answer the questions below.

1. Why were steel frames important in building skyscrapers?

2. How did electricity help people move in and around cities?

CHALLENGE What kinds of transportation have replaced the electric streetcar today?

1. Steel frames could hold up the weight of the building. **2.** Electricity powered streetcars, making it possible for cities to spread out. **CHALLENGE** Electric and diesel trains, subways, buses, and cars

Section 2 Immigrants From Asia and Latin America

Words to Know

nativism	a feeling of citizens who are against immigrants
exclusion	keeping a person or a group from coming in

Getting Started Write the following quote on the chalk board: "We are one and all, immigrants or sons and daughters of immigrants." —President Dwight D. Eisenhower. Discuss the meaning of this quotation.

As immigrants poured into the United States, some Americans feared that they would not fit in with the American way of life. Other people worried that the new immigrants would take away their jobs.

From Asia to America

Almost 300,000 immigrants from Asia arrived during the second half of the 1800s. These immigrants came mostly from China, Japan, and the Philippine Islands.

Chinese Immigrants

Remember
Many Chinese immigrants came to California near the start of the gold rush.

When Chinese workers came to California in 1849, they first found work in gold mines and on farms. As mining jobs became harder to get, Chinese workers found jobs building the transcontinental railroad. When the railroad was finished, most Chinese people chose to settle in San Francisco, California.

Some Chinese immigrants living in cities became factory workers. Others opened small businesses. Still others opened eating places or stores that sold cloth and other Chinese goods.

Japanese Immigrants

Immigrants from Japan were the second group of Asian immigrants to arrive in the United States. Many traveled first to Hawaii, where American businesses owned sugar cane fields. Japanese workers could earn six times the pay in Hawaii that they could in their homeland.

Some Japanese people immigrated to California. They worked on farms. Some worked on railroads or in food-packing plants. Many Japanese immigrants were able to buy farmland. The warm and sunny climate of California was perfect for growing fruits and vegetables. By the early 1900s, some of the fruits and vegetables shipped to the east coast had been grown on Japanese-owned farms in California.

The success of Japanese farmers did not please some Americans. Some newspapers said that Japanese immigrants and other Asians were a danger to the United States. They said that Japanese farmers would take control of American farms. That worried American farmers.

Geography Fact Have students locate the Philippine Islands on the world map in the back of their books.

Filipino Immigrants

The United States took control of the Philippine Islands in 1898. In 1903, the U.S. government invited the first Filipino immigrants to come to the United States. The newcomers were young students. They came to finish their education in American universities.

Geography Fact

More than 7,000 islands make up the Philippines. They are located about 500 miles off the southeast coast of Asia.

The U.S. government paid for their education. The students were expected to go back to the Philippines. They were to become leaders there and teach others what they had learned.

In the early 1900s, most of the Filipino immigrants were men who came to find work, not to go to school. Most Filipinos worked outside under the hot sun. Some worked on sugar cane plantations in Hawaii. Others worked on farms in California. Their plan was to return to the Philippines after they had earned a lot of money.

Where did most Chinese immigrants and Japanese immigrants settle? Most Chinese immigrants: California; Japanese: Hawaii, California

Feelings Against Immigrants

Many Americans wanted to keep Asian immigrants from entering the United States. They believed that the newcomers were taking jobs from them. Immigrants were willing to work long hours for low pay. This led to feelings of **nativism.** Nativism is a feeling of citizens who are against immigrants.

The U.S. government took steps to limit immigration. Lawmakers passed the Chinese Exclusion Act of 1882. **Exclusion** means keeping a person or a group from coming in. This act banned Chinese immigration for ten years.

In 1908, the United States and Japan made a "Gentleman's Agreement." The agreement limited the number of Japanese immigrants entering the United States. Only the children, wives, and parents of Japanese people already living in the United States were allowed to enter.

How did nativism hurt Asian immigrants? Led to the passing of the Exclusion Act in 1882 and the "Gentleman's Agreement"

A Treaty With Mexico

Until 1848, Mexico controlled much of the land in the southwestern part of the United States. In that year, the United States and Mexico signed the Treaty of Guadalupe Hidalgo. The treaty ended the war between the United States and Mexico. The treaty settled the boundary between the United States and Mexico. In the treaty, the United States gained about one million square miles of land.

Many Mexicans continued to live on the land the United States gained. The Mexicans still spoke Spanish. Many of their customs were from Mexico, which was their homeland.

What did the United States gain from the Treaty of Guadalupe Hidalgo? The United States gained territory from Mexico, boundary between U.S. and Mexico settled

Immigrants From Mexico

During the late 1800s, immigrants from Mexico came to live in the Southwest. Most came to find freedom and jobs, like other immigrants before them.

Some Mexicans had family and friends already living in the Southwest. These people got together to help the new immigrants. They helped the newcomers find jobs in the mines of Utah and Nevada. Many Mexicans found work building railroads.

Many Mexicans became farm workers. They worked long hours every day on huge farms, planting and packing crops such as tomatoes, lettuce, and grapes.

What kinds of jobs did the Mexican immigrants find? Jobs in mines, building railroads, farm work

1. In 1903, when the U.S. government invited them to come.
2. The government passed the Chinese Exclusion Act of 1882.
3. They brought new customs and languages, developed different neighborhoods.
4. Student letters should mention jobs found, how they are treated, language and customs.

Section 2 Review

1. When did the first Filipino immigrants arrive in the United States?
2. How did the U.S. government attempt to limit immigration?
3. **Critical Thinking** How did the immigrants of the 1800s change American society?
4. **Write About Citizenship** You are a Mexican immigrant settling in the Southwest. Write a short letter home describing what life is like.

More Review is provided in Exercise 57 of the Workbook.

Section 3 African Americans Move North

Words to Know

migration	a movement of people within a country or area
racism	feelings against people because of their skin color

Getting Started Point out to students that some of them have relatives from other countries. Other students have relatives from states in this country. Discuss why their relatives relocated.

African Americans had first been brought to the Americas as enslaved people. Hundreds of years later, slavery was ended. However, African Americans were faced with discrimination and violence. From the late 1800s to the 1920s, many African Americans migrated from the South to the North.

Leaving the South

After Reconstruction, African Americans faced serious problems in the South. Southern states had passed laws that kept the races apart. African Americans could not vote. Those who protested the laws could be beaten or lynched.

There also were few jobs, poor schools, and violence. This made African Americans look to the North. Between 1890 and 1900, more than 200,000 African Americans migrated from the South to the North. A **migration** is a movement of people within a country or a certain area. By 1920, more than one million African Americans lived in northern cities such as Chicago, Detroit, and New York City.

Once African Americans moved North, they faced discrimination and **racism** there as well. Racism is a feeling against a people because of their skin color.

Migration of African Americans, 1910–1920

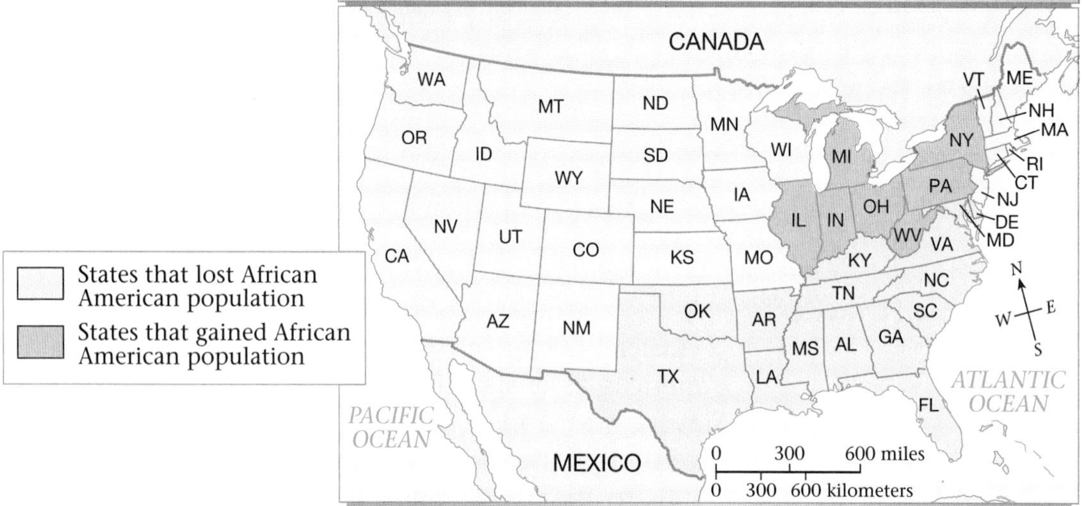

Map Study

1. Which states gained in African American population between 1910 and 1920?
2. Why do you think that most of the states that gained in African American population bordered southern states?

Map Some African Americans moved north because of the promise of better wages and living conditions. Others moved because they had struggled for years in the South to build successful farms.

1. Michigan, Illinois, Indiana, Ohio, Pennsylvania, New York, West Virginia
2. Student responses might include that African Americans did not have the money to travel to faraway states.

African Americans faced other problems as well.

1. Business owners refused to hire African Americans.
2. Business owners who hired African Americans gave them the worst jobs.
3. African Americans were unable to live in neighborhoods where white people lived.

Sometimes the difficulties between whites and African Americans led to violence. In Chicago in 1919, fighting broke out between mobs of African Americans and white people. Thirty-eight people were killed.

How did racism in the North affect the lives of African Americans? Businesses would not hire them; gave them the worst jobs; kept out of white neighborhoods

Fighting for Rights

African Americans continued their fight for equal education. They opened their own schools. Howard University opened its doors in 1867. Hampton Institute opened in 1868. Booker T. Washington, an African American leader, started Tuskegee Institute in 1881.

Another important African American leader was W.E.B. DuBois. In 1905, DuBois and 28 other leaders met in Niagara Falls, Canada. The group decided to protest until they received equal treatment as Americans. However, equal treatment did not come easily.

In 1909, a group of African Americans and white Americans formed the National Association for the Advancement of Colored People (NAACP). This group became one of the strongest groups in the fight for equal rights for African Americans. The NAACP helped African Americans to fight the racism they faced on their jobs, in housing, and in education.

What group helped African Americans fight for equal rights? The National Association for the Advancement of Colored People helped African Americans fight for equal rights.

Section 3 Review

1. How did life for African Americans remain the same after Reconstruction ended?
2. Why did many African Americans migrate north?
3. **Critical Thinking** Do you think the lives of African Americans improved after they moved to the North? Explain.
4. **Write About Citizenship** Write an editorial that may have appeared in a northern newspaper discussing the importance of the beginning of the NAACP.

More Review is provided in Exercise 58 of the Workbook.

1. Even though slavery was abolished, African Americans still faced obstacles in the South. They could not vote and they did not receive equal treatment.
2. There was violence in the South, few jobs, and poor schools.
3. Student responses might mention that African Americans continued to face discrimination and violence as they protested against racism.
4. Students should show an understanding of an organization that openly worked to improve the lives of African Americans. This did not happen before. African Americans now had a place to go for help.

Chapter 14 Review

Summary Have students use this graphic organizer to outline the main ideas and details of the chapter.

Summary: After the Civil War, immigrants arrived in America from many different countries. Cities grew quickly as more people came to the United States. African Americans moved north.

Section 1: Many immigrants from eastern and southern Europe came to the United States after 1880. Living and working conditions were poor. Steel and electricity changed city life.

Section 2: Many immigrants from Asia arrived. They faced nativism. Immigrants also came from Mexico.

Section 3: African Americans living in the South moved north in great numbers, beginning in the late 1800s. They worked together to fight for equal rights.

More Vocabulary Review is provided in Exercise 89 of the Classroom Resource Binder.

Vocabulary Review

Write *true* or *false*. If the statement is false, change the underlined term to make it true.

1. Keeping a group of people out of a country is called <u>migration</u>. False: exclusion

2. People may choose to live in a <u>skyscraper</u>, where they can share the same customs and traditions. False: ghetto

3. Citizens of a country who are against people because they are immigrants are showing <u>nativism</u>. True

4. A <u>tenement</u> may be part of a poor, crowded, run-down neighborhood. True

1. Most immigrated to the U.S. to make better lives for themselves. p. 254 2. Education, jobs, could live in communities inhabited by people from their homeland pp. 257, 259 3. Wanted a chance to work and save money before returning to their homeland p. 262 4. Possible answer: Some Americans might have thought immigrants would take their jobs; Americans might have felt threatened by this. p. 263 5. Possible answer: Some African Americans still had to face racism and still had to fight for their rights. pp. 265–266

Chapter Quiz

Write your answers in complete sentences.

1. In what ways were old immigrants and new immigrants alike?
2. What opportunities did cities offer to immigrants?
3. Why did some immigrants from Asia choose to stay in the United States for a short time?
4. **Critical Thinking** What feelings did some Americans have toward immigrants? Explain why.
5. **Critical Thinking** What struggles did African Americans have after they moved north?

Test Tip
To prepare for a test, list all of the topics you need to review.

Writing Tip
Make sure every sentence has a subject and a verb.

Using the Timeline

Use the timeline on page 252–253 to answer the questions.

1. What two structures changed the way New York City looked in the 1880s? The Brooklyn Bridge in 1883 and the Statue of Liberty in 1886
2. What event controlled the number of Chinese immigrants coming to the United States? The Chinese Exclusion Act in 1882

Group Activity See the Teacher's Planning Guide for a scoring rubric for this activity.

Group Activity

With your group, write five new laws that will protect the health and safety of people living in cities today. Include laws for both living and working areas.

Critical Thinking 1. They wanted to keep the land they had been living on for generations. 2. The country's population grew, raising the demand for beef. 3. He predicted steel would be in demand, began buying small steel companies. 4. Racism, limited rights, sought a better life in the North

Unit 4 Review

Critical Thinking

Give one reason why each of the following events happened.

1. Native Americans fought against U.S. troops.
2. The beef industry grew.
3. Andrew Carnegie controlled almost all of the steel industry.
4. African Americans left the South for northern cities.

Building Your Skills

Write *F* next to each statement that is a fact. Write *O* next to each statement that is an opinion.

__F__ 1. The first transcontinental railroad in the United States was finished in 1869.

__O__ 2. Chief Joseph was the bravest man in the history of the United States.

__O__ 3. Thomas Alva Edison worked harder than any other inventor in the United States.

__F__ 4. Workers in many industries went on strike.

__O__ 5. Asian immigrants wanted to take the jobs of American citizens.

Where Is It?

Write the name of the place where each event below happened.

1. This was the place where immigrants entered the United States. Ellis Island
2. This state was where the transcontinental railroad was joined. Utah
3. Custer's Last Stand took place here. Little Bighorn River, Montana

Writing an Essay

Answer one of the following essay topics.

See the Answer Key for a detailed answer.

1. Describe the treatment of Native Americans by the U.S. government during the 1860s.
2. Identify reasons why the steel industry became important to the United States.
3. Explain how African Americans worked to improve their lives during the late 1800s and early 1900s.

Linking Past and Present

Discuss how some newcomers to the United States today are treated. Point out the differences between treatment today and in the past. Is it better or worse? Explain.

Student responses should mention rights afforded to new immigrants today and that prejudices today may be less overt.

Unit Opener Use the titles, visual, and caption to engage students in a discussion of the time period.

Unit 5 Becoming a World Leader

Ships in the Great White Fleet showed the strength of the U.S. Navy. Why is a strong navy important to a world power? A strong navy allows a country to move weapons and troops anywhere in the world.

> *"There is a [common saying]: 'Speak softly and carry a big stick; you will go far.' If . . . America will speak softly and build . . . a [strong] navy, the Monroe Doctrine will go far."*
>
> —Theodore Roosevelt, speech in Chicago, Illinois, in 1903

Primary Source Theodore Roosevelt was fond of using the West African proverb "Speak softly and carry a big stick; you will go far." He referred to this saying many times in his writings and speeches, especially when discussing his foreign policies. In this excerpt, Roosevelt is expressing his intention to make the United States a strong international power, ready to defend its interests around the world.

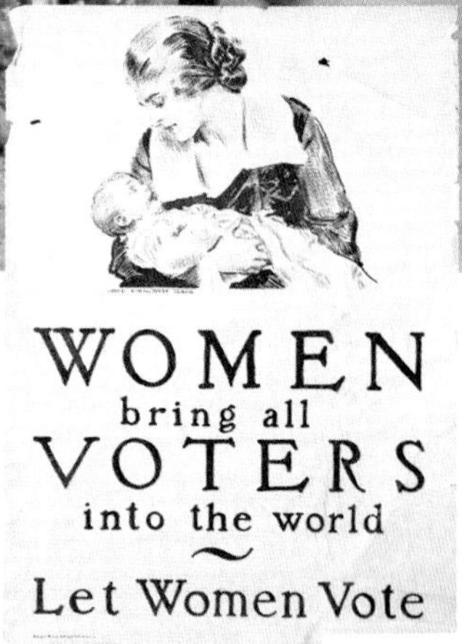

These women tried to gain the right to vote. Posters, like the one shown, were used in the cause for voting rights for women. What did women do to gain support for their cause? Women organized, had meetings, tried to encourage men to join their fight

The Age of Reform

1872 Ulysses S. Grant reelected

1881 James Garfield assassinated; Chester A. Arthur takes office

1883 Civil Service Act becomes law

1884 Grover Cleveland elected

1888 Benjamin Harrison elected

1892 Cleveland reelected

1901 William McKinley assassinated; Theodore Roosevelt takes office

1870 | 1875 | 1880 | 1885 | 1890 | 1895 | 1900

Additional activities and strategies to customize lessons can be found in the Teacher's Planning Guide.

Chapter 15 The Reformers 1870–1920

ESL Note To help students understand the concept of reform, have partners discuss problems that face society today. Explain that in the late 1800s, reformers tried to solve problems in society and correct injustice.

Words to Know

bribe

civil service

kickback

capitalism

muckraker

trust

income tax

Prohibition

Words to Know These words are defined in the section in which they appear, as well as in the Glossary. Point out that the terms *bribe* and *kickback* have to do with using power to help oneself or one's friends rather than working for the public good.

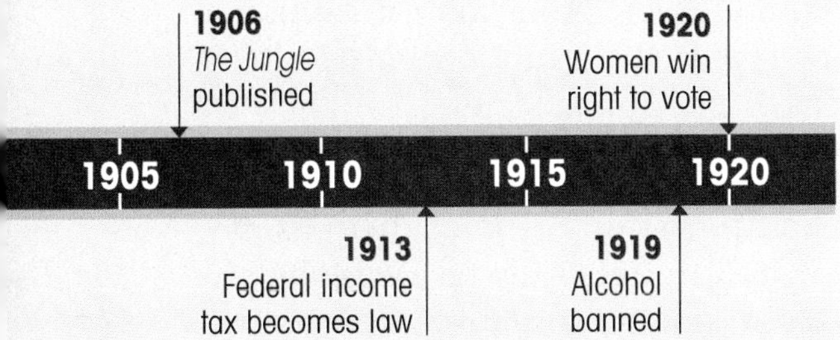

Learning Objectives

- Describe early reforms in business and government.
- Identify the goals of the Progressive movement.
- Explain how muckrakers brought change to government, business, and society.
- Describe reforms passed under Presidents Roosevelt, Taft, and Wilson.
- Discuss the struggle for women's suffrage.
- Identify cause and effect.

Project Have students research the person they chose at the library or on the Internet.

Portfolio Project

This chapter is about people who worked to solve problems in the United States. Choose one person you would like to write about. At the end of the chapter, write an essay about what that person did. Explain how the person helped to change the lives of people in the United States.

Timeline The timeline is divided into 5-year intervals. The events take place over a period of 48 years. Point out the reforms noted on the timeline.

Section 1 Early Reforms

Words to Know

bribe	money paid to get someone to do something against the law
civil service	system that includes most government workers who are appointed rather than elected
kickback	an illegal payment of money made in return for a favor or service

Getting Started Talk about what can happen to people who get too much power.

In the years after the Civil War, the United States grew strong. Millions of immigrants came to the United States to find work in factories, in steel mills, and on the railroad. Yet growth also brought problems. Some people used their wealth and power to change laws for their own gain. On the other hand, many Americans began working to reform, or change and improve, business and government.

The Power of Big Business

The Gilded Age was a time when wealthy people lived very well and spent a great deal of money. Gilded means covered with gold. During this time, many wealthy people did not care about the problems of poor people or society. However, there were problems. Corruption, or dishonesty, was one problem. Corruption spread through many areas of the United States.

During the Gilded Age, some leaders of big business became very rich and powerful. Many of them used their money to do good things. They created jobs, helped poor people, and built museums and other public places. However, a number of very wealthy businesspeople tried to use the government for their own gain. Some of them even gave **bribes** to government officials to get what they wanted. A bribe is money paid to get someone to do something against the law.

Leaders of big business felt that they should have laws that helped their businesses. Usually, they were successful in having laws passed. Some people joked that John D. Rockefeller owned the best legislatures, or lawmaking groups, money could buy. Cornelius Vanderbilt was a business leader who wanted to control the railroads. He bribed lawmakers to pass laws to help his railroads. He did not care if the laws hurt other railroads. Someone once told Vanderbilt he was breaking a law. "What do I care about law?" he asked. "Haven't I got the power?" Vanderbilt spoke for many other leaders of big business.

Remember
John D. Rockefeller controlled the oil industry.

What did some big business leaders try to get government to do? Change laws for their own gain

Corruption in Government

During the Gilded Age, from about 1870 to 1900, many government officials were corrupt. In national, state, and city governments, some officials lied and cheated. Officials took bribes from wealthy business leaders who wanted to control their votes. Officials also bribed voters to vote for their candidates.

There was a lot of corruption in the government of New York City. Some city leaders were called political bosses because they controlled city government. William Tweed was a political boss in New York City. He was called Boss. Like other bosses, Tweed controlled elections by giving gifts, jobs, and favors to voters in exchange for their votes. In return, Tweed got a **kickback.** A kickback is an illegal payment of money made in return for a favor or service.

Tweed also padded, or added to, city bills. He took the extra money himself. In six years, Boss Tweed cheated New York City out of as much as $200 million.

Tweed paid police officers and workers in the mayor's office to keep quiet about his corrupt practices. However, he was finally arrested and sent to jail. After escaping once, he was returned to jail. He remained there for the rest of his life. In time, reformers started new forms of city government that limited the powers of the bosses.

How did big city bosses control elections? By giving gifts, jobs, and favors to voters in exchange for their votes

Civil Service Reform

Remember
President Andrew Jackson used the spoils system when he was President in the 1830s.

Many Americans called for reforms. Some lawmakers decided to reform **civil service.** Civil service is a system that includes most government workers who are appointed rather than elected. During the 1870s and 1880s, civil service jobs were filled according to the spoils system. Government jobs were

A Closer Look

POLITICAL CARTOONS

A political cartoon is a drawing that shows an artist's point of view about an issue. Artists use humor to get their point across. Political cartoons appear in newspapers and magazines.

Thomas Nast created political cartoons about Boss Tweed. Many people in New York City in the late 1800s could not read. They did not know how dishonest Boss Tweed was. Nast's cartoons were easy to understand. After the people in New York City saw Nast's cartoons, they demanded that the police stop Boss Tweed.

In this political cartoon, Boss Tweed shows that he is not afraid of the police.

Critical Thinking Are political cartoons a good way to show opinions? Explain. Yes, because people who can't read can understand cartoons. No, because cartoons do not give reasons or details about the opinions.

given to supporters. For example, a new President would give jobs to people who helped the President get elected.

In the late 1870s, President Rutherford Hayes decided to speak out against the spoils system. However, some lawmakers in Congress decided that they did not want to reform the system.

In 1880, James Garfield was elected President. During his first few months in office, people kept asking him for government jobs. In 1881, a man was angry because Garfield did not give him a job. The man shot and killed Garfield.

After Garfield died, Vice President Chester Arthur became President. In 1883, Congress passed the Civil Service Act, which Arthur eventually supported. The act said that people who wanted government jobs had to take a test. The test would show whether or not job seekers had the skills needed for a certain job. The act provided the basis for the civil service system in place today.

What was the Civil Service Act? Congress required job seekers to take a test for a job. An elected official could no longer reward supporters with jobs unless they were qualified.

Section 1 Review

1. How did Rockefeller and Vanderbilt try to change laws?
2. How did bosses like Boss Tweed cheat cities and make themselves rich?
3. **Critical Thinking** Why do you think some leaders of big business thought they had a right to get what they wanted from government?
4. **Write About Economics** Write a paragraph about the Civil Service Act of 1883. Explain why you think the law is fair or unfair.

More Review is provided in Exercise 61 of the Workbook.

Economics Fact

Today writers, artists, printers, scientists, air traffic controllers, geographers, park rangers, historians, and others have civil service jobs.

Economics Fact The term civil service was first used to designate the British administration in India. It was extended to Great Britain in 1854.

1. By using their money to bribe lawmakers
2. By bribing voters, taking kickbacks, padding bills, and paying people to keep quiet about what they were doing
3. Student responses may include these ideas: They thought what was good for them was good for the country; they were focused totally on their businesses; they had become selfish and self-centered.
4. Fair: Only people with the right skills get the job. Unfair: Officials cannot reward those who worked hard for them.

BUILDING YOUR SKILLS
Identifying Cause and Effect

When you study history, it is important to understand the difference between a cause and an effect. A *cause* is an action that leads to an event. An *effect* is the outcome of the action. Here is an example of cause and effect.

European explorers wanted to find a shorter route to Asia. This is a cause.

European explorers landed in the Americas. This is an effect.

To understand cause and effect, ask why it happened and what happened. *Why* it happened tells you the cause. *What* happened tells you the effect.

Read the following pairs of sentences. In each pair, decide which sentence gives the cause and which sentence gives the effect.

a. Cornelius Vanderbilt wanted to control the railroads. **b.** Cornelius Vanderbilt bribed lawmakers to make laws that helped his railroads and hurt others.
c. Thomas Nast drew cartoons to show his opinions about Boss Tweed. **d.** Many people in New York City could not read.
e. President Garfield was assassinated. **f.** A man was angry because President Garfield did not give him a job.

CHALLENGE Choose the effect from sentences **e** and **f.** Write what happened next.

Apply the Skill

Find another cause and effect in this section. Write a pair of sentences on a separate sheet of paper. Exchange papers with a partner. Discuss what you have written.

a. cause **b.** effect **c.** effect **d.** cause **e.** effect **f.** cause **CHALLENGE** Student responses might point out that Garfield's assassination caused the passage of the Civil Service Act.

Section 2 The Progressives

Words to Know

capitalism	a system in which private businesses, farms, and factories compete with one another to make a profit
muckraker	a writer who brings attention to corruption
trust	a giant corporation, or group of companies

Getting Started Discuss with students a time when they may have worked together with someone or a group of people to improve a situation. For example, maybe they helped to clean up a neighborhood park, or collect money for a cause. As students read the section, compare reform efforts from the Progressive Era with those of the present.

As the 1900s began, the United States faced a number of problems. They included poverty, unsafe working conditions, and unclean food. Some Americans blamed rich people for these problems. Some Americans said **capitalism** did not work. Capitalism is a system in which private businesses, farms, and factories compete with one another to make a profit. Many Americans, called Progressives, thought they could improve the system by working together with government.

Making Improvements

Progressives believed that many problems were caused by the fast growth of industry and cities. They wanted laws to regulate, or control, business and to improve working conditions. They also felt that laws were needed to improve health and education in poor neighborhoods. Progressives felt that these laws would lead to better lives.

Writers became part of the Progressive movement. In newspapers, magazines, and books, these writers brought attention to corruption in business and government.

These men are workers in a meatpacking factory.

Visual *The Jungle* described unclean practices in the meatpacking industry. Upton Sinclair often said that when he wrote the book, he aimed for the heart and by accident hit the stomach.

The writers came to be known as **muckrakers,** or writers who bring attention to corruption. They were named for a character in a novel who spent his time raking up muck, or dirt, from the floor.

Upton Sinclair wrote about unclean practices in the meatpacking industry. Sinclair's book *The Jungle* described what he saw in meatpacking plants. The book sickened and angered Americans.

Ida Tarbell wrote about corruption in the oil industry. She found out that John D. Rockefeller had made secret deals with railroad companies. These deals made Rockefeller's oil cheaper. Cheap prices helped to force other oil companies out of business. This created an oil monopoly for Rockefeller.

Lincoln Steffens wrote about corruption in local government. He showed how bosses took bribes from big businesses to allow them to break safety laws.

How did the muckrakers help the Progressives? They wrote about corruption and unsafe conditions.

Roosevelt and the Coal Miners' Strike

Vice President Theodore Roosevelt became President in 1901, after President William McKinley was assassinated. Roosevelt supported many Progressive ideas.

In 1902, more than 100,000 Pennsylvania coal miners went on strike. They wanted an eight-hour work day and a pay raise. They complained that they were forced to live in company towns. However, wealthy mine owners would not talk to the miners or to leaders of their union, the United Mine Workers.

Citizenship Link

MODERN PROGRESSIVES

The Progressives changed the way citizens thought about their responsibilities. Organized groups of volunteers began to work together to improve their communities.

Workers in a community garden

The National Neighborhood Coalition (NNC) and Habitat for Humanity are both modern-day progressive groups. Both work with neighborhood groups to solve community problems.

The NNC helps neighborhood groups get information about programs that help communities. It also helps them contact government officials. The NNC believes that it is important for the government to work with the people to solve neighborhood problems.

Critical Thinking How are modern progressive groups like the Progressives of the early 1900s? They still believe government should work for the good of the people.

The strike continued for several months. Without coal, there would be no heat. Finally, Roosevelt warned that he would have U.S. troops take control of the mines. That warning forced the owners to talk. The owners gave the miners some of what they went on strike for.

What did Theodore Roosevelt do to end the coal miners' strike of 1902? Warned that he would have U.S. troops take over the mines

Trust Busting and Other Reforms

Some leaders of big business had organized giant corporations, or groups of companies, called **trusts.** President Roosevelt felt that it was against the law for trusts to force smaller companies out of business. Roosevelt took several trusts to court. The courts ordered that the trusts be broken up into smaller companies.

In 1904, Roosevelt was easily elected to office. Roosevelt got Congress to pass laws that cleared run-down areas of cities and made factories safer. Laws were also passed to control the power of railroads and allow health officials to inspect meatpacking plants.

What were some of President Roosevelt's reforms? He broke up trusts, made factories safer, controlled railroads

Section 2 Review

1. According to the Progressives, what was the purpose of government?
2. What did the muckrakers write about?
3. **Critical Thinking** Why did President Roosevelt want to end the coal miners' strike?
4. **Write About History** Write a short essay about Theodore Roosevelt as the first Progressive President.

1. To do good for people
2. Corruption in the oil industry and in local government, unclean practices in meatpacking plants
3. Student responses may show an understanding of the importance of coal for fuel, the plight of the miners, and the need for the President to assert the government's authority over business.
4. Students' essays may emphasize Roosevelt's progressive ideas and tell about the coal miners' strike, trust busting, and other reforms.

More Review is provided in Exercise 62 of the Workbook.

Section 3 Reform Continues

Words to Know

income tax	a tax paid on the money a person earns
Prohibition	a time period when making, selling, and transporting alcohol was unlawful in the United States

Getting Started Remind students that African American men had been legally granted voting rights by the Fifteenth Amendment in 1870. Women, however, had not been given the vote. Discuss why they think women's suffrage took so long.

After Theodore Roosevelt left office in 1908, there were still many reforms that Progressives wanted. William H. Taft and Woodrow Wilson, the Presidents who followed Roosevelt, continued to support reforms in business and government. The Progressives worked for social reforms too. Social reforms affected the way people lived. The Progressives thought social reforms would make life better for poor people, immigrants, women, children, and other groups.

William Taft's Reforms

Visual William Taft was the first President to start the custom of a President throwing out the first ball in the baseball season.

This 1908 campaign poster shows William H. Taft and James S. Sherman.

Theodore Roosevelt did not want to run for a second full term as President in 1908. Instead, he supported William H. Taft. Because most Americans liked Roosevelt, they voted for Taft.

Taft and Roosevelt shared many of the same beliefs about the purpose of government. However, Taft was not as forceful a leader as Roosevelt. Some Progressives felt that Taft made decisions that favored big business. Others felt that he did not do enough to protect the national parks and forests.

However, Taft's four years in office did bring a number of reforms. For example, Taft took twice as many trusts to court as Roosevelt had.

Taft supported a federal **income tax**, or a tax paid to the government on the money a person earns. In the 1890s, farmers and laborers, or workers, had joined together to create the Populist party. This party wanted a federal income tax, with the wealthy paying more than the poor to support the government. The Sixteenth Amendment was passed just before Taft left office. It authorized the federal income tax. Taft also supported passage of the Seventeenth Amendment. It was approved by the states shortly after he left office. It said that U.S. senators must be directly elected by voters, not chosen by state lawmakers.

What were some reforms under President Taft? Took trusts to court; supported income tax, and direct election of senators

History Fact

The Progressive party was called the Bull Moose party because of a remark by Theodore Roosevelt. At the start of the presidential race of 1912, Roosevelt said he felt as strong as a bull moose.

History Fact Theodore Roosevelt also popularized the phrase "My hat's in the ring," during his campaign of 1912. It meant he had declared himself a political candidate. Originally, it was a boxing term, meaning a person was ready to fight.

The Election of 1912

The election year of 1912 was unusual. There were three men running for President. William Taft was the Republican candidate. Woodrow Wilson, the governor of New Jersey, was the Democratic candidate. For the first time, the Progressive party, also known as the Bull Moose party, ran a candidate for President. That candidate was Theodore Roosevelt. Roosevelt decided to run again because he felt that Taft had not been progressive enough as President.

The split between Taft and Roosevelt helped Wilson win. Roosevelt came in second. Many Americans saw the election as a sign that progressive ideas were spreading across the country.

Why was 1912 an unusual election year? Three people ran for President.

Woodrow Wilson's Reforms

As President, Wilson supported business and banking reforms. These are laws passed while President Wilson was in office.

1. There were lower tariffs, or taxes, on foreign goods, to make all goods cheaper for Americans to buy.

2. A graduated income tax began so wealthy people would pay taxes at a higher rate.

3. Price-fixing, or companies working together to raise or lower prices of an item, ended.

4. The rights of unions and workers were protected.

President Wilson started two government agencies that are still important today. One is the Federal Reserve System, which gave the federal government control over banks. Another is the Federal Trade Commission, which gave the federal government power to uncover unfair business practices and take businesses to court.

Many Americans felt that Wilson was good at reforming business and government. However, he was not as strong on social reform. For example, African Americans felt that Wilson treated them unfairly. Under Wilson, government offices were segregated. African American workers had to use separate offices, shops, and rest rooms.

History Fact Rankin served two terms in the House of Representatives. During her second term (1941–1943), she was the only legislator to vote against declaring war on Japan after Pearl Harbor. This unpopular stand ended her political career in Washington.

What were some reforms under President Wilson?
Lower tariffs, graduated income tax, end of price-fixing

Women's Suffrage

During President Wilson's first term in office, he angered many women because he did not support women's suffrage, or their right to vote. In 1916, when Wilson ran for a second term, he came closer to supporting women's right to vote. Women's groups joined a parade to celebrate his victory. However, once in office, Wilson did not act quickly. He did not take action to pass a national women's suffrage law.

As a result, women's groups protested in front of the White House. Some protesters were put in jail. The protests brought the suffrage movement to the attention of the nation.

History Fact

Jeannette Rankin of Montana was the first woman to serve in the U.S. Congress. She was elected in 1916, four years before women were given the right to vote in all states.

Map Point out to students that this map identifies those states giving equal suffrage to women before the Nineteenth Amendment was adopted.

1. 1912

2. Partial suffrage

Women's Suffrage, 1919

Map Study

1. In what year did Arizona became a full suffrage state?

2. Was Iowa a full, partial, or no suffrage state?

President Wilson did not support the suffrage movement. However, women continued to fight for voting rights. Groups such as the National Woman Suffrage Association and the National Woman's Party organized to protest. They went on hunger strikes and walked on picket lines. One woman who led the movement was Carrie Chapman Catt. She argued that women voters were needed to bring about progressive reforms. Catt and her followers decided the best plan was to gain suffrage in each state. They felt this should make it easier to get an amendment passed.

By 1919, 15 states had full suffrage. Women could vote in all elections. In 14 states, women had partial suffrage. That meant women were allowed to vote in state and town elections only. Finally, in 1920, the Nineteenth Amendment gave women throughout the United States the right to vote.

What did the Nineteenth Amendment do? Gave women throughout the United States the right to vote

Prohibition

Many women were against the use of alcohol. They felt that alcohol was a dangerous and deadly drug that destroyed people and families. Since the 1870s, the Woman's Christian Temperance Union had been trying to teach people about the dangers of alcohol. By 1917, many people agreed that something needed to be done.

As a result, in 1919 the Eighteenth Amendment was approved by the states. It made it illegal to sell or transport alcohol in the United States. The time period when this amendment was in effect is called **Prohibition.** Prohibition means "not allowed." During Prohibition, many people obeyed the law. Many others did not. They found secret ways to make, sell, and move alcohol. There was a great deal of money to be made in the unlawful alcohol business. Gangs and crime grew rapidly, especially in cities. In 1933, the Twenty-first Amendment repealed, or did away with, the Eighteenth Amendment. Prohibition ended.

Why were many women united against alcohol?
They said it was dangerous, deadly, destroyed people and families.

Section 3 Review

1. What did the Sixteenth Amendment give the federal government the right to do?
2. Why were African Americans and women angry with President Wilson?
3. **Critical Thinking** Why were the women who worked for women's suffrage unhappy with partial suffrage?
4. **Write About Citizenship** You live in a city during Prohibition. Make a sign to help people obey the law. Remember, some people cannot read. Use both words and pictures on the sign.

1. Allowed government to tax people on their income
2. African Americans were angry because they were segregated from white government workers. Women were angry because Wilson did not support women's suffrage.
3. Student responses should show an understanding that women wanted to vote in all elections, including presidential elections.
4. Signs should include pictures and words and warn people not to make, sell, drink, or transport alcohol.

More Review is provided in exercise 63 of the Workbook.

Chapter 15 Review

Summary Have students use this graphic organizer to outline the main ideas and details of the chapter.

Summary: From 1870 through 1920, Americans with progressive ideas worked for reforms.

Section 1: During the Gilded Age, there was more corruption in big business and government. Some reforms included new forms of city government and testing for civil service jobs.

Section 2: The Progressives believed they could work with government to solve the problems of society. Writers called *muckrakers* called attention to corruption. President Theodore Roosevelt supported progressive reforms.

Section 3: Presidents Taft and Wilson continued progressive reforms. Women led the fight for reforms in suffrage and Prohibition.

More Vocabulary Review is provided in Exercise 97 of the Classroom Resource Binder.

Vocabulary Review

Write *true* or *false*. If the statement is false, change the underlined term to make it true.

1. A kickback is money paid to affect a person's vote. False: bribe
2. Muckrakers wrote about corruption in business and politics. True
3. To get a government job in the civil service, a person must take a test. True
4. President Theodore Roosevelt busted many trusts, or large corporations. True
5. During capitalism, people were not allowed to use alcohol. False: Prohibition

1. Business leaders wanted laws for their own benefit, used bribes, accepted kickbacks, gave jobs to their friends p. 275 **2.** Improve society, solve problems, work for the good of the people p. 279 **3.** The wealthy had to pay more, or at a higher rate. p. 284 **4.** Possible answer: Women wanted better lives for themselves and their families; many wanted the right to vote pp. 285–286 **5.** Possible answer: Civil service reform, changes in city government, income tax laws, right to vote for women, trust busting, changes in food industry pp. 279–287

Chapter Quiz

Write your answers in complete sentences.

1. What were some corrupt practices in business and government during the late 1800s?
2. What did the Progressives, including President Roosevelt, think government could do for people?
3. Presidents Taft and Wilson supported a federal income tax. How did the income tax laws affect wealthy people?
4. **Critical Thinking** Why do you think women were so interested in progressive ideas?
5. **Critical Thinking** Do you think the Progressives were able to bring about change in people's lives? Explain your answer.

Test Tip
To prepare for a test, look for words that show a *cause* and words that show an *effect*.

Writing Tip
Use the words *some* or *many* when writing about something not many people agree with.

Using the Timeline

Use the timeline on pages 272–273 to answer the questions.

1. Which happened first, the Civil Service Act or the federal income tax law? Civil Service Act
2. Which two Presidents took office after assassinations? Arthur and Roosevelt

Group Activity See the Teacher's Planning Guide for a scoring rubric for this activity.

Group Activity

Form groups of three or four. With your group, write a list of reforms you would support for your school or community. Choose one problem to discuss with the class and tell how it might be solved.

The first ship sailed through the Panama Canal in 1914. This is the cover of a souvenir booklet that talks about the canal. How would you describe the canal? Long, narrow

United States Expansion

- **1890**
- **1892** Grover Cleveland elected
- **1895**
- **1896** William McKinley elected
- **1898** Battleship *Maine* explodes in Cuba
- **1900**
- **1901** McKinley assassinated; Theodore Roosevelt becomes President
- **1904** Theodore Roosevelt elected
- **1905**
- **1907** Great White Fleet begins world tour

Chapter 16 Expansion Overseas 1890–1914

ESL Note To help students understand the concept of imperialism, discuss the role they think the United States should play in other countries' affairs. Discuss whether or not the United States should promote democracy in other countries, intervene to stop wars, or aid in times of disaster.

Words to Know

isolationist

protectorate

annex

yellow journalism

imperialism

foreign policy

isthmus

corollary

Words to Know These words are defined in the section in which they appear, as well as in the Glossary. Point out that *yellow journalism* and *imperialism* end with the suffix *-ism* which means "the act or result of." Explain that it is sometimes easier to try to guess the meaning of a word by removing the *-ism* ending.

Learning Objectives

- Discuss how the United States became involved in Asia.
- Explain why the United States needed a port in the Pacific.
- Discuss the role of the United States in the Spanish-American War.
- Describe Theodore Roosevelt's foreign policy.
- Explain why the Panama Canal was built.
- Explore the political views of José Martí.

Project Students may work individually, writing headlines for each event as they read each section. Allow time for students to complete the work after they finish reading the chapter.

Portfolio Project

During the 1890s and early 1900s, most people got the news from newspapers. As you read about each event in this chapter, write a headline about that event. Remember that many headlines of the time were shocking. When you finish reading the chapter, your headlines should tell a story of the main events of the time.

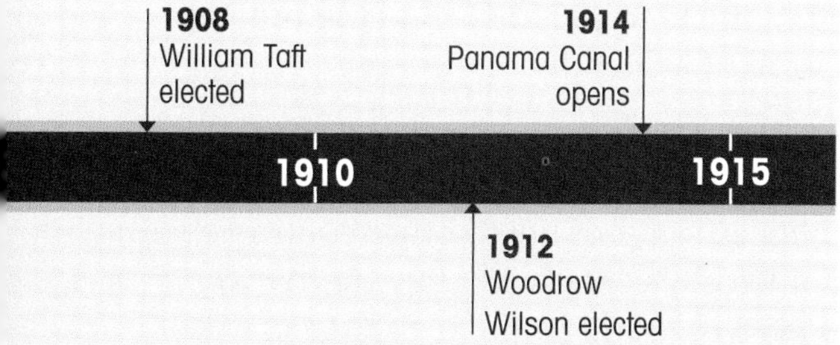

Timeline The timeline is divided into 5-year intervals. The events take place over a period of 22 years. Point out events that cover the emergence of the United States as a world power.

Section 1 Looking Toward Asia

Words to Know

isolationist	a person or country that wants to stay out of the political affairs of other countries
protectorate	a country that is partly controlled and protected by a more powerful country
annex	to add or take possession of a smaller country

Getting Started Have students discuss a time in their lives when they wanted something more or different from what they already had. What happened? Explain that the United States felt that way and began to seek new colonies.

During the 1890s, many Americans began to pay more attention to other parts of the world. Americans had expanded the borders of the United States to the Pacific Ocean. The United States had bought Alaska from Russia in 1867. The West had been settled. Some Americans thought that now was the time to look overseas, especially to Asia. The United States would become a world power through trade and military force.

Different Ideas in the United States

Not all Americans agreed about the need for expansion. Many Americans felt that it was wrong to try to control other countries. Some Americans were **isolationists.** An isolationist is a person or country that wants to stay out of the political affairs of other countries. U.S. isolationists were afraid of being pulled into a war on the side of a friendly country.

However, the number of Americans in favor of expansion was growing. For one thing, some Americans wanted to take American ways of life to other countries. For another thing, a strong feeling was growing that the United States needed to expand in order to increase its economic strength.

Around the nation, farms and businesses were producing more than ever. However, farms were growing more crops than people in the United States could eat. Factories were making more products than people in the United States could use. Farms and businesses needed to sell more of their goods to other countries. It seemed that the United States needed more foreign trade.

What were the arguments for and against U.S. expansion? For: Spread American customs, increased trade; Against: Wrong to control other countries

Opening Trade With Japan

For many years, American businesses wanted to trade with Asia. However, the people of China and Japan had little interest in trading with the United States.

In Japan, ideas about trade began to change during the 1850s. In 1853, Commodore Matthew Perry led U.S. warships to Japan. Perry convinced the Japanese emperor to open the country to trade. Later, a new emperor opened trade to the West even more. Japan began to build factories like those in the West. Japan also began to build up its navy. Now Japan needed U.S. steel and oil for Japanese ships. In return, the United States could buy cloth and other products from Japan.

After Japan became a U.S. trading partner, other Asian countries began trading with the United States. However, thousands of miles separated the west coast of the United States from Asian countries. U.S. ships needed a place in the Pacific Ocean to stop for fuel. U.S. leaders decided that Pearl Harbor was the best stop. Pearl Harbor was a port on Oahu, one of the Hawaiian Islands.

Why did the United States need a port in the Pacific Ocean? So ships could refuel between the west coast of the United States and Asia

Taking Control of Hawaii

Geography Fact

Hawaii is a group of islands in the Pacific Ocean. It is over 2,000 miles from California.

Geography Fact Hawaii's islands are the tops of volcanoes rising from the ocean floor.

Today, Hawaii is a state. However, in the 1800s, Hawaii was a free nation. The climate and farmlands of this island nation were perfect for growing sugarcane plants. Because of that, American planters bought large areas of land from the Hawaiian people. The king of Hawaii gave the United States the use of the Hawaiian port of Pearl Harbor.

American planters in Hawaii wanted to control the government of Hawaii. When Queen Liliuokalani became the ruler of Hawaii in 1891, she did not like the Americans' having so much power over the islands. She did not agree that the United States had the right to use Pearl Harbor.

American planters and traders in Hawaii feared they would lose a great deal of money. In 1893, the Americans led a revolt against Queen Liliuokalani. U.S. Marines

A Closer Look

SEWARD'S FOLLY

After opening trade with Japan, Americans wanted to continue expanding overseas. However, when Secretary of State William Seward purchased, or bought, Alaska from Russia, many people laughed at him. They felt the land was worthless and that Seward's purchase was a foolish act. They called it Seward's Folly and Seward's Ice Box.

The purchase was an important one. Alaska added nearly 600,000 square miles to the area of the United States. Alaska also had natural resources such as timber, furs, oil, and minerals. The discovery of gold in Alaska nearly 30 years later convinced people of the value of the land.

This is a Russian church in the state of Alaska.

Critical Thinking Why do you think Seward felt that buying Alaska was a good opportunity? Americans still believed in Manifest Destiny, and now this idea meant expanding beyond the borders of the United States.

joined the fight against the queen. After the planters won, they asked Congress to make Hawaii a U.S. **protectorate.** A protectorate is a country that is partly controlled and protected by a more powerful country.

In 1898, the United States **annexed** Hawaii. To annex means to take possession of a smaller country. Hawaii became part of the United States.

What did the United States do when Queen Liliuokalani tried to take back control of Hawaii? Led a revolt, made Hawaii a U.S. protectorate.

Relations With China

The United States now controlled a port on the way to Japan. The United States wanted to trade with China, a large country in Asia. During the 1800s, China was a weak nation with little industry. Fighting wars had hurt its economy. A number of nations had divided China into areas where they had control of trade. Countries such as Japan and Russia wanted to make colonies out of their areas in China.

The United States and Great Britain, however, had other ideas. They asked Chinese rulers to make an Open Door Policy for trade. An Open Door Policy meant that all countries should be free to trade with China. The U.S. Secretary of State, John Hay, sent letters called Open Door Notes to all the foreign countries involved in China. Most countries accepted the Open Door Policy.

Many Chinese people did not like foreign countries making decisions for China. In 1900, an organization called the Boxers tried to get rid of foreigners during the Boxer Rebellion. The United States and several other countries used force to end the Rebellion.

The United States was changing. It was starting to play a new, more forceful role in the world.

How did the United States and Great Britain try to open trade in China? By the Open Door Policy, which said that all countries would have a chance for trade in all areas of China

Queen Liliuokalani ruled Hawaii from 1891 to 1893.

Visual Queen Liliuokalani was the last reigning queen of Hawaii. She wrote many songs, including the popular "*Aloha Oe*," and "Farewell to Thee."

The Great White Fleet

Between 1880 and the early 1900s, the United States began to enlarge its navy. If trade with foreign countries increased, the United States would need navy ships to protect its merchant ships.

In 1907, President Theodore Roosevelt wanted to show the world that the United States was becoming a great power. He sent 16 battleships, called the Great White Fleet, on a world tour. At every port, people welcomed the fleet. Around the world, people could see the power of the U.S. Navy.

Why did President Roosevelt send the Great White Fleet on tour? To show the world the power of the U.S. Navy

Section 1 Review

1. What made many Americans think the United States needed more foreign trade?
2. Why did Japan start trading with the United States?
3. **Critical Thinking** Why did the U.S. Marines fight with the planters against Queen Liliuokalani?
4. **Write About Economics** Write a dialogue between two people in the 1890s. One person is an isolationist. The other person supports U.S. expansion. What might these two people say about the Boxer Rebellion in China?

More Review is provided in Exercise 65 of the Workbook.

1. American farms and businesses were producing more than people in the United States could buy, so farms and businesses needed to look elsewhere for buyers.
2. Japan needed U.S. steel and oil to build up its navy.
3. Student responses should show an understanding that the interests of the planters dovetailed with the interests of the U.S. government, which supported increased trade and the need for a refueling stop.
4. Student answers should show an understanding that the reason for U.S. involvement in putting down the Boxer Rebellion was the desire of the United States for trade with China. Isolationists might argue that the United States should not be in China, might side with the Boxers.

Section 2 The Spanish-American War

Words to Know

yellow journalism	the publishing of exaggerated or made-up news stories to attract readers and influence their ideas
imperialism	the policy of one nation gaining control over other lands and using them to build an empire

Getting Started Discuss with students the general reasons why nations might go to war (economic, religious, nationalist). Explain that Americans went to war in Cuba to seek control of the Western Hemisphere.

By the late 1800s, Spain was no longer a world power. Its empire had grown smaller and smaller. In the Americas, only Cuba and Puerto Rico were under Spain's control.

For many years, American leaders were interested in the affairs of Cuba. The island of Cuba was just 90 miles off the coast of Florida. After Cubans rebelled against Spain in 1868, some Cuban leaders, including José Martí, fled to New York City.

Cubans Revolt Against Spain

After the rebellion of 1868, Cubans fought the Spaniards off and on for nearly 30 years. In 1895, José Martí returned to Cuba to fight against Spain.

In the United States, many Americans sided with the Cubans. The Cuban revolt reminded some Americans of their own fight for independence against Great Britain. U.S. newspapers printed shocking stories about what was happening in Cuba. These newspapers practiced **yellow journalism**, or the publishing of exaggerated or made-up news stories to attract readers and influence their ideas.

Why did many Americans side with the Cubans in their fight against Spain? Americans remembered their fight for independence; yellow journalism

Explosion of the Maine

In early 1898, fighting started in Havana, Cuba. President William McKinley sent the U.S. battleship *Maine* to Havana. McKinley wanted to protect Americans in Cuba. However, on February 15, 1898, the *Maine* exploded in Havana Harbor. There were 260 American sailors killed.

Most Americans blamed the explosion on Spain. News stories said that a bomb had been planted on the ship. The headline "Remember the *Maine!*" increased Americans' anger against Spain. Years later, a study showed that the blast had been an accident. However, at the time, Americans were ready to fight. On April 25, 1898, the United States declared war on Spain.

Visual In 1976, Admiral Hyman Rickover of the U.S. Navy reopened the investigation into the cause of the *Maine* explosion. His team of experts believed the explosion was probably the result of a coal bunker fire and, therefore, not caused by an external attack.

Why did U.S. newspapers print the headline "Remember the *Maine!*"? To build up American anger against Spain

This is a picture of the explosion of the U.S. battleship Maine.

Fighting the War

The Spanish-American War lasted for less than three months. The war was fought in the Philippines and in Cuba. In the Philippine Islands, Commodore George Dewey destroyed the Spanish fleet at Manila Bay. Then Dewey sent weapons to a Filipino leader named Emilio Aguinaldo and his followers. Filipino and U.S. forces quickly won almost all of the islands.

In Cuba, Theodore Roosevelt became a hero. He was the leader of a special army unit called the Rough Riders. They won a major battle at San Juan Hill. Soon after, the U.S. Navy defeated the Spanish fleet at Santiago.

When the war ended, Spain was no longer the great power it had once been. The Treaty of Paris ended the war in 1898. It gave the United States control of Cuba and Puerto Rico in the Caribbean, and the Philippines and other islands in the Pacific.

What areas did the United States gain in the war against Spain? Control of Cuba and Puerto Rico in the Caribbean; the Philippines; and other islands in the Pacific

Theodore Roosevelt and the Rough Riders are shown after their victory in Cuba.

Visual Although Teddy Roosevelt had a "rough" exterior, he had a soft side. The "teddy bear" was named for Roosevelt after he refused to shoot an old, injured bear on a hunting trip.

The United States, a World Power

The U.S. victory over Spain made the United States a world power. The United States now controlled lands from the Caribbean Sea to the Pacific Ocean. U.S. control of the Philippines gave American businesses more chances for trade in Asia.

Americans still had mixed feelings about controlling other countries. Some Americans wanted a United States empire like the British Empire. Others were against **imperialism.** Imperialism is the policy of one nation gaining control over other lands and using them to build an empire. Still other Americans did not want U.S. troops to be stationed thousands of miles from home, keeping the peace in faraway places.

How did the United States become a world power? By winning the Spanish-American War

New Responsibilities

As a world power, the United States had to make decisions about how they would govern the areas they now controlled. Often, the decisions did not please the people living in the areas.

Cuba became a protectorate. After the war, the United States kept troops in Cuba. A large U.S. naval base was built at Guantanamo Bay, in Cuba.

At first, the United States gave Puerto Rico limited independence. Then, the Jones Act of 1917 made Puerto Rico a U.S. territory. The United States appointed a governor for Puerto Rico. Puerto Rico could have a representative in Congress. However, the representative could not vote.

A U.S. government was set up in the Philippines. For several years, the Filipinos fought U.S. troops to gain their independence. The Filipinos lost their fight in 1901.

What decisions were made about Cuba, Puerto Rico, and the Philippines? Cuba–Protectorate; Puerto Rico–limited independence; Philippines–limited government

1. The newspapers said the Spaniards had planted a bomb on the *Maine.*
2. In the Philippines and in Cuba
3. Student responses should show an understanding of yellow journalism. Some students may refer to sensational stories about celebrities, violence, drugs.
4. Student paragraphs should show an understanding that the Treaty of Paris gave the United States control over their lands.

Section 2 Review

1. Why did many Americans think the Spaniards were responsible for the explosion of the *Maine*?
2. Where was the Spanish-American War fought?
3. **Critical Thinking** What kinds of stories might be called yellow journalism today? Describe at least two kinds of stories.
4. **Write About Citizenship** How do you think the people of Cuba, Puerto Rico, and the Philippines felt about the Treaty of Paris? Write a paragraph that describes how they might have felt.

More Review is provided in Exercise 66 of the Workbook.

VOICES FROM THE PAST
José Martí

José Martí was one of the most famous fighters in Cuba's battle for freedom. In 1869, at age 16, he had already joined the fight against Spanish forces. He was captured and spent more than a year in jail.

José Martí

From 1881 to 1895, Martí lived mostly in New York City. He wrote poems and news stories about the fight for Cuban independence. Martí's writing was so powerful that Cubans living in the United States began to give money to help the fight for freedom.

In 1895, fierce fighting began again in Cuba. Martí put down his pen and returned to Cuba. He was killed at age 42, a month after joining the fight. Here are some of Martí's most famous words.

"Let us rise up so that freedom will not be endangered [put at risk] by apathy [lack of interest]. Let us rise up for the true republic [country], those of us who . . . with our habit of hard work will know how to preserve it [save it]. And let us place around the star of our new flag this motto [saying]: *With all, and for the good of all.*"

1. Where did Martí do most of his writing?

2. How did Martí's writing help Cuban freedom fighters?

CHALLENGE What do you think Martí meant by the motto "With all, and for the good of all"?

1. Martí did most of his writing in New York City. **2.** Martí's writing was so powerful that people began to support Cubans fighting for freedom. **CHALLENGE** Student responses should show an understanding that the motto probably meant that a free nation would come about through the rising up of all Cubans and that the nation would work for the good of all Cubans.

Section 3 The "Big Stick" and the Panama Canal

Words to Know

foreign policy	the way a country deals with other countries
isthmus	a narrow strip of land that connects two larger-sized lands
corollary	an addition to a document

Getting Started Have students brainstorm a list of people they believe have power and influence in their school, community, nation, or in the world. Discuss how these people came to power. Explain how the United States gained power and influence through trade.

President Theodore Roosevelt believed that the United States should take action in the world. He often repeated an African saying, "Speak softly and carry a big stick." Roosevelt meant that the United States should use the threat of force to carry out its **foreign policy.** Foreign policy is the way a country deals with other countries.

The Need for a New Route

For hundreds of years, ships had to make the long trip around the tip of South America to travel between the Pacific Ocean and the Atlantic Ocean. During the Spanish-American War, it took the battleship *Oregon* 98 days to sail from San Francisco to Cuba. The battleship almost missed the war.

President Theodore Roosevelt wanted to build a canal across Central America that would shorten the trip from the Pacific to the Atlantic oceans. In 1881, a French company tried to build a canal in Panama. After eight years the company gave up. Disease and lack of money forced the project to end. This did not stop Roosevelt. His plan was to build a canal through Panama. However, Panama was a part of the country of Colombia. When Roosevelt made an offer for the right to build a canal,

Colombia said "no." President Roosevelt was not a person who liked to take no for an answer.

Why did Roosevelt want to build a canal across Central America? To shorten the trip between the Pacific and Atlantic oceans

Building the Canal

In 1903, the people of Panama rebelled against Colombia. President Roosevelt sent ships and troops to help the rebels. Colombia was not strong enough to fight the United States, so Colombia gave Panama its independence. After Panama was free, it agreed to give the United States a ten-mile right-of-way across the Isthmus of Panama. An **isthmus** is a narrow strip of land that connects two larger-sized lands. In return the United States agreed to pay Panama $10 million and $250,000 a year in rent.

Many Latin Americans and others did not like the way Roosevelt had acted toward Colombia. However, Roosevelt was proud of what he had done.

Before work on the Panama Canal could begin, the United States had to get rid of the mosquitoes that carried both malaria and yellow fever. Colonel William C. Gorgas had the job of improving the sanitary conditions in the area. Under Gorgas's leadership, the Army Medical Corps cleared the land and drained the swamps where mosquitoes lived.

Building the Panama Canal was one of the biggest construction projects anyone had ever done. Thousands of men worked for nine years to build it. In the hot, steamy weather, they dug ditches and cut through rocky hills. They used huge steam shovels to load the dirt and rock onto trains, which hauled it away to dumps. Later the workers used the dirt and rocks to build a dam. This dam made a lake called Lake Gatun.

How did President Roosevelt get the right to build the Panama Canal? Helped Panama rebel against Colombia; Panama agreed to U.S. terms

History Fact

President Theodore Roosevelt was the first President to visit a foreign country while in office. In 1906, he visited Panama to see the construction of the canal for himself.

History Fact After the canal was built, Theodore Roosevelt was reported to have called it "the greatest task of its own kind that has ever been performed in the world."

The Panama Canal

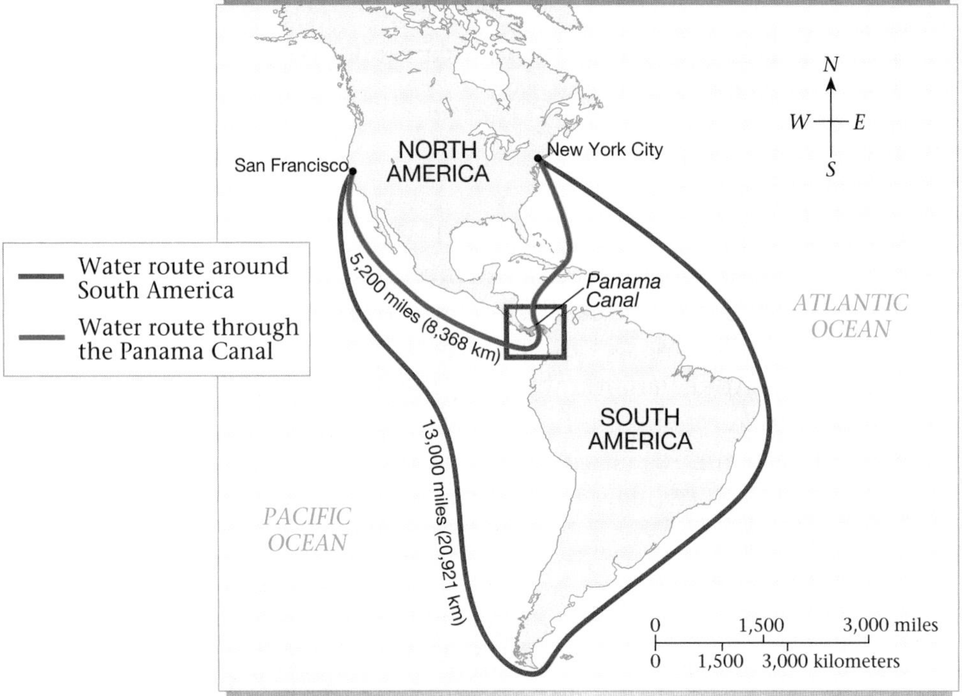

Map This map shows the travel miles from New York City to San Francisco with and without the Panama Canal. Tell students that the Panama Canal shortened the trip between New York City and San Francisco by 7,800 miles.

1. 5,200 miles
2. Atlantic and Pacific oceans

Map Study

1. How many miles is it between New York City and San Francisco by way of the canal?
2. What two oceans does the canal link?

The Canal Opens

In 1914, the first ship passed through the Panama Canal. The United States now controlled the shortest route between the Atlantic and Pacific oceans. The canal helped make the United States one of the most powerful nations on earth.

From the opening of the canal until 1979, many Americans lived and worked in the Panama Canal Zone. In 1979, however, a treaty gave Panama control of most of the area known as the Panama Canal Zone.

The treaty said Panama could take control of the canal on December 31, 1999.

How did the opening of the Panama Canal affect the United States? United States became more powerful; United States sent Americans to live and work in the Panama Canal Zone

The Roosevelt Corollary

President Roosevelt wanted the United States to be able to do whatever was necessary to settle problems in countries in the Western Hemisphere. In 1904, the Roosevelt Corollary was added to the Monroe Doctrine. A **corollary** is an addition to a document. It said that only the United States had the right to act in countries in the Western Hemisphere.

Remember
The Monroe Doctrine warned European powers against taking action in countries in the Western Hemisphere.

For the next 30 years, the United States used the Roosevelt Corollary as an excuse to interfere in the affairs of Latin American countries.

What was the Roosevelt Corollary? An addition to the Monroe Doctrine that said the United States was the only country that could take action in countries in the Western Hemisphere

Section 3 Review

1. How would a canal across Panama affect ships sailing from the West coast to the East coast of the United States?
2. Why was it important to control mosquitoes on the Isthmus of Panama?
3. **Critical Thinking** Why do you think Latin American countries criticized the United States in the early 1900s?
4. **Write About Citizenship** You are preparing a report to the U.S. Congress in 1901. List reasons for and against choosing the Isthmus of Panama as the place for a canal.

More Review is provided in Exercise 67 of the Workbook.

1. It cut the trip by thousands of miles.
2. They carried the diseases malaria and yellow fever.
3. Student responses should mention intervention in Latin American affairs, Colombia and Panama, Roosevelt Corollary.
4. For: Location between Pacific and Atlantic oceans; isthmus is narrow. Against: Colombia doesn't want to give permission; weather is hot and steamy; need to control disease

Chapter

16 Review

Summary Have students use this graphic organizer to outline the main ideas and details of the chapter.

Summary

Between 1890 and 1914, the United States began to expand its trade power in the world.

Section 1

Trade with Asian countries grew after Japan opened its ports. The United States took control of Hawaii to gain a port on the way to Asia. The United States opened trade in China.

Section 2

The United States fought with the Cubans against Spain in the Spanish-American War. At the end of the war, the United States gained control of lands in the Caribbean and the Pacific.

Section 3

President Roosevelt believed the United States had the right to use the threat of force to get what it wanted. The United States built the Panama Canal to increase its trade.

More Vocabulary Review is provided in Exercise 104 of the Classroom Resource Binder.

Vocabulary Review

Write *true* or *false*. If the statement is false, change the underlined term to make it true.

1. Yellow journalism helped build strong feelings in the United States against Spain. True

2. In 1898, the United States annexed, or took possession of, Hawaii. True

3. A protectorate is a narrow strip of land that connects two larger lands. False: isthmus

4. A nation that practices foreign policy is trying to build an empire. False: imperialism

1. Sent Perry to Japan, sent Open Door Notes to European countries involved in China, helped defeat the Boxers in China pp. 293, 295 **2.** The United States needed to use Pearl Harbor. p. 294 **3.** Sympathized with Cuban revolt; angered by *Maine* explosion pp. 297–298 **4.** Possible answer: New markets for American products and raw materials p. 293 **5.** Possible answer: Roosevelt's view of foreign policy; the United States was part of the Western Hemisphere; the United States was the strongest country in the Western Hemisphere p. 305

Chapter Quiz

Write your answers in complete sentences.

1. What did the United States do to expand trade with Japan and China?
2. Why did the United States need to control Hawaii?
3. Why did the United States declare war on Spain?
4. **Critical Thinking** Why do you think some Americans were interested in trade with other countries in the late 1800s?
5. **Critical Thinking** President Roosevelt felt that the United States should be the only country with the right to take action in countries in the Western Hemisphere. Why do you think he felt that way?

Test Tip
To study for a test, write a short summary of each chapter.

Writing Tip
Make some notes before you begin to write. In your notes, include the points you want to make.

Using the Timeline

Use the timeline on pages 290–291 to answer the questions.

1. When did Theodore Roosevelt first become President? 1901
2. Who was President when the Panama Canal opened? Woodrow Wilson

Group Activity

Form groups of four to debate this question: Should the United States take action in other countries today? Two students in your group should prepare to answer *yes*. Two students should prepare to answer *no*. Before you begin your debate, list some reasons the United States has recently sent planes or troops to other countries.

Group Activity See the Teacher's Planning Guide for a scoring rubric for this activity.

NEW YORK JOURNAL

EIGHTH EDITION

House by a Vote of 373 to 50 Passes Joint Resolution

WAR IS DECLARED BY U. S.

Interned German Ships Seized by Customs Authorities

Washington, April 6.—After a debate of nearly seventeen hours, the House early to-day passed the resolution previously adopted in the Senate, declaring a state of war against the Government of Germany. The vote was 373 to 50.

The resolution now goes to Vice-President Marshall, who must sign it in formal session of the Senate. It will then be taken before the President for his signature.

VESSELS IN ALLIES REST

Amendments to prevent the use of United States military forces in Europe, Asia or Africa unless directed by Congress were voted down. The resolution adopted by the Senate on Wednesday was approved by the House without the crossing of a "t" or the dotting of an "i."

A German bomb attack destroyed buildings in a city in Belgium in 1914. Newspaper headlines reported that the United States entered the war. How do you think the lives of these people were affected? Devastated, frightened, determined to rebuild their cities

World War I

1914 | 1915 | 1916 | 1917 | 1918

- **1914** World War I begins
- **1915** German submarine sinks *Lusitania*
- **1916** Woodrow Wilson reelected
- **1917** Zimmermann telegram printed in U.S. newspapers
- **1917** U.S. enters the war
- **1918** World War I ends

Additional activities and strategies to customize lessons can be found in the Teacher's Planning Guide.

Chapter 17 World War I 1914–1920

ESL Note To help students understand the concept of world war, have pairs share their ideas and experiences about a war that involves many countries. As a group, compare the ideas.

Words to Know

arms race
terrorist
stalemate
propaganda
ambassador
victory garden
bond
communism
armistice

Words to Know These words are defined in the section in which they appear, as well as in the Glossary. Point out to students that two of these words (*propaganda* and *bond*) may be familiar. They took on new meanings during the war.

1919	1920
1919 President Wilson and other Big Four leaders sign Treaty of Versailles	**1920** Warren Harding elected

Learning Objectives

- Describe the causes of World War I.
- Identify the events that led the United States to enter the war.
- Discuss how the war changed the lives of Americans at home.
- Explain how the United States helped the Allies win the war.
- Describe the Treaty of Versailles.
- Explore how propaganda is used.

Project Students can begin their charts when they begin the chapter. To help them get started, assist them in finding headings.

Portfolio Project

As you read the chapter, make a chart about World War I. To begin, skim the chapter and write some headings for the chart. Here are a few ideas for headings: Causes, Nations, Events, Weapons, Lives Lost, Cost, Making Peace. After you finish the chart, write five questions the chart can answer. Exchange charts with a partner. Answer each other's questions.

Timeline This timeline is divided into 1-year intervals. The events take place over a period of 7 years. Point out to students the outbreak of war in Europe and the end of the war.

Section 1 A World War Begins

Words to Know

arms race	a contest to build weapons and military power
terrorist	a person who uses violence for a political cause
stalemate	a situation in which neither side wins nor loses

Getting Started Discuss with students how technology has accelerated the pace of our lives. For example, cite the difference between sending a letter through the U.S. mail and sending it via e-mail. Explain that the many new weapons and strategies used during World War I, such as stealth bombs and trench warfare, changed the nature of war.

In 1914, war broke out in Europe. The war was called the Great War. Later it was called World War I. These names showed that this war was different from earlier wars. Whole nations, including soldiers and civilians, suffered in the war. The Great War affected people all over the world.

Causes of War in Europe

The war had many causes. One cause was that many people felt their group or nation was better than other groups or nations. This is called extreme nationalism. A second cause was the contest between nations for trade and for colonies. A third cause was the growth of alliances. An alliance is a group of nations that promise to protect one another. In alliances, strong countries could protect weak countries.

Many European countries did not trust one another. Also, they felt that a big armed force showed their greatness. For those reasons, they started an **arms race.** An arms race is a contest to build weapons and military power. Germany built the biggest army. Great Britain built the biggest navy.

? **Why did an arms race develop in Europe?** No trust between countries; thought a large armed force showed greatness

The Archduke and the Terrorist

In 1914, Austria-Hungary was a weak nation in Europe. Austria-Hungary included groups of people from many different backgrounds. Some of these groups wanted to be free nations. For example, Austria-Hungary controlled Bosnia. The Serbs in Bosnia wanted to join the nearby nation of Serbia.

Archduke Franz Ferdinand was next in line to be emperor, or ruler, of Austria-Hungary. In June 1914, the archduke visited Sarajevo, in Bosnia. While there, he was assassinated by a Serbian. The killer, Gavrilo Princip, was a **terrorist.** A terrorist is a person who uses violence for a political cause. Princip wanted Bosnia to break away from Austria-Hungary and join Serbia.

Within six weeks, war broke out. Austria-Hungary declared war on Serbia because a Serbian had shot the archduke. Other countries that had agreed to protect one another were pulled into the war.

How did Austria-Hungary's declaration of war on Serbia cause other countries to declare war? Countries that had agreed to protect one another were pulled into the war.

The Central Powers and the Allied Nations

The two sides in the war were the Central Powers and the Allied Nations, or Allies. You can see the nations of the two sides as well as the neutral nations, on the map on page 312. Germany, Austria-Hungary, and the Ottoman Empire were the major Central Powers. Great Britain, France, and Russia were the leaders of the Allies.

The war was fought on land, at sea, and in the air. The main battleground was in Europe. The longest fighting took place on the Western Front, in France and Belgium. A front is a line of battle. When the war began, both sides hoped for a quick end to the fighting.

What nations were the leaders of the two sides in the war? Central Powers: Germany, Austria-Hungary, Ottoman Empire; Allies: Great Britain, France, Russia

Geography Fact

Bosnia is in the Balkan Peninsula. This is the same area where violence broke out in the 1990s.

Geography Fact Have students turn to the world map in the atlas in the back of the book to find Bosnia and Serbia.

Europe at the Beginning of World War I, 1914

- Allied nations
- Central Powers
- Neutral nations
- • City

Map Study

1. What groups does the map key show?
2. Which Central Powers nation borders, or touches, France?

1. Allied nations, Central Powers, neutral nations
2. Germany

Map Point out that when the war started the major Allies were Russia, Great Britain, and France. The major Central Powers included Germany, Austria-Hungary, and the Ottoman Empire.

The First Years of the War

The war did not go as planned for either side. Each side won some battles and lost some. Neither side was close to victory. Neither side was ready to give up. At the end of 1914, the war reached a **stalemate.** A stalemate is a situation in which neither side wins or loses.

As the war reached a stalemate, the soldiers on both sides dug trenches, or ditches, in the ground. Soldiers took cover in these trenches. The trenches were 6 to 8 feet wide and about 5 feet deep. Hundreds of miles of trenches stretched along the Western Front. Millions of soldiers would live and die in these muddy ditches in the coming years. The trenches were filthy. They were filled with rats and bugs carrying disease.

Between the trenches of the two sides, there was an empty area. It was known as "no-man's land." In order to attack, soldiers crawled out of the trenches and crossed over no-man's land to the other side. Battles could last for months. One battle was at the Somme River in France, on the Western Front. It lasted from July to November 1916. In that time, more than one million soldiers were killed or wounded. Yet neither side could defeat the other.

How did soldiers attack along the Western Front?
They crawled out of their trenches and crossed no-man's land to the other side.

A Closer Look

AIR WAR

The airplane was invented about ten years before World War I began. The frames of the airplanes used during the war were made of wood. The coverings were made of cloth. Pilots flew in seats called cockpits that were open to the air. The fastest planes traveled only about 140 miles per hour.

A pilot who shot down more than five enemy planes was called an ace. Eddie Rickenbacker was the leading U.S. war ace. He shot down 22 enemy planes and four balloons in just a few months. Baron Manfred von Richtoffen was the leading German ace. Von Richtoffen was known as the Red Baron because his plane was once painted red. The Red Baron shot down 80 enemy planes.

Eddie Rickenbacker

Critical Thinking How are most planes today different from most World War I planes? Planes today have metal frames and coverings. The cockpits are closed and the planes are faster.

Soldiers wore gas masks to protect themselves from poison gas.

Visual Germany was the first country to use poison gas, in April 1915. The Allies began to use poison gas soon afterward.

1. Extreme nationalism, the contest for colonies, the growth of alliances, and an arms race
2. A terrorist shot Archduke Franz Ferdinand.
3. Student responses might mention that soldiers become discouraged. As casualties mounted, more and more soldiers were needed.
4. Student responses might mention fear that the country will be invaded or defeated, that property will be destroyed, that people will be killed.

Weapons of War

On both sides, soldiers had weapons that were new or had been used very little in earlier wars. The machine gun was one new weapon. It could fire up to 600 bullets a minute. Machine guns were heavy, so they were usually kept at the top of a trench.

Other new weapons of war were also used. These included tanks, poison gas, submarines, and airplanes.

Weapons killed and hurt civilians too. Some fighting took place in villages and towns. Civilians were attacked, and their property was destroyed. Civilians on both sides were killed in cities by bombs and cannon fire. Many civilians also died from starvation, disease, and lack of shelter.

What were some new weapons used in World War I? Machine guns, tanks, poison gas, submarines, and airplanes

Section 1 Review

1. What were the causes of the war in Europe?
2. What event in Bosnia in 1914 dragged many European nations into war?
3. **Critical Thinking** Explain how a stalemate might affect soldiers in a war.
4. **Write About History** You live in Europe during 1914. What are some of your fears for your country? Choose the European country where you live. Then write a letter to cousins in the United States. Tell them how you feel.

More Review is provided in Exercise 69 of the Workbook.

Section 2 From Neutral to Declaration of War

Words to Know

propaganda	the spreading of ideas, information, and beliefs to help or hurt a cause
ambassador	a person sent to another country to speak for the government of his or her own country

Getting Started Discuss with students a time when friends had an argument and one person would not take sides. What happened? Explain that remaining neutral in World War I was a position that the United States eventually could no longer afford to hold.

President Woodrow Wilson wanted to keep the United States out of the war. However, Germany's actions made many Americans angry, including the President. Finally, in 1917 the United States was drawn into the war.

Not all Americans wanted the United States to enter the war.

Visual Woodrow Wilson created the Committee on Public Information (CPI) on April 13, 1917. The CPI used newsreels, newspapers, films, posters, and other media to disseminate government propaganda about the war.

The United States Is Neutral

When the war began, President Wilson said the United States would remain neutral. He felt that, by not taking sides, the United States could help bring the Allies and the Central Powers together. Many Americans agreed. Other Americans disagreed with Wilson. They had family ties to Europe. Many Americans wanted the United States to fight for the Allies. Others wanted the United States to fight for the Central Powers.

Both the Allies and the Central Powers used **propaganda** to try to get Americans to join their side. Propaganda is the spreading of ideas, information, and beliefs to help or hurt a cause. Propaganda may include true or false information. It may support good or bad causes.

What did Wilson say about the United States and the war? The United States would remain neutral.

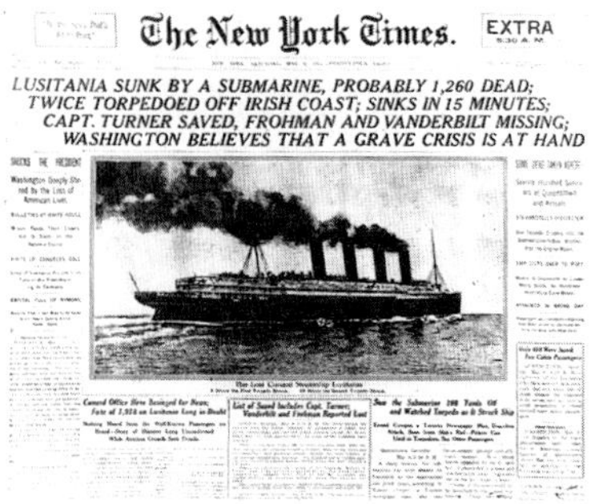
The New York Times. EXTRA

LUSITANIA SUNK BY A SUBMARINE, PROBABLY 1,260 DEAD;
TWICE TORPEDOED OFF IRISH COAST; SINKS IN 15 MINUTES;
CAPT. TURNER SAVED, FROHMAN AND VANDERBILT MISSING;
WASHINGTON BELIEVES THAT A GRAVE CRISIS IS AT HAND

***This newspaper headline tells about the sinking of the ship* Lusitania.**

Visual The *Lusitania* sank in less than 20 minutes. It went down in 295 feet of rough water about 12 miles off the southern Irish port of Kinsale. During the late 1990s, legal debate on ownership rights to the *Lusitania* went all the way to the Supreme Court.

The Sinking of the *Lusitania*

Great Britain set up a blockade of German ports early in the war. Food and other supplies could not reach Germany. The German navy was not large enough to blockade British ports. Germany decided to use submarines called U-boats to hurt the British navy. Traveling underwater, the submarines could sneak up on British ships.

In 1915, Germany said it would use its submarines to sink any ships coming to or going from Great Britain. The Germans said their submarines would not attack ships of neutral countries. However, they warned that they could not prevent accidents.

The German government placed ads in U.S. newspapers warning Americans not to sail on British ships. Not many Americans listened to the German warnings. Then on May 7, 1915, a German submarine sank the British ocean liner *Lusitania*. About 1,200 people died when the ship sank. Of those killed, 128 were Americans. The sinking of the *Lusitania* turned many Americans against Germany.

President Wilson was reelected in 1916. He kept trying to get the Allies and the Central Powers together to make peace. However, both sides still felt they could win the war. No one wanted to talk about peace.

By early 1917, German submarines were sinking any ships that came near Britain. In one three-week period, submarines sank 134 ships. Thousands of sailors and civilians were killed.

What happened to the *Lusitania*? A German submarine sank the *Lusitania* and killed 1,200 people, including 128 Americans.

The Zimmermann Telegram

In February 1917, the British gave the United States a secret telegraph message they had overheard. A German foreign minister named Arthur Zimmermann had sent the message to the German **ambassador** in Mexico. An ambassador is a person sent to another country to speak for the government of his or her own country. The Zimmermann telegram told the German ambassador in Mexico to get Mexico into the war on the side of the Central Powers. It also promised that Germany would help Mexico take back lands in Texas, Arizona, and New Mexico.

Newspapers in the United States printed the Zimmermann telegram. Most Americans were very angry with Germany. In early April 1917, President Wilson asked Congress to declare war on Germany and the Central Powers.

What was the purpose of the Zimmermann telegram?
To get Mexico into the war on the side of the Central Powers

Section 2 Review

1. Why did President Wilson want the United States to remain neutral in the war?
2. How did the sinking of the *Lusitania* change American feelings toward Germany?
3. **Critical Thinking** Explain why the Zimmermann telegram had such a big effect on the way Americans felt about the war.
4. **Write About Citizenship** Many European Americans had family members still living in Europe. Write a short essay describing how you think these Americans may have felt about the neutral position of the United States.

More Review is provided in Exercise 70 of the Workbook.

1. He felt that by not taking sides, the United States could help bring the Allies and the Central Powers together.
2. Most Americans turned against Germany.
3. Student responses should show an understanding that the Zimmermann telegram showed Americans that the war could come close to home. They saw that Germany might try to control the United States, as well as the rest of the world.
4. Student responses should show an understanding that European Americans would be concerned about family members and the fate of their homeland. Essays might defend or oppose involvement in the war.

CONNECTING HISTORY AND LANGUAGE
Propaganda

The U.S. government needed to gain American support for entering the war. To do this, the U.S. government used propaganda. The government formed a group called the Committee on Public Information (CPI). The CPI wrote news stories and made posters to encourage Americans to support the war effort.

CPI propaganda included facts and opinions about the war. In propaganda, opinions are usually presented as facts.

This poster asks Americans to support the war effort.

Look at the statements below. Which statements are facts? Which are opinions?

1. The United States has declared war on Germany. Fact
2. We can't win without you! Opinion
3. Food will win the war. Opinion
4. The Allies have asked for American troops. Fact
5. Millions die in battle. Fact
6. With hard work, we will win! Opinion

Answer the questions below.

1. Why do governments use propaganda?
2. Which of the statements above may have been used on a CPI poster?

CHALLENGE Sometimes propaganda includes statements that are not true. Do you think it is right to use false statements to help a good cause?

1. To gain support for government actions **2.** Statements 2, 4, 6 **CHALLENGE** Using false statements is unnecessary; often fails. Using false statements is morally wrong.

Section 3 The Home Front

Words to Know

victory garden	a garden in which citizens raised their own food during World War I
bond	a paper that shows debt, or money owed

Getting Started Have students brainstorm a list of the ways in which civilians can help in a time of war.

The United States prepared to enter World War I. Men began leaving their jobs and families to go to a faraway war. Americans at home helped to support the war effort in many ways. Men, women, and children all did their part.

Raising the Troops

Remember
A draft is a way of selecting people for required military service.

The United States had only a small army. Some men quickly volunteered for the army. However, President Wilson felt that a draft was the best way to create a large armed force. If men are selected for the draft, in most cases they must serve.

In 1917, Congress passed a draft law known as the Selective Service Act. The law said that all men between the ages of 21 and 30 had to sign up for the draft. By 1918, that was extended to men from 18 to 45. Within 18 months, almost three million Americans had been drafted. Also, more than one million men had volunteered to join the armed forces.

Americans from many groups were drafted into the armed forces. Some were immigrants to the United States. They were quickly taught to speak and read English.

What was the Selective Service Act of 1917? A law that said all men between 21 and 30 had to sign up for the draft

Changes in the Economy

The war changed the U.S. economy and American lives. Everyone's help was needed to produce supplies for U.S. and Allied troops. Millions of men left their jobs to fight in the war. This meant there were not enough workers to make goods for the troops.

Women replaced men in some jobs. They did factory work, drove trucks, and took railroad jobs. Mexican immigrants worked on farms, on railroads, and in factories. Many African Americans left the South to find work in northern cities. They worked in factories, mines, and other businesses.

How did the war change the United States economy? Many supplies needed to be produced.

Citizenship Link

PAYING FOR THE WAR

Fighting the war cost the United States billions of dollars. New taxes helped pay for some of the costs. The new taxes were based on people's income. Goods such as tobacco and movie tickets were also taxed.

The government borrowed money to pay for the war. To do that, the government sold pieces of paper called war bonds. A bond is sold to raise money for a government or a business. The seller promises to pay back the money that is borrowed plus some extra money called interest.

The U.S. government encouraged Americans to buy bonds to support the war. The bonds were called Liberty bonds. By the end of the war, Americans had lent $21 billion to the government.

Posters asked people to buy bonds.

Critical Thinking How do you think Americans who owned bonds felt about the war? Student might say that many Americans were proud that they could support the war.

Supporting the Troops

The U.S. government asked men, women, and children to support the troops. Soldiers needed most of the food the farmers produced. The government used news articles, posters, and cookbooks to show families how to save food for the troops. Families went without meat on certain days of the week. Families also grew their own food in gardens called **victory gardens.**

Women and children sewed clothing and knitted socks and sweaters for the troops. They wrote letters and gathered books for soldiers to read. Children took care of victory gardens. Not everyone supported the war, but most Americans wanted to do their part. Americans also supported the war by buying **bonds.** A bond is a paper that shows debt, or money owed.

How did people at home support the war? They went without meat on certain days, grew their own food, made things for soldiers, wrote letters, gathered books.

Section 3 Review

1. How did President Wilson plan to get enough men to fight the war?
2. Why did women have more chances for jobs during the war?
3. **Critical Thinking** Think about how Americans at home supported the troops. How do you think this support affected the troops and the people at home?
4. **Write About Citizenship** Describe the feelings of a soldier leaving home to fight in World War I.

More Review is provided in Exercise 71 of the Workbook.

1. He wanted a draft.
2. Many men were away from their jobs, fighting in the war.
3. Student responses may include the following: troops got food, equipment, clothing; felt that people at home had not forgotten them. People at home felt good doing what they could.
4. Student responses should show an understanding that soldiers were leaving their loved ones, their jobs, and familiar surroundings. Some students may mention a spirit of adventure and feelings of fear, anxiety, and excitement.

Section 4 The War to End All Wars

Words to Know

communism	an economic system in which the government owns all property and businesses
armistice	an agreement to stop fighting

Getting Started Have students think of a place from their past that they may have gone back to visit. Discuss how the place might have seemed different. Explain that the United States and Europe were changed places after the war.

When the first U.S. troops arrived in Europe, the war had already killed millions of people. A revolution in Russia had put France and Great Britain in danger. American troops would play a large role in winning the war with the Allies.

Revolt in Russia

From 1914 to 1917, Russian troops were an important part of the Allied forces. The Russians fought the Germans along the Eastern Front. At that time, a powerful ruler, called a tsar, ruled Russia. The tsar and his family were wealthy. However, most of the Russian people were poor. The people were unhappy with the way the war was going. The Russians had suffered huge casualties.

As the fighting in Europe continued, a revolution broke out in Russia. In November 1917, the Communists took power. Communists believe in **communism**, an economic system in which the government owns all property and businesses. The Communists took control of all farms, banks, and industry in Russia. During the revolution, many people died. The tsar of Russia and his family were murdered in 1918.

The Communist government signed a peace agreement with Germany and the Central Powers.

The agreement meant that the Allies would not have millions of Russian troops on their side. The Central Powers could turn most of their force against the French and the British. The Allies badly needed more troops to join the fight.

What group took power in Russia in 1917?
The Communists

U.S. Troops Arrive

Once U.S. troops were trained, they had to cross the Atlantic Ocean to reach Europe. However, crossing the Atlantic Ocean was very dangerous. More than 100 German submarines moved quietly beneath the water. To carry troops safely across the Atlantic, the U.S. Navy traveled in convoys. In this system, warships traveled along with ships carrying troops.

The first American troops arrived in France in June 1917. Over the next months, more than one million U.S. soldiers came to France to fight.

In early 1918, German forces planned to attack Paris, the capital of France. They broke through the Allied lines and came within 50 miles of Paris. However, there they were stopped by French and U.S. troops.

Why did U.S. ships travel to Europe in convoys?
For safety from German submarines

The Allies Push Ahead

American troops fought two very important battles in France that helped end the war.

Belleau Wood

Belleau Wood was a thick forest. For 24 hours a day for two weeks, U.S. troops fought their way through the forest. German machine guns hidden in trees fired down on the Americans. Finally, the Americans took control of Belleau Wood. However, about 8,000 Americans were killed or wounded in the battle.

Geography Fact

After Russia left the war, Germany could focus on the Western Front. It no longer had to fight on the Eastern Front.

Geography Fact Have students turn back to the map "Europe at the Beginning of World War I" on page 312. Students should identify which nations made up the Central Powers.

The Argonne Forest

The Argonne Forest was a large area along the Western Front. The Germans controlled the area. The Germans had machine guns, barbed wire, and big cannons waiting for the Allies. On September 26, 1918, more than one million Americans attacked at dawn. A heavy fog covered the forest. Many Americans walked into German positions. However, the Americans kept fighting. More than 100,000 Americans were killed or wounded in the Argonne Forest. The battle lasted for 47 days until the Americans pushed through enemy lines. At about the same time, British, French, and Belgian forces also won battles along the Western Front.

By November 1918, the German army began to retreat, or fall back. Other Central Powers could no longer fight without the power of Germany behind them. Finally, on November 11, in a railroad car in northern France, the Allies and the Central Powers signed an agreement to end the war. World War I was over. Germany accepted the terms of the **armistice**. An armistice is an agreement to stop fighting.

How did the United States help the Allies? U.S. troops provided the extra forces the Allies needed, especially at Belleau Wood and the Argonne Forest.

World War I, 1914–1918

Number of soldiers from all countries killed	8,528,831
Number of soldiers from all countries wounded	21,189,154
Number of American soldiers killed	126,000
Number of American soldiers wounded	204,002
Cost to United States	$33.7 billion

Chart Study

1. What was the cost of World War I to the United States?
2. What was the total of all wounded soldiers in World War I?

Chart Point out that the majority of soldiers injured or killed in World War I were not from the United States. More than half the dead were non-battle deaths.

1. $33.7 billion
2. 21,189,154

American troops fought many battles along the Western Front.

The Cost of War

The United States had been in the war for less than a year. U.S. troops had provided the extra forces needed by the Allies. Although U.S. losses were great, they were far fewer than those of other countries in the war.

The war had taken a terrible toll in Europe. As many as 13 million civilians and soldiers had died. Much of northern France was destroyed. In Germany, millions of people were starving. Between 1918 and 1919, more people died from a flu epidemic. An epidemic is a sudden spread of disease that affects many people at one time. The flu epidemic killed 20 million people.

What conditions did Europe face after the war?
Disease and starvation

Visual While fighting France, 63,000 Americans died from disease, not combat. Most of them were struck down by the flu epidemic.

Europe After World War I, 1919

Map Study

1. Which new independent nation borders Russia and Germany? Poland

2. After World War I, how many new independent nations were there? 9

Map Use the transparency map "Europe at the Beginning of World War I" in the Classroom Resource Binder to review the changes that took place as a result of the war.

The Allies' Plan for Peace

Wilson wanted World War I to be the "war to end all wars." He already had a plan for peace called The Fourteen Points. He presented his plan to Congress in January 1918. Wilson's plan included a League of Nations where countries could meet to solve their problems without fighting.

In January 1919, President Wilson met with the leaders of Italy, Great Britain, and France. They met at the Palace of Versailles outside Paris, France. The leaders were called the Big Four. Wilson and the European leaders disagreed over punishment for Germany. The European leaders wanted to punish Germany for the suffering their countries had gone through.

The leaders signed the Treaty of Versailles in June 1919. President Wilson did not like all the parts of the treaty. For example, the treaty forced Germany to take all the blame for the war. In addition, Germany had to pay billions of dollars in damages to Allied countries. Germany did not have enough money to pay.

However, the treaty did include some of Wilson's Fourteen Points. The treaty provided for a League of Nations. The U.S. Senate refused to approve the treaty. Some senators were afraid the League would drag the United States into another war. The United States never became a member of the League of Nations. Wilson fought for the League, but he grew tired and sick. He died in 1924.

How did the European Allies plan to punish Germany? They wanted to make Germany pay damages to Allied countries and take all the blame for the war.

Section 4 Review

1. How did the revolution in Russia affect the Allies?
2. What happened at the Battle of the Argonne Forest?
3. **Critical Thinking** Do you think it was right to punish Germany for the war? Explain.
4. **Write About Citizenship** You are about to give a speech in favor of the League of Nations. Make some notes for your speech. Include some lessons the world has learned from World War I.

More Review is provided in Exercise 72 of the Workbook.

1. The Communists gained power. They signed a peace agreement with Germany and left the war. The Allies no longer had the Russians on their side. The Allies did not have enough soldiers.
2. The Americans fought the Germans. The battle lasted 47 days. More than 100,000 Americans were killed or wounded. The Americans finally pushed through enemy lines.
3. Students may answer yes or no. Some students may feel that the winner has the right to ask for damages. Other students may realize that the German people suffered in the war and should not suffer more.
4. Student responses should show an understanding that world war might have been avoided if a League of Nations had been in place rather than a system of alliances.

Chapter 17 Review

Summary Have students use this graphic organizer to outline the main ideas and details of the chapter.

Summary	When World War I started in Europe, the United States tried to stay neutral. As the war went on, most Americans supported the Allies. The United States entered the war in 1917.
Section 1	The war had many causes. Most of the countries in Europe lined up on two sides. At the end of the first year, there was a stalemate.
Section 2	The United States remained neutral for the first years of the war. Then the Germans sank the *Lusitania*. Finally, in 1917, the United States joined the Allies.
Section 3	During the war, women, Mexican Americans, and African Americans worked in farms, factories, and other businesses.
Section 4	U.S. troops fought in two important battles, Belleau Wood and the Argonne Forest. After these battles, the German army retreated. The Treaty of Versailles ended the war.

More Vocabulary Review is provided in Exercise 110 of the Classroom Resource Binder.

Vocabulary Review

Write *true* or *false*. If the statement is false, change the underlined term to make it true.

1. In a <u>stalemate</u> neither side wins or loses. True
2. <u>Ambassadors</u> believe government should own property and businesses. False: Communists
3. <u>Propaganda</u> tries to make people support certain causes. True
4. A paper showing money owed is a <u>bond</u>. True

1. The sinking of the *Lusitania* and the Zimmermann telegram pp.316–317 **2.** Bought bonds, planted victory gardens; African Americans, Mexican immigrants, women had better job opportunities p.320 **3.** Won many battles including Belleau Wood and Argonne Forest. pp. 323–324 **4.** No: U.N. and fear of nuclear weapons will prevent wars. Yes: There will always be some nations that want power over others. **5.** Allied countries in Europe lived closer to Germany, wanted to be sure Germany could never become too strong again. pp. 326–327

Chapter Quiz

Write your answers in complete sentences.

1. Why did the United States change from neutral to declaring war on Germany?
2. How did the war affect Americans at home?
3. How did U.S. troops help the Allies win the war?
4. **Critical Thinking** Do you think there could ever be a war that would end all wars? Explain your answer.
5. **Critical Thinking** Why do you think European leaders were more eager to punish Germany than President Wilson was?

Test Tip
To prepare for a test, look for key words. The Words to Know are key words. Find them in the chapter. Be sure you know what they mean.

Writing Tip
Always leave enough time to reread what you have written before handing it in. Check for correct grammar and spelling.

Using the Timeline

Use the timeline on pages 308–309 to answer the questions.

1. What events happened in 1917? Zimmermann telegram printed in U.S. newspapers; U.S. entered war
2. How many years after the start of World War I did the United States enter the war? Three

Group Activity See the Teacher's Planning Guide for a scoring rubric for this activity.

Group Activity

Form groups of four or five. In your group, make a booklet about World War I. Ask one person to make the cover. Have other group members make two pages each. Write the most interesting things you have learned. Also, draw pictures to show what happened. Then staple the pages together to make a booklet.

Critical Thinking 1. Sinclair's book, *The Jungle,* described unclean meatpacking practices. 2. To shorten the sea route between the Atlantic and the Pacific oceans 3. To get the United States on their side 4. To save food grown on farms for the troops

Unit 5 Review

Critical Thinking

Give one reason why each of the following events happened.

1. Americans became upset about unclean meat.
2. The United States built the Panama Canal.
3. Germany and Great Britain used propaganda.
4. Americans planted victory gardens.

Building Your Skills

Write one effect of each cause listed below.

1. The Civil Service Act was passed.
2. The battleship *Maine* exploded in Cuba.
3. Mosquitoes in Panama carried diseases.
4. Many American men left their jobs to go to war.
5. The Communists took power in Russia in 1917.

Building Your Skills 1. People had to take a test for civil service jobs. 2. Americans got angry at Spain. 3. Americans destroyed places where mosquitoes lived. 4. Women, Mexican immigrants, and African Americans had more chances for jobs. 5. The Communist government took over farms, banks, and industry. Russia left the war.

Who Is It?

Write the name of the person who took each action below.

1. She wrote about corruption in the oil industry. Ida Tarbell
2. He said the United States should carry a big stick. Theodore Roosevelt
3. He had the idea for the League of Nations. Woodrow Wilson

Writing an Essay

Answer one of the following essay topics. See the Answer Key for a detailed answer.

1. Discuss the reasons why Americans wanted to reform government in the late 1800s and early 1900s.
2. Identify the events in the late 1800s and early 1900s that made the United States a world power.
3. Describe the peace treaty that ended World War I.

Linking Past and Present

Think of the way newspapers covered the Spanish-American War. Do you think newspapers cover wars the same way today? Explain your answer.

Student responses may be yes or no. Students should refer to coverage of a recent conflict.

Unit Opener Use the chapter titles and dates to set up a unit timeline.

Unit 6 Years of Uncertainty

Chapter 18 **The Roaring Twenties** 1920–1929

Chapter 19 **The Great Depression** 1929–1934

Chapter 20 **The New Deal** 1933–1941

During the early 1930s, many people lost their jobs. They could not afford many things. Why do you think these people are waiting in line?
They are waiting for free food.

> *"I am the mother of seven children and they are hungry, and [we] have only 65 cents. Oh, President, my heart is breaking."*
>
> —from a letter from Mrs. H. L. to President Franklin Roosevelt in 1934

Primary Source Point out that the quotation was part of a letter that Roosevelt received during the Great Depression. During his first week in office, nearly half a million U.S. citizens wrote to him. Point out that the brackets around *we* indicate that the word was not part of the original quote.

The 1920s is often called the Jazz Age. A new kind of music called jazz became popular. Many jazz songs, like the title of the one shown here, were written. What kind of instruments did these musicians use? Drums, piano, trumpet, clarinet, sliding trombone, banjo

The Roaring Twenties

1920 Warren G. Harding elected

1920 First radio station begins broadcasting

1921 Law limiting immigration passed

1923 President Harding dies

1923 Calvin Coolidge takes office

1924 First woman becomes governor of a state

1920 — 1921 — 1922 — 1923 — 1924 — 1925

Additional activities and strategies to customize lessons can be found in the Teacher's Planning Guide.

Chapter 18 The Roaring Twenties 1920–1929

ESL Note To help students understand the concept of the Roaring Twenties, discuss the meaning of the term. Explain that the 1920s was a time of wild stunts and increased spending, as well as a celebration of leisure activities. Americans needed to express their relief that the world had survived World War I.

Words to Know

assembly line

installment plan

mass media

jazz

renaissance

inflation

deport

Words to Know These words are defined in the section in which they appear, as well as in the Glossary. Point out to students that the prefix *de-*, as in the word *deport*, indicates "removal" or "undoing."

Learning Objectives

- Describe how the U.S. economy changed after World War I.
- Discuss how cars affected American life.
- Describe how culture changed during the 1920s.
- Explain why immigration was limited after World War I.
- Identify the causes of the Great Migration.
- Compare ideas on a chart.

Project There are many important people in this chapter. If time allows, have students research the person they chose at the library or on the Internet.

Portfolio Project

In this chapter, you will read about musicians, writers, sports stars, and other talented people who changed the way Americans viewed the world. Create your own "Top 10" list of outstanding Americans of the 1920s. Tell why you chose each person.

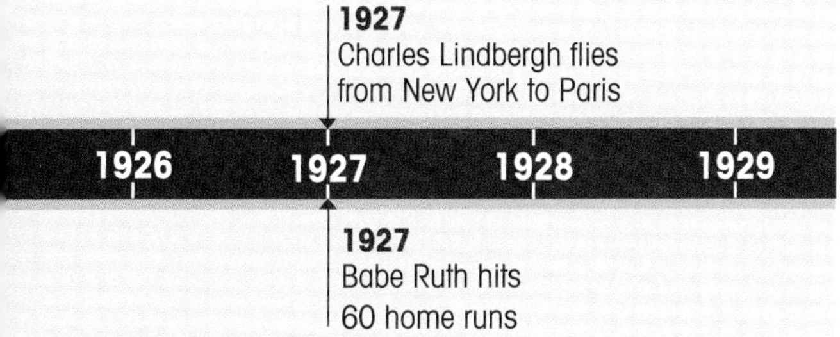

Timeline The timeline is divided into 1-year intervals. The events take place over a period of 8 years. Point out that great strides in the technology of sound happened during this time.

Section 1 A Time of Prosperity

Words to Know

assembly line	a system in which each worker does a different job in putting together a product
installment plan	the payment of money over time toward the total cost of an item
mass media	the communications that reach large numbers of people

Getting Started Discuss with students the ways in which they are consumers. Explain that the 1920s was a time of prosperity and that many Americans wanted to buy new things.

In 1920, the United States had come out of World War I. The nation was at peace. The economy was healthy. Americans were beginning to enjoy good times.

A Short Term as President

Warren G. Harding was elected President in 1920. For the American people, he was a good choice. Americans had survived World War I and great sorrow. Now they wanted an ordinary man who could return the country to prewar times. President Harding was a man from a small town in Ohio.

Once President Harding was elected, he had to choose his Cabinet. Some of the men Harding chose were very honest and capable. However, President Harding also chose men because they were his friends.

By the summer of 1923, Congress was about to examine some of the decisions that President Harding and his friends had made. The President was worried. Later that summer, President Harding became ill. He died on August 2, 1923. Vice President Calvin Coolidge became President.

In the months that followed, several scandals were reported. The Teapot Dome scandal involved Albert Fall, the Secretary of the Interior. Fall had accepted bribes from private oil companies. After being found guilty, Fall went to jail.

Why did Americans elect Warren G. Harding in 1920? Americans wanted an ordinary President who would return the country to prewar times.

Cars Change the Economy

When Calvin Coolidge became President in 1923, the American people wanted to build a new and prosperous, or rich, country. Congress passed laws that helped businesses grow larger. As a result, salaries went up and prices came down. People were able to buy more things.

One item that many Americans wanted was the "Tin Lizzie," or Model T Ford. Henry Ford owned a large automobile company. It was Ford's idea to have workers in his automobile factories build cars on an **assembly line.** An assembly line is a system in which each worker in a factory does a different job in putting together a product. As parts are sent down the line, each person adds a part to the product. When the product reaches the end of the line, it is finished.

The assembly line allowed Ford to build cars faster and more cheaply than ever before. The cars could be sold at a low cost because so many could be built in one day.

Here is how the growth of the automobile industry changed the American way of life and the American economy.

1. The steel, rubber, glass, and oil industries grew to supply the needs of automobile builders.

2. Americans found new jobs selling, repairing, parking, and driving cars.

Economics Fact

By 1929, almost one out of every five Americans owned a car.

Economics Fact From 1920 to 1930, the number of cars on the road grew from 9.2 million to 26.7 million.

Workers built Ford cars on an assembly line.

Visual 15 million Model T cars were built. Ford ended production of them in 1927, when sales began to drop.

3. Thousands of miles of new roads were built.
4. Small businesses, such as diners, motels, and stores, were built where motorists might stop.
5. As roads spread across the country, people began to move from the cities to the suburbs.

How did the automobile industry change the American economy? By adding to the growth of industries; by giving more people automobile-related and road-building jobs

Americans Spend More

During the 1920s, more and more products were built on assembly lines. Products such as washing machines, toasters, and refrigerators became part of

American life. Sometimes, these products, like cars, cost more than most people could afford.

Yet, even people who did not have enough money for certain products could buy them. These people bought goods through **installment plans.** On an installment plan, a person pays money over time toward the total cost of the item. A new radio, record player, or kitchen tool could be bought for $5 down and as little as $5 a month.

During the 1920s, Americans began to spend their money. One industry that grew as Americans spent more was advertising. Ads tried to convince people that they needed certain products. The ads promised people that the products would make them happier, wealthier, or smarter.

Before the 1920s, most ads had been in newspapers. During the 1920s, ads began to appear in other kinds of **mass media.** Mass media refers to the communications that reach large numbers of people. Advertisers used radio, billboards, and magazines to sell products.

Why did the advertising industry grow in the 1920s?
As people began to spend more money, the advertising business expanded as it tried to convince people to spend even more money.

Section 1 Review

1. How did Henry Ford change the way goods were produced in the United States?

2. How did people use the installment plan?

3. **Critical Thinking** Why is the price of certain goods lower if they are made on an assembly line?

4. **Write About Economics** Write an ad for a household product. Explain to buyers how they can pay a little money down and take an expensive item home.

1. Henry Ford introduced the assembly line for the mass production of goods.
2. People could pay for an item over a period of time.
3. The cost of making goods on an assembly line is lower than the cost of individually crafting goods; therefore, the goods can be sold at a lower price.
4. Student responses should include the idea of the installment plan and the advantages of being able to enjoy an item immediately.

More Review is provided in Exercise 75 of the Workbook.

BUILDING YOUR SKILLS
Comparing on a Chart

When you compare things on a chart, you can see how they are alike and how they are different.

Follow these steps to compare on a chart.

- Read the title on each side of the chart to see what you are comparing.
- Read across each row to see how the items are the same or different.

Automobiles in the 1920s	Automobiles Today
1. They cost under $500	**1.** They cost thousands of dollars
2. Top speed of 50 miles an hour	**2.** Top speed of 100 miles an hour
3. Used oil and gas	**3.** Use oil and gas

Answer the questions using the information from the chart.

1. In what ways were cars in the 1920s different from cars today?

2. In what way were cars in the 1920s the same as cars today?

CHALLENGE Complete the chart. Add information that compares automobiles in the 1920s and today.

Apply the Skill

Create a chart that compares popular entertainment in the 1920s and today.

1. Cars today are faster and cost more money today. **2.** Both use oil and gas
CHALLENGE Student responses might include such items as styling and comfort.

Section 2 Good Times for Many

Words to Know

jazz	a kind of music created by African Americans in the South in the early 1900s
renaissance	a time of new interest and activity in the arts

Getting Started Ask students whether or not they feel celebrities such as sports figures and movie personalities should be role models. Point out that in the 1920s many people looked at stars of sports and stage as heroes.

Bessie Smith was a well-known singer.

Visual The African American public bought millions of Bessie Smith's records during the years of her greatest fame, from 1923 to 1928.

The 1920s was a time of prosperity, or good times, and change for many people. More people enjoyed wealth and luxury. Americans lived with high hopes for the future.

Popular Entertainment

Cars were something new in the 1920s. There was new music too. Families had radios in their homes. People could go to movies and be entertained. For many people, the 1920s was simply a time to enjoy life. People called those carefree times the Roaring Twenties. Another nickname was the Jazz Age.

Music

Jazz was a kind of music created by African Americans in the South in the early 1900s. African American musicians first started playing jazz in New Orleans. Horns, drums, piano, and banjo were used in playing jazz.

Jazz became well known as musicians traveled first from New Orleans to Chicago and then to other northern cities. Jazz clubs opened in New York, Chicago, St. Louis, and other large cities. Jazz musicians like Louis Armstrong and Jelly Roll Morton were popular with both African American music lovers and white music lovers.

History Fact

The first scheduled radio program was on November 2, 1920. The election returns were announced. Warren Harding had won.

History Fact Warren Harding was the first President to give a speech over the radio.

Radio

Americans heard the first radio program from Pittsburgh, Pennsylvania, in 1920. By 1922, there were more than 500 radio stations in the United States.

At first, music was heard during most of the time a radio program was on. However, there were also news reports and children's stories. Sporting events quickly became popular.

Movies

In the 1920s, movies had no sound. There were a few movies, though, with background music. Sometimes when the actors spoke, the words were written on the screen.

At other times, the viewers had to guess what the actors were saying. In 1927, the first "talkie" was produced. From that time on, all movies had sound.

Books and Magazines

Reading was another leisure-time, or free-time, activity for Americans. F. Scott Fitzgerald became a favorite writer for many adults. The people in Fitzgerald's stories were always looking for wealth and success. Ernest Hemingway wrote stories about wartime experiences, sports, and travel.

Many famous magazines were first published in the 1920s. People read such magazines as *Time* for its news. They read the *Saturday Evening Post* for its stories.

Sports

Sports were so popular that the 1920s became an age of sports heroes. What American of that day had not heard of the baseball player Babe Ruth? In 1927, Ruth hit a then-record 60 home runs.

Nearly everyone knew about the heroes of other sports too. Red Grange was college football's outstanding player during the 1920s. Jack Dempsey was the boxing champion. Gertrude Ederle was the first woman to swim the English Channel.

Hero of the 1920s

The greatest hero of the 1920s was a pilot named Charles Lindbergh. On May 20, 1927, Lindbergh climbed into his one-seat plane called the *Spirit of St. Louis* in New York. Lindbergh was trying to become the first person to fly alone across the Atlantic Ocean to Europe. After $33\frac{1}{2}$ hours, he landed in Paris, France. Soon after Lindbergh's flight, planes began carrying passengers and mail between Chicago and San Francisco. His flight opened the door to a new world of flight.

Charles Lindbergh was the first person to fly alone across the Atlantic Ocean.

Visual Charles Augustus Lindbergh was born on February 4, 1902, in Detroit, Michigan. The press named him "Lucky Lindy" after his solo nonstop flight across the Atlantic Ocean, which covered more than 3,600 miles.

What kinds of popular entertainment were there in the 1920s? Jazz music, radio, movies, books, magazines, sports

The Harlem Renaissance

Many young African Americans who moved to the North in the 1920s came to a part of New York City called Harlem. Many African American artists, writers, and musicians settled in Harlem. African Americans who lived in this community were free to express themselves.

African Americans had been artists, writers, and musicians long before 1920. African American writers and artists created books, plays, poems, and paintings. This period was known as the Harlem Renaissance. A **renaissance** is a time of new interest and activity in the arts. African Americans used literature and art to show their racial pride. They also spoke out against racial discrimination.

Writer Langston Hughes was one of the leaders of the Harlem Renaissance. Countee Cullen, Claude McKay, and Zora Neale Hurston also wrote of their African American experiences.

What was the Harlem Renaissance? A time when many African Americans settled in Harlem, which became an important cultural center.

Women in the 1920s

For women, the 1920s became a time of new freedom. Many young women turned away from the beliefs and styles of their mothers. They cut their hair short and wore short dresses. They began to speak out. There were several reasons for the changes.

1. The Nineteenth Amendment gave all women the right to vote in all elections.

2. Women could hold public offices. In 1924, Nellie Tayloe Ross became governor of Wyoming. In 1925, Miriam A. Ferguson became governor of Texas.

Women's Jobs

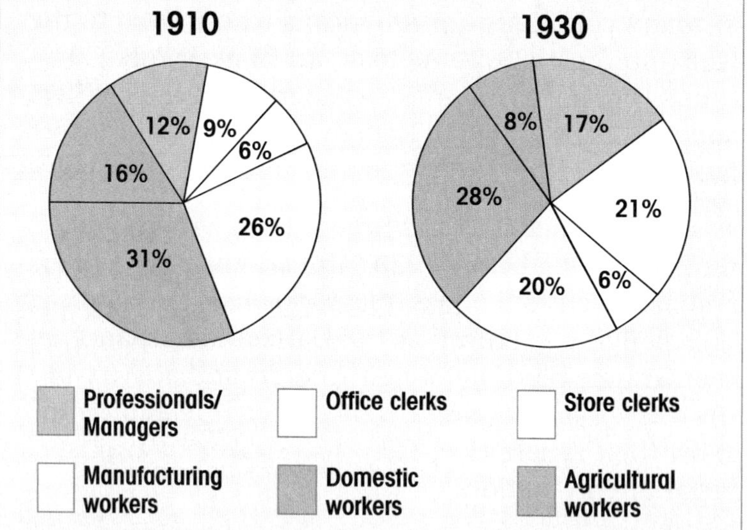

Chart Study

1. What percentage of workers were store clerks in 1910 and 1930?

2. What job had more workers in 1930 than in 1910, office clerks or agricultural workers?

Chart Explain that the pie charts compare the type of jobs that women held in 1910 and 1930. Point out that more women participated in a wider variety of jobs in 1930.

1. 6%

2. Office clerks

3. After World War I, many women continued to work outside their homes.

4. Household tools made women's lives easier. New books, music, and art helped them to think differently. More women decided to go to college.

Even though women began to gain more rights, they were not always treated the same as men. More women had jobs during the 1920s. However, employers thought they would work until they got married. As a result, employers did not train women for some jobs.

Women were still paid less than men. More women were becoming doctors and lawyers. However, many hospitals and law offices refused to hire women.

In what ways were the 1920s a time of change for women? Right to vote; hold public office; work outside home; household conveniences

Section 2 Review

1. What big changes took place in the 1920s?
2. How did the Nineteenth Amendment change women's lives?
3. **Critical Thinking** Why do you think the Harlem Renaissance was called a rebirth of African American culture?
4. **Write About History** Write a paragraph in which you explain why you would or would not like to have lived during the 1920s.

More Review is provided in Exercise 76 of the Workbook.

1. The automobile, radio, movies, books, and magazines opened doors to the world.
2. Gave women the right to vote in all elections.
3. Possible answer: Artists and writers in Harlem defined racial pride and praised African American traditions.
4. Possible answer: There was the excitement and adventure of the 1920s. Life was just going too fast in the 1920s.

Section 3 A Time of Change

Words to Know

inflation	a sharp rise in the price of goods
deport	to force a person who is not a citizen to leave the country by government order

Getting Started Have students debate the following questions: Should returning veterans get their old jobs back? If so, what happens to the people who have been doing those jobs? Explain that some people who had lost their jobs took out their anxiety on the new immigrants who filled their places.

Although the 1920s was a new and exciting time, there were problems too. Many Americans were without jobs. Prices were rising. A growing fear of immigrants led to violence. Violence against African Americans continued in the South.

Economic Problems

The men who fought in World War I returned home as heroes. However, many men did not return to jobs. There were fewer jobs than before the war. Factories did not need as many workers to make weapons or military supplies. In addition, the economy faced other problems.

1. People who had jobs were eager to spend the money they earned. Businesses had trouble making products fast enough.

2. Prices began to rise sharply because there were fewer goods. This price rise is called **inflation.**

3. Bad feelings between workers and owners grew. Workers demanded higher pay to keep up with inflation. Many workers went on strike.

Why did men returning from World War I have problems finding jobs? Fewer workers were needed to make weapons and military supplies.

Growing Fears

As the economy grew worse, many Americans began to fear workers who went on strike. They believed that strikers were under the control of Communists.

Communists had taken control of Russia in 1917. They believed that the government should control all businesses and property. Many Americans feared that strikes were the start of a Communist takeover in the United States. These fears led the U.S. government to take action. In 1920, about 6,000 people were arrested across the United States.

A Closer Look

THE SACCO AND VANZETTI CASE

The growing fear that Americans had toward immigrants is shown in the case of Nicola Sacco and Bartolomeo Vanzetti. In April 1920, robbers stole a payroll from a shoe factory near Boston, Massachusetts. A guard was killed. The police blamed Sacco and Vanzetti. These two Italian immigrants were charged with murder. The men said that they had nothing to do with the crime.

Nicola Sacco and Bartolomeo Vanzetti

Some people believed Sacco had handed out papers that said things against the U.S. government. Many Americans feared that the men were planning to destroy the government. They thought that Sacco and Vanzetti were Communists.

Both Sacco and Vanzetti were found guilty and put to death in 1927. Fifty years later, in 1977, the governor of Massachusetts stated that the men had not been fairly tried.

Critical Thinking Why do you think the governor of Massachusetts admitted in 1977 that Sacco and Vanzetti had not been fairly treated? Since a fair trial is one of the rights guaranteed by the U.S. Constitution, the governor might have wanted to publicly recognize that fact.

The government believed these people were Communists. Hundreds of people were **deported.** To deport someone is to force a person who is not a citizen to leave the country by government order.

Feelings against immigrants began to grow. Some people believed that immigrants were taking jobs from Americans. They asked the U.S. government to pass laws that would control the number of immigrants allowed into the country. In 1921, the government passed a law that allowed only 357,000 immigrants into the United States each year.

The new immigration laws were a huge change from the past. The door to the United States, which was once wide open, was now almost shut.

What huge change did the immigration law of 1921 make in the United States? The immigration law closed the door of the United States to many immigrants.

The Great Migration

Between 1910 and 1930, more than two million African Americans migrated, or moved, from the South to the North. The migration of African Americans to cities in the North was known as the Great Migration. African Americans settled in the cities of New York, Philadelphia, Chicago, and Detroit. They left the South for many reasons.

1. There were unfair working conditions in the South. Many African Americans were sharecroppers. They had to pay for the right to farm lands.
2. In the 1920s, the South was hit by floods and then long spells of dry weather. This made farming difficult.
3. Laws in the South forced African Americans to attend separate schools and use separate restaurants, restrooms, and drinking fountains.

Many African Americans hoped for better lives in the North. African Americans could earn higher pay at factory jobs in the North than they could earn at any job in the South. African Americans were often paid less than white workers for doing the same jobs.

Feelings against African Americans led to violence in some places. The Ku Klux Klan was a terrorist group that started after Reconstruction. In the 1920s, it continued to spread fear among African Americans. White men in hoods attacked African Americans in the South, Midwest, and West.

African Americans fought back against racism by forming groups that increased their racial pride. Churches, social clubs, and businesses owned by African Americans helped them depend less on white people.

Remember
The NAACP was formed in 1909 to gain equal rights and opportunities for African Americans.

Some African Americans formed groups that hoped to build a new homeland in Africa. A homeland was never set up in Africa. However, African Americans became proud of their heritage during the 1920s.

What was the Great Migration? The movement of African Americans to northern cities by the thousands to get industrial jobs

Section 3 Review

1. What economic problems did the country face after World War I?
2. Why did African Americans leave the South?
3. **Critical Thinking** Why do you think the Ku Klux Klan gained more members during the 1920s?
4. **Write About Citizenship** Write a paragraph to express your opinion of the immigration law passed in 1921.

More Review is provided in Exercise 77 of the Workbook.

1. Inflation, not enough jobs, strikes, businesses could not keep up with the demands for goods
2. Unfair working conditions, poor farming conditions, racism
3. Student responses should mention growing fear that immigrants and African Americans were taking jobs white Americans felt belonged to them.
4. Student responses might mention a sense of disappointment that Americans would want to deny other people the opportunity to live in the United States.

Chapter

18 Review

Summary Have students use this graphic organizer to outline the main ideas and details of the chapter.

Summary
In the 1920s, cars, music, movies, and the radio became part of everyday life. Problems in the economy led to strikes, anti-immigration feelings, and discrimination.

Section 1
The automobile industry changed the way people lived. Household goods were produced to improve life.

Section 2
The 1920s was a time of new music, art, literature, and entertainment. People had more leisure time.

Section 3
Men returning from World War I had problems finding work. Strong feelings against immigrants began to grow. Many African Americans migrated north.

deport
installment plan
mass media
assembly line
inflation

More Vocabulary Review is provided in Exercise 118 of the Classroom Resource Binder.

Vocabulary Review

Write the term from the list that matches each definition below.

1. Radio, newspapers, magazines, and books mass media

2. A sudden and sharp rise of prices inflation

3. To order someone who is not a U.S. citizen out of the country because of an action against the government deport

4. A way that people can buy an item without having the money to pay for it at that time installment plan

5. A way of making huge amounts of the same product quickly assembly line

1. Different jobs, people traveled more, more roads, new businesses pp. 335–336 **2.** Many African American writers, musicians, and artists moved from the South. p. 341 **3.** They feared Communists would take control of all businesses and property in the U.S. pp. 345–346 **4.** Possible answer: People bought more, more products needed pp. 336–338 **5.** Possible answer: Women became more aware of injustices against women and learned about others advancing the cause of equal rights. pp. 342–343

Chapter Quiz

Write your answers in complete sentences.

1. How did the automobile change the lives of Americans?
2. Why was Harlem the center of a renaissance in the 1920s?
3. Why did many people fear communism in the 1920s?
4. **Critical Thinking** How did advertising help the economy?
5. **Critical Thinking** How do you think the mass media affected women in their struggle for equal rights?

Test Tip
To prepare for a test, answer the review questions in your book.

Writing Tip
When writing a paragraph, state the purpose of the paragraph in the beginning. You can support the purpose with facts and examples.

Using the Timeline

Use the timeline on pages 332–333 to answer the questions.

1. In what year did the first radio broadcast take place? 1920
2. What timeline entry shows that immigrants were not welcome in the United States? Immigration Law of 1921

Group Activity See the Teacher's Planning Guide for a scoring rubric for this activity.

Group Activity

With your group, create a poster for a movie, musical, or sports event. Give the event a title. Add the date and time of the event. Hang your posters around the classroom.

During the Great Depression, some people lived in shacks made of wood and tin. Some people sold apples to earn money. What does the photograph above show about people's lives during the Great Depression? People were having a difficult time. They lived in shacks.

The Great Depression

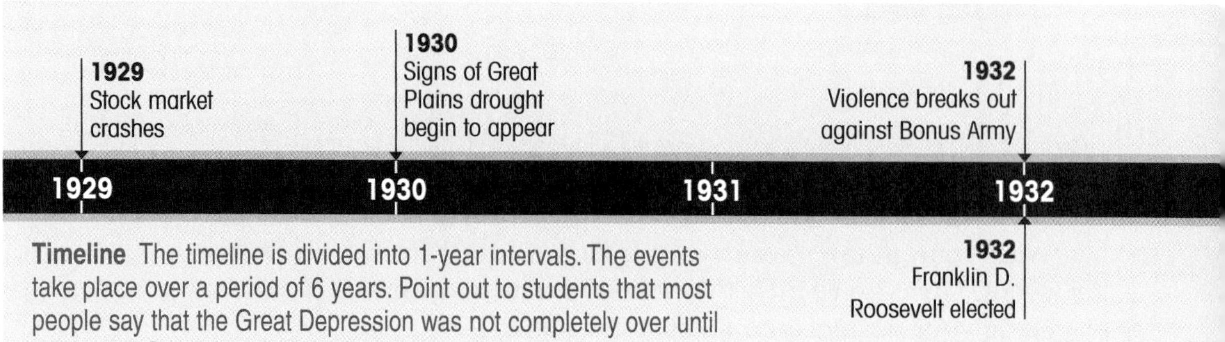

Timeline The timeline is divided into 1-year intervals. The events take place over a period of 6 years. Point out to students that most people say that the Great Depression was not completely over until the United States entered World War II in 1941.

Additional activities and strategies to customize lessons can be found in the Teacher's Planning Guide.

Chapter 19 The Great Depression 1929–1934

ESL Note To help students understand the concept of economic depression, discuss difficult economic times they, or people they know, may have experienced in other countries. What were the causes and effects?

Words to Know

stock market

depression

default

foreclose

bonus

drought

migrant worker

public works

relief

Words to Know These words are defined in the section in which they appear, as well as in the Glossary. Point out to students that the suffix *-ion* indicates a state of being. In this case, it indicates the state of being *depressed*, or lowered.

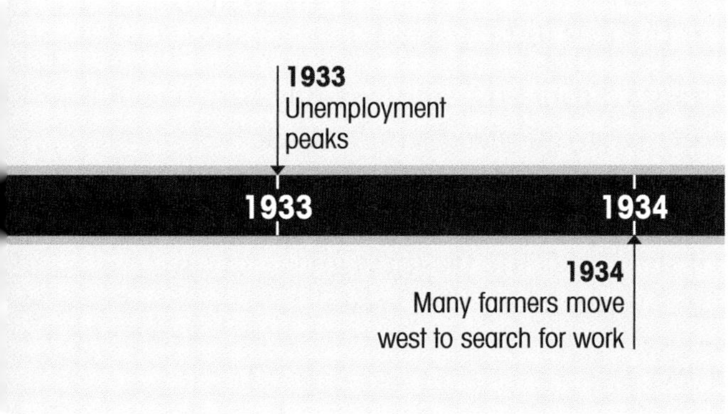

Learning Objectives

- Explain the causes of the Great Depression.
- Describe how the Great Depression changed the lives of Americans.
- Discuss the hardships suffered by farmers, African Americans, and Mexican Americans during the Great Depression.
- Explain President Hoover's approach to helping Americans during the Great Depression.
- Explore how the Dust Bowl affected Americans.

Project Students will be able to begin the project after they have finished reading the chapter. Students may need to do additional research.

Portfolio Project

You have been asked to help prepare a television documentary on the Great Depression. Choose a group of people whose lives were affected by that event. Take notes on the ways that their lives changed. Write an article describing what happened.

Section 1 The Nation's Troubled Economy

Words to Know

stock market	a place where stocks, or shares in businesses, are bought and sold
depression	a time when the economy of a nation falls sharply
default	to fail to pay a loan when it is due
foreclose	to take the property of someone who has failed to pay back a loan
bonus	money given in addition to what is owed

Getting Started Discuss with students how they would feel if their money suddenly disappeared. Explain that at this time in history many people all over the United States actually lost all their money.

In the 1920s, the media often made the times seem carefree and exciting. Yet, many people had barely enough money to pay their bills. When the U.S. economy began to fall apart, the nation suffered.

Telegraphic ticker machines were used in stock markets during the 1920s.

The Stock Market Crash

In the 1920s, fewer than five percent of Americans were wealthy. Most Americans lived on a yearly income of $3,000 or less. They worked long hours for low pay. When Americans needed something that cost a lot, some people borrowed money that they could not pay back. Some paid on the installment plan.

To solve their money problems, some people turned to the **stock market.** That is a place where stocks, or shares in businesses, are bought and sold. When people bought stocks, they became part owners of a business. They hoped to become rich as the business grew. In the late 1920s, businesses were doing very well.

Visual In 1869, Thomas Edison invented an improved ticker machine called the Edison Universal Stock Printer. He sold the rights for $40,000.

People made money in the stock market, and they wanted to make even more money. Many people borrowed money to buy more stocks.

In the autumn of 1929, however, the stock prices began to drop. People did not want to lose their money, so they began to sell their stocks. As a result, the prices dropped even more. On October 29, 1929, stock prices plunged. Many stocks became worthless. People who had borrowed money to buy stocks had suddenly lost all their money.

What caused the stock market to crash in 1929? As people tried to sell their stocks, the value of the stocks dropped.

The Great Depression

Soon after the stock market crash, the United States entered a **depression.** A depression is a time when the economy of a nation falls sharply. It was called the Great Depression.

As the 1920s ended, millions of people were out of work. Farmers were losing their farms. Banks began to go out of business because they had used their customers' savings to buy stocks.

Other things were happening in the country that helped bring about the Great Depression. During World War I, many farmers had sold food crops to the armed forces. They earned a lot of money. After the war, fewer crops were needed. Prices fell. Many farmers who had borrowed money for farm machines began to **default** on their payments. To default is to fail to pay back a loan when it is due.

The clothing and coal-mining industries grew smaller as big businesses grew larger. Thousands of factory workers in small industries lost their jobs.

Who was affected by the Great Depression? The Great Depression affected everyone, including factory workers, bankers, and farmers.

Economics Fact

The day on which the New York Stock Market crashed was called Black Tuesday.

Economics Fact Tell students that after Black Tuesday, stock values fell steadily for the next three years. Between 1930 and 1933, stock prices went down 80 percent.

Hard Times

By the beginning of 1932, the U.S. economy had almost fallen completely apart. Thousands of businesses had closed. Factory owners could not afford to pay their employees. Many people lost their jobs. As a result, most Americans could not afford to buy all the goods that were being made.

Unsold goods began to pile up. Some factories made fewer goods, so the factories needed fewer workers. Even more people lost their jobs. The workers who had jobs were paid very little. Families sometimes had less than $1.50 a day to buy food.

A Closer Look

TEENAGERS IN THE GREAT DEPRESSION

During the Great Depression, millions of Americans did not have a place to live. About 250,000 of those homeless Americans were under 21.

One reason teenagers left home was that there were no jobs. Others felt that they were a burden to their families. Some took to the road for the adventure.

Some teenagers traveled on top of boxcars. A boxcar is a type of railroad car. This ride was thrilling, but dangerous. Many died or were injured. Others died from disease or hunger. Sometimes, teenagers on the road would not eat for days.

Some teenagers found work on farms where they picked crops. Many did not find jobs until after the Great Depression came to an end.

Some teenagers left home to find jobs.

Critical Thinking How was life difficult for a teenager during the Great Depression? Teenagers died from boxcar accidents, hunger, and disease. It was hard to find jobs.

Farm families were deeply hurt by the Great Depression. When farmers began to default on the payments, banks were forced to **foreclose** on their property. Foreclose means to take the property of someone who has failed to pay back a loan. In one day in 1932, banks foreclosed on one fourth of all the farms in Mississippi.

The Great Depression grew even worse. Many Americans lost their homes as well as their jobs. In every large city, people stood in line for hours for free loaves of bread. Families sold apples to earn a few cents. Hungry children picked through garbage pails for scraps of food.

This woman sold apples to earn money.

Visual By 1933, one in four Americans who wanted to work was unable to find a job.

What are two examples of hard times in the United States during the Great Depression? People lost their homes and jobs, waited for handouts, and rummaged for food.

Jobless and Hopeless

The Great Depression continued, and the government and business leaders had no answers. Americans asked President Hoover for help. Of course, Hoover wanted to end the Great Depression. However, he felt that help from government charity was not the answer. Hoover felt that Americans had to help themselves.

The failure of the government and big business to help people made many Americans angry. These are some of the things that people did to express their anger.

1. Some workers without jobs joined the Communist party.
2. Some farmers destroyed their crops rather than sell them at unfair prices.
3. Some farmers joined together to stop banks from taking their property.
4. Many World War I veterans marched on Washington, D.C., in 1932.

World War I veterans were especially angry with the government. After World War I, Congress had voted to give veterans a **bonus**. A bonus is money given in addition to what is owed.

When the Great Depression hit, the veterans asked for the bonus, but Congress refused to pay it. During the summer of 1932, 15,000 veterans formed what became known as the Bonus Army. They camped out in the nation's capital. The veterans promised to remain there until they received their bonuses.

President Hoover feared that there might be violence. He ordered U.S. troops to drive out the Bonus Army. Armed soldiers attacked the veterans' camps. The sight of American soldiers attacking men who had fought for their country sickened many people. To many Americans, it meant that a change was needed in government.

How did President Hoover feel about the government helping Americans during the Great Depression?
President Hoover felt that government charity was not the answer to the problem.

Section 1 Review

1. How would buying stocks help people to become rich?
2. What happened to many businesses in the late 1920s?
3. **Critical Thinking** How do you think the U.S. government might have avoided the violence against the Bonus Army?
4. **Write About History** Choose one change in people's lives caused by the Great Depression. Write a newspaper article about the change.

1. The value of stocks would increase as businesses grew. When the price of the stocks went up, they could be sold at a profit.
2. Businesses lost money and had to let workers go.
3. Possible answer: Both sides might have met to discuss possible solutions and work out compromises.
4. Student responses might describe a specific hardship in people's daily life.

More Review is provided in Exercise 79 of the Workbook.

Section 2 Hard Times for Americans

Words to Know

drought	a long period of very dry weather
migrant worker	a worker who travels from place to place to harvest crops

Getting Started Discuss with students a time when they could not fix a problem and had to start over again. Explain that for many families during the Great Depression, employment was so scarce that they had no choice but to try again somewhere else.

The Great Depression affected Americans in different ways. However, the people who suffered most were farmers, immigrants, African Americans, and unskilled workers. These Americans had difficult lives to begin with. During the Great Depression, their suffering was even greater. Unemployment for African Americans was twice the national average.

Changes in Family Life

The Great Depression brought many changes to American families. Some families who worked together to survive grew closer. However, in many cases, having no job or home tore families apart. Many men who felt hopeless left their wives and children. Many teenagers felt that they should support themselves, so they left home.

Millions of young children had to work to help their families survive. Children as young as seven years old sold newspapers, did yard work, and ran errands for a few pennies a day. Many children had to leave school to work or watch younger children while their parents looked for work.

How did the Great Depression change American family life? Some families split up. In other families, children often helped out.

The Dust Bowl

Map This map shows the area affected by the Dust Bowl. Students might be surprised to learn how far east the dust blew.

1. North Dakota, South Dakota, Nebraska, Kansas, Oklahoma, Texas, New Mexico, Colorado, Wyoming, and Montana
2. The area west of the Rocky Mountains

During World War I, farmers of the Great Plains made huge profits growing food for the armed forces. After World War I, falling prices made farming a difficult way to earn a living. Then shortly after the Great Depression began, a **drought** turned much of the Great Plains into a dusty, dry land. A drought is a long period of very dry weather. The Great Plains became a dust bowl.

By 1934, thousands of farmers decided to leave their farms. They packed everything they could into old cars

The Dust Bowl, 1930s

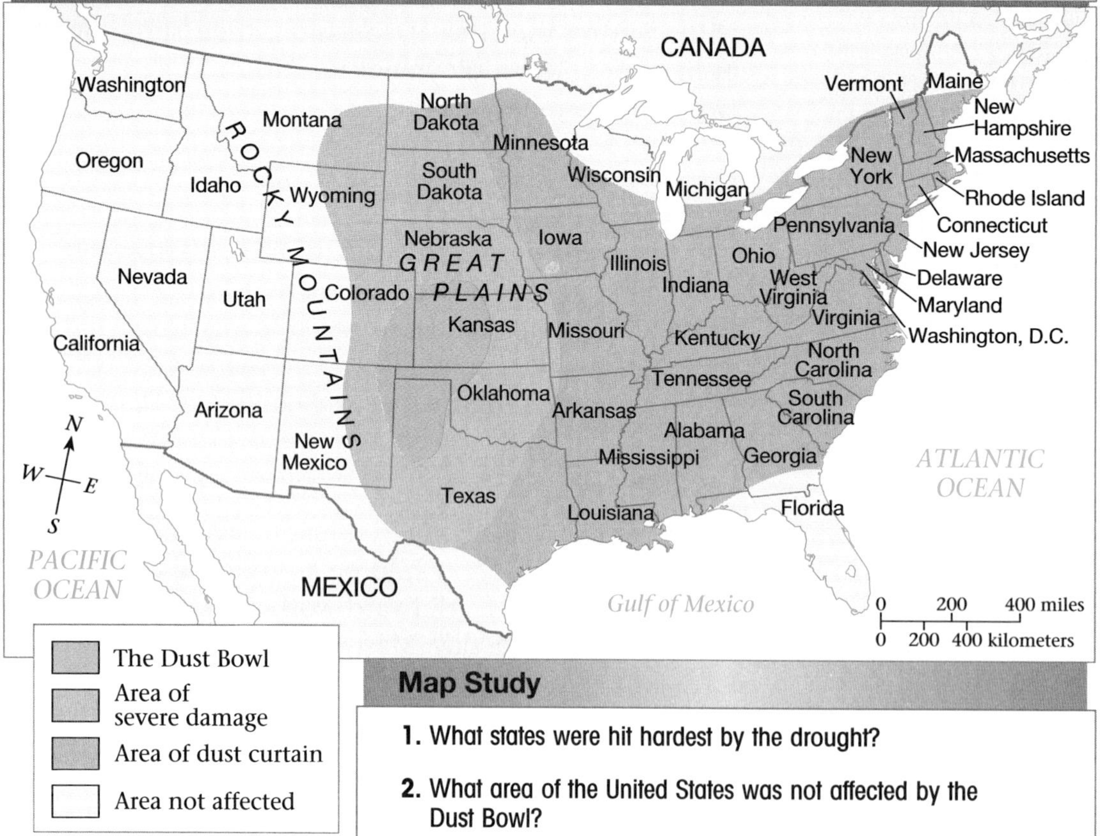

Map Study

1. What states were hit hardest by the drought?
2. What area of the United States was not affected by the Dust Bowl?

and trucks. They headed west on a long journey to California in search of work.

The newcomers were not welcome in California. The people there were suffering too. One sign at the California border said, "No Jobs in California. If you are looking for work—Keep Out."

Many newcomers worked for vegetable and fruit growers, picking crops. Whole families worked as **migrant workers.** A migrant worker travels from one place to another to harvest crops.

Working all day, a person might earn $1.50. That was barely enough to keep someone alive. At night, people crowded into tents and slept on the ground. When the job was finished, they moved on to pick the next crop.

Economics Fact

During the Great Depression, a quart of milk sold for 10 cents. A loaf of bread cost 5 cents.

Economics Fact A six-room house could cost under $3,000.

? **Why did farmers on the Great Plains decide to leave their farms?** They left in search of work after their farms had been destroyed by drought.

African Americans and the Great Depression

African Americans had been among the poorest Americans for a long time. When the Great Depression hit, their lives became even harder.

As the economy grew worse, African Americans were the first workers to be fired. Many bosses lowered the pay of African Americans to save money. Many African Americans, who often had the most dangerous and dirty jobs, lost their jobs to white people. By 1932, one half of all African Americans had no jobs.

Life in the South was even harder for African Americans. Most were farmers who worked the land of white owners. Whole families worked to grow cotton. They raised animals and a few crops to feed themselves.

Falling cotton prices in the early 1930s created terrible hardships. African Americans lived in shacks.

Jobs were hard to find. These African Americans drove from Tennessee to Arkansas to work for a day in the cotton fields.

Visual Some African American churches started free "soup kitchens" to feed the hungry. In some cities, African Americans joined together to buy large amounts of food at lower prices.

These shacks had no heat or plumbing. The people lived on corn meal, pork scraps, and even weeds. Some families lived on less than $250 a year.

The hard times in the South also brought a rise in violence. Lynchings of African Americans by white people were always a threat.

How did the Great Depression affect the lives of African Americans? When the Great Depression hit, many African Americans were the first to lose their jobs.

Mexican Americans and the Great Depression

During the 1920s, many Mexican immigrants and Mexican Americans moved to large U.S. cities. Some came to work in factories. Others found work outside the city on large farms. Mexican immigrants and Mexican Americans suffered during the Great Depression.

As the Great Depression became worse, farm workers complained that Mexican immigrants and Mexican Americans were taking jobs from other Americans. Factory workers in the cities said that Mexican immigrants and Mexican Americans worked for lower pay and were taking their jobs.

Mexican immigrants and Mexican Americans were forced to live in the poorest areas. Yet Mexican immigrants continued to settle in the United States even though they were not welcome. Local authorities ordered thousands of Mexican immigrants to leave the country.

Remember
In 1921, the government passed a law limiting the number of immigrants allowed into the United States.

What problems did Mexican immigrants and Mexican Americans face during the Great Depression?
Mexican Americans and Mexican immigrants worked for lower pay, lived in the poorest areas, and faced prejudices.

Section 2 Review

1. Why did the Great Depression affect farmers, Mexican immigrants, African Americans, and unskilled workers so much?
2. During the Great Depression, how was the treatment of African Americans and Mexican Americans alike?
3. **Critical Thinking** Why do you think there was violence against African Americans in the South during the Great Depression?
4. **Write About Geography** You are leaving the family farm on the Great Plains. Describe what the land looks like as you drive away in a rundown truck.

1. They had the fewest resources to begin with. They found it harder to get jobs; their living conditions got worse.
2. Both groups were targets of prejudice and blame. They were forced to live in the poorest areas.
3. People were frustrated by poverty and looked for someone to blame.
4. Student responses might use details to describe the Dust Bowl they are leaving behind.

More Review is provided in Exercise 80 of the Workbook.

CONNECTING HISTORY AND THE ENVIRONMENT: The Dust Bowl

Early in the 1930s, a drought set in on the Great Plains. With no rainfall, the soil in the fields dried out. Grass, which was needed to protect the soil, could not grow in the sun-baked fields. Soon, the soil turned to dust and was blown away. Roads were covered with huge mounds of dust. Houses and barns were buried in sand. Some mounds of sand were 30 feet high. The Great Plains became a dust bowl.

Soil turned to dust and was blown away.

Strong winds blew over the dry, bare fields. They carried the dust from the Great Plains eastward across the United States. The dust that drifted to the East coast was called a dust curtain.

In 1934, President Franklin Roosevelt ordered that trees be planted on millions of acres of farmland. Lines of trees called windbreaks were planted to protect the fields. This plan took many years to work. By then, most farmers had lost their land.

Answer the questions below.

1. Why was the Great Plains called the Dust Bowl in the early 1930s?

2. What did President Franklin Roosevelt do to stop the damage done by the drought and wind?

CHALLENGE How can citizens today help care for the environment?

1. Because tons of the region's soil blew away in strong winds, creating clouds of dust **2.** He ordered millions of acres of farmland to be planted with trees to create windbreaks. **CHALLENGE** Possible answer: By knowing and following recycling rules, conserving natural resources, educating citizens in caring for the environment

Section 3

The U.S. Government and the Great Depression

Words to Know

public works	construction projects paid for by public funds
relief	help given to poor people

Getting Started Discuss with students how a government might help hungry, jobless people. Explain that the people in the United States were in a situation so bad that the government needed to help them.

History Fact

Herbert Hoover was the first President to be born west of the Mississippi River. He was born in West Branch, Iowa.

History Fact After Hoover's election to the presidency, the ordinary cottage he grew up in became a tourist attraction. Grant Wood, the American artist, portrayed this image in his painting, *The Birthplace of Herbert Hoover, West Branch, Iowa.*

By 1932, most Americans blamed President Hoover for not doing enough to fight the Great Depression. Many people were surprised that Hoover had no answers. They felt it was time to look to another leader.

President Hoover's Actions

Herbert Hoover was a smart businessman who was a millionaire by the age of 40. During World War I, he had headed the government bureau that sent food and clothing to people in need in Europe.

When the Great Depression hit, Americans wondered why a smart businessman had so few plans for helping the U.S. economy. They also wondered why a man who helped Europeans in need could not find a way to help Americans.

In fact, some of President Hoover's actions made the problems in the economy worse. In 1930, Hoover signed a law that hurt trade with foreign countries. As a result, fewer goods came into the United States. American businesses were not able to sell goods overseas. The slowing of trade meant that European countries had to default on money they owed to the United States.

Once President Hoover understood how serious the Great Depression was, he did take some action. President Hoover asked Congress to pass several laws to help people in the United States.

1. One law started **public works** to put people to work. Public works are construction projects paid for by public funds, such as building roads, docks, and canals.
2. A second law cut taxes.
3. Another law lent money to banks and other businesses.

Most of Hoover's actions came too late to be helpful. Hoover's main belief was that helping people would destroy their freedom. It would make them depend too much on the government. Hoover believed the government should not be responsible for solving the problems of the economy.

Visual Roosevelt was a very popular President. He was elected four times, in 1932, 1936, 1940, and 1944. He served longer than any other President, more than 12 years.

What actions did President Hoover take to fight the Great Depression? He asked Congress to pass laws to support public works, cut taxes, and lent money to banks and other businesses.

Franklin D. Roosevelt won the election of 1932.

A New President

President Hoover was not able to solve the problems caused by the Great Depression. Yet, he ran for a second term. Hoover tried to show that he should be chosen over Franklin Delano Roosevelt, who ran against him in the election for President.

Roosevelt believed that the government should do more to help Americans during this difficult time. Hoover believed that Roosevelt's plan was a danger to the American way of life. According to Hoover, Roosevelt's plan would give the U.S. government too much power. Hoover saw danger in a government that was too strong.

In 1932, Americans elected a new President, Franklin Delano Roosevelt. Roosevelt won easily. The American people felt a change had to be made. They hoped a new leader could do something to help the nation.

For many Americans, Roosevelt's speeches were filled with hope. He called for strong government programs to care for suffering families. He called for **relief** payments. Relief is help given to poor people. Roosevelt said the government had a duty to "see that no citizen shall starve."

When he took office, Franklin D. Roosevelt said it was the government's job to end the Great Depression. "Our greatest task is to put people to work," he said.

Why did Franklin D. Roosevelt win the election of 1932 so easily? Americans wanted a change, and Franklin D. Roosevelt offered hope. He wanted to involve the government in ending the Great Depression.

Section 3 Review

1. How did President Hoover feel about offering relief to people during the Great Depression?
2. What did Franklin D. Roosevelt call for in helping Americans during the Great Depression?
3. **Critical Thinking** What did the election of 1932 show about Americans' response to President Hoover's policies?
4. **Write About Citizenship** You plan to vote for Roosevelt in 1932. Write a radio commercial telling why people should vote for Roosevelt.

More Review is provided in Exercise 82 of the Workbook.

1. President Hoover believed that the government should not interfere with the problems of the economy.
2. He called for strong government programs to care for Americans.
3. Americans wanted relief; were tired of empty promises. They felt government should intervene.
4. Possible answer: Roosevelt gave people hope; was ready to take action; needed a change from Hoover's inaction.

Chapter

19 Review

Summary Have students use this graphic organizer to outline the main ideas and details of the chapter.

Summary

During the Great Depression, many Americans were not able to find work. The Great Depression lasted about 10 years and affected every part of American life.

Section 1

The good times of the 1920s ended. When the stock market crashed in 1929, the Great Depression followed. It brought hard times to most Americans.

Section 2

Most Americans, especially African Americans, Mexican Americans, and Mexican immigrants, suffered in the Great Depression. The Dust Bowl forced thousands of farm families to move west.

Section 3

President Herbert Hoover was not able to get the nation out of the Great Depression. Franklin D. Roosevelt promised to help Americans. He was elected in 1932.

bonus
migrant worker
public works
default
drought

More Vocabulary Review is provided in Exercise 125 of the Classroom Resource Binder.

Vocabulary Review

Fill in the blank with a term from the list.

1. Building a canal to join two rivers is a ___project. public works
2. People who ___on their car payments may get into trouble. default
3. Workers who work hard and bring more business to their company may be given a ___. bonus
4. No rain for a long time may cause a ___. drought
5. A ___may pick apples in one part of the country and oranges in another part. migrant worker

1. Stock market crash, bank failures, unemployment, farmers' problems, installment buying p. 353
2. Jobless workers joined the Communist party; farmers destroyed their crops; joined to stop bank takeover of their property. p. 355 **3.** Work hard to get; workers constantly traveling; wages low pp. 358–359 **4.** They worked on farms or were migrant workers pp. 359–361 **5.** His policies made problems worse. The country couldn't do much trading with foreign countries; less money made; less selling of goods. p. 363

Chapter Quiz

Write your answers in complete sentences.

1. What were two causes of the Great Depression?
2. How did jobless workers and farmers express their anger?
3. Why was life difficult for a migrant worker?
4. **Critical Thinking** Why did the failure of farms hurt African Americans, Mexican Americans, and Mexican immigrants so much?
5. **Critical Thinking** How did Hoover's trade policies affect the economy during the Great Depression?

Test Tip
To prepare for a test, write a list of questions you think will be asked. Then answer them.

Writing Tip
Do not begin sentences with *but* or *and*.

Using the Timeline

Use the timeline on pages 350–351 to answer the questions.

1. In what year were the most Americans out of work? 1933
2. How many years after the stock market crash did farmers move west to search for work? Five

Group Activity See the Teacher's Planning Guide for a scoring rubric for this activity.

Group Activity

With your group, discuss the steps that you think President Roosevelt should take to begin to help Americans recover from the Great Depression. Make a list of your ideas. Check it against the steps you will read about in the next chapter.

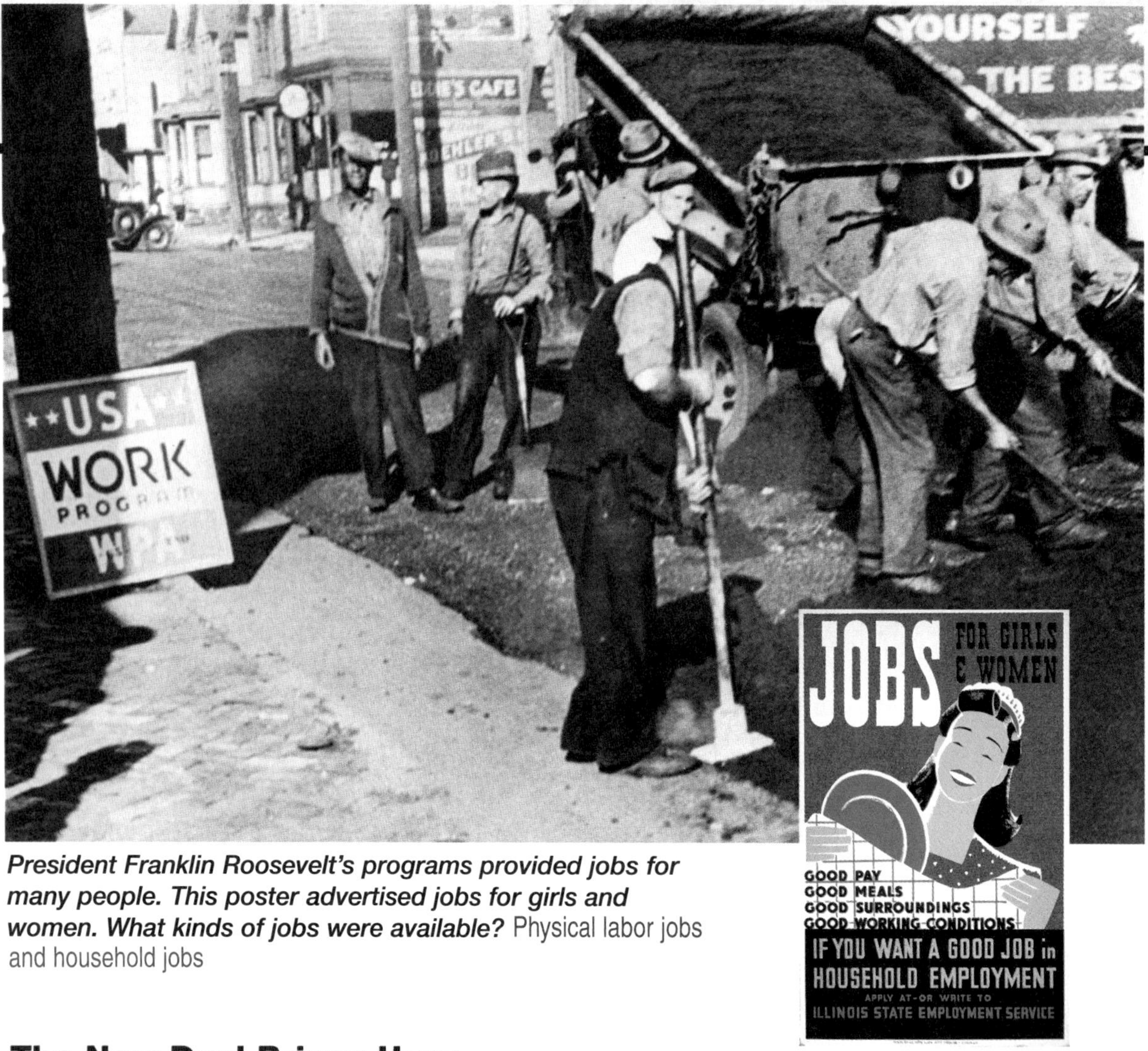

President Franklin Roosevelt's programs provided jobs for many people. This poster advertised jobs for girls and women. What kinds of jobs were available? Physical labor jobs and household jobs

The New Deal Brings Hope

1933
Roosevelt's fireside chats begin

1933
Civilian Conservation Corps established

1934
Indian Reorganization Act passed

1935
Social Security Board established

1935
National Labor Relations Board established

1936
Jesse Owens wins four Olympic medals

1936
Franklin Roosevelt reelected

1933 1934 1935 1936 1937 1938

Additional activities and strategies to customize lessons can be found in the Teacher's Planning Guide.

Chapter 20 The New Deal 1933–1941

ESL Note To help students understand the concept of government programs, ask pairs of students to discuss how the government in their families' countries either helps or does not help their citizens. If appropriate, students can share ideas with the class.

Words to Know

New Deal

fireside chat

conservative

liberal

soap opera

anti-Semitism

Words to Know These words are defined in the section in which they appear, as well as in the Glossary. Point out to students that *New Deal*, *fireside chat*, and *soap opera* are open compound words.

Timeline The timeline is divided into 1-year intervals. The events take place over a period of 8 years. Point out that for the first, and only time, a President was elected for more than two terms.

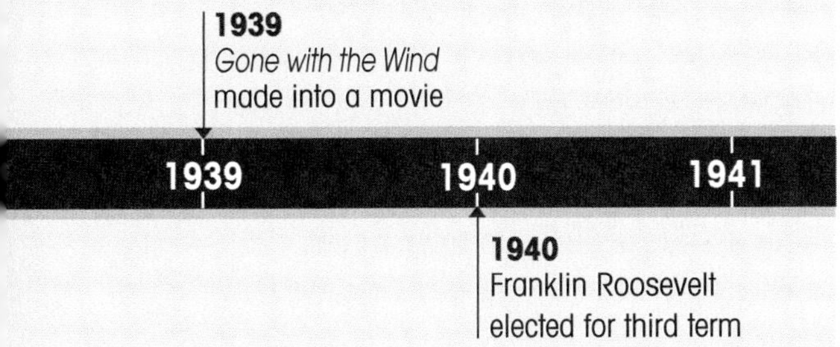

Learning Objectives

- Describe the steps that Franklin D. Roosevelt took to end the Great Depression.
- Identify the programs developed during the New Deal.
- Explain why some people were against the New Deal.
- Describe how the New Deal affected the lives of Americans.
- Identify how Americans spent their free time during the 1930s.
- Explore how Franklin D. Roosevelt's speeches brought hope to a nation.

Project Students will be able to begin work on the project after completing Section 3. Students should take notes throughout the chapter to help them prepare.

Portfolio Project

During the Great Depression, the U.S. government started projects for many artists, writers, and musicians. Decide how you could express your feelings about the Great Depression. Create a poster, a poem, or a song about the Great Depression and the changes it brought to the United States.

Section 1 The New Deal Begins

Words to Know

New Deal	Franklin D. Roosevelt's plan for helping the U.S. economy during the Great Depression
fireside chat	a radio speech to Americans given by President Franklin Roosevelt

Getting Started Discuss with students times when people need help. Discuss how people looked for solutions to their problems. Explain that during the Great Depression many Americans needed help and turned to their new President for solutions.

History Fact

Franklin D. Roosevelt was a cousin of Theodore Roosevelt, the twenty-sixth President.

History Fact Theodore and Franklin were fifth cousins. Both were descendents of Klaes Martensen Van Roosevelt, a Dutch landowner who in the 1640s settled in what is now New York City.

By 1932, about 12 million Americans were without jobs. Most were also without money and without hope. They were looking for a new leader. They found that leader in Franklin D. Roosevelt.

Roosevelt Takes Charge

When Franklin D. Roosevelt ran for President in 1932, he promised "a new deal for the American people." The **New Deal** was the name of Roosevelt's plan for helping the U.S. economy during the Great Depression.

Many voters supported Roosevelt's plan. In the election of 1932, Roosevelt won most of the votes in 42 of the 48 states. His election was a landslide, or a huge victory.

Franklin D. Roosevelt took office on a gray day in March 1933. For many Americans, the cloudy sky seemed to capture the feelings of the country. When Franklin Roosevelt gave his first speech as President, he spoke to millions of Americans. His words were carried across the country by radio. They gave Americans new hope. "The only thing we have to fear is fear itself," said Roosevelt.

Roosevelt's strong words helped Americans feel that the problems caused by the Great Depression could be solved. His plan became known as the Three R's. The Three R's stood for *relief, recovery,* and *reform*. This was how President Roosevelt's Three R's plan worked.

1. Relief—give help immediately to jobless workers who were in need.
2. Recovery—give help to banks, businesses, farmers, and workers to recover from the Great Depression.
3. Reform—make long-term changes in the economy so that a depression would never happen again.

Why did Franklin D. Roosevelt have such a huge victory in the election of 1932? Many voters supported him because of his promise of "a new deal for the American people."

Visual Someone once asked Eleanor Roosevelt if she thought her husband's illness had changed him. She said anyone who has suffered greatly is bound to have greater sympathy for and an understanding of the problems of mankind.

Many Americans were happy to support President Roosevelt.

The Brain Trust

President Roosevelt asked several men and women who were experts in certain areas to put his plans into action. College teachers, experts on the economy, and people who had worked with the poor joined the group known as the Brain Trust.

Frances Perkins was the first female Cabinet member.

Visual Early in her career, Frances Perkins lobbied for better conditions for workers. After witnessing the Triangle Shirtwaist Company Fire, Perkins worked to make factories safer.

Roosevelt chose Frances Perkins to join his Cabinet. For many years, Perkins had found ways to help people who were out of work. She had also worked for child labor reform. When Perkins became the secretary of labor, she was the first woman to hold a Cabinet position.

What was the Brain Trust? A group of experts in certain areas who President Roosevelt asked to help execute his New Deal.

The Hundred Days

Five days after Franklin Roosevelt became President, he called a special meeting of Congress. The President and Congress began to work on his plan for the nation.

President Roosevelt wanted to explain his plans to the American people as soon as possible. On March 12, 1933, he spoke on the radio to the nation from a chair near a fireplace in the White House. This was the first of his famous **fireside chats.** Roosevelt explained his goals in simple terms to millions of Americans.

Soon, President Roosevelt and Congress began working together to end the Great Depression. Never before had Congress passed so many laws so quickly. The period during which these bills were passed was from March 9 to June 16. It was called the Hundred Days.

The chart on the next page shows the first of several new changes that were made. Since there were so many programs, people often used the initial letters of the program name to describe it.

Why did President Roosevelt use the radio to speak to the nation? He wanted to personally explain his plans for the nation to the American people.

Early New Deal Programs

Program	Date	Purpose
Civilian Conservation Corps (CCC)	March 1933	Provided jobs, such as planting trees and building small dams, for young men from needy families
Agricultural Adjustment Administration (AAA)	May 1933	Paid farmers not to grow crops so that farm prices would rise
Federal Emergency Relief Administration (FERA)	May 1933	Helped families needing food, housing, clothes
Tennessee Valley Authority (TVA)	May 1933	Built dams on the Tennessee River to control flooding and to help produce hydroelectricity, or electricity produced by the power of quickly moving water
National Industrial Recovery Act (NIRA)	June 1933	Made sure all businesses worked together

Chart Study

1. **Which program controlled flooding in the Tennessee River?** Tennessee Valley Authority (TVA)
2. **Which program provided jobs for young men?** Civilian Conservation Corps (CCC)

Section 1 Review

1. What was the name of President Franklin Roosevelt's plan to get the nation out of the Great Depression?
2. What were the Hundred Days?
3. **Critical Thinking** Why were people ready to support President Roosevelt when he first took office?
4. **Write About History** Write an interview that you had with someone in President Roosevelt's Brain Trust. Ask about their area of knowledge.

More Review is provided in Exercise 83 of the Workbook.

Chart Point out to students that all Presidents have a 100-day honeymoon period with Congress. During that time, they set forth the agenda for their term.

1. The New Deal
2. The period during which many bills for the New Deal program were passed.
3. Student responses should mention that Roosevelt initiated relief and recovery programs right away. He took action, unlike Hoover.
4. Possible answer: Discuss how the person contributed to the Brain Trust; ideas given.

VOICES FROM THE PAST
Franklin D. Roosevelt

Eleven years before Franklin Roosevelt was elected President, he was paralyzed by polio. Polio was one of the most feared diseases of the time. Roosevelt worked hard to learn to walk again. However, he never was able to walk without help. He continued to be interested in government. He was not a man to be stopped by difficulties.

Years later, as President, Franklin Roosevelt often spoke to the American people. His speeches made people feel that the problems they faced could be solved. His words, written below, came at a time when many people were out of work and out of hope.

President Roosevelt often spoke to the American people on the radio.

"It is common sense to take a method and try it. If it fails, admit it frankly and try another. But above all, try something."

"Let us unite in banishing [getting rid of] fear. . . . Together we cannot fail."

"I never forget that I live in a house owned by all the American people and that I have been given their trust."

Answer the questions below.

1. What advice did President Roosevelt give to people who did not succeed the first time they tried something?

2. What "house" is Roosevelt speaking of in the last statement?

CHALLENGE How do you think Franklin Roosevelt's battle against polio helped him to understand the struggles Americans faced in the Great Depression?

1. His advice was to admit failure and try another method. **2.** President Roosevelt lived in the White House. **CHALLENGE** Roosevelt knew about adversity, determination, and hard work in his personal life. That helped him to empathize with others and to encourage them in hard times.

Section 2 Social Reform and the New Deal

Words to Know

conservative	a person who wants the government to do less for its citizens
liberal	a person who wants the government to do more for its citizens

Getting Started Discuss with students some changes, or reforms, they would like to see at school. Would everyone agree with these reforms? Explain that not everyone agreed with President Roosevelt's New Deal reforms.

Franklin Roosevelt's first plans to end the Great Depression helped some people. However, after two years, the U.S. economy was still in serious trouble. Many people were still unemployed. Roosevelt made even stronger plans. Not everyone agreed with those plans.

Disagreement Over the New Deal

After two years of the New Deal, millions of Americans were still jobless. Many people wondered whether the United States would ever get out of the Great Depression. Roosevelt decided to make further plans. The economy remained in trouble and some people began to attack Roosevelt's programs.

Conservatives felt Roosevelt was asking the government to do too much. A conservative is a person who wants the government to do less for its citizens. These are the reasons conservatives did not like the New Deal.

1. The New Deal hurt businesses because the programs raised taxes.
2. The New Deal interfered too much in people's lives and in business.
3. The New Deal spent too much money to help people without jobs.

On the other hand, **liberals** felt that Roosevelt was not asking the government to do enough. A liberal is a person who feels the government must do more for its citizens. These are the reasons liberals did not like Roosevelt's New Deal.

1. The New Deal was not strong enough to solve the problems of the Great Depression.

2. The New Deal was just more of the same ideas that had failed in the past.

Conservatives formed groups against Roosevelt. Liberals spoke out about making a new system of government that helped the average person.

In 1936, Roosevelt won another election by a landslide. Although the problems of the Great Depression remained, Roosevelt believed that the American people were behind him.

President Roosevelt had already done a lot to help the American people. He continued to work for them. The chart on the next page shows some of the programs that President Roosevelt and Congress put into action.

Why did conservatives and liberals disagree over the New Deal? Conservatives: government already doing too much; Liberals: government not doing enough

Roosevelt and the Supreme Court

Most Americans supported President Roosevelt's plans. However, the Supreme Court disagreed with the President. It felt that the President's programs gave the government too much power. It thought some New Deal programs were against the Constitution.

The opinion of Supreme Court members shocked President Roosevelt. He decided to do something. He said that the country needed more and younger judges. Six of the nine judges had reached the age of 70. Roosevelt felt the President should have the power

New Deal Agencies

Agency	Year	Purpose
Federal Deposit Insurance Corporation (FDIC)	1933	To protect savings in banks
Home Owners Loan Corporation (HOLC)	1933	To give long-term loans at low cost to homeowners
Federal Communications Commission (FCC)	1934	To set rules for radio, telephone, and telegraph systems
Securities and Exchange Commission (SEC)	1934	To regulate stocks and to give stock information
National Labor Relations Board (NLRB)	1935	To give workers the right to start unions
Social Security Board	1935	To care for older Americans, disabled people, jobless people, and children who needed help through the Social Security Act
Works Progress Administration (WPA)	1935	To provide work relief on public projects, especially fine and performing arts

Chart Study

1. **Which agency gave workers the right to start unions?** National Labor Relations Board
2. **Which two agencies assisted individuals who needed help?** The Home Owners Loan Corporation and the Social Security Board

Chart Point out that five of the seven agencies deal with businesses.

to add six judges to the Supreme Court. That would make a total of 15 judges, up from nine.

Many Americans did not agree with President Roosevelt's plan. They said he was "packing" the Supreme Court. However, the Supreme Court began to back many of his programs. Older judges began to retire. President Roosevelt was finally able to get judges on the Supreme Court who believed in the New Deal.

How did the Supreme Court feel about many of President Roosevelt's plans? The Supreme Court thought that many of President Roosevelt's plans were against the Constitution.

People and the Government

As the 1930s came to an end, many of the problems of the Great Depression remained. However, the new laws and programs of President Roosevelt gave the government a new role in the lives of Americans. In addition, some Americans played a larger role in government than ever before.

1. Women had a larger part in political decisions. Some became judges. Some also represented the United States in other countries.
2. African Americans were given new hope by President Roosevelt. The President called together a group of African Americans to advise him. The group was called the Black Cabinet. Mary McLeod Bethune was a member of this group. The

Great Names in History

ELEANOR ROOSEVELT

Some people called First Lady Eleanor Roosevelt the "eyes and ears" of the President. As the President's wife, she traveled to many places. She went to areas hit hard by the Great Depression. She visited coal mines, factories, schools, and hospitals.

Eleanor Roosevelt and Marian Anderson

In the past, most First Ladies had quietly supported their husbands. Eleanor Roosevelt, however, took an active part in solving the problems of the American people. She strongly believed in the equal treatment of all people. She spoke out in favor of civil rights laws and against racial segregation in public places. Eleanor Roosevelt was one of the most active reformers ever to live in the White House.

Critical Thinking Why do you think Eleanor Roosevelt took an active part in solving the problems of the American people? Possible answer: She strongly believed in civil rights and wanted to promote the cause of equal justice for all.

President asked her to serve as the head of the National Youth Administration, which helped young people find work.

3. Native Americans were helped by the Indian Reorganization Act in 1934. Under this act, ways were provided to help Native Americans keep their customs and ways of life. Lands were returned to Native Americans, and thousands were given jobs on their lands.

Remember
The Dawes Act in 1887 tried to force Native Americans to give up their way of life.

To some people, Roosevelt's programs made government seem more responsible for average Americans. To others, the programs gave the government too much power over people's lives. However, most people agreed that the years of the New Deal were some of the most important in America's history.

What did Americans think of the New Deal? Some thought it made government more responsible for the people. Others thought that it gave government too much power.

Section 2 Review

1. Why were some people against the New Deal?
2. Why did Roosevelt want to add six judges to the Supreme Court?
3. **Critical Thinking** Why might people worry that the government might gain too much power over people's lives?
4. **Write About History** You are a newspaper reporter. Ask some people what they think of the "alphabet" of names in the Roosevelt programs. Write a short newspaper column.

More Review is provided in Exercise 85 of the Workbook.

1. Some people thought that the New Deal was giving the U.S. government too much power.
2. He needed judges who would support his New Deal programs.
3. Student responses should mention that America was a democracy. Many people feared that a strong government would limit their freedoms.
4. Student responses might mention that the acronyms make it easy to remember the programs, especially the ones that mean the most to them.

Section 3 Americans at Leisure

Words to Know

soap opera	a daytime radio show that was paid for by soap companies
anti-Semitism	the practice of hating Jewish people simply because they are Jewish

Getting Started Discuss with students ways they take their minds off their problems. Explain that during the Great Depression, Americans used entertainment to try to forget their problems.

As bad as the Great Depression was, most people found ways to get through it. They even found ways to have fun during the hard times.

Movies and Radio

During the 1930s, people often felt the need to escape from their problems. That need to escape made movies, radio shows, and books popular.

For most people in the 1930s, movies were the best way to forget about the world around them. There were many reasons why people went to the movies during the Great Depression. One reason was that for 25 cents, people could sit through two full-length movies.

Another reason why people went to the movies was to see handsome leading men and beautiful actresses on the screen. Such actors as Errol Flynn, Clark Gable, Cary Grant, and Spencer Tracy became very popular with female movie fans. Actresses like Joan Crawford, Greta Garbo, Jean Harlow, and Katherine Hepburn became the favorites of male movie fans.

Radio from the 1930s

Visual In the 1930s, many radio programs were only 15 minutes long. About half of radio programming was music.

Hollywood turned out movies for just about everyone to enjoy. There were comedies with Stan Laurel and Oliver Hardy, the Marx Brothers, and

W.C. Fields which made people laugh and forget their troubles. There were also action films like *King Kong* and *The Adventures of Robin Hood,* which gave people the chance to escape to distant places. Musicals, with the dancers Fred Astaire and Ginger Rogers, made people want to dance themselves. Dramas such as *Gone with the Wind* and *The Wizard of Oz* took people to another place and another time.

Listening to the radio was another way for people to spend their free time. Families gathered around the radio to listen to comedy shows, westerns, and **soap operas.** A soap opera is a daytime radio show that was paid for by soap companies. Men, women, and children followed the lives of the characters on the soap operas.

Why did people go to movies? People went to the movies to forget about their problems for a short time.

Books of the 1930s

In the 1930s, many people read books for the same reasons that they watched movies or listened to the radio. They wanted to escape from the hardships of their everyday lives. A popular book was *The Good Earth* by Pearl S. Buck. It told the story of a Chinese farmer fighting to keep alive just before the revolution in China. *Gone with the Wind* by Margaret Mitchell sold over one million copies in its first year. It was a story of the loves of a Southern woman during and after the American Civil War. The book was made into a movie in 1939.

Some writers used the Great Depression as a theme in their works. John Steinbeck wrote *The Grapes of Wrath* in 1939. The book tells the story of Dust Bowlers who leave their farm in Oklahoma and move to California. Once there, they become migrant workers.

Why were books popular during the 1930s? People wanted to escape from the hardships of their everyday lives.

In the 1930s, many people went to see musical films like this one starring Fred Astaire and Ginger Rogers.

Visual Fred Astaire was known as a great dancer; but when he auditioned at Paramount, an executive wrote that Astaire "Can't act. Can't sing. Balding. Can dance a little."

Athletes as Heroes

Athletes were heroes to many people in the 1930s. Thousands of Americans cheered such baseball players as Lou Gehrig, Joe DiMaggio, and J. H. "Dizzy" Dean. Football became a popular sport with the help of "Whizzer" White, Sid Luckman, and "Bronko" Nagurski.

Some of the most admired athletes of the 1930s were African Americans. African Americans were not allowed to play major league baseball. Instead, they played in the "Negro" Leagues. African Americans cheered such players as Leroy Robert "Satchel" Paige and Josh Gibson.

In 1932, many people wondered whether the Olympic Games would be held in Los Angeles. They questioned whether anyone would have the money to spend on the games. However, the games were held and people did come.

A Closer Look

JESSE OWENS AND THE 1936 OLYMPIC GAMES

The 1936 Summer Olympics were held in Berlin, Germany. Jesse Owens was a young member of the U.S. Olympic Team. He had entered the track and field events.

Jesse Owens

Adolf Hitler, the German leader, was hoping the German athletes would prove themselves to be much better than all other athletes. However, Jesse Owens became the hero of the games. He won four gold medals.

Hitler was angry. Not only was Jesse Owens an American, but he was also an African American. However, the German people cheered Owens. Almost 20 years later, a street in Berlin was named for Jesse Owens.

Critical Thinking Why do you think the German people cheered Jesse Owens? German people appreciated Jesse Owens's talents as an athlete, which transcended race.

More than 100,000 watched the colorful parade on the opening day. Americans cheered Mildred "Babe" Didrikson. She won the gold medal and set records for women in both the 80-meter hurdles and the javelin throw.

In 1936, the Olympic Games were held in Berlin, Germany. Adolf Hitler, the leader of Germany, was spreading **anti-Semitism** in his country. Anti-Semitism is the practice of hating Jewish people simply because they are Jewish.

Adolf Hitler also believed that white athletes were much better than African American athletes. Runner Jesse Owens, an African American, won four gold medals. He proved that Hitler's beliefs were wrong.

How did many people treat athletes in the 1930s?
They were treated as heroes.

Section 3 Review

1. In the 1930s, how did many people spend their leisure time?
2. What popular book also became a popular movie in the 1930s?
3. **Critical Thinking** Why do you think African Americans were not allowed to play major league baseball?
4. **Write About History** Write a fan letter to your favorite star or athlete of the 1930s.

More Review is provided in Exercise 86 of the Workbook.

1. Went to movies, listened to the radio, read books, and attended sports events
2. Margaret Mitchell's *Gone with the Wind*
3. Possible answer: Continuing racism and segregation during the 1930s
4. Student responses could mention the relief from everyday worries offered by the star's movie or show or the athlete's game.

Chapter 20 Review

Summary Have students use this graphic organizer to outline the main ideas and details of the chapter.

Summary	The New Deal, started by President Franklin D. Roosevelt, helped the United States recover from the Great Depression.
Section 1	President Roosevelt began programs to help people who were hurt by the Great Depression. His radio talks encouraged people to feel more hopeful about the future.
Section 2	The Great Depression did not disappear quickly. Not everyone agreed with Roosevelt's plans. Some New Deal programs became a permanent part of U.S. government.
Section 3	In the 1930s, Americans turned to movies, radio, books, and sports to escape from their problems.

- liberal
- anti-Semitism
- fireside chat
- New Deal
- conservative

More Vocabulary Review is provided in Exercise 131 of the Classroom Resource Binder.

Vocabulary Review

Complete the sentence with a term from the list.

1. A person who wants government to do less for its citizens is known as a ____. conservative
2. President Franklin Roosevelt often spoke to the American people in what was called a ____. fireside chat
3. A person who would like to see government do more for its people is known as a ____. liberal
4. People who treat Jewish people badly just because they are Jewish are guilty of ____. anti-Semitism
5. Franklin Roosevelt's plan to help the U.S. economy was called the ____. New Deal

1. New Deal programs provided people with jobs. p. 371 **2.** The Supreme Court worried that Roosevelt's programs gave the government too much power and were unconstitutional. pp. 376–377 **3.** Indian Reorganization Act returned land to Native Americans; provided jobs. p. 379 **4.** Possible answer: Some people believed that accepting help in time of need is a sign of weakness. pp. 375–376. **5.** Possible answer: The glamorous lives of movie stars and athletes were different from people's everyday lives. pp. 380–383

Chapter Quiz

Write your answers in complete sentences.

1. How did New Deal programs help people during the Great Depression?
2. Why did the Supreme Court oppose some of President Roosevelt's programs?
3. How did an act of Congress help Native Americans in the 1930s?
4. **Critical Thinking** What reasons might some people give for not supporting the New Deal?
5. **Critical Thinking** Why would many people look up to movie stars and athletes?

Test Tip
To prepare for a test, write important vocabulary words in a sentence.

Writing Tip
Once you decide on your main topic, stick to it. You may come up with other interesting thoughts. Use those that are important to your main topic.

Using the Timeline

Use the timeline on pages 368–369 to answer the questions.

1. How many years after the Civilian Conservation Corps was established was the Social Security Board established? Two years
2. What sports event took place while Franklin Roosevelt was in office? 1936 Olympics

Group Activity See the Teacher's Planning Guide for a scoring rubric for this activity.

Group Activity

Divide your group into liberals and conservatives. Each group disagrees in some way with the New Deal. List your disagreements. Then see if you can compromise. Write down your compromise and share it with the class.

1. People had come through World War I. 2. Women had become accustomed to working during World War I. 3. Many African Americans wanted a better life through opportunities offered in the North. 4. President Hoover's plan to end the Great Depression was not effective.

Unit 6 Review

Critical Thinking

Give one reason why each of the following events happened.

1. In the early 1920s, many people wanted to enjoy life.
2. In the 1920s, many women were working outside their homes.
3. The Great Migration took place.
4. President Franklin Roosevelt promised the American people a New Deal.

Building Your Skills

Make a chart comparing the lives of women before and after 1920. Then add information of your own.

- Women began to think differently.
- Most women worked in the home.
- Women could not vote in most states.
- Women followed the beliefs of their mothers.
- Nellie Tayloe Ross became governor of Wyoming.
- Women could not hold public office.
- Women worked outside the home.
- The Nineteenth Amendment was passed.

Who Did It?

Write the name of the person who took each action below.

1. He owned the largest automobile company in the United States. Henry Ford
2. She was one of the most active First Ladies in U.S. history. Eleanor Roosevelt
3. He won four gold medals at the 1936 Olympics. Jesse Owens

Writing an Essay

Answer one of the following essay topics.

See the Answer Key for a detailed answer.

1. Explain how changes in the automobile industry led to installment-plan buying.
2. Identify events that led to the Great Depression.
3. Explain how African Americans and immigrants were affected by the Great Depression.

Linking Past and Present

Discuss the types of problems a modern-day New Deal might try to solve. Student responses should show an understanding of social and economic issues affecting citizens today.

Unit Opener Use the primary source to set the tone for the time period.

Unit 7 The United States in Crisis

Chapter 21 Leading Up to War 1922–1941

Chapter 22 A World at War 1941–1945

Chapter 23 The Cold War 1945–1960

During the battle at Iwo Jima in World War II, U.S. Marines raised the American flag. Why do you think it was important for the soldiers to raise the flag after winning the battle? The soldiers were proud of what they had done. They wanted to let everyone know that they had won the battle.

> *"When peace has been broken anywhere, the peace of all countries everywhere is in danger."*
>
> —from a radio address by President Franklin Roosevelt, September 3, 1939

Primary Source This radio address, "On the European War," was Franklin Roosevelt's fourteenth fireside chat. "Fireside chats" were Roosevelt's radio addresses that were broadcast to U.S. citizens while he sat by the fireside in the White House.

Members of the Nazi party came together at this rally, or large meeting. The poster is from Nazi Germany. It says "Leader, We Follow You!" What does the number of people at the rally tell you about the Nazi party? Many people supported the cause of the Nazi party.

The Road to War

- **1920**
- **1922** Mussolini becomes prime minister of Italy
- **1925**
- **1930**
- **1931** Japan attacks Manchuria
- **1932** Franklin D. Roosevelt elected
- **1933** Adolf Hitler becomes chancellor of Germany
- **1935**
- **1936** Franklin D. Roosevelt reelected

Additional activities and strategies to customize lessons can be found in the Teacher's Planning Guide.

Chapter 21 Leading Up to War 1922–1941

ESL Note To help students understand what a dictator is, have small groups discuss leaders from countries around the world today who have complete power over citizens. Ask if people they know, or have read about, came to this country to escape such leaders.

Words to Know

dictator

Fascist

Nazi

appeasement

militarism

puppet state

cash-and-carry policy

lend-lease plan

Words to Know These words are defined in the section in which they appear, as well as in the Glossary. Point out to students that the suffix *-ism* has several meanings. One meaning is a "belief in." The word *militarism* is a belief in using the military.

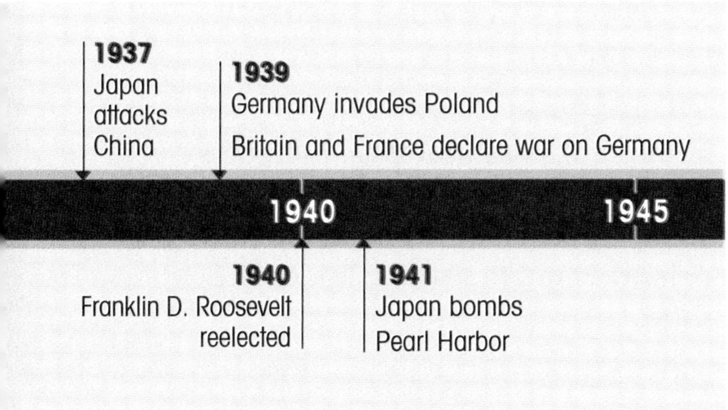

Learning Objectives

- Discuss the rise of dictators in Europe.
- Describe how Japan expanded during the 1930s.
- Explain how Americans felt about becoming involved in another world war.
- Describe why the United States was drawn into war.
- Identify ways to recognize a point of view.

Project Students may begin their project after completing Section 3. To help them get started, have students review the reasons why some Americans wanted to stay out of World War I.

Portfolio Project

Write a dialogue between two groups of Americans taking sides on the question of whether the United States should enter or stay out of the war in Europe in 1939. Have members of each group give strong reasons for what they believe.

Timeline The timeline is divided into 5-year intervals. The events take place over a period of 20 years. Point out the events that caused the United States to be drawn into world affairs.

Section 1 Dictators in Europe

Words to Know

dictator	a ruler with complete power in a country
Fascist	a member of a political party who supports extreme nationalism and a dictator
Nazi	a member of a political party in Germany led by Adolf Hitler
appeasement	the policy of giving in to someone's demands in order to keep peace

Getting Started Ask students to describe a situation in which they felt stronger because they were supported by a large group. Explain that the Europeans turned to strong leaders to help lead their nations' recoveries.

The U.S. economy started out strong in the 1920s. However, countries in Europe were still repairing the damage from World War I. Europeans turned to strong leaders to help their nations become strong again.

The Rise of Dictators

In the 1920s, many countries in Europe were still torn apart by World War I. They faced serious economic problems. Some countries with a strong belief in freedom tried to solve their problems without changing governments. Others turned to **dictators** for answers to their problems. A dictator is a ruler with complete power in a country.

Communism in the Soviet Union

In 1917, a revolution broke out in Russia. Members of the Communist party led the revolution. After the Communist revolution, Russia changed its name to the Union of Soviet Socialist Republics (U.S.S.R.), or the Soviet Union for short.

In 1924, a dictator named Joseph Stalin was in a position of power. Stalin was a cruel leader. Most Soviet people did not dare go against him. At least 10 million Soviet citizens were killed under Stalin's rule.

Fascism in Italy

Italy was one of the countries that was not defeated in World War I. Yet, the government and economy of Italy had been weakened by the war. There were labor strikes and riots in the country. Many people turned to a politician named Benito Mussolini for change and hope.

In 1919, Mussolini started the Italian Fascist party. A **Fascist** is a member of a political party who supports the rule of a dictator. Mussolini often spoke to his followers about the glories of war. He became prime minister of Italy in 1922.

A Closer Look

TOTALITARIAN GOVERNMENT

Not everyone in Russia or Italy believed that dictators could find answers to their problems. Some people tried to speak out against Communism in the Soviet Union and Fascism in Italy. Many of these people were arrested, beaten, or even killed.

Communist Soviet Union and Fascist Italy established totalitarian governments. A totalitarian government has complete control over the everyday lives of its citizens. In a totalitarian government, the individual has no right to think, speak, or write freely. This kind of government has a network of spies watch and report on every citizen.

Critical Thinking How might your life be different under a totalitarian government? Students may answer that a totalitarian government would be in control of every aspect of their life.

Benito Mussolini established a totalitarian government in Italy.

Jewish people over the age of six in Germany were forced to wear a yellow star that said "Jude," or Jew.

Visual The Star of David is a symbol of Judaism. The star allowed the Nazis to immediately identify Jews.

Nazism in Germany

Germany suffered more than any other country after World War I. In order to solve its problems, a political party called the National Socialist Party took over. A **Nazi** was a member of this political party in Germany that was led by Adolf Hitler.

In 1933, Adolf Hitler became the chancellor, or leader, of Germany. He reminded the German people that the treaty that ended World War I punished Germany more than any other country. He pointed out that the Allies expected Germany to pay the cost of the war.

Hitler had other opinions too. He said Germans were better than other people. According to Hitler, the Germans were so much better than all other people that they should rule the world. He called Germans the master race.

Hitler also said that there were groups of people who were lower than the Germans. He said that these people had caused Germany's problems. Hitler blamed Jews and the Communists for Germany's economic problems.

In 1935, Hitler said that Jews could no longer be German citizens. Jewish children were not allowed to go to German schools. In addition, all Jews were forced to wear yellow badges which showed the six-pointed Star of David. That way, they could be easily identified as Jews.

How did dictators come to power in Europe after World War I? People turned to dictators, or all-powerful leaders, to help make their nations strong again.

The Road to War

Hitler believed that Germany could become the most powerful country in the world. In 1936, Hitler decided to move beyond Germany's boundaries. First, his army crossed into an area between France and Germany known as the Rhineland.

France and Great Britain complained. However, neither France nor Great Britain took action against the Germans. These two countries followed a policy of **appeasement.** Appeasement is the policy of giving in to someone's demands in order to keep peace.

In 1938, Germany took control of Austria. Next, Hitler demanded that Czechoslovakia hand over the Sudetenland. About three million Germans lived there.

France and Great Britain had signed treaties to protect Czechoslovakia. The leaders of the two countries met

Map This map shows which European countries were controlled by Germany.

German Advances, 1939–1941

Map Study

1. What countries separate Germany and Italy? Switzerland, Austria, Czechoslovakia
2. How many countries were controlled by the Axis Powers in 1941? 13 countries

with Hitler and Mussolini in Munich, Germany, in 1938. They signed a pact, or agreement. Hitler could keep the Sudetenland.

What areas did Hitler take over between 1936 and 1938? The Rhineland, Austria, the Sudetenland

War Breaks Out Again

In 1939, German forces took control of all of Czechoslovakia. Hitler's next target was Poland. In August 1939, Adolf Hitler and Joseph Stalin of the Soviet Union agreed to attack Poland and divide the country between them. On September 1, 1939, German forces struck Poland. Great Britain and France now realized that appeasement would no longer work. Both countries immediately declared war on Germany.

In 1940, German forces invaded Denmark, Norway, the Netherlands, Belgium, Luxembourg, and finally France. Great Britain now faced Hitler's forces alone.

Why did Great Britain and France immediately declare war on Germany? They realized that appeasement would no longer work, that Germany was determined to fight.

Section 1 Review

1. Why did Europeans want strong leaders after World War I?
2. What did Great Britain and France do to keep war from breaking out?
3. **Critical Thinking** Why do you think Hitler and Stalin became allies?
4. **Write About History** You are a news reporter at the meeting in Munich in 1938. Write a news headline for a German and a British newspaper.

1. Europeans wanted leaders who could help their countries grow strong again.
2. They followed a policy of appeasement.
3. Both were dictators and wanted to take over other lands without interference.
4. Possible answers: Germany is optimistic, Britain is suspicious of Germany's plans.

More Review is provided in Exercise 88 of the Workbook.

BUILDING YOUR SKILLS
Recognizing a Point of View

When you read something or listen to information, it is important to understand the writer's or speaker's point of view. A point of view is a person's opinion about an event, a problem, or another person. The information below will help you to recognize a point of view.

- The writer or speaker should have enough knowledge about the topic.
- The writer or speaker may use phrases such as "I believe" or "I think."
- The writer or speaker has a particular opinion.

Read statements A and B below. Then answer the questions that follow.

A. "Should we not appreciate that we cannot right every wrong in this world? We cannot police this world. . . ."

—Congressman James F. O'Connor (1914)

B. "This is not a European war. Only people who . . . fight and sacrifice for their freedom and rights can survive."

—Major General John F. O'Ryan (1914)

1. What point of view does Congressman O'Connor give?

2. What point of view does General O'Ryan give?

CHALLENGE How could O'Ryan persuade O'Connor to view things differently?

Apply the Skill

Some Americans felt that the United States had a responsibility to help keep world peace in the 1930s. Use facts from the chapter to support this point of view.

1. O'Connor feels the United States cannot fix every problem in the world. **2.** O'Ryan feels the United States has a responsibility to protect its freedom. **CHALLENGE** O'Ryan could tell O'Connor that the United States needs to help the countries in Europe fight to keep their freedom.

Section 2 Japan Rises to Power

Words to Know

militarism	the policy of strong military actions taken by the leaders of a country
puppet state	a government that is under the control of another, stronger power

Getting Started Have students locate Asia and Southeast Asia on the world map in the back of their book. Ask students where Japan might move its forces if it wanted to expand its territory. Ask why the United States might shy away from conflicts in the region.

For most of the 1920s, Japan had been a peaceful democracy. However, military leaders took control of the country in the early 1930s. Japan began to rise as a military power.

Japan Expands Its Empire

Adolf Hitler was not the only dictator who wanted more land. On the other side of the world, military leaders were gaining control in the island nation of Japan, in Asia.

The military leaders set out to make Japan the most feared military force in Asia. They began a plan called **militarism.** Militarism is the policy of strong military actions taken by the leaders of a country.

In the 1930s, Japan needed natural resources to keep its industries running. A natural resource is material made by nature that people can use. Coal and oil are natural resources. Japan did not have many natural resources.

In 1931, Japan attacked Manchuria in the north of China. Manchuria was rich in coal and other minerals. A year later, Japan established the **puppet state** of Manchukuo in Manchuria. A puppet state is a government that is under the control of another, stronger power. Six years later, in 1937, Japan started a full-scale attack on China. The United States became worried, but it did not send military help to China.

Why did Japan's leaders decide to attack China? Japan wanted China's natural resources for its industries.

The Seeds of War

In 1937, Japan's attack on China led to a full-scale war. By the following year, Japanese forces controlled most of eastern China.

Japanese military leaders were planning to bring all of eastern Asia under Japan's control. Many European colonies in Asia had natural resources. The most important resource was oil. Japan needed oil to run its industries and armies. Japan was now becoming friendly with Nazi Germany and Fascist Italy. Soon, the three countries would sign an anti-Communist agreement. Japan planned to become a world power with Germany and Italy.

Why did Japan become friendly with Germany and Italy? By becoming friendly with Germany and Italy, Japan hoped to join those two nations in becoming a world power.

Section 2 Review

1. Why did Japan set out to become the strongest military power in Asia?
2. What natural resources could Japan get from countries in Asia?
3. **Critical Thinking** Why do you think the United States refused to help China?
4. **Write About Economics** Write a paragraph describing how Japan's need for natural resources led to the use of force in Manchuria and other regions of China.

1. Japan wanted to become a world power and to control eastern Asia. Japan could use the resources in Asia.
2. Coal and oil
3. Possible answer: The United States wanted to stay out of international affairs. It felt that the country was not in any immediate danger.
4. Possible answer: Japan needed natural resources to boost its industries. It invaded nearby areas that had large supplies of the materials Japan needed.

More Review is provided in Exercise 90 of the Workbook.

Section 3 From Isolation to Pearl Harbor

Words to Know

cash-and-carry policy a plan that let nations at war buy goods that they could pay cash for and then carry home

lend-lease plan to lend or lease supplies to a country whose defense is needed to protect the United States

Getting Started Discuss what action could possibly cause an isolationist country like the United States to change its mind and get involved in a war. As they read, ask students to look for the answer.

Remember
The United States was in the middle of the Great Depression when World War II began.

Many Americans agreed with the message on this poster.

Visual Share with students that President Franklin Roosevelt didn't believe that the United States could remain "a lone island" while the rest of the world was at war.

After World War I, most Americans feared that alliances, or unions, with other nations would pull the United States into another war. Yet, Americans could see the growing signs of war in Europe and Asia. Many Americans asked whether the United States had a duty to help other countries.

Staying Out of War

Between 1935 and 1937, the U.S. Congress passed several laws to keep the country out of war. Many Americans backed these laws because they wanted the United States to remain a peaceful nation. However, some Americans backed the laws because they were isolationists. Isolationism is the policy of staying out of the problems of another country. These people said the United States had plenty of problems of its own.

Congress passed a law that started a **cash-and-carry policy.** Under this plan, nations at war could buy goods that they could pay cash for and then carry home.

President Roosevelt did not agree with isolationism. He believed that the United States should be a good neighbor to countries around the world. President Roosevelt also believed that the United States should stand up to the dictators in Europe. However, Roosevelt had a huge problem to solve at home. He spent most of his time trying to end the Great Depression.

Why were many Americans isolationists? They believed that the U.S. had problems of its own.

The End of Isolation

Before 1940, no President of the United States had ever run for a third term. The election of 1940 was different. The reason was the war in Europe. Many Americans felt Roosevelt's experience as a leader was necessary if the United States did go to war.

President Roosevelt promised the American people that if he were elected for a third term, he would keep the United States out of the war.

In 1940, Franklin Roosevelt was reelected for a third term as President. He was the first American President ever to serve more than two straight terms.

The American people could now see how dangerous Hitler really was. President Roosevelt said that the United States had to keep Hitler out of the Western Hemisphere. Roosevelt asked for the first peacetime draft in U.S. history.

Soon after the election of 1940, Winston Churchill, the leader of Great Britain, asked the United States for help against Nazi Germany. Britain did not have enough money to buy weapons.

To help Great Britain, President Roosevelt asked Congress to pass a **lend-lease plan.** This plan gave the President the power to lend or lease supplies to a country whose defense was needed to protect the United States. Many isolationists disliked Roosevelt's plan. However, in early 1941, Congress agreed to the lend-lease plan.

Sending ships, guns, and other supplies to Britain became very dangerous. German submarines began

Geography Fact

The Western Hemisphere is the hemisphere in which all of North America and South America are located.

Geography Fact Have students use the transparency map of the Americas in the Classroom Resource Binder to locate North America and South America.

attacking American ships. In October 1941, German submarines sank a U.S. Navy ship, killing 115 sailors. To many Americans, it seemed that war was coming closer each day.

What did President Roosevelt do to prepare for war?
He ordered a peacetime draft and sent military supplies to Britain.

Pearl Harbor

In September 1940, Japan became an ally of Germany and Italy. At the same time, Japan continued to expand into Asia. In protest, Roosevelt, in 1941, stopped trade with Japan. He banned oil shipments to Japan. Japan needed oil to keep its military tanks, trucks, and airplanes working.

Japan and the United States started talks in November 1941. Neither side would compromise. While the talks continued, Japan was busy making

Chart Point out to students that the chart shows that the Nazis had gained power in Germany by the early 1930s. They were creating political alliances and invading their neighbors.

1. Mussolini
2. Germany had already annexed Austria, made a pact with the Soviet Union, and invaded Poland.

Events Leading to World War II

October	1922	Mussolini gains power in Italy.
September	1931	Japan invades Manchuria.
January	1933	Hitler becomes leader of Germany.
July	1937	Japanese move farther into China.
March	1938	Germany annexes Austria.
September	1938	Munich Conference is held.
August	1939	Nazi-Soviet Pact is signed.
September	1939	Germany invades Poland.

Chart Study

1. Who was the first dictator to gain power?
2. Late in 1939, why did countries in Europe fear Germany?

plans to attack the U.S. navy base in Pearl Harbor, Hawaii, in the Pacific Ocean. These islands belonged to the United States. Japan felt it would take the United States a while to rebuild its forces after an attack.

Before dawn in Hawaii on Sunday, December 7, 1941, Japanese pilots headed toward the U.S. Navy base at Pearl Harbor, on the Hawaiian island of Oahu. There, Japanese planes destroyed 19 American ships and killed more than 2,400 Americans.

The next day, December 8, 1941, President Roosevelt asked Congress to declare war on Japan. Congress agreed, and the United States once again joined its allies to fight a war.

What happened when Japan attacked Pearl Harbor?
The United States declared war on Japan.

Section 3 Review

1. In what ways were the views of many members of Congress different from President Roosevelt's on isolationism?

2. Why did Americans elect President Roosevelt for a third term in 1940?

3. **Critical Thinking** Why were some isolationists against the lend-lease plan?

4. **Write About History** Members of your family are isolationists. You have just heard the news about the attack on Pearl Harbor. Describe in writing the discussion that takes place in your home.

More Review is provided in Exercise 91 of the Workbook.

1. Many members of Congress backed isolationism. Roosevelt believed that the U.S. should be a good neighbor to other countries.
2. They were confident that Roosevelt would be a good leader in the event of war.
3. Student responses might mention that lending or renting supplies indirectly involved the U.S. in the war, which they opposed.
4. Student responses might include a change of opinion now that American lives have been lost.

Chapter

21 Review

Summary Have students use this graphic organizer to outline the main ideas and details of the chapter.

Summary	In the 1920s, some dictators took power in Europe. In Asia, Japan turned to militarism. Later, the United States became involved in world events.
Section 1	Some countries in Europe turned to dictators to help solve the problems that followed World War I. Adolf Hitler in Germany pushed his country toward war.
Section 2	Leaders of Japan took over parts of China. Then Japan joined Nazi Germany and Fascist Italy in their search for world power.
Section 3	The United States tried to stay out of Europe's problems. However, it offered to help as events in Europe became worse. The attack on Pearl Harbor pushed the United States into World War II.

More Vocabulary Review is provided in Exercise 139 of the Classroom Resource Binder.

Vocabulary Review

Write *true* or *false*. If the statement is false, change the underlined term to make it true.

1. A <u>dictator</u> has complete control of a country. True

2. <u>Cash-and-carry</u> was a plan to loan supplies to a country. False: Lend-lease plan

3. The Jews were badly treated by <u>militarism</u>. False: Nazis

4. A President who wants to stay out of the problems of other countries believes in <u>appeasement</u>. False: isolationism

5. Benito Mussolini was a <u>Fascist</u>. True

1. Joseph Stalin in the Soviet Union, Benito Mussolini in Italy, Adolf Hitler in Germany, a group of military leaders in Japan. pp. 391–392, 396 2. Germany had been punished more than any other country; the Allies expected Germany to pay for the cost of World War I p. 392 3. To show its disapproval of Japan's taking over more of Asia p. 400 4. Possible answer: Dictators assume absolute power and control; often look upon appeasement as weakness. p. 393 5. Possible answer: The U.S. naval base at Pearl Harbor was much closer to Japan than the west coast of the United States. p.401

Chapter Quiz

Write your answers in complete sentences.

1. Which rulers came to power in the Soviet Union, Italy, Germany, and Japan in the 1920s and 1930s?
2. What did Adolf Hitler keep pointing out to the German people after World War I?
3. Why did the United States cut off exports to Japan?
4. **Critical Thinking** Why was appeasement a poor way to treat dictators?
5. **Critical Thinking** Why do you think the Japanese chose to attack Pearl Harbor rather than the west coast of the United States?

Test Tip
Make flashcards for studying key words and phrases. Use index cards. Write a word or phrase on one side and the definition on the other.

Writing Tip
Always use quotation marks around words that come directly from a speaker.

Using the Timeline

Use the timeline on pages 388–389 to answer the questions.

1. How many years after Adolf Hitler became the leader of the Nazi Party was Franklin Roosevelt reelected the first time? 3 years
2. What two countries attacked or invaded other countries? Japan attacked Manchuria and China. Germany invaded Poland.

Group Activity See the Teacher's Planning Guide for a scoring rubric for this activity.

Group Activity

With your group, discuss the good points of isolationism. Then discuss whether it is possible for a powerful country like the United States to remain isolated. Write your ideas in a paragraph. Share them with the class.

Allied soldiers landed in Normandy, France, for the largest land and sea attack in history. Soldiers wore metal identification tags called "dog tags," like the ones shown here. What dangers do you think these soldiers faced? The troops had to move into waist-high water; they were going to fight in a place they were unfamiliar with and against an enemy they had never fought before.

A Second World War

1941
Japan bombs Pearl Harbor
U.S. enters World War II

1942
Japanese Americans sent to internment camps

1944
General MacArthur returns to Philippines
D-day

1941 — 1942 — 1943 — 1944

1942
Allies invade North Africa
Battle of Midway

Timeline The timeline is divided into 1-year intervals. The events take place over a period of 5 years. Point out to students that the timeline covers some of the important events of the war.

Additional activities and strategies to customize lessons can be found in the Teacher's Planning Guide.

Chapter 22 A World at War 1941–1945

ESL Note To help students understand which countries were involved in World War II, have them use the world map at the back of their books to locate Germany, Japan, Italy, Great Britain, France, Russia, and the United States. Explain that after World War I, the United States was drawn back into another world war.

Words to Know

- Axis Powers
- mobilize
- siege
- partisan
- amphibious landing
- rationing
- internment camp
- Holocaust
- genocide
- atomic bomb

Words to Know These words are defined in the section in which they appear, as well as in the Glossary. Point out to students that the words *rationing*, *internment camp*, *Holocaust*, and *genocide* deal with the effects of war on innocent civilians.

1945
Franklin D. Roosevelt dies
Harry S. Truman becomes President

1945

1945
U.S. drops atomic bombs on Hiroshima and Nagasaki
World War II ends

Learning Objectives

- Explain the Allies' plan for winning World War II.
- Discuss ways in which the U.S. government controlled the economy during the war.
- Describe how the war affected women, African Americans, and Latinos.
- Discuss the treatment of Japanese Americans during the war.
- Describe the effect of the Holocaust.
- Explain how the United States forced Japan to surrender.
- Explore the life of a Japanese family during the war.

Project Students will be able to begin work on the project after completing Section 4. To get started, they can take notes as they read the chapter.

Portfolio Project

Prepare a time capsule that will hold items relating to World War II. In your time capsule, include items such as newspaper headlines, maps, and a rationing book. Make a list of the items you want in the capsule.

Section 1 A World at War Again

Words to Know

Axis Powers	the countries that fought the Allies in World War II
mobilize	to get ready for war
siege	a military blocking of a city to force its surrender

Getting Started Remind students that up until now, the United States had not entered the war. Discuss what kinds of events they think would have to happen to cause this country to go to war again.

On December 7, 1941, Japanese planes attacked Pearl Harbor, Hawaii. The following day, the United States found itself at war for the second time in less than 25 years. As the war spread, few places were left untouched.

The United States Declares War

Americans were shocked by the surprise attack on Pearl Harbor. The day after the attack on Pearl Harbor, the United States declared war on Japan. The United States had now joined Great Britain and the Soviet Union. In June 1941, Germany attacked the Soviet Union, bringing the Soviet Union into the war. Now the United States, the Soviet Union, and Great Britain were allies fighting against the **Axis Powers**. The Axis Powers is the name given to the countries that fought the Allies in World War II. Three days later, on December 11, Germany and Italy declared war on the United States.

As soon as war was declared, the United States began to **mobilize** its forces. To mobilize is to get ready for war. More than ten million men were drafted. Another six million American men and women volunteered.

Why did the United States declare war on Japan?
Because of the bombing of Pearl Harbor

Japan Grows More Powerful

Within hours of the attack on Pearl Harbor, Japanese bombers attacked other U.S. bases. The Japanese leader, Hideki Tojo, was certain that Japan would become the most powerful empire in the world. By May 1942, Tojo's hope seemed to be coming true. Japan had taken control of Hong Kong and Singapore in Asia. Its forces had also taken control of the U.S. islands in the Pacific Ocean and the Philippine Islands. The Japanese takeover of the Philippine Islands was a great loss for the United States. American troops had been stationed there since the Spanish-American War of 1898.

In the battle for control of the Philippines, Filipino troops fought bravely along with the Americans. They were all were under the command of General Douglas MacArthur.

The Japanese pushed the American and Filipino troops farther into the Philippines. The area was known as Bataan. Once there the Japanese trapped the Americans and put them under **siege**. A siege is a military blocking of a city to force its surrender.

As the situation got worse, President Roosevelt ordered General MacArthur to go to Australia. The President wanted MacArthur to take command of all the Allied forces there. As MacArthur was leaving the Philippines, he said, "I shall return."

The starving Americans and Filipinos soon had to surrender. The Japanese forced them to march about 65 miles to prison camps. The prisoners had no food or water. The journey came to be known as the Bataan Death March.

What areas did Japan take control of by 1942? The Japanese took the U.S. islands in the Pacific Ocean; Hong Kong and Singapore in Asia; and the Philippines.

General Douglas MacArthur

Visual MacArthur's father, General Arthur MacArthur, Jr., helped defeat the Spanish in the Philippines during the Spanish-American War. He also served as military governor of the Philippines.

The Allies Make Plans

While the Axis Powers were taking over Europe and Asia, the three most powerful Allied leaders were planning to fight back. They were Franklin Roosevelt of the United States, Winston Churchill of Great Britain, and Joseph Stalin of the Soviet Union. These Allied leaders were called the Big Three.

The Big Three agreed that they would first have to defeat the Axis forces in Europe. Each leader presented his plan. Stalin said the United States and Britain should attack the west coast of Europe. Roosevelt said the United States and Britain should start the attack in France. Churchill said the United States and Britain should attack Italy first through North Africa.

The three leaders agreed that the defeat of Germany was the most important goal. Finally, they decided to attack North Africa first, where German forces were the weakest. Then they would attack the west coast of Europe. Finally, they would attack the Pacific area.

What plan did the Allies decide to use to fight the Axis powers? They decided to attack North Africa first, the west coast of Europe second, and the Pacific area third.

Section 1 Review

1. How did the United States mobilize for war?
2. How were Americans and Filipinos on Bataan treated by the Japanese forces?
3. **Critical Thinking** Why did the Allied leaders decide to attack North Africa first?
4. **Write About History** You are a reporter for an American newspaper. Write a story describing the meeting of the Allied leaders.

1. Drafted more than ten million men
2. They were treated brutally. They were forced to march without food or water to a prison camp.
3. German forces were weakest in North Africa.
4. Student responses should include who they were, why they met, what their plans were.

More Review is provided in Exercise 92 of the Workbook.

Section 2 The Allies Strike Back

Words to Know

partisan	a person who strongly believes in a cause
amphibious landing	a planned movement of troops from the sea

Getting Started Discuss what advantages and disadvantages the United States might have had by entering the war after it had already begun. Talk about the importance of strong leaders.

History Fact

General Rommel was named the Desert Fox because of his clever tactics in tank warfare during the fighting in North Africa.

History Fact Rommel was implicated in a plan to kill Hitler in 1944.

By mid-1942, the Germans controlled most of Europe. The Japanese had taken large parts of Asia. Then, quite suddenly, it seemed that American and British soldiers gained major victories over the Germans.

Fighting in North Africa and Italy

The Allies wanted to control North Africa. From there, they would prepare for an Allied attack on Italy. Germany and Italy were also interested in controlling North Africa. For nearly three years, the Allies and the Axis Powers fought hard for North Africa. They faced a new kind of warfare. They were fighting in a desert.

A major Allied attack in North Africa took place against the German general Erwin Rommel. In late October 1942, British troops entered the desert areas from the east and hit Rommel's forces. About two weeks later, American troops under General Dwight D. Eisenhower landed in North Africa and headed for Rommel. By May 1943, Rommel's forces were defeated.

From North Africa, the Allies moved north across the Mediterranean Sea. They attacked Italy, the weakest of the Axis Powers. By that time, many Italians had turned against Mussolini and the Fascists. They also did not like the Nazis. They joined groups of **partisans** who were fighting the Germans. A partisan is a person who strongly believes in a cause.

Hitler's troops went to Italy to fight the Allies. Thousands of Allied soldiers lost their lives while driving the Nazis from Italy. However, by June 1944, the Allied forces had won. They had fought a hard fight.

How did the Allies defeat Rommel in North Africa?
Rommel was trapped between British and American forces.

War in the Pacific

In the spring of 1942, the Allies began to move across the Pacific Ocean. An aircraft carrier moved within 700 miles of Japan. On the carrier were 16 lightweight American bombers. The bombers took off from the carrier and headed for Tokyo. They flew low over Tokyo, bombing factories, railroad yards, and a navy base. The Japanese were shocked. No enemy had ever attacked their homeland.

After the bombings, the Japanese decided to push closer to U.S. territory. The huge Japanese fleet headed for Midway Island. The U.S. fleet sailed to meet the Japanese.

A Closer Look

NAVAJO CODE TALKERS

More than 400 Navajos served in the U.S. Marines as "code talkers" during World War II.

The Navajo language worked well as a code. It was difficult for anyone who was not familiar with it to understand it. Every sound in the language means something. The meaning can change if a speaker's voice is low or high.

The Navajo code was never broken. It was one of the war's most secure communications system.

Navajos served as code talkers during World War II.

Critical Thinking Why was it important to make a code that the enemy could not break? So that the enemy would not learn about the Allied battle strategy

World War II in the Pacific, 1942–1945

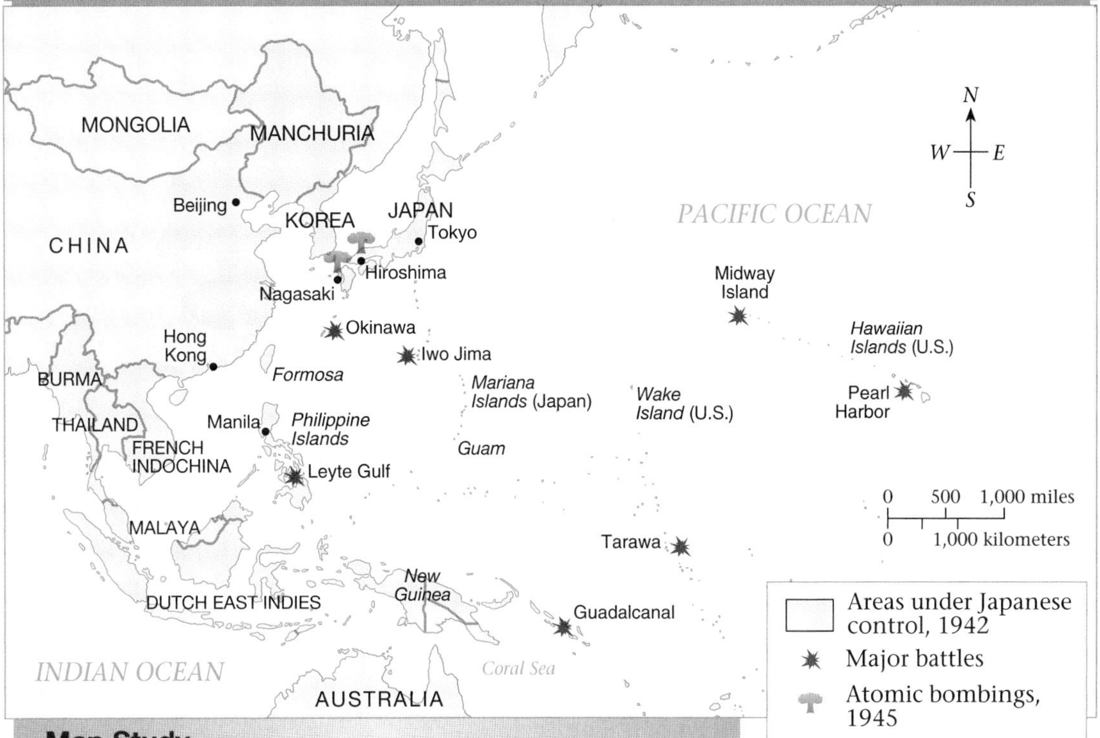

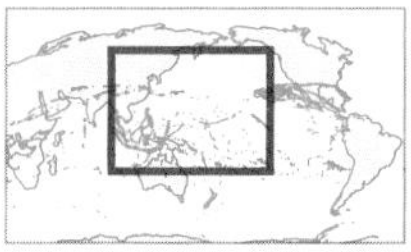

Map Study

1. About how many miles is Tokyo from Pearl Harbor?
2. What were the major battles in the Pacific?

Map Have students locate battles on this map as they read about them in the text.

1. About 4,000 miles

2. Okinawa, Iwo Jima, Leyte Gulf, Midway Island, Pearl Harbor, Tarawa, Guadalcanal

Even before the battle began, navy code experts were able to figure out the secret messages being sent between Japanese ships. U.S. ships always knew where the enemy ships were going to be.

At dawn on June 4, 1942, American planes attacked Japanese planes. The Japanese were caught by surprise. They suffered great losses. The Battle of Midway was the first big defeat for the Japanese.

Why was the Battle of Midway important? The Battle of Midway was the first major defeat for the Japanese.

Island-hopping in the Pacific

The Japanese still held many islands in the Pacific Ocean. The Americans realized that if they captured the islands, they could use them to attack other Japanese bases. They could also cut off the Japanese from needed supplies.

The Americans decided on a plan. They called the plan island-hopping. They would use Marines to make **amphibious landings** on certain islands. An amphibious landing is a planned movement of troops from the sea. Land, sea, and air forces work together for an invasion.

Under the island-hopping plan, the islands that were taken became air and supply bases for attacks on other islands. Between late 1943 and the fall of 1944, the United States was moving across the Pacific Ocean. Japanese forces were being pushed back to Japan.

Why was island-hopping a good plan? Island-hopping gave American troops an opportunity to take Japanese islands one at a time and use the islands as bases for further attacks.

Section 2 Review

1. How did the Allies defeat General Rommel's forces?
2. Why were the bombings of Tokyo in 1942 important?
3. **Critical Thinking** Why were American forces able to defeat the Japanese in the Pacific?
4. **Write About History** You have been asked to make a film about the Battle of Midway. Write a paragraph describing the opening scene of your film.

More Review is provided in Exercise 93 of the Workbook.

1. British troops attacked Rommel first. U.S. troops, under General Eisenhower, attacked Rommel two weeks later.
2. The Japanese people were shocked that an enemy was attacking their homeland.
3. Possible answer: American island-hopping, which the Japanese were unable to stop
4. Possible answer: The excitement of American pilots as they begin the mission in planes and their anticipation of Japanese responses.

Section 3 The War at Home

Words to Know

rationing	limiting the amount of something that each person can buy
internment camp	a prisonlike place in which people are held during a war

Getting Started Discuss how Americans at home behaved during World War I. Based on that, discuss how they might behave during World War II.

The U.S. forces needed huge supplies of weapons to defeat the Axis Powers. This need for supplies helped the economy and pulled the United States out of the Great Depression. Many other changes also took place at home between 1941 and 1945. Some were good, but others were not.

War Effort at Home

In 1939, American factories were making almost 6,000 airplanes each year. However, after the attack on Pearl Harbor, President Roosevelt felt more airplanes were needed. He talked of producing 50,000 planes a year.

Within months, the American work force was mobilized to get the job done. Many factories remained open around the clock and divided the work time into three 8-hour shifts. By 1944, workers were turning out more than 90,000 planes a year. By the end of the war, here is what American men and women had made.

1. over 70,000 ships
2. about 44 billion bullets
3. almost $2\frac{1}{2}$ million army trucks

American workers made more materials than all of the factories of the Axis countries put together.

Many Americans who were too young or too old for the armed forces provided other needed services. Some worked for the Red Cross. Some knitted sweaters and socks for the troops. Some donated blood. Many families planted vegetable gardens called victory gardens.

Remember
During World War I, Americans planted victory gardens to make more food available for people in the armed forces.

People bought war bonds to help pay for the war. Many children bought savings stamps to paste in a war bond book. By saving a dime a week, a child could buy a war bond in a few years.

How did Americans help on the home front during World War II? Americans worked in factories, did volunteer work, purchased war bonds, and planted victory gardens.

Mobilizing the Economy

During World War II, the U.S. government set up various agencies, or offices, to direct the war effort. A fuel agency had to get fuel to the armed forces. It encouraged civilians to cut back on the use of fuel. A wage-and-price agency controlled food prices and workers' pay. No prices or wages were raised during the war.

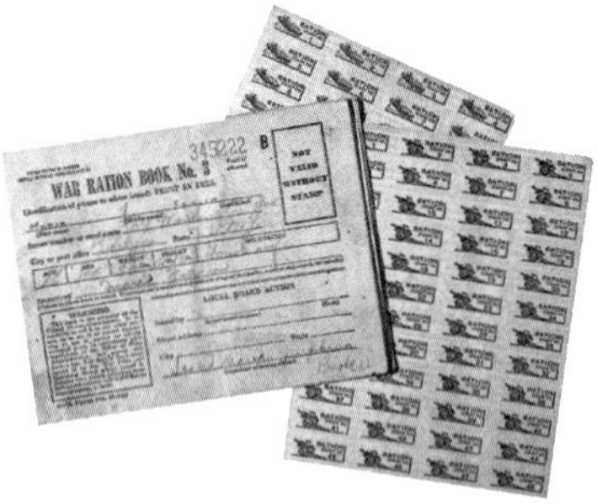

Americans at home received ration coupons to buy things like food and gasoline.

Visual Americans could earn extra rationing stamps by turning in leftover grease from cooking. These fats were used to make explosives.

The government also used **rationing** during the war. Rationing is limiting the amount of something that each person can buy. With rationing, a person received a month's supply of coupons. The coupons allowed people to buy products that were hard to get, such as meat, sugar, butter, or coffee.

Some items were difficult or impossible to buy. Some clothing was scarce because cloth was needed for uniforms for the armed forces.

How did rationing work? Under rationing, people were given coupons. This allowed them to purchase a certain amount of goods.

Opportunities for Women

During the war, women made up about one third of all factory workers. In the past, women who worked had most often been young and unmarried. By 1944, more married women than unmarried women held jobs in factories. Many women workers were over the age of 35.

The war changed women's lives in other ways too. They gained a new sense of freedom. American magazines carried drawings of "Rosie the Riveter," a homemaker turned factory worker who stood for all women workers.

American women took on many new responsibilities. These are some of the responsibilities.

Visual About 6.5 million women entered to workforce between 1941 and 1945.

This photograph shows women making bombers during World War II.

This poster shows "Rosie the Riveter," one of more than six million women who worked on the home front during World War II.

Visual Rose Will Monroe was the model for "Rosie the Riveter." Monroe was working as a riveter and building military airplanes when she was asked by the government to star in a promotional movie about women during the war. She was also featured on posters.

Economics Fact

More than 2 million African Americans worked in factories during World War II.

Economics Fact African Americans said they were working for a "Double V"—victory against the Axis Powers and victory against inequality at home.

1. Women served in the armed forces in great numbers. All branches of the service had separate women's units.
2. Women worked in military offices so that more men could serve in battle.
3. Women flew supply planes so that men could fly fighters and bombers.
4. Women served as nurses. They often lived under the same dangerous conditions as the soldiers.

The U.S. government needed the work of women. However, women were paid 40 percent less than men in the same jobs.

How did the role of women change during the war? Women took factory jobs and served in the armed forces. They gained a new sense of freedom by helping in the war effort.

African Americans During the War

More than 27 million Americans moved during the war. It was the largest migration of people in U.S. history. Many African Americans moved to cities in the Northeast, in the Midwest, and on the West coast to work in factories.

For African Americans, World War II brought many changes. Many African Americans left low-paying farm jobs in the South for better-paying factory jobs. President Roosevelt signed an order to make sure African Americans were treated fairly in defense plants.

About a million African Americans served in the armed forces during World War II. However, even in the armed forces, African Americans faced discrimination. Those who joined the armed forces were given jobs as cooks, waiters, or workers in supply units. In spite of this, many African Americans still wanted to be part of the fighting.

In 1941, one group of African Americans trained to serve as fighter pilots. The 332nd Fighter Group was formed. All the pilots in the 332nd were African American. They were known as the Tuskegee Airmen.

The Tuskegee Airmen carried out missions, or special assignments, during the war. They protected bombers flying over Europe. The fighter group shot down 103 enemy planes and destroyed 298 enemy planes on the ground. No bomber protected by the Tuskegee Airmen was ever shot down.

Who were the Tuskegee Airmen? A group of African Americans trained to serve as pilots during World War II

Latinos During the War

During World War II, more Latinos volunteered for service than any other group in the United States. Still, they faced discrimination in the armed forces and at home.

More than 300,000 Latinos served in the armed forces during the war. Many were Mexican Americans and Puerto Ricans. About one in four of the men on the Bataan Death March was a Mexican American.

Latinos also joined the effort on the home front. When farm workers and railroad workers went off to fight in the war, Latinos took over their jobs. Many became shipyard workers in the huge factories on the West coast.

Like African Americans, Latinos fought two battles. One was against prejudice. The other was against the Axis Powers.

How did Latinos help out during the war? They served in the armed forces, worked on farms and railroads, in shipyards and factories.

Japanese Americans During the War

After Pearl Harbor, some Americans feared that the Japanese Americans on the West coast might help Japan. In 1942, President Roosevelt ordered the army to take Japanese Americans from their homes to **internment camps.** An internment camp is a prisonlike place in which people are held during a war.

More than 100,000 Japanese Americans had to give up their farms, their homes, and their businesses. In spite of this experience, thousands of Japanese Americans served in segregated units of the armed forces. One group was the Japanese Americans of the 442nd Infantry. It was a highly decorated unit in World War II.

There was never any reason to believe that Japanese Americans were not loyal. After the war, the U.S. government paid some Japanese Americans for the loss of their property. However, the payment they received covered no more than 10 percent of their losses.

History Fact

Japanese Americans from western Washington, Oregon, California, and parts of Arizona were sent to internment camps.

History Fact In 1988, the U.S. government apologized to Japanese Americans who had been forced into internment camps. Survivors were also given $20,000.

Why were many Japanese Americans moved to internment camps? Many Americans thought that the Japanese Americans would help Japan to win the war.

Section 3 Review

1. How was World War II "fought on the factory floor"?
2. How did the war change the lives of American women?
3. **Critical Thinking** How did Japanese Americans show that they were loyal Americans?
4. **Write About History** Write a news report about the role of the 332nd Fighter Group in World War II.

1. Factories remained open around the clock seven days a week. Workers produced an incredible amount of war supplies for the Allies.
2. They enjoyed a new sense of freedom and importance. Women filled factory jobs and served in the armed forces.
3. Many served with distinction in the 442nd Infantry.
4. Possible answer: The group's loyalty to its country and beliefs, its members training as fighter pilots, and its success rate

More Review is provided in Exercise 95 of the Workbook.

VOICES FROM THE PAST
Yuri Tateshi

Yuri Tateshi was a Japanese American woman. On April 26, 1942, the Tateshi family was ordered to move from their home in Los Angeles, California, to an internment camp. The camp was in a desert wasteland of California known as Manzanar. These are her words.

These Japanese Americans brought their belongings to the internment camp on a wheelbarrow.

"It was terrible because you had to sell everything. Of course, we got nothing for it, because we had such a short time to go. The day before we left, we all slept on the floor, cooked on the floor, and ate on the floor.

When we first got to Manzanar, we were given numbers. We went to the mess hall, and we were given meals in tin plates and tin cups. It was canned hot dogs and canned spinach.

After eating, we were taken to our room. The floors were boarded, but you could see the ground below. What hurt most was seeing hay mattresses. We were used to a regular home. All of us were in one room. We felt like prisoners."

Answer the questions below.

1. Why did the Tateshi family sleep on the floor the day before they left their home?

2. Why did the living conditions in the internment camp hurt Yuri Tateshi?

CHALLENGE Why do you think Yuri Tateshi wrote about her experience?

1. They were forced to sell their belongings. **2.** She and her family had been used to a regular home. **CHALLENGE** To describe the unfair treatment by the U.S. government, to let people know about the conditions of the camps, to show she survived the indignity

Section 4 Winning the War

Words to Know

Holocaust	the mass murder of millions of Jews by the Nazis
genocide	the planned murder of an entire people
atomic bomb	a nuclear bomb with enormous power to harm

Getting Started Discuss with students the lengths some people would go to win something. Explain that President Truman had to go to great lengths to win World War II. He decided to use a new weapon—the atomic bomb.

By early 1944, the Allies were pushing German and Japanese forces back to their homelands. However, many battles remained to be fought. Many lives would be lost in battle and in Nazi death camps. The most powerful weapon ever used in battle would bring the war to an end.

The D-Day Invasion

To end the war, there had to be an Allied invasion, or attack, of Western Europe. For more than six months, Allied troops prepared to land on the coast of Europe. General Dwight D. Eisenhower of the U.S. Army planned the invasion. Later, he would lead all Allied troops to victory in Europe.

The Germans were expecting an invasion. They planted land mines and put up barbed wire to stand in the way of the Allied troops.

June 6, 1944, was D-day. On that day, an invasion took place. Over 170,000 Allied soldiers crossed the English Channel from Britain. They landed on the coast of Normandy in northern France. Within a week, the Allies had landed tons of supplies and hundreds of thousands of soldiers in France.

The attack was possible because the Allies had tricked Hitler. He thought that the landing was going to be at a spot farther up the French coast. Hitler had sent his best soldiers there.

Why was D-day planned? D-day was planned to start the Allied invasion of Europe.

End of the War

The Allies wanted to force Hitler to surrender, so they began to bomb German cities day and night. Germany's defeat seemed certain. However, the Nazis made one final attack on the Allies in December 1944. But the Allies forced the German troops to retreat toward Berlin, the capital of Germany.

History Fact

On May 8, 1945, the Allies celebrated VE Day (Victory in Europe).

History Fact In the skies above Paris, two searchlight beams formed a V for victory to celebrate V-E Day.

Soon, millions of Allied soldiers were closing in on the German capital from all directions. Finally, on May 7, 1945, Germany surrendered. The war in Europe was over.

What made the Germans surrender? Berlin was captured, German cities were destroyed.

The Holocaust

Allied troops moved into Germany and into lands that Germany had controlled. Soon, they found evidence of one of the most horrible acts of the war. It was the **Holocaust.** The Holocaust was the mass murder of millions of Jews by the Nazis.

During his rise to power, Hitler had blamed Jewish people for most of Germany's problems. Before long, the Nazis decided on a "final solution" for the Jews. The solution was **genocide.** Genocide is the planned murder of an entire people.

To do this, the Nazis built death camps, where they sent Jews from around Europe. These death camps had specially built gas chambers. The Nazis killed thousands of people a day. Their bodies were burned in huge ovens. In all, the Nazis killed six million Jews.

Children were among the victims of the Holocaust.

Visual About 15,000 Jewish children were sent to Theresienstadt, a concentration camp. Fewer than 100 survived.

Several million other people were also murdered in the death camps.

The Allies had heard reports of death camps during the war, but few people believed them. When the Allied troops freed the people left in the camps, they were shocked by what they saw.

After the war, the Allies put some Nazi leaders on trial for war crimes. The Allies wanted to make sure that the people who had helped plan the Holocaust were punished. At the trials, 12 Nazi leaders were sentenced to death.

Why did the Allies put the Nazi leaders on trial? Felt they should be punished for planning the Holocaust

Victory Over Japan

After Germany surrendered, the Allies turned all their attention toward the Pacific Ocean. By that time, Allied forces had retaken the Philippines. Also, General MacArthur returned. He had kept his promise.

The last two islands under Japanese control fell to Allied forces in 1945. The Allied leaders did not want to send troops to attack Japan. They feared that one million soldiers could be lost in such an attack. Instead, they ordered bombers to drop bombs over Japanese cities day and night. They caused terrible destruction.

Victory over Japan was now in sight. President Roosevelt had begun to serve his fourth term in March 1945. He was planning to meet with Winston Churchill of Great Britain and Joseph Stalin of the Soviet Union. He wanted to work with the two leaders to find a way to end war forever.

President Roosevelt had been in poor health for some time. He died on April 12, 1945. His Vice President, Harry S. Truman, became President.

Why did the Allied leaders decide against sending troops to Japan? They feared one million soldiers would be lost in an attack.

A New Weapon

President Truman immediately faced a huge decision. For years, scientists had worked in secret to develop a powerful new weapon, the **atomic bomb.** An atomic bomb is a nuclear bomb with enormous power to harm. In July 1945, the scientists successfully tested the bomb. President Truman would have to decide whether to use this terrible new weapon.

President Truman got advice from scientists and government leaders. Scientists who developed the bomb did not want Truman to use it. Other people said using the bomb would save the lives of thousands of Allied troops.

At last, President Truman made a decision to use the deadly weapon. On August 6, 1945, the first atomic bomb was dropped over the Japanese city of Hiroshima. Three days later the United States dropped a second atomic bomb on the city of Nagasaki. The Japanese agreed to end the war on August 14, 1945. World War II was over at last.

Why did President Truman order the atomic bomb to be dropped? President Truman did not want to risk the lives of thousands of Allied troops in a ground war against the Japanese.

Section 4 Review

1. What was D-day?

2. Why did Adolf Hitler start the Holocaust?

3. Critical Thinking Why do you think the decision about the atomic bomb was so difficult for President Truman?

4. Write About History You are a radio announcer. Prepare a short radio broadcast about the Allied victory over Japan.

More Review is provided in Exercise 96 of the Workbook.

History Fact

More than 60 million people throughout the world died in World War II. Of those, about 300,000 were Americans.

History Fact When the war ended, Europe and Japan were in ruins. Millions of people were homeless, food was scarce, and factories were destroyed. In the United States, however, the war strengthened the economy and ended the Great Depression.

1. The day on which the Allied invasion of Europe took place
2. Hitler wanted to rid Germany of the Jews and other people whom he considered to be "undesirable."
3. Possible answer: Advisers on both sides of the question had powerful arguments, but Truman had to think of the good of the country rather than his own personal view.
4. Possible answer: Broadcast should include why Allied leaders did not send troops, what happened.

Chapter

22 Review

Summary Have students use this graphic organizer to outline the main ideas and details of the chapter.

Summary
In 1941, the United States entered World War II on the side of the Allies. The atomic bomb ended the war.

Section 1
In 1941, the United States declared war on Japan. It joined the Allied forces against Germany and Japan. The Allies made a plan for war.

Section 2
Allied forces attacked the Axis Powers in North Africa and then moved into Europe. In the Pacific, the Battle of Midway was a major defeat for the Japanese.

Section 3
Making war supplies created more jobs. African Americans and Latinos fought bravely in the war. The internment of Japanese Americans was a serious mistake.

Section 4
The landing at Normandy brought the Allies into Western Europe. There, they saw the horrors of the Holocaust for the first time. Dropping the atomic bomb on Hiroshima and Nagasaki ended World War II.

More Vocabulary Review is provided in Exercise 146 of the Classroom Resource Binder.

Vocabulary Review

Write *true* or *false*. If the statement is false, change the underlined term to make it true.

1. During World War II, Germany and Japan fought on the side of the <u>Allies</u>. False: Axis Powers
2. Many Japanese Americans were forced to move to <u>amphibious landings</u>. False: internment camps
3. <u>Rationing</u> was a way to distribute scarce goods fairly. True
4. People still remember the <u>siege</u> with its death camps and cruel treatment of millions of people. False: Holocaust

1. The attack on Pearl Harbor p. 406 **2.** The Americans figured out the secret messages being sent between Japanese ships, so they knew where the Japanese were. p. 411 **3.** African Americans and Latinos faced prejudice in the armed forces. pp. 416–417 **4.** Possible answer: The suspicion that they were disloyal citizens p. 418 **5.** Possible answer: The evil of the Holocaust experience continues to fill people with horror today. pp.421–422

Chapter Quiz

Write your answers in complete sentences.

1. What event led the United States to declare war on Japan in 1941?
2. How were the Americans able to win the Battle of Midway against the strong Japanese fleet?
3. How were African Americans and Latinos discriminated against during World War II?
4. **Critical Thinking** What do you think caused Japanese Americans more sorrow than the loss of property?
5. **Critical Thinking** Why do you think the Holocaust is still remembered?

Test Tip
Before studying each section, look at the photos, charts, and maps. Read the captions of the photos to get an idea about the topic.

Writing Tip
Before you begin writing, think about your purpose for writing. Do you want to persuade someone, give a point of view, or tell a story?

Using the Timeline

Use the timeline on pages 404–405 to answer the questions.

1. How many years after the Battle of Midway did World War II end? 3 years
2. Which cities were nearly destroyed by the atomic bomb during the war? Hiroshima and Nagasaki

Group Activity See the Teacher's Planning Guide for a scoring rubric for this activity.

Group Activity

With your group, make a storyboard showing how one of the people named in the chapter took part in World War II. Include what the person did during the war and why the person is remembered.

After World War II, the United States continued to build and test atomic bombs. Signs, such as this one, appeared at the entrance to every public fallout shelter. How would you describe the force of an atomic explosion? It is very powerful.

The Cold War

1945
Harry S. Truman becomes President
World War II ends
United Nations formed

1947
Truman Doctrine

1948
Harry S. Truman elected
Berlin Airlift
Marshall Plan

1949
NATO formed

1950
Korean War begins

1952
Dwight D. Eisenhower elected

1953
Korean War ends

1945 — 1948 — 1951 — 1954

Additional activities and strategies to customize lessons can be found in the Teacher's Planning Guide.

Chapter 23 The Cold War 1945–1960

ESL Note To help students understand the concept of a cold war, discuss the difference between a "cold" and a "hot" war. Have students consider how a war could be fought without the use of military weapons. Have students consider what some of the weapons used during the cold war might have been.

Words to Know

satellite

iron curtain

cold war

containment

superpower

demilitarized zone

blacklist

McCarthyism

fallout

space race

Words to Know These words are defined in the section in which they appear, as well as in the Glossary. Point out to students that *iron curtain* and *cold war* are idioms—terms that mean something other than their literal meaning.

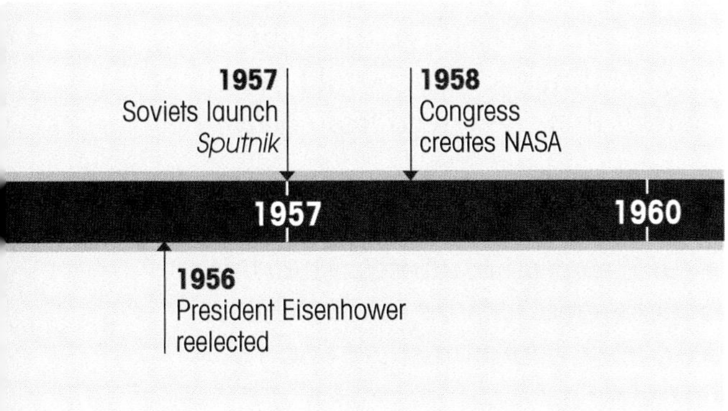

Learning Objectives

- Describe how communism spread in Eastern Europe.
- Explain attempts to stop the spread of communism.
- Explain how communism spread in Asia.
- Describe the reasons why the United States was drawn into the arms race.
- Explore how the United Nations began.

Project Students will be able to begin work on the project after they have finished reading Section 3. To help them get started, have them take notes on the images from the cold war.

Portfolio Project

Many of the events in this chapter have been shown in photos, in books, on television, and in newsreels. As you read, make a list of the pictures that tell the story of the cold war. At the end of the chapter, you will be able to create a news broadcast. Point to pictures, and explain what took place in each event.

Timeline The timeline is divided into 3-year intervals. The events take place over a period of 14 years. Point out to students that many events deal with the United States and its relations with other countries.

Section 1 The Cold War Begins

Words to Know

satellite	a country controlled by a more powerful country
iron curtain	an imaginary wall, or dividing line, separating the Soviet nations from the rest of Europe
cold war	a sharp conflict between countries without actual war
containment	a policy of preventing a country from expanding its power and threatening other countries

Getting Started Discuss with students what life would be like if television, the Internet, radio, and all print media were controlled by the government. Explain that Communists in Europe made it illegal for citizens to receive information from the rest of the world after World War II.

Even before World War II ended, world leaders hoped to bring a lasting peace to the world. However, after the war was over, the spread of communism led to conflicts between the United States and the Soviet Union.

Communism in Eastern Europe

While battles were still going on during World War II, Allied leaders were already thinking of peace. They hoped to start an international organization that would keep world peace. In 1945, the United Nations was formed.

The Allied leaders agreed that after the war they would give the countries under Nazi rule the right to choose their own governments. They would hold elections in each country that they freed from Nazi rule.

After the war, the United States and the Soviet Union were very strong countries. Each wanted to see its own kind of government in European countries. The United States wanted to see democratic governments. The Soviet Union wanted to see Communist governments.

The United States held free elections in the countries freed by American troops. The Soviet Union refused to hold free elections in the countries freed by its troops. Instead, it used force to set up Communist governments.

The Soviets made the countries they freed **satellites** of the Soviet Union. A satellite is a country controlled by a more powerful country. Poland, Romania, Bulgaria, Hungary, and Czechoslovakia became the chief satellites of the Soviet Union.

The Soviet Union kept a tight grip on its satellite countries. Secret police watched and listened everywhere. People were not free to speak out against their own governments. Few people were allowed either in or out of their countries. People were not able to get news about the outside world.

The spread of communism worried the leaders of democratic countries. Winston Churchill, the leader of Great Britain, described what the Soviet Union was doing in a speech in 1946. He declared that "an **iron curtain** had been drawn down" on Soviet-held lands.

The iron curtain that Churchill spoke about was an imaginary wall, or dividing line, separating the Soviet nations from the rest of Europe.

Why were free elections not held in the countries freed by Soviet troops? The Soviet Union wanted to keep those countries under Communist control.

A New Kind of War

Within a few months after the end of World War II, a new kind of war began. It became known as the **cold war.** A cold war is a sharp conflict between countries without actual war. A cold war is fought mostly with angry words and threats. In 1945, the United States felt that the Soviet Union was trying to spread communism throughout the world.

History Fact

Winston Churchill gave his famous Iron Curtain Speech on March 5, 1946, in Fulton, Missouri.

History Fact In this speech, Churchill said "that the people of any country have the right, and should have the power by constitutional action, . . . to choose or change the character or form of government under which they dwell; that freedom of speech and thought should reign."

On the other hand, the Soviet Union felt that the United States was trying to rule other countries. Neither country trusted the other. This was just the beginning of several showdowns between the United States and the Soviet Union.

Why did the United States and the Soviet Union become enemies after World War II? The U.S. resented the Soviets taking over other countries; Soviet Union resented U.S. power.

The Truman Doctrine

President Truman believed that the Soviet Union would slowly conquer the world with its political ideas. He wanted to stop the spread of communism. In 1947, President Truman promised to help any nation that wanted to act against communism.

Just the year before, in 1946, Communists in Greece had revolted against the Greek government. Great Britain had been giving Greece help. However, the British said that they could no longer give Greece all the help it needed.

President Truman thought that if Greece fell to Communist control, its neighbor, Turkey, would be next. Truman sent military advisers to help the Greeks fighting against communism.

President Truman adopted a policy of **containment.** Containment is the policy of preventing a country from expanding its power and threatening other countries. The United States promised that it would not allow communism to spread to other countries. Truman's plan to help countries fight against communism became known as the Truman Doctrine. It became the basis for the United States' cold war policy.

What did the Truman Doctrine promise to other countries? To help countries facing a Communist takeover

The Marshall Plan

After World War II, much of Europe had been destroyed. Factories were shut down. There were short supplies of food, fuel, and medicine. President Truman asked George C. Marshall, the U.S. secretary of state, to draw up a plan to help Europeans rebuild their countries.

In 1948, Marshall put together a plan that became known as the Marshall Plan. U.S. dollars paid for

1. new factories, schools, hospitals, and bridges in Europe to replace the ones that had been destroyed during World War II.
2. supplies to help England, France, and West Germany.
3. a huge market for American goods, which kept the U.S. economy booming.
4. protection to democratic nations against the Soviet Union.

How did the Marshall Plan help Europeans? Built factories, gave supplies, gave protection against Soviet Union

The Berlin Airlift

At the end of World War II, the Allies divided Germany among themselves. The United States, Great Britain, France, and the Soviet Union each controlled an area, or zone. Berlin, which had been the capital of Germany, was divided into four zones. The United States, Great Britain, and France held West Berlin. The Soviet Union held East Berlin.

In 1948, the United States, Great Britain, and France wanted to rebuild Germany by forming one country called West Germany. They did not want the Communists to make Germany another Soviet satellite.

Under the Marshall Plan, the United States sent goods to Europe.

Visual Congress required items shipped under the Marshall Plan to be labeled. "For European Recovery—Furnished by U.S.A." was the first label. Congress wanted there to be no mistake about who had supplied the assistance.

The Cold War in Europe, 1955

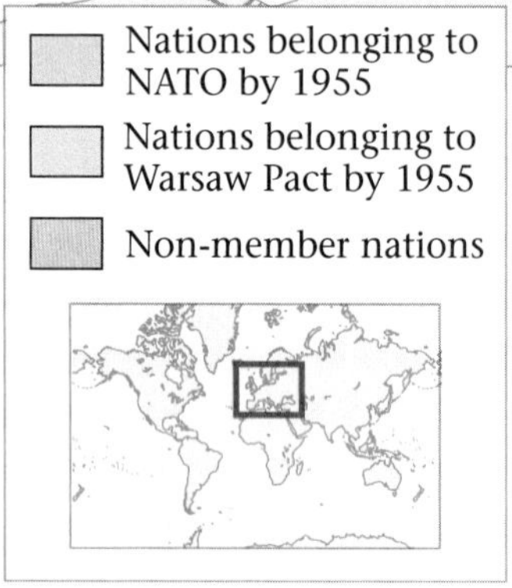

Map Study

1. To what group did Greece belong, NATO or the Warsaw Pact nations?
2. What nations belonged to the Warsaw Pact by 1955?

Map This map shows NATO, Warsaw Pact, and nonmember nations of Europe. Point out to students that Sweden, Switzerland, Austria, Spain, and Yugoslavia did not join with any other nation.

1. Greece belonged to NATO.
2. Soviet Union, Poland, East Germany, Czechoslovakia, Romania, Bulgaria, Albania, Hungary

The Soviets saw what was happening. Immediately, they closed all railroad and road traffic between West Berlin and the American, British, and French zones. The people of West Berlin were soon trapped with very little food, medicine, or heating fuel.

President Truman and the other Allied leaders did not want war. However, they did not want to allow the Soviets to take over West Berlin either. The Allies decided there was only one way to get supplies to West Berlin. They started the Berlin airlift to send in supplies by air.

For more than a year, American and British planes carried food and other supplies to the people of West Berlin. Finally, in 1949, the Soviets called off the siege.

Why was the Berlin airlift important? The Berlin airlift provided supplies to the people of West Berlin.

North Atlantic Treaty Organization

In 1949, the United States and Canada joined ten countries in Western Europe. Together, they signed a treaty. In the treaty, they set up the North Atlantic Treaty Organization. It became known as NATO. The treaty said that if a member nation were attacked, all other member nations would help that nation. General Dwight D. Eisenhower became the commander of NATO.

In 1955, the Soviet Union and its satellites formed their own military group. This group was known as the Warsaw Pact. As the cold war continued, Europe again became a divided area. The NATO nations were on one side. The Warsaw Pact nations were on the other side.

What was the purpose of NATO? Group of countries joined together to fight communism

Section 1 Review

1. Why were the United States and the Soviet Union no longer friends after World War II?
2. What was the purpose of the Truman Doctrine?
3. **Critical Thinking** How do you think the Marshall Plan helped the U.S. economy?
4. **Write About Geography** Write a paragraph describing why it was important to the United States for Canada to join NATO.

More Review is provided in Exercise 97 of the Workbook.

1. The countries had opposing views on how the countries freed after World War II should be governed. The United States wanted democratic governments. The Soviet Union wanted Communist governments.
2. To prevent the spread of communism
3. Possible answer: Provided a market for American goods, kept economy going strong
4. Possible answer: It was important for the security of the United States that Canada join NATO. Canada is the northern neighbor of the United States. The two countries share a boundary.

CONNECTING HISTORY AND GOVERNMENT
The United Nations

On April 25, 1945, delegates, or representatives, from 50 nations met in San Francisco, California. They met to write a charter, or constitution, for a new organization. This organization was called the United Nations, or the UN. It was formed to keep peace in the world.

In a way, the United Nations is a system of government for the world. Its charter says all member nations belong to the General Assembly. In this group, nations discuss problems and suggest actions. However, the General Assembly has no power to carry out the actions.

The United Nations building in New York City

The Security Council has the job of carrying out actions. It is made up of five permanent members. In 1945, the permanent members were the United States, the United Kingdom (Great Britain and Northern Ireland), France, China, and the Soviet Union. Ten other nations are chosen for two-year terms on the Security Council. The Security Council can take action against nations. Only the five permanent nations can veto, or stop, any council action.

Answer the questions below.

1. What can the General Assembly do?

2. How long do countries that are not permanent members serve on the Security Council?

CHALLENGE Why might a member nation veto an action of the Security Council?

1. The General Assembly can discuss issues and suggest actions to take against member countries. **2.** They serve for two years. **CHALLENGE** The council member country might have good relations with the country in question. The proposed actions might hurt the member country.

Section 2 Communism in Asia

Words to Know

superpower	a country that is a top world power
demilitarized zone	an area where no military forces are allowed

Getting Started Discuss with students the reasons that sometimes turn enemies into friends, and friends into enemies. Explain that after World War II, Japan became a friend to the United States and China became an enemy.

The United States was able to contain communism in Europe after World War II. Containment also worked in parts of Asia and the Middle East. However, in the small country of Korea, a war began.

Changes in Japan and China

After defeating Japan in World War II, the United States decided to help that country to rebuild. The United States sent money to Japan. Japan formed a new democratic government with free elections. By the time the U.S. forces left the country in 1952, Japan had repaired its cities. Factories were making goods.

Remember
Japan had started a war with China in 1937 and had controlled most of eastern China.

A civil war began in China in 1946. Chiang Kai-shek, the leader of China's Nationalist party, led his army against Mao Zedong, the leader of China's Communist party. The United States supported the Nationalists. It tried to get the two sides to share power. However, both sides refused.

In 1949, the Communists won the civil war. They took control of China. The Nationalists, led by Chiang Kai-shek, were forced onto the island of Formosa. Later, Formosa became known as Taiwan.

The United States said that the government on Taiwan was the real government of China. It used its

As U.S. soldiers marched into South Korea, South Korean citizens rushed to leave.

Visual About 54,000 American soldiers died in the Korean War. Nearly three million Korean and Chinese troops and civilians died.

veto power to keep Communist China out of the United Nations. Communist China formed an alliance with the Soviet Union.

Why was China kept out of the United Nations? The U.S. used its veto power to keep China out of the UN.

The Korean War

Korea is a small country on the east coast of Asia. From 1910 until 1945, Korea was under the control of Japan. After World War II, Korea was divided into two parts. Communist troops controlled North Korea. American troops controlled South Korea.

Neither the United States nor the Soviet Union could agree on a plan to unite Korea. Both countries had become **superpowers**, and neither wanted to allow the other to become more powerful. A superpower is a country that is a top world power.

In June 1950, North Korean troops attacked South Korea. Their plan was to unite Korea under a Communist government. Americans were angry about the attack. President Truman immediately sent U.S. troops to Korea under the command of General MacArthur. The newly formed United Nations also sent troops.

Americans made up about 90 percent of the fighting force. Suddenly, the Korean War became an American war. However, President Truman never asked Congress to declare war. The fighting was called a police action.

The Korean War lasted until 1953. Neither side was able to defeat the other. Finally, the two sides agreed to set up a **demilitarized zone.** A demilitarized zone is an area where no military forces are allowed.

How did the Korean War become an American war?
In 1950, President Truman sent American troops to South Korea to defend it against communism.

Section 2 Review

1. How did the United States help Japan after World War II?
2. Who did the United States support in China's civil war?
3. **Critical Thinking** Why was it important for both sides in the Korean War to set up a demilitarized zone?
4. **Write About History** Write a paragraph explaining how communism affected Asia after World War II.

1. The United States sent money to Japan.
2. Chiang Kai-shek and the Nationalist party
3. So that the fighting would stop and not easily start again
4. Possible answer: Civil war in China; Korea divided; Americans become involved in Korea.

More Review is provided in Exercise 99 of the Workbook.

Section 3 The Cold War at Home

Words to Know

blacklist	a list of people who are not approved for employment
McCarthyism	term named for Senator Joseph McCarthy's campaign of accusing people of being Communists
fallout	the radioactive waste from a nuclear blast
space race	the competition among countries to be first in exploring space

Getting Started Discuss ways that fear can affect people or entire countries. Explain that after World War II an unseen fear between the United States and the Soviet Union became a way of life.

During the 1950s, the bad feelings between the Soviet Union and the United States increased. Many Americans feared that Communist spies were operating in the United States. The fear of communism caused problems for many people.

A Hunt for Spies Begins

In 1938, Congress formed a group to look into secret Nazi and Communist activities in the United States. The group was called the House Un-American Activities Committee, or HUAC.

HUAC began to look into communism in the American motion picture industry in 1947. HUAC hunted for writers, actors, and directors who once belonged to the Communist party.

Many people in the movie industry were called to Washington, D.C. Once there, they were questioned by HUAC. Those who refused to testify were put on a **blacklist.** A blacklist is a list of people who are not approved for employment. Just being called before HUAC could ruin a person's career.

Julius and Ethel Rosenberg were not in the motion picture industry. However, in 1951, they were accused of helping Communists. They were charged with giving atomic secrets to the Soviets during World War II. The Rosenbergs said they were not guilty. However, a jury found them guilty. They were put to death in 1953.

Why were many people in the movie industry blacklisted in the 1950s? They were thought to be members of the Communist party.

The McCarthy Era

One member of Congress who became famous during the 1950s was Senator Joseph McCarthy of Wisconsin. He claimed to have secret knowledge of Communists working in the U.S. government. In a speech in 1950, McCarthy said he had a list of names of 205 Communists in the State Department. He did not have such a list.

Senator Joseph McCarthy was seen on television saying that many Communists worked in the U.S. government.

Visual The term *McCarthyism* was first used in 1950 in a cartoon in the *Washington Post*, a newspaper published in Washington, D.C.

Many Americans feared the spread of communism. They believed that McCarthy was trying to save the United States from a Communist takeover. Many other people thought that McCarthy was a danger to the United States. Americans saw Joseph McCarthy speak on television. The term **McCarthyism** began to be used. The term means accusing people of being Communists.

In 1954, McCarthy claimed that there were Communists in the U.S. Army. None of McCarthy's charges were ever proven. Many Americans believed him anyway. The fear that he created remained throughout the 1950s.

What information did Senator McCarthy tell people he had? He said that he had the names of Communists in the State Department and that there were Communists in the U.S. Army.

The Race for Arms and Space

In 1949, the Soviet Union tested its first atomic bomb. Americans were shocked. No one expected the Soviets to have atomic weapons so soon. In 1952, American scientists exploded the first hydrogen bomb. It was a weapon many times more powerful than the atomic bomb that was dropped on Hiroshima, Japan, in 1945. The new President, Dwight D. Eisenhower, ordered the military to build up its supply of nuclear bombs.

Atomic weapons did not have to be used in war to be dangerous. Test explosions of the bombs formed large clouds of **fallout.** Fallout is the radioactive waste from a nuclear blast.

Many scientists feared that atomic testing would poison the earth's environment. The superpowers met during the 1950s to talk about banning tests. However, no agreement was reached.

A Closer Look

THE SPACE RACE

The space race between the United States and the Soviet Union started on October 4, 1957. On that day, the Soviet Union sent into orbit the first satellite made by people. It was named *Sputnik*. *Sputnik* orbited the earth in 96 minutes.

Many Americans were concerned that the Soviet Union's technology was better than that of the United States. They feared that *Sputnik* would be used to carry nuclear weapons.

This is the Sputnik *stamp issued by the Soviet Union.*

The next month, the Soviet Union launched a second satellite. It was called *Sputnik 2*. *Sputnik 2* weighed 1,120 pounds. It stayed in orbit for almost 200 days. After *Sputnik 2* was launched, the United States sped up its own space efforts.

Critical Thinking How do you think the space race affected the lives of Americans? Americans became more concerned about the power of the Soviet Union, the spread of communism; took greater interest in technology and science.

In 1957, people around the world were shocked again by news from the Soviet Union. The Soviets sent *Sputnik*, the first satellite, into space.

Soon, the United States and the Soviets were in a **space race.** The space race was a competition among countries to be first in exploring space. In 1958, the United States launched its first satellite, named *Explorer 1*. The same year, Congress set up the National Aeronautics and Space Administration, or NASA. It was formed to control the U.S. space program.

Many Americans were worried that the Soviets were ahead of the United States in the space race. In 1958, Congress passed the National Defense Education Act. This act helped to improve education in the United States. It gave money so that students who needed money to go to college could get loans. Schools could build more science labs, and teachers could take courses to keep up with science and math. Finally, states could buy better teaching supplies.

Why did the United States build a hydrogen bomb?
The United States wanted to have more powerful weapons than the Soviet Union.

Section 3 Review

1. How did blacklisting hurt people?

2. Why was the House Un-American Activities Committee started?

3. Critical Thinking Why did many Americans feel that McCarthyism was a danger?

4. Write About History You have just heard the news that the Soviet Union has sent *Sputnik* into space. Write about the discussion that takes place in your class the next day.

More Review is provided in Exercise 100 of the Workbook.

1. Blacklisting limited many people's opportunities to find work.
2. The House Un-American Activities Committee was started to investigate the spread of Nazism and communism in the United States.
3. Possible answer: McCarthyism limited Americans' freedom of expression and pitted Americans against one another.
4. Possible answer: Disappointment and alarm that Americans were not first; possibilities for the future; hope that America would be the first nation to send humans into space; fear of the Soviet Union's controlling space; fear of a nuclear arms race in space.

Chapter 23 Review

Summary Have students use this graphic organizer to outline the main ideas and details of the chapter.

Summary
After World War II, the Soviets controlled most of Eastern Europe. A cold war developed between the United States and the Soviet Union. The fear of communism spread.

Section 1
After World War II, the United States and the Soviet Union did not get along well. The Western world hoped the United Nations and NATO would keep world peace.

Section 2
The United States helped Japan rebuild after World War II. The attempt to expand communism in Asia led to wars in China and Korea.

Section 3
Many U.S. citizens feared communism. This led to an investigation of the motion picture industry and the rise of McCarthyism. The space race became important.

- satellite
- blacklist
- superpower
- space race
- containment

More Vocabulary Review is provided in Exercise 152 of the Classroom Resource Binder.

Vocabulary Review

Write a term from the list to match each definition.

1. Competition among countries to be the first in exploring space space race
2. A list of people who are not approved for employment blacklist
3. A policy of preventing the expansion of power by one country over another country containment
4. Country controlled by a more powerful country satellite
5. Country that is a top world power superpower

1. With secret police, by limiting people's personal freedoms p. 429 **2.** Possible answer: Truman Doctrine, policy of containment, Marshall Plan, Berlin Airlift, joining the NATO alliance pp. 430–433 **3.** North Korea planned to unite Korea by force. pp. 436–437 **4.** Possible answer: The disapproval by most Americans of communism pp. 438–439 **5.** Possible answer: Scientists would be interested in providing more advanced science and math courses for both teachers and students and giving all students an opportunity for a better education. p. 441

Chapter Quiz

Write your answers in complete sentences.

1. How did the Soviet Union keep its satellite nations under its control?
2. In what ways did the United States react to the spread of communism in other countries?
3. Why did the Korean War start?
4. **Critical Thinking** Why did Americans feel threatened by the spread of communism at home and overseas?
5. **Critical Thinking** Why would scientists have supported the National Defense Education Act in 1958?

Test Tip
Each time you begin studying for a test or quiz, list the main ideas as you read.

Writing Tip
List all the facts and details you want to include in your answer before you start writing.

Using the Timeline

Use the timeline on pages 426–427 to answer the questions.

1. Who was President when the Korean War began? Harry S. Truman
2. What was one U.S. response to the launching of *Sputnik*? NASA

Group Activity See the Teacher's Planning Guide for a scoring rubric for this activity.

Group Activity

With your group, choose a world problem that you would like to see the United Nations act on. Discuss how you would bring the problem to the attention of the United Nations. Decide what you would ask the United Nations to do about it. Make a list of questions.

Critical Thinking 1. Some countries believed that a dictator would solve their postwar problems. 2. Hitler and Stalin wanted to take control of Poland. 3. The United States wanted to avoid sending troops into Japan and possibly losing thousands of American lives. 4. Allied leaders wanted an organization to keep world peace.

Unit 7 Review

Critical Thinking

Give one reason why each of the following events happened.

1. Dictators came to power in Europe in the 1930s.
2. Germany invaded Poland.
3. The United States dropped atomic bombs on Japan.
4. The United Nations was formed.

Building Your Skills

Write *I* next to the statements below that show an isolationist's point of view. Write *NI* if it shows the point of view of a person who is not an isolationist.

1. We have problems of our own. I
2. Freedom and democracy must be saved throughout the world. NI
3. We must stand up to the Nazi's power. NI
4. American boys should not have to fight in faraway wars. I

Who Did It?

Write the name of the person who took each action below.

1. This African American team was part of the 332nd Fighter Group. Tuskegee Airmen
2. He said that "an iron curtain had been drawn down" on Soviet-held lands. Winston Churchill
3. He started the Italian Fascist party. Benito Mussolini

Writing an Essay

Answer one of the following essay topics.

See the Answer Key for a detailed answer.

1. Discuss what might have happened if the United States had not taken part in World War II.
2. Explain what the U.S. government did to control the economy at home during World War II.
3. Describe how the fear of communism affected Americans in the 1950s.

Linking Past and Present

Before the Japanese bombed Pearl Harbor, many Americans were isolationists. The debate over whether the United States should get involved in the problems of other countries continues today. How do you feel about this? Explain.

Affirmative—United States is a superpower, has responsibilities to keep peace and to help other countries; Negative—United States needs to work to solve its own problems.

Unit Opener Use the titles, visual, and caption to engage students in a discussion of the time period.

Unit 8 A Changing Society

Chapter 24 **Changing Ways of Life** 1945–1960

Chapter 25 **The Struggle for Equality** 1947–1965

Chapter 26 **A New Frontier and a Great Society** 1960–1968

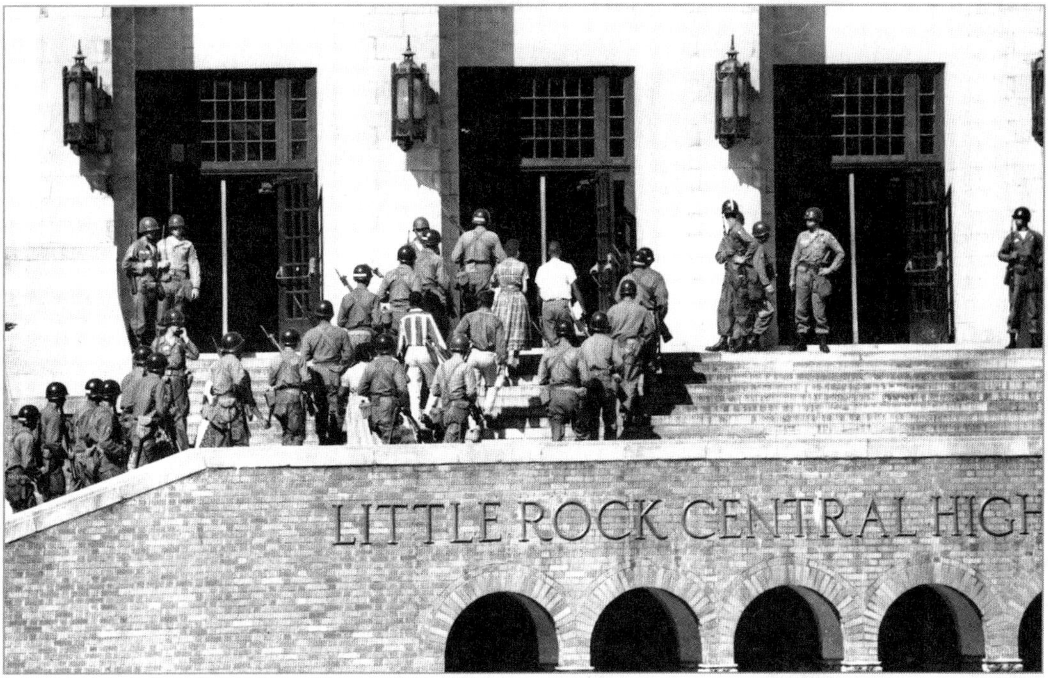

In 1957, nine African American students entered Central High School in Little Rock, Arkansas, under the guard of U.S. troops. Why do you think these students needed protection by U.S. troops? Some people wanted to prevent the students from attending school. Some of those people might have tried to hurt the students.

> *"I have a dream that my four little children will one day live in a nation where they will not be judged by the color of their skin, but by the content of their character."*
>
> —Reverend Dr. Martin Luther King, Jr., speaking at the March on Washington, August 28, 1963

Primary Source Dr. Martin Luther King, Jr., was awarded the Nobel Peace Prize in 1964 for his work in civil rights. He was the second African American to win the award. King was assassinated on April 4, 1968.

Many families bought homes in Levittown, a new suburb in Long Island, near New York City. During the 1950s, frozen TV dinners that could be heated in the oven, like the one shown here, were popular. What do you notice about the streets and houses in Levittown? The streets are straight, and the houses all look alike.

The Years After World War II

- ***1945*** World War II ends
- **1948** Harry S. Truman elected
- **1950** Polio strikes 33,300 Americans
- **1951** Disc jockey invents term *rock 'n' roll*
- **1952** Dwight D. Eisenhower elected
- **1954** Polio vaccine tested

1945 — 1948 — *1951* — 1954

Additional activities and strategies to customize lessons can be found in the Teacher's Planning Guide.

Chapter 24 Changing Ways of Life 1945–1960

ESL Note To help students understand the concept of the "American Dream," discuss why many people have come to America. Point out that these reasons, or dreams, were for a better life. Ask students what their own "American dream" is.

Words to Know

automation

service industry

baby boom

suburb

consumer

generation gap

recession

interstate highway system

Words to Know These words are defined in the section in which they appear, as well as in the Glossary. Point out to students that four terms (*automation*, *service industry*, *consumer*, and *recession*) are business and economics terms.

Learning Objectives

- Explain how veterans were treated after World War II.
- Describe the economy after World War II.
- Describe how American life changed during the 1950s.
- Describe the growth of popular culture during the 1950s.
- Discuss the policies of President Eisenhower.
- Identify how bar graphs give information.

Project Students will be able to begin work on the project after completing Section 3. Students should take notes throughout the chapter to help them prepare.

Portfolio Project

As you read, collect information about life during the 1950s. Find information about television, music, advances in medicine, and changes in the way people worked and lived. Make a booklet that shows scenes from life during this time.

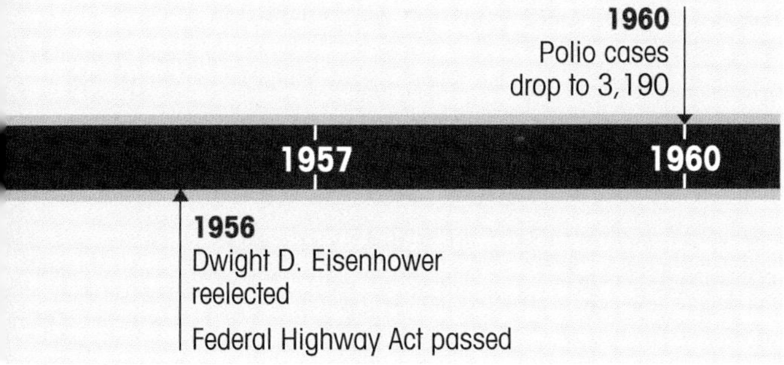

Timeline The timeline is divided into 3-year intervals. The events take place over a period of 16 years. Point out to students that 3 of the events deal with polio, a paralyzing disease that affected mostly children.

Section 1 Progress and Change

Words to Know

automation	the use of machines to do jobs once done by people
service industry	a business that provides a service for others
baby boom	a large increase in births, especially in the United States, after World War II
suburb	a community at the edge of a city

Getting Started Discuss ways that a government could show appreciation to veterans who fought for their country. What would students suggest?

After World War II, the United States changed in many ways. The economy grew to meet the needs of Americans in peacetime. The population grew quickly too. Americans found new kinds of work, new places to live, and new ways of doing things.

Helping Veterans

History Fact

In 1944, every member of Congress voted in favor of the GI Bill of Rights.

History Fact Of the ten million veterans who returned home, about eight million used the GI Bill to further their education.

President Harry Truman and many other Americans wanted to help veterans, or soldiers who had fought in the war. Veterans needed an education, jobs, and housing. To help veterans, Congress passed an act called the GI Bill of Rights. *GI* is a term for soldiers and veterans. Here is what the GI Bill of Rights of 1944 provided.

1. unemployment pay for one year to each veteran unable to find a job
2. special loans to buy houses or farms, or to start businesses
3. $500 a year to pay for a college education, plus money for rent and food

The GI Bill helped millions of veterans get a college degree. Many of them would not have been able to attend college any other way. The GI Bill also helped the economy. Veterans were able to earn and spend money.

What was the purpose of the GI Bill of Rights? To help veterans returning from the war

A Growing Economy

President Truman helped change the U.S. economy after World War II. He knew that factories must start making cars, refrigerators, and other things families needed. The money spent for these goods helped the economy grow. During the late 1940s and the 1950s the following changes took place.

1. Americans began to spend the money they had saved during the war. They bought cars, clothing, food, and houses. They also bought appliances, or machines, for the home.
2. U.S. businesses created more jobs to make the goods Americans wanted to buy.
3. U.S. businesses spent money on factories and machines to make more goods. Farmers also spent money on machines to grow more food.
4. American workers got more work done and made more money each year. Unions helped workers get higher pay. Workers had more money to spend.

U.S. workers built more than eight million cars a year.

Visual In 1940, more than 3.7 million passenger cars were sold in the United States. By 1950, that number had almost doubled to 6.6 million.

The U.S. economy became the biggest in the world. This meant that the value, or worth, of all the goods made and services performed in the United States was more than that of any other country. The government played a large role in the economy. For example, the U.S. government spent huge amounts of money on the arms race and the space race.

What happened to the U.S. economy after World War II? Government, business, and the American people spent lots of money. The economy grew.

Changes at Work

As the economy grew, work changed in many ways. One change was **automation.** Automation is the use of machines to do jobs once done by people. Automation helped factories make goods faster. For example, automation cut the time needed to make a car from 310 hours to 155 hours. Automation helped U.S. farmers too. With new machines, they could produce more meat, wheat, and corn than ever before. The use of machines meant that workers had to work fewer hours.

A second change was the kind of work that most people did. Before the 1950s, most workers had blue-collar jobs. They worked in factories, on farms, and in mines. The name *blue-collar* came from the blue work shirts or uniforms that many of the workers wore. However, in the 1950s, more workers began to have white-collar jobs. They worked in **service industries,** such as offices, banks, schools, and stores. A service industry is a business that provides a service for others. The name *white-collar* came from the white shirts that most male office workers wore.

This 1950 ad showed a woman doing housework.

Visual Even though advertisements were geared to housewives, more and more women began to work outside the home. By 1960, women made up one third of the work force.

A third change was the number of jobs held by women. During the war, many women worked outside the home. After the war, however, the government wanted veterans to get their old jobs back. Veterans often had first chances for new jobs. Government, businesses, and unions wanted women to stay at home. Many women left the workplace to raise their families. Later, during the 1950s, some women returned to work.

How did automation change the way people worked?
Machines made goods faster; people worked fewer hours.

Changes in Family Life

World War II veterans and other Americans wanted to get on with their lives. Millions of veterans and other Americans started families. The large increase in births,

During the 1950s, these teenagers enjoyed life in the suburbs.

especially in the United States, after World War II was known as the **baby boom**. Between 1946 and 1964, the U.S. population had one of its highest growth rates.

Visual As the suburbs grew, a new American lifestyle emerged. Teenagers began to gather at drive-ins, diners, and bowling alleys. By 1955, there were about 5,000 drive-in movie theaters in the U.S.

Growing American families needed homes. With help from the GI Bill, many veterans were able to get loans to buy homes. However, there were not enough homes for them to buy. In cities, there was not enough space for building. Builders like William Levitt looked outside the cities to nearby areas that became known as **suburbs.** A suburb is a community at the edge of a city. There they built developments, or large groups of houses. In suburbs, many workers commuted, or traveled back and forth, to their jobs in the city. As more Americans moved to the suburbs, businesses followed. Huge indoor shopping centers, or malls, were built.

As the suburbs grew, cities began to lose some of their population. Many skilled and educated workers moved out of the cities. On the other hand, many poor and unskilled people moved to cities to find work. Poor people often lived in tall apartment buildings built by city and federal governments. Many of the buildings were poorly built, and they were allowed to become run-down. People often tried to work with the government to improve the places where they lived. However, poor people in cities were one group left out of the growing U.S. economy. Many of these people were African Americans who had moved north to find jobs.

Why did people first move to the suburbs? There was not enough housing in the cities.

Great Names in History

DR. JONAS SALK AND DR. ALBERT SABIN

During the late 1940s and early 1950s, people lived in fear of a disease called polio. This disease paralyzed, or caused a loss of movement, in some part of a person's body. Franklin Roosevelt had polio as a young man. He could not walk completely on his own for the rest of his life. As thousands of people came down with polio, Americans raised money to find a way to prevent it.

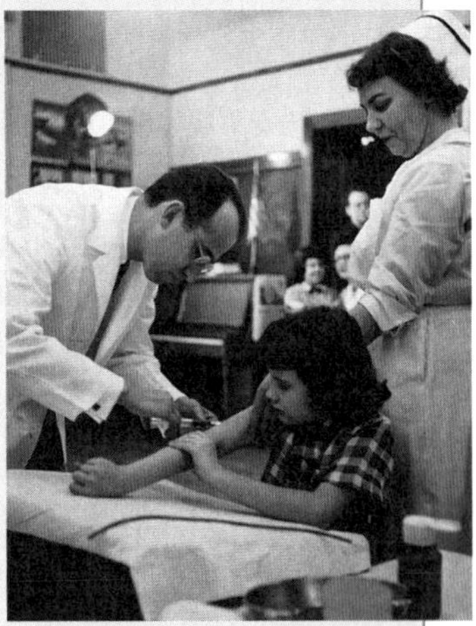

This is Dr. Jonas Salk giving the polio vaccine he developed.

Jonas Salk was a medical scientist. He developed the first vaccine against polio. It was an injection, or a shot. First, he tested the vaccine on himself and his family. Then, he tested it on about 400,000 American children. In 1955, the vaccine was declared a success. In most cases, it prevented polio.

In 1959, Albert Sabin developed another vaccine for polio. Sabin's vaccine was taken by mouth. By 1960, only 3,190 new polio cases were reported in the United States. Soon, polio was nearly wiped out in the United States.

Critical Thinking Why do you think Jonas Salk tested the vaccine on himself and his family first? Possible answer: Salk wanted to show that he believed the vaccine was safe enough to give his own children.

Changes in Health Care

Many American families were living a good life, but they were afraid of a terrible disease. The disease was polio. Polio left some children unable to walk. During the 1950s, Dr. Jonas Salk and Dr. Albert Sabin finally found a way to prevent polio.

During this time, health care in the United States improved for most people. New antibiotics such as penicillin could cure diseases caused by bacteria. New vaccines could prevent, or stop, some diseases from developing. New ways of doing surgery could transplant a part of an eye and move bone and skin.

Many advances in medicine that were developed during the war were now used to help all Americans.

How did health care change during the 1950s?
Antibiotics, new vaccines, new methods of surgery were developed

Section 1 Review

1. What three things did the GI Bill of Rights of 1944 provide to veterans?
2. How did work change during the late 1940s and the 1950s?
3. **Critical Thinking** Why do you think there were so many advances in health care after World War II?
4. **Write About Geography** Levittown was a planned community. Make your own planned community. List all the things the community needs. Then draw a map or picture to show where streets, parks, and buildings will be.

More Review is provided in Exercise 101 of the Workbook.

1. Unemployment pay, special loans, money for college
2. Automation was used in factories and on farms. More people got white-collar jobs. Women left the work force after the war. Some women began returning to the work force during the 1950s.
3. Student responses may show an understanding that new surgeries and medicines were often developed to help wounded and sick soldiers.
4. Student maps or pictures should include streets, parks, houses, stores, places of worship, recreational facilities, and so on.

BUILDING YOUR SKILLS
Reading A Graph

Graphs are drawings that make some facts easier to understand. There are many kinds of graphs. Bar graphs help you compare information.

The Growth of the Suburbs, 1921–1960

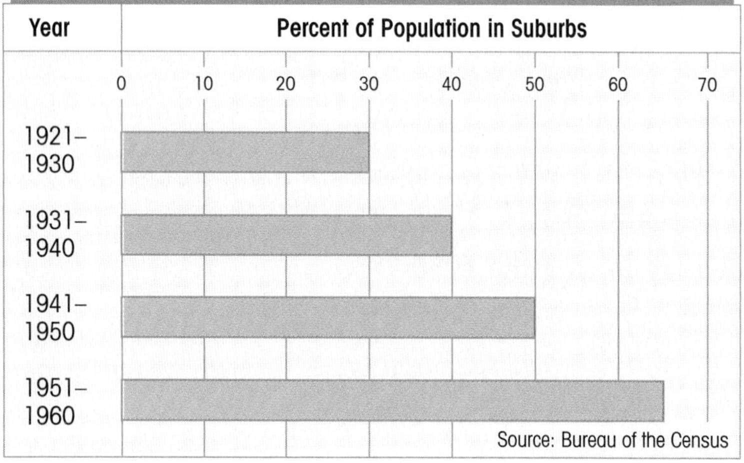

Follow these steps to read a bar graph.

1. Read the title to learn what the graph is about.

2. Read the label and the numbers across the top and side of the graph.

3. Draw conclusions from the graph.

Answer the questions using the graph.

1. What does each bar stand for?

2. Look at the bars for 1921–30 and 1931–40. What happened?

CHALLENGE What was the population growth between 1921 and 1950?

Apply the Skill

Make a graph with two bars. Show information about your class. For example, you might make a graph to show the number of female and male students in the class.

1. The percent of the population that lived in suburbs in 1921–60 **2.** The percent of Americans living in suburbs increased about 10 percent in between those periods. **CHALLENGE** 20%

Section 2 The Growth of Popular Culture

Words to Know

consumer	a person who buys and uses products
generation gap	a large difference in taste and values between young people and their parents

Getting Started Discuss with students how many hours they spend watching television or listening to music. Do their parents approve of their choices? Explain that teenagers in the 1950s had similar issues.

During the 1950s, television began to affect American life. Television brought the same programs, music, advertisements, and political messages to Americans all over the country. Television created a popular American culture. However, teenagers and adults began to like different things.

Television Changes American Life

The first television sets were sold to Americans in the late 1940s. Most families, however, did not get their own television sets until the 1950s. These early sets were small boxes with even smaller black-and-white screens. Still, television was exciting. For the first time, people across the United States could watch the same programs. By 1950, about four million American homes had television sets. By 1960, most American families owned a television set.

Television changed family life. Before television, families made their own fun. They read, sang, listened to the radio, or played games. Sometimes, they just talked about the day's events. By 1956, however, many adults were spending as much time each week watching television as they spent working. Children were also spending many hours watching television.

Graph Point out to students that the number of TV sets in the U.S. increased by almost 900 percent during the 1950s.

1. 35 million

2. Between 1950 and 1952

Homes With Television Sets, 1950–1960

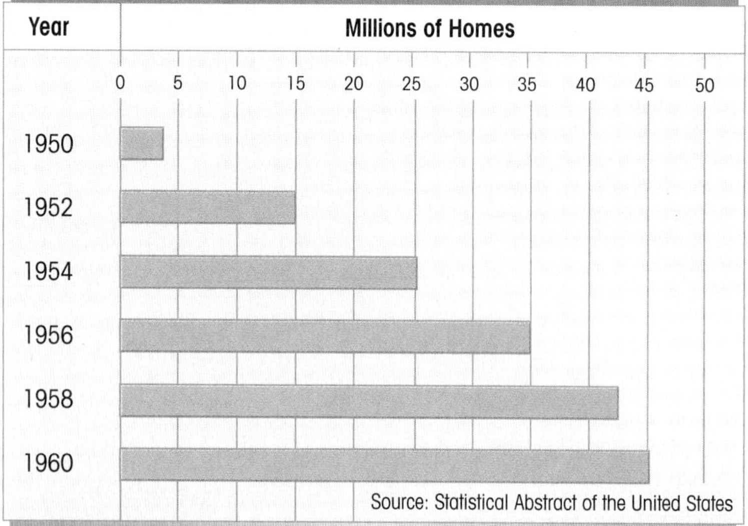

Source: Statistical Abstract of the United States

Graph Study

1. How many homes had TV sets in 1956?

2. When did the number of homes with TV sets increase the most?

Television changed politics too. During the 1952 race for President, the candidates gave speeches on television for the first time. On television, candidates could speak to millions of people at one time. The way candidates looked and sounded on television could affect who won or lost the race. Candidates with the most money could pay for more ads on television.

Since 1952, the way candidates use television has played a large part in American politics. Many Americans get most of their information about candidates from television.

How did television change family life? Families watched television instead of making their own fun together.

A Society of Consumers

Television made another important change. It affected the buying habits of people. Television ads reached millions of people at a time. Suddenly, people who lived in different parts of the United States were buying the same kinds of food, clothes, and washing machines. Companies spent millions of dollars to put their ads on television because they could reach so many people at one time.

The United States was becoming a society of **consumers.** A consumer is a person who buys and uses products. Everywhere Americans looked, there were ads encouraging them to buy more. There were more ads in magazines, in newspapers, on billboards, and on television. To adults who had been through the Great Depression and a war, it seemed wonderful to be able to buy things. Teenagers also became large consumers.

Why did companies spend so much money on television ads? Television allowed companies to reach much larger audiences than they had ever been able to before.

Rock and Roll

Rock 'n' roll had started in the 1940s and 1950s. Many African Americans moved from the South to the North and brought this new kind of music with them. It was called rhythm and blues. Rhythm and blues mixed a jazz beat with a sad kind of music called the blues. Radio stations in the North started playing this music. Alan Freed, a white disc jockey, gave rhythm and blues a new name. He called it rock 'n' roll.

Soon African American musicians were recording top-selling rock 'n' roll hits. Then, in 1955, a new singer by the name of Elvis Presley appeared. Like many African American musicians, Elvis had grown up in the South. However, Elvis was white. He became a big rock 'n' roll star.

History Fact

The word *teenager*, means "a person between the ages of 13 and 19." The word was invented in the United States.

History Fact Teenagers were the fastest-growing consumer group in the 1950s. They were responsible for fads like 3-D glasses.

Elvis Presley opened the door for a new group of rock 'n' roll musicians. Jerry Lee Lewis, Buddy Holly, and the Everly Brothers were white Southerners who made top-selling hits. Chuck Berry, an African American, wrote songs about the problems of young people. He was the first great rock 'n' roll guitar player.

Chuck Berry

Visual Both rhythm and blues and rock 'n' roll had its earliest roots in gospel music.

How did rock 'n' roll begin? It began as rhythm and blues. African Americans from the South brought it to the North.

The Generation Gap

Many adults did not like the new American music or its stars. They liked their own softer, gentler music. Rock 'n' roll songs were often loud and fast. The lyrics, or words, were about being young in the 1950s. Some rock stars were not the role models parents wanted for their teenagers. People began to talk about a **generation gap.** A generation gap is a large difference in taste and values between young people and their parents.

The generation gap included differences over clothes, hairstyles, dances, movies, books, and ideas.

What caused the generation gap between young people and their parents. Rock 'n' roll, clothes, hairstyles, dances, movies, books, ideas

Section 2 Review

1. How did television change politics?
2. How did television affect buying habits in the United States?
3. **Critical Thinking** Why did rock 'n' roll become such an important part of young people's lives?
4. **Write About History** Write a scene in which teenagers tell their parents why they like rock 'n' roll. Have parents tell why they do not like it.

More Review is provided in Exercise 102 of the Workbook.

1. Candidates could talk to millions at one time.
2. Ads reached across the United States. People all over the country bought the same products.
3. Possible answer: Young people could be part of a teenage culture across the United States; rock 'n' roll was a way to rebel against their parents.
4. Possible answer: Teenagers—rock 'n' roll is new, exciting, different; Parents—music is too loud, stars are bad role models, words are silly.

Section 3 Eisenhower as President

Words to Know

recession	a period when the economy slows down
interstate highway system	a network of roads built and cared for by the U.S. government

Getting Started Discuss with students people they admire. What leadership qualities do these people show? Explain that General Eisenhower's leadership qualities in World War II made many Americans vote for him for President.

In 1952, Americans elected Dwight D. Eisenhower as President. Most Americans were happy with the direction in which the country was going. The cold war, however, continued to take much of the President's time.

Eisenhower's Policies at Home

For 20 years, U.S. Presidents had been Democrats. In 1952, many Americans felt it was time for a change in the White House. The Republicans chose Dwight D. Eisenhower to run for President. Eisenhower, nicknamed Ike, was well known to most Americans. He had led the Allied forces in Europe during World War II.

In 1952, Eisenhower won a landslide election over Adlai Stevenson of Illinois. In a landslide election, one candidate wins by a huge number of votes. Eisenhower was in office for two terms. In 1956, he defeated Stevenson again.

To please Republicans, Eisenhower promised to control government spending. To please Democrats, Eisenhower said he would keep some of Franklin Roosevelt's New Deal programs.

Eisenhower approved the building of public housing in poor city neighborhoods. He also created the

History Fact

The Twenty-second Amendment to the Constitution was passed in 1951. It limited Presidents to two terms in office. President Eisenhower was the first President affected by the law.

History Fact The 22nd Amendment was proposed by Congress after FDR's four terms broke the precedent of George Washington that a President should serve only two terms.

Department of Health, Education, and Welfare. This department ran programs on food and drug safety, health, and education. The department also ran a social security program for older Americans.

During most of Eisenhower's terms in office, the economy did well. However, there was a **recession** during his second term. A recession is a period when the economy slows down. People spend less, and there are fewer jobs.

How did Eisenhower's policies at home help Americans? There was public housing in poor neighborhoods; Department of Health, Education, and Welfare ran special programs

The Interstate Highway System

Eisenhower felt the United States needed better roads. He sponsored a law to create the **interstate highway system.** The interstate highway system is a network of roads built and cared for by the U.S. government. Along these roads, people can drive across the country without stopping for traffic lights.

In 1956, Congress passed the Federal-Aid Highway Act. The act provided nearly $31 billion to build 41,000 miles of new highways. It started the interstate highway system.

The interstate highway system changed the U.S. economy and the way many people lived. Some big changes included trucks becoming the fastest and cheapest way to carry goods. More people drove their cars to work. More people also drove their cars to places where they spent their vacations. New businesses, such as restaurants and motels, grew up near the interstate highways.

These changes caused other things to happen. For example, railroads lost business. Some railroads had to quit or cut back on their service. Communities near the interstates grew. Those far away from the interstates lost business. More people moved to the suburbs

Geography Fact

Alaska and Hawaii became states in 1959. These would be the only states without an interstate highway.

Geography Fact Although Alaska is geographically the largest state, it has the smallest population of any state.

because it became easier to drive to work. Pollution increased, as the air became dirty from car fumes.

How did the interstate highway system change the way people lived? More people used their cars for driving to and from work and for vacations. More people moved to the suburbs.

Eisenhower's Foreign Policy

The cold war continued while Eisenhower was President. Eisenhower ended the Korean War. He met with the leaders of the Soviet Union and other countries.

Remember
The cold war between the United States and the Soviet Union started shortly after World War II ended.

During the 1950s, fighting broke out in several parts of the world. In 1956, citizens in Hungary revolted against Soviet rule. Many Hungarians were killed before the Soviets stopped the revolution. Americans sided with the Hungarians. However, Eisenhower decided not to send U.S. troops to Hungary. In 1959, Communists took power in Cuba. Since Cuba is so close to the United States, Eisenhower tried everything he could to stop the Communist takeover. He cut off relations with Cuba.

What problems developed in other countries while Eisenhower was President? Revolt in Hungary, Communist takeover of Cuba

Section 3 Review

1. Why did Americans like Eisenhower?
2. How did the recession affect life in the United States in the 1950s?
3. **Critical Thinking** If you lived in the 1950s, how would you feel about the new interstate highway system? Explain.
4. **Write About History** Choose one problem in the world when Eisenhower was President. Tell why the event was important.

1. He was well known to them. Some students may mention that people wanted a change.
2. There were fewer jobs; people spent less.
3. Possible answer: Most families liked the new system. However, there were negative effects on people who worked for railroads or lived far away from the interstates.
4. Possible answer: Understanding that the United States was in a cold war against communism

More Review is provided in Exercise 103 of the Workbook.

Chapter 24 Review

Summary Have students use this graphic organizer to outline the main ideas and details of the chapter.

Summary	American ways of life changed after World War II ended. The economy and the population grew. Many Americans moved to the suburbs.
Section 1	The GI Bill of Rights helped returning veterans. An increase in spending and the creation of jobs helped the economy grow. Families moved to the suburbs. Fewer women worked outside the home.
Section 2	Television changed American culture in the 1950s. Family life, people's buying habits, and politics changed. A teenage culture developed, based mostly on the new music called rock 'n' roll.
Section 3	Americans elected Dwight Eisenhower as President in 1952. He tried to limit federal spending. Eisenhower and Congress created the interstate highway system. Eisenhower dealt with many foreign policy issues related to the cold war.

consumer
automation
suburb
generation gap
recession

More Vocabulary Review is provided in Exercise 160 of the Classroom Resource Binder.

Vocabulary Review

Fill in the blank with a term from the list.

1. Using machines instead of workers is called ______. automation
2. A ______ is a community just outside a city. suburb
3. Differences between teenagers and adults is usually called a ______. generation gap
4. Someone who buys something is a ______. consumer
5. ______ is a time when the economy slows down. Recession

1. Veterans had money to spend for school, homes, farms, and businesses. pp. 448–449 2. Cities lost population, and suburbs gained population. pp. 451–452 3. To make goods quickly to meet growing demands p. 450. 4. Possible answer: Both TV and computers changed the lives of teenagers. Answers should include at least one difference or similarity. p. 455 5. Possible answer: Yes or no. Consider issues such as added air and noise pollution. pp. 460–461

Chapter Quiz

Write your answers in complete sentences.

1. How did the GI Bill help the economy grow?
2. What happened to the population of cities and suburbs?
3. Why did factories need automation?
4. **Critical Thinking** Television changed the lives of teenagers in the 1950s. Computers changed the lives of teenagers in the 1990s. Compare the ways television and computers have affected teenagers.
5. **Critical Thinking** Many highways today are crowded with cars and trucks. Do you think the United States should build more highways? Why or why not?

Test Tip
Some words and phrases show a contrast between ideas. Watch for words and phrases such as *although, but, however,* and *while.*

Writing Tip
If necessary, research your topic before you begin writing. Try to find opinions that will support your point of view.

Using the Timeline

Use the timeline on pages 446–447 to answer the questions.

1. What two Presidents were in office in the years following World War II? Truman and Eisenhower
2. What two events show that important medical research took place? 1954—Polio vaccine tested; 1960—Polio cases drop to 3,190.

Group Activity See the Teacher's Planning Guide for a scoring rubric for this activity.

Group Activity

With your group, discuss some ways television ads try to get you to buy a product. Are the ads always fair? Do they tell the whole truth about a product? Then choose a product your group likes. Create a TV ad for it. Present your ad to the class.

Dr. Martin Luther King, Jr., spoke at the civil rights march in Washington, D.C., in 1963. The march supported the Civil Rights Act. The sign at the right is from a protest march for better jobs. How do you think the people at the march felt about the Civil Rights Act? The size of the crowd shows that people supported it.

Working for Equal Rights

1945 · 1950 · 1955 · 1960

- **1947** Jackie Robinson breaks baseball's color barrier
- **1952** Dwight D. Eisenhower elected
- **1954** Supreme Court rules against public school segregation
- **1955** Montgomery bus boycott begins
- **1956** Dwight D. Eisenhower reelected
- **1957** Federal troops sent to Little Rock, Arkansas
- **1960** Sit-ins begin

Additional activities and strategies to customize lessons can be found in the Teacher's Planning Guide.

Chapter 25 The Struggle for Equality 1947–1965

ESL Note To help students understand the concept of "the struggle for equality," point out that in the U.S. all people are supposed to be equal under the law and entitled to the same opportunities. Remind students that a struggle is a kind of fight. Discuss why people might need to fight for things they are entitled to.

Words to Know

- integrate
- executive order
- appeal
- desegregate
- boycott
- sit-in
- civil disobedience

Words to Know These words are defined in the section in which they appear, as well as in the Glossary. Point out to students that *boycotts*, *sit-ins*, and acts of *civil disobedience* are all ways to protest peacefully.

Timeline The timeline is divided into 5-year intervals. The events take place over a period of 19 years. Point out that this was an active period in the struggle for equal rights.

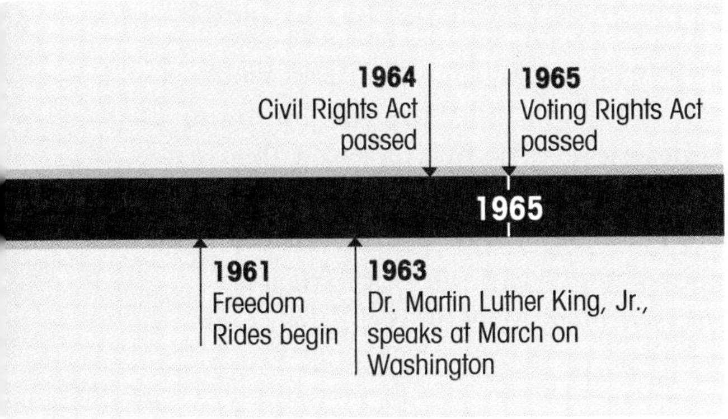

Learning Objectives

- Explain the importance of the integration of the armed forces.
- Discuss the Supreme Court decision in *Brown* v. *Board of Education of Topeka.*
- Discuss the ways in which the federal government took steps to integrate southern schools.
- Identify the events that led to the passing of the Civil Rights Act of 1964.
- Explain how Americans used nonviolence to end segregation.
- Explore the views of Dr. Martin Luther King, Jr., on social protest.

Project Students can complete this project in school or as a homework assignment or as they read each section.

Portfolio Project

There were many heroes in the struggle for equal rights. As you read, make a list of heroes in the civil rights movement. Arrange the entries in alphabetical order. Write at least one thing each person did to make a difference in the lives of others.

Section 1 Early Gains for Equal Rights

Words to Know

integrate	to open to people of all backgrounds; to bring together
executive order	a rule made by the President

Getting Started Discuss with students ways that African Americans were denied equal rights in the U.S. Point out how segregated schooling, the armed forces, sports, and entertainment kept these citizens from participating in the predominantly white society.

The civil rights movement in the United States became very powerful after World War II. African Americans led the fight for equality. The first victories for civil rights were in the armed forces. Other victories were in sports and entertainment.

Segregation in the North and the South

More than one million African American soldiers served in World War II. They were kept in segregated units. White officers led these units. After the war, many African American veterans felt their service to the nation was forgotten. African American veterans did not have equal chances to take part in the growing economy.

In both the North and the South, African Americans faced discrimination in jobs, housing, and education. In the South, there were unfair laws called Jim Crow laws.

Remember
In the late 1800s, the South passed Jim Crow laws that segregated African Americans and white Americans.

Many southern whites felt the Jim Crow laws were lawful. They pointed to a decision by the U.S. Supreme Court in 1896. This decision came from a case called *Plessy* v. *Ferguson*. The case was about separate railroad cars for African Americans and white people. The Court said that "separate but equal" treatment of African Americans was legal. However, many Americans knew that separate treatment was always unequal.

There were no Jim Crow laws in the North. However, most African Americans lived segregated lives there, too. In the North, most African Americans lived in poor city neighborhoods. They had a hard time getting good jobs. Most African American children went to segregated schools.

What was wrong with the "separate but equal" idea in *Plessy* v. *Ferguson?* Where there was separate treatment, the treatment was almost always unequal.

Integrating the Armed Forces

After World War II, many white Americans began to disagree with the unfair treatment of African Americans. They joined with African Americans to work for civil rights, or equal treatment and fair laws for everyone.

One of the first victories for civil rights came in the U.S. armed forces. Civil rights leaders spoke out against segregation in the armed forces. They wanted to **integrate** the military, or open it to people of all backgrounds.

In 1948, President Truman signed an **executive order.** An executive order is a rule made by the President. The order said that the armed forces must integrate. The President's rule made all jobs in the armed forces open to African Americans. African Americans could serve in the same units as whites. Finally, African American officers could command white soldiers.

In 1954, the Defense Department made an announcement. It said that there were no longer any African American units in the armed forces.

What did President Truman's executive order do? It integrated the armed forces.

Integrating Sports and Entertainment

Another victory for civil rights was the integration of major league baseball. In the 1940s, baseball was the favorite sport of most Americans. However, the major league teams had a color barrier. This was an unwritten

History Fact

In 1954, Benjamin Davis, Jr., became the first African American Air Force major general. Later, he was promoted to lieutenant general.

History Fact Benjamin Davis, Jr., retired in 1970 as lieutenant general and went on to serve as assistant secretary in the department of transportation.

Visual Point out that this is a collectors coin.

This coin shows Jackie Robinson. He was the first African American baseball player on a major league team.

1. African Americans in the North lived in poor neighborhoods. Schools were segregated. Whites had the best jobs.
2. In time, all jobs were open to African Americans; African Americans could serve in the same units as whites; and African American officers could command white soldiers.
3. Student responses might include the following: Robinson felt it was important to be strong, stay focused, and avoid trouble so that he could open the way for other African American players.
4. Student responses should mention the *Plessy* v. *Ferguson* decision, which Southerners used to support Jim Crow laws.

rule that allowed discrimination against African Americans. There were no African Americans on major league teams.

In 1947, Jackie Robinson broke the color barrier. The Brooklyn Dodgers signed Jackie Robinson to play for the team. During Robinson's first season with the Dodgers, some people behaved in hateful ways. Some players from other teams tried to hurt Robinson. However, Robinson's great skills helped make the Dodgers a winning team. Soon he had white and African American fans cheering for him. In 1962, Jackie Robinson became the first African American elected to the Baseball Hall of Fame.

Throughout the late 1940s and early 1950s, African Americans won small victories. African American musicians became popular with both whites and African Americans. African American writers wrote books that were read by all Americans. However, few laws that allowed discrimination against African Americans were changed.

How did Jackie Robinson change major league baseball in 1947? He broke the color barrier and integrated baseball.

Section 1 Review

1. In what ways was the North segregated?
2. How did integration change the U.S. armed forces?
3. **Critical Thinking** Jackie Robinson faced many people who were not happy with him in the major leagues. Why do you think Robinson chose not to become angry with these people?
4. **Write About History** Write a brief paragraph explaining how the Supreme Court supported southern segregation.

More Review is provided in Exercise 105 of the Workbook.

Section 2 Fighting for an Equal Education

Words to Know

appeal	to ask a higher court to review the decision of a lower court
desegregate	to end segregation, or separation of the races

Getting Started Ask students if they have ever taken a stand on an issue that was both unpopular and dangerous. Explain that some African American students in the 1950s had the courage to brave dangerous mobs of angry whites to do what they believed in.

Since 1935, the National Association for the Advancement of Colored People (NAACP) had been working to end segregation. The NAACP wanted equal treatment for African Americans everywhere in the United States. In the 1950s, the NAACP fought hard to integrate schools. Thurgood Marshall led the fight.

Unequal Schools

Southern states sent white children and African American children to different schools. Southern lawmakers said the schools were equal.

The schools, however, were not equal. Many African American children had to walk miles to their schools. They had to share books because there were not enough for all students. Teachers were poorly trained. Classes were overcrowded.

For white children, things were different. For the most part, they lived closer to their schools. Each child had a book. Teachers were better trained. Classes were smaller.

In the North, schools were not equal either. Most children went to segregated schools. Often, African American schools were worse than all-white schools.

How were schools set up in the South? They were segregated; schools were not equal.

Map Point out to students that the entire Southeast was segregated by law. Remind students that this region also favored slavery during the 1800s.

Segregated Schools, 1952

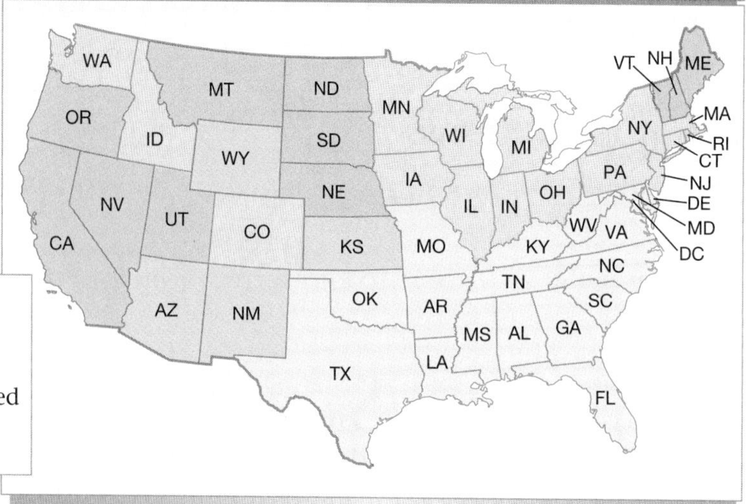

Map Study

1. What year does the map show?
2. Which states did not allow segregated schools?

1. 1952
2. WA, ID, CO, MN, IA, WI, IL, MI, IN, OH, NY, PA, MA, RI, CT, NJ

Parents Fight for Equal Schools

In Topeka, Kansas, in 1950, Oliver Brown was worried about his daughter, Linda. She had to walk a mile and cross railroad tracks to get to the African American school. However, an all-white school was seven blocks from her home. Brown tried to enroll her there, but he was refused. Brown went to the NAACP for help. He decided to sue the Board of Education of Topeka, or take the board to court.

The court in Topeka ruled against Brown and the NAACP. The judge said that the Supreme Court had ruled that separate but equal schools were legal. However, Brown and the NAACP did not give up. They decided to **appeal** the case to the U.S. Supreme Court. To appeal is to ask a higher court to review the decision of a lower court. Other African American parents joined the fight.

Why did Oliver Brown sue the Board of Education of Topeka? The board would not allow his daughter to attend an all-white school close to her home.

Victory in the Supreme Court

Thurgood Marshall was the lawyer who argued the case for the African American parents and the NAACP. He told the Supreme Court judges that the idea of "separate but equal" was impossible. The court agreed. This is what Chief Justice Earl Warren wrote.

1. The fact that a school was segregated meant that it was unequal.

Great Names in History

THURGOOD MARSHALL

For 60 years, Thurgood Marshall fought to gain civil rights for all Americans. Marshall was a lawyer for the NAACP. Marshall and the NAACP worked to end discrimination and segregation. They asked the Supreme Court to end laws that limited African Americans' rights. Marshall also traveled in the South. He helped African Americans who had been wrongly accused of crimes.

Thurgood Marshall

Marshall's most famous case was *Brown* v. *Board of Education of Topeka*. He argued the case before the U.S. Supreme Court. Marshall said that racial segregation in public schools was against the Constitution. The Supreme Court agreed.

In 1967, Marshall became the first African American to serve on the Supreme Court. He was a Supreme Court justice for nearly 24 years.

Critical Thinking Why do you think Thurgood Marshall was appointed to the Supreme Court? Had a great deal of legal experience; needed to represent the diversity of the nation

2. Separate schools went against the Fourteenth Amendment to the Constitution, which promised "equal protection under the law."

In May 1954, the Supreme Court announced its decision. The *Brown* v. *Board of Education of Topeka* decision said that in public schools "separate but equal" has no place. The Court said that public schools must **desegregate**, or end the separation of the races.

What did the Supreme Court decide in the *Brown* v. *Board of Education of Topeka* case? In public schools, "separate but equal" does not work; public schools must desegregate.

Problems at Little Rock

An angry crowd yelled at Elizabeth Eckford as she walked to Central High School.

Visual Point out that the African American students who went to Central High School in Little Rock were heroes to some because of their bravery as they faced the hatred of white students and white adults.

The Supreme Court ordered all schools to desegregate as soon as possible. In many places, schools desegregated with only a few problems. However, in some places, political leaders and other citizens tried to stop desegregation.

In 1957, a court in Little Rock, Arkansas, decided to integrate Central High School, which was an all-white school in Little Rock. Arkansas Governor Orval Faubus did not want schools to integrate. He called out the Arkansas National Guard to stop it. On the second day of school in 1957, nine African American students went to the school. They became known as the Little Rock Nine. Crowds yelled ugly names at the teenagers. When they tried to enter school, National Guardsmen stopped them.

The desegregation of Central High School became a national news story. Photographs of crowds yelling at the nine African American students appeared in newspapers across the country.

Who were the Little Rock Nine? African American students who tried to enter an all-white high school in Little Rock, Arkansas

The Federal Government Sends Help

President Eisenhower was upset by the news from Little Rock. He sent U.S. troops to Little Rock to protect the students. At the end of September, the nine African American students entered Central High School. Central High was desegregated. However, for several weeks, armed troops had to take the students to class. Some white students kicked, shoved, and cursed at the African Americans. Eight of the Little Rock Nine finished the school year. Ernest Green became the first African American to graduate from Central High.

The governor of Arkansas kept fighting desegregation. At one point, he closed Central High. When the courts forced Little Rock's schools to open, two other members of the Little Rock Nine graduated from Central High. As the 1950s ended, many schools in the South began to desegregate. Americans knew that the federal government stood behind the right of African Americans to an equal education.

How did President Eisenhower help desegregate Central High School? He sent U.S. troops to protect the Little Rock Nine so they could attend the all-white high school.

Section 2 Review

1. In what ways were African American and all-white schools unequal?
2. How did *Brown* v. *Board of Education of Topeka* change schools across the country?
3. **Critical Thinking** Would you have chosen to be a member of the Little Rock Nine? Explain.
4. **Write About Citizenship** Choose a person from this section who made a difference to our nation. Write a thank-you note to that person.

More Review is provided in Exercise 106 of the Workbook.

1. Many African American children had to walk miles to their schools. They had to share old books. Teachers were poorly trained, and classes were overcrowded.
2. The Court ruled that separate but equal went against the Fourteenth Amendment. Schools had to desegregate.
3. Possible answer: An opportunity to make a difference; understand the dangers in the situation.
4. Students may choose Marshall, Warren, Eisenhower, Brown, the Little Rock Nine, Ernest Green. Notes should show an understanding of the individual's contribution.

Section 3 Protests and Marches for Equality

Words to Know

boycott	a nonviolent protest in which people refuse to buy products or use services
sit-in	a nonviolent protest in which people sit down and refuse to get up
civil disobedience	a nonviolent refusal to obey laws or government demands in order to cause change

Getting Started Ask students if they think it is right to disrupt the lives of people who may not have any opinion or involvement in a particular issue. Explain that during the 1950s and 1960s, new types of nonviolent protests disrupted the lives of everyday people to help the cause of civil rights.

This is Rosa Parks after she was arrested.

Visual Rosa Parks later spoke about her refusal to give up her seat. She said, "The only tired I was, was tired of giving in."

On December 1, 1955, Rosa Parks, an African American, got on a bus in Montgomery, Alabama. What she did next would lead to huge changes in American society. Many African Americans and others would take part in nonviolent, or peaceful, protests. They would use these protests to change laws and gain equal rights for all Americans.

The Montgomery Bus Boycott

Rosa Parks was tired when she got on the bus. She took a seat in the first row of the African American section of the bus. As the bus became more crowded, there were no more seats for white people in the front. The white bus driver ordered Parks to give her seat to a white passenger. She refused. The bus driver called police. Parks was arrested.

News of Parks's arrest spread through the African American community in Montgomery. The Reverend Dr. Martin Luther King, Jr., a young minister in Montgomery, presented a list of demands for the bus company. These were the demands.

1. African Americans must be treated politely by bus drivers.
2. African Americans should not have to give up seats to white passengers.
3. The bus company must hire African American drivers for bus routes used by large numbers of African Americans.

Dr. King said African Americans would not ride the buses until the demands were met. African Americans would **boycott** the buses. A boycott is a nonviolent protest in which people refuse to buy products or use services. Soon, most buses in Montgomery were empty. Instead of taking buses, African Americans walked or got rides. At first, the white citizens of Montgomery fought back. Employers said they would fire their African American workers. The police would stop African American drivers and ask to see their licenses.

The boycott lasted more than a year. White business owners in Montgomery lost shoppers. The bus company lost riders. Finally the U.S. Supreme Court ruled that segregation on Alabama buses was illegal.

Why was Rosa Parks arrested? Parks was arrested because she refused to give her seat on the bus to a white passenger.

Sit-ins Across the South

The success of the bus boycott brought attention to Martin Luther King, Jr. People began to believe that nonviolent protests could bring down segregation in other places. Soon people began nonviolent protests against restaurants, movie theaters, and other segregated places.

In 1960, four African American college students in Greensboro, North Carolina, went to a lunch counter and sat down. That might not seem like such a brave act. However, the lunch counter was for "whites only." The students continued to sit at the counter after the waitress refused to serve them.

History Fact

African Americans made up 75 percent of bus riders in Montgomery.

History Fact One African American woman turned down the offer of a ride during the bus strike by saying, "I'm not walking for myself, I'm walking for my children and my grandchildren."

Crowds threw food at these sit-in protesters in Greensboro, North Carolina.

Visual After a student in North Carolina was refused service at a "whites only" lunch counter, he returned with other students to sit at the counter each day. More students—African American and white—joined the protest.

The next day 20 more students went back to the lunch counter and took seats. Again they refused to leave. The protests continued every day for six months. Finally, the lunch counter was desegregated.

This kind of protest came to be known as a **sit-in.** A sit-in is a nonviolent protest in which people sit down and refuse to get up. To protest segregation, African Americans took seats in segregated areas. Soon hundreds of sit-ins were taking place across the South. African American and white protesters had sit-ins in movie theaters, libraries, and drugstores.

Some protesters were thrown from their seats. However, the protesters never fought back. If they were knocked down, they got up and took their seats again. If police arrested them, another group of protesters took their places.

By 1961, more than 70,000 African American and white students had taken part in sit-ins. By that time, segregated lunch counters and other segregated places had almost disappeared in the South.

Why did sit-ins take place across the South? To desegregate places such as lunch counters, movie theaters, libraries, and drugstores

The Freedom Riders

In 1961, other African American and white protesters rode buses through southern states. They wanted to end segregation on interstate buses, or buses that travel from one state to another, and in bus stations. The protesters became known as Freedom Riders. African American and white riders sat together on buses. They broke segregation rules in restaurants, waiting rooms, and restrooms in bus stations. This kind of protest is called **civil disobedience.** Civil disobedience is a nonviolent refusal to obey laws or government demands in order to cause change.

Like other protesters, the Freedom Riders faced violence. In Alabama, a crowd beat the riders and burned a bus. The Freedom Riders were put in jail in Mississippi. However, their efforts made people aware of the unfair conditions on buses and in bus stations in the South. As a result, the U.S. government made tougher rules against segregation on interstate buses.

What did the Freedom Riders hope to change? They hoped to desegregate interstate buses and bus stations.

Protests in Birmingham

In 1963, Dr. Martin Luther King, Jr., went to Birmingham, Alabama, to protest Jim Crow laws. Birmingham was one of the most segregated cities in the United States. Dr. King believed that if protesters could end Jim Crow laws in Birmingham, the laws could be ended elsewhere too.

In April 1963, Dr. King and other leaders organized sit-ins and other protests across Birmingham. Dr. King and other leaders were arrested and spent a week in jail. From jail, Dr. King wrote a famous letter, "Letter from Birmingham Jail."

In May, 25,000 protesters, including many children and young people, marched in Birmingham. Police and firefighters attacked the protesters with hoses and attack dogs. Police and police dogs even attacked protesters trying to enter a church.

Pictures of the violence appeared on television news programs. Many Americans were shocked. In the North and the South, people were very upset by the violence against children. Finally, Birmingham businesses agreed to desegregate and to hire more African Americans.

Why did Dr. King go to Birmingham? To try to end Jim Crow laws in one of the most segregated cities in the United States

The March on Washington

In 1963, civil rights leaders planned a march on Washington, D.C. The purpose of the march was to urge, or push, Congress to pass a civil rights bill that was in Congress. On August 28, 1963, more than 200,000 African Americans and other Americans gathered in Washington, D.C. There they heard Martin Luther King, Jr., give one of the most famous speeches in American history. It came to be called the "I Have a Dream" speech.

In July 1964, President Lyndon Johnson worked with Congress to pass the Civil Rights Act.

1. The act protected the right of all citizens to vote.
2. It made segregation in public places illegal.
3. It made discrimination in hiring illegal.

The Civil Rights Act did not end the Civil Rights Movement. There was still the fight to give African Americans the right to vote. Laws had been passed giving African Americans this right. However, it could not be carried out in the South.

What was the purpose of the march on Washington, D.C., in 1963? To push Congress to pass a civil rights bill

Action for Voting Rights

The summer of 1964 became known as Freedom Summer. As soon as the Civil Rights Act was signed, volunteers headed to the South. Many volunteers were college students. They planned to work all summer to register African Americans to vote. Some southern lawmakers and hate groups tried to stop them.

In July, three young volunteers disappeared. Andrew Goodman and Michael Schwerner were white. James Chaney was African American. The three young men were arrested for speeding. They were held in jail in Mississippi. No one ever saw them alive again. Federal agents found their bodies a month later. Chaney had been beaten, and all three were shot to death.

Americans were again shocked by the ugly actions of some people opposed to, or against, equal rights. African Americans were even more determined to use the power of the vote.

Throughout Freedom Summer, the Ku Klux Klan attacked civil rights volunteers. By the end of the summer, more than 35 African American churches had been burned. More than 30 houses were also destroyed. However, by the end of the summer, more than 170,000 African Americans had registered to vote.

What was Freedom Summer? The summer of 1964, when civil rights workers helped African Americans register to vote

Visual In 1966, the number of registered African American voters in Mississippi rose to 175,000 from only 22,000 in 1960. It was a 695.4% increase.

Volunteers worked to get African Americans registered to vote.

The Voting Rights Act of 1965

In 1965, Congress passed the Voting Rights Act. The act said the states could not prevent African Americans from registering to vote. The federal government would take over registration in any states that tried to stop African Americans from voting. By the end of the year, more than 2.5 million African Americans were registered to vote. Since then, many African Americans have been elected to political office.

What would happen to states that did not follow the Voting Rights Act of 1965? The U.S. government would take over registration in the state.

Section 3 Review

1. Why did African Americans boycott buses in Montgomery?
2. What change did sit-ins bring about?
3. **Critical Thinking** Do you think nonviolence was the best way for African Americans to cause change in the South? Explain.
4. **Write About Citizenship** Dr. King's dream was about freedom and equality. Write a poem about your dream for a better world.

More Review is provided in Exercise 108 of the Workbook.

1. To get the bus company to meet Dr. Martin Luther King, Jr.'s, demands for equal treatment of African Americans
2 Lunch counters, restaurants, movie theaters, libraries, and drugstores were desegregated.
3. Possible answer: Nonviolence produced pressure for change in the South and at the federal level.
4. Possible answer: Students should describe a world that seems better to them.

VOICES FROM THE PAST
Dr. Martin Luther King, Jr.

Dr. Martin Luther King, Jr., was one of the most important leaders in the fight for civil rights. He was the minister of a church in Montgomery, Alabama, in the early 1950s. Later, Dr. King led protests against segregation in the South.

Dr. Martin Luther King, Jr.

In 1963, Dr. King was arrested in Birmingham, Alabama, for leading a protest march. From jail, Dr. King wrote a letter to eight white religious leaders in Birmingham. In a Birmingham newspaper, these leaders had called Dr. King a troublemaker. They blamed him for using "extreme measures" that led to hatred and violence between the races. These religious leaders thought African Americans should work slowly for change. Dr. King answered them with his famous "Letter from Birmingham Jail." Here are some words from his letter.

"We have waited for more than 340 years for our . . . rights . . . Perhaps it is easy for those who have never felt . . . segregation to say 'Wait.' This wait has almost always meant 'Never.'

But when you have seen vicious mobs lynch your mothers and fathers . . . when you have seen hate-filled policemen curse, kick, and even kill your black brothers and sisters. . . . when you are . . . living constantly at tip-toe stance [position] never quite knowing what to expect next, then you will understand why we find it difficult to wait."

1. Why did Dr. King write his letter?

2. How does Dr. King feel about waiting for equal rights?

CHALLENGE Why did Dr. King say, "We have waited more than 340 years"?

1. As a response to religious leaders who accused him of making trouble between the races. **2.** He feels that African Americans have waited long enough for equality, that "Wait" usually means never. **CHALLENGE** African Americans had waited to be free since colonial times.

Chapter 25 Review

Summary Have students use this graphic organizer to outline the main ideas and details of the chapter.

Summary	**After World War II, African Americans demanded equal opportunities in jobs, housing, the military, and education. Nonviolent protesters worked for civil rights.**
Section 1	After World War II, returning African American veterans felt left out of the economy. The armed forces were integrated. African Americans made gains in sports and entertainment.
Section 2	The 1954 Supreme Court decision in *Brown* v. *Board of Education of Topeka* ended segregation in public schools.
Section 3	Nonviolent protests helped end segregation. Martin Luther King, Jr., became an important civil rights leader. The Civil Rights and Voting Rights Acts were passed.

- executive order
- desegregate
- sit-in
- civil disobedience
- boycott

More Vocabulary Review is provided in Exercise 167 of the Classroom Resource Binder.

Vocabulary Review

Fill in the blank with a term from the list.

1. Disobeying a law to cause change is called ____. civil disobedience

2. President Truman gave an ____ to integrate the armed forces. executive order

3. The Little Rock Nine wanted to ____ Central High School. desegregate

4. Refusing to buy a product or use a service is called a ____. boycott

5. Students held a ____ at a "whites only" lunch counter. sit-in

1. African Americans in the military did not have equal opportunities. p. 467 2. Against the Fourteenth Amendment; segregated schools were unequal pp. 471–472 3. Support the Civil Rights Act; push Congress to pass the bill p. 478 4. Yes: Truman ordered integration of armed forces; Eisenhower sent troops to Little Rock. No: Earlier action may have prevented some segregation. pp. 467, 473 5. Possible answer: Most Americans were outraged after seeing nonviolent protesters being hosed, beaten, and attacked by dogs on TV news. p. 478

Chapter Quiz

Write your answers in complete sentences.

1. Why was it important to integrate the armed forces?
2. In *Brown* v. *Board of Education of Topeka*, what did the Supreme Court say about separate but equal schools?
3. Why did thousands of people march on Washington in 1963?
4. **Critical Thinking** Do you think that Presidents Truman and Eisenhower did enough to help desegregate American society? Explain.
5. **Critical Thinking** How do you think television affected Americans' ideas about the fight for civil rights?

Test Tip
Be sure you know how to spell the names of people and events in the chapter. Practice writing each of them several times.

Writing Tip
Always reread written answers to check for words that may have been left out.

Using the Timeline

Use the timeline on pages 464–465 to answer the questions.

1. Who was President when Federal troops were sent to Little Rock, Arkansas? Dwight D. Eisenhower
2. What two laws were important in the struggle for equality? Civil Rights Act, Voting Rights Act

Group Activity See the Teacher's Planning Guide for a scoring rubric for this activity.

Group Activity

With a partner, prepare a TV news report on one of the events in this chapter. One of you can be the person who gives the report to the television audience. The other can be the reporter on the scene. Give the news report to the class.

John Kennedy gave a speech as he took office in 1961. This is a Kennedy-Johnson campaign button from the 1960 election. How do you think people might feel when they hear a newly elected President speak? Hopeful, excited, ready to support the person they have elected; ready to make important changes

The 1960s

1960 John F. Kennedy elected

1961 Peace Corps started

1961 Bay of Pigs invasion

1962 John Glenn orbits Earth

1962 Cuban Missile Crisis

1963 JFK assassinated

Lyndon B. Johnson becomes President

1964 Civil Rights Act passed

Economic Opportunity Act passed

1964 Lyndon B. Johnson elected

1965 Voting Rights Act passed

Additional activities and strategies to customize lessons can be found in the Teacher's Planning Guide.

Chapter 26 A New Frontier and a Great Society 1960–1968

ESL Note To help students understand the concept of a new frontier, explain that a frontier is usually a newly settled area just outside an area of older settlements. Point out that in the 1960s in the U.S., it refers to new ideas that can take you to new places in your thinking.

Words to Know

- New Frontier
- urban renewal
- exile
- quarantine
- Great Society
- Medicare
- Medicaid

Words to Know These words are defined in the section in which they appear, as well as in the Glossary. Point out to students that, in the tradition of Franklin Roosevelt, programs and goals were given memorable names, such as *New Frontier, Great Society, Medicare,* and *Medicaid.*

Timeline The timeline is divided into 1-year intervals. The events take place over a period of 9 years. Point out to students the events that show that African Americans continued fighting for civil rights.

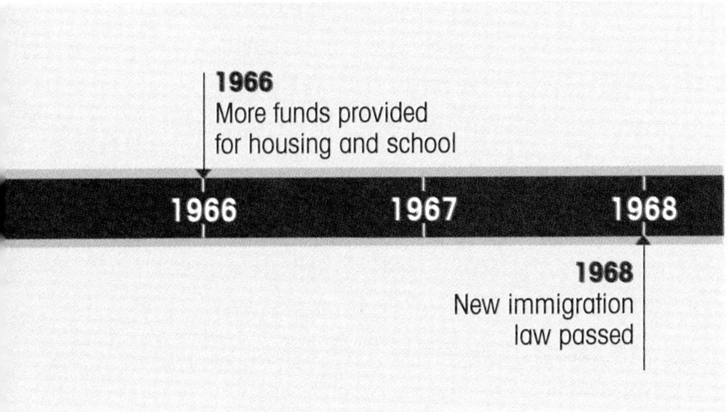

Learning Objectives

- Describe the goals and programs of President Kennedy's New Frontier.
- Discuss U.S. relations with Cuba and the Soviet Union during the 1960s.
- Describe President Kennedy's assassination and the reactions of the American people.
- Describe the goals and programs of President Johnson's Great Society.
- Explore the role of the United States in the space race.

Project This project cannot be completed until students have finished Section 3. Throughout the chapter, students should take notes to help them compare and contrast programs.

Portfolio Project

President Kennedy and President Johnson created many programs that are still working today. As you read, make a list of Kennedy's and Johnson's programs. At the end of the chapter, compare and contrast the programs of Kennedy's New Frontier and the programs of Johnson's Great Society on a chart.

Section 1 The New Frontier

Words to Know

New Frontier	President Kennedy's ideas, goals, and programs for America's future
urban renewal	a program to rebuild run-down areas of cities

Getting Started Ask students if they have ever seen a political ad on TV. Discuss how a candidate's TV appearance affects a voter's decision on election day. Explain that the first televised debates played an important part in the 1960 presidential election.

By the end of the 1950s, Americans were again ready for a change. Many wanted equal rights for all Americans. Others wanted the United States to become a stronger power.

The Election of 1960

In 1960, the Republicans chose Richard M. Nixon as their candidate for President. He had been Vice President under Dwight D. Eisenhower. Nixon was known for his strong feelings against the Soviet Union and communism.

The Democrats chose John F. Kennedy to run for President. He had served in the House of Representatives. At the time he was chosen to run, Kennedy was a senator from Massachusetts. He was 43 years old. Some people felt he was too young to be President. If elected, Kennedy would also be the first Catholic to become President. Kennedy, often called JFK, chose Lyndon Johnson to run for Vice President. Johnson was a powerful leader in the U.S. Senate.

Kennedy told Americans that the United States faced many challenges. He said the United States was at "a **New Frontier.**" New Frontier became the name of Kennedy's ideas, goals, and programs for America's future. Kennedy promised support for civil rights, laws to protect the environment, and programs to help urban areas.

During the campaign, Richard Nixon reminded Americans that the 1950s had been good for the country. He promised to follow Eisenhower's policies. Nixon also promised to keep the U.S. military strong.

John Kennedy said that the Republicans had not spent enough on the military. He promised to spend more on defense and on science education in schools. Kennedy also said that Republicans had not done enough for health care or to help poor Americans.

The Kennedy-Nixon debates were watched by millions of Americans.

Visual The series of televised debates between Nixon and Kennedy was the first time presidential candidates discussed issues face to face on TV. Between 85 and 120 million Americans watched the debates.

Who were the Republican and Democratic candidates for President in 1960? Richard M. Nixon was the Republican candidate. John F. Kennedy was the Democratic candidate.

The Television Debates

Nixon and Kennedy met face to face to debate their ideas on television. In a debate, people give arguments for their points of view. On television, Kennedy seemed calm and friendly. Nixon seemed tired and nervous. Before the television debates, people liked both candidates. After the debates, more people liked Kennedy.

People who listened to the debates on the radio thought the two candidates came out even. People who saw the debates on television thought Kennedy had won them. Clearly, the way candidates looked and acted on television counted.

In the end, almost 69 million Americans voted in the 1960 election. Kennedy won by fewer than 120,000 votes. The election of 1960 was the closest election in U.S. history.

Who did Americans think had won the debates? Americans who listened to the radio thought the two candidates came out even. Americans who watched on TV thought Kennedy had won.

The Presidential Election of 1960

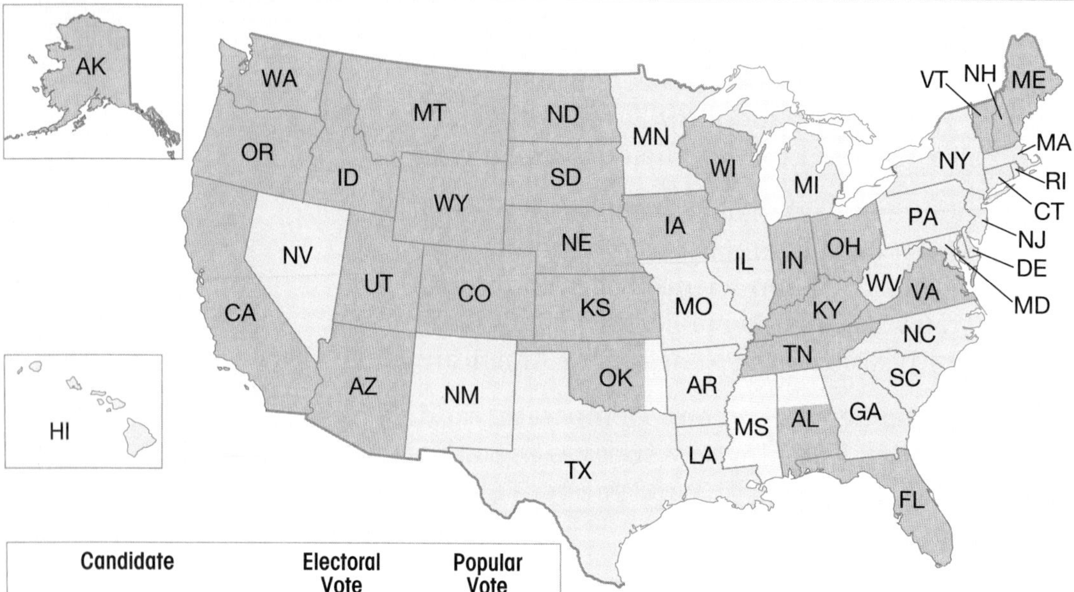

Candidate	Electoral Vote	Popular Vote
John F. Kennedy (Democrat)	303	34,227,096
Richard M. Nixon (Republican)	219	34,107,646
Harry F. Byrd (Independent)	15	501,643

Map Study

1. Which candidate won the states of Minnesota, Nevada, and Texas?
   John F. Kennedy
2. Look at the electoral votes for Kennedy and Nixon. How many more votes did Kennedy get? 84

Map Point out to students that, with the exception of Nevada, the entire Northwest voted for Nixon. Students should identify their state on the map and for whom the majority voted.

The Kennedy Years

John F. Kennedy became President in January 1961. He gave a speech the day he took office. Kennedy asked Americans to make the country better. His words became famous. This is part of what he said: "And so, my fellow Americans: ask not what your country can do for you—ask what you can do for your country."

Kennedy had a hard time getting Congress to pass new laws. Most southern Democrats in Congress did not support Kennedy's programs. They felt Kennedy wanted to pass laws that would involve the federal government in business, housing, and education.

However, Kennedy did get some of his bills passed. These are the bills Congress voted to pass during the first months of Kennedy's term.

1. It voted to send money to places where people were jobless.

2. It voted to give money to or build housing for older Americans.

3. It made it easier for young people to get loans for college.

Citizenship Link

BECOMING A VOLUNTEER

John F. Kennedy started programs that gave Americans a chance to help others. Volunteers, or people who choose to help, took part in these programs. Some of these programs continue to help people today.

Kennedy started the Peace Corps in 1961. Today nearly 6,700 volunteers work in the Peace Corps in 77 countries around the world.

After the Peace Corps, Kennedy started the Alliance for Progress in 1961. The Alliance helped people in Latin America. The volunteers helped build homes, schools, and hospitals. The Alliance lasted until 1974.

Peace Corps workers help people in countries around the world.

In 1964, VISTA (Volunteers In Service To America) was organized. This group worked in neighborhoods to find ways to end poverty. Over 120,000 Americans have volunteered to work in VISTA.

Critical Thinking How useful do you think volunteer organizations are?

Possible answer: Very useful—people who care are given a chance to help and share their talents; Not useful—organizations may not reach enough people.

4. It passed laws to control pollution.

5. It passed laws to give more Americans social security benefits.

Kennedy also got Congress to approve money for **urban renewal.** An urban renewal program rebuilds run-down areas of cities.

Kennedy started programs that would help people in other countries too. In 1961, he started the Peace Corps. Many young people volunteered for the Peace Corps. They went to poor countries to give people new ideas for farming and business. They also taught classes and worked in health-care centers.

In 1961, Kennedy promised that the United States would put a man on the moon before 1970. To do this, the United States would have to spend billions of dollars. However, President Kennedy believed the United States should get to the moon before the Soviet Union. Many Americans agreed.

What laws did Kennedy get Congress to pass? Send money to poor areas, give money for housing for older Americans, help college students, control pollution, provide Social Security benefits

Section 1 Review

1. What did each candidate promise in his campaign in 1960?

2. How did television change political campaigns in the United States?

3. **Critical Thinking** Do you think Kennedy's programs changed the lives of Americans? Explain.

4. **Write About Citizenship** Kennedy wanted Americans to think of what they could do for their country. List three things you can do for your country today.

More Review is provided in Exercise 109 of the Workbook.

1. Nixon: continue Eisenhower programs; keep military strong. Kennedy: support education, health care, poverty programs
2. People could watch the candidates debate their ideas. The way candidates looked and acted became important.
3. Student responses may include urban renewal programs to improve cities, money for older Americans, improving the environment, helping students get college loans.
4. Possible answer: Working hard in school, being informed about politics and government, registering to vote when old enough, helping to keep the community clean and safe.

CONNECTING HISTORY AND SCIENCE
The Space Race

In 1961, the Soviet astronaut Yuri Gagarin became the first human to orbit, or circle, Earth. Many Americans were worried that the Soviet Union would someday control space. Those worries led to a space race.

Both the United States and the Soviet Union wanted to be the first to reach the moon. In February 1962, John Glenn became the first American to orbit Earth. From that time on, both countries spent billions of dollars to win the space race.

Not all Americans supported the space program. Some scientists felt that robots and instruments could provide information about space. They felt that sending humans into space was too dangerous. Other people felt that the money spent on the space program should be used to help Americans on Earth instead.

Astronauts Neil Armstrong (left), Michael Collins (center), and Edwin Aldrin (right) made up the Apollo 11 *crew.*

However, on July 20, 1969, U.S. astronauts Neil Armstrong and Edwin "Buzz" Aldrin landed on the moon. They set the U.S. flag on the moon. This was a sign to the world that the United States had won the space race. The landing of the spaceship *Apollo 11* was the result of years of work. When Armstrong finally stepped on the moon, he said, "That's one small step for a man, one giant leap for mankind."

Answer the questions below.

1. How did the space race begin?

2. Why did some Americans question the space race?

CHALLENGE What did Armstrong mean when he said, "That's one small step for a man, one giant leap for mankind"?

1. After a Soviet and an American orbited Earth, the U.S. and the Soviet Union raced to become the first to reach the moon. **2.** Felt money spent on the space race could be better used on Earth
CHALLENGE That his own small step on the moon was a great advancement for all humans.

Section 2 Kennedy's Foreign Policy

Words to Know

exile	a person who lives away from his or her home country
quarantine	to isolate, or cut off, from other countries

Getting Started Discuss with students what it means to "pay any price, bear any burden, meet any hardship" to assure the survival of a cause. Explain that this was John F. Kennedy's foreign policy promise to the nation in his inaugural address of 1960.

From the 1950s on, the cold war affected much of U.S. foreign policy. During the 1960s, there were many problems between the Soviet Union and the United States. Communism was spreading in some poor countries of the world. The United States took action to stop communism.

Trouble in Cuba

President Kennedy believed in fighting communism by making the U.S. military stronger than the Soviet military. He also felt that the United States should give money, technology, and advice to help developing countries.

Remember
Rebels took over the government of Cuba in 1959.

The first serious trouble between the Soviet Union and the United States took place in Cuba. Fidel Castro was the Communist leader of rebel forces in Cuba. Castro's Cuba and the Soviet Union were close allies. Castro took over U.S. businesses in Cuba. Castro was afraid the United States would attack Cuba. He asked the Soviet Union for weapons to defend Cuba.

President Eisenhower made secret plans to train Cuban **exiles** to invade Cuba and overthrow Castro. An exile is a person who lives away from his or her home country. Eisenhower felt the Cuban people would rise up against Castro. He felt they would help the exiles.

When Kennedy became President, he decided to go ahead with the invasion plan. On April 17, 1961, the exiles landed at the Bay of Pigs, in Cuba. However, the Cuban people did not rise up against Castro. When the Cuban people learned the United States had planned the invasion, they attacked the exiles. More than 100 were killed, and the rest were put in prison. In fact, Kennedy took the blame for the failed invasion.

What happened at the Bay of Pigs? The invasion and planned overthrow of the Castro government failed.

The Berlin Wall

Feelings between the United States and the Soviet Union grew worse in the early 1960s. In 1961, Kennedy went to Europe to meet with the Soviet leader, Nikita Khrushchev. The two leaders talked about Berlin, the former capital of Germany. Khrushchev told Kennedy that the Communists should control all of Berlin.

Kennedy refused to let the Communists control all of Berlin. Both leaders left the meeting ready to build up their countries' military power.

Late that summer, the East German government began building a wall between East Berlin and West Berlin. The wall was 12 feet high and more than 100 miles long. It had barbed wire on top. The wall was built to keep East Germans from escaping to freedom in West Berlin. After the wall was built, few people were able to leave East Berlin. Many died trying to escape.

The Berlin Wall divided East and West Berlin.

Visual Point out that Western countries, such as the United States, Britain, and France, were against the construction of the Berlin Wall. However, their protests were ignored.

Why was the Berlin Wall built? To keep East Germans from escaping to freedom in West Berlin

The Cuban Missile Crisis

In 1962, the Soviet Union decided to send missiles to Cuba. Because Cuba was close to the United States, the missiles could easily hit U.S. cities.

On October 22, Kennedy announced that Cuba was under **quarantine.** This meant that Cuba was isolated, or cut off, from all other countries. Kennedy also said that if missiles based in Cuba were used to attack the United States, the United States would attack the Soviet Union.

People around the world feared war would break out. Finally, on October 24, Khrushchev agreed to remove the missiles from Cuba if the United States promised never to invade Cuba.

Visual After Johnson was sworn in, he thanked Mrs. Kennedy for being present. He said to her, "You're so brave to do this."

What did President Kennedy say the United States would do if Cuba attacked the United States? The United States would attack the Soviet Union.

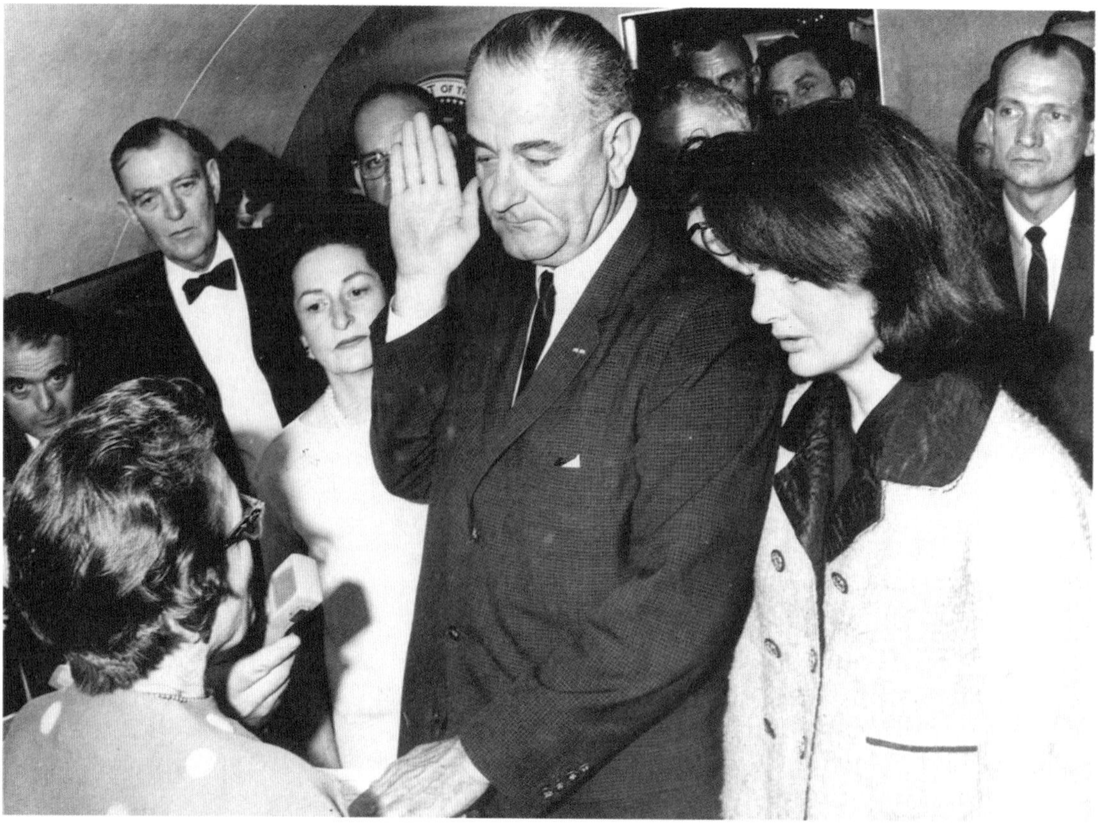

Lyndon Johnson takes office with Mrs. Kennedy by his side.

The Death of a President

On November 22, 1963, President Kennedy and Mrs. Kennedy went to Dallas, Texas. He was planning to run for a second term. Kennedy was shot dead while riding through Dallas in an open car. Later a plane carried President Kennedy's body back to Washington, D.C. On that same plane, Vice President Lyndon Johnson was sworn in as President.

Lee Harvey Oswald was arrested and charged with the assassination of President Kennedy. Two days later, millions of Americans saw Oswald on television. He walked through a police station guarded by officers. Suddenly a nightclub owner named Jack Ruby shot and killed Oswald. Ruby went to prison for the murder.

The assassination of President Kennedy shocked Americans. Schools and businesses closed. Soon after the assassination, a special commission, or committee, studied what had happened. Many people wondered if Oswald had acted alone. However, no proof was ever found that others took part in the assassination.

What happened to President Kennedy in Dallas?
President Kennedy was assassinated by Lee Harvey Oswald.

Section 2 Review

1. In what way did President Kennedy fight communism?
2. Why did the United States quarantine Cuba?
3. **Critical Thinking** Why do you think the assassination of President Kennedy shocked Americans?
4. **Write About History** It is 1961. You live in East Berlin. Write a paragraph describing how you feel about the building of the Berlin Wall.

More Review is provided in Exercise 111 of the Workbook.

History Fact

President Johnson set up the Warren Commission to determine if Oswald had acted alone.

History Fact Point out that Chief Justice Earl Warren headed the commission.

1. Kennedy wanted to build up U.S. military strength and offered aid to developing countries.
2. Kennedy quarantined Cuba because the Soviet Union sent missiles there, posing a threat to the nearby United States.
3. Possible answer: Americans were shocked by the violent nature of the event and the lack of evidence about it.
4. Possible answer: Mention the feeling of hopelessness; the difficulty of living in a Communist state

Section 3 President Johnson and the Great Society

Words to Know

Great Society	President Johnson's ideas, goals, and programs for America's future
Medicare	medical insurance and hospital care for older Americans
Medicaid	medical insurance for low-income people and people with disabilities

Getting Started Ask students to describe their own idea of what a Great Society might include. Explain that the legislative programs Lyndon Johnson created in the 1960s, such as Medicare, Medicaid, and Head Start, continue to benefit Americans today.

Lyndon B. Johnson's first speech to Americans calmed the fears of many citizens. He expressed sadness at the death of President Kennedy. Then Johnson spoke about the policies he supported. He asked Congress to pass Kennedy's civil rights bill.

Action on Civil Rights

Lyndon B. Johnson, who was often called LBJ, was a Southerner. He was born in Texas and grew up there. However, unlike some Southerners, Johnson had fought for civil rights for many years.

Johnson made many lawmakers from the South angry. They felt that he, as a Southerner, should stay out of the civil rights battle. On the other hand, many civil rights leaders did not trust Johnson. They believed that because he was a Southerner, he would not take strong action on civil rights.

Johnson introduced a civil rights bill to Congress in late January, 1964. Johnson worked hard to get votes for the bill. Finally, Congress passed it in July. The bill became the Civil Rights Act of 1964. This act desegregated public places and gave African Americans a better chance at getting jobs. The act also gave government the power to protect the voting rights of African Americans. The Voting Rights Act was passed in 1965. Johnson also helped to get this act passed by Congress.

What action did Johnson take on civil rights? Worked to get Civil Rights Act and Voting Rights Act passed

War on Poverty

The U.S. economy had been changing since the end of World War II. Most people had jobs. However, many people had trouble finding jobs. Machines had replaced people in some jobs. Other jobs needed people with special skills and education. The young, the elderly, and new immigrants were more likely to be poor and without jobs. In addition, many African Americans were unable to get jobs because of unfair hiring practices.

President Johnson felt he could fight poverty by giving federal money to help people without jobs until they found work. He also wanted to offer programs to help poor people learn useful job skills. In August 1964, lawmakers passed Johnson's Economic Opportunity Act. These were some of the programs created by the Economic Opportunity Act.

1. The Job Corps: It paid young people while they learned new job skills.
2. Project Head Start: It helped preschool children from low-income families get ready for elementary school.
3. VISTA: This was a program in which young people worked in cities and on Indian reservations.

How did President Johnson decide to fight poverty? With federal money to jobless people until they found work

President Johnson shook hands with Dr. Martin Luther King, Jr., after signing the Civil Rights Act.

Visual Explain to students that the Civil Rights Act was not universally popular. The Senate approved the act only after a debate that lasted 74 days.

Federal Funding for Public Schools, 1960–1970

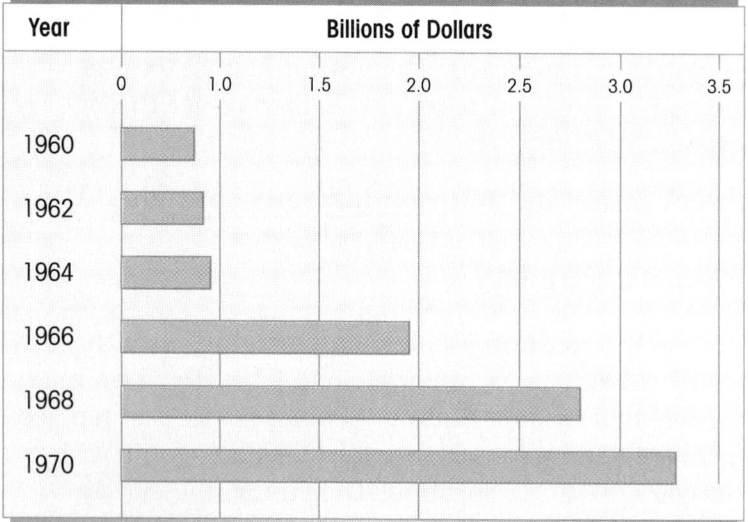

Graph Study

1. How much federal money went to public schools in 1960?
2. When did federal funding for public schools increase the most?

Graph The graph shows the amount spent on funding public schools.

1. Less than $1 billion
2. Between 1964 and 1966

Planning the Great Society

Johnson ran for reelection in 1964. Many Americans supported Johnson. They felt that he had guided the country well after Kennedy's death. Johnson had also been able to get Congress to pass important laws.

Johnson won a landslide election against Republican Barry Goldwater. Many people thought Goldwater was too conservative. Conservatives often like to see things stay the same.

Johnson called his ideas, goals, and programs for America's future the **Great Society.** Johnson wanted to help homeless people, older Americans, low-income people, and new immigrants.

Johnson reached most of his goals for the Great Society. By 1966, he had won more funds for housing and for public schools. Johnson was also able to get immigration laws changed. In 1968, a new immigration law allowed more immigrants from Asia, Latin America, and Eastern Europe into the United States. This law would change the population of the United States. The law no longer favored Western Europeans over other groups.

What were President Johnson's goals for the Great Society? To help homeless people, older Americans, low-income people, and new immigrants

Health Care Programs

Two of Johnson's Great Society programs still help people today. **Medicare** is a health insurance program for people over 65. It helps them pay for doctors' services and hospital bills. **Medicaid** helps low-income people and people with disabilities pay for many kinds of health care. Under Medicaid, federal and state governments pay for doctors, drugs, dental care, and eyeglasses.

How do Medicare and Medicaid help many Americans? By helping them pay for health-care costs

Section 3 Review

1. How did the Civil Rights Act of 1964 help African Americans?
2. What is Project Head Start?
3. **Critical Thinking** How do you think older Americans felt about Johnson's Great Society programs?
4. **Write About Citizenship** President Johnson felt that government money should be spent to help people make their lives better. Write three things you think government money should be used for today.

More Review is provided in Exercise 112 of the Workbook.

1. Desegregated public places; gave African Americans better chance at finding jobs
2. It helped preschool children from low-income families get ready for elementary school.
3. Possible answer: Mention how Medicaid and Medicare helped older Americans.
4. Possible answer: Funds for the military, for health research, social security, Medicare, Medicaid, education, safety

Chapter

26 Review

Summary Have students use this graphic organizer to outline the main ideas and details of the chapter.

Summary

In 1960, John Kennedy defeated Richard Nixon for the presidency. There were problems between the Soviet Union and the United States.

Section 1

Congress passed some of President Kennedy's New Frontier programs. He set a goal of putting a man on the moon by 1970.

Section 2

The Cuban Missile Crisis caused trouble between the United States and the Soviet Union. Kennedy was assassinated on November 22,1963. Lyndon Johnson became President.

Section 3

Lyndon Johnson worked with Congress to pass the Civil Rights Act of 1964. Johnson's Great Society programs helped many Americans.

More Vocabulary Review is provided in Exercise 173 of the Classroom Resource Binder.

Vocabulary Review

Write *true* or *false*. If the statement is false, change the underlined term or terms to make it true.

1. The effort to rebuild cities was called <u>urban renewal</u>. True
2. Lyndon Johnson's program was the <u>New Frontier</u>. False: Great Society
3. A low-cost health care program for people over 65 is called <u>Medicare</u>. True
4. Cubans forced to live in the United States were <u>exiles</u>. True
5. A country under <u>quarantine</u> cannot trade with other countries. True

1. Gave money to areas where people did not have jobs p. 489 2. To stop people from East Berlin from escaping to West Berlin p. 493 3. The economy had been changing; jobs had been lost to machines; people did not have the skills and training needed for good jobs. p. 497 4. Possible answer: Soviets believed what Kennedy said; they did not want a war with the United States. p. 494 5. Possible answer: Programs like the Peace Corps, Head Start, Medicare, and Medicaid improve people's lives and are too popular for Congress to cut. pp. 489, 490, 497, 499

Chapter Quiz

Write your answers in complete sentences.

1. How did President Kennedy and Congress help Americans with lower incomes?
2. Why did the Communists build the Berlin Wall?
3. Why did President Johnson decide to fight a war on poverty?
4. **Critical Thinking** Why do you think Khrushchev decided to remove the missiles from Cuba?
5. **Critical Thinking** Why do you think some of Kennedy's and Johnson's programs have lasted for many years?

Test Tip
In a multiple-choice test, cross out answers that you know are not correct.

Writing Tip
A paragraph should have unity. Every sentence should give information about the topic.

Using the Timeline

Use the timeline on pages 484–485 to answer the questions.

1. Which happened first, the Bay of Pigs invasion or the Cuban Missile Crisis? Bay of Pigs invasion
2. Who was President when the Civil Rights Act was passed? Johnson was President.

Group Activity See the Teacher's Planning Guide for a scoring rubric for this activity.

Group Activity

With your group, create a poster to teach other students about the space program. Include pictures and words about famous astronauts and events in space. Show your ideas about the future in space. Give your poster a title.

Critical Thinking 1. New interstate highways were built. Most people used cars rather than trains to commute. 2. Sit-ins and other nonviolent protests called attention to segregation. 3. Cuba had missiles with nuclear warheads from the Soviet Union.

Unit 8 Review

Critical Thinking

Give one reason why each of the following events happened.

1. Some railroads went out of business during the 1950s.
2. More and more businesses became desegregated.
3. President Kennedy said that if Cuba attacked the United States, the United States would attack the Soviet Union.

Building Your Skills

Make a bar graph to show the number of hours you spend doing homework. One bar should show hours for a weekday. Another bar should show hours for Saturday or Sunday. Give your graph a title.

Student graphs should include a title, two bars, and appropriate labels and numbers.

Who Did It?

Write the name of the person who took each action below.

1. He tested the first successful polio vaccine on almost two million children. Dr. Jonas Salk
2. Her refusal to give up her seat led to a bus boycott. Rosa Parks
3. He took over Cuba in 1959, turning it into the United States' closest Communist neighbor. Fidel Castro

Writing an Essay

Answer one of the following essay topics

See the Answer Key for a detailed answer.

1. Discuss the effects of television on people in the United States.
2. Describe the methods African Americans used to protest segregation and discrimination.
3. Identify the ways Kennedy and Johnson tried to help poor Americans with low incomes.

Linking Past and Present

Think about the work of civil rights leaders and volunteers of the 1950s and 1960s. Explain how their work affects Americans today.

Student responses should show an understanding of the goals and accomplishments of the civil rights movement. Students may feel that there is more equality today than in the past but that a great deal remains to be done.

Unit Opener Use the chapter titles and dates to set up a unit timeline.

Unit 9 Years of Change

Chapter 27 **Working for Change** 1960–1975

Chapter 28 **The Vietnam War** 1960–1973

Chapter 29 **Entering a New Decade** 1970–1975

Many Americans, like this protester putting flowers into the gun, had different ways of showing their feelings about the Vietnam War. What was the protester trying to say with his action? Student responses might mention that the flowers symbolize beauty, gentleness, and peace rather than the ugliness and cruelty of war.

> *"The world will not be the same for our children or even for ourselves . . . because ours is a time of change."*
>
> —from the Inaugural Address of Lyndon B. Johnson, January 20, 1965

Primary Source Tell students that Johnson greatly increased the number of U.S. combat troops that were sent to Vietnam in 1965. U.S. involvement in Vietnam's war was so complicated and overwhelming that Lyndon Johnson chose not to run for a second presidential term.

These people were marching for racial and economic equality. At the right is the cover of Ms. *magazine. This was the first magazine to report on topics important to women. Why do you think the men joined the women in this march?* The men probably felt the cause was important for all people.

Challenges at Home

1962 National Farm Workers Association formed

1963 Equal Pay Act passed

1964 Civil Rights Act passed

1965 Malcolm X assassinated

1966 Black Panther party formed

National Organization for Women founded

1968 Dr. Martin Luther King, Jr. assassinated

AIM organized

1960 — 1965 — 1970

Additional activities and strategies to customize lessons can be found in the Teacher's Planning Guide.

Chapter 27 Working for Change 1960–1975

ESL Note To help students understand the concept of working to change society, ask pairs of students to discuss ways the societies of their friends or families in other countries are different from society in the U.S. How could people work together to make them better?

Words to Know

black power

Black Panther party

gender

feminism

lobby

bilingual

life expectancy

nisei

Words to Know These words are defined in the section in which they appear, as well as in the Glossary. Point out to students the qualities of a panther, such as its strength, ferocity, and violence. Have students predict why the Black Panther party might have chosen to be represented by a panther.

Learning Objectives

- Discuss the rise of the black power movement.
- Identify the causes and effects of riots in the cities during the mid-1960s.
- Discuss the steps women took to gain equal treatment.
- Describe the political and social gains of Latinos.
- Explain the struggle of Native Americans and Asian Americans to gain civil rights.
- Learn how to write an essay.

Project Students will be able to begin working on the project after they have completed Section 3. Have them work on the project as a homework assignment.

Portfolio Project

In the 1960s, several groups of people had reasons to protest. Choose one group from the chapter that interests you. Create a flyer that you think members of the group could have given out at a protest march. Make your message clear.

1972 Congress recommends ERA

1975

1975 Military academies train women Army officers

Timeline The timeline is divided into 5-year intervals. The events take place over a period of 14 years. Point out that two African American leaders were assassinated during this time period.

Section 1 African American Protests

Words to Know

black power	a movement among African Americans to gain political and economic power
Black Panther party	a political party formed to work for the rights of African Americans

Getting Started Discuss with students the frustration of working toward a goal that seems to be moving ahead very slowly, if at all. What kinds of action might be taken? Explain that many African Americans believed the pace of the civil rights movement was too slow. They thought it was time to have their voices heard at any cost.

By 1964, the civil rights movement had brought many changes to American society. However, many African Americans thought the changes had come too slowly. Some leaders of the civil rights movement were looking for a new way to gain equality. They felt nonviolence was no longer the answer.

Angry Voices for Change

By 1964, Dr. Martin Luther King, Jr., was one of the most respected men in the world. His plans for nonviolent, or peaceful, protest had won many victories for African Americans. However, not all African Americans agreed with Dr. King.

For many African Americans, gaining fair treatment was taking too long. Many young leaders in the fight were angry. Some believed that African Americans would be better off living separately from whites.

Many African Americans in the North felt that white society would never treat them fairly. They were angry about white landlords who owned poorly kept buildings in African American neighborhoods and charged high rents. They were also angry with white store owners who charged high prices in African American neighborhoods.

They spoke out against white city officials who ignored their problems. They also demanded that white police officers begin to treat them fairly.

One person who spoke out against the slow progress of the civil rights movement was Malcolm X. As a young man, Malcolm X joined the Black Muslims. The Black Muslims believed African Americans and white Americans should live separately.

After a trip to Africa, Malcolm X felt that all people should work together for equality.

Visual Malcolm X's family name was Little. He later took the name X to show that he did not accept his slave name.

In 1964, Malcolm X traveled to the city of Mecca in Saudi Arabia. There, he saw that people of all races lived and worked together. When Malcolm X returned to the United States, he spoke out against separation. He now said that all people should work together for freedom and equality.

Some African Americans did not like Malcolm X's new message. In February 1965, Malcolm X was assassinated. Three African Americans went to prison for his murder.

In the 1960s, what did many African Americans believe about white society? That white society would never treat them fairly

Black Power

In 1966, James Meredith set out from Memphis, Tennessee, on a march. He hoped to make people aware of the rights African Americans should have. On his way to Jackson, Mississippi, Meredith was shot and wounded by a white man.

When James Meredith was able to continue on his march again, several African Americans joined him. Among the leaders of the march were Dr. Martin Luther King, Jr., and a young civil rights leader named Stokely Carmichael. The march ended in a rally of 15,000 people at the state capital in Jackson, Mississippi.

During the march Carmichael and others began to use the term **black power.** They chose a raised fist as the symbol of black power. Black power was a movement among African Americans to gain political and economic power. Black power included these goals.

1. To develop African American political parties.
2. To help African Americans become business owners rather than workers.
3. To build self-respect and pride among African Americans with slogans such as "Black is beautiful."
4. To fight against white people in power.

What was the main goal of the black power movement? To gain political and economic power for African Americans

Visual The Black Panther party was formed in Oakland, California, in 1966. The party's influence weakened in the 1970s because of many internal disputes in the party.

A black panther became the symbol of the Black Panther party.

The Black Panthers

The **Black Panther party** began in Oakland, California, in 1966. The political party worked for the rights of all African Americans. Members of the Black Panther party believed in black pride.

The Black Panther party drew up a list of demands. It wanted more and better jobs for African Americans and better housing in African American neighborhoods. It also demanded better education and an end to cruel treatment by the police. Finally, it demanded that African Americans on trial be judged by African American juries.

The Black Panthers said that black violence was the answer to white violence. This led to battles in many cities between Black Panthers and the police.

Members of the Black Panther party started programs to help its communities. It began day-care programs for children of working parents. It offered breakfast to school-age African American children.

Some civil rights leaders felt that black power would hurt the cause of equality for African Americans. The

National Association for the Advancement of Colored People (NAACP), in particular, was against black power.

Why was the Black Panther party formed? It was formed to gain and protect rights for African Americans.

Violence and an Assassination

By the mid-1960s, many white Americans had moved to the suburbs. Many businesses and industries followed white Americans to the suburbs. That meant fewer tax dollars went to cities. Schools, hospitals, and other city services suffered huge budget cuts.

Many African Americans were left in cities without enough services. This led to violence. African Americans could no longer hold in their anger. They were tired of the daily problems of racial discrimination, lack of jobs,

Visual In 1969, James Earl Ray was convicted of assassinating Dr. King. Ray was sentenced to a 99-year prison term. He died in prison in 1998.

Many people came to the funeral march for Dr. Martin Luther King, Jr.

and poor housing. Riots broke out in several cities. In 1965, a riot broke out in Watts, a section of Los Angeles, California. It started when an African American was arrested by a white police officer. After the riot, 34 people were dead, and 4,000 people had been arrested. In Detroit, a riot in 1967 left 43 people dead. Army tanks had to be brought in to stop the violence. Later, in Chicago, whites threw rocks and bottles at Dr. King and other marchers.

In 1968, Dr. King went to Memphis, Tennessee. He planned to support a strike by African American workers. There Dr. King spoke about the future. "I may not get there with you," he said, "but I . . . know . . . we as a people will get to the promised land."

That was Dr. King's last speech. On April 4, 1968, he was shot as he stood on the porch of the Lorraine Motel. The death of the man who had believed in nonviolence led to riots in more than 100 cities. For many people, Dr. King's murder was the end of the civil rights movement.

Why did riots break out in many cities during the 1960s? Many African Americans became angry about the lack of services in the cities.

Section 1 Review

1. What was the goal of the Black Panther party?
2. Why did some civil rights leaders disagree with the black power movement?
3. **Critical Thinking** What programs of the Black Panthers do you think most African Americans agreed with?
4. **Write About History** Write a list of questions you might have asked Malcolm X if you had interviewed him.

More Review is provided in Exercise 113 of the Workbook.

1. To work for the rights of African Americans
2. Black power leaders believed in violence to advance their cause. Many civil rights leaders believed in nonviolence.
3. Teaching African American children to take pride in themselves, the breakfast program, the day-care program
4. Student responses might include asking Malcolm X what he most admired about the people in Mecca, how difficult it was for him to change his opinion on separateness, how he felt about the idea of black power.

BUILDING YOUR SKILLS
Writing an Essay

An essay is a piece of writing in which you tell what you know about a topic. To do that, you need to choose a topic, use facts to explain the topic, and draw conclusions about the ideas in your essay.

Follow these steps to write an essay.

1. Choose a topic.
2. List all the ideas that you want to put in your essay.
3. Write one sentence that gives the main idea of your essay.
4. Make an outline of information that will support the main idea.
5. Write a rough copy of your essay. Follow your outline.
6. Carefully rewrite your essay. Check grammar and spelling.

Answer these questions.

1. What is the first thing you need to do to write an essay?
2. A rough copy of your essay follows what step?

   CHALLENGE What topic would you choose when writing an essay about a person or event in this chapter?

1. Choose a topic **2.** Your outline
CHALLENGE Answers will vary.

Apply the Skill
Follow the steps above to write a short essay. Then read your essay to your classmates. Together discuss what you have learned from your essay.

Section 2 Women Demand Equality

Words to Know

gender	whether a person is male or female
feminism	a political and social movement that favors equal rights for women
lobby	to try to make lawmakers pass certain laws

Getting Started Have students discuss the various images of women that they have seen on TV or in magazines. Explain that in the 1960s, women's groups challenged the way society portrayed women at home and at work.

Remember
Women first organized a movement for equal rights at the Seneca Falls Convention in 1848.

The strength of the civil rights movement spread to other groups in the 1960s. Many people who felt that society treated them unfairly began to protest. American women of all races began to demand equal treatment.

Gaining Equal Rights

Before the 1960s, the term *woman's work* meant cooking, cleaning, and caring for children at home. Outside the home, woman's work meant jobs such as nursing, teaching, and office or sales work.

In the 1960s, more women went to college than ever before. After they finished college, many looked for high-paying jobs. However, women were shut out of many jobs. Only a few women became business leaders. Even fewer women became lawyers, doctors, or scientists. There were almost no women judges or governors. Those women who did get jobs in business and science were often paid less than men who held the same jobs. Few women were promoted to top positions. Many women felt they were being treated unfairly.

Congress passed two laws to help women. The first was the Equal Pay Act of 1963. That law said there had to be equal pay for men and women doing the same job.

The second was the Civil Rights Act of 1964. That law said there could not be job discrimination on the basis of color, race, **gender**, or religion. Gender is whether a person is male or female.

In the 1960s, why did many women think that they were treated unfairly? Many women were being shut out of certain jobs. They were not receiving pay equal to that of men.

National Organization for Women

Women's struggles in the 1960s for equal rights led to the movement called **feminism.** Feminism is a political and social movement that favors equal rights for women. In 1966, the leaders of feminism formed the National Organization for Women, called NOW. The organization had several goals. These are some of its goals:

1. More job opportunities for women in government, industry, and business.
2. Equal shares of work at home for men and women.
3. Fewer ads that showed women only as homemakers.
4. Political candidates who supported women's rights.
5. A woman's right to choose an abortion.

To reach these goals, NOW decided to **lobby** lawmakers in states and in Congress. To lobby is to try to make lawmakers pass certain laws. NOW supported two pieces of legislation. One was the Educational Amendments Act of 1972. This act banned discrimination on the basis of gender in educational programs. The other was the Equal Credit Opportunity Act. This act helped women get loans and credit cards in their own names.

What was the chief goal of NOW? The chief goal of NOW was to gain true equality for all women.

During the 1960s and 1970s, women joined together to demand equal rights.

Visual The term *feminism* was first used in 1895.

Equal Rights Amendment Ratification, 1972–1977

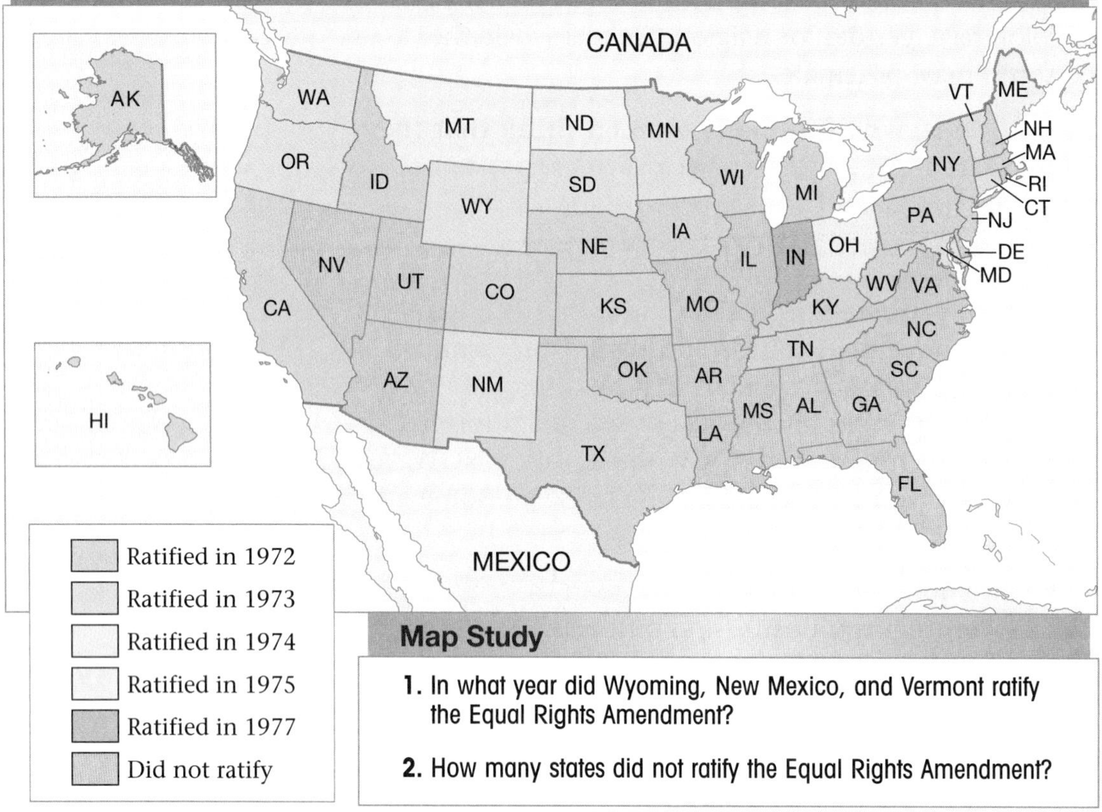

Map Study

1. In what year did Wyoming, New Mexico, and Vermont ratify the Equal Rights Amendment?
2. How many states did not ratify the Equal Rights Amendment?

Map This map shows which states ratified the ERA, and when. Point out that Indiana and North Dakota were the last states to ratify.

1. 1973

2. 15

Steps Forward

In the 1970s, the women's movement gave women a new place in American society. Women were hired for jobs such as FBI agents, airline pilots, astronauts, and religious leaders. In 1975, U.S. military academies began to train women as army officers. Women also became reporters on television news programs.

Gloria Steinem began a new magazine in 1972. It was called *Ms.* Steinem believed in feminism. Her magazine pointed out that men and women should be equal. Many women began to call themselves Ms. instead of Miss or Mrs.

In 1972, Congress passed the Equal Rights Amendment, or the ERA. That amendment to the Constitution declared that men and women must be treated equally under the law.

Not everyone felt the same about the Equal Rights Amendment. Those in favor of the ERA felt that women's rights had to be guaranteed by the U.S. Constitution. Those against the ERA said that it was unnecessary because women were already protected by federal laws. They also felt that under the ERA women would be forced to serve in the armed forces.

Before the Equal Rights Amendment could become law, 38 states had to approve it within 10 years. However, only 35 states approved the ERA by 1982. The amendment was dropped.

What was the Equal Rights Amendment? A constitutional amendment stating that men and women must be treated equally

Section 2 Review

1. How did the 1960s women's movement help women?
2. What happened to the Equal Rights Amendment?
3. **Critical Thinking** Why do you think some women felt they needed an organization such as NOW?
4. **Write About History** You are working to have the lawmakers in your state ratify the Equal Rights Amendment. Write a paragraph explaining why it should be ratified.

1. New career opportunities became available to women; women's pay became closer to men's pay.
2. It was not ratified by 38 states within 10 years, so it was dropped.
3. Possible answer: Women felt they could achieve more by working together.
4. Possible answer: Mention that the ERA declared that men and women must be treated equally by law.

More Review is provided in Exercise 114 of the Workbook.

Section 3 Rights for All Americans

Words to Know

bilingual	able to speak two languages very well
life expectancy	the number of years a person can expect to live
nisei	second-generation Japanese Americans

Getting Started Discuss what makes different nationalities unique. Explain that, during the 1960s, groups of people began to speak out about what makes them unique and why they should be treated fairly by the law.

In the 1960s, a period of change took place for many groups in the United States. Latinos, Native Americans, and Asians followed the example of African Americans as they fought for their civil rights.

Latinos Demand Rights

In the 1960s and 1970s, the largest Latino groups in the United States came from Mexico, Puerto Rico, and Cuba. The Latino population grew faster than any other group in the country. Like other newcomers, they faced problems in finding jobs and housing.

Chicanos

During the 1960s, Mexican Americans saw that they had many of the same struggles that African Americans had. They saw how African Americans united in their struggle for equal rights.

Mexican Americans began to use the word *Chicano* to describe the pride they felt in their culture and background. Leaders of the Chicano movement demanded respect and justice. They demonstrated against police brutality. The most famous leader of the Chicano movement was César Chávez. He led the movement for farm workers' rights.

Mexican Americans fought for **bilingual** schools in their neighborhoods. Bilingual means being able to speak two languages very well. Schools with bilingual programs have teachers who can speak both English and Spanish. In this way, students could learn English and keep up with their regular school work.

Puerto Ricans

Puerto Ricans faced many problems when they arrived in the United States. Prejudice against them was strong, even though they were U.S. citizens. Many could find only unskilled jobs at low wages. However, many Puerto Ricans found ways to improve their lives. One way was ASPIRA. ASPIRA, meaning "Hope" in Spanish, was formed in 1969. Its aim was to improve

Great Names in History

CÉSAR CHÁVEZ

In the 1960s, Mexican American farm workers worked in the fields for 14 to 16 hours a day. Some workers only received five dollars for this work.

César Chávez wanted to help farm workers get a better life. He came from a family of migrant workers. He knew how hard it was to make a living that way. In 1962, Chávez began the National Farm Workers Association (NFWA), a union for migrant farm workers.

Later, Chávez organized a strike against wealthy grape growers. The NFWA called for a national boycott of California grapes. About 17 million Americans stopped buying grapes. Eventually, California grape pickers won the wages they wanted.

César Chávez believed in nonviolence.

Critical Thinking Why did César Chávez think that only a union could help the farm workers? Possible answer: Unions have more power to bring about change than individuals.

Geography Fact

Cubans settled in Miami because it is the closest large city to Cuba. Ninety miles separates Cuba from the United States.

Geography Fact According to the U.S. Census Bureau, more than one million people of Cuban origin live in the United States. Cuban Americans represent nearly five percent of the total Hispanic population. Sixty-five percent of Cuban Americans are Florida residents.

education among Latinos. Puerto Ricans also sponsored clubs to help newcomers. They set up bilingual education programs. They organized labor unions and started businesses. They worked to increase the number of Puerto Rican teachers, police officers, and firefighters.

Cubans

When Fidel Castro became the leader of Cuba in 1959, he brought in Communist ideas. Many Cubans did not want communism. Many educated Cubans left their homes and came to Miami, Florida. The drain of middle-class people who had money and special skills hurt Cuba's economy. As a result, Castro banned Cubans from going to the United States.

Cubans brought new businesses to Florida, especially in banking and trade. In recent years, they have gained political power.

What problems did both Chicanos and Puerto Ricans face in the United States? They were discriminated against; not fluent speakers of English, unskilled workers.

Native Americans Call for Action

In the 1960s, living conditions on Native American reservations were among the worst in the United States. Alcohol abuse and violence had lowered the **life expectancy** of Native Americans. Life expectancy is the number of years a person can expect to live.

In 1968, the American Indian Movement, or AIM, was formed in Minneapolis, Minnesota. Its goal was to improve the lives of Native Americans in that city. It also wanted to protect Native Americans from unfair treatment by the police.

Soon there were branches of AIM in other cities. During the 1970s, AIM worked to improve schools for Native Americans and help young people on reservations understand Native American culture and traditions. AIM wanted to create health-care programs and get the U.S. government to focus on the land rights of Native Americans. Finally, it hoped to get the U.S. government to improve conditions on Native American reservations.

What kind of help did Native Americans want from the U.S. government? Native Americans wanted help in gaining land rights and improving conditions on reservations.

Asian Americans Seek Civil Rights

Before 1960, most Asians came to the United States from China, Japan, and the Philippines. A change in immigration laws in 1965 brought Koreans, Indians, and Vietnamese to the United States. Many Asians settled in large cities on the West coast. Like most newcomers, Asian immigrants faced problems in finding jobs and decent housing and in getting an education.

Second-generation Japanese Americans, called **nisei**, formed the Japanese American Citizens League (JACL). The JACL supported the civil rights movement. The JACL also wanted the U.S. government to pay the Japanese Americans who had been sent to internment camps during World War II.

What group worked to get civil rights for Japanese Americans? The Japanese American Citizens League

Section 3 Review

1. Why was ASPIRA an important organization?
2. How did AIM try to improve life for Native Americans?
3. **Critical Thinking** Why might some Americans be against bilingual schools?
4. **Write About Citizenship** Write a brief essay describing how Latinos, Native Americans, and Asian immigrants worked to gain their civil rights.

1. Puerto Ricans organized ASPIRA to improve education among Latinos.
2. It worked to improve education and health-care services.
3. Possible answer: Some Americans might think that people who live in the United States should be required to speak the language of the country.
4. Possible answer: Organizations founded, such as ASPIRA, formed by Puerto Ricans; the NFWA, by Mexican Americans; AIM, by Native Americans; and JACL, by Japanese Americans. Political platforms included demands for better education, housing, health care.

More Review is provided in Exercise 116 of the Workbook.

Chapter

27 Review

Summary Have students use this graphic organizer to outline the main ideas and details of the chapter.

Summary

In the 1960s and 1970s, many Americans felt that they were being denied their civil rights. Immigrants also felt that they had to fight for civil rights.

Section 1

Some African Americans rejected Dr. Martin Luther King, Jr.'s, belief in nonviolence. They joined the Black Panther party. Some protested because they felt conditions did not change quickly enough.

Section 2

Women felt that they were treated unfairly at home and in the workplace. The National Organization for Women (NOW) was formed to fight for equal treatment of women.

Section 3

Latinos, Asian Americans, and Native Americans organized to gain social, economic, and political rights.

lobby
bilingual
feminism
life expectancy
black power

More Vocabulary Review is provided in Exercise 181 of the Classroom Resource Binder.

Vocabulary Review

Complete each sentence with a term from the list.

1. Many people who came to the United States from Mexico wanted ___ education for their children. bilingual

2. The ___ of people is not the same throughout the world. life expectancy

3. Women and NOW tried to ___ to have new laws passed. lobby

4. For some African Americans, ___ was a way of gaining self-respect. black power

5. The movement to gain equal rights for women is called ___. feminism

1. Young civil rights workers were not happy with progress of civil rights movement; wanted changes sooner; wanted to improve economic and social opportunities for African Americans. pp. 507–508 **2.** Women organized NOW; lobbied to have legislation passed. p. 513 **3.** To improve the lives of Native Americans p. 518 **4.** As owners, African Americans would have more power. They could provide opportunities for other African Americans. pp. 507–508 **5.** Possible answer: The U.S. should pay for the suffering the Japanese people went through. p. 519

Chapter Quiz

Write your answers in complete sentences.

1. What caused the rise of the black power movement?
2. What two ways did women use to gain equal rights during the 1960s?
3. What was the purpose of AIM?
4. **Critical Thinking** Why would leaders of black power have encouraged African Americans to become owners of businesses rather than workers in a business?
5. **Critical Thinking** Why do you think the nisei demanded payment by the U.S. government for the treatment of the Japanese people during World War II?

Test Tip
As you read, try to state the main idea of a paragraph in your own words.

Writing Tip
The subject and verb in a sentence should always agree.

Using the Timeline

Use the timeline on page 504–505 to answer the questions.

1. How many years after the Equal Pay Act was passed was the Equal Rights Amendment recommended by Congress? 9 years
2. What two African Americans with different views were assassinated in the 1960s? Malcolm X and Dr. Martin Luther King, Jr.

Group Activity See the Teacher's Planning Guide for a scoring rubric for this activity.

Group Activity

With your group, compare and contrast the goals of different civil rights groups during the 1960s. Decide what methods each group used to achieve these goals. Chart your results.

U.S. troops head into battle in Vietnam. Many people who were against the Vietnam War wore peace symbols like this one. Why might people be against a war in which the soldiers from their own country are fighting? Student responses might mention that Americans should not be sent to protect a foreign country or solve its problems.

Timeline The timeline is divided into 1-year intervals. The events take place over a period of 14 years. Point out to students the national and world events related to the Vietnam War.

The United States in Vietnam

1960 John F. Kennedy elected

1963 President Kennedy assassinated; Lyndon B. Johnson becomes President

1964 Gulf of Tonkin incident

1965 Bombing of North Vietnam begins

1968 Tet offensive

1968 My Lai massacre; Richard Nixon elected

1960 | 1961 | 1962 | 1963 | 1964 | 1965 | 1966 | 1967 | 1968 | 1969

Additional activities and strategies to customize lessons can be found in the Teacher's Planning Guide.

Chapter 28 The Vietnam War 1960–1973

ESL Note To help students understand why war is waged, discuss the reasons why countries go to war. Explain that most people believe they know right from wrong. However, war often complicates moral issues.

Words to Know

- domino theory
- Viet Cong
- guerrilla warfare
- depose
- napalm
- Agent Orange
- conscientious objector
- deferment
- Vietnamization
- censor

Words to Know These words are defined in the section in which they appear, as well as in the Glossary. Point out to students that *Agent Orange* is the name of a chemical. It was called Agent Orange because it was stored in barrels painted with large orange stripes.

1970 | 1971 | 1972 | 1973

1970 Four Kent State University students killed in antiwar protest

1971 Pentagon Papers published

1972 Richard Nixon reelected

1973 Last U.S. troops leave Vietnam

Learning Objectives

- Explain the political situation in Vietnam during the 1960s.
- Discuss how the United States became involved in Vietnam.
- Identify the reasons why many Americans were against the war.
- Discuss President Richard Nixon's actions during the war.
- Identify the events that led to the end of the Vietnam War.
- Explore the rise of protest music during the Vietnam years.

Project Students can complete this project individually (as a homework assignment) as they read each section. When the projects are completed, encourage students to share their surveys with one another.

Portfolio Project

The Vietnam War was a war unlike any other war in U. S. history. Many Americans supported the war, but many Americans were against the war. Take a survey to find out how six people you know felt or even still feel about the Vietnam War. Prepare the questions that you want to ask so that you can put together the results. Write a report of your survey.

Section 1 A Distant War Divides a Nation

Words to Know

domino theory	belief that if one country falls to communism, others nearby will fall, one after the other
Viet Cong	Communist Vietnamese in South Vietnam
guerrilla warfare	fighting by troops who are not members of a regular army, using surprise attacks
depose	to remove from office

Getting Started Ask students if they have ever played the game of dominoes. Discuss how lightly touching the first piece sets all the pieces in motion. Explain that U.S. political leaders believed that if Vietnam fell to communism, then other countries would quickly follow, like dominoes.

Remember
U.S. forces had already tried to stop the spread of communism in Korea. Korea is also in Southeast Asia.

During the cold war in the 1950s, the United States tried to stop the spread of communism. By the 1960s, the United States would face a bigger challenge in Vietnam. The United States did not want to become too involved. Yet, U.S. leaders wanted to stop the spread of communism in Vietnam.

War in Vietnam

Before the early 1950s, few Americans had ever heard of Vietnam. The United States had hardly any contact with that small country in Southeast Asia. Vietnam was more than 10,000 miles away.

France controlled Vietnam for many years. In 1946, the people of Vietnam fought a war against France. They wanted to gain their independence. Ho Chi Minh was the leader of the war for independence. Ho Chi Minh was a Communist.

In May 1954, Ho Chi Minh's forces won a great victory over the French. The war ended two months later. Vietnam won its independence. According to the peace treaty, Vietnam was divided into two parts.

There was North Vietnam and South Vietnam. National elections were to be held in 1956. The people of Vietnam would vote for one leader to bring the country together.

In the months before the elections, Ho Chi Minh took over North Vietnam. He set up a Communist government there. Ngo Dinh Diem became the leader of South Vietnam. He was against communism.

The United States worried that Ho Chi Minh would win the elections. American leaders felt that if he won the elections, the Communist government would take over all of Vietnam. Then, if Vietnam took over neighboring countries, they would become Communist. One nation after another would fall under Communist control, like a row of dominoes. The United States called this the **domino theory.** The United States saw Ho Chi Minh's Communist government as a threat to all of Asia.

How was Vietnam divided after the French left?
Vietnam was divided into two parts: North Vietnam and South Vietnam.

An Unpopular Leader

In 1956, Ngo Dinh Diem called off the national elections. He decided to form an independent non-Communist country in the southern part of Vietnam. The United States agreed with Diem's decision. President Dwight D. Eisenhower promised to help Diem.

However, many people in South Vietnam did not like Diem. They thought that he ruled South Vietnam like a dictator. Diem did not allow freedom of speech. He put people who went against him into prison. He did not allow some people to practice their religion.

In 1957, people who were against Diem formed a group called the **Viet Cong.** They were South Vietnamese Communists. In 1959, the Viet Cong joined the North Vietnamese army to fight Diem's forces. This was the beginning of the Vietnam War.

Who was Ngo Dinh Diem? Ngo Dinh Diem was a Vietnamese anti-Communist leader who became the leader of South Vietnam.

History Fact People who were against Diem were called Viet Cong by their opponents. Their organization was called the National Liberation Front (NLF).

History Fact

Ngo Dinh Diem was offered a position in Ho Chi Minh's government. He refused.

Help From the United States

When John F. Kennedy became President in 1961, he continued helping South Vietnam. He sent military advisers to South Vietnam to train the South Vietnamese fighters. The U.S. trainers were not supposed to fight. However, many trainers did fight battles against the Viet Cong and the North Vietnamese.

Fighting the Viet Cong was not easy. The Viet Cong used **guerrilla warfare.** Guerrilla warfare is fighting by troops who are not members of a regular army. They use surprise attacks and then quickly disappear before the enemy can respond.

As the fighting continued, Diem became more and more unpopular. In 1963, South Vietnamese military leaders decided to **depose** Diem. To depose means to remove from office. On November 1, 1963, Diem was killed by his own generals. Military officers took control of South Vietnam.

Three weeks later, President Kennedy was assassinated. Lyndon Johnson, the Vice President, became President. He was now in charge of the Vietnam War.

? **How did President Kennedy help South Vietnam?** He sent military advisers to train South Vietnamese fighters.

The Fighting Continues

President Johnson believed that it was important for the United States to fight communism in Vietnam. He believed that North Vietnam could be defeated if the United States helped South Vietnam.

The question of how to fight communism was not easy to answer. Most of the Vietnamese people lived in South Vietnam. They farmed in the Mekong River delta. However, most people in that area supported the Viet Cong.

In addition, North Vietnam regularly sent supplies to the Viet Cong. These troops used the Ho Chi Minh Trail that passed through Cambodia, the country west of Vietnam. The trail was named after the North Vietnamese leader.

Secretary of Defense Robert MacNamara told the American people that the war in Vietnam could be won. However, he told President Johnson that more American help was needed.

Where did most of the Vietnamese people live? Most Vietnamese people lived in the Mekong River valley in South Vietnam.

North and South Vietnam, 1964–1965

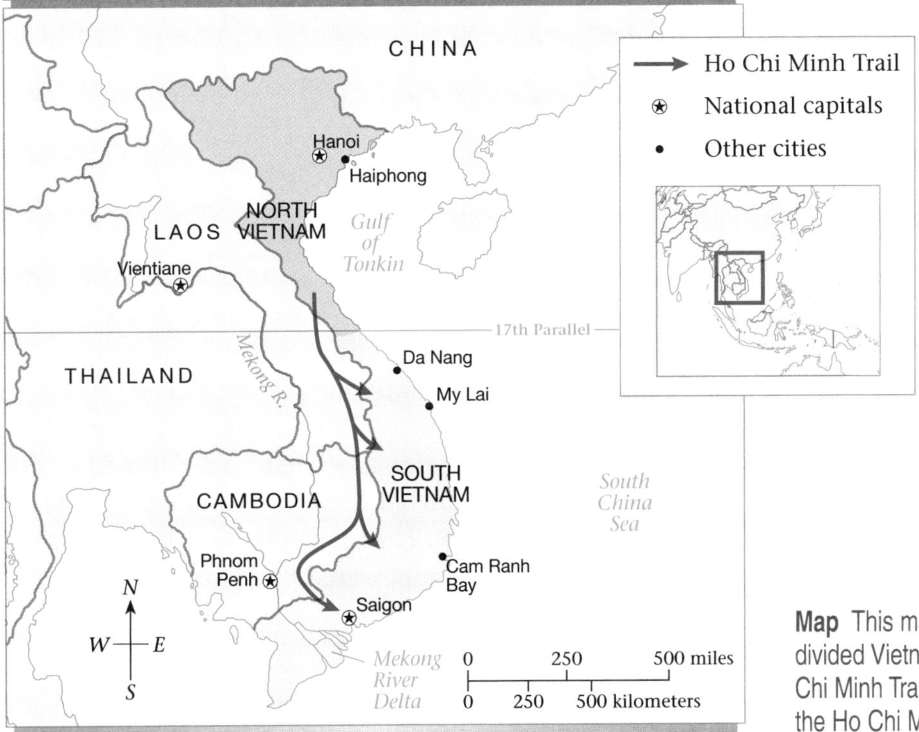

Map Study

1. What are the capitals of South Vietnam and North Vietnam?
2. According to the domino theory, what other countries might fall to communism?

Map This map shows a divided Vietnam and the Ho Chi Minh Trail. Point out that the Ho Chi Minh Trail passes through the countries of North Vietnam, Laos, Cambodia, and South Vietnam.

1. Saigon; Hanoi
2. Cambodia, Laos, Thailand

President Johnson spoke to the American people about the Gulf of Tonkin.

Visual In 1965, President Johnson defended U.S. involvement in the war. He said, "We fight this war because we must fight if we are to live in a world where every country can shape its own destiny."

The Gulf of Tonkin Incident

The Vietnam War took an important turn in August 1964. On August 2, a U.S. warship reported that it had been attacked by North Vietnamese gunboats. It was in the Gulf of Tonkin, off the coast of North Vietnam.

President Johnson spoke on television to the American people about what had happened. He described the attack. He said that American forces would fight back.

President Johnson asked Congress to give him the power to order U.S. forces into South Vietnam. Congress allowed Johnson to do this. The Tonkin Gulf Resolution was passed on August 7. From then on, the President could send troops to Vietnam without declaring war.

What did President Johnson ask for after the Gulf of Tonkin attack? President Johnson asked Congress to give him the power to order U.S. forces into South Vietnam.

The Bombing of North Vietnam

In 1964, President Johnson won a landslide victory in the election. He defeated Barry Goldwater, the Republican candidate. Johnson had now been elected President on his own. The American people liked Johnson's strong stand against communism. Johnson had promised that American soldiers would not be sent to Vietnam. However, while Johnson was making his promise, plans were being made to bomb North Vietnam.

In February 1965, Viet Cong forces attacked a military base in South Vietnam. Eight Americans were killed. After that attack, President Johnson ordered the bombing of North Vietnam to begin. For more than three years, the United States dropped 500 tons of bombs a day on North Vietnam. The bombs destroyed many areas in North Vietnam. However, it made the

North Vietnamese and the Viet Cong want more than ever to continue their fight against the United States.

Many Americans supported the President's actions. However, many other Americans knew that Johnson had gone against his promises. He continued to send soldiers to Vietnam. By June 1965, more than 50,000 U.S. soldiers were in Vietnam.

What did President Johnson promise the American people in 1964? He promised that he would not send American troops to Vietnam.

Section 1 Review

1. Why was the United States worried about Ho Chi Minh's takeover of North Vietnam?
2. Why was Ngo Dinh Diem unpopular?
3. **Critical Thinking** Why do you think President Johnson believed that the United States could defeat North Vietnam?
4. **Write About History** President Johnson felt the United States needed to send troops to Vietnam. Write a paragraph telling why you agree or disagree with his decision.

More Review is provided in Exercise 117 of the Workbook.

1. The United States felt other countries would be taken over by Communists.
2. Many South Vietnamese people thought that Diem was a dictator.
3. Possible answer: President Johnson believed in the superior strength of the U.S. military.
4. Possible answer: Agree; President Johnson was preventing another world war. Disagree; President Johnson was only involving the United States in the problems of a foreign nation.

VOICES FROM THE PAST
Protest Songs

By the mid-1960s, many Americans felt that the Vietnam War was a mistake. Many musicians wrote songs to protest the presence of U.S. troops in Vietnam. Some of these musicians were Bob Dylan, Buffy Sainte Marie, and Neil Young.

Folksinger Phil Ochs wrote a song protesting all wars. His song was called "I Ain't Marching Anymore." This is one verse of the song.

"For I marched to the battles of the German trench. In a war that was bound to end all wars. Oh I must have killed a million men. And now they want me back again. But I ain't marchin' anymore."

Protest music did not help end the war. However, it did help make the antiwar movement strong.

1. According to Ochs, what would happen after the last war he fought in?

2. What does the line "And now they want me back again" mean?

CHALLENGE Why do you think protest music is written?

Bob Dylan wrote many popular protest songs during the 1960s.

1. It was supposed to be the war that would end all wars. **2.** The government wants soldiers to fight another war. **CHALLENGE** Possible answer: This is another way to voice an opinion about social and political issues; it can reach many people; the message is simple.

Section 2 The Conflict Grows

Words to Know

napalm	a sticky gasoline jelly used in bombs
Agent Orange	a powerful chemical that kills all plant life where it is sprayed
conscientious objector	a person whose beliefs do not let him or her take an active part in war
deferment	putting off, or delaying, having to serve in the armed forces

Getting Started Point out to students that a turning point is an incident that changes the expected outcome of a situation. Have them give examples from their own lives.

Visual Radios were also used in Vietnam for air-to-air communications between flight crews.

U.S. troops often used two-way radios to communicate.

By 1966, U.S. troops were fighting hard in Vietnam. Each day thousands of Americans were killed or wounded. Yet winning the war did not seem near. The United States was being pulled deeper and deeper into an unpopular war.

A Difficult Fight

By 1966, U.S. military leaders knew that the Vietnam War would not end soon. The enemy was not like any other enemy that Americans had ever faced.

To find the hiding places of the Viet Cong, U.S. forces used two weapons that were dropped from planes. One was **napalm,** a sticky gasoline jelly that is used in bombs. It destroys plants and also sticks to flesh. The other was **Agent Orange.** This is a powerful chemical that kills all plant life in areas where it is sprayed.

Napalm was put into bombs. American troops dropped napalm bombs on areas where they could not easily reach the Viet Cong. Napalm bombs killed or injured millions of Vietnamese civilians.

Chart Point out to students that U.S. soldiers and the Viet Cong had different styles of warfare. The Viet Cong's style was better suited to the geography of the land.

1. The Viet Cong did not wear uniforms.
2. They knew the land and waterways; they knew where to plant traps and small bombs.

American airplanes sprayed Agent Orange over large areas of forest to kill the leaves. With the leaves destroyed, the Americans could see and attack the Viet Cong from helicopters. The Viet Cong had no place to hide.

By the end of 1966, there were more than 385,000 American troops in Vietnam. Yet the Viet Cong seemed more determined than ever to win.

Why did U.S. troops spray Agent Orange? Wanted to make the Viet Cong easier to see and attack

The Tet Offensive

Tet is the name of the most important Vietnamese holiday. It marks the beginning of the Vietnamese New Year. Traditionally, the Vietnamese celebrate this holiday for several days.

American Forces in Vietnam

Weaknesses of American Forces	Strengths of Viet Cong Forces
They defended an unpopular goverment.	They fought to unite their country.
They helped a weak army that could not defend its own government.	They were experienced fighters who believed in communism.
They fought in a country they did not know.	They knew the land and waterways.
They had a hard time recognizing the Viet Cong, who did not wear uniforms.	They could easily recognize American troops.
They had been trained in modern warfare.	They were experts in guerrilla warfare.
They used long-range weapons, like guided missiles, that easily strayed off target.	They used booby traps, small bombs called land mines, and sharpened metal that fell from trees as weapons.

Chart Study

1. Why were the Viet Cong hard to recognize?
2. What advantage did the Viet Cong have in fighting in their own country?

In 1968, the Viet Cong, the South Vietnamese, and the Americans agreed to stop fighting briefly on Tet. Most South Vietnamese troops went on holiday leave.

Late one evening, sounds of firecrackers, laughter, and song filled the air in Saigon, the capital city of South Vietnam. Then suddenly, there was the sound of rifle fire. The Viet Cong had made a surprise attack. The Viet Cong also struck nearby South Vietnamese towns and villages. The U.S. embassy in Saigon and a U.S. military base were also badly damaged. About 84,000 Viet Cong and North Vietnamese troops took part in what became known as the Tet offensive.

In the United States, Americans watching the evening news on television were shocked and angry. Much of what Americans learned about the Vietnam War came from what they saw on television. For several years, they had been hearing that U.S. forces were slowly winning the war in Vietnam.

Americans now saw that things were worse than they had imagined. Enemy forces were no longer hiding in the country and fighting in the thick forests. They were attacking cities, towns, and villages in Vietnam. After the Tet offensive, fewer Americans supported the Vietnam War.

However, some Americans believed that it was important for the United States to stop communism anywhere it spread. They believed that the Soviet Union and Chinese Communists controlled Ho Chi Minh. They feared that allowing the Communists to win would hurt the United States.

What was the chief effect of the Tet offensive on the United States? Fewer Americans supported the war.

Vietnamese civilians ran for safety during the Tet offensive.

Visual To prepare for the Tet offensive, North Vietnamese troops smuggled weapons into Saigon by holding fake funerals. Their weapons were hidden in coffins.

Voices Against the War

Many young people in the United States wanted peace. Some were college students. Others were high school students. People who were against the war were **conscientious objectors.** A conscientious objector is a person whose beliefs do not let him or her take an active part in war. All of these people believed that the United States was wrong to fight in Vietnam.

To express their feelings about the war, people attended antiwar protests. These protests often had huge crowds. As many as 50,000 people might attend an antiwar protest.

Many of the Vietnam protests were peaceful. However, sometimes protests ended in violence. There were fights between people who supported the war and those against the war. Sometimes there were fights between the police and protesters.

History Fact

The average age of Americans fighting in Vietnam was 22 years old.

History Fact The average age of a U.S. soldier who fought in World War II was 26. In Vietnam, no U.S. soldier killed in action was younger than 20 years of age. The oldest man killed was 62 years old.

In May 1970, students at Kent State University in Ohio were protesting the war. National Guard troops were protecting the university buildings. Rocks were thrown from the crowd. The troops fired shots. Four college students were killed and nine were wounded.

Americans against the war also protested the draft. All men had to register for the armed forces when they turned 18. However, college students could get a **deferment.** A deferment is putting off, or delaying, having to serve in the armed forces.

People against the draft said it was unfair. Poor white men, African Americans, and other minorities were drafted. Most middle-class and wealthy students were in college, so they got deferments. Some people who did not support the war burned their draft cards in protest. Others moved to Canada rather than serve in Vietnam.

Why did some people protest the draft? They were against the war; believed the draft was unfair.

Four students were killed during an antiwar protest at Kent State University in 1970.

Visual Reaction across the country to the Kent State shooting was swift. Protests were held at more than 1,000 colleges. More than 500 campuses were shut down. At more than 100 schools, National Guard troops were called in to maintain order.

The Election of 1968

By 1968, President Lyndon Johnson had lost a lot of support among Americans. He became much less popular than he had been earlier. Many people who liked his Great Society programs did not like his support of the war. Finally, on March 31, 1968, Johnson surprised the American people. He announced that he would not run again for President. After he announced his decision, two other Democrats who had entered the race were left. Senator Eugene McCarthy was one. Robert Kennedy, President John F. Kennedy's brother, was another. Both spoke out against the war.

On June 5, 1968, two months after Dr. Martin Luther King, Jr., was killed, Robert Kennedy was shot. He died the next day. A year that had begun with the Tet offensive was now half over. Thousands of troops were dead. Two famous Americans had been assassinated.

In August, the Democrats met in Chicago to choose a candidate to run for President. Many antiwar protesters came to Chicago, too. Fights broke out between the protesters and the police. Americans watched on television as Chicago was torn by antiwar riots. Finally, Vice President Hubert Humphrey was nominated for President.

The Republicans met a short time later in Miami. Few protesters showed up there. Richard Nixon was chosen to run for President. Nixon promised to end the Vietnam War. Richard Nixon was elected in 1968. He defeated Hubert Humphrey in a close race.

What did Richard Nixon promise at the Republican convention in Miami? He promised to end the war in Vietnam.

Section 2 Review

1. What was the Tet offensive?
2. Why were there antiwar protests during the Vietnam War?
3. **Critical Thinking** Why do you think Lyndon Johnson chose not to run for a second term as President?
4. **Write About History** U.S. soldiers were not used to guerrilla warfare. Write a paragraph describing the problems they faced.

More Review is provided in Exercise 119 of the Workbook.

1. A surprise attack by the Viet Cong on Saigon during a Vietnamese holiday called Tet.
2. Some Americans thought that the war was wrong and that the United States should withdraw its troops.
3. Possible answer: Lyndon Johnson felt that he would lose the election or that there was no solution to the Vietnam War.
4. Possible answer: The lack of knowledge about the land, fear of stepping on land mines and bombs, fear of surprise attacks, not trusting people in villages.

Section 3 The War Ends

Words to Know

Vietnamization	President Nixon's plan for turning over the fighting of the Vietnam War to the South Vietnamese
censor	to make changes in or to take parts out

Getting Started Discuss with students the responsibility a U.S. President has to tell the truth to the American people. Explain that at times the U.S. government was not completely honest with the American people about Vietnam.

Richard Nixon's election gave people hope that the Vietnam War would soon end. However, even though President Nixon promised a quick end to the war, it lasted four more years.

The War Spreads

In early 1969, President Nixon ordered U.S. planes to begin bombing the Ho Chi Minh Trail that ran through Vietnam, Laos, and Cambodia. Nixon believed this would stop the North Vietnamese from sending troops and supplies to the Viet Cong in the South. Cambodia had not taken sides in the war. However, the North Vietnamese had stored materials there.

History Fact

By April 1970, about 150,000 American troops had returned to the United States.

History Fact The United States spent $150 billion to fight the Vietnam War.

The bombing was planned to last for only a short time. However, the bombing lasted more than a year. During that time, the attacks were kept secret. American government papers were changed to say the bombings had taken place in Vietnam, not in Cambodia.

In 1969, President Nixon announced a plan called **Vietnamization.** This was President Nixon's plan for turning over the fighting of the Vietnam War to the South Vietnamese. This would force the South Vietnamese to do most of the fighting in the war. The United States would give aid, but no more troops, to South Vietnam.

Americans wanted the United States out of Vietnam. They remembered that in 1971, newspapers printed part of a secret report called the Pentagon Papers. It showed that President Johnson was planning to enter the war in the same year he promised not to send U.S. troops to Vietnam. The U.S. government tried to stop the printing of the Pentagon Papers. However, the owners of the newspapers went to court. They said that, under the U.S. Constitution, the government could not **censor** their newspapers. To censor is to make changes in or to take parts out. The court agreed.

The fighting lasted two more years. In January 1973, a peace agreement was signed in Paris, France.

What was President Nixon's Vietnamization plan?
To turn over the fighting in Vietnam to the South Vietnamese.

Great Names in History

MAYA YING LIN

In 1981, the Vietnam Veterans Memorial Fund held a contest. They were looking for someone to design a memorial to Vietnam veterans. Maya Ying Lin was an architecture student at Yale University. She entered the contest. People were surprised when 22-year-old Lin won the contest.

Maya Ying Lin

Lin designed two black granite walls. The names of the 58,156 Americans killed in Vietnam were carved into the memorial. Some people thought the design was beautiful. Others felt it was too simple to honor the soldiers who died in battle. They wanted Lin to change the design.

Lin refused. She said the focus of the design should be on the names of the people who died during the Vietnam War.

Critical Thinking Why do you think Maya Ying Lin refused to change her design? Possible answer: Lin was convinced that a simple wall gave her an opportunity to honor all the veterans; it was a noble look.

After the War

All U.S. troops left Vietnam by the end of March 1973. Without United States support, the South Vietnamese forces were soon defeated. Two years later, the North Vietnamese took over Saigon. Vietnam became a country united under Communist rule.

Not all veterans returning from the war were treated as veterans from other wars had been treated. Many veterans felt that Americans who protested the war did not respect the sacrifices they had made.

It was not until the 1980s that Americans recognized the courage and sacrifice of the men and women who had served in Vietnam. More than 58,000 Americans died in the Vietnam War. In 1982, the Vietnam Veterans Memorial was built in Washington, D.C. Maya Ying Lin, a Chinese American woman, designed the memorial.

How did many veterans feel when they returned after the war? Many veterans felt that the American people did not appreciate the sacrifices they had made during the war.

The names of all the men and women killed and missing in Vietnam are on the Vietnam Veterans Memorial.

Visual It was the idea of a Vietnam Veteran named Jan Scruggs to have a memorial erected for Vietnam veterans. Congress approved his idea.

Section 3 Review

1. Why did President Nixon order the bombing of the Ho Chi Minh Trail?
2. What happened in Vietnam after U.S. troops left?
3. **Critical Thinking** Why do you think President Nixon wanted to keep the bombing of Cambodia a secret?
4. **Write About Citizenship** You have been asked to print the Pentagon Papers in your newspaper. Write a paragraph explaining how you might defend your decision to print or not to print the papers.

More Review is provided in Exercise 120 of the Workbook.

1. President Nixon hoped that the bombing would stop the North Vietnamese from sending troops and supplies to the Viet Cong.
2. South Vietnamese forces crumbled; North Vietnamese took over Saigon.
3. Possible answer: President Nixon might have feared the negative reaction of many Americans.
4. For: The government does not have the right to deceive the American people; Against: Confidential government information should remain the property of the government

Chapter

28 Review

Summary Have students use this graphic organizer to outline the main ideas and details of the chapter.

Summary	Between 1960 and 1973, the United States was involved in a war to stop communism in Vietnam.
Section 1	The United States was afraid the Communists would take over Vietnam. At first, the United States sent advisers to help the South Vietnamese. Later it sent supplies and troops.
Section 2	The United States realized that fighting the Viet Cong would not be easy. Many Americans protested against the draft.
Section 3	President Nixon announced a plan called Vietnamization. The peace agreement in 1973 ended the role of the United States in Vietnam.

More Vocabulary Review is provided in Exercise 188 of the Classroom Resource Binder.

Vocabulary Review

Write *true* or *false*. If the statement is false, change the underlined term to make it true.

1. <u>Agent Orange</u> was the name of the Communist Vietnamese who hid in villages in South Vietnam. False: Viet Cong
2. Some college students who did not want to serve in the Vietnam War asked for a <u>deferment</u>. True
3. Viet Cong troops knew a lot about the <u>domino theory</u>. False: guerrilla warfare
4. A person who does not take an active part in a war is a <u>Vietnamization</u>. False: conscientious objector

1. U.S. government wanted to prevent a Communist takeover of Vietnam; U.S. offered advice, then participation in Vietnam. pp. 524–526 **2.** U.S. warships said they were attacked by North Vietnamese gunboats. p. 528 **3.** Nixon turned the fighting over to the South Vietnamese; the U.S. withdrew; South Vietnam lost to Communist North Vietnam. pp. 537–539 **4.** Yes: freedom of speech; No: It hurt the war effort; should support your country. p. 534 **5.** The Veterans served in an unpopular war; they had not been told the complete truth about the war. p. 539

Chapter Quiz

Write your answers in complete sentences.

1. How did the United States become involved in Vietnam?
2. What happened at the Gulf of Tonkin?
3. How did President Nixon's plan of Vietnamization help to bring about the end of the Vietnam War?
4. **Critical Thinking** Many Americans openly protested against the war. Do you think this should have been allowed?
5. **Critical Thinking** Why do you think some Vietnam veterans were angry with their government leaders?

Test Tip
Try to check all your answers before handing in your test paper.

Writing Tip
Reread your answers to make sure you have used enough facts, details, and examples to support the main idea.

Using the Timeline

Use the timeline on page 522–523 to answer the questions.

1. How many years after the beginning of the bombing of North Vietnam did the Tet offensive take place?
   3 years
2. Which event shows how some Americans felt about the war? Kent State protest

Group Activity See the Teacher's Planning Guide for a scoring rubric for this activity.

Group Activity

With your group, plan a time capsule to describe to future generations the antiwar protests of the Vietnam War years. You might include such items as antiwar songs, posters, news headlines, and letters from and to members of the armed forces. Make a list of what you will include.

Richard Nixon was the first American President to visit Communist China. These headlines announced Nixon's visit. How do you think Americans felt about Nixon's visit to China? Student responses might mention that Americans were probably pleased that the countries were trying to work together.

A Difficult Decade

1971
Supreme Court decides on school busing plan

1972
President Nixon reelected

President Nixon visits China and Soviet Union

1973
Arabs ban oil exports to United States

Watergate trial begins

1970 | **1971** | **1972** | **1973**

Additional activities and strategies to customize lessons can be found in the Teacher's Planning Guide.

Chapter 29 Entering a New Decade 1970–1975

ESL Note To help students understand the concept of scandal, have pairs discuss a time when their image of someone famous changed from positive to negative. Explain that in some countries, some of the actions Americans would consider as wrong are acceptable because of a difference in values.

Words to Know

normalize

détente

revenue sharing

affirmative action

stagflation

executive privilege

perjury

Words to Know These words are defined in the section in which they appear, as well as in the Glossary. Point out to students that *détente* is a French word meaning "to loosen or relax."

Learning Objectives

- Explain how President Nixon improved relations with China.
- Discuss how President Nixon handled the social and economic problems of the 1970s.
- Describe the steps that led to the Watergate scandal and the resignation of President Nixon.
- Explore how inflation affects the economy.

Project The project can be completed after students have finished Section 3. Students may wish to refer to the timeline to help place events in order.

Portfolio Project

Prepare ten short statements that describe the events of the 1970s. The statements will be used in a bulletin-board display. Place the statements in the order in which they happened. Mark those statements describing events that greatly changed peoples' daily lives.

1974
President Nixon resigns
Gerald Ford becomes President
President Ford pardons Nixon

1974 — 1975

1975
Communist forces take control of Cambodia

Timeline The timeline is divided into 1-year intervals. The events take place over a period of six years. Point to entries that show that President Nixon made great achievements in foreign affairs. Watergate, however, seriously damaged his presidency.

Section 1 Ending the Cold War

Words to Know

normalize	to continue normal dealings with a country, or begin again
détente	an easing of tension between nations

Getting Started Explain to students that conflicts can be resolved by negotiation. Explain that the United States renegotiated its relations with other countries after the Vietnam War.

As the Vietnam War came to an end, President Nixon turned his attention to other world problems. He searched for ways to have better relations with China, the Soviet Union, and other countries.

New Feelings Toward China

When Richard Nixon became President in 1969, the United States and China had been enemies for nearly 20 years. However, in 1971, China hinted that it wanted to improve relations with the United States. President Nixon agreed that it was time for the two countries to become friends. He and Secretary of State Henry Kissinger planned to **normalize** relations between the United States and Communist China. To normalize is to continue normal dealings with a country, or begin again.

Economics Fact

One fifth of the world's population lives in China.

In 1972, Richard Nixon became the first American President to visit China while in office. To Americans, this was one sign that the cold war was beginning to end.

Economics Fact In 1979, China introduced a one-child policy. Couples can have one child only. There have been 250 million fewer births since 1979.

Why was President Nixon ready to change relations with China? Nixon felt it was time for the United States and China to become friends.

Ties to the Soviet Union

The possibility of a friendship between the United States and China worried the Soviet Union. Soviet leaders feared that the United States and China might somehow work against them. They decided to try to improve relations with the United States.

In May 1972, a few months after returning from China, President Nixon went to the Soviet Union. No American President had ever visited the Soviet Union. Nixon's goal was to build **détente** between the United States and the Soviet Union. Détente means an easing of tension between nations.

President Nixon met with Soviet leader Leonid Brezhnev. They talked about nuclear weapons. Nixon and Brezhnev agreed to limit the number of new weapons each country would build. In addition, the United States agreed to sell wheat and other grains to the Soviet Union. The agreement helped bring food to the Soviet people and money to American farmers.

Why did Soviet leaders worry about the friendship between the United States and China? They feared that the U.S. and China might work together against the Soviet Union.

President Nixon is shown here with Soviet leader Leonid Brezhnev.

Visual When in the Soviet Union, Nixon visited Red Square. In Russia, the square is called *Krasnaya Ploschad.* The word *krasnaya* means both "red" and "beautiful."

Relations With Other Countries

President Nixon's trips to Communist countries made him popular in the United States. However, problems in other countries concerned many Americans.

In 1970, the people of Chile elected Salvador Allende, a leader who followed Communist ideas. The United States spent millions of dollars helping people in Chile fight Allende's government. In 1973, Allende was overthrown. However, the leaders who came into power were dictators. They murdered thousands of people and took away the civil rights of many others. Still the United States remained a friend of the new leaders. Many Americans felt this was wrong.

Remember
President Nixon secretly ordered the bombing of Cambodia in 1969.

The Vietnam War brought Vietnam and Cambodia to the attention of Americans. Once the Communists gained control of South Vietnam, thousands of anti-Communists tried to escape. In Cambodia, Communist forces took control in 1975. More than one million Cambodians were killed. By the end of the 1970s, thousands of Cambodian people had come to the United States.

How did the U.S. government help the people of Chile and Cambodia? Spent money to help people fight in Chile; accepted thousands of Cambodian immigrants

Section 1 Review

1. What did President Nixon's visit to China mean to Americans?
2. What did President Nixon and Leonid Brezhnev decide about nuclear weapons?
3. **Critical Thinking** Why do you think some Americans were angry about the U.S. support of dictators in Chile?
4. **Write About Economics** You are a wheat farmer in the Midwest. Write an article for a farm journal, giving your opinion of President Nixon's meeting with Brezhnev.

1. It was a sign that the cold war was ending.
2. They decided to limit the number of weapons each country could build.
3. Even though Salvador Allende followed Communist ideas, the leaders who replaced him were dictators who murdered thousands of people and took away many of their rights.
4. Student responses might mention optimism about the future of farming and suggestions for increasing profits.

More Review is provided in Exercise 121 of the Workbook.

Section 2 Changes at Home

Words to Know

revenue sharing	a program in which the federal government shares its income from taxes with state and local governments
affirmative action	a program for correcting the effects of discrimination
stagflation	a rise in prices together with a drop in business activity and more unemployment

Getting Started Ask students if they have ever managed a budget. Discuss how they would manage a budget that was no longer able to cover all the items they needed to buy. This is the problem many people faced in the early 1970s because of inflation and high unemployment.

President Nixon was mainly interested in how the United States and other nations got along. However, there were economic and social problems in the United States that he had to deal with as well. Nixon had plans for solving some of these problems.

New Plans for the United States

President Nixon believed that the major problems of the nation should be handled by the federal government in Washington, D.C. He believed that all other problems should be handled by state and local governments. In August 1969, Nixon told Americans of his new plan for the government.

Nixon's plan was to give the states more control. Housing programs, job training, and education would be controlled by the states. To help pay for the programs, the President developed a plan called **revenue sharing.** Revenue sharing is a program in which the federal government shares its income from taxes with state and local governments.

Over a five-year period, Nixon sent more than $30 billion in government money to the states.

Leaders of the states were free to spend the money on the programs that they felt would best help the people in their state. This plan showed Nixon's belief that states and local governments knew more about the needs of their people than the national government did.

Why did Nixon's revenue sharing plan give money to state and local governments? Nixon believed that state and local governments knew more about the needs of their people.

New Direction in Civil Rights

President Nixon put into action the policy of **affirmative action** that President Johnson had ordered in 1965. Affirmative action is a program for correcting the effects of discrimination.

Affirmative action programs increased opportunities in employment and education for minorities and women. Some businesses, schools, and government agencies had kept women, African Americans, Hispanic Americans, and other people out. Now they were required to give everyone the same opportunity.

Also during Richard Nixon's presidency, the Supreme Court made two important decisions that increased equal opportunities for Americans.

1. In 1969, the Supreme Court declared that segregated schools must be desegregated "at once." All-white schools and all-African American schools were no longer legal.
2. In 1971, the Supreme Court declared that a plan for busing students would start. Busing students to schools in other neighborhoods was a way to keep a racial balance.

What program did President Nixon order to give all people equal rights at work and in school? President Nixon ordered a program of affirmative action.

Other Problems at Home

The biggest problem Nixon faced was the economy. The Vietnam War was costing the United States billions of dollars a year. The government was spending more money than it collected in taxes. Money had to be borrowed to pay for the war.

The number of jobless, or unemployed, Americans rose in the early 1970s. At the same time, there was inflation, or the steep rise in the price of goods. Most experts felt that if unemployment was up, prices should fall. However, that did not happen.

Adding to the problems of the economy was an oil shortage. In 1973, Israel fought a war with Egypt and Syria. The United States supported Israel. This angered the Arab states in the Middle East. As a result, they banned oil shipments to the United States. Suddenly Americans faced a gasoline shortage.

Visual Tell students that many states rationed gasoline in the early 1970s. Whether the last digit in a license plate was an odd or even number determined the day on which a person could buy gasoline.

In the early 1970s, Americans often waited for hours to buy gas.

Americans suffered from the gas shortage in many ways. The price of a gallon of gas went up 40 percent. People could buy gas for their cars only on certain days. Sometimes there was no gas at all.

The cost of travel by car, bus, and airplane also went up. The cost of food went up too because everything cost more to make and carry. The price of home heating oil also increased. These rising prices increased inflation.

In the 1970s, inflation continued. Unemployment increased and business activity dropped. This became known as **stagflation.**

What were the biggest economic problems facing the United States in the early 1970s? Unemployment and inflation

Section 2 Review

1. What programs was revenue sharing used for?
2. Whom did affirmative action programs help?
3. **Critical Thinking** How do you think the state governments felt about President Nixon's revenue sharing?
4. **Write About Economics** Prepare a chart with the following two headings: *The Vietnam War* and *1973 War in the Middle East*. Under each heading, list the ways that these foreign affairs changed the daily lives of Americans.

More Review is provided in Exercise 123 of the Workbook.

1. Revenue sharing was used for such programs as housing, job training, and education.
2. Affirmative action programs helped women, African Americans, Hispanic Americans, and other people who had not been treated fairly.
3. Possible answers: States were happy to control their own programs; states were concerned about money for other programs not covered by revenue sharing; concerned about running out of money.
4. Vietnam: inflation, fewer jobs; Middle East: oil shortage, higher prices for gas, higher prices for bus and airplane tickets, higher price for heating homes

CONNECTING HISTORY AND ECONOMICS
Inflation

Inflation is a rise in prices. If the amount you pay for groceries is $5.00 more than it was for the same groceries last year, it probably is the result of inflation. With inflation, the purchasing power of the dollar drops. This means that you are spending more money for fewer goods. Spending $50.00 during inflation brings in fewer goods than spending $50.00 during better economic times.

A little inflation in an economy is a sign that business is doing well. People are working and spending money. However, too much inflation is not good for an economy. Usually, wages that people earn do not increase as prices rise. People have a difficult time paying for basic needs, such as food, clothing, and shelter.

It takes more money to buy goods during inflation.

During the time President Nixon was in office, several things were done to control inflation. One plan was a freeze on wages and prices for 90 days. That meant that salaries and prices for goods could not go up for 90 days. This did not work. Problems with inflation continued while Nixon was in office.

Answer the questions below.

1. What does inflation do to the value of a dollar?

2. What did President Nixon do to control inflation?

CHALLENGE How might inflation make it difficult to plan future spending?

1. Inflation lowers the value of the dollar. **2.** President Nixon put a freeze on wages and prices for 90 days. **CHALLENGE** Possible answer: With inflation, people are not sure of the future value of their money.

Section 3 Watergate

Words to Know

executive privilege	the right of a President to withhold important information from other branches of the government
perjury	lying in court while under oath

Getting Started Ask students what a role model is and if they expect the President of the U.S. to be a role model. How would they feel if the President broke the law? Explain that President Nixon resigned from office because he was about to be impeached.

Richard Nixon accomplished a great deal as President. However, for almost two years, Americans heard about dishonesty and corruption in the President's office. The events caused Nixon to become the first President to resign from office.

Shocking News

In June 1972, the media reported that five men had been arrested in Washington, D.C. They had broken into the headquarters of the Democratic National Committee in a building called the Watergate.

The news shocked many Americans. The shock grew worse when it was discovered that the men worked for the committee to reelect the President. They had been hired to break into the headquarters.

At first, not many people connected the Watergate break-in to President Nixon. Some people knew that the President wanted to serve a second term. They also knew that he had asked his close advisers to help get him reelected. That was not unusual.

Soon Nixon's office reported that what happened had been investigated. It was only a break-in. In November 1972, President Nixon was reelected in a landslide victory over Senator George McGovern.

Even after the election, the media was not satisfied. Reporters kept digging up facts. Two reporters, Bob Woodward and Carl Bernstein, continued to investigate the scandal. Finally, on January 8, 1973, five people involved in the break-in were brought to trial. At their trial, they admitted that they had been trying to put special listening wires into the phones to listen in on Democratic party plans. They tried to steal information that could be used to help get Nixon reelected. They also admitted that they gave untrue information about certain candidates to the media.

Early in 1973, Americans learned more about the break-in. The Watergate group had been paid with Republican campaign money to break into the Watergate. An attempt was made to cover up the burglars' connection to President Nixon. Then, in May 1973, the Senate began to investigate the Watergate situation. Many people who had worked at the White House told their stories.

Great Names in History

WOODWARD AND BERNSTEIN

Bob Woodward and Carl Bernstein were reporters for the *Washington Post*. In June 1972, they heard about a break-in at the Democratic campaign headquarters. They learned that men working on President Nixon's reelection campaign were behind the break-in.

At first, no one listened to Woodward and Bernstein. After Nixon was reelected, they continued to research the story. They made sure everything they wrote was true. In the end, their stories brought attention to the Watergate scandal.

Critical Thinking Why do you think Woodward and Bernstein continued to write about the Watergate scandal? They probably felt it was their duty as journalists to report the truth to the American people.

Bob Woodward and Carl Bernstein

One man who had advised the President was John Dean. Dean told the senators that Nixon had known about the cover-up. He also said the White House had a list of people whom it called political enemies. Dean said Nixon planned to hurt his political enemies by having their tax returns investigated and by spreading false stories about them in the media.

Why did a group of men break into the Democratic headquarters in the Watergate building? To learn about the Democratic party campaign plans

The Office Tapes

During the Senate investigation, it came out that there was a tape-recording system in the Oval Office at the White House. The President had secretly put in a system to tape people in his office or on the phone. Senators then asked for copies of the tapes.

At first, President Nixon did not want to hand over the tapes. He said that he had **executive privilege** to keep them. Executive privilege is the right of a President to withhold important information from the other branches of the government.

Several members of the executive branch tried to get Nixon to give up the tapes. Finally, the case went to the Supreme Court. While the case was in Court, it was clear that a vote to impeach Nixon could not be avoided. It would be the first time that such charges had been brought against a U.S. President since 1868. In that year, the House of Representatives voted to impeach President Andrew Johnson.

The Watergate scandal lasted for more than a year. Some of Nixon's advisers went on trial for such crimes as **perjury.** Perjury is lying in court while under oath. In the end, about 40 people in Nixon's administration were charged with crimes.

In the summer of 1974, the Supreme Court ordered Nixon to release the tapes. The tapes proved that Nixon knew about the cover-up. He had even helped to plan the cover-up.

Nixon was in serious trouble. Most Americans no longer believed him. Members of his own party could not defend his actions. On August 9, 1974, Richard Nixon became the first U.S. President to resign.

After Nixon resigned, Gerald Ford became President. In 1974, President Ford granted a pardon to Richard Nixon. Many Americans were not happy with this decision. It meant that Nixon could not be taken to trial. He would not be punished for any of his crimes.

What did the tapes that President Nixon was asked to release prove? The tapes proved that President Nixon had helped to plan the cover-up.

Section 3 Review

1. What events led up to the Senate investigation of Watergate?
2. Who decided that Nixon did not have executive privilege to keep his tapes?
3. **Critical Thinking** Why do you think it was important to find out when the President knew about the Watergate break-in?
4. **Write About Citizenship** Write a paragraph in which you describe the kind of person a leader of a community or of a country should be.

1. The media reported that five men had been arrested for breaking into the Watergate building.
2. The Supreme Court
3. Possible answer: So that the extent of the President's guilt might be properly evaluated
4. Possible answer: A person who is honest, trustworthy, fair, and courageous, in addition to having the knowledge and experience needed for leadership

More Review is provided in Exercise 124 of the Workbook.

Chapter 29 Review

Summary Have students use this graphic organizer to outline the main ideas and details of the chapter.

Summary	**President Nixon worked toward building friendships with China and the Soviet Union. After the Watergate scandal, Nixon resigned as President.**
Section 1	Nixon wanted the United States to change its feelings toward China and the Soviet Union.
Section 2	Nixon introduced revenue sharing as a way to give the state and local governments more control. He supported affirmative action.
Section 3	Nixon wanted to be reelected. He and his advisers used unlawful means to do this. This led to an investigation. Nixon resigned in 1974.

affirmative action
perjury
executive privilege
détente
revenue sharing

More Vocabulary Review is provided in Exercise 194 of the Classroom Resource Binder.

Vocabulary Review

Fill in the blank with a term from the list.

1. ___ is an easing of tensions between nations. Détente

2. Because of ______ , many groups were able to get ahead. affirmative action

3. ___ helps state governments provide for the needs of their citizens. Revenue sharing

4. The President can claim the right of ___ . executive privilege

5. People who knowingly lie in court are guilty of ___. perjury

1. President Nixon's plan for improving relations with the Soviet Union p. 545 2. President Nixon felt the federal government should handle major problems of the nation. p. 547 3. Nixon knew about the cover-up; the White House had a list of political enemies; Nixon planned to hurt those enemies. pp. 552–555 4. Possible answer: President Nixon was much more successful in foreign relations than in domestic relations. pp. 544–546; 549–550 5. Possible answer: Americans learned that their leaders do not always act in an honorable way. pp. 552–555

Chapter Quiz

Write your answers in complete sentences.

1. What was the policy of détente?
2. According to President Nixon, what was the role of the federal government?
3. What did the Senate investigation of Watergate reveal?
4. **Critical Thinking** Why might some people say that Nixon was more interested in dealing with other nations than with problems at home?
5. **Critical Thinking** What do you think Americans learned from the Watergate incident?

Test Tip
To prepare for a test, write key points on index cards.

Writing Tip
A written piece that persuades is one in which the writer gives his or her opinion about a topic. The writer tries to make the reader agree with his or her opinion.

Using the Timeline

Use the timeline on pages 542–543 to answer the questions.

1. How many years after his reelection did President Nixon resign? 2 years
2. What event led to an increase in gas prices?
The Arab ban on oil exports

Group Activity See the Teacher's Planning Guide for a scoring rubric for this activity.

Group Activity

With your group, make a chart in which you trace the steps in the Watergate incident that proved that justice was done.

Critical Thinking 1. Many African Americans felt nonviolence was no longer the best way to gain civil rights. 2. The United States hoped to stop communism there. 3. He wanted better working conditions for grape pickers. 4. President Nixon was about to face charges of impeachment.

Unit 9 Review

Critical Thinking

Give one reason why each of the following events happened.

1. Black power becomes a new slogan for many African Americans.
2. The United States sends help to South Vietnam.
3. César Chávez called for a boycott of California grapes.
4. President Nixon resigns.

Building Your Skills

Put the following essay-writing steps in the order in which they should be followed.

1. Write a rough draft. 4
2. Carefully rewrite your essay. 5
3. Write one sentence that gives the main idea of your essay. 2
4. Make an outline. 3
5. Choose a subject. 1

Who Did It?

Write the name of the person who took each action listed.

1. He was an African American who came to believe that all people could work together for equal rights. Malcolm X
2. She designed the Vietnam Veterans Memorial. Maya Ying Lin
3. As President of the United States, he visited China and the Soviet Union. Richard Nixon

Writing an Essay

Answer one of the following essay topics.

See the Answer Key for a detailed answer.

1. Discuss the goals of such groups as Latinos or African Americans during the 1960s and 1970s.
2. Explain how the Vietnam War was different from other wars in U.S. history.
3. Describe how you think future generations might judge President Nixon.

Linking Past and Present

Discuss how veterans from World Wars I and II were treated. How did this compare to the way Vietnam War veterans were treated?

Veterans from World Wars I and II felt proud, supported. Vietnam veterans returned to a country in which they were treated indifferently. They did not feel they were supported or respected.

Unit Opener Use the primary source to set the tone for the time period.

Unit 10 Forward to the Future

This photograph shows the Oval Office at the White House. President George W. Bush is holding a meeting with his advisers. In the Oval Office, the U.S. President makes many important decisions. Why are the decisions of the U.S. President important to both Americans and people around the world?
The decisions of the U.S. President impact both the United States and the world.

> *"I ask you to be citizens: citizens, not spectators; citizens, not subjects; responsible citizens, building communities of service and a nation of character."*
>
> —from the Inaugural Address of George W. Bush, January 20, 2001

Primary Source The outcome of the 2000 presidential election, which took 35 days to resolve, favored George W. Bush, Texas governor and son of George Herbert Walker Bush, the forty-first President.

President Jimmy Carter helped Egyptian leader Anwar Sadat and Israeli leader Menachem Begin reach a peace agreement. President Carter appeared on the cover of a national news magazine. How would you describe the actions of the leaders?
The leaders are smiling, their hands are clasped in a handshake.

Changes at Home and Far Away

1976 Jimmy Carter elected

1979 American hostages taken in Iran
Camp David Accords

1980 Ronald Regan elected

1981 Hostages freed

1982 U.S. Marines sent to Lebanon

1984 Reagan reelected

1976 | 1978 | 1980 | 1982 | 1984

Additional activities and strategies to customize lessons can be found in the Teacher's Planning Guide.

Chapter 30 Changes at Home and Abroad 1976–1988

ESL Note Point out to students that *contras* and *glasnost* are foreign words that come to English from other languages. *Contra* is Spanish for "against." *Glasnost* is Russian for "openness."

Words to Know

human rights

dissident

hostage

federal deficit

national debt

contra

special prosecutor

glasnost

Words to Know These words are defined in the section in which they appear, as well as in the Glossary. Point out to students that four of the words are open compound words. To understand them, think of the two words that make up each one.

Learning Objectives

- Identify successes and problems President Carter faced at home.
- Explain how President Carter helped bring peace between Egypt and Israel.
- Describe the Iran hostage crisis.
- Discuss President Reagan's social and economic policies.
- Describe President Reagan's foreign policy.
- Identify tips for taking a test.

Project This project cannot be done until Section 3 is completed. However, students can note the interesting events as they read.

Portfolio Project

In this chapter, you will read about some fairly recent events. You or older members of your family may remember some of these events. Interview an older person about an event in this chapter. Write your questions first. Take notes during the interview. Record answers later.

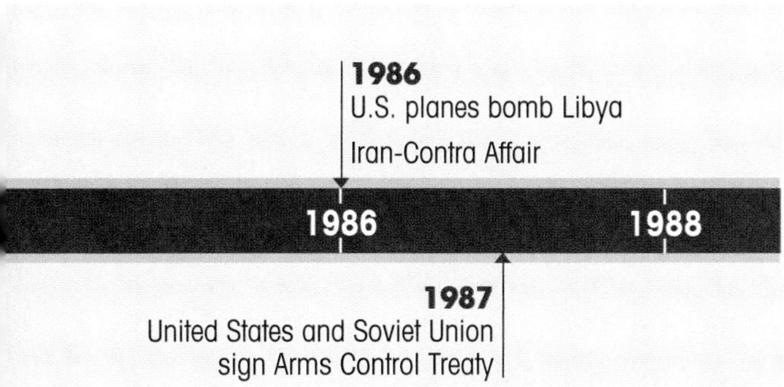

Timeline The timeline is divided into 2-year intervals. The events take place over a period of 12 years. During this time period, foreign affairs kept U.S. Presidents busy.

Section 1 A New Kind of Leader

Words to Know

human rights	the basic freedoms that all people should have
dissident	a person who strongly disagrees with government policies or its rule
hostage	a person who is held captive until certain demands are met

Getting Started Discuss the meaning of a peace negotiator. Ask students to write a job description for such a person. Explain that Jimmy Carter met with several international leaders to achieve peace during his presidency. How do you think he did?

In 1976, Jimmy Carter was the Democratic party's candidate for President. Carter had never held national office before. That was fine with many Americans. They were tired of scandal in Washington, D.C. They wanted an outsider in the White House. President Gerald Ford was the Republican candidate. Some Americans felt Ford should not have pardoned Nixon. They also blamed Ford for the poor economy.

This is a campaign button that supports Jimmy Carter for President.

Visual Jimmy Carter won 297 electoral votes in the 1976 election. Gerald Ford won 241.

Successes and Problems at Home

Jimmy Carter had been an officer in the U.S. Navy, a peanut farmer, and the governor of Georgia. He was known for his business success and his concern for equal rights. Jimmy Carter promised that he could be trusted. "I'll never lie to you," he told Americans. Many Americans believed him. In 1976, Carter defeated Ford in a close election.

One of Carter's first acts was to pardon young men who had avoided the draft during the Vietnam War. In addition, he created the Department of Education and the Department of Energy. He named women, Latinos, and African Americans to his Cabinet and staff. He also named several women as judges.

During Carter's first year, the economy improved. Then inflation and joblessness increased again. Carter tried different ways to slow down inflation and create more jobs. For example, Carter tried spending more government money. Then he tried spending less government money. He asked businesses to agree to keep prices and wages down. None of these policies worked.

High oil and gasoline prices were a big part of inflation. Carter tried to get Americans to use less oil and gasoline. However, the demand for oil stayed high. The oil-producing countries of the Middle East kept raising their prices. Many people wondered whether Carter could solve the nation's economic problems.

What were some early successes of the Carter presidency? He created new departments, named diverse groups to his Cabinet and staff, and named women as judges.

Relations with the Soviet Union

In foreign policy, Carter had strong ideas. Carter believed that all nations should give **human rights** to their citizens. Human rights are the basic freedoms that all people should have. For example, human rights include the right to life, liberty, and equality. However, many nations did not permit basic freedoms. Carter limited or stopped trade with some countries that did not give basic freedoms to everyone. Most of the countries were in Africa, Asia, and Latin America.

Relations between the Soviet Union and the United States became worse while Carter was President. First, the Soviets did not like the way Carter openly supported **dissidents** in the Soviet Union. A dissident is a person who strongly disagrees with government policies or its rule. Dissidents in the Soviet Union wanted greater freedom to speak out.

Then, in 1979, Carter made two decisions after the Soviet Union invaded the country of Afghanistan. To

Remember
An embargo is a government order that stops trade with other countries.

punish the Soviets, he put an embargo on selling U.S. grain to the Soviet Union. Also, Carter announced that U.S. athletes would not be allowed to take part in the summer Olympics in the Soviet Union. These decisions pleased some Americans but made others angry.

How did relations with the Soviet Union change while Carter was President? Relations between the United States and the Soviet Union became worse.

The Camp David Accords

Carter's biggest success in foreign policy was with Israel and Egypt, in the Middle East. Israel became a nation in 1948. Since that time, its Arab neighbors refused to accept Israel as a nation. Fighting between Israel and Arab countries often broke out.

In 1978, President Carter helped bring the countries of Egypt and Israel together to make an important agreement. Anwar el-Sadat was the leader of Egypt. Menachem Begin was the leader of Israel. These two leaders and President Carter met at Camp David, in Maryland. Begin and Sadat signed the Camp David Accords, or agreement. It said Egypt would enter into peaceful relations and trade with Israel. Israel would remove troops from land that belonged to Egypt.

The Camp David Accords could not bring peace in the Middle East. However, it was a step toward ending years of hatred.

What happened at Camp David? Leaders agreed to peaceful relations. Israel would remove troops from Egyptian land.

The Iran Hostage Crisis

In another part of the Middle East, Carter did not have success. In 1979, a religious leader called the Ayatollah Khomeini led a successful revolution against the government of Iran and its leader, the shah. The shah asked to come to the United States for cancer treatment. The United States said, "Yes."

On November 4, 1979, followers of the Ayatollah took over the U.S. embassy in Tehran, Iran's capital. They were angry that the United States had helped the shah. These revolutionaries took about 50 Americans as **hostages.** A hostage is a person who is held captive until certain demands are met. The Iranians said the hostages would not be let go until the shah was returned to Iran. The shah had treated his enemies badly when he was in power. Now they wanted to put him on trial.

Carter would not send the shah back to Iran. He tried to use diplomacy, or talking between countries, to end the crisis. Carter even ordered a rescue mission to Iran. However, the mission failed. A rescue helicopter crashed, and eight men were killed.

The hostage crisis continued for more than a year. The shah died in July 1980. However, the Iranians would

Visual At the beginning of the crisis, 66 Americans were held hostage. The revolutionaries released most of the women and all African American hostages.

These men are returning home to America after being held hostage in Iran for 444 days.

not let the hostages go. In 1980, as the crisis continued, President Carter ran for reelection against Ronald Reagan.

Reagan felt that Carter did not handle the hostage crisis well. He said the hostage crisis made the United States seem like a helpless giant. On top of that, he pointed to the poor economy, which Carter had not been able to fix.

Carter lost the election to Reagan in a landslide. After the Reagan victory, the hostage crisis ended. After 444 days, the Iranians freed the American hostages. The Americans left Iran on January 20, 1981. That was the same day Ronald Reagan took office.

Why did Iranian revolutionaries take over the U.S. embassy? They were angry that the United States had allowed the shah into the country for cancer treatment. They wanted the shah to return to Iran to face trial.

Section 1 Review

1. What happened to the economy while Carter was President?

2. What was one of Carter's major foreign policy successes?

3. **Critical Thinking** Do you think the shah of Iran should have been allowed to come to the United States for treatment? Explain your answer.

4. **Write About Citizenship** President Carter supported Soviet dissidents. Write a letter to the President explaining why you agree or disagree with his position.

More Review is provided in Exercise 125 of the Workbook.

1. Inflation and joblessness increased.
2. Camp David Accords between Egypt and Israel
3. Possible answer: The decision was difficult because the shah had been friendly with the United States, and he was in trouble. On the other hand, this action was sure to anger the new government of Iran.
4. Possible answer: Agree—Students may point out that the Soviet dissidents wanted freedoms that U.S. citizens already had. Disagree—Students may point out that Carter should not have interfered with another country's problems.

BUILDING YOUR SKILLS
Taking a Test

When you take a test, you have to answer questions in a certain amount of time. Some tests have essay questions that need longer answers. Other tests have short questions, such as true or false, multiple choice, fill in the blank, and matching. Some tests have both essay questions and short questions.

These tips can help you do well on a test. Use them the next time you take a test.

1. Quickly look over the whole test. Try to get an idea of how much time you will need to finish each part of the test.
2. Read the directions carefully.
3. Look for key words in an essay question, such as *compare, contrast, define, describe, explain, evaluate,* or *review.*
4. Answer the easiest questions first.
5. In multiple-choice tests, read all of the choices before you answer. First, decide which answers are wrong. Then, if you are still not sure of the answer, make your best guess from the remaining choices.
6. Try to leave some time to check over your work.

Apply the Skill

Write five test questions about Section 1. Use key words to write two essay questions. Then write three short questions, such as true or false or fill in the blank. Answer your questions and trade questions with a partner. Check each other's answers.

Section 2 Turning Toward Conservatism

Words to Know

federal deficit	the difference between the amount of money the government spends and what it collects
national debt	the amount of money the federal government owes

Getting Started Have students brainstorm a list of high-paying jobs and low-paying jobs today. Discuss the kinds of jobs that pay the most. Point out that some people became very wealthy during the 1980s, but not everyone shared in the good times.

When Ronald Reagan became President, the United States faced serious problems. The nation faced high inflation, a recession, and joblessness. Relations with the Soviet Union were at a low point. However, Reagan wanted Americans to feel good about themselves and their country. He had a gift for talking to Americans. He often told stories from his past. Reagan came to be called the "Great Communicator."

A Difficult Beginning

President Ronald Reagan

Visual Ronald Reagan had appeared in 50 films and became interested in politics during his six terms as president of the Screen Actors Guild.

Ronald Reagan had been a movie and television star, a union leader, and the governor of California. At age 69, he was the oldest person to become President.

Two months after Reagan took office, a disturbed man named John Hinkley, Jr., tried to kill him. James Brady, Reagan's press secretary was also shot. Reagan's good humor after the shooting won the hearts of many Americans. Since Reagan was a Republican, he said to his surgeons, "Please tell me you're Republicans." Reagan recovered after the shooting. However, James Brady never walked again without help.

What happened to Reagan two months after he took office? He was shot by a man and had to have surgery.

Ideas About Government and Society

President Reagan felt the federal government should be smaller. He said the government took too much tax money away from people and made too many rules for businesses. In 1981, Reagan said, "Government is not the solution to our problems; government is the problem." Many Americans agreed.

Conservative groups helped Reagan win the election. These groups came to be called the New Right. Many members of the New Right were business leaders who wanted lower taxes and fewer laws on business.

Remember
A conservative is a person who wants the government to do less for its citizens.

Other groups in the New Right, such as the Moral Majority, were new to politics. They included religious groups that had never supported a candidate before. Many people in the religious right followed televangelists or preachers who had radio or television shows. The Reverend Jerry Falwell and the Reverend Pat Robertson were two of these preachers. The religious right did not feel that special programs for minorities and women were needed. They wanted a return to traditional family life. Many groups wanted prayer in public schools.

During the 1980s, the New Right elected many conservative candidates to Congress. These lawmakers and their programs became known as the Reagan Revolution.

What was Reagan's idea about the role of the federal government? It should be small, not take so much money from people, not make too many rules for businesses.

Ideas About the Economy

President Reagan had new ideas for fixing the economy. He believed that cutting taxes on people and businesses would make the economy grow. The tax cut would mean that people would have more money to buy goods and services. Businesses would create jobs to provide those goods and services.

Reagan felt that if the economy improved, people would be able to get jobs, health care, food, and shelter without government help. Reagan and Congress worked quickly to accomplish these goals. They cut taxes on people and businesses. They increased spending for defense. Finally, they cut spending on many education and social programs.

Reagan's programs both helped and hurt the economy. Inflation and joblessness fell, and many businesses did well. However, **federal deficits** grew. A federal deficit is the difference between the amount of money the government spends and what it collects. When there is a deficit, the government has to borrow money. Each year there is a federal deficit, the **national debt** grows. The national debt is the amount of money the federal government owes.

What did President Reagan believe would help the economy grow? If people paid less taxes and had more money to spend, businesses would grow.

Citizenship Link

GERALDINE FERRARO

The Equal Rights Amendment (ERA) was not ratified in 1982. After its defeat, women's groups worked hard to get women elected to public office. More women began to run for public office. In 1984, the Democratic presidential candidate, Walter Mondale, chose Geraldine Ferraro to run for Vice President. Ferraro was a member of Congress from New York. She was the first woman to run as a major party candidate.

A Geraldine Ferraro campaign button

Ferraro knew she was making history. During the 1984 Democratic Convention in San Francisco, she said, "By choosing an American woman to run for our nation's second-highest office, you send a powerful message to all Americans. There are no doors we cannot unlock. We will place no limits on achievement."

Critical Thinking Why do you think women's groups felt it was important to get more women elected to public office? Possible answer: If more women were in public office, then they could pass more laws to protect women's rights.

The 1984 Election

Reagan was a popular President. Many Americans shared his strong belief that the government should not help poor people. These Americans thought churches, charities, and families should provide help. Some women, African Americans, and other groups felt Reagan's programs hurt them. However, most people trusted him to run the country.

In 1984, Democrats tried to win back the White House. They chose Walter Mondale to run for President. Mondale chose Geraldine Ferraro to run for Vice President. Ferraro was the first woman from a major political party to run for this office.

Reagan and his Vice President, George Bush, won the election easily. Reagan's economic policies continued. However, in 1987, the stock market crashed, or lost a great deal of value. After the crash, Reagan and Congress agreed to raise taxes. The tax increase was mostly on wealthy people and on businesses.

Why was President Reagan such a popular President?
Many Americans agreed with his ideas and trusted his leadership.

Section 2 Review

1. What did the New Right want?
2. What two things did Reagan and Congress do quickly after Reagan took office in 1981?
3. **Critical Thinking** Do you think it is the job of government to help poor people? Explain.
4. **Write About Economics** During the time Reagan was President, the federal budget was not balanced. Why do you think it is important to balance the federal budget? Explain your answer in writing.

1. Less government money for special programs, a greater emphasis on religion and traditional family values
2. Cut taxes, increased defense spending
3. Some students may think that only government can help; other students may favor family and other private help.
4. Possible answer: Should show an understanding of keeping budgets balanced. When there is not enough money, the government will borrow to get enough money.

More Review is provided in Exercise 126 of the Workbook.

Section 3 Acting in a Changing World

Words to Know

contra	a rebel fighting the Sandinista government in Nicaragua
special prosecutor	an investigator who looks into the actions of the President and other high officials
glasnost	a policy that allows open discussion about Soviet life and politics

Getting Started Discuss with students whether or not the United States should send U.S. troops to help other countries. Some people felt that the powerful role of the United States in the world came with the responsibility of helping other countries.

President Reagan believed the United States should play an active role in the world. Reagan wanted to fight communism around the world. He also wanted to keep peace in the Middle East and other areas. Many Americans agreed with Reagan's policies. Others protested against them.

Sending the Troops

Reagan took military action in many parts of the world. Sometimes the United States acted alone. At other times, U.S. troops were part of a UN peacekeeping force.

Remember
The domino theory says that if one country falls to communism, nearby countries will fall next.

Reagan was afraid that countries in nearby Central America would become Communist. He felt the domino theory might work in Central America.

In the 1980s, Reagan decided to help anti-Communist groups in Nicaragua and El Salvador. In Nicaragua, the United States gave weapons and supplies to the rebels, or **contras.** A contra was a rebel fighting the Sandinista government. The Sandinista government had Communist leaders. Reagan blockaded ports in Nicaragua to stop supplies to the Sandinistas from the Soviets and Cuba.

In El Salvador, the United States helped the government, too. Reagan felt the rebels were Communists. The U.S. military trained special groups of soldiers from El Salvador. These soldiers kidnapped and killed suspected Communist rebels. In 1980, they kidnapped and killed four American women who worked with the Catholic Church.

Many Americans disagreed with U.S. actions in Central America. These Americans wrote letters and protested against U.S. policies in Central America. They said the United States was fighting against poor people in Central America.

Chart Point out to students that only the conflict in Libya was an act of retaliation. No other conflict affected U.S. citizens directly.

Why did Reagan help the contras in Nicaragua?
Reagan felt the Sandinista government was Communist.

Trouble Spots Around the World, 1982–1987

Place	Location	Problem	U.S. Action
Lebanon	Middle East	Fighting broke out between groups in Lebanon. Earlier, Israel and the Palestinians in Lebanon had fought.	In 1982, U.S. Marines were sent as part of a UN peacekeeping force.
Grenada	Caribbean	The Prime Minister died. Reagan feared Communists might take over the country.	In 1983, U.S. troops helped the non-Communist government come to power.
Libya	Africa	Terrorists killed an American soldier in Germany. Libya was a training center for terrorism.	In 1986, U.S. planes bombed Libya.
Persian Gulf	Middle East	Iran and Iraq were at war. Iran tried to stop shipping in the Persian Gulf.	In 1987, U.S. ships were sent to protect trade in the Persian Gulf. They were ordered to fire when fired upon.

Chart Study

1. When and where were the U.S. Marines part of a UN peacekeeping force? 1982, Lebanon
2. Why did U.S. planes bomb Libya? It was a center of terrorism. Terrorists killed an American soldier in Germany.

History Fact

The first case for a special prosecutor was the Watergate scandal. Since that time, special prosecutors have looked into the actions of Presidents Carter, Reagan, Bush, and Clinton.

History Fact In June 1999, Congress did not renew the special prosecutor law. Some people felt that the independent counsel had too much power. Others felt that the office was supposed to increase trust in government, but, in reality, it had had the opposite effect.

Iran-Contra Affair

Since the Iran hostage crisis, Congress had outlawed selling weapons to Iran. In the mid-1980s, Congress also outlawed military aid to the contras in Nicaragua. However, in 1986, Americans found out that some of Reagan's advisers had been secretly selling weapons to Iran. They had been using the money to buy weapons for the contras.

Many Americans were angered by the news. They still felt that Iran was an enemy because of the hostage crisis. They also felt that the contras were cruel and corrupt.

Reagan said that he did not know about the weapons or the aid. However, Congress voted to have a **special prosecutor** look into the Iran-Contra affair. A special prosecutor is an investigator who looks into the actions of the President and other high officials.

The special prosecutor found that Reagan's advisers had broken the law. The prosecutor had no proof that Reagan had broken the law. However, the Iran-Contra affair hurt Reagan's reputation in America.

What was the Iran-Contra affair? Reagan's advisers sold weapons to Iran and gave the money to contras in Nicaragua.

Changes in the Soviet Union

When President Reagan took office in 1981, Communist governments in Europe were still strong. The United States and the Soviet Union were still the superpowers of the world. Reagan called the Soviet Union an "evil empire." He raised defense spending, knowing that the Soviets would have to match it. The Soviets would need to spend money they did not really have.

By the middle of the 1980s, the Soviet Union was in trouble. The economy could not meet people's everyday needs. Soviet citizens spent much of their days waiting in line for poorly made goods.

In 1985, Mikhail Gorbachev, the Soviet leader, knew he must do something to improve the economy. He called for a policy of **glasnost.** This policy allowed open discussion about Soviet life and politics. He tried to be more friendly with the United States, too. Gorbachev and Reagan met several times. In 1987, they signed an arms control treaty. In 1989, Gorbachev withdrew troops from Afghanistan.

Gorbachev wanted to reform, or change, the Communist government in the Soviet Union. However, Gorbachev did not want to end Communist rule. He did not know that Eastern Europeans were about to overthrow Communist governments. Soon, the Soviet Union would break apart. The cold war was about to end.

What did Gorbachev want to do in the Soviet Union? Reform the Communist government in the Soviet Union, have better relations with the United States

President Reagan and Soviet leader Mikhail Gorbachev

Visual Mikhail Gorbachev won the Nobel Peace Prize in 1990 for the significant role he played in reducing East-West tensions.

Section 3 Review

1. What did Reagan think might happen in Central America?
2. Why did many Americans get angry about the Iran-Contra affair?
3. **Critical Thinking** Why do you think Gorbachev wanted to be friends with the United States?
4. **Write About Geography** You are an adviser to President Reagan. List steps to show how the domino theory might work in Central America.

More Review is provided in Exercise 127 of the Workbook.

1. Communists might take over and then other countries close to the United States might become Communist. **2.** They felt Iran was the enemy because of the hostage crisis and the contras were cruel and corrupt. **3.** Possible answer: Gorbachev wanted to spend less money on defense. Therefore, he would need to be friendlier with the United States. 4. Possible answer: Should show an understanding of the position of Central America relative to Mexico and the United States

Chapter

30 Review

Summary Have students use this graphic organizer to outline the main ideas and details of the chapter.

Summary	Presidents Carter and Reagan faced problems at home and abroad. These problems included the economy, communism, and keeping peace in the Middle East.
Section 1	President Carter had successes and failures. He helped bring peace between Israel and Egypt. However, he could not fix the economy or end the Iran hostage crisis. Carter lost the election of 1980 to Ronald Reagan.
Section 2	President Reagan changed the U.S. economy. He cut taxes and social programs and increased defense spending.
Section 3	President Reagan believed in an active foreign policy. During Reagan's presidency, the Soviet Union weakened.

glasnost
hostage
dissident
contra
federal deficit

More Vocabulary Review is provided in Exercise 202 of the Classroom Resource Binder.

Vocabulary Review

Write the term from the list that matches each definition below.

1. A person who strongly disagrees with the government dissident
2. Greater freedom in the Soviet Union glasnost
3. A person who is captured and held until some demand is met hostage
4. What happens when the U.S. government spends more than it collects federal deficit
5. A group of rebels in Nicaragua contras

1. They were high and added to inflation. p. 563 **2.** He emphasized human rights; supported Soviet dissidents; disliked Soviets for invading Afghanistan; put an embargo on grain; skipped the summer Olympics in Moscow. pp. 563–564 **3.** He thought cutting taxes would improve the economy; social programs wouldn't be needed. pp. 569–570 **4.** Camp David: Began a move toward peace in the MIddle East; Iran hostage crisis: Led to Carter losing election in 1980 pp. 564–566 **5.** The Soviet Union now wanted to communicate with Western countries. pp. 574–575

Chapter Quiz

Write your answers in complete sentences.

1. How did oil and gas prices affect the economy during Carter's presidency?
2. Why did relations with the Soviet Union get worse when Carter was President?
3. Why did President Reagan cut taxes and social programs?
4. **Critical Thinking** Think about the Camp David Accords and the Iran hostage crisis. Write one effect of each of these events.
5. **Critical Thinking** How do you think the policy of glasnost showed that the Soviet Union was changing?

Test Tip
As you study, read and review material carefully. Ask yourself questions to explore main ideas and important details.

Writing Tip
In a descriptive paragraph, a writer uses many details to describe a person, place, or thing.

Using the Timeline

Use the timeline on pages 560–561 to answer the questions.

1. How many times was Carter elected President? One time
2. In what year did President Reagan send marines to Lebanon? 1982

Group Activity See the Teacher's Planning Guide for a scoring rubric for this activity.

Group Activity

Form a group of three or four. Talk about the reasons people voted for Carter and Reagan. Then brainstorm a list of reasons why people vote for a presidential candidate today. Include good and bad reasons. Make a numbered list. Put a star next to each of the reasons you think is best.

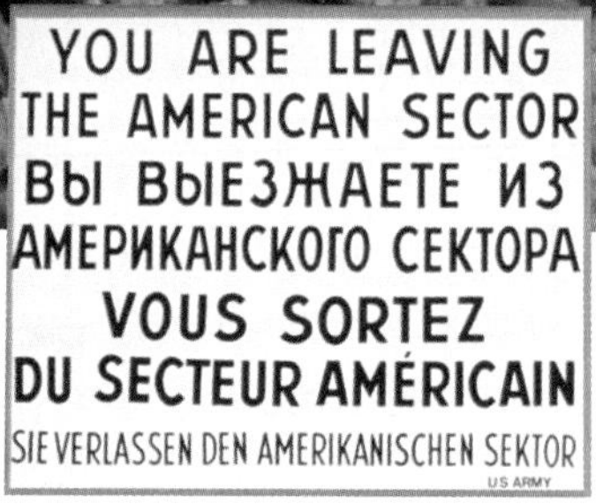

In Germany, people celebrated the fall of the Berlin Wall. The border between East and West Berlin, called Checkpoint Charlie, was marked by the sign shown here. How did the people celebrate the fall of the Wall? One man is giving a victory sign; crowds are gathered on both sides.

New Role for America

1988 George Bush elected

1989 Berlin Wall comes down

1990 Americans with Disabilities Act

1991 Gulf War

1992 William Clinton elected

1995 Terrorist bombs Federal Building, Oklahoma City

1996 Welfare reform passed; Clinton reelected

1988 — 1990 — 1992 — 1994 — 1996

Additional activities and strategies to customize lessons can be found in the Teacher's Planning Guide.

Chapter 31 Progress and Problems 1988–2000

ESL Note To help students understand the concept of progress and problems, help them brainstorm examples of progress and problems in their community.

Words to Know

primary

downsize

budget surplus

grand jury

ethnic cleansing

coalition

underclass

workfare

Words to Know These words are defined in the section in which they appear, as well as in the Glossary. Point out to students that the terms *downsize*, *budget surplus*, *workfare*, and *underclass* are about economics.

Learning Objectives

- Describe the elections of 1988, 1992, and 1996.
- Discuss the economy during the Bush and Clinton presidencies.
- Explain the importance of the end of the cold war and the Persian Gulf War.
- Identify areas where U.S. troops helped keep peace during the 1990s.
- Describe new opportunities for minorities and women.
- Explore Maya Angelou's message.

Project Students can begin work on their charts after reading Section 1. To help them get started, identify improvements in the economy as progress. Identify job losses to other countries as a problem.

Portfolio Project

In this chapter, you will learn about changes in the United States and the world during the 1990s. As you read, make a list of these changes. Then make a chart with two headings: *Progress* and *Problems*. Write your list of items on the chart.

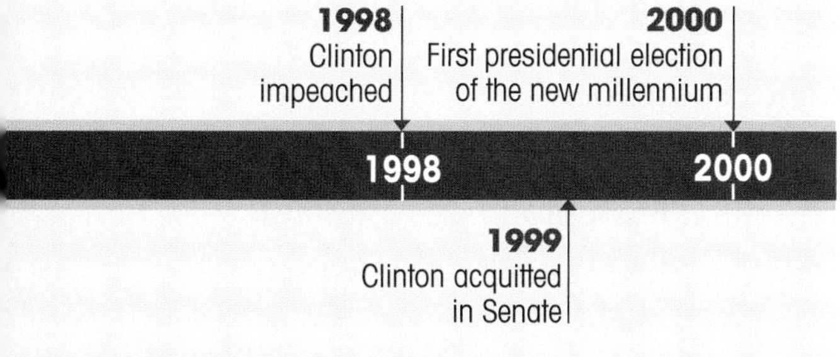

Timeline The timeline is divided into 2-year intervals. The events take place over a period of 13 years. Point out that during those years, the United States participated in conflicts around the world.

Section 1 Politics and Presidents

Words to Know

primary	an early election that helps a political party choose its candidate
downsize	to make smaller, to reduce the size of the workforce
budget surplus	the amount of money that is left over after spending
grand jury	a jury that decides if charges against a person are strong enough to go to trial

Getting Started Discuss the role of the economy in a country. Explain how the state of the economy affects students and their families.

President Reagan had finished two terms in office. By law, he could not run again. Americans still worried about the economy. They worried that a new President would try to fix the economy by raising taxes.

The 1988 Election

Jesse Jackson won several Democratic primaries in 1988.

Visual As a young man, Jesse Jackson worked closely with Dr. Martin Luther King, Jr.

In 1988, the Republicans chose George H. W. Bush, who was Reagan's Vice President, to run for President. Jesse Jackson, a civil rights leader from Chicago, won several Democratic **primaries.** A primary is an early election that helps a political party choose its candidate. For a time, it looked as though Jackson might be the Democratic candidate. He won primaries in Mississippi, Alabama, and Louisiana. However, Michael Dukakis, the popular governor of Massachusetts, became the Democratic candidate for President.

During the election campaign, Bush said Dukakis had been "soft" on crime. Bush promised again and again not to raise taxes. "Read my lips," he said. "No new taxes."

Who were the candidates in the 1988 election?
George Bush and Michael Dukakis

Taxes and the Economy

Bush won the election. Many Americans expected him to continue Reagan's policies. Like Reagan, Bush wanted people to help themselves. However, he wanted the country to be "a kinder, gentler nation." Bush wanted to spend more government money on public schools. He also wanted to fight a war on drugs.

While Bush was President, federal budget deficits were still a big problem. Many Americans were beginning to worry about the huge national debt. Finally, Bush decided to cut spending and raise taxes. Some Americans understood the need for new taxes. Others felt that Bush had broken a promise to them.

In 1991, the U.S. economy began to get worse. Many companies moved jobs to other countries where workers were paid less. Many banks and businesses closed. Still other businesses began to **downsize.** To downsize means to make smaller, or to reduce the size of the workforce. When businesses got smaller, people lost their jobs.

Why did President Bush raise taxes? The national debt was growing, and no other remedies were working.

George Bush raised taxes. This made many Americans angry.

Visual Point out that candidates cannot always predict the circumstances they will face as President. In some cases, to stick to a campaign promise might hurt the country.

The Clinton Years

By the time of the 1992 election, Americans were really concerned. They were not sure that either the Republican or Democratic candidate could fix the economy. President George Bush was the Republican candidate. Governor William Clinton of Arkansas was the Democratic candidate. Ross Perot, a successful business leader, ran as a third-party candidate. Perot said that the federal government was wasteful. He said he could change it and get rid of federal deficits.

Clinton convinced the voters that he could improve the economy. He and his running mate, Albert Gore, Jr., won the 1992 election.

During the 1992 election, Bill Clinton held town meetings for people to discuss different issues.

Visual John F. Kennedy was a role model for Bill Clinton, who decided to go into politics after meeting Kennedy in 1963.

At age 46, Clinton was the youngest President since John F. Kennedy. He had never served in Washington, D.C. In 1996, President Clinton ran for office again. He defeated Republican Robert Dole, a former senator from Kansas.

During his presidency, Clinton's personal life and past business dealings were concerns. Yet Clinton could make people feel that he cared about them. Many Americans believed him when he said, "I feel your pain."

Under Clinton, the economy improved. Joblessness fell and inflation stayed low. In 1997, Clinton and Congress agreed to a plan to balance the budget by 2002. However, in 1998 there was a **budget surplus.** A budget surplus is the amount of money left over after spending.

During the 1992 election, what did Clinton convince voters he could do? Improve the economy

Impeachment and Acquittal

In 1998, Clinton became the first U.S. President to testify in front of a **grand jury** about his own actions. A grand jury decides if charges against a person are strong enough to go to trial. A special prosecutor, Kenneth Starr, thought Clinton had lied to the grand jury. He sent a report about lying and other wrongdoing to the House of Representatives.

On December 19, 1998, Clinton became the second President to be impeached by the House of Representatives. At a trial in the Senate in early 1999, Clinton was acquitted, or found not guilty. In spite of his problems, Clinton continued his work. Many world events needed his attention.

Remember
Andrew Johnson was the first President to be impeached in 1868.

What happened to Clinton in the House of Representatives and in the Senate? He was impeached in the House and acquitted in the Senate.

Section 1 Review

1. What happened to many jobs while Bush was President?
2. Who were the three candidates for President in the 1992 election?
3. **Critical Thinking** How do you think the federal government should use budget surpluses?
4. **Write About Citizenship** Write a news article about the 1988 or 1992 election. Include the main issue and the candidates.

More Review is provided in Exercise 129 of the Workbook.

1. Many companies moved jobs to other countries. When companies went out of business or downsized, people lost their jobs.
2. Bill Clinton, George Bush, and Ross Perot
3. Possible answer: If there is a debt, it needs to be paid. Some students may favor tax cuts or spending on programs they like.
4. Possible answer: Should identify economics as the major issue. They should correctly identify the candidates in the election.

Section 2 A New Role in the World

Words to Know

ethnic cleansing	the removal of one group of people by another group in the same region
coalition	a temporary alliance of nations for a special action

Getting Started Discuss what it means to be free. Explain that this word has different meanings from country to country. Point out that in the late 1980s and 1990s, people in Eastern Europe and South Africa fought for and won their freedom.

While George Bush was President, the Soviet Union broke apart. The cold war ended. However, peace did not come to the world. Instead, many conflicts broke out. The United States was the only superpower left. No other country had enough power and money to try to end conflicts around the globe.

The End of the Cold War

In the late 1980s, the Soviet Union was moving toward reform, or change. The Soviet Union, however, could not change fast enough to hold onto Eastern Europe.

In Poland, Czechoslovakia, Hungary, and other countries, the people said "no" to communism. In 1989, East Germans forced out the Communist government. East and West Berliners broke down the Berlin Wall. Soon East and West Germany would be reunited as one country. Communist leaders could do nothing to stop those who wanted freedom.

The republics of the Soviet Union wanted their freedom too. The central government in Moscow, could not hold them together. In 1991, some Communist officials tried to take over the government and turn back Gorbachev's reforms. Russians, led by Boris Yeltsin, stopped the takeover. In the months that followed, the Soviet republics broke free. Gorbachev resigned, or quit. The Soviet Union was no more.

Russia was the biggest and most powerful republic of the old Soviet Union. The United States and other democracies tried to help Russia and Boris Yeltsin. Yeltsin was the new leader of Russia. However, the Communists had controlled the people and the economy of Russia for a long time. Many Russians had a difficult time changing to a new way of life.

After the cold war, the United States and Russia worked together. One area was in the exploration of space. Also, the United States tried to help Russia and other republics figure out what to do with old weapons.

What happened to the Soviet Union in 1991? It broke apart and ended.

Yugoslavia After the Cold War

Yugoslavia was a country in Eastern Europe. After the cold war ended, Yugoslavia broke apart. Each republic of Yugoslavia gained independence. However, violence and civil war broke out in several areas. The republic of Serbia attacked Bosnia, another republic. Once they were there, the Serbs practiced **ethnic cleansing.** This means the Serbs forcibly removed the Bosnians from their homes. The United States helped bring about an agreement between Bosnia and Serbia.

In 1998, Serbs began the ethnic cleansing of 1.5 million Albanians living in Kosovo, another republic. In 1999, the United States and other NATO countries bombed Serbia and Serbian forces in Kosovo. They did so to force the Serbs to allow the Kosovars, or the natives of Kosovo, to return to Kosovo. Later, the United States joined other NATO countries and Russia in a peacekeeping force in Kosovo.

What happened to Yugoslavia after the cold war? Broke apart; republics gained independence

Russians who supported Gorbachev carried a giant Russian flag in Red Square.

Visual A few days after this demonstration, Gorbachev resigned and Yeltsin became leader of Russia.

Geography Fact

Kuwait is 6,880 square miles, only slightly larger than Hawaii.

Geography Fact Twenty percent of the world's oil fields are in Kuwait.

The Persian Gulf War

In the 1980s, Iran and Iraq, two countries in the Persian Gulf, fought against each other. After the war ended, Saddam Hussein, the leader of Iraq, continued to build up his military weapons. In 1990, Hussein sent 100,000 troops to invade the neighboring country of Kuwait. Hussein wanted to make Kuwait and its oil fields part of Iraq. Within hours, he controlled Kuwait. What happens in the Middle East is important to the security of the United States. The United States buys oil from countries in the Middle East.

President George Bush was afraid Iraq would invade Saudi Arabia next. He went to the United Nations. He formed a **coalition** of nations that disagreed with the actions of Iraq. A coalition is a temporary alliance of nations for a special action. The coalition of over 25 nations included the United States, Egypt, Saudi Arabia, Syria, France, Italy, Great Britain, and others.

The coalition sent troops to the Middle East to protect Saudi Arabia. This mission was called Operation Desert Shield. The United Nations warned Hussein that Iraqi troops had to leave Kuwait by January 15, 1991, or the United Nations would have to "use all necessary means" to remove them.

What was Operation Desert Shield? The mission to send troops to the Middle East to protect Saudi Arabia from Iraq

Operation Desert Storm

Saddam Hussein did not remove his troops from Kuwait. President Bush asked Congress for permission to go to war with Iraq. On January 17, 1991, the allies attacked Iraq from the air. The air attack was called Operation Desert Storm. The allies bombed military targets in Iraq. Most of Iraq's air force was destroyed.

On February 24, a ground war began. U.S. and coalition forces smashed through Iraqi lines. On

The Persian Gulf War, 1991

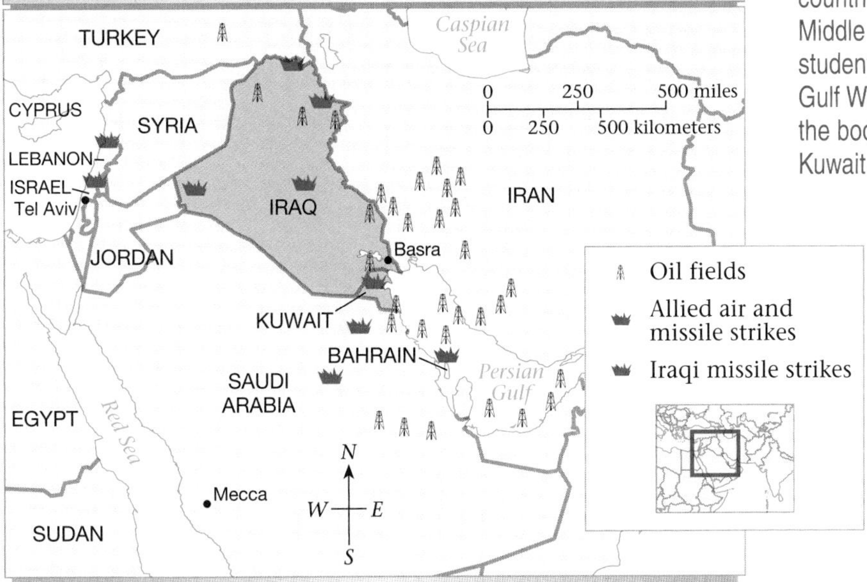

Map This map shows the countries that make up the Middle East. Point out to students that the Persian Gulf War was so named for the body of water bordering Kuwait.

Map Study

1. What six countries border Iraq?
2. What body of water does Kuwait border?

1. Iran, Kuwait, Saudi Arabia, Jordan, Syria, Turkey
2. Persian Gulf

February 27, President Bush issued a cease-fire, or an order to stop fighting.

About 540,000 U.S. forces served in the Gulf War. About 40,000 of them were women. Women did jobs they had never done before in war. About 150 Americans were killed in the war. Later, however, many suffered serious health problems called the Gulf War Syndrome. About 100,000 Iraqis were killed.

Two American heroes of the Persian Gulf War were Norman Schwarzkopf and Colin Powell. Schwarzkopf was the commanding general of the American troops. Powell was Chairman of the Joint Chiefs of Staff.

What was Operation Desert Storm? Air attack on Iraq; the allies dropped bombs on military targets

Results of the Gulf War

When the war ended, the United Nations did not want Hussein to build up a strong military again. The United Nations wanted to put limits on the types of weapons Iraq could have. Later, the United Nations sent inspection teams to Iraq to make sure Hussein was not building more weapons. Hussein tried to stop the United Nations teams from coming.

The Gulf War did not remove Saddam Hussein from power in Iraq. However, the war showed that the United States could bring nations together.

Why did the United Nations send inspection teams to Iraq? To keep Hussein from building a strong military again; to be sure he was not building certain types of weapons

Great Names in History

COLIN POWELL

General Colin Powell was the first African American to become Chairman of the Joint Chiefs of Staff. The Chairman of the Joint Chiefs of Staff is the highest military position in the United States. The Chairman advises the President on important defense issues.

Powell served as Chairman of the Joint Chiefs of Staff during the Persian Gulf War. He helped develop the plan to remove Iraqi troops from Kuwait. Powell's role in the Persian Gulf War made him a national hero. As a result, many people wanted him to run for President.

Colin Powell

In 1993, Powell retired from the Joint Chiefs of Staff. He became the chairman of America's Promise: The Alliance for Youth. Powell traveled around the country speaking about the importance of young people getting involved with volunteer work. In 2001, Powell became Secretary of State.

Critical Thinking Why is Powell a good model for young people to follow? He has been successful in both war and peace. As an African American, he knows that people can overcome difficulties in life. As a national hero, he had many opportunities, and yet he chose to do something to make people's lives better.

Conflict and Change Around the World, 1983–1994

Country	Problem	U.S. Action
Panama (1983)	In 1983, General Noriega took over Panama. He helped get illegal drugs into the United States.	In 1990, President Bush sent U.S. troops to capture Noriega. He was tried in the United States and sent to jail.
China (1989)	In 1989, Chinese students and workers protested against the Communist government. The government crushed the protest.	Relations between China and the United States got worse. Later, President Clinton visited China.
Haiti (1990)	In 1990, the military overthrew the elected leader, Jean-Bertrand Aristide.	In 1990, U.S. troops forced military leaders to accept Aristide as Haiti's leader.
Somalia (1991)	In 1991, fighting broke out between two armies. Somalian people were caught in the middle. Many starved or were murdered.	U.S. troops joined a peacekeeping force. In 1993, Somalia fighters killed several U.S. soldiers. President Clinton withdrew U.S. soldiers in 1994.
Israel (1993)	Fighting between the Israelis and Palestinians continued.	In 1993, President Clinton helped arrange a meeting between Prime Minister Rabin of Israel and Yasir Arafat of the PLO. They signed an agreement.

Chart Study

1. **How did relations between the United States and China change in 1989?** Relations became worse after the Chinese government crushed student worker protests.
2. **In what ways does the United States become involved in other countries?** The United States uses diplomacy, military action, or peacekeeping forces.

Conflict and Change Around the World

At the end of the cold war, the United States was the only superpower. The Soviet Union was no longer a threat to the security of the United States. However, the United States still faced challenges from conflicts and changes in other countries. Since the 1980s, some of the problems included civil wars in Asia, the Middle East, Africa, and Europe.

The United States also helps countries after natural disasters. For example, U.S. soldiers and navy ships helped in Turkey, in the Middle East, after the earthquake in August 1999.

Chart This chart shows U.S. involvement in various conflicts that erupted around the world between 1983 and 1994. Point out to students that U.S. peacekeeping efforts were not always successful.

During the 1980s and 1990s, the United States used sanctions, or punishments, to try to make change. In South Africa, black Africans fought apartheid, or separation of the races, for many years. In the 1960s, the white government jailed leaders of the anti-apartheid movement. One leader, Nelson Mandela, spent 27 years in jail. However, he still worked to help the anti-apartheid movement.

Americans protested against apartheid in South Africa for many years. Finally, in 1986, the U.S. government used sanctions on U.S. companies doing business with South Africa. In 1990, the South African government freed Mandela. In 1994, Mandela became president of South Africa. The United States and South Africa began to rebuild their relationship.

What conflicts in other countries have been a challenge to the United States since the 1980s? Civil wars in Asia, the Middle East, Africa, and Europe

Section 2 Review

1. What happened to the Berlin Wall in 1989?
2. What did the United States do to help the former republic of Yugoslavia?
3. **Critical Thinking** Why was the Persian Gulf War important to the United States?
4. **Write About Citizenship** Draw a poster either for or against U.S. sanctions on U.S. companies in South Africa. List reasons to support your position.

More Review is provided in Exercise 130 of the Workbook.

1. East Germans and West Germans tore it down.
2. Tried to stop ethnic cleansing; tried to get Serbs to allow Kosovars to return home
3. Possible answer: The United States depends on oil from the Middle East; the United States cannot allow a leader like Saddam Hussein to take a country for himself; the war showed that the United States could organize a coalition and keep it together.
4. Possible answer: For—Equal Rights for everyone; companies doing business are supporting apartheid. Against—U.S. has no right to interfere.

Section 3 New Rights and Opportunities

Words to Know

underclass a group of people with few job skills and little education

workfare a government program in which people have to work to receive aid

Getting Started Discuss with students how women, members of minority groups, and people with disabilities have advanced in U.S. society. Explain that in the 1980s and 1990s much progress was made toward greater equality.

The 1980s and 1990s were a time of gains and losses in American society. The gap between rich and poor people became wider. Throughout the 1990s, the number of homeless people grew. However, many groups gained rights and opportunities they had never had before.

Toward Greater Equality

During the 1980s, the government cut back on programs to help women, poor people, and minorities. However, during the 1980s and 1990s, many African Americans, Latinos, Native Americans and other minorities entered politics and gained political office.

In Politics

There were several "firsts." Douglas Wilder of Virginia became the first African American governor. In 1992, Ben Nighthorse Campbell became the first Native American U.S. senator in more than 60 years. Also in 1992, Nydia Velazquez became the first Puerto Rican woman elected to Congress.

In Civil Rights

In the 1980s, African Americans were determined to make the birthday of Martin Luther King, Jr., a national holiday. In 1994, President Clinton declared a federal holiday in honor of King's birthday.

Jesse Jackson won several Democratic primaries in the 1988 election for President. He formed the Rainbow Coalition to create more opportunities for minorities.

Discrimination continued to be a serious problem. In 1992, Los Angeles police officers beat an African American man named Rodney King. A videotape of the beating was shown on television. When a jury refused to convict the officers, riots broke out in Los Angeles. Later, another jury convicted two of the officers for violating King's civil rights. In New York City, between 1997 and 1999, there were more cases of police brutality toward minorities.

By the 1990s, women had made many gains. Although they still held only a small percentage of elected offices, there were now two women Supreme Court Justices. They were Sandra Day O'Connor and Ruth Bader Ginsburg. On average, women did not receive the same pay as men. They made about 70 percent of the pay men received for the same work. One issue that came up during the 1990s was sexual harassment in the workplace. Some women won lawsuits against employers who asked women for special favors.

What gains took place for minorities and women during the 1980s and 1990s? Political and civil rights gains

New Programs and Laws

In the 1990s, new programs and laws changed the lives of millions of people in the United States.

Americans with Disabilities Act (ADA)

In 1990, people with disabilities worked for a law that would give them equal rights. This law made more buildings and transportation accessible to people with disabilities. Accessible means that people can get into a place and use it. The law also outlawed discrimination against people with disabilities.

The ADA helped many people with disabilities go to school and get jobs. It helped them become part of the mainstream of American life.

Welfare Reform

During the 1980s, some Americans felt the welfare system did not work. They felt welfare payments made people lose interest in working. They said welfare had created an American **underclass.** An underclass is a group of people with few job skills and little education.

In 1996, a new welfare reform plan changed the welfare system. It encouraged states to set up **workfare** instead of welfare. Workfare is a government program in which people have to work to receive aid. Those who did not work would not receive welfare payments. The law also said a person could receive welfare benefits for up to five years. Some critics worried that welfare reform would cause more people to be homeless. They were also concerned that single mothers with jobs would have problems finding someone to take care of their children.

Visual Before becoming the First Lady of the United States, Hillary Rodham Clinton served as First Lady of Arkansas for twelve years. She is also a lawyer and a mother.

Hillary Rodham Clinton campaigned for health care.

Health Care Reform

Millions of Americans do not have health insurance. Early in Clinton's presidency, he named his wife, Hillary Rodham Clinton, to lead a study of health care reform. Hillary Clinton and her team advised that lawmakers form a national health care program. However, the program did not gain approval among lawmakers.

Clinton, however, won passage of some laws that affect medical care. One law provided health care for children. Another gave millions of workers the right to stay home to care for a baby or for sick family members. Workers would not be paid, but they would keep their health insurance and their jobs.

How did the welfare reform plan change the welfare system? Workfare program; limits on the time a person could receive welfare payments

Visual Jim Brady was press secretary to President Reagan. Brady was shot during the assassination attempt on Reagan. He suffered paralysis and became a gun control supporter.

Jim Brady gave a victory sign after the Brady Bill was passed.

Fighting Violence and Crime

During the 1990s, there were violent events in government buildings, at abortion clinics, in schools, and at businesses.

At this time, Americans saw the first major acts of terrorism inside the United States. In 1993, a bomb exploded in the World Trade Center in New York City. In 1995, a blast killed 168 people at the Federal Building in Oklahoma City.

Terrorism made Americans sad and angry. Many schools and government buildings had to increase security. Many Americans discussed the need for gun control. Others talked about how violence on television, in movies, and in video games affected young people.

In 1993, the Brady Bill was passed. The bill required a waiting period and background checks for gun buyers. Other gun-control measures failed in Congress. President Clinton and Congress did pass laws to put more police officers in communities and to build more prisons.

What was the purpose of the Brady Bill? Before a person could buy a gun, he or she had to follow the waiting period and go through a background check.

Section 3 Review

1. What political gains did minorities make during the 1980s and 1990s?
2. How did the Americans with Disabilities Act help people with disabilities?
3. **Critical Thinking** Do you think workfare helps or hurts people? Explain your answer.
4. **Write About Citizenship** Write an editorial for or against a national health-care program for all Americans.

1. Mention Douglas Wilder, Ben Nighthorse Campbell, Nydia Velazquez
2. It helped them get into and use buildings and public transportation. It also helped them go to school and get jobs.
3. Possible answers: Some people would be helped and some hurt. Some would get jobs, but others might have too many responsibilities and too little experience.
4. Possible answer: Everyone is entitled to the best health care. Now poor people suffer the most. Or, students might say, it is the responsibility of the states and of the individual to find good health-care programs.

More Review is provided in Exercise 132 of the Workbook.

VOICES FROM THE PAST
Maya Angelou

Maya Angelou is a poet. President Clinton asked Angelou to write a poem for his inauguration in 1993. An inauguration is a ceremony when an elected official is sworn into office. The poem Angelou wrote was "On the Pulse of the Morning." Here is part of Angelou's poem.

Maya Angelou

"Lift up your eyes upon
This day breaking for you.
Give birth again
To the dream.
Women, children, men,
Take it into the palms of your hands.
Mold it into the shape of your most
Private need. Sculpt it into
The image of your most public self.
Lift up your hearts.
Each new hour holds new chances
For a new beginning.
Do not be wedded [attached] forever
To fear . . ."

Answer the questions below.

1. What do you think Angelou meant when she wrote "Each new hour holds new chances for a new beginning"?

2. What do you think Angelou meant when she wrote "Do not be wedded forever to fear"?

CHALLENGE Why was Angelou's poem good for an inauguration of a President?

1. Students may say that you can always start again in life. **2.** Students may say that even if you are fearful now, you can conquer your fears. **CHALLENGE** Possible answer: The inauguration is a new start, or new day, for the United States.

Chapter 31 Review

Summary Have students use this graphic organizer to outline the main ideas and details of the chapter.

Summary: During the late 1980s and the 1990s, George H. W. Bush and William J. Clinton were Presidents. The role of the United States in the world changed after the cold war ended.

Section 1: George Bush won the election of 1988. Bill Clinton won in 1992 and 1996. The economy improved during Clinton's presidency. Clinton became the second President to be impeached. He was acquitted in the Senate.

Section 2: The Soviet Union broke apart in 1991. The cold war ended. The United States was the remaining superpower.

Section 3: During the late 1980s and the 1990s, many groups made progress. A major new law helped people with disabilities.

More Vocabulary Review is provided in Exercise 209 of the Classroom Resource Binder.

Vocabulary Review

Write *true* or *false*. If the statement is false, change the underlined term or terms to make it true.

1. A primary is a kind of election. True
2. Downsize is a new social program of the 1990s. False: Workfare
3. A coalition is a group of nations. True
4. A group of people who decides if a court case should be tried is called the underclass. False: grand jury
5. A budget surplus means the government has collected more money than it needs to spend. True

1. Bush: Budget deficits, downsizing; Clinton: Economy improves, inflation low, more jobs, budget surplus pp. 581–582 **2.** To free Kuwait and stop Hussein from building up his military weapons p. 586 **3.** ADA, welfare reform pp. 592–593 **4.** Possible answer: Yes, the United States felt world peace was threatened and the United States is the only superpower; No, the United States should have let other countries work out their own problems pp. 584–587 **5.** Possible answers: Yes: Takes longer to get a gun, might stop people; No: People can find other ways to get a gun p. 594

Chapter Quiz

Write your answers in complete sentences.

1. What changes occurred in the economy during the Bush and Clinton administrations?
2. Why did the United States fight the Persian Gulf War?
3. What new programs and laws in the 1990s changed the lives of Americans?
4. **Critical Thinking** Do you think the United States should have become involved in the problems of other countries?
5. **Critical Thinking** Do you think the Brady Bill helped to stop some of the violence and crime in America?

Test Tip
Try studying with a friend. Ask one another questions from your textbook.

Writing Tip
Use phrases to show that something is important. Some examples are *most important* or *to sum up.*

Using the Timeline

Use the timeline on pages 578–579 to answer the questions.

1. Who was President when the Berlin Wall came down? George Bush
2. Who was President when the Federal Building in Oklahoma City was bombed? Bill Clinton

Group Activity See the Teacher's Planning Guide for a scoring rubric for this activity.

Group Activity

Form groups of three or four. Think of some ways to stop violence in the United States and around the world. Consider other ways to resolve conflicts. Write a group poem about it. Practice saying the poem aloud. Present it to the class.

People celebrated the beginning of a new century on January 1, 2000. The next year many Americans wore ribbons like this one after the tragedy of September 11, 2001. Why do you think photographs about these two events were chosen for the beginning of this chapter?
The events were two of the most important that have happened so far in the twenty-first century.

Challenges for Today and the Future

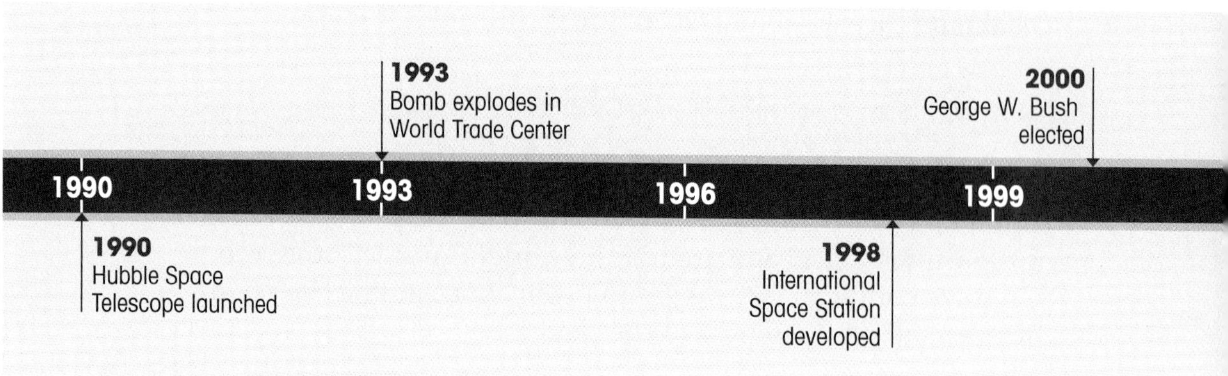

Additional activities and strategies to customize lessons can be found in the Teacher's Planning Guide.

Chapter 32 A New Century
1990–the future

ESL Note To help students understand the word *millennium*, point out that it is based on the prefix *mil-*, meaning "a thousand" in many languages, including Spanish, French, and Italian. Make the connection between *mil-* and *-ennium*, which refers to *year* in the Romance languages.

Words to Know

millennium

popular vote

electoral vote

resolution

acid rain

global warming

recycling

Words to Know These words are defined in the chapter, as well as in the Glossary. Point out to students that the terms *popular vote* and *electoral vote* pertain to presidential elections. The terms *acid rain*, *global warming*, and *recycling* pertain to the environment.

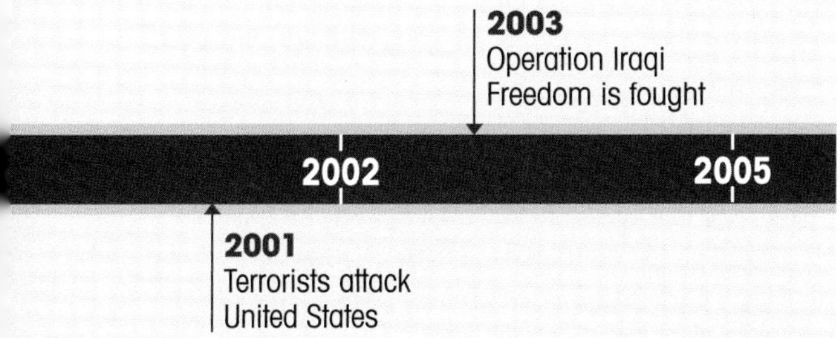

Learning Objectives

- Discuss the 2000 presidential election and how it was decided.
- Describe the terrorist attacks of September 11, 2001, and the U.S. response to the attacks.
- Discuss the environmental issues that challenge Americans in the twenty-first century.
- Explore how technology has improved space exploration and health care.

Project Help students to see how chapter information on the environment, space technology, and medical care can help them create futuristic settings.

Portfolio Project

As you read this chapter, think about what you would like the future of the United States to be. Plan the setting for a story in 2050. Describe the outdoors and the places where your characters live, work, and play. If you wish, draw a picture of your setting. Label the objects in it and write how they will be used.

Timeline The timeline is divided into three-year intervals. The events take place over a period of 14 years. Point out that the timeline includes challenges Americans faced in a new century.

Section 1 Challenges for a New President

Words to Know

millennium	a period of 1,000 years
popular vote	a vote cast by a citizen in a presidential election
electoral vote	a vote cast by a chosen elector in a presidential election
resolution	an official statement of opinion

Getting Started Ask students how they would describe life in the twenty-first century. What do they think will be our greatest challenges as a nation? What hopes do they have for the future? What fears and concerns do they have?

On January 1, 2000, people around the country celebrated the start of a new **millennium**. A millennium is a period of 1,000 years. The presidential campaign had begun. The country was looking toward the future with a new President.

George W. Bush, shown with his wife, Laura Bush, was elected President in 2000.

Visual George W. Bush was the first U.S. President to be elected in the twenty-first century.

The Election of 2000

In the election of 2000, Vice President Albert Gore, Jr., ran against the governor of Texas, George W. Bush. George W. Bush is the son of the forty-first President, George Herbert Walker Bush.

The election of 2000 made history. Gore received the majority of the nation's **popular votes**, or votes by citizens. However, the **electoral votes**, or votes by chosen electors, were very close. When citizens vote for a U.S. President, they are actually picking electors. Electors then vote for a candidate.

When all the votes were counted, the results depended on the state of Florida. The winner of Florida's electoral votes would win the election. Many people believed that the voting machines in Florida had not counted the ballots, or votes, correctly. They thought that some ballots should be counted again.

A legal battle about counting the votes by hand lasted for five weeks. On December 12, 2000, the U.S. Supreme Court made a decision. The Court stopped the recounting of votes in Florida. George W. Bush had the most popular votes in Florida, so he won Florida's electoral votes. George W. Bush then became the forty-third President.

How was the election of 2000 different from other elections? The U.S. Supreme Court decided the election by stopping the recounting of votes in Florida and George W. Bush became President.

The United States Under Attack

George W. Bush took office in January 2001. At that time, one of the biggest issues he faced was a weak economy. Eight months later, that changed. On September 11, 2001, foreign terrorists hijacked, or took over by force, four U.S. passenger planes.

The first two planes crashed into the Twin Towers of the World Trade Center in New York City. The explosions sent the burning 110-story buildings crashing to the ground. The third plane struck the Pentagon building near Washington, D.C. The Pentagon is the headquarters for the U.S. Department of Defense. About one-half hour after that, the fourth plane crashed outside of Pittsburgh, Pennsylvania. Passengers on this plane had fought with the hijackers to try to stop another attack.

Foreign terrorists had attacked U.S. interests in the past. In 1998, U.S. embassy buildings in Kenya and Tanzania in Africa were bombed. In 2000, terrorists attacked the Navy destroyer USS *Cole* in Yemen in the Middle East.

However, September 11 brought the worst acts of terrorism against the United States. Thousands of people were killed in these attacks. Osama bin Laden

The World Trade Center burned and fell to the ground after two hijacked planes struck the Twin Towers on September 11, 2001.

Visual The World Trade Center symbolized trade and the business success of the United States. The terrorists wanted to show that despite U.S. wealth the country could still be attacked.

Remember
In 1993, a bomb exploded in the World Trade Center. This was one of the first acts of foreign terrorism in the United States.

was the main suspect. He and his group of al Qaeda terrorists in Afghanistan hated the United States. They were against U.S. policies in the Arab world.

What happened on September 11, 2001? Thousands of people died after foreign terrorists hijacked four planes, which crashed.

Protecting Americans at Home

President Bush and other leaders tightened U.S. security right away. On September 11, passenger planes could not be flown. Important buildings were closed. The National Guard was sent to airports across the country. Military ships and aircraft guarded many U.S. cities.

On October 8, President Bush created a new presidential Cabinet position. This position was the Director of Homeland Security. This job included planning ways to make Americans safe at home.

How did the government respond to the terrorist attacks at home? The government increased security.

A Closer Look

THE HEROES OF SEPTEMBER 11, 2001

President Bush spoke to the nation on September 20, 2001. He thanked the American people for their courage and unity on September 11.

He praised the passengers and crew of the fourth hijacked plane for fighting with the terrorists. These citizens lost their lives trying to stop one of the planned attacks.

He also thanked the many police officers, fire fighters, and other citizens who rescued people in the World Trade Center and the Pentagon. Many of these rescuers put their own lives in danger to help others.

Rescue teams at the World Trade Center

Critical Thinking What does the photograph of the World Trade Center tell about the rescue work?
Many groups of people worked hard to rescue survivors after the terrorist attack.

Fighting Terrorism Abroad

On September 20, 2001, President Bush spoke to the world. He said the United States would punish terrorists and the governments that protect them. He told all countries to decide whether "you are with us, or you are with the terrorists." Great Britain and other countries promised to support the United States.

The war on terrorism started in Afghanistan. There, the Taliban government protected Osama bin Laden and his al Qaeda followers. On October 7, 2001, Operation Enduring Freedom began. The United States bombed parts of Afghanistan. U.S. troops were sent in to defeat the Taliban. These military actions were successful. Early in 2002, the Taliban was driven from power in Afghanistan. The al Qaeda group of terrorists was weakened.

What was Operation Enduring Freedom? the U.S. effort to defeat the al Qaeda terrorists and the Taliban government in Afghanistan

In 2001, U.S. soldiers were sent to Afghanistan to defeat the Taliban and al Qaeda.

Visual The U.S. mission in Afghanistan offered humanitarian relief to the people of that country. Millions of U.S. aid packages were dropped from planes to help the Afghan people.

Preventing Future Attacks

The fight against terrorism continued after the defeat of the Taliban. The President identified Iraq, Iran, and North Korea as dangerous to the United States. He said they threatened the peace of the world.

The U.S. government focused on Iraq. Officials believed that Iraq's leader, Saddam Hussein, had deadly chemical and biological weapons. They knew that he had used them against his own people. They feared that he might use them against U.S. interests.

Remember
Saddam Hussein invaded Kuwait in 1991. The United States led a UN coalition of more than 25 countries. The coalition attacked Iraq and removed Iraqi troops from Kuwait.

Which nations did President Bush identify as dangerous to the United States? Iraq, Iran, and North Korea

History Fact

After the Persian Gulf War in 1991, a UN resolution stated that Saddam Hussein must destroy his deadly chemical and biological weapons.

History Fact In the decade after the Persian Gulf War, Iraq challenged the United Nations by not cooperating with UN weapons inspectors.

UN Weapons Inspections

In 2002, President Bush spoke to members of the United Nations before the United States began its attack of Iraq. Bush hoped to gain a new UN **resolution**. A resolution is an official statement of opinion. On November 8, the United Nations passed a resolution demanding that Iraq destroy all of its deadly weapons. The UN sent inspection teams to Iraq to make sure this happened.

President Bush was not satisfied with the inspections. He and others believed that Iraq was not cooperating with the inspectors. Bush started to send U.S. troops into the Persian Gulf region. Some members of the United Nations, such as France, Germany, and Russia, did not approve. They wanted the inspections to continue.

What did the UN resolution demand from Iraq?

It demanded that Iraq destroy all of its weapons.

Visual Many statues of Saddam Hussein were brought down during Operation Iraqi Freedom. Taking down these statues sent a message to the Iraqi people and the world that Hussein's rule had ended.

This statue of Saddam Hussein in Baghdad, Iraq, was taken down in 2003.

Operation Iraqi Freedom

Without UN support, a coalition of nations led by the United States and Great Britain prepared for war. The main goal now was to remove Saddam Hussein from power and free the Iraqi people from his harsh rule. President Bush promised the American people, "We will bring freedom to others. And we will prevail."

On March 17, 2003, President Bush gave Saddam Hussein and his two sons a warning: Leave Iraq within 48 hours or face war. They did not leave. An hour after the deadline passed, U.S. cruise missiles and bombs hit Baghdad, the capital of Iraq. The war, called Operation Iraqi Freedom, had begun. Within weeks, President Bush announced the fighting was over. As a result of the war, Saddam Hussein was removed from power.

What was the main goal of Operation Iraqi Freedom? The main goal was to remove Saddam Hussein from power.

Section 1 Review

1. What role did the U.S. Supreme Court play in the 2000 presidential election?
2. Who was held responsible for the terrorist attacks in the United States on September 11, 2001?
3. **Critical Thinking** How did the goals of the UN inspection teams differ from the goals of the coalition of nations led by the United States and Great Britain?
4. **Write About History** You are an American journalist in Baghdad, Iraq. Operation Iraqi Freedom has just begun. Write a brief article describing the first signs of military action. Tell how you feel as war begins in Iraq.

More Review is provided in Exercise 133 of the Workbook.

1. The U.S. Supreme Court ordered the hand counting of ballots in Florida to stop, thereby deciding the election in Bush's favor.
2. Osama bin Laden and his group of al Qaeda terrorists
3. The UN's goals were to disarm Iraq and destroy its weapons. The goal of the coalition of nations led by the United States and Great Britain was to remove Saddam Hussein from power and free the Iraqi people from his rule.
4. Students' responses should include a description of bombs and missiles exploding in Baghdad and of the feelings that U.S. journalists might experience.

Section 2 Challenges for All Americans

Words to Know

acid rain	rain that is polluted by harmful chemicals
global warming	the theory, or idea, that Earth's temperature is slowly rising
recycling	using a product more than once

Getting Started Have students brainstorm a list of practical things that they can do at home or at school to help protect the environment. Point out that over the last few decades, people have become more careful about how they use natural resources.

The United States is always changing. We cannot know just what tomorrow will bring. One thing is certain: Working together, Americans will meet the challenges of the future.

Reducing Pollution

The environmental movement began in the 1960s and has remained strong. In 1970, environmental groups planned the first Earth Day. It is now celebrated every year. Also, in 1970, the Environmental Protection Agency (EPA) was formed. It made new laws to control pollution and protect the environment.

One problem is **acid rain**. Acid rain is rain that is polluted by harmful chemicals. These chemicals are released into the air. These chemicals come from coal-burning power plants and exhaust fumes from cars. Acid rain kills plants and animals. It is harmful to people and even to buildings. Environmental laws have helped reduce acid rain in the United States. However, all countries must agree to new laws to reduce acid rain around the world.

Another concern is **global warming**. Global warming is the theory, or idea, that Earth's temperature is slowly rising. Gases from factories and homes trap the heat from the Sun and keep it close to Earth. This excess heat could melt the ice at the North and South Poles. This would raise the levels of the oceans. Global warming could turn green areas into deserts.

During the 1980s, scientists found holes in the ozone layer. The ozone layer protects Earth from dangerous rays from the Sun. Certain gases in spray cans, refrigerators, and air conditioners caused the problem. Nations around the world have agreed to reduce their use of these products.

Many communities have run out of places to put garbage. They are **recycling** to cut down on waste. Recycling means using a product more than once. Items such as cans, bottles, and paper are now recycled in many areas.

Recycling bins are used to hold bottles, cans, and newspapers.

Visual The recycle logo (shown on the side of the bin) was created for the first Earth Day in 1970. In 1997, November 15 was proclaimed America Recycles Day.

How did Americans work to protect the environment? Americans made laws, stopped using some products, and started recycling.

Using Energy Wisely

Today, the United States uses more energy than any other nation in the world. Most of that energy comes from oil and coal. These are nonrenewable resources. This means that they will run out one day. Much of the oil Americans use comes from countries in the Middle East. Oil can be expensive to buy, especially when problems arise between the United States and some Middle Eastern countries.

Americans have begun to look elsewhere for energy. Water, wind, and the sun provide energy. These are renewable resources that can be replaced by nature. In the 1970s and 1980s, nuclear power plants were built to provide energy.

What are renewable resources? Resources that will not run out, such as the sun, wind, and water

Geography Fact

Some scientists say one of the best renewable energy resources is the water and steam beneath Earth's surface. It is called geothermal energy.

Geography Fact
Geothermal energy plants currently provide enough electricity to power 3.5 million homes.

In November 2000, space shuttle Endeavour *carried a crew of astronauts on a mission to the International Space Station.*

Visual Space shuttle *Endeavour* lifted off at night from Kennedy Space Center in Florida. One shuttle can be used for a number of missions.

Improving Space Technology

In the 1970s, researchers at the National Aeronautics and Space Administration (NASA) built the space shuttle. The space shuttle is a reusable rocket and spacecraft. On space shuttle flights, astronauts conduct experiments about the space environment. The first successful U.S. space shuttle, *Columbia*, was launched in April 1981.

Two major tragedies have occurred since the space shuttle was first created. In January 1986, space shuttle *Challenger* exploded after liftoff. All seven astronauts on the shuttle, including one schoolteacher, were killed. In February 2003, space shuttle *Columbia* broke apart just minutes before it was supposed to land. All seven astronauts on board were killed.

In 1990, the Hubble Space Telescope was launched into space. This telescope sends pictures of events and objects in space back to Earth. In 1998, the United States began working with 14 other countries to build an International Space Station (ISS). Astronauts take space shuttles to the station. There, they conduct experiments and undertake space walks. They develop technologies for the future in communications, medicine, and other areas.

How has the ISS affected technology? It is a laboratory for research in which astronauts can develop technologies for the future.

Improving Health Care

Advances in science and medical technology have helped Americans to live longer, healthier lives. Special computers allow doctors to check areas of bones, skin, and organs that X-rays cannot show. Better instruments, high sound waves, and lasers make surgery safer and more comfortable.

Scientists continue to search for better treatments and cures for diseases such as cancer, Alzheimer's disease, and AIDS. Alzheimer's disease usually affects older people. It causes memory loss. AIDS destroys the body's ability to fight disease. Treatment and prevention for many diseases have improved over the years.

Why do doctors use special computers to look at the human body? To find and treat disease; to see areas that X-rays cannot show

Working Together

The United States is a country of invention and change. Again and again, Americans have faced and solved difficult problems. With each problem solved, the country has become stronger.

The United States entered the twenty-first century as the only superpower in the world. Yet the United States depends on the friendship and resources of other countries. Nations must cooperate, or work together, to ensure a peaceful and prosperous world.

Why is it important for nations to work together in the twenty-first century? To ensure worldwide peace and economic strength

Section 2 Review

1. How does acid rain hurt the environment?
2. How have computers improved health care?
3. **Critical Thinking** Why does the United States need the friendship of other countries?
4. **Write About Economics** Saving energy often means saving money. Make a list of ways to save energy. Put a check mark next to the ones that also save money.

More Review is provided in Exercise 134 of the Workbook.

1. Acid rain kills plants and animals. It is harmful to people.
2. They allow doctors to see parts of the body more closely than are shown in X-rays, which can help to prevent and treat illnesses.
3. Possible Answer: The United States needs to trade resources with other countries and needs allies to fight violence in the world.
4. Possible answers: Turning off lights, walking instead of driving, using less air conditioning or heat. Probably all items will be checked.

Chapter 32 Review

Summary Have students use this graphic organizer to outline the main ideas and details of the chapter.

Summary
Soon after the new century began, the 2000 presidential election made history. Terrorism against the United States brought changes in security at home. Wars in Afghanistan and Iraq followed. Americans continued to work to protect the environment and improve space technology and medical care.

Section 1
In the presidential election in 2000, George W. Bush defeated Albert Gore, Jr. On September 11, 2001, foreign terrorists attacked the United States. The war against terrorism abroad began in Afghanistan and Iraq.

Section 2
Caring for the environment continued to be a concern. Space technology advanced with the International Space Station. This station was built by 15 countries, including the United States. Medical advances improved the lives of Americans.

acid rain
popular vote
recycling
global warming
millennium

More Vocabulary Review is provided in Exercise 215 of the Classroom Resource Binder.

Vocabulary Review

Write the term from the list that matches each definition below.

1. A vote cast by a citizen in a presidential election popular vote
2. Rain that hurts living things and buildings acid rain
3. An idea that Earth's temperature is rising global warming
4. A period of 1,000 years millennium
5. The process of using things more than once recycling

1. When the U.S. Supreme Court decided that the counting of votes by hand in Florida had to stop, George W. Bush had the most popular votes. He won Florida's electoral votes and the election. pp. 600–601 2. The United States sent troops into Afghanistan in response to the terrorist attacks of September 11, 2001. p. 603 3. Nonrenewable resources will run out one day. p. 607 4. Possible answer: Because weapons inspections in Iraq had failed before following a UN resolution in 1991 p. 604. 5. Possible answer: Protecting against future terrorist attacks at home and abroad pp. 603–604.

Chapter Quiz

Write your answers in complete sentences.

1. How was the winner of the 2000 presidential election decided?
2. Why did the United States send troops into Afghanistan?
3. Why do Americans need to look for renewable resources of energy?
4. **Critical Thinking** Why do you think President George W. Bush believed that the weapons inspections in Iraq would fail?
5. **Critical Thinking** Think about the present and the future of the United States. What is the most important challenge for the future? Explain why.

Test Tip
Always look up the correct answers to any questions that you got wrong on a test.

Writing Tip
Correct any grammar and spelling mistakes you made on a test. Keep the test in a portfolio so that you can look at it again.

Using the Timeline

Use the timeline on pages 598–599 to answer the questions.

1. In what year was George W. Bush elected? 2000
2. In what year was Operation Iraqi Freedom fought? 2003

Group Activity See the Teacher's Planning Guide for a scoring rubric for this activity.

Group Activity

Form groups of four or five. Prepare a television news report on one of the events in this chapter. Work as a group to write the report. Then, select one or two people to report the event to the class.

Critical Thinking **1.** President Carter allowed the shah to come to the United States. **2.** To force the Soviet Union to spend money it didn't have **3.** To defeat the Taliban who had protected Osama bin Laden, the main suspect of the September 11 terrorist attacks against the United States **4.** People with disabilities wanted equal rights.

Unit 10 Review

Critical Thinking

Give one reason why each of the following events happened.

1. Iran took American hostages.

2. President Ronald Reagan raised defense spending.

3. President George W. Bush sent troops to Afghanistan in 2001.

4. The Americans with Disabilities Act was passed.

Building Your Skills

Complete the following skill.

You have learned the best way to take a test. Answer the remaining questions in this Unit Review as if it were a test. Check your answers with the information in the chapters.

Who Did It?

Write the name of the person who took each action below.

1. He stopped American athletes from going to the Olympics in the Soviet Union. President Jimmy Carter

2. She led a national study of health care. Hillary Rodham Clinton

3. He was the Chairman of the Joint Chiefs of Staff during the Persian Gulf War. Colin Powell

Writing an Essay

Answer one of the following essay topics.

See the Answer Key for a detailed answer.

1. Discuss President Reagan's ideas about the role of the federal government.

2. Discuss the advantages and disadvantages of the welfare reform plan.

3. Discuss the U.S. response to the terrorist attacks of September 11, 2001.

Linking Past and Present

President Reagan believed the United States should take an active role in the world. He sent the U.S. military to many trouble spots. Should the U.S. military go to trouble spots today? Defend your answer with examples from newspapers and television news reports.

Answers will vary.

Reference Center

The World

West Africa

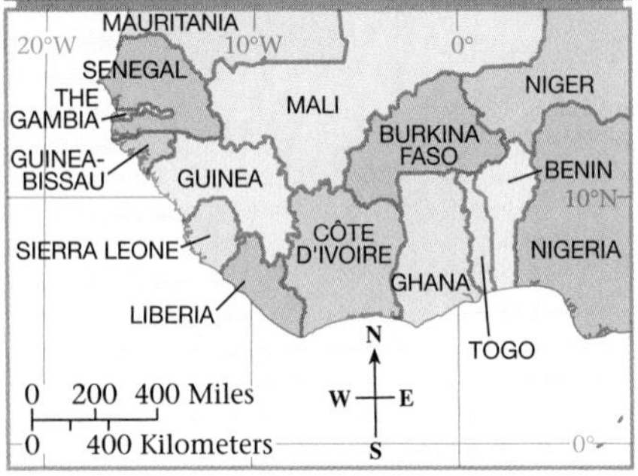

West Indies and Central America

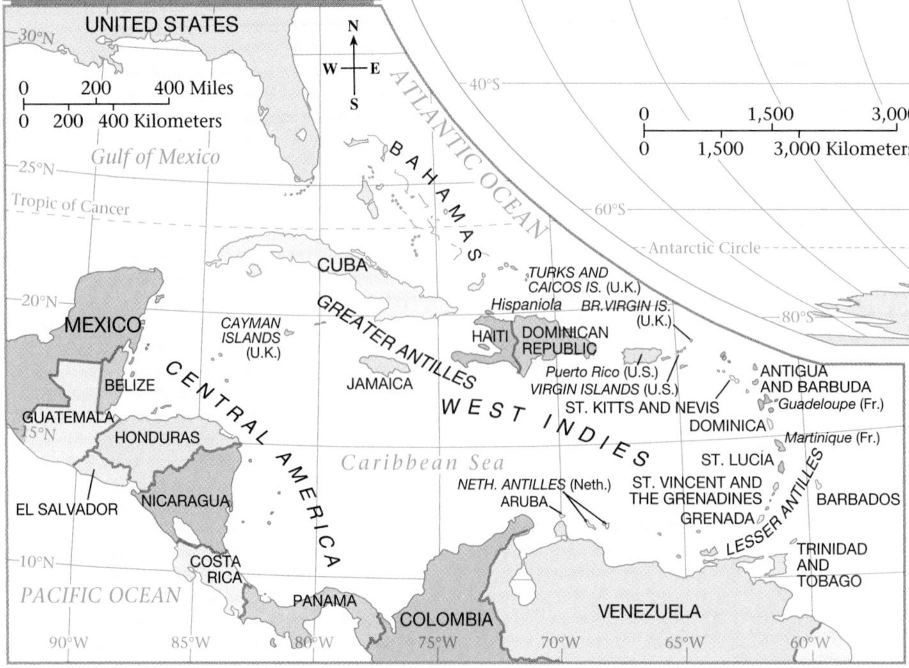

ARCTIC OCEAN
Arctic Circle
ICELAND
Europe
RUSSIA
KAZAKHSTAN
MONGOLIA
GEORGIA
ARMENIA
UZBEKISTAN
TURKMENISTAN
KYRGYZSTAN
TAJIKISTAN
TURKEY
AZERBAIJAN
CHINA
N. KOREA
S. KOREA
JAPAN
PACIFIC OCEAN
CYPRUS
SYRIA
LEB.
MALTA
ISRAEL
IRAQ
IRAN
AFGHANISTAN
NEPAL
BHUTAN
MOROCCO
ALGERIA
LIBYA
EGYPT
JORDAN
KUWAIT
BAHRAIN
QATAR
PAKISTAN
SAUDI ARABIA
OMAN
BANGLADESH
INDIA
MYANMAR (BURMA)
LAOS
Hong Kong
TAIWAN
WESTERN SAHARA (Mor.)
MALI
MAURITANIA
NIGER
West Africa
CHAD
ERITREA
YEMEN
UNITED ARAB EMIRATES
THAILAND
VIETNAM
PHILIPPINES
NORTHERN MARIANA IS. (U.S.)
GUAM (U.S.)
MARSHALL IS.
SUDAN
DJIBOUTI
CAMBODIA
NIGERIA
CENTRAL AFRICAN REP.
ETHIOPIA
SOMALIA
MALDIVES
SRI LANKA
BRUNEI
MALAYSIA
PALAU
FEDERATED STATES OF MICRONESIA
CAMEROON
UGANDA
KENYA
RWANDA
EQUATORIAL GUINEA
SÃO TOMÉ & PRÍNCIPE
GABON
CONGO
DEM. REP. OF THE CONGO
BURUNDI
TANZANIA
COMOROS
MAYOTTE (Fr.)
SEYCHELLES
SINGAPORE
INDONESIA
PAPUA NEW GUINEA
NAURU
KIRIBATI
TUVALU
SOLOMON ISLANDS
CABINDA (Ang.)
ANGOLA
ZAMBIA
MALAWI
INDIAN OCEAN
VANUATU
FIJI
MADAGASCAR
ZIMBABWE
NAMIBIA
MAURITIUS
BOTSWANA
RÉUNION (Fr.)
MOZAMBIQUE
SWAZILAND
AUSTRALIA
NEW CALEDONIA (Fr.)
ATLANTIC OCEAN
SOUTH AFRICA
LESOTHO
NEW ZEALAND
ANTARCTICA
20°W
0°
20°E
40°E
60°E
80°E
100°E
120°E
140°E
160°E
Europe
ALB.= ALBANIA
BELG.= BELGIUM
B. H.= BOSNIA AND HERZEGOVINA
CRO.= CROATIA
EST.= ESTONIA
LAT.= LATVIA
LIECH.= LIECHTENSTEIN
LITH.= LITHUANIA
LUX.= LUXEMBOURG
MAC.= MACEDONIA
MON.= MONACO
NETH.= NETHERLANDS
RUS.= RUSSIA
SERB.-MONT.= SERBIA AND MONTENEGRO
SLOV.= SLOVENIA
S. M.= SAN MARINO
SWITZ.= SWITZERLAND
0 200 400 Miles
0 400 Kilometers
20°E
30°E
40°E
10°E
0°
10°W
Arctic Circle
60°N
50°N
40°N
N
E
S
W
FINLAND
NORWAY
SWEDEN
EST.
RUSSIA
LAT.
North Sea
Baltic Sea
UNITED KINGDOM
IRELAND
DENMARK
LITH.
RUS.
NETH.
BELARUS
GERMANY
POLAND
BELG.
LUX.
CZECH REP.
UKRAINE
FRANCE
LIECH.
SLOVAKIA
MOLDOVA
SWITZ.
AUSTRIA
HUNGARY
ATLANTIC OCEAN
SLOV.
CRO.
ROMANIA
S. M.
B.H.
Black Sea
ANDORRA
SERB.-MONT.
BULGARIA
MON.
ITALY
PORTUGAL
SPAIN
MAC.
ALB.
TURKEY
GREECE
Mediterranean Sea

United States: Political

United States: Physical

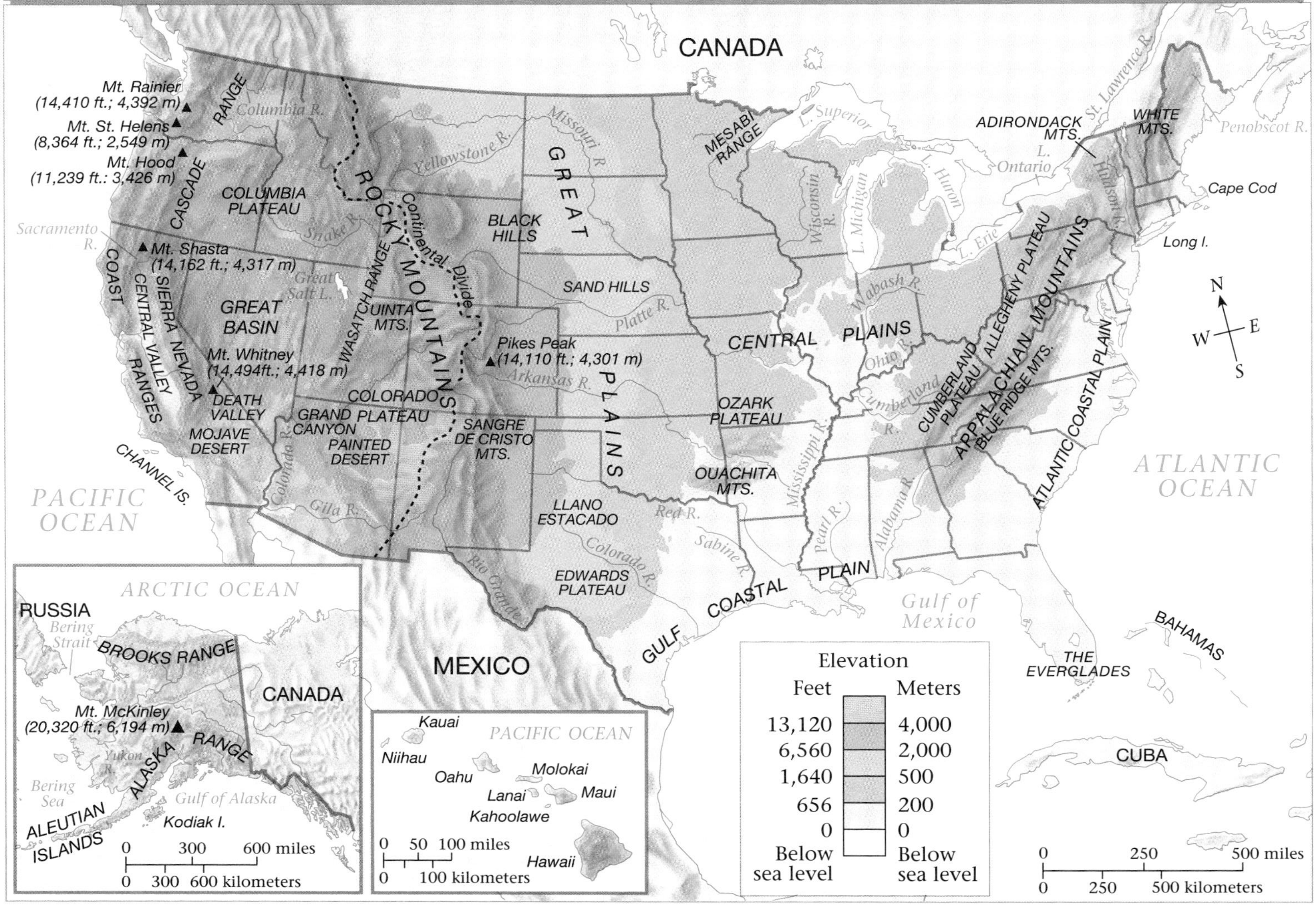

Primary Source Document

The Declaration of Independence

In Congress July 4, 1776

The Unanimous Declaration of the Thirteen United States of America

Why the Declaration of Independence Was Written
The Declaration of Independence was written because the American colonies decided to break away from Great Britain.

When in the course of human events, it becomes necessary for one people to dissolve the political bands which have connected them with another, and to assume among the powers of the earth, the separate and equal station to which the laws of nature and of nature's God entitle them, a decent respect to the opinions of mankind requires that they should declare the causes which impel them to the separation.

Political Theory of the Declaration

Purposes of Government
The colonists wanted a government that protected the rights of the people. These rights included the rights of life, liberty, and the chance to seek happiness.

We hold these truths to be self-evident, that all men are created equal, that they are endowed by their Creator with certain unalienable rights, that among these are life, liberty, and the pursuit of happiness. That to secure these rights, governments are instituted among men, deriving their just powers from the consent of the governed. That whenever any form of government becomes destructive of these ends, it is the right of the people to alter or to abolish it, and to institute new government, laying its foundation on such principles and organizing its powers in such form, as to them shall seem most likely to effect their safety and happiness. Prudence, indeed, will dictate that governments long established should not be changed for light and transient causes; and accordingly all experience hath shown, that mankind are more disposed to suffer, while evils are sufferable, than to right themselves by abolishing the forms to which they are accustomed. But when a long train of abuses and usurpations, pursuing invariably the same object evinces a design to reduce them under absolute despotism, it is their right, it is their duty, to throw off such government, and to provide new guards for their future security.

Grievances Against the King

Such has been the patient sufferance of these colonies; and such is now the necessity which constrains them to alter their former systems of government. The history of the present King of Great Britain is a history of repeated injuries and usurpations, all having direct object the establishment of an absolute tyranny over these states. To prove this, let facts be submitted to a candid world.

Reasons for Independence
The Declaration lists 27 reasons why the colonists wanted to be free of the king's government. The people believed this government had denied them their basic human rights.

He has refused his assent to laws, the most wholesome and necessary for the public good.

He has forbidden his governors to pass laws of immediate and pressing importance, unless suspended in their operation till his assent should be obtained; and when so suspended, he has utterly neglected to attend to them.

He has refused to pass other laws for the accommodation of large districts of people, unless those people would relinquish the right of representation in the legislature, a right inestimable to them and formidable to tyrants only.

He has called together legislative bodies at places unusual, uncomfortable, and distant from the depository of their public records, for the sole purpose of fatiguing them into compliance with his measures.

Charges Against the King
King George III was charged with not letting the colonies have the laws they needed, stopping laws that would set up courts, and making taxes go up.

He has dissolved representative houses repeatedly, for opposing with manly firmness his invasions on the rights of the people.

He has refused for a long time, after such dissolutions, to cause others to be elected; whereby the legislative powers, incapable of annihilation, have returned to the people at large for their exercise; the state remaining in the meantime exposed to all the dangers of invasion from without, and convulsions within.

He has endeavored to prevent the population of these states; for that purpose obstructing the laws for naturalization of foreigners, refusing to pass others to encourage their migrations hither, and raising the conditions of new appropriations of lands.

He has obstructed the administration of justice, by refusing his assent to laws for establishing judiciary powers.

He has made judges dependent on his will alone, for the tenure of their offices, and the amount and payment of their salaries.

He has erected a multitude of new offices, and sent hither swarms of officers to harass our people, and eat out their substance.

He has kept among us, in times of peace, standing armies without the consent of our legislatures.

He has affected to render the military independent of and superior to the civil power.

He has combined with others to subject us to a jurisdiction foreign to our constitution, and unacknowledged by our laws; giving his assent to their acts of pretended legislation:

For quartering large bodies of armed troops among us;

For protecting them, by a mock trial, from punishment for any murders which they should commit on the inhabitants of these states;

For cutting off our trade with all parts of the world;

For imposing taxes on us without our consent;

For depriving us, in many cases, of the benefits of trial by jury;

For transporting us beyond seas to be tried for pretended offenses;

For abolishing the free system of English laws in a neighboring province, establishing therein an arbitrary government, and enlarging its boundaries so as to render it at once an example and fit instrument for introducing the same absolute rule into these colonies;

For taking away our charters, abolishing our most valuable laws, and altering fundamentally the forms of our governments;

For suspending our own legislatures; and declaring themselves invested with power to legislate for us in all cases whatsoever.

He has abdicated government here, by declaring us out of his protection and waging war against us.

He has plundered our seas, ravaged our coasts, burned our towns, and destroyed the lives of our people.

He is at this time transporting large armies of foreign mercenaries to complete the works of death, desolation, and tyranny, already begun with circumstances of cruelty and perfidy scarcely paralleled in the most barbarous ages, and totally unworthy, the head of a civilized nation.

Charges Against Parliament
The king and Parliament working together were charged with making colonists keep British soldiers in their homes, cutting off colonial trade with other countries, forcing taxes, and not allowing trials by jury in many cases.

He has constrained our fellow citizens taken captive on the high seas to bear arms against their country, to become the executioners of their friends and brethren, or to fall themselves by their hands.

He has excited domestic insurrections amongst us, and has endeavored to bring on the inhabitants of our frontiers, the merciless Indian savages, whose known rule of warfare, is an undistinguished destruction of all ages, sexes, and conditions.

In every stage of these oppressions we have petitioned for redress in the most humble terms. Our repeated petitions have been answered only by repeated injury. A prince whose character is thus marked by every act which may define a tyrant is unfit to be the ruler of a free people.

Nor have we been wanting in attentions to our British brethren. We have warned them from time to time of attempts by their legislature to extend an unwarrantable jurisdiction over us. We have reminded them of the circumstances of our emigration and settlement here. We have appealed to their native justice and magnanimity, and we have conjured them by the ties of our common kindred to disavow these usurpations, which would inevitably interrupt our connections and correspondence. They too have been deaf to the voice of justice and of consanguinity. We must, therefore, acquiesce in the necessity, which denounces our separation, and hold them, as we hold the rest of mankind, enemies in war, in peace friends.

Cry for Freedom
The colonists state they are left with no other choice than to become free. They have asked the king and the British people to listen to them. Neither has responded.

A Proclamation of Independence

We, therefore, the representatives of the United States of America, in General Congress, assembled, appealing to the Supreme Judge of the world for the rectitude of our intentions, do, in the name, and by the authority of the good people of these colonies, solemnly publish and declare, that these united colonies are, and of right ought to be free and independent states; that they are absolved from all allegiance to the British Crown, and that all political connection between them and the state of Great Britain, is and ought to be totally dissolved; and that as free and independent states, they have full power to levy war, conclude peace, contract alliances, establish commerce, and to do all other acts and things which independent states may of right do. And for the support of this declaration, with a firm reliance on the protection of Divine Providence, we mutually pledge to each other our lives, our fortunes, and our sacred honor.

Signed by John Hancock of Massachusetts, President of the Congress, and by the fifty-five other Representatives of the thirteen United States of America.

Colonists Declare Their Independence
The final paragraph actually proclaims independence. It says that the United States can make war or make peace, make friends with other countries, and do business with other countries.

Signers of the Declaration
The signers of the Declaration of Independence pledged their lives and all they owned to the cause of independence.

Primary Source Document

The Constitution of the United States of America

Preamble
This Constitution was written to see that all citizens are treated fairly, to keep the country safe, and to keep people free for all times.

Preamble

We the people of the United States, in order to form a more perfect Union, establish justice, insure domestic tranquility, provide for the common defense, promote the general welfare, and secure the blessings of liberty to ourselves and our posterity, do ordain and establish this Constitution for the United States of America.

Article I

The Legislative Branch

SECTION 1. All legislative powers herein granted shall be vested in a Congress of the United States, which shall consist of a Senate and House of Representatives.

House of Representatives

SECTION 2. (1) The House of Representatives shall be composed of members chosen every second year by the people of the several states, and the electors in each state shall have the qualifications requisite for electors of the most numerous branch of the state legislature.

Section 2. (2)
To be a member of the House of Representatives, a person must:
- Be at least 25 years old.
- Be a U.S. citizen for at least seven years.
- Live in the state he or she represents.

(2) No person shall be a representative who shall not have attained to the age of twenty-five years, and been seven years a citizen of the United States, and who shall not, when elected, be an inhabitant of that state in which he shall be chosen.

(3) Representatives *~~[and direct taxes]~~ shall be apportioned among the several states which may be included within this Union, according to their respective numbers, ~~[which shall be determined by adding to the whole number of free persons, including those bound to service for a term of years, and excluding Indians not~~

* The blue lines indicate portions of the Constitution changed by amendments to the document.

taxed, three-fifths of all other persons]. The actual enumeration shall be made within three years after the first meeting of the Congress of the United States, and within every subsequent term of ten years, in such manner as they shall by law direct. The number of representatives shall not exceed one for every thirty thousand, but each state shall have at least one representative; [and until such enumeration shall be made, the state of New Hampshire shall be entitled to choose 3, Massachusetts 8, Rhode Island and Providence Plantations 1, Connecticut 5, New York 6, New Jersey 4, Pennsylvania 8, Delaware 1, Maryland 6, Virginia 10, North Carolina 5, South Carolina 5, and Georgia 3.]

(4) When vacancies happen in the representation of any state, the executive authority thereof shall issue writs of election to fill such vacancies.

(5) The House of Representatives shall choose their speaker and other officers; and shall have the sole power of impeachment.

Senate

SECTION 3. (1) The Senate of the United States shall be composed of two senators from each state, [chosen by the legislature thereof,] for six years; and each senator shall have one vote.

Section 3. (1)
All states are represented by two senators. Senators serve six-year terms.

(2) Immediately after they shall be assembled in consequence of the first election, they shall be divided as equally as may be into three classes. [The seats of the senators of the first class shall be vacated at the expiration of the second year, of the second class at the expiration of the fourth year, and of the third class

at the expiration of the sixth year,] so that one-third may be chosen every second year; [and if vacancies happen by resignation, or otherwise, during the recess of the legislature of any state, the executive thereof may make temporary appointments until the next meeting of the legislature, which shall then fill such vacancies].

(3) No person shall be a senator who shall not have attained to the age of thirty years, and been nine years a citizen of the United States, and who shall not, when elected, be an inhabitant of that state for which he shall be chosen.

Section 3. (4)
The Vice President of the United States is the lead officer in the Senate. However, the Vice President can only vote in case of a tie.

(4) The Vice President of the United States shall be president of the Senate, but shall have no vote, unless they be equally divided.

(5) The Senate shall choose their other officers and also a president pro tempore, in the absence of the Vice President, or when he shall exercise the office of President of the United States.

(6) The Senate shall have the sole power to try all impeachments. When sitting for that purpose, they shall be on oath or affirmation. When the President of the United States is tried, the Chief Justice shall preside; and no person shall be convicted without the concurrence of two-thirds of the members present.

(7) Judgment in cases of impeachment shall not extend further than to removal from office, and disqualification to hold and enjoy any office of honor, trust, or profit under the United States; but the party convicted shall nevertheless be liable and subject to indictment, trial, judgment, and punishment, according to law.

Organization of Congress

SECTION 4. **(1)** The times, places, and manner of holding elections for senators and representatives, shall be prescribed in each state by the legislature thereof; but the Congress may at any time by law make or alter such regulations, except as to the places of choosing senators.

(2) The Congress shall assemble at least once in every year, ~~[and such meeting shall be on the first Monday in December, unless they shall by law appoint a different day]~~.

SECTION 5. **(1)** Each house shall be the judge of the elections, returns, and qualifications of its own members, and a majority of each shall constitute a quorum to do business; but a smaller number may adjourn from day to day, and may be authorized to compel the attendance of absent members, in such manner, and under such penalties as each house may provide.

(2) Each house may determine the rules of its proceedings, punish its members for disorderly behavior, and, with the concurrence of two-thirds, expel a member.

Section 5. (2)
Each house is responsible for making its own rules. Each house must also keep a record of its daily activities.

(3) Each house shall keep a journal of its proceedings, and from time to time publish the same, excepting such parts as may in their judgment require secrecy; and the yeas and nays of the members of either house on any question shall, at the desire of one-fifth of those present, be entered on the journal.

(4) Neither house, during the session of Congress, shall, without the consent of the other, adjourn for more than three days, nor to any other place than that in which the two houses shall be sitting.

Section 6. (1)
Members of Congress are paid by the government. No one in Congress can be punished or questioned for anything they said while Congress is in session.

SECTION 6. (1) The senators and representatives shall receive a compensation for their services, to be ascertained by law, and paid out of the treasury of the United States. They shall in all cases, except treason, felony, and breach of the peace, be privileged from arrest during their attendance at the session of their respective houses, and in going to and returning from the same; and for any speech or debate in either house, they shall not be questioned in any other place.

(2) No senator or representative shall, during the time for which he was elected, be appointed to any civil office under the authority of the United States, which shall have been created, or the emoluments whereof shall have been increased during such time; and no person holding any office under the United States, shall be a member of either house during his continuance in office.

Section 7.
All tax bills must start in the House of Representatives. Bills have to be passed by both houses of Congress.

SECTION 7. (1) All bills for raising revenue shall originate in the house of Representatives; but the Senate may propose or concur with amendments as on other bills.

(2) Every bill which shall have passed the House of Representatives and the Senate, shall, before it becomes a law, be presented to the President of the United States; if he approves he shall sign it, but if not he shall return it, with his objections to that house in which it shall have originated, who shall enter the objections at large on their journal, and proceed to reconsider it. If after such reconsideration two-thirds of that house shall agree to pass the bill, it shall be sent, together with the objections, to the other house, by which it shall likewise be reconsidered, and if approved by two-thirds of that house, it shall become a law. But in all such cases the votes of both houses shall be determined by yeas and

nays, and the names of the persons voting for and against the bill shall be entered on the journal of each house respectively. If any bill shall not be returned by the President within ten days (Sunday excepted) after it shall have been presented to him, the same shall be law, in like manner as if he had signed it, unless the Congress by their adjournment prevent its return, in which case it shall not be a law.

(3) Every order, resolution, or vote to which the concurrence of the Senate and House of Representatives may be necessary (except on the question of adjournment) shall be presented to the President of the United States; and before the same shall take effect, shall be approved by him, or being disapproved by him, shall be repassed by two-thirds of the Senate ad House of Representatives, according to the rules and limitations prescribed in the case of a bill.

Powers of Congress

SECTION 8. The Congress shall have power: **(1)** To lay and collect taxes, duties, imposts, and excises, to pay the debts and provide for the common defense and general welfare of the United States; but all duties, imposts, and excises shall be uniform throughout the United States;

(2) To borrow money on the credit of the United States;

(3) To regulate commerce with foreign nations, and among the several states, and with the Indian tribes;

(4) To establish a uniform rule of naturalization, and uniform laws on the subject of bankruptcies throughout the United States;

Section 8.
The powers and duties of Congress are listed here.

(5) To coin money, regulate the value thereof, and of foreign coin, and fix the standard of weights and measures;

(6) To provide for the punishment of counterfeiting the securities and current coin of the United States;

(7) To establish post office and post roads;

(8) To promote the progress of science and useful arts, by securing for limited times to authors and inventors the exclusive right to their respective writings and discoveries;

(9) To constitute tribunals inferior to the Supreme Court;

(10) To define and punish piracies and felonies committed on the high seas, and offenses against the law of nations;

(11) To declare war, ~~[grant letters of marque and reprisal,]~~ and make rules concerning captures on land and water;

(12) To raise and support armies, but no appropriation of money to that use shall be for a longer term than two years;

(13) To provide and maintain a navy;

(14) To make rules for the government and regulation of the land and naval forces;

(15) To provide for calling forth the militia to execute the laws of the Union, suppress insurrections and repel invasions;

(16) To provide for organizing, arming, and disciplining the militia, and for governing such part of them as may be employed in the service of the United States, reserving to the states respectively, the appointment of the officers, and the authority of training the militia according to the discipline prescribed by Congress;

(17) To exercise exclusive legislation in all cases whatsoever, over such district (not exceeding ten miles square) as may, by cession of particular states, and the acceptance of Congress, become the seat of the government of the United States, and to exercise like authority over all places purchased by the consent of the legislature of the state in which the same shall be for the erection of forts, magazines, arsenals, dockyards, and other needful buildings; and

(18) To make all laws which shall be necessary and proper for carrying into execution the foregoing powers, and all other powers vested by this Constitution in the government of the United States, or in any department or officer thereof.

Section 8. (18)
The Constitution says that Congress has the power to make any laws it needs to carry out the powers listed in Section 8.

Powers Denied to Congress

SECTION 9. (1) ~~[The migration or importation of such persons as any of the states now existing shall think proper to admit, shall not be prohibited by the Congress prior to the year one thousand eight hundred and eight, but a tax or duty may be imposed on such importation, not exceeding ten dollars for each person.]~~

Section 9.
These are actions that Congress may not take.

(2) The privilege of the writ of habeas corpus shall not be suspended, unless when in cases of rebellion or invasion the public safety may require it.

(3) No bill of attainder or ex post facto law shall be passed.

(4) No capitation, ~~[or other direct,]~~ tax shall be laid, unless in proportion to the census or enumeration herein before directed to be taken.

(5) No tax or duty shall be laid on articles exported from any state,

(6) No preference shall be given by any regulation of commerce or revenue to the ports of one state over those of another; nor shall vessels bound to, or from, one state, be obliged to enter, clear, or pay duties in another.

(7) No money shall be drawn from the treasury, but in consequence of appropriations made by law; and a regular statement and account of the receipts and expenditures of all public money shall be published from time to time.

(8) No title of nobility shall be granted by the United States; and no person holding any office of profit or trust under them, shall, without the consent of the Congress, accept of any present, emolument, office, or title, of any kind whatever, from any king, prince, or foreign state.

Powers Denied to the States

Section 10.
The states cannot:
- Make treaties with other countries.
- Print money.
- Declare war.

SECTION 10. (1) No state shall enter into any treaty, alliance, or confederation; grant letters of marque and reprisal; coin money; emit bills of credit; make anything but gold and silver coin a tender in payment of debts; pass any bill of attainder, ex post facto law, or law impairing the obligation of contracts, or grant any title of nobility.

(2) No state shall, without the consent of the Congress, lay any imposts or duties on imports or exports, except what may be absolutely necessary for executing its inspection laws; and the net produce of all duties and imposts, laid by any state on imports or

exports, shall be for the use of the treasury of the United States; and all such laws shall be subject to the revision and control of the Congress.

(3) No state shall, without the consent of Congress, lay any duty of tonnage, keep troops, or ships of war in time of peace, enter into any agreement or compact with another state, or with a foreign power, or engage in war, unless actually invaded, or in such imminent danger as will not admit of delay.

Article II

The Executive Branch

SECTION 1. (1) The executive power shall be vested in a President of the United States of America. He shall hold his office during the term of four years, and, together with the Vice President, chosen for the same term, be elected, as follows:

Section 1. (1)
The executive branch is made up of the President and the Vice President. They are elected to four-year terms.

(2) Each state shall appoint, in such manner as the legislature thereof may direct, a number of electors, equal to the whole number of senators and representatives to which the state may be entitled in the Congress; but no senator or representative, or person holding an office of trust or profit under the United States, shall be appointed an elector.

(3) ~~[The electors shall meet in their respective states, and vote by ballot for two persons, of whom one at least shall not be an inhabitant of the same state with themselves. And they shall make a list of all persons voted for, and of the number of votes for each; which list they shall sign and certify, and transmit sealed to the seat of the government of the United States, directed to the president of the Senate. The president of the~~

Senate shall, in the presence of the Senate and House of Representatives, open all the certificates, and the votes shall them be counted. The person having the greatest number of votes shall be the President, if such number be a majority of the whole number of electors appointed; and if there be more than one who have such majority, and have an equal number of votes, then the House of Representatives shall immediately choose by ballot one of them for President; and if no person have a majority, then from the five highest on the list the said House shall in like manner choose the President. But in choosing the President, the votes shall be taken by states, the representation from each state having one vote; a quorum for this purpose shall consist of a member or members from two-thirds of the states, and a majority of all the states shall be necessary to a choice. In every case, after the choice of the President, the person having the greatest number of votes of the electors shall be the Vice President. But if there should remain two or more who have equal votes, the Senate shall choose from them by ballot the Vice President.]

(4) The Congress may determine the time of choosing the electors, and the day on which they shall give their votes; which day shall be the same throughout the United States.

Section 1. (5)
The President must:
- Have been born a citizen of the United States.
- Be at least 35 years old.
- Have been a resident of the United States for at least 14 years.

(5) No person except a natural-born citizen, or a citizen of the United States at the time of the adoption of this Constitution, shall be eligible to the office of President; neither shall any person be eligible to that office who shall not have attained to the age of thirty-five years, and been fourteen years a resident within the United States.

(6) In case of the removal of the President from office, or of his death, resignation, or inability to discharge the powers and duties of the said office, the same shall devolve on the Vice President, and the Congress may by law provide for the case of removal, death, resignation or inability, both of the President and Vice President, declaring what officer shall then act as President, and such officer shall act accordingly, until the disability be removed, or a President shall be elected.

Section 1. (6)
If the President dies, resigns, or is removed from office, the Vice President becomes President.

(7) The President shall, at stated times, receive for his services, a compensation, which shall neither be increased nor diminished during the period for which he shall have been elected, and he shall not receive within that period any other emolument from the United States, or any of them.

(8) Before he enter on the execution of his office, he shall take the following oath or affirmation:—"I do solemnly swear (or affirm) that I will faithfully execute the Office of President of the United States, and will to the best of my Ability, preserve, protect, and defend the Constitution of the United States."

SECTION 2. (1) The President shall be commander in chief of the Army and Navy of the United States, and of the militia of the several states, when called into the actual service of the United States; he may require the opinion, in writing, of the principal officer in each of the executive departments, upon any subject relating to the duties of their respective offices, and he shall have power to grant reprieves and pardons for offenses against the United States, except in cases of impeachment.

Section 2. (1)
The President is the commander of all the armed forces.

(2) He shall have power, by and with the advice and consent of the Senate, to make treaties, provided two-

thirds of the senators present concur; and he shall nominate, and by and with the advice and consent of the Senate, shall appoint ambassadors, other public ministers and consuls, judges of the Supreme Court, and all other officers of the United States, whose appointments are not herein otherwise provided for, and which shall be established by law; but the Congress may by law vest the appointment of such inferior officers, as they think proper, in the President alone, in the courts of law, or in the heads of departments.

(3) The President shall have power to fill up all vacancies that may happen during the recess of the Senate, by granting commissions which shall expire at the end of their next session.

SECTION 3. He shall from time to time give to the Congress information of the state of the Union, and recommend to their consideration such measures as he shall judge necessary and expedient; he may, on extraordinary occasions, convene both houses, or either of them, and in case of disagreement between them, with respect to the time of adjournment, he may adjourn them to such time as he shall think proper; he shall receive ambassadors and other public ministers; he shall take care that the laws be faithfully executed, and shall commission all the officers of the United States.

Section 4.
The President and Vice President can be removed from office by impeachment and conviction by a Senate trial.

SECTION 4. The President, Vice President, and all civil officers of the United States, shall be removed from office on impeachment for, and conviction of, treason, bribery, or other high crimes and misdemeanors.

Article III

The Judicial Branch

SECTION 1. The judicial power of the United States shall be vested in one Supreme Court, and in such inferior courts as the Congress many from time to time ordain and establish. The judges, both of the Supreme and inferior courts, shall hold their offices during good behavior, and shall, at stated times, receive for their services, a compensation, which shall not be diminished during their continuance in office.

Section 1.
The judicial branch is made up of the Supreme Court and lower courts. The Supreme Court is the highest court in the land.

SECTION 2. (1) The judicial power shall extend to all cases, in law and equity, arising under this Constitution, the laws of the United States, and treaties made, or which shall be made, under their authority;—to all cases affecting ambassadors, other public ministers and consuls;—to all cases of admiralty and maritime jurisdiction;—to controversies to which the United States shall be a party;—to controversies between two or more states; ~~[between a state and citizens of another state;]~~ between citizens of different states;—between citizens of the same state claiming lands under grants of different states, ~~[and between a state, or the citizens thereof, and foreign states, citizens or subjects]~~.

(2) In all cases affecting ambassadors, other public ministers and consuls, and those in which a state shall be party, the Supreme Court shall have original jurisdiction. In all other cases before mentioned, the Supreme Court shall have appellate jurisdiction, both as to law and fact, with such exceptions, and under such regulations as the Congress shall make.

Section 2. (2)
The Supreme Court hears cases involving foreign ministers and state governments. The Supreme Court can also decide if it wants to hear appeals of other cases.

(3) The trial of all crimes, except in cases if impeachment, shall be by jury; and such trial shall be held in the state where the said crimes shall have been committed; but when not committed within any state, the trial shall be at such place or places as the Congress may by law have directed.

Section 3.
Treason is the act of making war against the United States or helping its enemies. A person can be convicted of treason by the testimony of two witnesses, or the person confesses in court.

SECTION 3. (1) Treason against the United States, shall consist only in levying war against them, or in adhering to their enemies, giving them aid and comfort. No person shall be convicted of treason unless on the testimony of two witnesses to the same overt act, or on confession in open court.

(2) The Congress shall have power to declare the punishment of treason, but no attainder of treason shall work corruption of blood, or forfeiture except during the life of the person attainted.

Article IV

Relations Among States

Sections 1–2.
All states must accept acts, records, and laws of other states. Citizens of each state must have the same rights as citizens of other states when visiting those states.

SECTION 1. Full faith and credit shall be given in each state to the public acts, records, and judicial proceedings of every other state. And the Congress may by general laws prescribe the manner in which such acts, records, and proceedings shall be proved, and the effect thereof.

SECTION 2. (1) The citizens of each state shall be entitled to all privileges and immunities of citizens in the several states.

(2) A person charged in any state with treason, felony, or other crime, who shall flee from justice, and be found in another state, shall on demand of the executive authority of the state from which he fled, be

delivered up, to be removed to the state having jurisdiction of the crime.

(3) [~~No person held to service or labor in one state, under the laws thereof, escaping into another, shall, in consequence of any law or regulation therein, be discharged from such service or labor, but shall be delivered up on claim of the party to whom such service or labor may be due.~~]

Federal-State Relations

SECTION 3. (1) New states may be admitted by the Congress into this Union; but no new state shall be formed or erected within the jurisdiction of any other state; nor any state be formed by the junction of two or more states, or parts of states, without the consent of the legislatures of the states concerned as well as of the Congress.

(2) The Congress shall have the power to dispose of and make all needful rules and regulations respecting the territory of other property belonging to the United States; and nothing in this Constitution shall be so construed as to prejudice any claims of the United States, or any particular state.

SECTION 4. The United States shall guarantee to every state in this Union a republican form of government, and shall protect each of them against invasion; and on application of the legislature, or of the executive (when the legislature cannot be convened) against domestic violence.

Sections 3–4.
Congress has the power to admit new states. The United States government will protect all states from enemies.

Article V
The Constitution may be amended, or changed.

Article V

Provisions for Amendments

The Congress, whenever two-thirds of both houses shall deem it necessary, shall propose amendments to this Constitution, or, on the application of the legislatures of two-thirds of the several states, shall call a convention for proposing amendments, which, in either case, shall be valid to all intents and purposes, as part of this Constitution, when ratified by the legislatures of three-fourths of the several states, or by conventions in three-fourths thereof, as the one or the other mode of ratification may be proposed by the Congress; provided ~~[that no amendment which may be made prior to the year one thousand eight hundred and eight shall in any manner affect the first and fourth clauses in the ninth section of the first article; and]~~ that no state, without its consent, shall be deprived of its equal suffrage in the Senate.

Article VI
The Constitution is the highest law in the United States. Elected officials must take an oath to support the Constitution.

Article VI

National Debts

(1) All debts contracted and engagements entered into, before the adoption of this Constitution, shall be as valid against the United States under this Constitution, as under the Confederation.

Supremacy of National Law

(2) This Constitution, and the laws of the United States which shall be made in pursuance thereof, and all treaties made, or which shall be made, under the authority of the United States, shall be the supreme law of the land; and the judges in every state shall be

bound thereby, anything in the constitution or laws of any state to the contrary notwithstanding.

(3) The senators and representatives before mentioned, and the members of the several state legislatures, and all executive and judicial officers, both of the United States and of the several states, shall be bound by oath or affirmation, to support this Constitution; but no religious test shall ever be required as a qualification to any office or public trust under the United States.

Article VII

Ratification of Constitution

The ratification of the conventions of nine states, shall be sufficient for the establishments of this Constitution between the states so ratifying the same.

Done in convention by the unanimous consent of the states present the seventeenth day of September in the year of our Lord one thousand seven hundred and eighty-seven and of the independence of the United States of America the twelfth. In witness whereof, we have hereunto subscribed our names,

George Washington—President and deputy from Virginia

Attest: William Jackson—Secretary

Delaware
George Read
Gunning Bedford, Jr.
John Dickinson
Richard Bassett
Jacob Broom

Maryland
James McHenry
Daniel of St. Thomas Jenifer
Daniel Carroll

Virginia
John Blair
James Madison, Jr.

Article VII
The Constitution will go into effect after nine of the thirteen states ratify, or adopt, it.

North Carolina
William Blount
Richard Dobbs Spaight
Hugh Williamson

South Carolina
John Rutledge
Charles Cotesworth Pinckney
Charles Pinckney
Pierce Butler

Georgia
William Few
Abraham Baldwin

New Hampshire
John Langdon
Nicholas Gilman

Massachusetts
Nathaniel Gorhan
Rufus King

Connecticut
William Samuel Johnson
Roger Sherman

New York
Alexander Hamilton

New Jersey
William Livingston
David Brearley
William Paterson
Jonathan Dayton

Pennsylvania
Benjamin Franklin
Thomas Mifflin
Robert Morris
George Clymer
Thomas FitzSimons
Jared Ingersoll
James Wilson
Gouverneur Morris

Amendments to the Constitution

(The first ten amendments are the Bill of Rights)

First Amendment—1791
Congress may not make rules to take away freedom of religion, freedom of speech, freedom of the press, or the right of people to assemble peaceably.

Amendment 1 *Freedom of Religion, Speech, and the Press; Rights of Assembly and Petition*

Congress shall make no law respecting an establishment of religion, or prohibiting the free exercise thereof; or abridging the freedom of speech, or of the press; or the right of the people peaceably to assemble, and to petition the government for a redress of grievances.

Second Amendment—1791
In order to have a prepared military, people have the right to keep and bear arms.

Amendment 2 *Right to Bear Arms*

A well-regulated militia, being necessary to the security of a free state, the right of the people to keep and bear arms shall not be infringed.

Amendment 3 *Housing of Soldiers*

No soldier shall, in time of peace, be quartered in any house, without the consent of the owner; nor in time of war, but in a manner to be prescribed by law.

Third Amendment—1791
In peacetime, the government cannot make citizens feed and house soldiers in their homes.

Amendment 4 *Search and Arrest Warrant*

The right of the people to be secure in their persons, houses, papers, and effects, against unreasonable searches and seizures, shall not be violated; and no warrants shall issue, but upon probable cause, supported by oath or affirmation, and particularly describing the place to be searched, and the persons or things to be seized.

Fourth Amendment—1791
People or their homes may not be searched without a good reason. Search warrants can only be issued if witnesses give good reasons under oath.

Amendment 5 *Rights in Criminal Cases*

No person shall be held to answer for a capital, or otherwise infamous crime, unless on a presentment or indictment of a grand jury, except in cases arising in the land or naval forces, or in the militia, when in actual service in time of war or public danger; nor shall any person be subject for the same offense to be twice put in jeopardy of life or limb; nor shall be compelled in any criminal case to be a witness against himself; nor be deprived of life, liberty, or property, without due process of law; nor shall private property be taken for public use, without just compensation.

Fifth Amendment—1791
Only a grand jury can accuse people of a serious crime. People cannot be forced to give evidence against themselves. People cannot be tried twice for the same crime if found not guilty.

Amendment 6 *Rights to a Fair Trial*

In all criminal prosecutions, the accused shall enjoy the right to a speedy and public trial, by an impartial jury of the states and district wherein the crime shall have been committed, which district shall have been previously ascertained by law, and to be informed of the nature and cause of the accusation; to be confronted

Sixth Amendment—1791
People have the right to a speedy and public trial. They must be told what they are accused of, have the right to a lawyer, and can see and question those who accused them.

with the witnesses against him; to have compulsory process for obtaining witnesses in his favor, and to have the assistance of counsel for his defense.

Seventh Amendment—1791
Judges cannot overturn the decision of a jury, unless they find that mistakes were made.

Amendment 7 *Rights in Civil Cases*

In suits at common law, where the value in controversy shall exceed twenty dollars, the right of trial by jury shall be preserved; and no fact tried by a jury, shall be otherwise re-examined in any court of the United States, than according to the rules of the common law.

Eighth Amendment—1791
Punishment must not be cruel and unusual.

Amendment 8 *Bails, Fines, and Punishments*

Excessive bail shall not be required, nor excessive fines imposed, nor cruel and unusual punishments inflicted.

Ninth Amendment—1791
The people may have rights that are not listed in the Constitution.

Amendment 9 *Rights Retained by the People*

The enumeration in the Constitution of certain rights shall not be construed to deny or disparage others retained by the people.

Tenth Amendment—1791
States and people have powers not clearly given to the government or denied to the states.

Amendment 10 *Powers Reserved to the States and the People*

The powers not delegated to the United States by the Constitution, nor prohibited by it to the states, are reserved to the states respectively, or to the people.

Eleventh Amendment—1795
The power of the judicial branch is limited to certain kinds of cases.

Amendment 11 *Lawsuits Against States*

The judicial power of United States shall not be construed to extend to any suit in law or equity, commenced or prosecuted against one of the United States by citizens of another state, or by citizens or subjects of any foreign state.

Amendment 12 *Election of the President and Vice President*

The Electors shall meet in their respective states and vote by ballot for President and Vice President, one of whom, at least, shall not be an inhabitant of the same state with themselves; they shall name in their ballots the person voted for as President, and in distinct ballots the person voted for as Vice President, and they shall make distinct lists of all person voted for as President, and of all persons voted for as Vice President; and of the number of votes for each, which lists they shall sign and certify, and transmit sealed to the seat of the government of the United States, directed to the president of the Senate;—the president of the Senate shall, in the presence of the Senate and House of Representatives, open all certificates and the votes shall then be counted;—the person having the greatest number of votes for President, shall be the President, if such number be a majority of the whole number of electors appointed; and if no person have such majority, then from the persons having the highest numbers not exceeding three on the list of those voted for as President, the House of Representatives shall choose immediately, by ballot, the President.
But in choosing the President, the votes shall be taken by states, the representation from each state having one vote; a quorum for this purpose shall consist of a member or members from two-thirds of the states, and a majority of all the states shall be necessary to a choice. And if the House of Representatives shall not choose a President whenever the right of choice shall devolve upon them, ~~[before the fourth day of March next following,]~~ then the Vice President shall act as President, as in the case of the death or other

Twelfth Amendment—1804
Electors vote for President and Vice President separately.

constitutional disability of the President. The person having the greatest number of votes as Vice President, shall be the Vice President, if such number be a majority of the whole number of electors appointed, and if no person have a majority, then from the two highest numbers on the list, the Senate shall choose the Vice President; a quorum for the purpose shall consist of two-thirds of the whole number of senators, and a majority of the whole number shall be necessary to a choice. But no person constitutionally ineligible to the office of President shall be eligible to that of Vice President of the United States.

Thirteenth Amendment—1865
Slavery is forbidden.

Amendment 13 *Abolition of Slavery*

SECTION 1. Neither slavery nor involuntary servitude, except as a punishment for crime whereof the party shall have been duly convicted, shall exist within the United States, or any place subject to their jurisdiction.

SECTION 2. Congress shall have power to enforce this article by appropriate legislation.

Fourteenth Amendment—1868
People born in or granted citizenship in the United States are citizens of the United States and the state they live in. No state can take away their rights as citizens.

Amendment 14 *Rights of Citizens*

SECTION 1. All persons born or naturalized in the United States, and subject to the jurisdiction thereof, are citizens of the United States and of the state wherein they reside. No state shall make or enforce any law which shall abridge the privileges or immunities of citizens of the United States; nor shall any state deprive any person of life, liberty, or property, without due process of law; nor deny to any person within its jurisdiction the equal protection of the laws.

SECTION 2. Representatives shall be apportioned among the several states according to their respective numbers, counting the whole number of persons in each state, ~~[excluding Indians not taxed]~~. But when the right to vote at any election for the choice of electors for President and Vice President of the United States, representatives in Congress, the executive and judicial officers of a state, or the members of the legislature thereof, is denied to any of the ~~[male]~~ inhabitants of such state, ~~[being twenty-one years of age,]~~ and citizens of the United States, or in any way abridged, except for participation in rebellion, or other crime, the basis of representation therein shall be reduced in the proportion which the number of such male citizens shall bear to the whole number of ~~[male]~~ citizens ~~[twenty-one years]~~ of age in such state.

SECTION 3. No person shall be a senator or representative in Congress, or elector of President and Vice President, or hold any office, civil or military, under the United States, or under any state, who, having previously taken an oath, as a member of Congress, or as an officer of the United States, or as a member of any state legislature, or as an executive or judicial officer of any state, to support the Constitution of the United States, shall have engaged in insurrection or rebellion against the same, or given aid or comfort to the enemies thereof. But Congress may by a vote of two-thirds of each House, remove such disability.

SECTION 4. The validity of the public debt of the Untied States, authorized by law, including debts incurred for payment of pensions and bounties for services in suppressing insurrection or rebellion, shall not be questioned. But neither the United States or any state shall assume or pay any debt or obligation incurred in aid of insurrection or rebellion against the

United States, or any claim for the loss or emancipation of any slave, but all such debts, obligations, and claims shall be held illegal and void.

SECTION 5. The Congress shall have power to enforce, by appropriate legislation, the provisions of this article.

Fifteenth Amendment—1870
No one can be denied the right to vote on the basis of race.

Amendment 15 *African American Suffrage*

SECTION 1. The right of citizens of the United States to vote shall not be denied or abridged by the United States or by any state on account of race, color, or previous condition of servitude.

SECTION 2. The Congress shall have power to enforce this article by appropriate legislation.

Sixteenth Amendment—1913
Congress is allowed to pass a tax on income.

Amendment 16 *Income Taxes*

The Congress shall have power to lay and collect taxes on incomes, from whatever source derived, without apportionment among the several states, and without regard to any census or enumeration.

Seventeenth Amendment—1913
Senators will be elected directly by the people.

Amendment 17 *Popular Election of Senators*

(1) The Senate of the United States shall be composed of two senators from each state, elected by the people thereof for six years; and each senator shall have one vote. The electors in each state shall have the qualifications requisite for electors of the most numerous branch of the state legislatures.

(2) When vacancies happen in the representation of any state in the Senate, the executive authority of such state shall issue writs of election to fill such vacancies: Provided, That the legislature of any state may empower the executive thereof to make temporary appointments until the people fill the vacancies by election as the legislature may direct.

(3) [This amendment shall not be so construed as to affect the election or term of any senator chosen before it becomes valid as part of the Constitution.]

Amendment 18 *Prohibition of Liquor*

[**SECTION 1.** After one year from the ratification of this article the manufacture, sale, or transportation of intoxicating liquors within, the importation thereof into, or the exportation thereof from the United States and all territory subject to the jurisdiction thereof for beverage purposes is hereby prohibited.

SECTION 2. Congress and the several states shall have concurrent power to enforce this article by appropriate legislation.

SECTION 3. This article shall be inoperative unless it shall have been ratified as an amendment to the Constitution by the legislatures of the several states; as provided in the Constitution, within seven years from the date of the submission hereof to the states by the Congress.]

Eighteenth Amendment — 1919
Liquor cannot be manufactured or sold in the United States.

Amendment 19 *Women's Suffrage*

SECTION 1. The right of citizens of the United States to vote shall not be denied or abridged by the United States or by any state on account of sex.

SECTION 2. Congress shall have power to enforce this article by appropriate legislation.

Nineteenth Amendment — 1920
Women are given the right to vote.

Amendment 20 *Terms of the President and Congress*

SECTION 1. The terms of the President and Vice President shall end at noon on the 20th day of January, and the terms of senators and representatives at noon on the third day of January, of the year in which such terms would have ended if this article had not been ratified; and the terms of their successors shall then begin.

Twentieth Amendment — 1933
Presidents start their new terms on January 20. Congress starts its new term on January 3.

SECTION 2. The Congress shall assemble at least once in every year, and such meeting shall begin at noon on the third day of January, unless they shall by law appoint a different day.

SECTION 3. If, at the time fixed for the beginning of the term of the President, the President elect shall have died, the Vice President elect shall become President. If a President shall not have been chosen before the time fixed for the beginning of his term, or if the President elect shall have failed to qualify, then the Vice President elect shall act as President until a President shall have qualified; and the Congress may by law provide for the case wherein neither a President elect nor a Vice President elect shall have qualified, declaring who shall then act as President, or the manner in which one who is to act shall be selected, and such person shall act accordingly until a President or Vice President shall have qualified.

SECTION 4. The Congress may by law provide for the case of the death of any of the persons from whom the House of Representatives may choose a President whenever the right of choice shall have devolved upon them, and for the case of the death of any of the persons from whom the Senate may choose a Vice President whenever the right of choice shall have devolved upon them.

SECTION 5. Sections 1 and 2 shall take effect on the 15th day of October following the ratification of this article.

SECTION 6. This article shall be inoperative unless it shall have been ratified as an amendment to the Constitution by the legislatures of three-fourths of the several states within seven years from the date of its submission.

Amendment 21 *Repeal of 18th Amendment*

SECTION 1. The eighteenth article of amendment to the Constitution of the United States is hereby repealed.

SECTION 2. The transportation or importation into any state, territory, or possession of the United States for delivery or use therein of intoxicating liquors, in violation of the laws thereof, is hereby prohibited.

SECTION 3. This article shall be inoperative unless it shall have been ratified as an amendment to the Constitution by conventions in the several states, as provided in the Constitution, within seven years from the date of the submission hereof to the states by the Congress.

Twenty-first Amendment—1933
This amendment repeals, or cancels, the Eighteenth Amendment.

Amendment 22 *Limitation of Presidential Terms*

SECTION 1. No person shall be elected to the office of President more than twice, and no person who has held the office of President, or acted as President, for more than two years of a term to which some other person was elected President shall be elected to the office of the President more than once. ~~[But this article shall not apply to any person holding the office of President when this article was proposed by the Congress, and shall not prevent any person who may be holding the office of President, or acting as President, during the term within which this article becomes operative from holding the office of President or acting as President during the remainder of such term.]~~

SECTION 2. ~~[This article shall be inoperative unless it shall have been ratified as an amendment to the Constitution by the legislatures of three-fourths of the several states within seven years form the date of its submission to the states by the Congress.]~~

Twenty-second Amendment—1951
A President cannot serve more than two terms.

Twenty-third Amendment—1961
Residents of Washington, D.C. have the right to vote for President.

Amendment 23 *Presidential Electors in the District of Columbia*

SECTION 1. The district constituting the seat of government of the United States shall appoint in such manner as the Congress may direct: A number of electors of President and Vice President equal to the whole number of senators and representatives in Congress to which the district would be entitled if it were a state, but in no event more than the least populous state; they shall be in addition to those appointed by the states, but they shall be considered, for the purposes of the election of President and Vice President, to be electors appointed by a state; and they shall meet in the district and perform such duties as provided by the twelfth article of amendment.

SECTION 2. Congress shall have power to enforce this article by appropriate legislation.

Twenty-fourth Amendment—1964
No state can deny a citizen the right to vote because of unpaid poll taxes or any other tax.

Amendment 24 *Poll Taxes*

SECTION 1. The right of citizens of the United States to vote in any primary or other election for President or Vice President, for electors for President or Vice President, or for senator or representative in Congress, shall not be denied or abridged by the United States or any state by reason of failure to pay any poll tax or other tax.

SECTION 2. The Congress shall have the power to enforce this article by appropriate legislation.

Amendment 25 *Presidential Disability and Succession*

SECTION 1. In case of the removal of the President from office or of his death or resignation, the Vice President shall become President.

SECTION 2. Whenever there is a vacancy in the office of the Vice President, the President shall nominate a Vice President who shall take office upon confirmation by a majority vote of both houses of Congress.

SECTION 3. Whenever the President transmits to the president pro tempore of the Senate and the speaker of the House of Representatives his written declaration that he is unable to discharge the powers and duties of his office, and until he transmits to them a written declaration to the contrary, such powers and duties shall be discharged by the Vice President as Acting President.

SECTION 4. Whenever the Vice President and a majority of either the principal officers of the executive departments or of such other body as Congress may by law provide, transmit to the president pro tempore of the Senate and the speaker of the House of Representatives their written declaration that the President is unable to discharge the powers and duties of his office, the Vice President shall immediately assume the powers and duties of the office as Acting President.

Thereafter, when the President transmits to the president pro tempore of the Senate and the speaker of the House of Representatives his written declaration that no inability exists, he shall resume the powers and duties of his office unless the Vice President and a majority of either the principal officers of the executive department or of such other body as Congress may by

Twenty-fifth Amendment—1967
If a President dies, resigns, or is removed from office, the Vice President becomes President. If the President becomes too sick to perform the duties of office, then the Vice President becomes the Acting President.

law provide, transmit within four days to the president pro tempore of the Senate and the speaker of the House of Representatives their written declaration that the President is unable to discharge the powers and duties of his office. Thereupon Congress shall decide the issue, assembling within forty-eight hours for that purpose if not in session. In the Congress, within twenty-one days after receipt of the latter written declaration, or, if Congress is not in session within twenty-one days after Congress is required to assemble, determines by two-thirds vote of both houses that the President is unable to discharge the powers and duties of his office, the Vice President shall continue to discharge the same as Acting President; otherwise, the President shall resume the powers and duties of his office.

Twenty-sixth Amendment—1971
Eighteen-year-olds are given the right to vote.

Amendment 26 *Suffrage for 18-Year-Olds*

SECTION 1. The right of citizens of the United States, who are eighteen years of age or older, to vote shall not be denied or abridged by the United States or by any state on account of age.

SECTION 2. The Congress shall have power to enforce this article by appropriate legislation.

Twenty-seventh Amendment—1992
Laws passed by Congress to increase their salaries do not take effect until after the next election of representatives.

Amendment 27 *Congressional Compensation*

No law, varying the compensation for the services of the senators and representatives, shall take effect until an election of representatives shall have intervened.

The Presidents of the United States

1

2

3

4

5

6

7

8

9

10

11

12

13

14

	Years in Office	Vice President
1. George Washington Born: 1732 Died: 1799	1789–1797	John Adams
2. John Adams Born: 1735 Died: 1826	1797–1801	Thomas Jefferson
3. Thomas Jefferson Born: 1743 Died: 1826	1801–1809	Aaron Burr, George Clinton
4. James Madison Born: 1751 Died: 1836	1809–1817	George Clinton, Elbridge Gerry
5. James Monroe Born: 1758 Died: 1831	1817–1825	Daniel D. Tompkins
6. John Quincy Adams Born: 1767 Died: 1848	1825–1829	John C. Calhoun
7. Andrew Jackson Born: 1767 Died: 1845	1829–1837	John C. Calhoun, Martin Van Buren
8. Martin Van Buren Born: 1782 Died: 1862	1837–1841	Richard M. Johnson
9. William Henry Harrison* Born: 1773 Died: 1841	1841	John Tyler
10. John Tyler Born: 1790 Died: 1862	1841–1845	None
11. James K. Polk Born: 1795 Died: 1849	1845–1849	George M. Dallas
12. Zachary Taylor* Born: 1784 Died: 1850	1849–1850	Millard Fillmore
13. Millard Fillmore Born: 1800 Died: 1874	1850–1853	None
14. Franklin Pierce Born: 1804 Died: 1869	1853–1857	William R. King

* died in office ** assassinated while in office *** resigned while in office

The Presidents of the United States

15

16

17

18

19

20

21

22, 24

23

25

26

27

28

29

	Years in Office	Vice President
15. James Buchanan Born: 1791 Died: 1868	1857–1861	John C. Breckinridge
16. Abraham Lincoln** Born: 1809 Died: 1865	1861–1865	Hannibal Hamlin, Andrew Johnson
17. Andrew Johnson Born: 1808 Died: 1875	1865–1869	None
18. Ulysses S. Grant Born: 1822 Died: 1885	1869–1877	Schuyler Colfax, Henry Wilson
19. Rutherford B. Hayes Born: 1822 Died: 1893	1877–1881	William A. Wheeler
20. James A. Garfield** Born: 1831 Died: 1881	1881	Chester A. Arthur
21. Chester A. Arthur Born: 1830 Died: 1886	1881–1885	None
22. Grover Cleveland Born: 1837 Died: 1908	1885–1889	Thomas A. Hendricks
23. Benjamin Harrison Born: 1833 Died: 1901	1889–1893	Levi P. Morton
24. Grover Cleveland Born: 1837 Died: 1908	1893–1897	Adlai E. Stevenson
25. William McKinley** Born: 1843 Died: 1901	1897–1901	Garrett Hobart, Theodore Roosevelt
26. Theodore Roosevelt Born: 1858 Died: 1919	1901–1909	Charles W. Fairbanks
27. William Howard Taft Born: 1857 Died: 1930	1909–1913	James S. Sherman
28. Woodrow Wilson Born: 1856 Died: 1924	1913–1921	Thomas R. Marshall
29. Warren G. Harding* Born: 1865 Died: 1923	1921–1923	Calvin Coolidge

* died in office ** assassinated while in office *** resigned while in office

The Presidents of the United States

30

31

32

33

34

35

36

37

38

39

40

41

42

43

	Years in Office	Vice President
30. Calvin Coolidge Born: 1872 Died: 1933	1923–1929	Charles G. Dawes
31. Herbert C. Hoover Born: 1874 Died: 1964	1929–1933	Charles Curtis
32. Franklin D. Roosevelt* Born: 1882 Died: 1945	1933–1945	John N. Garner, Henry A. Wallace, Harry S Truman
33. Harry S Truman Born: 1884 Died: 1972	1945–1953	Alben W. Barkley
34. Dwight D. Eisenhower Born: 1890 Died: 1969	1953–1961	Richard M. Nixon
35. John F. Kennedy** Born: 1917 Died: 1963	1961–1963	Lyndon B. Johnson
36. Lyndon B. Johnson Born: 1908 Died: 1973	1963–1969	Hubert H. Humphrey
37. Richard M. Nixon*** Born: 1913 Died: 1994	1969–1974	Spiro T. Agnew, Gerald R. Ford
38. Gerald R. Ford Born: 1913	1974–1977	Nelson R. Rockefeller
39. James E. Carter, Jr. Born: 1924	1977–1981	Walter F. Mondale
40. Ronald Reagan Born: 1911	1981–1989	George H. W. Bush
41. George H. W. Bush Born: 1924	1989–1993	J. Danforth Quayle
42. William J. Clinton Born: 1946	1993–2001	Albert Gore, Jr.
43. George W. Bush Born: 1946	2001–	Richard B. Cheney

* died in office ** assassinated while in office *** resigned while in office

The Fifty States

State (U.S. government abbreviation)	Date of Entry into Union (Order of entry)	Total Area in Square Miles (Rank)	Population (in thousands)	Capital City	State Nickname
Alabama (AL)	1819 (22)	52,423 (30)	4,447	Montgomery	Heart of Dixie
Alaska (AK)	1959 (49)	656,424 (1)	627	Juneau	The Last Frontier
Arizona (AZ)	1912 (48)	114,006 (6)	5,131	Phoenix	Grand Canyon State
Arkansas (AR)	1836 (25)	53,182 (29)	2,673	Little Rock	Natural State
California (CA)	1850 (31)	163,707 (3)	33,872	Sacramento	Golden State
Colorado (CO)	1876 (38)	104,100 (8)	4,301	Denver	Centennial State
Connecticut (CT)	1788 (5)	5,544 (48)	3,406	Hartford	Constitution State
Delaware (DE)	1787 (1)	2,489 (49)	784	Dover	First State
Florida (FL)	1845 (27)	65,756 (22)	15,982	Tallahassee	Sunshine State
Georgia (GA)	1788 (4)	59,441 (24)	8,186	Atlanta	Empire State of the South
Hawaii (HI)	1959 (50)	10,932 (43)	1,212	Honolulu	Aloha State
Idaho (ID)	1890 (43)	83,574 (14)	1,294	Boise	Gem State
Illinois (IL)	1818 (21)	57,918 (25)	12,419	Springfield	Prairie State
Indiana (IN)	1816 (19)	36,420 (38)	6,080	Indianapolis	Hoosier State
Iowa (IA)	1846 (29)	56,276 (26)	2,926	Des Moines	Hawkeye State
Kansas (KS)	1861 (34)	82,282 (15)	2,688	Topeka	Sunflower State
Kentucky (KY)	1792 (15)	40,411 (37)	4,042	Frankfort	Bluegrass State
Louisiana (LA)	1812 (18)	51,843 (31)	4,469	Baton Rouge	Pelican State
Maine (ME)	1820 (23)	35,387 (39)	1,275	Augusta	Pine Tree State
Maryland (MD)	1788 (7)	12,407 (42)	5,296	Annapolis	Old Line State
Massachusetts (MA)	1788 (6)	10,555 (44)	6,349	Boston	Bay State
Michigan (MI)	1837 (26)	96,705 (11)	9,938	Lansing	Wolverine State
Minnesota (MN)	1858 (32)	86,943 (12)	4,919	St. Paul	Gopher State
Mississippi (MS)	1817 (20)	48,434 (32)	2,845	Jackson	Magnolia State
Missouri (MO)	1821 (24)	69,709 (21)	5,595	Jefferson City	Show Me State
Montana (MT)	1889 (41)	147,046 (4)	902	Helena	Treasure State
Nebraska (NE)	1867 (37)	77,358 (16)	1,711	Lincoln	Cornhusker State
Nevada (NV)	1864 (36)	110,567 (7)	1,998	Carson City	Silver State
New Hampshire (NH)	1788 (9)	9,351 (46)	1,236	Concord	Granite State
New Jersey (NJ)	1787 (3)	8,722 (47)	8,414	Trenton	Garden State

The Fifty States

State (U.S. government abbreviation)	Date of Entry into Union (Order of entry)	Total Area in Square Miles (Rank)	Population (in thousands)	Capital City	State Nickname
New Mexico (NM)	1912 (47)	121,598 (5)	1,819	Santa Fe	Land of Enchantment
New York (NY)	1788 (11)	54,471 (27)	18,976	Albany	Empire State
North Carolina (NC)	1789 (12)	53,821 (28)	8,049	Raleigh	Tar Heel State
North Dakota (ND)	1889 (39)	70,704 (19)	642	Bismarck	Flickertail State
Ohio (OH)	1803 (17)	44,828 (34)	11,353	Columbus	Buckeye State
Oklahoma (OK)	1907 (46)	69,903 (20)	3,451	Oklahoma City	Sooner State
Oregon (OR)	1859 (33)	98,386 (9)	3,421	Salem	Beaver State
Pennsylvania (PA)	1787 (2)	46,058 (33)	12,281	Harrisburg	Keystone State
Rhode Island (RI)	1790 (13)	1,545 (50)	1,048	Providence	Ocean State
South Carolina (SC)	1788 (8)	32,008 (40)	4,012	Columbia	Palmetto State
South Dakota (SD)	1889 (40)	77,121 (17)	755	Pierre	Mount Rushmore State
Tennessee (TN)	1796 (16)	42,146 (36)	5,689	Nashville	Volunteer State
Texas (TX)	1845 (28)	268,601 (2)	20,852	Austin	Lone Star State
Utah (UT)	1896 (45)	84,904 (13)	2,233	Salt Lake City	Beehive State
Vermont (VT)	1791 (14)	9,615 (45)	609	Montpelier	Green Mountain State
Virginia (VI)	1788 (10)	42,777 (35)	7,079	Richmond	Old Dominion
Washington (WA)	1889 (42)	71,302 (18)	5,894	Olympia	Evergreen State
West Virginia (WV)	1863 (35)	24,231 (41)	1,808	Charleston	Mountain State
Wisconsin (WI)	1848 (30)	65,499 (23)	5,364	Madison	Badger State
Wyoming (WY)	1890 (44)	97,818 (10)	494	Cheyenne	Equality State
District of Columbia (DC)		68 (51)	572		
Commonwealths and Territories	**Total Area in Square Miles**	**Population (in thousands)**			**Capital**
Puerto Rico (PR)	3,508	3,809			San Juan
Guam (GU)	217	155			Agana
U.S. Virgin Islands (VI)	171	109			Charlotte Amalie
American Samoa (AS)	90	57			Pago Pago
N. Mariana Islands (MP)	189	69			Saipan

Glossary

abolitionist a person who wanted to end slavery (p. 162)

acid rain rain that is polluted by harmful chemicals (p. 606)

affirmative action a program for correcting the effects of discrimination (p. 548)

Agent Orange a powerful chemical that kills all plant life where it is sprayed (p. 531)

alliance a partnership (p. 96)

ally a nation that joins with other nations for the same cause (p. 61)

ambassador a person sent to another country to speak for the government of his or her own country (p. 317)

amendment a change or addition to a document (p. 92)

amphibious landing a planned movement of troops from the sea (p. 412)

annex to add or take possession of a smaller country (p. 295)

anti-Semitism the practice of hating Jewish people simply because they are Jewish (p. 383)

appeal to ask a higher court to review the decision of a lower court (p. 470)

appeasement the policy of giving in to someone's demands in order to keep peace (p. 393)

armistice an agreement to stop fighting (p. 324)

arms race a contest to build weapons and military power (p. 310)

assassinate to murder a political leader like a President (p. 192)

assembly line a system in which each worker does a different job in putting together a product (p. 335)

astronomy the study of stars and planets (p. 14)

atomic bomb a nuclear weapon with enormous power to harm (p. 423)

automation the use of machines to do jobs once done by people (p. 450)

Axis Powers the countries that fought the Allies in World War II (p. 406)

baby boom a large increase in births, especially in the United States, after World War II (p. 451)

barter to trade a product or service for another product or service (p. 48)

bilingual able to speak two languages very well (p. 517)

black codes a series of southern laws to limit the freedom of African Americans (p. 200)

Black Panther party a political party formed to work for the rights of African Americans (p. 508)

black power a movement among African Americans to gain political and economic power (p. 507)

blacklist a list of people who are not approved of for employment (p. 438)

blockade an action to keep supplies from getting into or out of an area (p. 70)

bond a paper that shows debt, or money owed (p. 321)

bonus money given in addition to what is owed (p. 356)

boom town a camp that grows into a town almost overnight (p. 230)

border state a slave state between the North and the South that remained in the Union during the Civil War (p. 176)

boycott a nonviolent protest in which people refuse to buy products or use services (p. 475)

bribe money paid to get someone to do something against the law (p. 275)

budget surplus the amount of money that is left over after spending (p. 582)

Cabinet a group of people chosen by the President to give advice (p. 93)

canal a human-made waterway (p. 125)

capitalism a system in which private businesses, farms, and factories compete with one another to make a profit (p. 279)

carpetbagger a name for a Northerner who went to the South after the Civil War (p. 205)

cash crop a crop grown for sale rather than for use by a farmer (p. 27)

cash-and-carry policy a plan that let nations at war buy goods that they could pay cash for and then carry home (p. 398)

casualty a person killed, injured, or captured in war (p. 179)

cede to surrender something (p. 62)

censor to make changes in or to take parts out (p. 538)

charter a written agreement giving certain rights (p. 26)

civil disobedience a nonviolent refusal to obey laws or government demands in order to cause change (p. 477)

civil rights rights belonging to all citizens (p. 200)

civil service a system that includes most government workers who are appointed rather than elected (p. 276)

civil war a war between regions or groups of people in the same country (p. 170)

civilian a person who is not a soldier (p. 181)

civilization the way of life of a people in one place and time (p. 7)

coalition a temporary alliance of nations for a special action (p. 586)

cold war a sharp conflict between countries without actual war (p. 429)

colony a settlement ruled by people from another land (p. 11)

common an open area shared by all villagers (p. 49)

communism an economic system in which the government owns all property and businesses (p. 322)

company town a community set up and run by a company for its workers (p. 246)

compass an instrument that shows direction (p. 14)

compromise a settling of differences where both sides give up something (p. 89)

conquer to take over and control (p. 22)

conscientious objector a person whose beliefs do not let him or her take an active part in war (p. 534)

conscription drafting of people for military service (p. 185)

conservative a person who wants the government to do less for its citizens (p. 375)

constitution the laws and plan of a nation's government (p. 84)

consumer a person who buys and uses products (p. 457)

containment a policy preventing a country from expanding its power and threatening other countries (p. 430)

contra a rebel fighting the Sandinista government in Nicaragua (p. 572)

convention a large gathering of people for a particular reason (p. 88)

convert to change from one religion or belief to another (p. 23)

corollary an addition to a document (p. 305)

corporation a large company formed by a group of investors (p. 240)

cotton gin a machine that separates cotton from its seed (p. 112)

debtor a person who owes money to others (p. 37)

declaration a public statement (p. 66)

default to fail to pay a loan when it is due (p. 353)

deferment putting off, or delaying, having to serve in the armed forces (p. 534)

demilitarized zone an area where no military forces are allowed (p. 437)

deport to force a person who is not a citizen to leave the country by government order (p. 346)

depose to remove from office (p. 526)

depression a time when the economy of a nation falls sharply (p. 353)

desegregate to end segregation, or separation of the races (p. 472)

détente an easing of tension between nations (p. 545)

dictator a ruler with complete power in a country (p. 390)

discrimination unjust treatment of a person based on false ideas about a particular group (p. 187)

dissident a person who strongly disagrees with government policies or its rule (p. 563)

doctrine a set of beliefs (p. 108)

domino theory belief that if one country falls to communism, others nearby will fall, one after the other (p. 525)

downsize to make smaller, to reduce the size of the workforce (p. 581)

drought a long period of very dry weather (p. 358)

economy the way goods, wealth, and services are created and used (p. 42)

elector a person selected to vote for the President and Vice President (p. 103)

electoral vote a vote cast by a chosen elector in a presidential election (p. 600)

embargo a government order that stops trade with other countries (p. 106)

empire the territories and people under the control of one ruler (p. 8)

equal rights rights that all people in a society should have (p. 142)

ethnic cleansing the removal of one group of people by another group in the same region (p. 585)

exclusion keeping a person or a group from coming in (p. 263)

executive branch the part of government that carries out laws (p. 90)

executive order a rule made by the President (p. 467)

executive privilege the right of a President to withhold important information from other branches of the government (p. 554)

exile a person who lives away from his or her home country (p. 492)

export to send goods to another region or country (p. 43)

extremist a person whose opinions are very different from those of most people (p. 166)

fallout the radioactive waste from a nuclear blast (p. 440)

famine a time when people in a place starve because there is not enough food (p. 140)

Fascist a member of a political party who supports extreme nationalism and a dictator (p. 391)

federal deficit the difference between the amount of money the government spends and what it collects (p. 570)

feminism a political and social movement that favors equal rights for women (p. 513)

fireside chat a radio speech to Americans given by President Franklin Roosevelt (p. 372)

foreclose to take the property of someone who has failed to pay back a loan (p. 355)

foreign policy the way a country deals with other countries (p. 302)

forty-niner a person who went to California in 1849 to find gold (p. 133)

free state a state in which slavery was not allowed (p. 156)

freedman a person freed from slavery (p. 206)

frontier a newly settled or lightly settled area just outside an area of older settlements (p. 44)

fugitive a person who runs away or escapes (p. 159)

gender whether a person is male or female (p. 513)

generation gap a large difference in taste and values between young people and their parents (p. 458)

genocide the planned murder of an entire people (p. 421)

geography the study of climates and land forms (p. 14)

ghetto a neighborhood where people of the same race, religion, or country live (p. 257)

glacier a huge sheet of moving ice (p. 4)

glasnost a policy that allows open discussion about Soviet life and politics (p. 575)

global warming the theory, or idea, that Earth's temperature is slowly rising (p. 607)

grand jury a jury that decides if charges against a person are strong enough to go to trial (p. 583)

Great Society President Johnson's ideas, goals, and programs for America's future (p. 498)

guerrilla warfare fighting by troops who are not members of a regular army, using surprise attacks (p. 526)

Holocaust the mass murder of millions of Jews and other people by the Nazis (p. 421)

homesteader a person who received land under the Homestead Act of 1862 (p. 220)

hostage a person who is held captive until certain demands are met (p. 565)

human rights the basic freedoms that all people should have (p. 563)

immigrant a person who comes to a country for the purpose of living there (p. 139)

impeach to accuse a high public official (like the President of the United States) of a crime (p. 204)

imperialism the policy of one nation gaining control over other lands and using them to build an empire (p. 299)

import an item brought into a country or region from another country or region (p. 49)

impressment the act of forcing a person into public service, especially into a navy (p. 106)

income tax a tax paid on the money a person earns (p. 284)

indentured servant a person who signs a contract to work for others (p. 27)

industry the making or producing of goods by businesses and factories (p. 109)

inflation a sharp rise in the price of goods (p. 344)

installment plan the payment of money over time toward the total cost of an item (p. 337)

integrate to open to people of all backgrounds; to bring together (p. 467)

interchangeable part a part that can be used in place of another part in manufactured products (p. 111)

internment camp a prisonlike place in which people are held during a war (p. 418)

interstate highway system a network of roads built and cared for by the U.S. government (p. 460)

iron curtain an imaginary wall, or dividing line, separating the Soviet nations from the rest of Europe (p. 429)

isolationist a person or country that wants to stay out of the political affairs of other countries (p. 292)

isthmus a narrow strip of land that connects two larger-sized lands (p. 303)

jazz a kind of music created by African Americans in the South in the early 1900s (p. 339)

joint-stock company a company in which people give money to share costs (p. 26)

judicial branch the part of government that settles differences about the meanings of laws (p. 90)

jury a group of people who decide whether a person on trial is guilty or innocent (p. 54)

kickback an illegal payment of money made in return for a favor or service (p. 275)

labor union a group of workers that tries to help its members (p. 247)

legislative branch the part of government that makes laws (p. 90)

lend-lease plan to lend or lease supplies to a country whose defense is needed to protect the United States (p. 399)

liberal a person who wants the government to do more for its citizens (p. 376)

life expectancy the number of years a person can expect to live (p. 518)

lobby to try to make lawmakers pass certain laws (p. 513)

Loyalist a colonist who remained loyal to Great Britain (p. 72)

martial law rule by an army instead of by elected officials (p. 176)

mass media the communications that reach large numbers of people (p. 337)

mass production a method of making large numbers of goods quickly and cheaply (p. 111)

McCarthyism term named for Senator Joseph McCarthy's campaign of accusing people of being Communists (p. 439)

Medicaid medical insurance for low-income people and people with disabilities (p. 499)

Medicare medical insurance and hospital care for older Americans (p. 499)

mercantilism the idea that a nation becomes stronger by building up its gold supply and increasing its trade (p. 54)

migrant worker a worker who travels from place to place to harvest crops (p. 359)

migration a movement of people within a country or area (p. 265)

militarism the policy of strong military actions taken by the leaders of a country (p. 396)

militia an army of citizens used in emergencies (p. 69)

millennium a period of 1,000 years (p. 600)

mission a settlement, built by a church, from which people teach their religion to others (p. 23)

mobilize to get ready for war (p. 406)

monopoly the complete control of an industry by one company or person (p. 243)

mountain man a fur trapper and trader who lived in the mountains and knew the wilderness (p. 126)

muckraker a writer who brings attention to corruption (p. 280)

napalm a sticky gasoline jelly used in bombs (p. 531)

national debt the amount of money the federal government owes (p. 570)

nationalism pride in one's country (p. 107)

nativism a feeling of citizens who are against immigrants (p. 263)

navigator a person who plans the direction of a ship (p. 11)

Nazi a member of a political party in Germany led by Adolf Hitler (p. 392)

neutral not favoring either side in a quarrel or war (p. 72)

New Deal Franklin D. Roosevelt's plan for helping the U.S. economy during the Great Depression (p. 370)

New Frontier President Kennedy's ideas, goals, and programs for America's future (p. 486)

nisei second-generation Japanese Americans (p. 519)

nomad a person who travels all the time in search of food (p. 4)

normalize to continue normal dealings with a country, or to begin again (p. 544)

overseer a person who watches over and directs the work of others (p. 113)

partisan a person who strongly believes in a cause (p. 409)

patent a government grant that allows only the inventor to make, use, and sell an invention for a certain time (p. 236)

Patriot a colonist who wanted independence from Great Britain (p. 72)

perjury lying in court while under oath (p. 554)

political rights rights given to people by the government (p. 54)

poll tax a tax paid before someone can vote (p. 210)

pollution damage to land, air, and water from harmful materials (p. 239)

popular sovereignty a system that allowed people in a territory to make their own decisions (p. 165)

popular vote a vote cast by a citizen in a presidential election (p. 600)

prairie a large area of level or slightly rolling land (p. 220)

primary an early election that helps a political party choose its candidate (p. 580)

proclamation an official government announcement (p. 63)

Prohibition a time period when making, selling, and transporting alcohol was unlawful in the United States (p. 287)

propaganda the spreading of ideas, information, and beliefs to help or hurt a cause (p. 315)

prospector a person who searches for gold, silver, or other valuable minerals (p. 230)

protectorate a country that is partly controlled and protected by a more powerful country (p. 295)

public works construction projects paid for by public funds (p. 364)

puppet state a government that is under the control of another stronger power (p. 396)

quarantine to isolate, or cut off, from other countries (p. 494)

racism feelings against people because of their skin color (p. 265)

ranch a large farm with grazing land for raising horses, cattle, or sheep (p. 133)

ratify to approve (p. 90)

rationing limiting the amount of something that each person can buy (p. 414)

recession a period of time when the economy slows down (p. 460)

Reconstruction the time period after the Civil War when the United States began to rebuild the South (p. 198)

recycling using a product more than once (p. 607)

reformer a person who works for a cause that improves the way something is done in a society (p. 147)

regulate to control (p. 54)

relief help given to poor people (p. 365)

renaissance a time of new interest and activity in the arts (p. 341)

repeal to end (p. 65)

representative a person selected to act for others (p. 64)

reservation public land set aside by the government for the use of a particular group of people (p. 222)

resolution an official statement of opinion (p. 604)

revenue sharing a program in which the federal government shares its income from taxes with state and local governments (p. 547)

revolution a sudden, complete change of government (p. 66)

rural having to do with the country (p. 138)

satellite a country controlled by a more powerful country (p. 429)

scalawag a name for a white Southerner who supported Reconstruction government (p. 205)

secede to break away from, as a state leaving the Union (p. 169)

sectionalism loyalty to one region of a country instead of to the whole country (p. 158)

segregation the separation of people by race (p. 204)

service industry a business that provides a service for others (p. 450)

sharecropping farming someone else's land while paying a share of the crops raised for rent (p. 208)

siege a military blocking of a city to force its surrender (p. 407)

sit-in a nonviolent protest in which people sit down and refuse to get up (p. 476)

skyscraper a very tall building with many floors, elevators, and a steel frame (p. 259)

slave state a state in which slavery was allowed (p. 156)

soap opera daytime radio shows that were paid for by soap companies (p. 381)

space race the competition among countries to be first in exploring space (p. 441)

special prosecutor an investigator who looks into the actions of the President and other high officials (p. 574)

spoils system the system of giving government jobs to people who had helped to get the winner elected (p. 121)

stagflation a rise in prices together with a drop in business activity and more unemployment (p. 550)

stalemate a situation in which neither side wins nor loses (p. 312)

stock market a place where stocks, or shares in businesses, are bought and sold (p. 352)

strike to refuse to work until certain demands, such as higher wages or better working conditions, are met (p. 248)

suburb a community at the edge of a city (p. 451)

suffrage the right to vote (p. 142)

superpower a country that is a top world power (p. 437)

tariff tax on goods brought into a country (p. 120)

tax money that must be paid to a government (p. 55)

temperance a reform movement that is against drinking alcohol (p. 149)

tenement an apartment house with poor safety, sanitation, and comfort conditions (p. 257)

territory land that belongs to a national government but is not a state (p. 86)

terrorist a person who uses violence for a political cause (p. 311)

textile woven cloth (p. 110)

total war the destruction of food, equipment, and anything else of use to soldiers and civilians (p. 190)

tradition the handing down of information, beliefs, and customs from one generation to another (p. 222)

transcontinental across a continent (p. 218)

treaty a written agreement between two or more nations (p. 36)

trust a giant corporation, or group of companies (p. 282)

underclass a group of people with few job skills and little education (p. 593)

Underground Railroad a network of secret escape routes enslaved African Americans followed to reach freedom in the North (p. 162)

urban having to do with the city (p. 138)

urban renewal a program to rebuild run-down areas of cities (p. 490)

veteran a person who has served in the armed forces (p. 193)

victory garden a garden in which citizens raised their own food during World War I (p. 321)

Viet Cong Communist Vietnamese in South Vietnam (p. 525)

Vietnamization President Nixon's plan for turning over the fighting of the Vietnam War to the South Vietnamese (p. 537)

workfare a government program in which people have to work to receive aid (p. 593)

yellow journalism the publishing of exaggerated or made-up news stories to attract readers and influence their ideas (p. 297)

Index

B

C

D

E

F

G

H

I

J

K

L

M

N

Q

R

S

Y

Z

Acknowledgments

Grateful acknowledgment is made to the following publishers, authors, and copyright holders:

Random House, Inc.: from ON THE PULSE OF THE MORNING by Maya Angelou. Copyright © 1993 by Maya Angelou. Reprinted by permission of Random House, Inc.

I AIN'T MARCHING ANYMORE, by Phil Ochs © (Renewed) Ballicade Music, Inc. (ASCAP). All reprint rights reserved Hal Leonard Corporation.

Note: Every effort has been made to locate the copyright owner of material used in this textbook. Omissions brought to our attention will be corrected in subsequent editions.

Grateful acknowledgment is made to the following for illustrations, photographs, and reproductions on the pages indicated:

Unit 1: p. 1: Christie's Images; p. 2: PhotoDisc, Inc.; p. 2: The Granger Collection; p. 6: Breton Littlehales, National Geographic; p. 11: Art Resource; p 12: The Granger Collection; p. 16: The Granger Collection; p. 20: The Granger Collection; p. 20: Courtesy of the Pilgrim Society, Plymouth, MA; p. 22: Victor Boswell, National Geographic Image collection; p. 23: Corbis/Bettmann; p. 26: The Library of Virginia; p. 28: Courtesy of The Pilgrim Society, Plymouth MA; p. 29: Courtesy of The Pilgrim Society, Plymouth MA; p. 31: The Granger Collection; p. 33: The Granger Collection; p. 36: The Historical Society of Pennsylvania; p. 40: The Granger Collection; p. 40: Christie's Images; p. 43: Culver Pictures, Inc.; p. 45: Library of Congress; p. 49: Peabody Essex Museum Salem, MA. Photo by Mark Sexton; p. 50: Philadelphia Free Public Library; p. 53: The Granger Collection; p. 59: The Granger Collection; p. 53 Colonial Williamsburg Foundation; p. 60: North Wind Pictures; p. 61 North Wind Pictures; p. 65: Courtesy, American Antiquarian Society; p. 69: Ted Speigel; p. 70: The Granger Collection; p. 72: Christie's Images; p. 73: Photograph Courtesy of the Concord Museum, Concord MA. And the archives of the Lexington Historical Society, David Bohl; p. 75 PhotoDisc, Inc.; p. 77: Bettmann/Corbis.

Unit 2: p. 81: The Granger Collection; p. 82: The Granger Collection; p. 82: Independence Hall, National Park Service; p. 84: National Archives and Records Administration; p. 85: The Granger Collection; p. 94: North Wind Archives; p. 100: The Granger Collection; p. 100: Museum of Textile History; p. 105: Missouri Historical Society; p. 110: North Wind Archives; p. 112: Scott Camazine, Photo Researchers, Inc.; p. 115: Smithsonian Institute; p. 118: The Bancroft Library; p. 118: Superstock; p. 121: The Granger Collection; p. 122: The Granger Collection; p. 125: The Granger Collection; p. 129: Courtesy of San Jacinto Museum of History, La Porte, TX; p. 132: Courtesy of Levi Strauss & Co.; p. 133: North Wind Archives; p. 136: Samuel B. Waugh, *The Bay and Harbor of New York* Museum of the City of New York, Gift of Mrs. Robert M. Littlejohn; p. 136: The Granger Collection; p. 139: The Granger Collection; p. 144: The Granger Collection; p. 147: The Granger Collection; p. 147: The Granger Collection; p. 148: The Granger Collection.

Unit 3: p. 153: The Granger Collection; p. 154: The Granger Collection; p. 154: The Granger Collection; p. 163: The Granger Collection; p. 163: The Granger Collection; p. 167: The Granger Collection; p. 170: The Granger Collection; p. 174: Library of Congress; p. 174: Larry Sherer/Time-Life Books, Inc./High Impact; p. 182: The Granger Collection; p. 184: The Granger Collection; p. 187: The Granger Collection; p. 189: Culver Pictures, Inc.; p. 196: The Library of Congress; p. 196: Museum of the Confederacy, Richmond, Virginia, Photo by Katherine Wetzel; p. 199: Andrew Johnson National Historic Site; p. 200: Harper's Weekly; p. 203: Library of Congress; p. 204: The Granger Collection; p. 207: The Granger Collection; p. 211: Library of Congress.

Unit 4: p. 215: The Granger Collection; p. 216: The Granger Collection; p. 216: Image Number 2.77.40, Courtesy of Old Sturbridge Village, photo by Henry E. Peach; p. 219: The Granger Collection; p. 220: The Granger Collection; p. 223: Superstock; p. 224: Library of Congress; p. 225: The Granger Collection; p. 228: The Granger Collection; p. 234: The Bridgemen Art Library International Ltd.; p. 234: PhotoDisc, Inc.; p. 236: The Granger Collection; p. 238: The Granger Collection; p. 240: Corbis/Bettmann; p. 241: A/P Wide World Photos; p. 242: The Granger Collection; p. 244: The Granger Collection; p. 247: Corbis; p. 248: The Granger Collection; p. 252: The Granger Collection; p. 252: Mark Burnett, Stock Boston; p. 256: The Granger Collection; p. 258: Courtesy of the New York Historical Society; p. 260: Brown Brothers.

Unit 5: p. 271: US Naval Academy Museum; p. 272: The Granger Collection; p. 272: North Carolina Museum of History; p. 276: The Granger Collection; p. 280: Brown Brothers; p. 281: Mark C. Burnett, Photo Researchers; p. 283: The Granger Collection; p. 290: Panama Canal; p. 290: Culver Pictures, Inc.; p. 294: Chris Arend, Alaska Stock; p. 295: The Granger Collection; p. 298: The Granger Collection; p. 299: Library of Congress; p. 301:

The Granger Collection; p. 308: Corbis/Bettmann-UPI; p. 308: Corbis/Bettmann-UPI; p. 313: The Granger Collection; p. 314: Index Stock Photography, Inc.; p. 315: Culver Pictures, Inc.; p. 316: AP/Wide World Photos; p. 318: The Granger Collection; p. 320: The Granger Collection; p. 325: National Archives.

Unit 6: p. 331: The Granger Collection; p. 332: Stock Montage; p. 332: The Granger Collection; p. 336: Henry Ford Museum & Greenfield Village; p. 339: Archive Photos; p. 341: The Granger Collection; p. 345: Corbis; p. 350: Archive Photos; p. 350: Silver Burdett and Ginn; p. 352: Courtesy of the New York Stock Exchange Archives; p. 354: Corbis; p. 355: Archive Photos; p. 360: The Granger Collection; p. 362: Wide World Photos; p. 364: Archive Photos; p. 368: National Archives; p. 368: The Granger Collection; p. 371: Corbis; p. 372: Culver Pictures, Inc.; p. 374: The Granger Collection; p. 378: Corbis; p. 380: Classic PIO Library; p. 381: The Granger Collection; p. 382: Corbis/Bettmann-UPI.

Unit 7: p. 387: AP/Wide World Photos; p. 388: Archive Photos; p. 388: Library of Congress; p. 391: AP/Wide World Photos; p. 392: Bettmann Corbis; p. 398: The Granger Collection; p. 404: Corbis/Bettmann; p. 404: Courtesy of the Hampel and D'Alessio Families; p. 407: The Granger Collection; p. 410: Archive Photos; p. 414: The Granger Collection; p. 415: Corbis Digital Stock; p. 416: Smithsonian Institute; p. 419: Wide World Photos; p. 422: Tony Stone Images; p. 426: National Archives; p. 426: PhotoDisc, Inc.; p. 431: Corbis/Bettmann; p. 343: United Nations; p. 436: Corbis-Bettmann-UPI; p. 439: Corbis; p. 440: Archive Photos.

Unit 8: p. 445: UPI-Corbis/Bettmann; p. 446: Van Bucher, Photo Researchers; p. 446: Index Stock; p. 449: Corbis/Minnesota Historical Society; p. 450: Corbis; p. 452: Archive Photos; p. 458: Archive Photos; p. 464: Archive Photos; p. 464: John Elk, III, Stock Boston; p. 468: AP/Wide World Photos; p. 471: The Supreme Court Historical Society; p. 472: UPI-Corbis/Bettmann; p. 474: AP/Wide World Photos; p. 476: AP/Wide World Photos; p. 479: Archive Photos; p. 481: FPG International LLC; p. 484: UPI-Corbis/Bettmann; p. 484: Archive Photos; p. 487: AP/Wide World Photos; p. 488: UPI-Corbis/Bettmann; p. 489: UPI-Corbis/Bettmann; p. 491: Archive Photos; p. 493: Archive Photos; p. 494: Corbis/Bettmann-UPI; p. 497: UPI-Corbis/Bettmann.

Unit 9: p. 503: Bernie Boston; p. 504: Martin Levick; p. 504: Reprinted by permission of Ms. Magazine © 1972; p. 507: John lanois, Black Star; p. 508: Corbis/Flip Schulke; p. 509: Michael Mauney, Black Star; p. 513: Archive Photos; p. 517: Ted Streshinsky/CORBIS; p. 522: Corbis/Tim Page; p. 522: Archive Photos; p. 528: Archive Photos; p. 530: Archive Photos; p. 531: Corbis; p. 533: Corbis/Bettmann; p. 535: Archive Photos; p. 538: AP/Wide World Photos; p. 539: Corbis/Steve Raymer; p. 542: Corbis; p. 542: AP/Wide World Photos; p. 545: Archive Photos; p. 549: Owen Franken, Stock Boston; p. 551: Silver Burdett Ginn; p. 553: Dennis Brack/Black Star.

Unit 10: p. 559: AP/Wide World Photos; p. 560: Pearson Education/PH College; p. 560: Courtesy of Time Life Syndication; p. 562: Courtesy of the Presidential Jimmy Carter Library; p. 565: Corbis; p. 568: The White House Photo Office; p. 570: Courtesy of The Democratic National Committee; p. 575: Courtesy of the Reagan Library; p. 578: AP/Wide World Photos; p. 578: Corbis/Vanni Archives; p. 580: Charles Tasnadi/AP Photo Wide World; p. 581: The White House Photo Office; p. 582: Corbis/Robert Maass; p. 585: Rueters/Bettmann; p. 588: AP/Wide World Photos; p. 593: Larry Downing, Sygma Photo News; p. 594: AP/Wide World Photos; p. 595: Corbis; p. 598: (l) ©Reuters; (r) Amos Morgan/Getty Images; p. 600: Getty Images; p. 601: Jim Collins/AP Wide World Photos; p. 602: AP/Wide World Photos; p. 603: Joel Nito/AFP/Corbis; p. 604: Robert Nickelsburg/Getty Images; p. 607: Tony Freeman, PhotoEdit; p. 608: Reuters/Corbis.

The Presidents Chart: 1: Corbis; 2: The Granger Collection; 3: Corbis; 4: Corbis; 5: Corbis; 6: Corbis; 7: Corbis; 8: Corbis; 9: Corbis; 10: Corbis; 11: Corbis; 12: Art Resource, NY; 13: Corbis; 14: The Granger Collection; 15: Corbis; 16: The Granger Collection; 17: The Granger Collection; 18: The Granger Collection; 19: Corbis; 20: Corbis; 21: The Granger Collection; 22: The Granger Collection; 23: The Granger Collection; 24: The Granger Collection; 25: Corbis; 26: The Granger Collection; 27: Corbis; 28: The Granger Collection; 29: National Portrait Gallery/Smithsonian Institute; 30: The Granger Collection; 31: Corbis; 32: The Granger Collection; 33: The Granger Collection; 34: Corbis; 35: AP/Wide World Photos; 36: Lyndon Baines Johnson Library Collection; 37: Corbis; 38: Corbis; 39: Corbis; 40: The White House Photo Office; 41: The White House Photo Office; 42: Corbis; 43: The White House Photo Office.

Cover: Space Shuttle: NASA; Stamp: Pearson Learning; Pottery: © Phil Schermeister/CORBIS; Train: © Bettmann/CORBIS; Flag: Gallery of the Republic; Button: Pearson Learning.